MW00876325

Partner with Us

Good day, we are a Christian based content creator influenced by the power of the holy-spirit. We believe that no Christian should be tormented by the devil provided they can pray and study the word. Prayer and the word are not just a means of 2 communications; it is our weapon of warfare against the power of the enemy. We have a website https://everydayprayerguide.com filled with numerous prayer and Bible study contents. These prayer points and Bible study contents were orchestrated by the spirit of God to help us in our daily lives. Also, we have a YouTube channel https://youtube.com/c/EveryDayPrayerGuideTV where you can find numerous prayer videos. With this, you can pray along with our head pastor and share your comments. All you need to do is visit the YouTube page, subscribe to our channel and turn on your notification to be notified when a new prayer video is released. Meanwhile, you can also catch up with us on our social media pages.

We are https://www.facebook.com/EveryDayPrayerGuide on Facebook, Instagram and Pinterest.

On Instagram @ https://www.instagram.com/everydayprayerguide Twitter @ https://twitter.com/prayerguide

On Pinterest @ https://www.pinterest.com/everydayprayerguide

You can contact me via email at everydayprayerguide@outlook.com as this is our way of evangelizing the gospel of Christ and setting people free from the power of darkness–we admonish that you partner with us on this course.

You can partner with us financially through our Patreon account https://www.patreon.com/everydayprayerguidetv **your partnership will help us in reaching our heterogeneous and diversified audience. For more prayers visit:** https://everydayprayerguide.com

Introduction

Like18:1, Then He spoke a parable to them that men always ought to pray and not lose heart.

Prayer is a communication channel with God that must be initiated all the time. As believers, our prayer life must be top-notch. This is because when we show laxity in place of prayer, the devil is just around the corner, waiting for the right time to strike.

God instructed that we pray all the time. The scripture says in the book of 1 Thessalonians 5:17 – Pray without ceasing.

Remember the scripture also stated in the book of 1Peter5:8 be sober, be vigilant; because your adversary, the devil, walks about like a roaring lion, seeking whom he may devour. One of the most effective ways to protect ourselves from the wrath of

3 the enemy is through prayer. I believe that the power of the enemy should not

Trample Christians, provided their prayer life is efficient.

When we look around us today, we see so many evil things happening. The enemy has gone on rampage already, and the target is mostly the people of God. Prayer is our only means of conquering the devil. That is why I have compiled a list of prayer topics in this book titled   PrayerGuideForEverydayLifeVolume1.   These prayer topics encompass different prayer categories needed for our everyday life to give us

Victory. These are prayer points that you can pray from anywhere at any time. And it is my prayer for you that God shall grant all your requests in Jesus name.

CHAPTER 1

POWERFUL MORNING PRAYERS MORNING DEVOTION

Good morning people of a great God, let us just repeat what God has said concerning us this morning.

> *"And this is my covenant with them," says the Lord. "My Spirit will not leave them, and neither will these words I have given you. They will be on your lips and on the lips of your children and your children's children forever. I, the Lord, have spoken!* - **Isaiah 59:21 NLT**

> *Therefore, the Lord is my strength and my song, and he has become my salvation; this is my God, and I will praise him, my father's God, and I will exalt him.* - **Exodus 15:2 ESV**

Oh, that you would burst from the heavens and come down! How the mountains would quake in your presence! As fire causes wood to burn and water to boil, your coming would make the nations tremble. Then your enemies would learn the reason for your fame! When you came down long ago, you did awesome deeds beyond our highest expectations. And oh, how the mountains quaked! For since the world began, no ear has heard and no eye has seen a God like you, who works for those who wait for him! You welcome those who gladly do good, who follow godly ways.

Therefore, associate yourselves o ye people, and ye shall be broken in pieces. *Give ear all ye of far countries; gird yourselves, take counsel together, it shall come to nought; speak the word, and it shall not stand: for God is with me.* **Isa. 8:9-10.**

As a result of my covenant with my God, and my praise and worship of my God, the Lord will make His face to shine upon me always, He shall be gracious unto me and mine. His

light will shine on my path and His Favor will encompass me all my days in Jesus name.

- From now, when I call upon the name of the Lord, He shall stretch forth His hand and lift me up above all my enemies and their works against me and He delivers me from all of them in Jesus name.

- Behold, every power/person /demon that are incensed against me shall be ashamed and confounded: they shall be as nothing; and the power and people that strive with me, shall perish. I shall seek them, and shall not find them even the powers contending with me and mine. They that war against me shall be as nothing in Jesus name.

- In this times and forever more, no weapon that is fashioned against me shall prosper, and every tongue that rises against me is already condemned, in Jesus name.

- The children of those who afflicted me, shall come bowing low to me, and all those who despised me, shall bow down at my feet, in Jesus name.

- When the enemy sees the blood of Jesus, they shall pass over, destroyers will not be able to enter into my household because of the blood of Jesus, in Jesus name.

- Lord we give you thanks for your word that never fails and for answering our prayers in Jesus name.

MORNING DEVOTION: REDEEMING THE TIME

ECCL. 3:1-8. TIME is the most valuable treasure given by God to man to trade with.

TIME could be a season marked by specific activities and events (Eccl. 3:1-8). Man is a product of how and what he uses his time for. Beloved, what time of your life are you now? Is it Morning, afternoon or evening? How much profit have you made with the time God gave you to trade with? How would you redeem your remaining allotted time, to avoid wastage or deficit? It is high time to conduct a heart-felt search about your life and see how you have fared with your God given time.

The 5 wise virgins knew that the bride groom was coming and they trimmed their lamps! Be prepared! It's not what you do once in a while. It's what you do minute owe minute that makes the difference. The time of the end is at hand, a time of trouble such as never was since there was a nation even to that time, God's people shall be delivered, everyone that shall be found written in the book of (Daniel 12:1) is your name written there?

LET US PRAY

- Any damage done to my destiny, be repaired in the name of Jesus

- O Lord, restore me to your original design for my life

- O Lord, bless me and enlarge my coast.

- I refuse to operate below my divine destiny in the name of Jesus

- O Lord anoint my eyes, hands and feet to locate my divine purpose in Jesus name

- Every power contending with my divine destiny, scatter unto desolation in the name of Jesus

- Let the spirit of excellence come upon me in Jesus name

- Thank you Jesus for answered prayers

  Bible reading: Isaiah 54- 58

  Memory verse: Rev. 2:7

MORNING DEVOTION: PRECIOUS

Matthew 26:26-29: And as they were eating, Jesus took bread, and blessed it, and breaks it, and gave it to the disciples, and said, Take, eat; this is my body. 26:27 and he took the cup, and gave thanks, and gave it to them, saying, Drink ye all of it; 26:28 for this is my blood of the new testament, which is shed for many for the remission of sins. 26:29 But I say unto you, I will not drink henceforth of this fruit of the vine, until that day when I drink it new with you in my Father's kingdom.

Today, we are going to be looking at the subject Precious in today's devotion. The fact that sin affected the blood of man (through Adam) made the virgin birth necessary. If Christ was to be the son of Adam, He would not have been a sinless man. He did not have a drop of Adam's blood in His veins because He did not have a human father. The seed of a man did not get Mary fertilized for Christ's birth. His body was of Mary, but His blood was of the Holy Ghost. And because he had no human father, He was a descendant of David according to the flesh.

Jesus body did not decompose after 3 days, but Lazarus body did after 4 days (PSALMS 16:10) every drop of blood that flowed in His body is still in existence and is as fresh as it was when it flowed from his wounds. The blood of Jesus is one of the most powerful weapons we can use in prayer. Plead the blood in prayer and it we speak for you (Heb. 12:24). It speaks life and forgiveness while Abel's blood cries for death and revenge. Whatever the blood of Jesus is applied or pleaded by faith, Satan cannot touch that person or situation to which is applied. He cannot pass by the blood of Jesus.

SATAN CANNOT WITHSTAND THE BLOOD OF JESUS.

As a believer in Jesus Christ, your protection and hiding place is under the blood. It is faith in the blood that gives you victory over the devil and every problem you may encounter. Apply it by faith and you will testify that" there is Power Mighty in the blood"

LET US PRAY

- Satan , I hold the blood of Jesus against you and declare that you have been defeated permanently in the name of Jesus

- I enter the Holy of Holies by the blood of Jesus , in the name of Jesus

- By the blood of Jesus, I disgrace the spirit of stagnant in any area of my life in the name of Jesus

- By the power in the blood of Jesus , I command all my delayed testimonies to manifest by fire in the name of Jesus

- Blood of Jesus, bring the judgment of death upon witchcraft power hindering my laughter and celebration in the name of Jesus

- Blood of Jesus, restore unto me every good thing the enemy had stolen from me in the name of Jesus

- I encircle my life and can't with the blood of Jesus, in the name of Jesus

- Thank you Lord Jesus for answered prayers

  Bible reading: Jeremiah 7:9

  Memory verse: Ephesians 1:7

DAILY MORNING PRAYER FOR EVERYONE

Psalm 59:16: But I will sing of thy power; yea, I will sing aloud of thy mercy in the morning: for thou hast been my defense and refuge in the day of my trouble.

It is a beautiful thing to start your day with your creator, those who seek Him early, will find Him early in life. Today we are going to be looking at daily Morning Prayer for everyone. Like the title suggests, this daily Morning Prayer is for everyone, you are encouraged to pray them before you leave your house daily. Why is this important? This is important because every day has enough evil of its own, Matthew 6:34. It is not cool for you to just walk out of the house in the morning without commuting your entire day to the Lord. When you don't engage in daily morning prayer, you become vulnerable to the attacks of the day, anything bad can happen to you at work, school, or anywhere you find yourself, also, there are also blessings that everyday carries, if you leave the house without praying to the Lord, the devil can easily distract you from the favour that can come to you on that day.

Engaging in daily Morning Prayer is also a show of gratitude to the Lord, the psalmist said ' I slept and I woke up this morning because the Lord sustained me' Psalms 3:5. We must recognize that even sleeping and waking up every morning is a miracle, many have died from their sleep, many cannot even sleep at all, it is called insomnia. Therefore we should not take this for granted we must develop an attitude of gratitude to Gods unmerited favour that He has showered on us. I believe as you make seeking God early through this daily Morning Prayer a lifestyle, you will never lack His presence in your life in Jesus name. I encourage you this day, always pray Morning Prayer daily, not because you want something from God, but because you love he and you want Him to continue to guide you every step of the way. I see the Lords favour overflowing in your life in Jesus name.

DAILY MORNING PRAYER

- Father, I thank you for sustaining me through the night, and for waking me up this morning in Jesus name.

- Father, I thank you for your mercies are new every morning in my life, thank you Lord for your great and unending faithfulness in my Life in Jesus name.

- Father, thank you for the gift of life and sound health that you have blessed me and my entire family with in Jesus name.

- Father, thank you for sustaining and waking up all my friends and loved ones this morning in Jesus name

- Father, thank you for fighting all my battles in the night and thus giving me a sound sleep in Jesus name.

- Father, I commit my day into your Holy hands in Jesus name

- Order my steps by the help of your holy spirit today in Jesus name

- Shield me from the arrows that flies by day in Jesus name

- As I go about my business this morning, cause me to be at the right place and at the right time in Jesus name.

- Father I declare that today all things will work out for my good in Jesus name

- No weapon fashioned against me shall prosper today in Jesus name

- I declare that I shall find favour with men that matter today in Jesus name

- I declare that my destiny helpers shall locate me today in Jesus name

- Father, make me a blessing to someone today in Jesus name

- Father, help me to win someone to Christ today in Jesus name

- Father, help me to put a smile on someone's face today in Jesus name.

- Father, lead me not into the temptations of today in Jesus name

- Father shield me from the wrong people in Jesus name

- I declare that all my expectations and daily goal or targets shall be met today and within record time in Jesus name

- I shall end well today in Jesus name.

- Father, I thank you for answering all my prayers this morning in Jesus name.

PRAYER POINTS FOR MORNING PROTECTION AND COVERING

Today we will be dealing with prayer points for morning protection and covering. The fact remains, life is filled with so much terror. The life of a man is like a breeze. You are here this moment, and the next moment, you are gone. One can't even tell what will would happen in the next minute. There are so many people who have died, not because it was time for them to answer the call but because they were stripped of the divine protection of the father.

As a man of God, I have experienced so many incredible miracles not to know that the grace of protection and the covering is not sufficient for everyone, every time and everywhere. This explains why you will see someone survive a ghastly accident that took the life of others. Little wonder the book of Ephesians 5:16 says, See then that you walk circumspectly, not as fools but as wise, redeeming the time, because the days are evil. We must be wise in our doings, and we must learn to redeem each day with the precious blood of Jesus because every day is filled with evil.

The truth remains, terrible things happen almost every second in a day. That's why we need to beg God for his protection especially in the morning before setting out. You are a young man or woman with huge aspirations. You wake up from bed each morning with your heads up high, ready to take on life until your goal unfolds. Well, I have seen young men and women who are fiercer than you caught up in the wind of life. They died before their aspirations were ripe enough to unfold. You don't joke with God's protection.

The children of Isreal would have died in the land of Egypt. They would have been wasted long before Moses was raised into a leader to bring them out of captivity. The intentions of the Egyptians were not to see the children of Isreal succeed or thrive. They went up against them every time they fear their number has grown tremendously. However, the protection of God Almighty was immensely upon the children of Isreal, and that's why none of the plagues affected any of them.

Every morning before you step out of your house, you must seek the face of God. You must activate the protection of God over your life. It gives the devil no joy that you are happy. It gives him no joy that you are alive and thriving. The devil's wish is to ensure that you are either dead or become a nonentity in life. This is why you must seek God early in the morning. Before you go out for your daily needs, say these prayers for protection and covering.

PRAYER POINTS:

- Lord Jesus, I thank you for another beautiful day. I thank you for your grace bestowed on me to see a new day that you have made. Lord, may your name be highly exalted in the name of Jesus.

- Lord God, the scripture says See then that you walk circumspectly, not as fools but as wise, redeeming the time, because the days are evil. I pray for your unwavering protection over my family and me. I ask that your angels will guide me in my ways today even as I step out for work.

- Lord Jesus, it has been written, the eyes of the Lord are always upon the righteous. Father, I pray that your eyes will always be upon me today. I pray that your spirit will guide me in the right way to go, in the name of Jesus.

- Lord, by virtue of the blood that was shed on the cross of Calvary, I cancel every evil manipulation that has been designed against me today. I break into pieces every trap of the enemy that would cost me my life today in the name of Jesus.

- Lord, for it, has been written, But the Lord is faithful, and He will strengthen you and protect you from the evil one. I pray for your strength today. I activate your powerful protection over my life today in the name of Jesus.

- Lord, as I step out this morning, I pray that the angel of the Lord will go before me and remove every dangerous vice of the devil on the road. I prophesy I shall not fall victim to an accident today in the name of Jesus.

- I declare that kidnappers shall not come my way today in the name of Jesus. I decree that by the mercy of the Lord, I shall not fall victim to a stray bullet in the name of Jesus.

- I redeem this day with the precious blood of Jesus. I direct every blood suckling demon that has vowed to take life today to the cross of Calvary, where there is abundant blood flow in the name of Jesus.

- Father, the scripture says be strong and courageous. Do not be afraid or terrified because of them, for the Lord your God goes with you; He will never leave you nor forsake you. I pray that you shall not forsake me today in the name of Jesus. I pray that the enemy will not triumph over me today in the name of Jesus.

- No weapon forged against you will prevail, and you will refute every tongue that accuses you. This is the heritage of the servants of the Lord, declares the Lord." Lord, I decree that every plan of the enemies to harm me today is nullified. I cancel their plans over my life today by the power in the name of Jesus.

- Father Lord, you have promised in your word that even if I pass through the fire, it shall not burn me. You promise to be with me when I pass through the waters of life. I activate this scripture over my life today in the name of Jesus.

- Even though I walk through the valley of the shadow of death, I fear no evil, for you are with me. Your rod and your staff comfort me. Father, I fear no evil today as I step for work. I put the angels of the lord in charge of my life; they will guide me in the right way to go today in the name of Jesus.

- Lord, I pray that your protection will be upon me this morning. As I'm leaving the house in peace, I shall not return dead. I sanctify this day with the precious blood of Jesus, and I decree that it is free from evil in the name of Jesus. Amen.

30 POWERFUL MORNING PRAYER POINTS TO COMMAND THE DAY

> *Psalm 63:1-2. O God, thou art my God; early will I seek thee: my soul thirsteth for thee, my flesh longeth for thee in a dry and thirsty land, where no water is; 2 to see thy power and thy glory, so as I have seen thee in the sanctuary.*

The morning hours are very crucial times in the realm of the spirit. The powers of darkness often seize the early hours of the morning, between 12.00 am and 3.00am GMT, to carry out their evil acts. The bible speaking in Matthew 13:25:25 But while men slept, his enemy came and sowed tares among the wheat, and went his way. As a child of God, you must understand the importance of Morning Prayer, if you only sleep all through the early hours of the day, you cannot control the rest of the day.

A lot of sleeping Christians today are victims of the enemies attack, but today we shall tell the devil no more!!!. I have compiled 30 powerful Morning Prayer points to command the day. Only those who take advantage of their early Morning Prayer times, can take control of the rest of their day.

This is an important lesson in the school of spiritual warfare, the morning hours are transitional hours, and it is a fertile time for the devil to strike. It is also a fertile time for believers to disarm the powers of darkness and prophesy blessings to their day. When we pray morning prayers, we cancel all the arrows of the devil that flies by day and all the pestilence that roam in darkness and all the destructions that wasteth at noon day, Psalms 91:5-6. When we seek God early, we find Him early in the day, when we engage in Morning Prayer, we command our day all through. I encourage you today to always take advantage of early morning prayers.

Use this early hours of the day to declare blessings over your day, give God quality praises, rebuke the hand of the enemy over your life and finally declare what you want to see in your life each day. The best time to engage in this kind of prayers in between the hours of 12.00am to 3.00 am GMT. Different time zones applies to different countries, but just know it's from midnight to the third hour of the day. As you engage this powerful Morning Prayer points to command the day, I see you commanding your day in Jesus name.

PRAYER POINTS

- I take authority over this day, in the name of Jesus.
- I draw upon heavenly resources today, in the name of Jesus.
- I confess that this is the day the Lord has made, I will rejoice and be glad in it, in the name of Jesus.
- I decree that all the elements of this day will cooperate with me, in Jesus' name.
- I decree that these elemental forces will refuse to cooperate with my enemies this day, in Jesus' name.
- I speak unto you the sun, the moon and the stars, you will not smite me and my family this day, in Jesus' name.
- I pull down every negative energy, planning to operate against my life this day, in Jesus' name.
- I dismantle any power that is chanting incantations to capture this day, in the name of Jesus.
- I render null and void, such incantations and satanic prayers over me and my family, in the name of Jesus.
- I retrieve this day from their hands, in the name of Jesus.
- Every battle in the heaven lies, be won by angels conveying my blessings today, in Jesus' name.
- My Father, let everything You have not planted in the heaven lies be uprooted, in Jesus' name.
- O Lord, let the wicked be shaken out of my heavens, in the name of Jesus
- O sun, as you are coming out today; uproot every wickedness targeted at my life, in the name of Jesus.

- I programme blessings into the sun for my life, in the name of Jesus.
- O sun, I have risen before you, cancel every evil programme projected into you against me by wicked powers, in the name of Jesus.
- You this day, you will not destroy my prosperity, in the name of Jesus.
- O sun, moon and stars, carry your afflictions back to the sender and release them against him, in Jesus' name.
- O God, arise and uproot everything You have not planted in the heaven lies that is working against me, in Jesus' name.
- O Lord, let the wicked be shaken out of the ends of the earth, in the name of Jesus.
- O sun, as you come forth, uproot all the wickedness that has come against my life, in the name of Jesus.
- I programme blessings into the sun, the moon and the stars for my life today, in the name of Jesus.
- O sun, cancel every daily evil programme drawn up against me, in the name of Jesus.
- O sun, torment every enemy of the kingdom of God in my life, in the name of Jesus.
- O sun, throw away those who spend the night pulling me down, in the name of Jesus.
- O elements, you shall not hurt me, in Jesus' name.
- O heaven lies, you shall not steal from my life today, in the name of Jesus.
- I establish the power of God over the heaven lies, in the name of Jesus.
- O sun, moon and stars, fight against the stronghold of witchcraft targeted at me today, in Jesus' name.
- O heaven lies, torment every unrepentant enemy to submission, in Jesus' name.

Thank you Jesus.

MORNING PRAYER FOR FINANCIAL MIRACLE

Today we will be dealing with morning prayer for a financial miracle. Why is it important to seek God in the morning for a financial miracle? When we pray to God early in the morning, our faith in Him is rekindled, and we get to invite him into the business of the day. Once God gets invited, we begin to see the manifestation of his hands in the affairs of our life. Little wonder the Psalmist said, O God, thou art my God; early will I seek thee. There is great importance in seeking God early in the morning.

Morning Prayer for Financial Miracle will have us talking to God on how we want our day to be designed financially. There is a blessing that is attached to each day. Morning Prayer for financial Miracle will help us key into the new day's blessing. There is nothing prayer cannot do, that debt that you have owed for long, God can settle it today, and all you need to do is ask for a financial miracle. The scripture says, declare a thing, and it shall be established. We must learn to design our day every morning. When we pray to God for a financial miracle in the morning before setting out for work, it unlocks the blessing of the day for us.

I decree by the authority of heaven, as you begin to use this prayer guide daily before you set out for business, may God continue to unlock the blessing of the day to you in the name of Jesus. Every power and principalities that may want to stand in your way, every power that may want to frustrate your efforts, I pray that the fire of the Holy Ghost comes upon them in the name of Jesus. In our lives as believers, we must understand the efficacy of morning prayers, especially for financial miracle. The scripture says we find God when he can be found. We should call upon him when he is near.

PRAYER POINTS

- Lord Jesus, I thank you for giving the grace to witness yet another day that you have made. I thank you because sparing my life to see this day means you have plans for me. I exalt your holy

18

name because you are God, Father, accept my Thanksgiving in the name of Jesus.

- Lord Jesus, as I will be stepping out into this new day, I pray that your grace will go with me. The scripture says, when Isreal was leaving Egypt, the house of Jacob out of people of strange language, Judah was his sanctuary and Isreal his dominion, the sea saw it and fled, Jordan was driven back. The mountains skipped like rams and the little hills like lambs. Lord, sea saw your power, Jordan saw your glory, the mountains, and small hills felt your presence; that was why they skipped. Jehovah, as I will be going out today, I decree that your glory goes with me in the name of Jesus. Every form of impossibility, every giant or stumbling block on my way to progress today, I decree that the fire of the most high come upon them in the name of Jesus.

- Lord Jesus, for it, has been written that I will be blessed when I come in and blessed when I go out. I unlock the blessing of this day by your power. I decree that by the authority of heaven, the blessing of today is released unto me in the name of Jesus. Lord, the scripture also says the blessing of the Lord brings riches without adding sorrow. I decree that your wealth of blessing become mine today in the name of Jesus.

- Father in heaven, everything I lay my hands upon today shall prosper. I announce this day that the anointing of prosperity is upon me. Everything that I have tried in the past and experienced failure, I decree that they are made possible today in the name of Jesus. The scripture says the heart of man and kings is in the hands of the Lord, and he directs it like the flow of waters. Lord, cause a man to bless me today. Let your favor go with me today when men see me let them bless me with their riches.

- For it has been written, "Blessed be the Lord, who daily loads us with benefits, the God of our salvation!" I tap into the blessings of today in the name of Jesus. I decree financial breakthrough today. I decree financial miracle in the name of Jesus. Lord, even where I never expect blessing, father cause men to bless me. I unlock the portal of wealth for today. I decree that the angel in charge of wealth go with me today, everything I lay my hands upon today shall yield fruits in the name of Jesus.

- The bible says Submit to God and be at peace with him; in this way, prosperity will come to you." Lord Jesus, as I will going out today, I submit myself to you. I pray that you will direct my ways; you will direct my path. I'm at peace with you, Lord Jesus, I pray that you will send prosperity my way today in the name of Jesus. Father you are the creator of all things, you are the God of prosperity, I decree that you will bless me abundantly in the name of Jesus.

- Father Lord, let me meet prosperity as I set out today. You said that the glory of the latter shall surpass the former. I do not care about the blessings and prosperity you gave me yesterday. I'm much more concerned about the one you will give to me today. Because I'm standing on the promises of your word that the glory of the latter shall surpass the former, this means that I shall never know a better yesterday. I decree that great portion of blessing I will receive today in the name of Jesus. As I will be making my way home at night, let songs of praise unto your holy name be my anthem. Amen

MORNING PRAYERS TO START YOUR DAY WITH GOD

Today we will be dealing with morning prayers to start the day with God. As believers, we must always learn to start a new day with God. We invite God into the business of the day through prayer. God, Himself would not invite himself, and until we recognize the fact that we cannot do anything without the help of God, we might not be getting things right.

Aside from giving thanks to God for seeing a new day when you wake up from sleep, there are prayers that you should say every morning to keep the right. When God is involved in the matter of men, things will work according to plans. Also, there is this confidence and satisfaction that we get whenever we pray over a specific issue before leaving home in the morning. This prayer article morning prayers to start your day with God will enlighten you on some important areas you should touch in prayer every morning to have a great day. I pray that as you follow this prayer, may God make himself manifest in your matter in the name of Jesus.

Another thing is that when we start our day with God, we are protected from evil. The scripture says the eyes of the Lord are always upon the righteous. When the eyes of the Lord upon a man, there is maximum security guaranteed for such a person, and the scripture says his ears are attentive to their prayers. This means that when we call on God in the morning, he would listen and Hearken to our prayers. I decree by the authority of heaven, that as you begin to start your day with this prayer article, the protection of God Almighty will come upon you.

Another set of people who will need a prayer like this are those who work for people. Maybe you work in a corporate organization where you are expected to meet a certain point every day. Even if where you work is not a corporate organization, but you want to meet a target each day, your best bet is to start your day with God in prayers. The scripture says I will lift my eyes to the hills, from where will my help come from? My help will come from God, the maker of heaven and earth.

Today, God will supply that help that you need to run the day in the name of Jesus. The bible says the steadfast love of God never ends; they are new every morning; this is why you must renew your prayer vows with God every morning. As you begin to follow this process, I pray for a supernatural turnaround in your life and business in the name of Jesus.

PRAYER POINTS:

- Father in heaven, I thank you for the grace you have bestowed on me to be among the living this morning, Lord, let your name be exalted in the name of Jesus. I magnify you because you are God over my life, I thank you for your eyes of protection that never sleeps concerning me, I thank you for the saving strength of your right hand that is always at work in my life, father let your name be exalted in the name of Jesus.

- The scripture makes me understand that it is more profitable to give thanks to God than to ask from him. Because of this, I thank you for your fatherly love, even when I don't merit it. Men may boast of their wealth and power, but only you can boast of your righteousness. You are faithful. I magnify your holy name in the name of Jesus.

- Lord God, as I will be setting out to work today, I come against every in my way. Everything that may want to stand in my way as a hindrance, I destroy them by the blood of the lamb in the name of Jesus. For the scripture says I will go before you and level up exalted places, I decree that your power goes before me this day in the name of Jesus. Everything that may want to hinder me from succeeding today, I destroy them by the fire of the holy ghost in the name of Jesus.

- Father Lord, a man is naked without your protection. I pray that the saving strength of your right hand will go with me today, as I will be stepping out of my house, the fire of the Holy Ghost will before me, and destroy every danger in my way in the name of

Jesus. I pray for the spirit of God, the Holy Ghost, that will tell me what to do and where to go. I pray that the spirit comes upon me in the name of Jesus. I exempt myself from every evil vices that the devil has staged for today. I separate myself by the blood of the lamb.

- Father in heaven, your word says the Lord is my shepherd, I shall not want. Lord, I decree that this day I shall not lack any good thing in the name of Jesus. The expectations of the righteous shall not be cut short; that is what the scripture says. I stand on the promises of this word, and I decree that every good thing or idea that I conceived in my mind this day shall be achieved in the name of Jesus. I pray for the help of God Almighty, the grace of Jehovah JIREH, that makes the struggle of a man smooth. I pray that such grace comes upon me today in the name of Jesus.

- Lord God, I pray that today you will help me fulfill the purpose of the day. Lord, I don't want to be carried away with the chanting noises around me that will make me lose focus on purpose for the day. I pray that you will help me achieve purpose today in the name of Jesus. I pray that as I set out in peace, I shall return in peace in the name of Jesus. Amen.

INSPIRATIONAL MORNING PRAYERS

Lamentations 3:22-23 *22 it is of the Lord's mercies that we are not consumed, because his compassions fail not. 23 They are new every morning: great is thy faithfulness.*

Behold, what manner of Love the father has given onto us, 1 John 3:1, God's love for His children is unconditional, unending, unquantifiable and much more. They are new every morning and inexhaustible every day. We are going to be engaging some inspirational morning prayers today. This inspirational morning prayers are inspired by our love for God which is triggered by His love for us. The best time to tell the Lord how much you love Him is in the morning, at the beginning of the day.

This inspirational morning prayers will help you strengthen the love bond between you and God, your father, it is a Father-Son bonding prayer, and you express your unconditional love for Him as you acknowledge His unconditional love for you. This inspirational morning prayers will also declare your stand as the beloved of God the bible tells us that through Christ we have been accepted into the beloved of God, Ephesians 1:6. This inspirational morning prayers will soak you more and more into the presence of God. I encourage you to always spend quality time every morning to pray this inspirational morning prayers, they more you appreciate the endless, excess and boundless love of God for you, the more you live in it and it lives through you to others. God bless your soul.

INSPIRATIONAL MORNING PRAYERS

- Father, I thank you for your endless and excess love in my life in Jesus name
- Father , I thank you for your practical manifestation of love in my life in Jesus name
- Father, I thank you for despite my imperfections your love for me is perfect in Jesus name
- Father, I thank you for despite my short comings your love never comes short in my life in Jesus name
- Father, I thank you for despite my gross unfaithfulness, your faithfulness is ever constant in my life in Jesus name
- Father, I appreciate your unusual love for me, if my body is full of mouths, it will not be enough to appreciate you.
- Father, I thank you for not treating me as I have deserved in Jesus name
- Father, I thank you for not paying me according to my own coin in life in Jesus name
- Father, I thank you for showing me mercy even when I clearly don't deserve mercy.
- Father, thank you for never abandoning me, even when I abandoned you on several occasions.
- Father, I thank you for being patient with me even when I am impossible to deal it
- Father, I thank you for understanding my frailty and my human weakness
- Father, I thank you for saving me by your grace (unmerited favour) and not by my own efforts
- Father, I thank you for sending your son Jesus Christ to die for my sins and save me from eternal destruction.
- Father, I thank you for giving me authority over all devils in the name of your Son Jesus Christ.

- Father, I thank you for sending the Holy Spirit into my life to help me live like Christ.
- Father, I thank you for making me more than conquerors in Christ Jesus
- Father, I thank you for the gift of righteousness that you have given me in Christ Jesus.
- Father, I thank you for my salvation in Jesus name
- Father, I thank you for this morning shall be great for me in Jesus name *(Use about five minutes to declare what you want to see this morning).*

Thank you Jesus for answering my prayers in Jesus name.

SIXTY DAILY MORNING PRAYER BEFORE WORK

Psalm 63:1-3: 1 O God, thou art my God; early will I seek thee: my soul thirsteth for thee, my flesh longeth for thee in a dry and thirsty land, where no water is; 2 to see thy power and thy glory, so as I have seen thee in the sanctuary. 3 Because thy loving-kindness is better than life, my lips shall praise thee.

Starting your morning with prayers, is the best way to kick start your day. God will only walk with those that invite Him into their hearts. Today we shall be looking at 60 daily Morning Prayer before work. We can also title it as daily Morning Prayer before school, for those of us who are students. The purpose for this prayers is to help you take charge of your day. Jesus said" every day has enough evil of its own" Matthew 6:34.

Therefore we must pray that the evil of each day shall not come near us and our loved ones. We must commit our days to God every morning in order for him to lead us to the right path. Psalm 91: 5, tells us that there are arrows that flies by that day, it will only take prayers to overcome those arrows. It could be arrows of failure, arrows of disappointment, arrows of sicknesses, arrows of death, and arrows of wrong business partners etc., which ever arrows the devil is targeting at you, you must return it back to him on the altar of prayers.

When we start our day with Morning Prayer, our strength is renewed, our day is secured as the host of angels walk with us. This daily Morning Prayer before work, will empower us with the grace of God to maximize our days. I encourage you this today, never leave your house without committing your ways to God, and always pray about everything to God, prayer is simply talking to God as one would talk to a friend. Commit your ways to Him and He will direct your path. When God is leading you, you will be unstoppable. No devil can ruin your day when you start it with Jesus. The reason I compiled up to 60 daily Morning Prayer is so that you will have more than enough things to pray about. When you hand over your mornings to Him in prayers, He takes care of the rest of your days. Today shall be a great day for you in Jesus name.

PRAYER POINTS

- Father, I thank you for waking me up this morning, in Jesus' name.
- O Lord, cause my whole heart to be at rest, trusting in You as I go about my day to day activities in Jesus name
- O Lord, keep me from leaning and relying on my own understanding and intelligence in Jesus name
- O Lord, deliver me from what seems right to me and deliver me to what is right to You in Jesus name
- O Lord, I pull down every imaginations and every high thing in my life that are not of You in Jesus name
- O Lord, purify my lips with Your holy fire in Jesus name
- O Lord, reveal to me those things that give my enemies advantage over me in Jesus name
- O Lord, let my fellowship with You become greater in Jesus name
- I draw upon heavenly resources today, in the name of Jesus.
- O Lord, engrave me to become the person You created me to be in Jesus name
- I surrender myself completely in every area of my life, in the name of Jesus.
- I stand against every satanic operation that will attempt to hinder my blessings today, in the name of Jesus.
- Satan, I refuse your involvement in my prayer life, in Jesus' name.
- Satan, I command you, to leave my presence with all your demons, in the name of Jesus.

- I bring the blood of the Lord Jesus Christ between me and you Satan in Jesus name
- Father Lord, open my eyes to see how great you are, in the name of Jesus.
- I declare that Satan and his wicked spirits are under my feet, in the name of Jesus.
- I claim the victory of the cross for my life today, in Jesus' name.
- Every satanic stronghold in my life, be dismantled by fire, in the name of Jesus.
- I put off all forms of weakness, in the name of Jesus.
- Lord Jesus, come into my life by fire. Break down every idol, and cast out every foe.
- Every wicked spirit planning to rob me of the will of God for my life, fall down die, in the name of Jesus.
- I tear down the stronghold of Satan against my life, in the name of Jesus.
- I smash every plan of Satan formed against me, in Jesus' name.
- I smash the stronghold of Satan formed against my body, in the name of Jesus.
- O Lord, let me be the kind of person that would please you.
- Holy Spirit, bring all the work of resurrection and Pentecost into my life today, in the name of Jesus.
- Every witchcraft power, I cast you into outer darkness, in the name of Jesus.
- I confound every stubborn pursuer, in the name of Jesus.
- I bind every power cursing my destiny into ineffectiveness, in the name of Jesus.
- I strike every evil power siphoning my blessing with chaos and confusion, in the name of Jesus.
- I nullify the incantations of evil spiritual consultants, in Jesus' name

- I turn the evil devices of household witchcraft upside down, in the name of Jesus.

- I render every local satanic weapon harmless, in the name of Jesus.

- I receive deliverance from the spirit of anxiety, in Jesus' name.

- I bind every spirit of mental stagnation, in the name of Jesus.

- I release myself from the power and authority of any curse, in the name of Jesus.

- I renounce any unholy covenants involving my life, in Jesus' name.

- I grab every stubborn problem and smash it against the Rock of my salvation, in the name of Jesus.

- I nullify every sacrifice to demons used against me, in Jesus' name.

- Every power cursing my destiny, be silenced, in the name of Jesus.

- I break the power of any incense burnt against me, in Jesus' name.

- Every serpentine spirit, go into the hot desert and be burned, in the name of Jesus.

- Let the blood of Jesus poison the roots of all my problems, in the name of Jesus.

- I go back to Adam and Eve on both sides of my bloodline, and I cut of every evil root, in the name of Jesus.

- I reverse every improper operation of body organs, in Jesus' name.

- Every evil contract working against my life, be rewritten by the blood of Jesus.

- I reverse every satanic calendar for my life, in the name of Jesus.

- Anything my ancestors have done to pollute my life, he dismantled now, in the name of Jesus.

- I refuse to be in the right place at the wrong time, in Jesus' name.

- I bind every negative energy in the air, water and ground working against me, in the name of Jesus.
- Anything from the kingdom of darkness that has made it their business to hinder me, I single you out right now and bind you, in the name of Jesus.
- I command every satanic opposition in my life to be bound with chains that cannot be broken, in the name of Jesus.
- I strip off all the spiritual armor of every strongman militating against my destiny, in the name of Jesus.
- I destroy the hold of every evil powers, standing on my way in the name of Jesus.
- I separate myself from evil today and forever in the name of Jesus.
- Lord Jesus, I thank you for the victory.
- I renounce any signing of my name over to Satan, in Jesus' name.
- I announce that my name is written in the Lamb's book of life, in the name of Jesus.
- Father, I thank you for answering my prayers in Jesus name.

THIRTY BEAUTIFUL MORNING PRAYER POINTS

Psalm 63:1:1 O God, thou art my God; early will I seek thee: my soul thirsteth for thee, my flesh longeth for thee in a dry and thirsty land, where no water is;

Glory be to God! We are in a new year. Seeking God early is the only way to command the affairs of your day. Only those who go on their knees before God early, enjoy early victories in the day. If you want to succeed as a Christian, you must always start your day with prayers. Today I have compiled 30 beautiful Morning Prayer points to kick start you on a platform of victory. This Morning Prayer will set the platform for divine intervention as you go about your fail activities.

Every day is full of good and bad things, we must pray that the bad things stay far from us and that the good come to us. The devil is always attacking Gods children daily, that is why this beautiful Morning Prayer points is timely. You must fortify yourself every day before you go out. You must ask the Holy Spirit to guide you and order your steps to the right places. You must pray for divine favour before everyone you meet on a daily basis, also you must ask for supernatural protection from all the attacks of the enemies. When you pray like this every morning, you have no choice but to walk in dominion over the devil.

I encourage you this day, never go out without fortifying yourself spiritually, the devil is not joking, he is out to destroy Gods children at any slight opportunity, this beautiful morning prayer points will serve as your daily spiritual fortification, as you pray it in faith, I see God crowning your days with His goodness and mercies. As you start your morning with Jesus, you shall always end your day with testimonies. God bless you.

PRAYER POINTS

- Father, I thank you for this beautiful morning, I slept and I woke up, because you preserved me. Thank you Jesus.

- Father, I thank you for all the benefits that you have loaded for me this day in Jesus name.

- Father, I thank you for your mercies that is new every morning in my life in Jesus name.

- Father, I commit all my activities in your able hand today in Jesus name.

- Father, grant me supernatural speed to achieve all my targets today in Jesus name.

- Father, order my steps by the help of your Holy Spirit this morning in the name of Jesus.

- Shield me oh Lord, from the arrows that flies by day in Jesus name

- I declare that no weapon fashioned against me this day shall prosper in Jesus name

- I declare that I shall be favoured by all who set their eyes on me today in Jesus name.

- The hand of God is upon my life, therefore I declare that I shall succeed today in Jesus name.

- All the plans of the enemy to frustrate my day today is hereby rendered null and void in Jesus name

- I declare that I shall never have a better yesterday in my life in Jesus name

- I declare that I am blessed in my going out this morning in Jesus name.

- I release the angels of the Lord to Go ahead of me this day and make all the crooked paths straight in Jesus name.

- Jesus is the captain of my ship, therefore I shall not sink in Jesus name

- Every satanic resistance on my path to greatness, be destroyed in Jesus name

- Every mountain standing between me and my breakthroughs be destroyed by fire in Jesus name.
- Every plans of household enemies to frustrate me in life in render their plans useless in Jesus name
- I declare that I am walking in favour in Jesus name
- I declare that I am walking in miracles in Jesus name
- I declare that my life is surrounded with signs and wonders in Jesus name
- I declare that I am far above principalities and powers in Jesus name.
- Every witchcraft power trying to stop me is destroyed forever in Jesus name
- Everyone that bless me is blessed by the Lord in Jesus name
- Everyone that curses me I cursed by God in Jesus name
- All those who have dug pits for me to fall into this day, they shall all be buried in that pit in Jesus name.
- Father, fight all my battles this morning in Jesus name.
- Father, I declare that my morning is blessed in Jesus name
- I declare that my entire day is blessed in Jesus name.
- Father, I thank you for answering my prayers in Jesus name.

THIRTY EARLY MORNING PRAYER POINTS FOR SPIRITUAL WARFARE

Psalms 5:2-3 hearken unto the voice of my cry, my King, and my God: for unto thee will I pray. 3 My voice shalt thou hear in the morning, O Lord; in the morning will I direct my prayer unto thee, and will look up.

Spiritual warfare are waged in the early morning hours of the day. What we usually call midnight prayers, are often early morning prayers. The following biblical events happened at midnight/early hours of the day. Israel was delivered from Egypt in the early hours of the day, Exodus 12:31-51, the king is Assyria was defeated in the midnight, 2 Kings 19:35, Peter was delivered from chains in prison in the night Acts 12:5-17, Paul and Silas was delivered in the midnight, Acts 16:25-34. You see, all this deliverance happened in the early hours of the day, if you want to see the hand of God in your life, you must engage in early morning prayers for spiritual warfare. You must arise in the midnight and wage spiritual warfare, you must attack the kingdom of darkness in prayers as you take your deliverance by force.

As a believer, the best time to call on the name of your God for deliverance is in the midnight or early morning. The psalmist understood the importance of seeking God early, Psalms 63:1-2. When we arise in the early hours of the day to wage spiritual warfare, heaven hears, and answers, this is because every day is like a blank slate, waiting for us to fill it with our declarations, when you begin to declare what you desire to see in a particular day, heaven begins to take note and see that it comes to pass in your life. My prayer for you is that you receive the grace to take advantage of this early Morning Prayer points for spiritual warfare. Pray this prayer points at midnight and expect to see the powers of darkness in your life totally destroyed in Jesus name.

PRAYER POINTS

- I take authority over this day, in the name of Jesus.

- I draw upon heavenly resources today, in the name of Jesus.
- I confess that this is the day the Lord has made; I will rejoice and be glad in it, in the name of Jesus.
- I decree that all the elements of this day will cooperate with me, in Jesus' name.
- I decree that these elemental forces will refuse to cooperate with my enemies this day, in Jesus' name.
- I speak unto you the sun, the moon and the stars: you will not smite me and my family this day, in Jesus' name.
- I pull down every negative energy, planning to operate against my life this day, in Jesus' name.
- I dismantle any power that is chanting incantations to capture this day, in the name of Jesus.
- I render such incantations and satanic prayers over me and my family null and void, in the name of Jesus.
- I retrieve this day from their hands, in the name of Jesus.
- Spirit of favour, counsel, might and power, come upon me, in Jesus' name.
- I shall excel this day and nothing shall defile me, in the name of Jesus.
- I shall possess the gates of my enemies, in the name of Jesus.
- The Lord shall anoint me with the oil of gladness above others, in the name of Jesus.
- The fire of the enemy shall not burn me, in the name of Jesus.
- My ears shall hear good news; I shall not hear the voice of the enemy, in the name of Jesus.
- My future is secured in Christ, in the name of Jesus.
- God has created me to do certain definite services. He has committed into my hands some assignments which He has not committed to anybody else. He has not created me for nothing. I shall do good. I shall do His work. I shall be an agent of peace. I

will trust Him in whatever I do and wherever I am. I can never be thrown away or downgraded, in the name of Jesus.

- There will be no poverty of body, soul and spirit in my life, in the name of Jesus.

- The anointing of God upon my life gives me favour in the eyes of God and men, all the days of my life, in Jesus' name.

- I shall not labour in vain, in the name of Jesus.

- I shall walk in victory and liberty of the spirit every day, in the name of Jesus.

- I receive the mouth and the wisdom, which my adversaries are not able to resist, in Jesus' name.

- Every battle in the heaven lies, be won in favour of the angels conveying my blessings today, in Jesus' name.

- My Father, everything which you have not planted in the heaven lies, let it be uprooted, in Jesus' name.

- O Lord, let the wicked be shaken out of my heavens, in the name of Jesus.

- O sun, as you are coming out today, uproot every wickedness targeted at my life, in the name of Jesus.

- I programme blessings into the sun for my life, in the name of Jesus.

- O sun, I have risen before you, cancel every evil programme, projected into you against my life by wicked powers, in the name of Jesus.

- You this day, you will not destroy my prosperity, in the name of Jesus.

- Thank you Jesus.

3 AM WARFARE PRAYER POINTS

2 Corinthians 10:3 For though we walk in the flesh, we do not war after the flesh: 10:4 (For the weapons of our warfare are not carnal, but mighty through God to the pulling down of strong holds;) 10:5 Casting down imaginations, and every high thing that exalted itself against the knowledge of God, and bringing into captivity every thought to the obedience of Christ;

Spiritual battles are real, and they are won or lost on the altar of prayers. Though we live in the flesh, but we do not war after the flesh, that is to say, that our battles in life are not with our fellow men, but they are with spiritual forces, forces fighting our lives and destiny. Every child of God that must overcome in life must learn how to wage spiritual warfare against these dark forces. Today we shall be engaging in 3am warfare prayer points. This warfare prayer points will empower you to overcome the strongholds of life and emerge a victor in your area of calling.

Why 3am warfare prayer points? Warfare prayer points are best done in the midnight or in the early hours of the morning that is between the hours of 12am and 3am. The devil and his agents always operate in the night, while men slept (See Matthew 13:25). If you must overcome the devil and his agents, you must be given to warfare prayers at midnight. When witches and wizards wants to attack you, they do it at the dead of the night, they know that mankind is at his most vulnerable state at night, the send there arrows at midnight hours. So if you want to take the battle to the camp of the enemies, you must also rise up at midnight hours to engage in warfare prayer points. This 3am warfare prayer points will empower you to overcome the power of darkness fighting your destiny.

PRAYER POINTS

- Every doorway and ladder to satanic invasion in my life, be abolished forever by the blood of Jesus.
- I loose myself from curses, hexes, spells, bewitchments and evil domination, directed against me through dreams, in the name of Jesus.
- You ungodly powers, release me by fire, in the name of Jesus.
- All past satanic defeats in the dream, be converted to victory, in the name of Jesus.
- All tests in the dream, be converted to testimonies, in Jesus' name.
- All trials in the dream, be converted to triumphs, in Jesus' name.
- All failures in the dream, be converted to success, in Jesus' name.
- All scars' in the dream, be converted to stars, in Jesus' name.
- All bondage in the dream, be converted to freedom, in Jesus' name.
- All losses in the dream, be converted to gains, in Jesus' name
- Any water spirit from my village or in the place of my birth, practicing witchcraft against me and my family, be amputated by the word of God, in the name of Jesus.
- Any power of witchcraft, holding any of my blessings in bondage, receive the fire of God and release it, in the name of Jesus.
- I lose my mind and soul from the bondage of marine witches, in the name of Jesus.
- Any witchcraft chain binding my hands and feet from prospering, break and shatter to pieces, in the name of Jesus.
- Every arrow, shot into my life from under any water through witchcraft, come out of me and go back to your sender, in the name of Jesus.
- Any evil material, transferred into my body through contact with any agent of darkness roast by fire, in the name of Jesus.
- Any evil done against me so far through witchcraft oppression and manipulation, be reversed by the blood of Jesus.

- I bind every witchcraft controlling and mind-blinding spirit, in the name of Jesus.
- I cast out every witchcraft arrow affecting my senses (sight, smell, taste, hearing), in the name of Jesus.
- I command every witchcraft arrow to depart from my body now in Jesus name
- I have come to Zion, my destiny must change, in Jesus' name.
- Every power derailing my destiny, fall down and die, in the name of Jesus.
- I refuse to miss my destiny in life, in the name of Jesus.
- I refuse to accept satanic substitute for my destiny, in the name of Jesus
- Anything programmed against my destiny in the heaven lies, be shaken down, in the name of Jesus.
- Every power, drawing powers from the heaven lies against my destiny, fall down and die, in the name of Jesus.
- Every satanic altar, fashioned against my destiny, crack asunder, in the name of Jesus.
- O Lord, take away my destiny from the hands of men.
- I revoke every satanic ownership of my destiny, in Jesus' name.
- Satan, you will not settle down on my destiny, in Jesus' name
- Thank You Jesus.

MORNING DEVOTION: IT WILL DISGRACE YOU

Numbers 20:7-12

In Today's Morning Devotion, We shall be looking at the topic: IT WILL DISGRACE YOU.

To whom much is given, much is expected. Moses was ordained by God with great power and authority to lead His people into the Promised Land. He communicated with God, however denied him entry into Canaan because of one act of disobedience. Moses even went to God to beg for forgiveness of sin, and asked for permission to enter into the Promised Land. God told Moses," do not ever pray about this again". Again and again Moses had made intercession for Israel before God, and God had forgiven their sins. But in this instance, Moses was not even allowed to intercede for himself! God was specific in His instruction. " speak to the Rock", but he struck the Rock instead because of his anger. God said what Moses did was an act of unbelief and as well as failure to demonstrate His holiness before His people (Num.20:12). If one disobeys God's laws and having been rendered in his likeness, succumbs to temptation, one denies God in himself.

We have learnt from the bible what consequences await those who contravene it. Identify any area of weakness in your life, those things that have become be setting sin to you and take them to Jesus today. He will deliver you. If you however decide to hold on to it, it will disgrace you

LET US PRAY

1. God, purge my heart from every deposit of disobedience, in the name of Jesus
2. O Lord, give me grace to be your faithful Stewart in Jesus name
3. Anointing of disobedience upon my life, dry up now in the name of Jesus
4 Satan, shall not use me against God in Jesus name
5. I refuse to walk out of the will of God in Jesus name
6. My Lord and my God, teach me to obey you, in Jesus name
7. Power to live for God till the end; overshadow my life in Jesus name
8. Thank you Jesus for answered prayers

Bible Reading: Zephaniah 1-3
Memory Verse: *Isaiah 1:19:19*
> *If you will only obey me, you will have plenty to eat.*

30 POWERFUL MORNING PRAYER POINTS

O God, thou art my God; early will I seek thee: my soul thirsteth for thee, my flesh longeth for thee in a dry and thirsty land, where no water is;

30 powerful Morning Prayer points to help you start your day with Jesus. As a born again believer, we must recognize the importance of committing our day to God before leaving our houses. Everyday carries its own blessings and divine opportunities. It is therefore important that we commit our ways to God and also ask for the leading of the Holy Spirit as we go out every morning.

The purpose of compiling this 30 powerful Morning Prayer points is to help believers engage in effective prayers every morning before leaving the house. This prayers cuts across every area of your endeavours therefore it is advised that you pray it every morning before going out.

PRAYER POINTS

1). Oh Lord, I thank you, as I go out this morning, let me encounter supernatural favour with my destiny helpers in Jesus name.

2). Oh Lord, as it was in the days of Moses and the children of Isreal in the wilderness, let your pillar of cloud continually go with me every morning in Jesus name.

3). Oh Lord, deliver me from all the arrows that fly by day and noon in Jesus name

4). Oh Lord, arise and defend me from all those who will attempt to attack me this morning in Jesus name.

5). Oh Lord, go ahead of me today and take away every obstacles that will make today a living hell for me in Jesus name.

6). Oh Lord, provide for me my daily bread today in Jesus name.

7). Oh Lord, lead me not into temptation and deliver me from all evil today in Jesus name.

8). I decree that those who lay in wait for me throughout the night in order to strike in the morning shall themselves not see the sunshine of today in Jesus name.

9). Oh Lord! Today, send your angels for the protection of my life in Jesus name.

10). I declare that any appointment of death targeted towards me today whether sent to me or through another person, be disappointed and torn to pieces in Jesus name.

11). Oh Lord, raise men and women to help me meet all my needs today in Jesus name.

12). Oh Lord, as I raise up the offering of praise to you this morning, let your rain of blessings follow me throughout today in Jesus name.

13). Oh Lord, Let me see favour today in Jesus name.

14). Lord, through the help of the holy spirit in me, guide my steps as I face the challenges of the day in Jesus name.

15). Oh Lord, sanctify me for the work of today in Jesus name.

16). Oh Lord, grant me my heart desires for today in Jesus name.

17). Oh Lord, may the disappointments and failure of yesterday not repeat itself in my life this morning in Jesus name.

18). I declare that I shall see your strange works and your strange acts in my life this morning in Jesus name.

20). Oh Lord, do not judge me by the measure of my faith today. Let the rain of your unmerited favour and mercy fall on me as I leave my house in Jesus name.

21). as I wake up this morning, I shall wake with my glory and with songs of praises that overshadow all sadness in Jesus name.

22). Oh Lord! As I wake this morning, send help from heaven and my destiny helpers throughout today in Jesus name.

23).Oh Lord, cause me to see your grace this morning and lead me in the way that I should go today in Jesus name.

24). Oh Lord, be my defender against every trouble of today in Jesus name.

25). I prophesy to my life this morning that as I arise, every dead thing around my life, my family, my business and career comes back to life in Jesus name.

26). Oh Lord, thank you for your steadfast love that is new every morning in Jesus name.

27). I prophesied that all the plots against my life today shall backfire in Jesus name.

28). Father grant me supernatural wisdom for my activities this morning in Jesus name

29). Father I declare that all my journeys today shall be accident free in Jesus name.

30). I declare that I shall hear good news today, beginning from this morning in Jesus name.

Thank you Jesus.

PRAYER POINTS FOR DOUBLE PORTION BLESSINGS

Isaiah 61:7 for your shame ye shall have double; and for confusion they shall rejoice in their portion: therefore in their land they shall possess the double: everlasting joy shall be unto them.

No child of God is ordained to suffer shame and reproach. Every child of God is ordained to enjoy unlimited blessings in life. Today we are looking at prayer points for double portion blessings. This prayer points shall empower you to take by force everything the devil has stolen from your life and destiny. As you engage this prayers today, expect to see the hand of God upon your life, crushing every powers of darkness fighting your destiny. Double portion blessings is Gods will for all His children, this prayers will bring your own double portion in Jesus name.

When we talk about double portion blessings, what do we mean? This simply means God showering you with your harvest of blessings. It means God giving you a crown of glory for all the shame you have suffered. Job received a double portion blessings after the reproach that he suffered, Job 42:12. I don't know what you are going through today, I don't care who is mocking you today, but the God of double portion blessings will change your story in Jesus name. The Lord your God will shut the mouths of all your enemies in the name of Jesus Christ. You shall emerge victorious in the name of Jesus. These prayer points for double portion blessings will give you double restoration after the order of Job in the name of Jesus.

I encourage you to pray this prayers with faith and great expectation. Affliction is over in your life today in Jesus name.

PRAYER POINTS

1. I break every hold of witchcraft working against my life, in the name of Jesus

2. I command a change to all unprofitable situations in my life, in the name of Jesus

3. I command my battles and challenges to change to double portion blessings in Jesus name

4. Let every mountain of satanic confrontation be disgraced, in the name of Jesus

5. Let every mountain of impossibility be dashed to pieces, in the name of Jesus.

6. Let new wells spring up in my desert places, in the name of Jesus.

7. Oh Lord, bear me up on eagle's wings before my enemies, in the name Jesus

8. Oh Lord, anoint my eyes to see my divine opportunities, in the name of Jesus

9. I refuse to allow my past to influence my future negatively in the name of Jesus

10. Let every satanic battle confronting me fall apart, in the name of Jesus

11. I bind every strongman of financial embarrassment, in the name of Jesus.

12. I declare myself free from every plagues of the devil in the name of Jesus

13. I command all challenged areas of my life to produce testimonies now in the name of Jesus

14. Let the Spirit of Excellence manifest in every area of my life in the name of Jesus

15. Let the fear of me fill my enemies and let them panic at the sound of my name in the name of Jesus

16. My years shall not be in struggle but in prosperity, in the name of Jesus

17. Let the oppressors of my life and destiny drown in their own red sea, in the name of Jesus

18. I receive power to leap over every wall that the enemy has built, in the name of Jesus

19. Let the enemy fall into his own trap, in the name of Jesus.

20. Oh Lord, make my miracles invisible to my enemies, in the name of Jesus.

Thank you Jesus.

30 PRAYER POINTS FOR DIVINE CONNECTION

Psalms 60:11 give us help from trouble: for vain is the help of man.

Divine connection is God linking you to men and women that are relevant to your glorious destiny in Life. No one succeeds in life without help. Everyone needs the help of God, and God helps people through destiny helpers, He sends you the right people that will catapult you to where He has ordained you to be. Today we shall be looking at 30 prayer points for divine connection. This prayer points will attract supernatural help your way in Jesus name. As you engage this prayers, any demonic veil shielding you from your destiny helpers will be erased and removed forever in Jesus name.

Divine connection is real; every child of God is entitled to divine connection. There are men and women that you need to connect with in life in order to get to the top in Life. This prayer points for divine connection is not a man dependent prayer, it is a God dependent prayer, and it is a prayer we pray when we depend on God to connect us to our destiny helpers. No man can help you, only God can. Man is created to disappoint, he does not have the capacity to be faithful that is why if you depend on man for help, you will be familiar with disappointments. On the other hand, when your faith is absolutely dependent on God, He will lead you to the right people to work with. This prayer points for divine connection is what you need to connect to the right people. Jesus prayed to God all through the night before He was led to pick the 12 apostles, Luke 6:12. As you pray this prayers today, God is going to lead you to your divine helpers in Jesus name.

PRAYER POINTS

1. Holy Spirit, do the work of deliverance in my life today, in the name of Jesus.

2. Every destiny destroyer, assigned against me, disappear, in the name of Jesus.

3. Blood of Jesus, remove every curse in my life, in the name of Jesus.

4. Holy Spirit, connect me with my destiny helpers in the name of Jesus.

5. Fire of God, explode in my life, in the name of Jesus.

6. Every satanic veil covering me from my destiny helpers, be burnt by fire in the name of Jesus.

7. Anointing for prosperity, fall upon me now, in the name of Jesus.

8. Grace for divine connection locate me now!!! In the name of Jesus.

9. Every demonic authority fighting my destiny be destroyed now! in the name of Jesus.

10. O Lord, let the heaven open upon me now, in the name of Jesus.

11). Oh Lord, I have no one here on earth that will help me. Help me for trouble is near. Deliver me so that my enemies will not cause me to weep in Jesus name.

12). Oh Lord, do not delay in helping me, send me help speedily and silent those who mock me in Jesus name.

13). Oh Lord! Do not hide your face from me at this trying period. Be merciful to me my God, arise and defend me in Jesus name.

14). Oh Lord, show me your loving kindness, raise helpers for me at this period of my life in Jesus name.

15). Oh Lord, a hope deferred makes the heart sick, there lord send me help before it's too late for me in Jesus name.

16). Oh Lord! Take hold of shield and buckler and stand up for my help in Jesus name.

17). Oh Lord, help me and use me to help others in Jesus name.

18). Oh Lord, fight against those who are fighting against my destiny helpers today in Jesus name.

19). Oh Lord, because of the glory of your name, help me on this issue (mention it) in Jesus name.

20). Oh Lord, from today, I declare that I shall never lack help in Jesus name.

21. I have come to Zion, my destiny must change, in Jesus' name.

22. Every power derailing my destiny, fall down and die, in the name of Jesus.

23. I refuse to miss my destiny in life, in the name of Jesus.

24. I refuse to accept satanic substitute for my destiny, in the name of Jesus

25. Anything programmed against my destiny in the heavenliest, be shaken down, in the name of Jesus.

26. Every power, drawing powers from the heavenliest against my destiny, fall down and die, in the name of Jesus.

27. Every satanic altar, fashioned against my destiny, crack asunder, in the name of Jesus.

28. O Lord, take away my destiny from the hands of men.

29. I revoke every satanic ownership of my destiny, in Jesus' name.

30. Satan, you will not settle down on my destiny, in Jesus' name. Thank You Jesus.

PRAYER POINTS TO SAY BEFORE GOING FOR INTERVIEW

Today we will be dealing with prayer points to say before going for interview. There are hundreds of thousands of graduates in Nigeria who don't have job. Quite a number of job adverts fly across the internet on daily basis, but only few people are able to secure an employment from the job adverts. There are graduates who has lost count on the number of times they have heard this popular sentence, you may go now we will get back to you.

While it is important to study hard and make necessary preparations before the interview, one must not neglect the place of prayer. There are quite a number of jobs that you one can't get by means of qualifications except for grace. The grace of God is such that long time existing protocols will be broken just because of an individual. When you understand the concept of grace, you will hold it dear and never take it for granted again.

When you want to go for an interview, it is important to know that you are not the only one who has got the invite for the job interview. Also, you are going there to meet a panel of expert who will be studying you with four eyes so they can know your area of strength and weaknesses. In a situation where there are multiple options to select from, you can't afford to be the less. You just have to be the best that you can be at that time. Meanwhile, the scripture says in the book of Isaiah 45:2 'I will go before you and make the crooked places straight; I will break in pieces the gates of bronze And cut the bars of iron. Regardless of the number of people who have been called out for the interview, when God goes before you, success is sure.

So many youths have experienced nothing but rejection all their life. Even in places where it seems their education qualification match the requirements needed for the position, they still meet disappointment. God is about to turn your story around. He will give you victory over rejection. I decree as an oracle of God, in every place that you have been rejected, may the hands of God change your story in the name of Jesus. Before you go out for that interview, use the following Bible verse and prayer points for prayers and expect miracle like never before.

PRAYER POINTS:

- Lord, I thank you for a new day. This is the day the lord has made and I will rejoice and be glad in it. I commit this day into your hands lord, let it end with joy in the name of Jesus.

- Father Lord, the scripture says for by grace you have been saved through faith. And this is not your own doing; it is the gift of God. Lord I pray that you will bless me with the gift of your grace in the name of Jesus.

- Father Lord, just like Esther saw favour in the sight of the king, I pray that you will let me find grace in the sight of the interviewee in the name of Jesus. I pray that your spirit will go before me and level up all the mountains that may want to arise against me at the interview in the name of Jesus.

- The scripture says if any man lacks wisdom let him ask from God that gives liberally without blemish. Lord, I pray that you will bless me with the wisdom to answers correctly in the name of Jesus. I pray that you will guard my tongue with diligence and grace to express myself with thoroughness and charm in the name of Jesus.

- Lord, regardless of my education qualification, I pray that your grace will speak for me today in the name of Jesus. As I open my mouth to utter words in response to the questions that I will be asked, I pray that you will bless the words of my mouth with power in the name of Jesus.

- Lord God, for it has been written in the book of Psalm 5:12 For You, O LORD, will bless the righteous; with favor you will surround him as with a shield. Lord I pray that you bless me with favour in the name of Jesus. I pray that your favour will be eminent in my life as I step out for the interview in the name of Jesus.

- Lord, I pray that among everyone that will be coming for the interview today, I pray that your mercy will single me out in the name of Jesus. I pray for the grace that will make me a moon among stars, I pray that you equip me with the grace in the name of Jesus.

- Lord, I come against every form of mistake in my response today. I rebuke the spirit of mistakes in the name of Jesus. I come against every demon of rejection today in the name of Jesus. The scripture says the sea saw it and fled, Jordan drew back, the young mountains, the little hills like lambs. I pray that problem will flee from my way in the name of Jesus.

- I pray that among people that will be called for the job, I pray that grace that will count me worthy to be on the list in the name of Jesus.

- For it has been written in the book Proverbs 16:7 when a man's ways please the LORD, He makes even his enemies to be at peace with him. Lord, I pray that you will make my way please you in the name of Jesus. I pray for divine favour in the sight of the interviewers in the name of.

- For it has been written, the heart of man and king is in the hands of the lord and He direct it like the glow of waters. I pray that you will touch the heart of the interviewers in the name of Jesus. I pray for a divine attraction of their hearts towards me in the name of Jesus.

5 PRAYER POINTS TO PRAY FOR YOUR HOME

Today we will be dealing with prayer points to pray for your home. It is so important to commit our families to God. The one who is able to do all things well for us. Prayer is the Power house of a Christian. As believers and individuals established in families, we cannot afford to be unserious with our prayer lives, it's our commitment to the Father.

We make things happen in the place of prayer, something's remain the same because we don't pray, and we pray to see changes in some things also. It's our responsibility to live a prayerful life. Parents should pray together, children should be taught how to pray by praying with the family and by extension, individually.

In this section, we are praying for spiritual growth, protection, abundance, progress and peace.

PRAYER POINTS

- Father in the name of Jesus Christ, thank you for your mighty hand upon us, we are your people and you are our God, Father we are grateful, blessed be your name Lord in the name of Jesus Christ.
- Father in the name of Jesus, thank you for your steadfast love and kindness over us, we glorify your Holy name, we exalt your majesty, thank you Blessed Redeemer in Jesus name.

PRAYER OF ABUNDANCE

- According to the Word of the Lord in Psa. 1:3, which says, "And he shall be like a tree planted by the rivers of water, that bringeth forth his fruit in his season, his leaf shall not wither and whatsoever he does shall prosper." In the name of Jesus, I pray for the abundance of God upon my home, my husband, my wife and my children, whatsoever we lay our hands upon; we shall prosper in the name of Jesus.

- According to Psa. 20:4 which says, "May He give you the desire of your heart and make your entire plan succeeds." Father in the name of Jesus, I commit my home into your able hands, for every of our projects and plans, we pray for success, we pray that you grant my husband, my wife and my children the desires of our heart according to your will in the name of Jesus Christ.

- According to Phil. 4:19 which says, " And my God will meet all your needs according to the riches of his glory in Christ Jesus" Father in the name of Jesus Christ, every need in my home is met, we have all that we need to eat, to drink and to give in the name of Jesus.

- According to Psa. 23:1 says, 'The Lord is my Shepherd; I shall not want.' Heavenly Father, you are the Shepherd in my home, we rest on you, we hope and trust in you that you shall be our supplier, whenever needs arise in my home, you will make them available for us in the name of Jesus Christ.

PRAYER OF PROTECTION

- According to 2 Tim. 1:7 which says 'For God hath not given us the Spirit of Fear; but of Power, and of love, and of a sound mind.' Father in the name of Jesus, I curse the spirit of fear in my home from the root, I decree your mighty hand of love shall rest upon my home and we are endured with the Spirit of sound mind and love from above in the name of Jesus Christ.

- Psa. 17:8 says, 'Keep me as the apple of your eye; hide me in the shadow of your wings' Father in the name of Jesus Christ, I commit my home into your hands Lord, I pray that you keep my wife, my husband, my children safe all day, all night, we pray that you keep us under the shadow of your wings in the name of Jesus Christ.

- Psa. 23:4 says, 'Even though I walk through the darkest valley, I will fear no evil, for you are with me; your rod and your staff, they comfort me.' Father in the name of Jesus, no matter what is going on in my environment, even when there is evil in the land, evil shall not come near me in the name of Jesus, we will fear no evil for you are our Rod and Staff, in the mighty name of Jesus.

- From Psa. 91: 1-7 Father in the name of Jesus, my wife dwells in your secret place, my husband's dwells in your secret place my children rest in your secret place, my home is protected from the snare of the fowler and from the noisome pestilence, my home is protected from all forms of evil, all forms of harm, all forms of accidents because we dwell in safety by you day in, day out in the name of Jesus Christ.

PRAYER OF PEACE

- Father in the name of Jesus Christ, I decree the Peace of God in my home on every side in the name of Jesus. My marriage experiences your peace in the name of Jesus Christ, the devil will have no place in my home in the name of Jesus Christ.

- Isa. 26:3 says, "You will keep him in perfect peace, whose mind is stayed on you, because he trusts in you."

- Heavenly Father, I pray in the name of Jesus Christ that you will keep my home in perfect peace as we trust in you in the name of Jesus Christ. Peace on every side, in the life of my husband, my wife, my children and to an extension, my relatives in the name of Jesus Christ.
- Col. 3: 15 says 'And let the Peace of God rule in your ears, to which also you were called in one body; and be thankful'
- Father in the name of Jesus Christ, the Peace and serenity from above will rule in my home by your power in the name of Jesus Christ.

PRAYER FOR SPIRITUAL GROWTH

- Eph. 1:18 says, 'The eyes of your understanding being enlightened; that ye may know what is the hope of his calling, and what the riches of the glory of his inheritance in the saints'.

- Father in the name of Jesus Christ, the eyes of our spirit man is continually flooded with light, we know what is ours in Christ, we are not tossed to and fro, and we know what our inheritance is in Christ daily in Jesus name.

- Psa. 69:9 which says, 'For the zeal of thy house has eaten me up, and the reproaches of them that reproached thee are fallen upon me' Father in the name of Jesus Christ, let the zeal of your kingdom fall upon my home heavily and make us tools for the expansion of your kingdom in the mighty name of Jesus Christ.

PRAYER OF PROGRESS

- Father in the name of Jesus, I decree progress in my business, promotion for my wife/husband and progress in the lives of my children in the name of Jesus.

- In my home, I come against every form of stagnation that might want to hold me down, my spouse and children, we are free from stagnation in the name of Jesus Christ.

- Heavenly Father I pray for all round favour in my home, for our business, career, favour in all of our endeavors, men see us and favour us, my children are favoured in Jesus Mighty name.

- Heavenly thank you because you always hear us, thank you for answered prayers in Jesus mighty name. Amen.

POWERFUL PRAYERS FOR EVERYDAY MIRACLES

Today we will be dealing with a powerful prayer for everyday miracles. Who doesn't want a miracle? A miracle is an event that happened when we least expected it. Have you ever been in a situation where all seemed to be working against you? Just when you think things could not get any better, help came from where you least expected.

The encounter between the widow of Zarephath and Prophet Elijah is nothing short of a miracle. The poor widow and her son were about to have their last food when the prophet came into their home. Elijah requested that the widow first prepare his meal. One thing we must understand about miracles is obedience. While we pray fervently for a daily miracle, it is also important that we learn how to obey given instructions. If the widow of Zarephath had not obeyed Elijah, she would not have been blessed so much. She prepared Elijah's meal, and just when she thought it was over for her, the Lord blessed her abundantly.

There are some of us that we have only experienced miracle maybe once or twice in our life. God is always set to perform his wonders in our lives each day. A daily miracle is such that you would not struggle to get things done; you would not suffer to obtain outstanding achievements. Even where others were rejected, you will be celebrated there. That is a miracle. Most importantly, as we enter the New Year, we would need all the miracles we can get.

The novel Covid-19 is currently increasing in virtually all countries of the world. Many countries are already thinking of going on a second lockdown as they expect the second wave of the virus to hit more than its first. We need God's miracle to live a comfortable life in the year 2021. I decree by the authority of heaven; God will always supply your needs in the name of Jesus. In every area of your life that you need a miracle, may the power of God Almighty surprise you in the name of Jesus.

PRAYER POINTS:

- Lord Jesus, I thank you for the gift of life, I thank you for the grace that you have bestowed upon me to see another beautiful day that you have made, Lord let your name be exalted in the name of Jesus.
- Father Lord, with all the evil happening around, the outbreak of a virus, economic meltdown, father, I pray that your grace will sustain me in the name of Jesus.
- Lord Jesus, in every way that my life deserves a miracle, father, I pray that you will perform your wonders in the name of Jesus. In every place that I have been rejected, Lord the grace to be celebrated, let it fall upon me in the name of Jesus.
- Lord Jesus, I pray that you will look down from heaven with mercy, and you will heal all my diseases in the name of Jesus. I pray that your power and grace will touch every area of my life that needs touching in the name of Jesus.
- Lord Jesus, you have carried all our infirmities to the cross. I pray that you will heal all my infirmities in the name of Jesus. Lord, every form of disease or sickness is taken away in the name of Jesus.
- Lord Jesus, I pray for a divine Job. The scripture says my God will supply all my needs according to his riches in glory through Christ Jesus. I speak my letter of employment into manifestation in the name of Jesus. In every organization that I have been rejected, the grace that will announce me for excellence let it come upon me in the name of Jesus.
- Lord, I pray that in every way that I need directions and guidance for my life, I pray that you will grant them to me in the name of Jesus. I refuse to run my life based on my human knowledge; I refuse to run my life based on trial and error; I pray that you will

endow me with your spirit that will teach and nurture me, let it come upon me in the name of Jesus.

- Lord Jesus, the scripture says When Israel went out of Egypt, the house of Jacob from a people of strange language; Judah was his sanctuary, and Israel his dominion. The sea saw it and fled: Jordan was driven back. The mountains skipped like rams, and the little hills like lambs. I decree by the power of the Most High, every problem in my way should flee in the name of Jesus. The fire of the Holy Ghost destroys every hindrance standing against me.

- Lord, I pray for marital Success. My kids are blessed in the name of Jesus. I decree in every way that I have been looking up to God for miracle concerning my marriage; God settle it right now in the name of Jesus.

- Lord Jesus, in every way that I'm looking up to you for blessings, father, I pray that you bless me abundantly in the name of Jesus. I decree for open heaven of blessing. I decree that your blessings fall on me in the name of Jesus.

- Father Lord, in every way that my life needs your favor, Lord favor me in the name of Jesus. When I face the east, let me find favor. When I face the west, let your blessing follow me when I go North, let your grace be with me in the name of Jesus.

- For it has been written, I will have mercy on whom I will have mercy on and compassion on whom I will have it upon. Father Lord, I pray that among those that will have your mercy Lord count me worthy in the name of Jesus.

- Lord Jesus, in every way that my life needs your miracle, whether concerning my health, marriage, career, or education, Lord, I pray that you will perform your wonders in the name of Jesus. God, you are a miracle-working God. I pray that the miracle of the eleventh hour happens in my life today in the name of Jesus.

- Lord Jesus, every day of my life, let your hands be upon me in the name of Jesus.

CHAPTER 2

PRAYER FOR CONCEPTION AND CHILDREN
PRAYERS FOR PARENT AND CHILDREN

Today we will be dealing with prayers for parents and children. The journey of every child into this world starts with the parent. It starts with a man and woman coming together as husband and wife. The scripture makes us understand that when God created man, he told them to be fruitful and multiply the earth. Marriage is a step towards fulfilling this mandate of multiplication. Meanwhile, the duty of every parent goes beyond producing offspring. They owe their children a duty of care both physically and spiritually.

The scripture in the book of Psalm 127:4 says like arrows in the hand of a warrior, So are the children of one's youth. The parents must take care of the children. Train your child in the way to go so that when he grows, he will not depart from it. This was the instruction of God to every parent. Parents have no excuse for laxity in bringing up their children. Let's take into account the life of Eli the Priest.

Eli was perfect as a priest, but he was so perfect as a parent. He was busy with things of the lord that he forgot to bring his children in the right way. The consequence was, however devastating as such, that Eli lost his life. While the parents owe their children a duty of care, the children also owe their parents a duty of care. Children must endeavor to obey their father and mother so their days may belong. It also goes beyond obeying their parents. They must endeavor to take care of their aged parents when they can no longer fend for themselves.

Within this prayer article, we will give several prayers that every parent and child must pray to God. We have only come to this world once. We must live right and fulfill our purposes.

PRAYER POINTS FOR PARENTS

- Father Lord, I thank you for the gift of children that you have blessed me with. May your name be highly exalted in the name of Jesus?

- Lord Jesus, I pray that you will give me the wisdom and understanding to raise my children in the right way. I refuse to fail on my children. I pray that you will equip me with the understanding to bring them up in the right way they should be in the name of Jesus.

- Lord, I pray that you will provide everything needed to bring up my children in the name of Jesus. The scripture says God will supply all my needs according to His riches in glory through Christ Jesus. I ask that you supply them all in the name of Jesus.

- Lord, the scripture says, here am I and the children whom the LORD has given me! We are for signs and wonders in Israel from the LORD of hosts, who dwells in Mount Zion. I pray that my children will signs and wonders for good in the name of Jesus.

- Lord, I pray for protection over my children. For it has been written, the eyes of the Lord are always upon the righteous, and his ears are always attentive to their prayers. Father Lord, I pray that your protection will always be upon my children, everywhere they go on this planet's surface, and your eyes will always be upon them in the name of Jesus.

- Lord, I pray that death shall not have power over my children in the name of Jesus. The death that take young people when they are at the corridor of greatness, I come against it over the lives of my children in the name of Jesus.

- I ask that the angel of the Lord will equip my children with the right power to overcome the devil in the name of Jesus. They shall not be swayed away from the lord in the name of Jesus. I ask for the grace for them to stand with you to the end; lord release it upon them in the name of Jesus.

- Lord, I know bad company corrupt sound mind, I ask for divine separation between my children and every evil friend that the enemy has programmed for them in the name of Jesus. Just like you cause a separation between Abraham and Lot, I pray that you shall separate my children from every evil friend in the name of Jesus.

- Lord, I come against every destiny hunter over my children. I curse them to death in the name of Jesus. Every arrow that destiny hunter has planned to shoot into my children's lives to kill their destiny, I pray that such arrow will not hit them in the name of Jesus.

☐

PRAYER POINTS FOR CHILDREN

- Father Lord, I thank you for the gift of life, I thank you particularly for the family you made me come through, I thank you for my mother and father, I thank you for how far you have helped them, may your name be highly exalted in the name of Jesus.

- Father Lord, I pray that you will help me to remain an excellent child to my parent and my community in the name of Jesus. I refuse to become a tool in the hands of the enemy to tarnish the image of my parents in the name of Jesus. I shall not become an object of ridicule to God and my parents in the name of Jesus.

- Lord, I pray that you will continue to bless my parents beyond measures. I ask that every of their heart desires shall be fulfilled in the name of Jesus. The scripture says the expectations of the righteous shall not be caught off, and I pray that their heart desires and every good thing they expect from the Lord shall be fulfilled in the name of Jesus.

- Lord, I pray that you shall bless my parents will good health and you will preserve their lives to witness my good deeds in the land of the living. I pray that they shall not be found wanting when it's time for them reap the fruits of their labour. This I pray in the name of Jesus.

PRAYER FOR CHILDREN'S SALVATION

Today we will be dealing with prayer for children's salvation. Train up a child in the way he should go: and when he is old, he will not depart from it.

We would be praying for our children. Glory to God this cuts across every individual, couples with children and expectant couples, singles who are looking forward to settling down as well. Irrespective of our status, we have one thing in common as Believers which is Christ.

We should not be so concerned about our children's pursuit in education, their future ambitions, their feeding, well-being and all that pertains to them that we forget to take responsibility for their Spiritual upbringing.

To abandon our children to external influence would do more harm than good. Taking a good look at the society we live in today. Times are changing and technology keeps evolving rapidly. We come across parents who are shocked at their children's behavioral pattern and wonder how and where they might have come across such.

As God empowers us in businesses and grants us career success on the long run, that we bear fruits financially, how they grow up, what they know, what they're being taught from home lies upon us.

They should not be left out during morning devotion. Talk to them about Jesus. Get them children Bible materials. Let them come to know God from home. The effect of this that, when there's a solid foundation, where children can strongly point to the love of God being taught and seen between their parents, nothing will be able to shake the foundation of the knowledge they have.

Values form in their hearts. Parents ought to teach godly values that would leave indelible mark on them. It forms how they choose their friends in school, it forms how they respond to ungodliness on the outside. Why? Because they have been trained and taught from home.

We can never run out of what to teach. There are Bible Personalities to study, to examine and learn from. King David, for example, let him get to know who that Bible personality is. These are conversations that could come up in the car, back from school, during their break time, after meals etc. It does not become a thing as there is never a time for such discussions, tiny bits here and there are seeds you plant in their hearts that would germinate into fruits, on the long run. They should not be asked outside the home who Esther is from the Bible and they are blank. In teaching and praying, we are setting our children on the right pedestal to go through life with boldness because they are equipped. JESUS should never be a strange name to children. The Bible records that Jesus welcomed children during his incarnate ministry.

Mark 10:13-16 And they brought young children to him, that he should touch them: and his disciples rebuked those that brought them.14 But when Jesus saw it, he was much displeased, and said unto them, Suffer the little children to come unto me, and forbid them not: for of such is the kingdom of God.15 Verily I say unto you, Whosoever, shall not receive the kingdom of God as a little child, he shall not enter therein.,16 And he took them up in his arms,, put his hands upon them, and blessed them.

Let them get to know that Jesus loves them, that He cares about them. Teach them to know that Jesus would always care for them every day. John 3:16,"For God so loved the world, that he gave his only begotten Son, that whosoever believeth in him should not perish, but have everlasting life.

Teach them about the works of Jesus and how saved their soul is in believing what He did for them. The Bible says that Faith comes by hearing and hearing by the Word of God. It is the Word they hear that they will be inclined to. *Acts 4:12, "Neither, is there salvation in any other: for there is none other name under heaven given among men, whereby, we must be saved." Teach children about Salvation.*

Matt.18:3-4 And, Verily I say unto you, Except ye be converted, and become as little children, ye shall not enter into the kingdom of heaven.4 Whosoever therefore shall humble himself as this little child, the same is greatest in the kingdom of heaven.

Jesus Christ speaking here was explaining that the hearts of children can be so tender and simple unlike the adults who might infuse rigidity into accepting the Goodness of Our Lord Jesus Christ. The child's mind from birth is a clean slate. The responsibility is on us to put in the work, talk to them about Jesus and the Love of the Father.

The strength to do all that is needed for us as Parents and intending Parents, the Lord will grant unto us in Jesus Name.

That is why it is important to pray for them. Prayer works. As we pray, we see remarkable results. Halleluiah.

PRAYER POINTS

- Father we thank you because over us, your goodness and your Mercy endures forever.
- Father we thank you for your unfailing love over our families, thank you because nothing can separate us from the love of the Father, in Jesus name.
- Father in the name of Jesus, we pray over our children, we declare the blessings and wisdom of God upon them in the name of Jesus.

- Heavenly Father, we thank you for the blessings of wonderful children that we have received from you in Jesus name.

- Father we pray that our children will come to know you better, day by day.

- Father we pray for wisdom for our children, we pray that they will make the right choices, do the right thing at the right time in Jesus name.

- Father we pray that you help them to grow in the knowledge of you every day as their desire and zeal to know you increases daily in Jesus name.

- Father in the name of Jesus, we pray that the hearts of our children are yielded to you, they respond to your love correctly in Jesus name.

- Heavenly Father we pray that our children are delivered from bad influences, evil association and ungodly company. They make the right choice of friends at each state of their lives in Jesus name.

- Father Lord we pray for every word taught, the Spirit of God will impart it upon their hearts in Jesus name.

- Father Lord, let Christ be continually formed in the lives of our children in the name of Jesus.

- Father we thank you for every seed that has proceeded and will proceed out of our wombs, we thank you because they are yours, thank you because you take charge of their lives from beginning to the end in Jesus mighty name.

DAILY PRAYER FOR MY CHILDREN

Today we will be dealing with daily prayer for my children. The scripture says children are the heritage of God, they are gifts and blessings of God unto their parents. The enemy knows that God always deposits some talents and gifts in the lives of children when they are born that is why the enemy is always at alert to attack any child. As parents, you do not only owe your children a duty of care by buying things for them, you always owe them a duty of prayer. The Success of every child lies in the hands of his/her parents. When there is a laxity in the place of prayer for the children, the enemies will not be too far to strike.

Let's take the life of Samuel as a case study. Before Hannah had Samuel, she was a barren woman. She was mocked for being barren and it really took a heavy turn on her. She resulted in praying for the fruit of the womb, Hannah never stopped praying until she got the result of her prayers and years of waiting. Meanwhile, even before Samuel was born, Hannah had made a covenant to God that if her shame and reproach is taken away and she conceived, the child will serve the Lord. Hannah was a typical fire branded mother who knows that the child she carries is a covenant and she never stopped praying for her child. The devil could have manipulated the destiny of Samuel if Hannah had relaxed in the place of prayer. I pray by the authority of heaven that the enemy will not have power over your children.

The children of Eli are a very good example of a manipulated destiny, their father was a priest but the children missed it. Eli was so carried away with priesthood duties that he forgot the care that he owed his children, the devil gained access into their lives and the end of them was a familiar history. Unfortunately, they didn't fall alone, they went down with their father, the great priest, Eli. This means that when we fail in our duty to pray for our children as parents, the enemy will strike us through the children we failed to pray for. For as many that are reading this prayer guide, I pray that the enemy will not have access to the life of your children in the name of Jesus. I counter the plans and agenda of the enemies concerning your children by the blood of the lamb, and I decree that the counsel of God alone will stand concerning your children in the name of Jesus.

Always remember that the success or failure of your children is in your hands as parents. When you fail to pray, the enemy will make a prey of your children. I decree that the devil will never make prey of your children in the name of Jesus.

PRAYER POINTS

- Lord Jesus, I come before today because of the children you gave me, as they will be going out today, I pray that your protection will be upon them. Said the eyes of the Lord are always upon the righteous and his ears are always attentive to their prayers. Lord Jesus, I pray that your eyes will be upon them in the name of Jesus. I decree that your hands of protection will upon my children even as they go out today in the name of Jesus.

- For it has been written that let no man trouble me because I carry the mark of Christ. I decree that as my children will be setting out today, they shall not be troubled. Whatever power or gang up of enemy against them is broken in the name of Jesus. You have promised in your word that I and my children are for signs and wonder, I pray that you will begin to manifest your glorious wonders in the lives of my children in the name of Jesus. No weapon fashion against my children will prosper in the name of Jesus.

- Lord Jesus, I pray over the destiny of my children, I decree that the enemies shall not power over it in the name of Jesus. Lord, every evil seer that has seen the brightness of my children and has decided to cause their lights to dim, I pray that you will render such enemy useless in the name of Jesus. Lord Jesus, every evil gang or meeting that is against the growth and development of my children, I scatter such gathering in the name of Jesus. Lord arise and let your enemies be scattered, let this who rise against my children in judgment be condemned in the name of Jesus.

- From henceforth, I pray that everything that my children lay their hands upon shall prosper in the name of Jesus. Those that are still in school, I for wisdom knowledge, and understanding for them to make exploit, I pray that you will give it to them in the name of Jesus. You are the creator of all thing through the source of light and wisdom, you are the founder of all things, and I decree that the light of your understanding will illuminate the darkness of my children's understanding, you will open their heads to assimilate faster in the name of Jesus.

- I pray for my children that have already ventured into the labor force, I pray that everything they lay their hands upon shall prosper in the name of Jesus. In every that they have been rejected, I decree that the mercy of the most high will go and announce them for success in the name of Jesus.

- Father Lord, what shall it profit a man that gains the whole world but lose his soul. The scripture recorded it that there is nothing that can be used for the exchange of a lost soul. I pray for my children that you will give them the grace to stand with you to the end, come what may, they will be steadfast in your presence in the name of Jesus.

PRAYER PARENTS SHOULD SAY FOR THEIR CHILDREN IN UNIVERSITY

Job 1:5 And it was so, when the days of their feasting were gone about, that Job sent and sanctified them, and rose up early in the morning, and offered burnt offerings according to the number of them all: for Job said, It may be that my sons have sinned, and cursed God in their hearts. Thus did Job continually.

Many parents don't know that it is important to always pray for their children in Colleges, Universities, Polytechnics and other tertiary institutions. Most times, all they do is pray for protection for their children when they are off to school and only remember to pray for them when they are about writing examination.

As much as it is important to pray for your children when they are writing exams, it is also very important to always pray for them daily. In the University, there are different type of people from different works of life, Little wonder, it is called a Universal City, it is a place where culture, belief and spiritual norms of most child is being melted down by evil friend causing them to adopt a new culture different to the one that you have brought them up with.

Have you not heard cases of some child turning from normal into strange when they gain admission into school, they started acting strange or start having a defiant behavior. They have been I influenced by another strong dominating character stronger than the one you trained them with. Also, some children are fortunate to meet good friends in school that will change them from bad to good. You will just discover that a child that barely pray for 10 minutes start praying well and constantly building up their relationship with God.

As parents, we owe our children a duty of prayer, the tertiary institution is a testing ground for all the pieces of training that you have given them since they were kids. This is because they will be coming home only once in a while, they will begin to spend most of their time in school, hostels or off-campus. Little wonder, the Bible says train up your child in the way of the Lord so that when he grows he won't depart from it. But it is not enough to just train them in the way of the Lord and leave them to face the trouble and challenges of life alone all by themselves, you as parents should make sure your altar of prayer for them keeps burning all the time.

A quick trip into the scripture just to establish how long an evil counsel can go in the life of a child. 2nd Samuel 15:31 Then someone told David, saying, "Ahithophel is among the conspirators with Absalom." And David said, "O LORD, I pray, turn the counsel of Ahithophel into foolishness!" It was the counsel of Ahithophel that helped Absalom take the throne away from David. David as a parent understands the power of evil counsel, instead of praying for a miracle to happen, he rather prayed that the counsel of Ahithophel become foolishness, which God granted. Lo and behold, David was able to take the throne again.

You as a parent must be able to design the life of your children in school through prayers, the type of friends they will keep, the hall of residence that they will stay, the lecturers that will take them.
We have highlighted some prayers that you should say for your children in the University and other tertiary institutions.
PRAY FOR WISDOM, KNOWLEDGE, AND UNDERSTANDING
The university is not a joking center. If a parent should capitalize on the fact that my child is very brilliant in secondary, he will surely do well in the institutions, well that may not be correct for all schools. The scripture made us understand that there is a spirit that will come upon a man, a spirit that will teach him in all workmanship, a spirit that reveal hidden things unto him, a spirit that will bring to his remembrance all that he has been taught in class and all that he read too.

The spirit of God is more powerful than Google, it searches all things, even to the deepest and innermost part. Ask God to grant your child His spirit. The spirit of God brings wisdom knowledge and understanding.

PRAY THAT THE PRESENCE OF GOD BE UPON YOUR CHILD

Armed with enough information from our article on how to pray, we mentioned that when praying, we should pray with the word of God. Be strong and steadfast! Do not fear nor be dismayed, for the Lord, your God, is with you wherever you go. (Joshua 1:9) Your first prayer should be that the presence of God should go with that child. When the presence of God goes with a man, protocols are broken, evil counsel does not stand, bad friends, do not come near such an individual. Remember the scripture in the book of Psalm 114 that talked about when is real were leaving Egypt. The scripture says Isreal was the sanctuary and Judah was the Lord's dwelling place. The subsequent verses talked about the Sea saw them and flees, how river Jordan was driven back. All of that was made possible because the presence of God Almighty went with the Israelites.

Of all our prayers as parents, we must endeavor to always seek that the presence of God Almighty goes with them.

PRAY THAT THE PROTECTION OF GOD BE UPON THAT CHILD

The scripture says no evil shall befall us nor come near our dwelling place. There is no doubt that the world is presently a hostile environment, with killings, implications, cultism and other vices happening every day. Many parents might even be scared to allow their children to go to school. A prayer of protection will go a long way. The eyes of the Lord is always upon the righteous and his ears are always attentive to their prayers. Pray that the protection of God Almighty is upon your child in that school.

30 PRAYERS FOR CHILDREN'S SUCCESS

Isaiah 8:18 Behold, I and the children whom the LORD hath given me are for signs and for wonders in Israel from the LORD of hosts, which dwelled in mount Zion.

Every caring parent will always desire the success of their children. A successful child will always bring joy to the parents. Today we shall be engaging in prayers for children's success. This prayers will empower our children with the spirit of excellence that will cause them to excel in all areas of their life. As a parent, I encourage you to pray this prayers with all your heart today and expect to see the glory of God radiate in the lives of your children in Jesus name.

Our Children need prayers, especially in this fast generation where both good and bad information are at our finger tips. We must raise our children in the way of the Lord, if we want to see them excel in life. We must point them in the direction of the Lord, if we want to see them succeed. A lot of parents today are too busy for their children, some of them are busy with their work, struggling to make ends meet, it's OK to work hard to take care of family, but we must understand that if our children fail us, there won't be any family to take care of, and all our efforts would have been wasted.

We must ask God for grace to raise our children in the way of the Lord that is why this prayers for the success of our children is timely. We must create time to pray for our children, we must ask God to reveal Himself to them even as children. I believe that as we engage in this prayer points today, our children shall make us proud in Jesus name.

PRAYER POINTS

- Father, thank you for children are your heritage and your reward in Jesus name.
- Father, I cover my children by the blood of Jesus

- Father, order the steps of all my children to the right direction in life in Jesus name
- Father, Let the angel of the Lord always protect my children from danger in Jesus name
- Father, let your wisdom rest upon my Children in the name of Jesus
- Father, arrest them as your arrested Saul who is known as Paul in Jesus name.
- Use my children mightily for your great purpose in Jesus name
- Father, lead not my children into temptation but deliver them from all evil in Jesus name
- Father, I separate my children from every ungodly influence in Jesus name
- Father, let your mercy prevail over judgment in the life of my children in Jesus name.
- You . . . (mention the name of the child), I dissociate you from any conscious or unconscious demonic groupings or involvement, in the name of Jesus.
- In the name of Jesus, I release my children from the prison of any strongman in Jesus name
- Let God arise and all the enemies of my home be scattered, in the name of Jesus.
- Every evil influence and activity of strange women on my children be nullified, in the name of Jesus.
- As I pray this prayer points for family let chains begin to fall from the hands of my children, my husband, wife, parents, and relatives in the mighty name of Jesus.
- As I pray this prayer points for family, because I am a son/daughter of Abraham, connected to the seed of David, let all that I have lost and all that have been captured from me be released, and recovered in double portion.

- Fire of the living God, like you, consumed Sodom and Gomorrah, consume the captors of my marital life as I pray this prayer points for my family.

- As the grave could not hold back Lazarus at the sound of the voice of Jesus. Because I am joint-heirs with Christ, as I pray this prayer points for family let the grave release everything it has held back from my family.

- Let there be mysterious earthquakes and tornados that will shake the foundations of where the success of my family has been kept as I pray this prayer points for family.

- Because there is nothing too hard for the lord that I serve, I declare that from today, every impossible situation that has been associated with my family is destroyed in the mighty name of Jesus.

- I command the angels that were assigned to me to comb the length and breadth of the earth and release every wealth that has the name of my family on it and deliver it to me today.

- Today, my family and I are delivered from the snare of the fowler and every noisome pestilence.

- This year every strong man from my father's house or every strong woman from my mother's side who have locked my children in the room of failure open the gates and be disgraced in the name of Jesus.

- Hailstones and fire for above begin to fall on every philistine that have captured, tortured, and ruptured the finance of my helpers today.

- Because Jesus, my savior, and lord, was resurrected and delivered from the hold of death after three days. I decree that within three days, my family and I are delivered from every strange spirit of death, haunting and trailing my family.1corinthians.

- Every territorial force of delay that is responsible for tying my children and me to a spot, thereby preventing us from being promoted and elevated, let thunder from heaven scatter them in the name of Jesus.

- Let the arrows from God begin to slay the guardians of every strange calabash, causing childlessness in my family.
- In the name of Jesus, let every principality and power standing on the way to my Children's success, wealth, and financial dominion this year be destroyed and put to shame.
- Let ballistic missiles visit the camp of any strange man or strange woman that has captured the hearts of my children and let them be bound with the same chains by which my family was bound.

30 PRAYER POINTS FOR OUR CHILDREN'S PROTECTION AND DELIVERANCE

Psalm 91:10. There shall no evil befall thee, neither shall any plague come nigh thy dwelling.

Today we are looking at 30 prayer points for our children's protection and deliverance. As parents, the importance of praying for the protection of our children can never be overemphasized. Our children needs our prayers now more than ever. We must always commit our children to the Lord continually as the grow up in this last days. The evil in the world today is at its peak, and the target is the younger generation. A lot of children join the bandwagon of sin as the grow into teenagers and young adults. We as parents must recognize that we are not capable of changing our children by our own power, we need the interventions of God in the life of our children and the only way to get Gods attention is to pray.

This prayer points for our children's protection and deliverance will destroy every plots of the enemy to lead our children astray. It will help them overcome sins that control the children of their age. As we pray for them the Holy Spirit will empower them to say no to evil and a! Ways say yes to Jesus. As we engage in this prayers, our children will not be victims of peer pressure. They will not be deceived by the Devil, instead they will find themselves in God. I encourage you to pray this prayer by faith, and expect a miracle as you pray in Jesus name.

30 PRAYER POINTS FOR OUR CHILDREN'S PROTECTION AND DELIVERANCE

- Father, thank you for children are your heritage and your reward in Jesus name.
- Father, I cover my children by the blood of Jesus
- Father, order the steps of all my children to the right direction in life in Jesus name

- Father, Let the angel of the Lord always protect my children from danger in Jesus name
- Father, let your wisdom rest upon my Children in the name of Jesus
- Father, arrest them as your arrested Saul who is known as Paul in Jesus name.
- Use my children mightily for your great purpose in Jesus name
- Father, lead not my children into temptation but deliver them from all evil in Jesus name
- Father, I separate my children from every ungodly influence in Jesus name
- Father, let your mercy prevail over judgment in the life of my children in Jesus name.
- Father deliver my children from sin in Jesus name.
- Father, I pray for the salvation of all my children, make there road rough till the find Jesus in Jesus name
- Father, I cause confusion between my children and any satanic influence in their life in Jesus name.
- Father, if my child is a satanic influence to other children, separate him from those innocent children and deliver him for me in Jesus name.
- Father deliver my child from formication
- Father deliver my child from adultery
- Father deliver my child from stealing
- Father deliver my child from smoking
- Father deliver my child from lying.
- Father deliver my child from drug addiction
- Father deliver my child from pornography
- Father deliver my child from bad company
- Father deliver my child from cultism
- Father deliver my child from disobedience
- Father deliver my child from laziness

- Father deliver my child from evil manipulation
- Father deliver my child from the hand of the enemies
- Father deliver my child from satanic strongholds
- Father , make me proud of my children in Jesus name
- Father, prosper my children and cause them to fulfill destiny in you in Jesus name
- Father thank you for answering my prayers.

DELIVERANCE PRAYERS FOR OUR CHILDREN'S PROTECTION

Psalm 127:1-5 Except the Lord build the house, they labour in vain that build it: except the Lord keep the city, the watchman waked but in vain. 2 It is vain for you to rise up early, to sit up late, to eat the bread of sorrows: for so he gives his beloved sleep. 3 Lo, children are a heritage of the Lord: and the fruit of the womb is his reward. 4 As arrows are in the hand of a mighty man; so are children of the youth. 5 Happy is the man that hath his quiver full of them: they shall not be ashamed, but they shall speak with the enemies in the gate.

Our children need our prayers now more than ever. The devil is after the younger generation because they are the future. We must stand in the gap to protect our children from the manipulations of darkness. In this last days, a lot of children are under the attack of the devil, a larger percentage of crimes we see in our world today are committed by underage kids. We must pray for the protection and preservation of our children in this end times. Today I have compiled some deliverance prayers for our children's protection. This deliverance prayers will guide us as we intercede for our children's protection. As we pray this prayers today God will deliver our children from all evil in Jesus name.

The bible tells us to train our children in the way they should go, (Proverbs 22:6)that way is the way if the Lord. If we want to see our children succeed and make us proud, we must raise them according to biblical standards. This deliverance prayers for our children's protection will break the hold of satanic bondage over our children, as we pray for them no matter how far gone they are, God will bring them back swiftly in Jesus name. I encourage you today, never stop praying for your children, they need your prayers and not your wishes, like Job, (Job 1:5), always stand in the gap for them in prayers and God will save them and you will become a proud parent in Jesus name.

DELIVERANCE PRAYERS FOR OUR CHILDREN'S PROTECTION

- Father, I rebuke every spirit, contrary to the Spirit of God, preventing me from enjoying my children, in the name of Jesus.
- I bind every spirit blinding their minds from receiving the glorious light of the Gospel of our Lord Jesus Christ, in the name of Jesus.
- Let all spirits of stubbornness, pride and disrespect for parents flee from their lives, in the name of Jesus.
- Father, destroy everything in my children preventing them from doing your will, in the name of Jesus.
- Every curse, evil covenant and all inherited problems passed down to my children, be cancelled and washed by the blood, in the name of Jesus.
- Prophecy over your children, call them by name one by one and speak into their future
- Let every association and agreement between my children and my enemies be scattered, in the name of Jesus.
- My children will not become misguided in life in Jesus' name.
- I release my children from the bondage of any evil domination, in the name of Jesus.
- Let all evil influences by demonic friends clear away, in the name of Jesus.
- You . . . (mention the name of the child), I dissociate you from any conscious or unconscious demonic groupings or involvement, in the name of Jesus.
- In the name of Jesus, I release my children from the prison of any strongman in Jesus name
- Let God arise and all the enemies of my home be scattered, in the name of Jesus.

- Every evil influence and activity of strange women on my children be nullified, in the name of Jesus.
- Thank God for answers to your prayer.

20 BIBLE VERSES ABOUT CHILDREN'S OBEDIENCE

The word of God is filled with bible verses about children's obedience. As believers, we must train our children in the way they should go, which is in the way of the Lord. These bible verses will guide us as we teach our children to be God fearing and to be like Christ. The world is filled with all manner of information, we must consciously educate our children in the way of the Lord in order for them not to go astray.

So I encourage you to read this bible verses, meditate on them, recite them to your children and encourage them to have those scriptures at heart. They word of God is the gateway to a glorious life, I see these bible verses about children's obedience helping you as you raise your children in the way of the Lord. Read and be blessed.

20 BIBLE VERSES ABOUT CHILDREN'S OBEDIENCE

1. Ephesian 6:1-4 Children, obey your parents in the Lord: for this is right. 2 Honor thy father and mother; which is the first commandment with promise; 3 that it may be well with thee, and thou mays live long on the earth. 4 And, ye fathers, provoke not your children to wrath: but bring them up in the nurture and admonition of the Lord.
2. Colossians 3:20: Children, obey your parents in all things: for this is well pleasing unto the Lord.
3. Matthew 15:4: For God commanded, saying, Honor thy father and mother: and, He that corset father or mother, let him die the death.
4. Proverbs 1:8: My son, hear the instruction of thy father, and forsake not the law of thy mother:
5. Exodus 20:12: Honor thy father and thy mother: that thy days may be long upon the land which the Lord thy God giveth thee.
6. Deuteronomy 21:18-21: If a man have a stubborn and rebellious son, which will not obey the voice of his father, or the voice of his mother, and that, when they have chastened him, will not hearken unto them: 19 Then shall his father and his mother lay

hold on him, and bring him out unto the elders of his city, and unto the gate of his place; 20 And they shall say unto the elders of his city, This our son is stubborn and rebellious, he will not obey our voice; he is a glutton, and a drunkard. 21 And all the men of his city shall stone him with stones that he die: so shalt thou put evil away from among you; and all Israel shall hear, and fear.

7. Proverbs 22:6: Train up a child in the way he should go: and when he is old, he will not depart from it.

8. Proverbs 13:24: He that spareth his rod hateth his son: but he that loveth him chasteneth him betimes.

9. Colossians 3:21 Fathers, provoke not your children to anger, lest they be discouraged.

10. Proverbs 13:1-25: A wise son heareth his father's instruction: but a scorner heareth not rebuke. 2 A man shall eat well by the fruit of his mouth: but the soul of the transgressors shall eat violence. 3 He that keepeth his mouth keepeth his life: but he that openeth wide his lips shall have destruction. 4 The soul of the sluggard desireth, and hath nothing: but the soul of the diligent shall be made fat. 5 A righteous man hateth lying: but a wicked man is loathsome, and cometh to shame. 6 Righteousness keepeth him that is upright in the way: but wickedness overthroweth the sinner. 7 There is that maketh himself rich, yet hath nothing: there is that maketh himself poor, yet hath great riches. 8 The ransom of a man's life are his riches: but the poor heareth not rebuke. 9 The light of the righteous rejoiceth: but the lamp of the wicked shall be put out. 10 Only by pride cometh contention: but with the well advised is wisdom. 11 Wealth gotten by vanity shall be diminished: but he that gathereth by labour shall increase. 12 Hope deferred maketh the heart sick: but when the desire cometh, it is a tree of life. 13 Whoso despiseth the word shall be destroyed: but he that feareth the commandment shall be rewarded. 14 The law of the wise is a fountain of life, to depart from the snares of death. 15 Good understanding giveth favour:

but the way of transgressors is hard. 16 Every prudent man dealeth with knowledge: but a fool layeth open his folly. 17 A wicked messenger falleth into mischief: but a faithful ambassador is health. 18 Poverty and shame shall be to him that refuseth instruction: but he that regardeth reproof shall be honoured. 19 The desire accomplished is sweet to the soul: but it is abomination to fools to depart from evil. 20 He that walketh with wise men shall be wise: but a companion of fools shall be destroyed. 21 Evil pursueth sinners: but to the righteous good shall be repaid. 22 A good man leaveth an inheritance to his children's children: and the wealth of the sinner is laid up for the just. 23 Much food is in the tillage of the poor: but there is that is destroyed for want of judgment. 24 He that spareth his rod hateth his son: but he that loveth him chasteneth him betimes. 25 The righteous eateth to the satisfying of his soul: but the belly of the wicked shall want.

11. Exodus 21:15: And he that smiteth his father, or his mother, shall be surely put to death.

12. Ephesians 6:2: Honour thy father and mother; which is the first commandment with promise;

13. Ephesians 6:4: And, ye fathers, provoke not your children to wrath: but bring them up in the nurture and admonition of the Lord.

14. Deuteronomy 5:16.16 Honour thy father and thy mother, as the Lord thy God hath commanded thee; that thy days may be prolonged, and that it may go well with thee, in the land which the Lord thy God giveth thee.

15. Proverbs 23:13-14: Withhold not correction from the child: for if thou beatest him with the rod, he shall not die. Thou shalt beat him with the rod, and shalt deliver his soul from hell.

16. Psalm 19:8: The statutes of the Lord are right, rejoicing the heart: the commandment of the Lord is pure, enlightening the eyes.

17. Proverbs 29:15 the rod and reproof give wisdom: but a child left to himself bringeth his mother to shame.

18. Proverbs 22:15: Foolishness is bound in the heart of a child; but the rod of correction shall drive it far from him.

19. Proverbs 10:1 the proverbs of Solomon. A wise son maketh a glad father: but a foolish son is the heaviness of his mother.

20. 1 Timothy 5:1-4: Rebuke not an elder, but entreat him as a father; and the younger men as brethren; 2 the elder women as mothers; the younger as sisters, with all purity. 3 Honour widows that are widows indeed. 4 But if any widow have children or nephews, let them learn first to show piety at home, and to requite their parents: for that is good and acceptable before God.

TOP 10 PRAYERS FOR OUR CHILDREN'S FUTURE SPOUSE

Genesis 24:3-4: And I will make thee swear by the Lord, the God of heaven, and the God of the earth, that thou shalt not take a wife unto my son of the daughters of the Canaanites, among whom I dwell: 4 But thou shalt go unto my country, and to my kindred, and take a wife unto my son Isaac.

Every godly parent knows the importance of praying for their children. We live in a world that is fast changing, in this era, it is more important than ever that we pray for our children's future. Today we shall be looking at top **10 prayers for our children's future spouse.** Who your children marry will determine a great deal how their lives will turn out. We must pray fervently for our children's marriage. The world is filled with godless people, people without the fear of God, we must pray that such individuals don't come near our children. God's word encourages us to marry godly people. The bible says do not be yoked with unbelievers 2 Corinthians 6:14, when we pray this prayers for our children's future spouse, God will direct them to godly people who will love and cherish them, people who will help them reach their greatest potential in life and destiny.

Engage this prayers with faith. Pray passionately for your children's future spouse. If your children are happy, you will be happy, if they are doing well in their marriage, you will be glad. But if they are frustrated and depressed or worse still divorced, you will never be happy as a parent. This prayers for our children's future spouse will also deliver your children from sexual perversion, the spirit of homosexuality and lesbianism. As you pray for your children's future today, I see God blessing your children beyond measure in Jesus name amen.

TOP 10 PRAYERS FOR OUR CHILDREN'S FUTURE SPOUSE

- Father, I thank you because you alone are the perfect matchmaker.
- Father, send the God ordained man/woman you have preordained as my daughter's/son's husband/wife.
- Lord, divinely connect my children to their God ordained spouse in Jesus name.
- Lord, let the spouse of my children be a God fearing person who loves you wholeheartedly in Jesus name.
- Lord, establish the marital destiny of my children with your word in Jesus name.
- Father, let all satanic barriers keeping my children from meeting there God ordained spouse be dissolved, in the name of Jesus.
- Lord, send forth your warring angels to protect the marriages of my children in Jesus.
- Lord, I believe you have created my daughter/son for a special man/woman of God. Bring it to pass, in Jesus' name.
- I call forth the God ordained spouse of my children to connect with them now in the name of Jesus.
- I reject the provision of counterfeit spouse by the enemy in the life of my children in the name of Jesus.

13 POWERFUL PRAYERS FOR OUR CHILDREN'S PROTECTION

Psalm 127:3-5: 3 Lo, children are a heritage of the Lord: and the fruit of the womb is his reward. 4 As arrows are in the hand of a mighty man; so are children of the youth. 5 Happy is the man that hath his quiver full of them: they shall not be ashamed, but they shall speak with the enemies in the gate.

Children are God's heritage, we should be proud of our children, support them and also pray for them. We live in a world today where sin and evil is now part of everyday living. Many of the abominations of the past are now legalized in today's world. Therefore we must arise as parents and pray for our children. We must pray that they don't get entangled I the lifestyle of this sinful world, we must pray for the Love of God to find its way into their hearts, we must pray for their salvation. We must pray for the protection of our children from every satanic influence of this last days, the list of prayers for our children's protection is endless. That is why we have compiled 15 powerful prayers for our children's protection. This prayers will guide us as we pray for our Children.

PRAYER POINTS

- Oh Lord! I declare that my Children are for signs and wonders in Jesus name.
- Oh Lord, let there be love among my children in Jesus name.
- Oh Lord, may none of my children trouble me in Jesus name.
- Oh Lord! Every curse of hatred and blood shedding in my family are washed by the blood of the Lamb in Jesus name.
- Oh Lord, save my children, turn the hearts of my children to you fully from today in Jesus name.
- Oh Lord, for thy faithfulness sake, keep all my children safe and sound in Jesus name.
- Oh Lord, give my children obedient hearts, a willing spirit and give them the grace to serve you all the days of their lives in Jesus name.

- Oh Lord, do not let my children be influenced by evil in Jesus name.
- Oh Lord, give my children a heart of flesh, take away the heart of stone from them so that they will hear your word, understand it, receive it and live by it in Jesus name.
- Oh Lord! Have mercy on my children, deliver them from their sins in Jesus name.
- Oh Lord, give my children the understanding to live good lives in Jesus name.
- Oh Lord, don't let my children turn their back on your Word in Jesus name.
- Prov. 8:32 – Oh Lord, give my children the grace to keep your word so that they will be blessed throughout the days of their lives in Jesus name.
- Oh Lord, let the lifestyle my children bring great joy to my heart in Jesus name.
- Oh Lord, through my children, let many be brought to the knowledge of Jesus Christ in Jesus name.

5 PSALM VERSES TO PRAY FOR YOUR KIDS AT BEDTIME

Today we will be dealing with 5 Psalm verses to pray for your kid at bedtime. We live in a world where corruption is been seen as civilized at the detriment of our growth of our young ones. Daily, the social media screams out loud the need for parents to take full responsibility for the upbringing of their children and not leave them to the influence of strangers where we begin to pray at a later time because we refuse to do what is expected of us as and when due. See the scriptures below:

Psa. 127:3-4 says, "Children are precious to God, they are God's blessings to families. We often hear people pray for newlyweds that may their marriages be blessed with fruits. So when we have been blessed with these fruits, in as much as children are from God, the onus is on the parents to do right by the children by training them in the way they should go.

Proverbs 22:6 says, 'Train up a child in the way he should go; and when he is old, he will not depart from it.'

We cannot afford to be nonchalant about the growth and training of our children because if we don't train them at a very early stage, such children become issues of concern to the parents and they start running from pillar to post when it's already late. May it not be late for us in the name of Jesus?

Children who receive trainings from home make it easy for their teachers in school and these ones become useful and productive citizens in the society, so also on the flip side, the ones who have no trainings from home make it difficult for the teachers in school and affect the society negatively. We decide what we want for our children, either they would bring honor to us or otherwise, we need to actively participate in the spiritual upbringing of our children.

It is the one who prioritizes the things of God that can make time for children at bedtime. We should not be too busy going here and there making money to sustain our family that we neglect the spiritual aspect of our children's lives. So it begins with acknowledging the place of God in our homes, by the things we do, in our speech, is God seen in how we relate to one another, mother to father?

In what we give our ears to, if David isn't used to listening to ungodly songs from home, it sinks into his consciousness that there is something much better than what is outside. So it is a reflection of what is being done in the home that is seen in what occurs at bedtime. In cases where this is otherwise, we can make changes, we can start something, and it is never too late.

In this section we would be praying from the book of Psalm for our children at their bedtime.

PRAYER POINTS

- Father in the name of Jesus, we thank you for the gift of life that you give to us, we say blessed be thy name in the name of Jesus Christ.
- Father in the name of Jesus, we thank you for preserving the life of each member of our families, we say, may your name be highly exalted in the name of Jesus.
- Father in the name of Jesus, we thank you for your daily load us with benefits, we are grateful Lord for the daily provisions, for sustenance, for protection, blessed be your name in the name of Jesus Christ.
- Father, thank for the blessings of children, we thank you for blessing our marriages with beautiful children, your word says children are your heritage, we acknowledge your doings in our homes, be thou exalted in the name of Jesus Christ.
- Spa 3:5 says, 'I laid me down and slept; I awaked; for the Lord sustained me.'

- Father in the name of Jesus, my child sleeps well and arises in the morning hale and hearty by your grace in the name of Jesus Christ.

- Following the verse in Psa. 3. Father in the name of Jesus, let your shield of covering be over my daughters and sons tonight in the mighty name of Jesus Christ.

- In the name of Jesus, I pray that the enemies shall not smite my fruits tonight and beyond, the plans of the enemy over my sons and daughters will fail in the name of Jesus Christ.

- Psa. 4:8 says, 'I will both lay me down in peace, and sleep; for thou, Lord, only makes me dwell in safety'.

- Father in the name of Jesus, I commit my children into your hands, as they lay in bed tonight, they lay in safety by your power in the name of Jesus, you are our Rock, Help and Fortress, keep them safe by your mighty hand in the name of Jesus Christ.

- Psa. 42:8 says, 'Yet the Lord will command his loving-kindness in the daytime, and in the night His song shall be with me and my prayer unto the God of my life'.

- Father in the name of Jesus Christ, I pray that your hand shall be upon my children both in the day as they go about their activities and in the noontime as they lay their head to sleep in the name of Jesus Christ.

- Psa. 91:11 says 'For he shall give his angels charge over thee, to keep thee in all thy ways.' Father in the name of Jesus, I ask that your angels shall keep watch over my children, the angels of God will keep them in all their ways, as they lay their head to sleep in Jesus name.

- Father in the name of Jesus, I ask that every night my children lay down to sleep, the angels of God are released to keep a guard roundabout them in the name of Jesus Christ.

- Psa. 121:7 says, 'The Lord shall preserve thee from all evil: he shall preserve thy soul.'

- Father in the name of Jesus Christ, my children is preserved in your care when they sleep at night and in the day in the mighty name of Jesus.

- Heavenly Father, you are the keeper of Israel who neither sleeps nor slumbers, do I pray that your mighty hand will keep my children from harm, you will keep them in your care, and they will dwell in safety by you in the name of Jesus Christ.

- Father in the name of Jesus, I pray that you protect my children from the eyes of the evil one, you will protect them from the arrows that fly by day and night in the mighty name of Jesus Christ.

- Father, I thank you for you always hear us, blessed be your name in the name of Jesus Christ. Amen.

BEDTIME PRAYER FOR KIDS

Today we will be dealing with bedtime prayers for kids. Parents must engage their kids in bedtime prayer before they retire to bed. Due to the nature of the kids, they might not remember or attach importance to bedtime prayer. It is in the doing of the parent to ensure that they get used to it.

Bedtime prayer for kids can take different forms or patterns. It can be for protection against some unseen spirit in the middle of the night to possess little children. And also, it could be a pattern for teaching the child in the way of the Lord so that when they grow up, they will not depart from it. Many children have lost their destinies simply because their parents relaxed in the place of prayer. The scripture was not making a mistake when it said that Christians should pray without season.

The Bible made it known that the devil doesn't rest. It goes about like a hungry beast looking for whom to devour. And the thief doesn't come during the day when the house owner is actively awake. The thief will instead come in the night when he is sure that the house owner has gone to sleep—our prayers as a defense mechanism to protect us from the vices of the devil. I decree as God lives and his spirit lives, the enemy shall not have power over your kids in the name of Jesus.

Another important reason why we must engage the children in bedtime prayer is to fulfill the words of the Lord that train your child in the way he should go so that when he grows up, he won't depart from it. When we continuously engage our children in prayers, it will give them a sense of consciousness that prayer is an integral part of their existence. I pray that the enemy will not have power over your kids in the name of Jesus. The evil spirit of the devil that possesses the lives of young children will never come near your children in the name of Jesus.

From now on, I assign the Seraphim's of glory to take charge of your children; they shall guide and protect them in the name of Jesus. Study and use this bedtime prayer for kids, and you are sure to protect the lives of your children.

You must let your kids repeat after you during the moment of prayer. Teach them how to pray so they can learn how to communicate with God.

PRAYER POINTS

- Dear Lord, I thank you for the success of my day. I thank you because you protected me all through the day. I appreciate you, Lord Jesus, because you stood by me every single minute of the day, and you did not allow any evil to befall. I thank you, Lord Jesus, for this, let your name be exalted.
- Father in heaven, I thank you for the lives of my parents, I thank you because you taught them to teach us in your way, I appreciate you because you never left them for a single moment, I thank you because you did not let any evil happen to them, let your name be exalted in the name of Jesus.
- Father Lord, I pray for the forgiveness of sin. In every way that I have childishly sin against you, in any way that I committed a crime and I do not know, Lord, please forgive me. For the sake and death of son Jesus Christ, I pray that you forgive me. And I promise never to do them again because your word says the sacrifices of the Lord are a broken spirit and a broken and a contrite heart will you not despise.
- Lord Jesus, I pray that as I'm going to sleep this night, I pray that your hands of protection be upon me. I protect myself from every arrow that flies by night. For the scripture says, children are a gift from God. As you have made me a gift from you to my parents, Lord, please do not allow the enemy to snatch away the gift in Jesus name.

- Father Lord, I come against every form of a scary dream that may contaminate the night. Every demonic dream that the enemy has staged to bring to my sleep to scare me, I destroy those dreams in the name of Jesus. The scripture says For God has not given us the spirit of fear but of son ship to cry Abba Father. Lord, I cry unto you today that you should destroy every evil dream from coming to my sleep tonight in the name of Jesus.

- Father Lord, for it, has been written that in for signs and wonders and the scripture also made to understand that I bear the mark of Christ so no one should trouble me. I come against every attack of the enemy with your power. I pray that you destroy their attacks in the name of Jesus.

- Lord Jesus, as I will be entering into a new day tomorrow, I sanctify tomorrow with your precious blood. I pray that every evil that is loaded is the blood of Jesus nullifies tomorrow. For it has been written that and they overcame him by the blood of the lamb and by the words of their testimonies. I decree in the name of Jesus that you will destroy every evil in tomorrow in the name of Jesus.

- Lord Jesus, I commit my education into your hands. I pray that you will give me the grace to excel excellently in the name of Jesus. And I decree into my future that it shall be great in the name of Jesus. In my sleep tonight, I want you to reveal deep things to me about myself. I decree that the heaven of revelations open for me in the name of Jesus. By tomorrow morning, let me have guts to glorify your name, in Jesus I pray.

PRAYER POINTS AGAINST BARRENESS

Today, we would be dealing with prayer points against barrenness. But let's do a quick study at the story of Simon Peter in Luke 5:1. And it came to pass, that, as the people pressed upon him to hear the word of God,, (2532) he stood, by the lake of Gennesaret, 2 And saw two ships standing by the lake: but the fishermen were gone out of them, and were washing their nets.3 And he entered into one of the ships, which was Simon's, and prayed him that he would thrust out a little from the land. And he sat down, and taught the people out of the ship.

Jesus was teaching and he needed to make use of Simon Peter's boat. If Peter had declined his request, maybe it would have been a different story today. What does that teach the believer today? Are we ready to make sacrifices?

Peter was all about making money and doing businesses but was he ready to give in what it takes to see fruitfulness in his business. Yes!!!
For us, are we ready to take that big step? Are we willing to sacrifice our time, energy and resources for God?
The Bible says that we've been created for His Pleasure. All that we have belongs to God. Why would we want to take it away from him? What have we that we've not received?
Let's read further.
Luke 5:4-5 now when he had left speaking, he said unto Simon, Launch out into the deep, and let down your nets for a draught.5 And Simon answering said unto him, Master, we have toiled, all the night, and have taken nothing: nevertheless at thy word I will let down the net.
Jesus speaking in verse 3 gave an instruction. That is to tell us that there's nothing we go through that God is not aware of. No situation or challenge catches God unawares. He knows about it all. There was an instruction. Do this. Do that.

It presents another question to the believer. Are you ready to follow God's instructions? In families, businesses, academics, as it were. Even after Jesus gave an instruction, Peter was still complaining.

Today, believers spend so much time complaining rather than doing what we are being told. Imagine being offered a solution and you're still complaining about the problem? Verse 5 of Luke 5 had it that Simon did as he was told. He said "nevertheless" When God speaks, nothing else matters. It doesn't matter what the situation looks like, it doesn't matter how long you've toiled and toiled, unfruitfulness is not of God. Halleluiah!

Our Father delights to see his Children proper on all sides, as we see in our opening verse above in Psa. 35:27

Believers, we are to shut our eyes to the challenges and focus on who can take care of those challenges. God is more able, responsible and ready to cater for our needs more than we ask Him. But are we willing to focus on God and stop complaining? Luke 5:5b "But at your word I will let down the nets." It means Peter had trust in the words of Jesus. For someone who wasn't a stranger to him, he knew Jesus words would not fail. He had been with him before then and had witnessed miracles by the hand of Jesus.

For believers, we say: But at thy word, I'll trust in you for marital fruitfulness, it doesn't matter what the Doctor reports, I hold onto what your Word reports. But at thy word, I'll trust in you for my business growth and expansion, it doesn't matter what the economy says.

But at thy word, I'll trust in you for career success, you'll make a way for me, on this path, I will be fruitful, and I'll prosper.

But at thy word, I'll trust in you for my academic progress, the odds will be in my favour. That's the language of the believer. When we know that we are of God, we know that God delights in our Prosperity and all round fruitfulness, it positions our utterance towards the situations around us.

Luke 5:6-9 and when they had this done, they enclosed a great multitude of fishes: and their net broke.7 and they beckoned unto their partners, which were in the other ship, that they should come and help them. And they came, and filled both the ships, so that they began to sink. 8 When Simon Peter saw it, he fell down at Jesus' knees, saying, Depart from me; for I am a sinful man, O Lord.9 For he was astonished,, and all that were with him, at the draught of the fishes which they had taken:

From these verses, we see that there was plenty, there was expansion, they were even astonished at the results, people saw and came to them.

Glory to God. God's Word never fails. So we are praying against barrenness in our land, our marriage, families, our academics, businesses, and careers and declaring fruitfulness on all sides.

PRAYER POINTS

- Heavenly Father we bless your name for you are Father to us. Thank you for your Grace and love over us in Jesus name.

- Father we thank you for your plan for us is of good and not of evil, thank you because you care for our needs, in Jesus name.

- Father we give you thanks because you're Will for us is to bear fruits on all sides and nothing shall be hindered in Jesus name.

- Father in the name of Jesus, every negative words spoken against us, we nullify their power in our lives in the mighty name of Jesus.

- Father we pray that every word of unfruitfulness sown by the complaining and nagging, they are cancelled and converted for fruitfulness in Jesus name.

- Father in the name of Jesus, every power that is not of God working against our fruitfulness in the lives of our children they are destroyed in Jesus name.

- Father we declare fruitfulness, in our businesses, our efforts shall yield increase in the name of Jesus.

- Father we pray for fruitfulness in our all of our projects, we will not fail, we shall bear fruits, our projects will success and yield fruits for us in Jesus name.
- Father in Jesus name, we pray for every one looking up to God for the fruit of the womb, in this year, they will carry their bundles of joy in the name of Jesus.
- Father, we come against barrenness in our marriages and we declare fruitfulness in the name of Jesus.
- Father, we declare plenty in every are if our lives in the name of Jesus.
- Father we pray, in our families, all through the year, our endeavors will yield fruits for us in the name of Jesus.
- Father we pray concerning our careers, you'll cause us to flourish in the name of Jesus.
- Father we pray that in our steps, plans, we plant seeds of growth and flourishing, so shall it be for us in the name of Jesus.
- Father in the name of Jesus, in our daily walk with you, our lives will bear fruits as we remain doers of your word in Jesus name.
- Father we pray that we shall bear fruits of righteousness unto your pleasing, we live as we ought to in Jesus name.
- Father we thank you because negative deeds are uprooted out of our lives in the name of Jesus.
- Father, we thank you for the year. We thank you because every month shall be marked with testimonies of fruitfulness in Jesus name.
- Father in Jesus name, we thank you for fruitfulness on all sides, blessed be your name Lord.
- Father we thank you for you hear us. All through the year, we thank you for the testimonies that abound for us, in our homes, our marriages and businesses, our careers and academics in the name of Jesus Christ we have prayed.

60 MFM PRAYER POINTS AGAINST THE SPIRIT OF BARRENNESS

Barrenness is not your portion. Exodus 23:25 tells as that as a servant of God barrenness can never be your portion. Barrenness is an affliction of the devil and can only be addressed on the altar of prayer. We have compiled 60 MFM prayer points against the spirit of barrenness. This prayer points is inspired by Dr Olukoya of mountain of fire and miracle ministries. The spirit of barrenness is real, they are called deserts spirits. They are responsible for all forms of unfruitfulness, including unfruitfulness of the womb. You must rise up and pray these MFM prayer points In order to deliver yourself from these evil spirits.

Pray this prayers in faith, be expectant and the God of fruitfulness shall visit you today in Jesus name. God visited Sarah, he visited Elizabeth, He has not change, and He will also visit you today. He said for your shame you shall have double. Expect your twins, triplets, quadruplets and more as you pour out your heart to the lord. These MFM prayer points against the spirit of barrenness will empower you to wage spiritual warfare. I see you sharing your testimonies today in Jesus name.

FIFTY-EIGHT MFM PRAYER POINTS AGAINST THE SPIRIT OF BARRENNESS.

1. Father, I thank you for delivering me from every form of bondage.
2. My Father, by the blood of your Son Jesus wash me of every sins in my life, including generational sins in Jesus name.
3. My Father, let your mercy prevail over every judgment in my life today in Jesus name.
4. Oh Lord, forgive me from any self-afflicting sin in my life in Jesus name...
5. Oh God, by the power in the name of Jesus, separate me from every sin of my fathers in Jesus name.
6. I renounce any evil dedication and satanic pronouncements placed upon my life, in Jesus' name.
7. I break every evil verdict and demonic ordination, over my life in the name of Jesus.
8. I renounce and loose myself from every negative dedication of my womb to the witch coven in the name of Jesus.
9. I command every evil altar speaking against my fruitfulness to crash by fire now in the name of Jesus Christ.
10. I take authority over all satanic powers fighting against my fruitfulness in the name of Jesus.
11. Lord, cancel the evil pronouncements against my fruitfulness in Jesus name.
12. I take authority over all the curses emanating from breaking the vows made by my ancestors that is now affecting my fruitfulness in the name of Jesus.
13. I command all demons associated with any broken evil parental vow and dedication to depart from me now, in the name of Jesus.
14. Oh God, I separate myself from the sins of my forefathers by the precious blood of Jesus.
15. I separate myself from every curse from my father's compound in Jesus name.

16. I command the curse of bareness to be broken, in the name of Jesus.

17. By the anointing of the Holy Spirit upon my life, I break every yoke of the curse of bareness in my family in the name of Jesus.

18. I command any demon afflicting my womb or causing miscarriages in my life to leave at once, in the name of Jesus.

19. Jesus my healer, heal all damages done to my body and reproductive organs in Jesus name.

20. I dismiss and disband from my heart every thought, image or picture of bareness in the name of Jesus.

21. I reject every spirit of doubt, fear and discouragement, in the name of Jesus.

22. I cancel all ungodly delays to the manifestations of my miracles, in the name of Jesus.

23. Let the angels of the living God roll away every stone of hindrance to the manifestation of my breakthroughs, in the name of Jesus.

24. O Lord, hasten your word to perform it in marriage in Jesus name.

25. O Lord, speedily avenge me of my adversaries in the name of Jesus.

26. I refuse to agree with the enemies of my fruitfulness, in Jesus' name.

27. O Lord I desire breakthroughs in the area of my fruitfulness in the name of Jesus.

28. O Lord, I desire to conceive this week, in the name of Jesus.

29. O Lord, I desire to have my miracle conception confirmed by the doctors this month, in the name of Jesus.

30. O Lord, I desire to carry my triplets this year, in the name of Jesus.

31. Let there be turbulence, re-arrangement, revision, re-organization Andre-routing' of situations and circumstances in order to give way to the manifestations of my desired miracles, in Jesus' name.

32. Let every loophole in my life that has enabled the enemies to afflict is declared close in the name of Jesus.

33. I declare that every monitoring demon monitoring my ovulation and conception, I commend them to go blind by fire in the name of Jesus.

34. The God of Elijah who answers by fire, answer me by fire, in the name of Jesus.

35. The God who answered Moses speedily at the Red Sea, answer me by fire, in the name of Jesus.

36. The God who changed the lot of Jabez, answer me by fire, in the name of Jesus.

37. The God which quickeneth and calleth those things that be not as if they are, answer me by fire today in Jesus name.

38. Let every area of my life become too hot for any evil to inhabit, in the name of Jesus.

39. You evil growth of fibroid in my body be uprooted and removed from my body in the name of Jesus.

40. Let my body reject every evil habitations of infections and STDs in my body in the name of Jesus.

41. O Lord, I declare that every affliction of low sperm count is healed now in Jesus name.

42. I reject all evil manipulations and manipulators, in Jesus' name.

43. I break the powers of the occult, witchcraft and familiar spirits over my life, in the name of Jesus.

44. Every satanic deposit in my intestine that is blocking my fruitfulness is thereby flushed by the blood of Jesus. I deliver and pass them out, in the name of Jesus.

45. I deliver and pass out any satanic deposit in my reproductive organs, in the name of Jesus.

46. I deliver and pass out any satanic deposit in my womb, in the name of Jesus.

47. In the Name of Jesus, I Declare before All the Forces of Darkness," I shall deliver all my babies (mention the numbers)

and the gates of hell shall be powerless to stop me" in the name of Jesus.

48. You foreign hand laid on my womb, release me by fire now!!! in Jesus' name

49. In the name of Jesus, I renounce, break and loose myself from all spirit husbands' ad spirit wives in the name of Jesus.

50. Father, do a creative miracle in my body today, replace every damaged organ in my body with news ones in the name of Jesus.

51. Father deliver me from every chronic infertility infection in Jesus name.

52. Father, heal me from every damage as a result of abortion in Jesus name.

53. Father wash my womb with your blood in the name of Jesus

54. Father was my fallopian tubes with your blood in Jesus name.

55. Let every enemy behind my fruitfulness be exposed and publicly disgraced in Jesus name.

56. Father just as I have gone for the child naming of many people, let people gather in my house today for my child naming in Jesus name.

57. Oh Lord, answer my mockers, by giving me my own children to the glory of your name in Jesus name.

58. Father thanks you for answering my prayers in Jesus name

MIDNIGHT PRAYERS FOR FRUIT OF THE WOMB

Genesis 21:1-2: And the Lord visited Sarah as he had said, and the Lord did unto Sarah as he had spoken. 2 For Sarah conceived, and bare Abraham a son in his old age, at the set time of which God had spoken to him.

The fruit of the womb is the reward of every marriage. It is the will of God that every marital union be blessed with children. Do you know that God does not expects us to pray for children? Children are supposed to come to us naturally especially in marriage. Whenever child bearing now becomes the issues of prayers, then you know that the devil is at work. That is why we are going to be engaging in midnight prayers for the fruit of the womb.

These midnight prayer points will break the hold of the devil over your fruitfulness in Jesus name. Do not be deceived, every sickness is an oppression of the devil, Acts 10:38. No matter the cause of your barrenness, it is from the devil, whether the doctor tells you its fibroid, or pelvic inflammation, or blocked tubes, or STDs, or STIs, it doesn't matter, they are all oppressions of the devil and prayers added with living a godly life can free you from all such ailments and make your fruitfulness a reality.

There are also scenarios where the doctors can't find anything wrong with the couples and yet conception is still not forth coming. These is a clear sign of demonic oppression and only violent midnight prayers can overcome these forces. I don't know how long you have been expecting your children, but I encourage you today, engage this midnight prayers for the fruit of the womb with all your heart, and all your faith. Pray your way out of barrenness into fruitfulness. As you pray this midnight prayers for the fruit of the womb tonight, I see God visiting you after the order of Sarah in Jesus name.

- Thou faith-weakening powers, loose your hold, in the name of Jesus.

- I refuse to become weak in the days of adversity, in the name of Jesus.
- Thou powers assigned to weaken my faith, die, in the name of Jesus.
- I reject and resist anything that would weaken my faith, in Jesus' name.
- Let my faith be barricaded by the fire of God, in the name of Jesus.
- Every strongman assigned to weaken my faith, catch fire, in Jesus' name.
- Every anti-miracle power, clear away, in the name of Jesus.
- I reject every opinion that weakens my faith or discourages, in the name of Jesus.
- I reject every man's negative opinion concerning my child-bearing, in the name of Jesus.
- Increasing age will not weaken my faith, in the name of Jesus.
- I shall believe the report of the Lord, in the name of Jesus.
- Impatience will not demote my faith, in the name of Jesus.
- I reject every spirit of frustration, in the name of Jesus.
- Medical reports will not weaken my faith, in the name of Jesus.
- I reject every negative medical report, in the name of Jesus.
- I reject every report of _ _ _ (pick from the under listed), in the name of Jesus.
  Abnormal ovaries
  Absence of ovaries
  Hormonal imbalance
  Absence of ovulation
  Bilateral blockage of fallopian tubes
  Abnormal womb (uterus)
  Surgical removal of the womb
  Congenital absence of the womb
  Previous occurrence of a miscarriage
  Tumour such as uterine fibroid

Low sperm count (oligospermia)

Absence of sperm (azoospermia)

Surgical removal or congenital absence of testis

Undescended testis or abnormal testis

- O God arise and overrule every negative report by Your divine supernatural verdict, in the name of Jesus.

- I cancel every spiritual or physical verdict contrary to the promises of God for my life, in the name of Jesus.

- O God, arise and transform my sperm to the ones that will supernaturally achieve a successful conception, in the name of Jesus.

- O God, arise and transform my sperm count to a supernatural sperm count that will divinely achieve a successful conception, in Jesus' name.

- O God, arise and replace every abnormal sperm with a normal sperm, in the name of Jesus.

- O God, arise and replace every non-motile sperm with a motile sperm, in the name of Jesus.

- O God, arise and replace every sluggish sperm with an active supernaturally energized

- Sperm, in the name of Jesus.

- O God, arise and replace every dead sperm with a living sperm, in the name of Jesus.

- Every strongman assigned to give me low sperm count be dismantled, in the name of Jesus.

- Every power that is responsible for low sperm count, die, in the name of

- Jesus.

- I command my semen stolen by the powers of darkness to be restored to me seven-fold, in the name of Jesus.

- I refuse to consider the deadness of the womb of my wife, in the name of Jesus.

- I reject every deadness of the womb of my wife, in the name of Jesus.
- I hereby command the womb of my wife to be converted from a functionally dead womb to a functionally reproductive womb, in the name of Jesus.
- I refuse to consider the negative medical report of infertile womb, in the name of Jesus.
- I reject and cancel every negative medical report of infertile womb, in the name of Jesus.
- O Lord, let the negative medical report of infertile womb be converted to God's own supernatural report of fertile womb, in the name of Jesus.
- I command my hormones to be balanced, in the name of Jesus.
- I refuse to consider the negative medical report of lack of ovulation, in the name of Jesus.
- I bind the spirit of lack of ovulation, in the name of Jesus.
- I command my ovaries to be ovulating normally, in the name of Jesus.
- I command my normal ovulation to be restored, in the name of Jesus.
- I command my ovaries to respond supernaturally to hormones that control ovulation, in the name of Jesus.
- O Lord, let every surgically or congenitally missing ovary be restored by your creative power, in the name of Jesus.
- I bind the spirit of blockage of fallopian tubes, in Jesus' name.
- I command the fire of God to burn to ashes everything that is blocking my fallopian tubes, in the name of Jesus.
- I command my fallopian tubes to be loosed and free from every pelvic adhesions, in the name of Jesus.
- I command the lumen (passages) of my fallopian tubes to be bilaterally patent and opened, in the name of Jesus.

- O Lord, let every surgically or congenitally missing fallopian tube be restored by your creative power, in the name of Jesus.
- I reject and cancel every negative medical report of abnormality of my womb, in the name of Jesus.
- I command every abnormality of my womb to be divinely and supernaturally corrected, in the name of Jesus.
- I command every evil growth in my womb such as uterine fibroid to die, in the name of Jesus.
- I reject and cancel every negative medical report of the congenital or surgical absence of the uterus, in the name of Jesus.
- O Lord, let every congenitally or surgically missing uterus be restored to me supernaturally and divinely, in the name of Jesus.
- Holy Spirit, create a conducive environment in my womb that would favour conception, in the name of Jesus.
- Holy Spirit, create a conducive environment in my womb that would favour the growth of my fetus to maturity, in Jesus' name.
- Every agenda of the power of darkness for my womb, die, in the name of Jesus.
- I break every witchcraft curse and spell on my womb, in Jesus' name.
- I break every ancestral curse on my womb, in the name of Jesus.
- I soak my womb in the blood of Jesus.
- I command the demon that has been assigned to give me a barren womb to loose its hold on me, in the name of Jesus.
- O Lord, let my womb be spiritually and physically compatible with the semen of my spouse, in the name of Jesus.
- Any component of my womb stolen by the powers of darkness to be restored to me now by fire, in the name of Jesus.
- I retrieve my blood hormones, ovaries, fallopian tubes, uterus and vagina from the coven of darkness, in the name of Jesus.
- I reverse the effects of the ageing process on my reproductive structures, in the name of Jesus.

- O Lord, as I grow older in age, let me become more fertile supernaturally, in the name of Jesus.

- Let every ovarian failure be converted to ovarian success, in the name of Jesus.

- Thou resurrection power of our Lord Jesus Christ, fall upon every deadness in my ovulation, in the name of Jesus.

- Thou resurrection power of our Lord Jesus Christ, fall upon every deadness in my ovaries, in the name of Jesus.

- You evil spirit guards at the doors of my fallopian tubes, I relieve you of your post, in the name of Jesus.

- Let every legal ground the enemy is claiming for closure of the doors of my fallopian tubes be withdrawn by fire, in Jesus' name.

- Let every clinical report of blocked fallopian tubes be cancelled over my life, in the name of Jesus.

- Let every blood supply to fibroids in my uterus be cut off, in the name of Jesus.

- Let the liquid fire of God flow into my uterus and melt away every fibroid, in the name of Jesus.

- Let the liquid fire of God flow into my uterus and dissolve every adhesion, in the name of Jesus.

- Let every negative effect of ageing on my uterus be nullified, in the name of Jesus.

- Holy Ghost fire, purge my womb from every satanic deposit, in the name of Jesus.

- Let all the doors of my womb become an expressway to conception, in the name of Jesus.

- Every power chanting anti-conception incantations into the heavenliest against me, die, in the name of Jesus.

- Let every barrenness programmed into my star be deprogrammed, in the name of Jesus.

- Age shall not limit my conception, in the name of Jesus.

- Every power accelerating my age towards premature menopause, loose your hold upon my life and die, in the name of Jesus.
- Every negative power battling to control the doors of my womb, be paralyzed, in the name of Jesus.
- Thou power of God that connected Zechariah and Elizabeth to their angel of breakthrough, connect me now to my angel of breakthrough, in the name of Jesus.
- By the power that directed angel Gabriel to Zechariah, let the angel of my miracle baby locate me now, in the name of Jesus.
- I command the strongman that has been assigned to give me miscarriage womb to fall down and die, in the name of Jesus.
- I reject miscarriages and abortion, in the name of Jesus.
- I reject bleeding in pregnancy, in the name of Jesus.
- I reject threaten-abortion, in the name of Jesus.
- I reject inevitable abortion and complete abortion, in Jesus' name.
- I reject complicated pregnancy, in the name of Jesus.
- I reject maternal and child death, in the name of Jesus.
- I reject every abnormal baby, in the name of Jesus.
- I reject every miscarriage able baby, in the name of Jesus.
- O Lord, let my baby be beautiful and normal, in Jesus' name.
- I reject every baby that is the product of the devil's workmanship, in the name of Jesus.
- I reject every abnormal chromosome, in the name of Jesus.
- I reject all babies that are prone to chromosomal abnormalities, in the name of Jesus.
- O Lord, grant unto me, babies that are resistant to every form of infection, in the name of Jesus.
- O Lord, let every abnormal structure in my womb be converted to normal structure, in the name of Jesus.
- I command the fire of God from heaven to burn every tumour in my womb to ashes, in the name of Jesus.

- O Lord, I repent of every personal damage done to my cervix in the past through a traumatic D & C, in the name of Jesus.
- I command anything in my womb that can cause ectopic pregnancy to die, in the name of
- Jesus.
- I command the strongman that has been assigned to siphon or drain away my progesterone and other hormones, to fall down and die, in the name of Jesus.
- I command the demon behind corpus luteum insufficiency to loose its hold on me now, in the name of Jesus.
- O Lord, remove every anxiety over old age from me, in the name of Jesus.
- I receive divine mandate to prayerfully enforce my right of conception, in the name of Jesus.
- Let every satanic road block mounted against the transport of my egg and spouse's sperm in my fallopian tube be dismantled by fire, in the name of Jesus.
- Let every satanic wall of partition between my egg and spouse's sperm be broken down by fire, in the name of Jesus.
- Let my fallopian tubes be freed from every adhesions, in the name of Jesus.
- I withdraw my fallopian tubes from every evil altar, in the name of Jesus.
- Let every inherited obstruction in my fallopian tubes, die, in the name of Jesus.
- Let every evil seed of barrenness in my foundation, die, in the name of Jesus.
- Let every infection in my fallopian tubes, die, in the name of Jesus.
- Let every microorganism causing infection in my womb be roasted, in the name of Jesus.
- Thou power of God that transformed the destiny of Hannah, fall upon me now and give me my own Samuel, in the name of Jesus.

- Thou power of the Holy Spirit, overshadow my life now and connect me to my own baby, in the name of Jesus.
- Holy Spirit, overhaul my womb by your fire to produce a divine conception, in the name of Jesus.
- Let every child formed in my womb be preserved by the fire of God and the Blood of Jesus, in the name of Jesus.
- Healing winds of God, blow upon all the organs of my body, in the name of Jesus.
- O God arise and withdraw my organs from every satanic blood bank, in the name of Jesus.
- Fire of God, boil infirmities out of my blood, in the name of Jesus.
- Thou creative power of God, work upon my life, in the name of Jesus.
- Glory of God, overshadow my body, soul and spirit, in the name of Jesus.
- Create new organs to replace sick or dead ones, in Jesus' name.
- O God supply organ spare parts to my body, in the name of Jesus.
- Heavenly surgeon, visit me now, in the name of Jesus.
- Power of God, pull down every stronghold of stubborn infirmities, in the name of Jesus.
- Fire of God, purge my organ for newness, in the name of Jesus.
- Let my youth be renewed as Eagle, in the name of Jesus.
- Every handwriting of darkness targeted against my health, be wiped off, in the name of Jesus.
- My organs receive creative miracles, in the name of Jesus.
- Spirit of God, move upon every organ in my body, in the name of Jesus.
- Creative power of God, work for me now, in the name of Jesus.
- I bind every spirit of death operating in my . . ., in the mighty name of Jesus.

- Let your resurrection power come upon my . . ., in the mighty name of Jesus.
- I command every dead bone in my . . . to come alive, in Jesus' name.
- You evil hand laid on my . . ., receive the thunder and the fire of God and be roasted, in the name of Jesus.
- I command every evil monitoring gadget fashioned against my . . . to be destroyed, in the name of Jesus.
- I breathe in the life of God and I reject every spirit of death and hell, in the name of Jesus.
- I recover every miracle that I have lost through unbelief, in the name of Jesus.
- Father, let your creative power operate afresh in . . . area of my life, in the name of Jesus.
- Father, let the fire of the Holy Ghost enter into my blood stream and cleanse my system, in the name of Jesus.
- I release my . . . from the cage of every household wickedness, in the name of Jesus.
- Let every information about my . . . be erased from every satanic memory, in the name of Jesus.
- I command every evil plantation in my life: Come out with all your roots, in the name of Jesus! (Lay your hands on your stomach and keep repeating the emphasized area.)
- Evil strangers in my body, come all the way out of your hiding places, in the name of Jesus.
- I cough out and vomit any food eaten from the table of the devil, in the name of Jesus. (Cough them out and vomit them in faith. Prime the expulsion.)
- Let all negative materials circulating in my blood stream be evacuated, in the name of
- Jesus.
- I drink the blood of Jesus. (Physically swallow and drink it in faith. Keep doing this for some time.)

- Lay one hand on your head and the other on your stomach or navel and begin to pray like this: Holy Ghost fire, burn from the top of my head to the sole of my feet. Begin to mention every organ of your body; your kidney, liver, intestine, blood, etc. You must not rush at this level, because the fire will actually come and you may start feeling the heat.
- I cut myself off from every spirit of . . . (mention the name of your place of birth), in the name of Jesus.
- I cut myself off from every tribal spirit and curses, in the name of Jesus.
- I cut myself off from every territorial spirit and curses, in Jesus' name.
- Holy Ghost fire, purge my life.
- I claim my complete deliverance, in the name of Jesus, from the spirit of . . . (mention those things you do not desire in your life).
- I break the hold of any evil power over my life, in Jesus' name.
- I move from bondage into liberty, in the name of Jesus.
- Thank God for answers to your prayer points

30 PRAYER POINTS FOR BABIES IN THE WOMB

Luke 1:41: And it came to pass, that, when Elisabeth heard the salutation of Mary, the babe leaped in her womb; and Elisabeth was filled with the Holy Ghost

Every expectant mother must pray for their unborn children. This is very important because we must recognize that every living thing responds to the power of prayers, and no prayer can be more powerful than the prayer of a mother to her baby in the womb. Today I have compiled 30 prayer points for babies in the womb. As a child of God, we must understand that the devil is after us and anything that will bring us joy, we must resist him steadfastly in prayers. Why must every mother or father pray for their babies in the womb?

The reasons are as follows:

1. **Safe Delivery:** Some babies die before, during and after delivery, this is not the will of God, every parent must pray for the safe delivery of their babies in the womb. They must take charge of the atmosphere in the realm of the spirit, they must pray against every form of complications in the womb and ask the Holy Spirit to continually protect their babies till the day of conception and even beyond. Also every expectant mother must always speak faith filled words to her baby in the womb, you must always make positive confessions concerning your child because Mark 11:23-24 tells us that you shall have what you say.

2. **Baby Illness:** Another effective prayer points for babies in the womb is to pray against baby illness. There are some babies that come into this world with one form of sickness or the other. Some babies are born with genetic anomalies, e.g., sickle cell, Siamese twins, disfigured body parts, down syndrome etc. all this are not the will of God for your baby. We must pray against all such illness. We must pray that the power of God overshadow our babies in the womb, giving them soundness of health, and protecting them from all forms of diseases that affect children.

We must pray this prayers by faith and daily, till the day of delivery.

3. **Babies Future:** God told Jeremiah, that" before I formed you in the womb I have chosen you" Jeremiah 1:5. Every parent must pray for the future and purpose of their child. Every child in this world has a destiny to fulfill. We must dedicate our babies in the womb to the Lord and pray that the fulfill there destinies in life. We must pray that God discover them quickly like he discovered Samuel (1 Samuel 3:6), Samson (Judges 13:16) Isaiah (Isaiah 6:1-8), Jeremiah (Jeremiah 1:5), Ezekiel (Ezekiel 1:17), John The Baptist (Luke 1:1-20), etc. It's impossible for you to pray like this and not have a successful child.

4. **Supernatural Provisions**: Every child carries favour, we must pray for financial favour to provide for our babies. We must ask the Lord to open doors of opportunities for us to excel financially so that we can give our babies the kind of future they deserve. When a parent is broke, they cannot take care if their children. Many children have suffered from premature death, teenage pregnancy, child abuse, gangsters, etc. because their parents had no money to give them proper training. We must ask God for supernatural provisions so that our children will not lack proper home training.

5. **Wisdom for Parenting:** We must pray for divine wisdom for parenting our children properly. Every parent needs wisdom on how to raise their babies, James 1:5, says if we lack wisdom in any areas of our life we should ask the Lord in faith and he will grant us wisdom. As God for the wisdom to be a great parent.

   2. The above listed are the very basic reasons we must pray for our children in the womb, this prayer points for babies in the womb will set the foundation for the success of our babies. Remember they will not be babies forever, we must build a great foundation for them, so that when they become adults, they will choose the right path.

30 PRAYER POINTS FOR BABIES IN THE WOMB

1. Father, I thank you for you are the giver of children in Jesus name
2. Father, I cover my babies in the womb with the blood of Jesus.
3. Father, I declare that no weapon formed against my babies shall prosper in Jesus name
4. Father, I cancel any satanic utterances concerning my babies in my womb in Jesus name
5. Father, I declare that there shall be no complications with my delivery in the name of Jesus
6. Father, I decree that my babies in the womb are well positioned in the name of Jesus
7. Father, I decree that my babies in the womb are developing properly in Jesus name
8. Father, I decree that the babies in my womb are unkillable in Jesus name
9. Father, I decree that the babies in my womb are super healthy in Jesus name
10. Father let your angels in chariots of fire surround my babies in my womb in Jesus name.
11. Fill my babies with the power of the holy ghost in Jesus name
12. I declare that my womb is super conducive for my baby delivery in Jesus name
13. I declare that every strength I need to push my babies successfully I receive it in Jesus name
14. Miscarriage is not my portion in Jesus name
15. Still birth is not my portion in Jesus name
16. Caesarian Section is not my portion in Jesus name
17. Prolonged labour is not my portion in Jesus name
18. Loss of blood during and after delivery is not my portion in Jesus name.
19. Deformed or disabled baby is not my portion in Jesus name
20. I declare that this baby shall bring me favour in Jesus name

21. I declare that there will be showers of blessings upon my life because of the arrival of these baby in the name of Jesus.
22. I declare that I shall be visited by important people with great gifts at the arrival of my baby in Jesus name
23. This baby shall bring prosperity to my family in Jesus name
24. All the enemies of my pregnancy shall be put to shame in Jesus name.
25. I declare that this baby/babies in my womb shall have a great future in Jesus name
26. No evil shall befall him/her as she grows up in Jesus name
27. My babies shall not die prematurely in Jesus name
28. My babies will not be a victim of children related sicknesses in Jesus name
29. My babies will grow in the wisdom of God in Jesus name
30. My babies will fulfill their God ordained purpose in life in Jesus name.

30 DELIVERANCE PRAYER POINTS AGAINST UNWANTED GROWTH IN THE WOMB

Exodus 23:26: There shall nothing cast their young, nor be barren, in thy land: the number of thy days I will fulfil.

Children are the heritage of the Lord, therefore no child of God is permitted to lose their child. This 30 deliverance prayer points against unwanted growth in the womb is for those who are finding it difficult to conceive due to certain growths in their womb or their body. This growth often lead to miscarriages or some other complications that prevents conception. You must understand that every sickness in the body is from the devil. Act 10:38. It is Gods ultimate will that you be free from every operations of the devil, including sicknesses and diseases.

As you pray this deliverance prayer points today, every growth in your womb or any part of your body will be dissolved in the name of Jesus. There is nothing that our God cannot do, pray this prayer with faith and expect instant miracles as you pray. God will through this deliverance prayer points against unwanted growth in your womb, cleanse your womb and your entire reproductive organ and cause you to conceive and carry your desired number of children today. Don't give up on God, Our God still answers prayers. Pray in faith today and receive your miracle.

30 DELIVERANCE PRAYER POINTS AGAINST UNWANTED GROWTH IN THE WOMB

1. Father, I thank you for the power to deliver me from any form of bondage.
2. I cover my womb with the precious blood of Jesus.
3. Father, let your purifying fire, purge my womb, in the name of Jesus.
4. Father, let every evil plot of the enemy against my life be return back to their heads in the name of Jesus.
5. By the blood of Jesus, I wash away every evil stamp of the enemy upon my life in Jesus name.
6. By your blood, I flush my system from every satanic deposits, in the mighty name of Jesus.
7. I break myself loose from the bondage of delayed conception, in the mighty name of Jesus.
8. Lord, destroy with your fire anything that stands between me and my breakthrough in the name of Jesus.
9. Let the blood, the fire and the living water of the Most High God wash my womb clean from unwanted growths in the name of Jesus
10. Let the blood, the fire and the living water of the Most High God wash my womb clean from evil plantations in the name of Jesus
11. Let the blood, the fire and the living water of the Most High God wash my womb clean from evil deposits from spirit husband in the name of Jesus
12. Let the blood, the fire and the living water of the Most High God wash my womb clean from impurities acquired from parental contamination in the name of Jesus
13. Let the blood, the fire and the living water of the Most High God wash my womb clean from evil spiritual consumption in the name of Jesus
14. Let the blood, the fire and the living water of the Most High God wash my womb clean from hidden sicknesses in the name of Jesus

15. Let the blood, the fire and the living water of the Most High God wash my womb clean from satanic remote control in the name of Jesus

16. Let the blood, the fire and the living water of the Most High God wash my womb clean from satanic poisons in the name of Jesus

17. I deliver and pass out any satanic deposit in my reproductive organs, in the name of Jesus.

18. I deliver and pass out any satanic deposit in my womb, in the name of Jesus.

19. In the name of Jesus, I declare that my body is the temple of the Lord, therefore no devil can prevail over me again in Jesus name.

20. I command every strange hand laid on my womb to wither now, in Jesus 'name.

21. In the name of Jesus, I renounce, break and loose myself from all demonic bonds in the name of Jesus

22. In the name of Jesus, deliver myself from all evil curses, chains, spells, jinxes, bewitchments, witchcraft or sorcery which may have been put upon me.

23. Let a creative miracle take place in my womb and reproductive system, in the name of Jesus.

24. Father, I declare that every weapon fashioned against me my conception shall not prosper in the name of Jesus.

25. I loose myself from every evil influence, dark spirit and satanic bondage, in the name of Jesus.

26. I confess and declare that my body is the temple of the Holy Spirit, redeemed, cleansed, and sanctified by the blood, I shall never be a victim of unfruitfulness in Jesus name

27. I bind, plunder and render to naught every strongman assigned to my womb, reproductive system and marital life, in Jesus' name.

28. God who quickens the dead, quicken my womb and reproductive system, in the name of Jesus.

29. I release myself from the hold of spirits of sterility, infertility and doubt, in the name of Jesus.

30. Father, let your angels of fire surround my womb, from conception to safe delivery in the name of Jesus amen.

25 POWERFUL PRAYER POINTS FOR THE FRUIT OF THE WOMB

1 Samuel 2:21: And the Lord visited Hannah, so that she conceived, and bare three sons and two daughters. And the child Samuel grew before the Lord.

It is Gods will that all His creatures be fruitful, from the beginning he commanded mankind to be fruitful and to replenish the earth. Every form of unfruitfulness whether in mankind or animals or plants is not from God. Therefore child of God we have compiled 25 powerful prayer points for the fruit of the womb, for you. This prayer points will guide you to prayer against every form of unfruitfulness in your womb. You are going to be crying in faith to the God of Fruitfulness and multiplication to intervene in your situation.

25 powerful prayer points for the fruit of the womb

1. Oh Lord, in the beginning, your declaration to mankind was to be fruitful, to multiply, and replenish the earth, I stand by your word this day and I declare my fruitfulness in Jesus name.
2. Our covenant fathers, Abraham, Isaac, and Jacob all had their children, therefore I declare that I shall have mine in Jesus name.
3. Oh Lord! I declare today that I shall be fruitful and multiply in Jesus name.
4. Gen. 15:5 – Oh God that visited Sarah with Isaac and Hannah with Samuel, father visit me today in Jesus name.
5. Oh Lord, under the new covenant, Jesus paid the prize for my fruitfulness, therefore I receive my Children today in Jesus name.
6. I believe that what man see as impossible is possible for God in my life. I shall be pregnant and deliver my own baby this year in Jesus name.
7. Oh Lord, I command every fertility related sickness in the body or blood of my wife, whether fibroid, pelvic inflammation disease'(PID), ovarian cyst, fallopian tube blockage, any other

chronic STDs or STIs whatever your names are I command you to disappear from my wife's body in Jesus name.

8. Oh Lord, remove whatever is the root cause of my barrenness today. Make me a mother this month in Jesus name.

9. My Father and My God, remember me even as you remembered Rachel and opened her womb, remember me today, listen to me today and open my womb today in Jesus name.

10. Oh Lord, bless me today with the blessing of the breasts and of the womb in Jesus name.

11. I prophesy that there shall be no other miscarriage in my life again in Jesus name.

12. Oh Lord, open my eyes to the Solution of my fruitfulness in Jesus name Amen

13. Oh Lord, by your mighty hand, I change my name from mother of barrenness to mother of many children in Jesus name.

14. Oh Lord, I declare to my womb today," Womb, Hear the Word of the Lord, Be Opened and carry my Children in" in Jesus name.

15. Father, grant me my on miracle children testimony in Jesus name

16. Oh Lord, heal my husband from any fertility related sickness in Jesus name.

17. Oh Lord, all my grief arising from barrenness has been nailed to the cross from today. It is now my turn to carry my babies in Jesus name.

18. All reproach of barrenness in my life shall come to an end this month in Jesus name.

19. I declare that all those that are mocking me today, shall soon come and celebrate with me in Jesus name.

20. Oh Lord, do not judge me by the measure of my faith over my prayers. Let the rain of mercy fall on me today and open my womb in Jesus name.

21. Oh Lord, cause my womb become fertile in Jesus name.

22. Oh Lord, settle me in my marriage, make me a joyful mother of my biological children in Jesus name.

23. Oh Lord, your word proclaim that you don't shut the womb! Anything that has shut my womb, I declare it open now!!! In the name of Jesus Christ

24. Oh Lord, save me from shame, give me my own children today in Jesus name.

25. I set myself free from every demonic spirit husband or spirit wife fighting against my Child bearing in Jesus name.

10 PRAYER POINTS FOR NEW BORN BABY

Today we will be dealing with 10 prayer points for new born baby. The level of excitement that elude a family cannot be quantified when a new baby we delivered in the family. The news of this practically brings joy to the face of every member of the family. The scripture says in the book of Psalm 127:3-5 Behold, children are a heritage from the LORD, The fruit of the womb is a reward. Like arrows in the hand of a warrior, so are the children of one's youth. Happy is the man who has his quiver full of them; they shall not be ashamed, But shall speak with their enemies in the gate. The Bible stated that children are the heritage of God. This means children are golden in the sight of the Lord.

The scripture went further to liken them to be like an arrow in the hands of a warrior and any man who have them in his quiver will be happy forever. This explains why it is the prayer of every family for the fruit of the womb. Every family pray for a new child. And it is always the prayer of the parents that have they have known the beginning of the new baby, they should not know his/her end too.

While it is one thing to have baby, it is another thing to raise the child in the way of the Lord. The scripture admonish that we should train out children in the way they would go so that when they grow up, they won't depart from it. There are some parents who have failed in their duty of rising a godly children. This didn't happen because they refuse to reprimand their kids anytime they do something wrong but because they refuse to pray for their children while they were growing. The truth is, when a child is born, the enemy is always on the watch to know the type of child that has been born. They get the news of the birth of a new child even people the news went abroad. Such is the story of Christ Jesus.

If care is not taken, they can destroy the destiny of the new child. This explains why parents should pray fervently for their new born babies. I have prepared 10 prayer points that every parents must pray for their new babies to rescue them from the fang of the enemies.

PRAYER POINTS:

1. Father Lord, I thank you for the gift of child that you have given to my family. I thank you because you cancelled our shame and reproach and blessed us with this gift. Lord, I dedicate this child to you. This child belongs to you. I pray that you will guide and nurture this child in the name of Jesus. The scripture says my children and I are for signs and wonders. I ask that you will use this baby for your glory in the name of Jesus. I pray that you will rescue this child from the snare of the Fowler in the name of Jesus.

2. Lord Jesus, the scripture says the eyes of the lord is always the righteous and his ears are always attentive to their prayers. Lord I pray that your eyes will be upon this baby in the name of Jesus. I pray that your mighty hands of protection will be upon him in the name of Jesus. I pray that the angel of the lord will be assigned to this baby to guide him and protect him from all evil in the name of Jesus.

3. Lord, I commit the destiny of this baby in your hands. I pray that you shall guide it from the prying eyes of the enemies in the name of Jesus. Lord, I come against every monitoring spirit that has been assigned to this baby to watch him/her in all ways, I break every demonic mirror that is used to for monitoring the destiny of this baby, in the name of Jesus.

4. Father Lord, the scripture says if any man lacks Wisdom let him ask from God that gives liberally without blemish. Father Lord, I ask for the right kind of wisdom to be able to guide, train and nurture this child in the right way to go. I pray for the wisdom to be able to be a good parent to this baby in the name of Jesus.

5. Father Lord, I pray for the grace for this new baby to wax in the strength of the lord. Every evil hands that has been assigned against him should wither away today in the name of Jesus. Every demonic hands that has been sent from the pit of hell to change the destiny of this baby should cut off in the name of Jesus.

6. Father Lord, I come against every evil friend or peer group that the enemy may have assigned to come the way of this baby, I cause an asunder between them today in the name of Jesus. This child belongs to the lord, every satanic friend that the enemy has programmed to become a bad influence on this baby, I come against such friend in the name of Jesus.

7. Lord God, I pray that you shall strengthen this baby to fulfill the purpose of his existence in the name of Jesus. He shall not fail purpose in the name of Jesus. I pray that you will grant him the grace to have the right standing with you, I pray he shall not fall away from your way in the name of Jesus.

8. I remove the name of this child from every ancestral curse or evil protocol that may want to work against him. I put the mark of Christ upon him and his destiny today in the name of Jesus. He shall not be moved in the name of Jesus. Every demonic covenant from the lineage where he has been born will have no power over his life in the name of Jesus.

9. Lord, just as the Bible has stated that children are like arrows in the hands of a warrior. I pray that this child will be an arrow I the hands of we the parents in the name of Jesus. He shall not be an object of ridicule in the name of Jesus. He shall continue to make us proud in the name of Jesus.

10. Lord, I pray that you will help this baby to make a great impact in this world in the name of Jesus. He shall not come and leave the world untraceable like a snake that walked the surface of a rock. I pray that you will help him to make a huge difference in the world in the name of Jesus.

POWERFUL PRAYER POINTS AGAINST PREGNANCY COMPLICATIONS

Today we will be dealing with powerful Prayer points against pregnancy complications. You know the joy that radiates in your heart the day you knew you would be a mother. That joy becomes overwhelming when you start having a big belly. You need to pray ahead of the day you will deliver the child. This is because not all expecting mothers live long to see the day their child will be delivered, and not all babies are delivered. The scripture admonishes that we pray without ceasing because God knows that our adversary, the devil goes about day and night looking for whom to devour.

Pregnancy complications can come in any form. The child might suddenly stop growing in the womb. Sometimes it could be that the child mysteriously changes position in the womb. It could be the inability of the expecting mother to give birth to her child by herself. The enemy can come in any form. There are several women whose pregnancy has never grown beyond a particular month. When they reach that month, they experience a miscarriage. I speak as an oracle of God. In every way the devil is making you cry over that pregnancy, I decree that your tears are over in the name of Jesus.

For you that suffer miscarriage during certain months of pregnancy, I decree by the authority of heaven, that demon that comes to kill your child at a specific time will die today in the name of Jesus. For some other people, it could be severe complications that will lead to the death of either the expecting mother or the child on the day of delivery. I speak as an oracle of God, every power and principality that has gone before you to the day of your delivery. I decree that the angel of the lord Strike such powers dead in the name of Jesus.

The scripture says, the effectual prayer of the righteous avail much. The lord is mighty to save you from the demon that torment you during pregnancy. If you ask some women, their worst nightmares usually occur when they are pregnant. For this reason, many women don't want to be pregnant. Despite the joy of carrying a child, most women prefer not to conceive because the demon torments them during pregnancy. For as many of you that suffers this type of fate, the lord will set you free today in the name of Jesus.

PRAYER POINTS

- Lord Jesus, I thank you for the grace you have bestowed on me to conceive a child. Thank you for counting me worthy to carry a baby in my womb. I thank you for blessing my womb with this precious gift. May your name be highly exalted in the name of Jesus.

- Father Lord, I pray that your hands of protection will be upon me and this precious gift growing in my womb. The scripture says, And Jesus increased in wisdom and stature, and favor with God and man. I ask that my child will continue to grow unhindered in my womb in the name of Jesus.

- Father Lord, I come against every form of complications that may arise against me in this stage of my life. I rebuke them today in the name of Jesus. I come against every demon that sucks the blood of a baby in the womb, and I set you such ablaze over my life today in the name of Jesus.

- Lord, every demonic agent that has been assigned to me from the kingdom of darkness to torment me during pregnancy, I decree that the angel of the Lord will destroy them today in the name of Jesus.

- I come against every evil arrow from the kingdom of darkness to kill the baby in my womb. For it has been written, no weapon fashion against me shall prosper. Every evil arrow sent from the Kingdom of darkness to harm the child and me in my womb, lose your power today in the name of Jesus.

- Lord, I sanctify the day of delivery with the precious blood of Jesus. I cover the hospital or maternity home that I will use on that day with the precious blood of Jesus. I decree that every demon that has been assigned to work against me that day die right now in the name of Jesus.

- Lord, for it, has been written 'I will go before you and make the crooked places straight; I will break in pieces the gates of bronze and cut the bars of iron. I decree that you will go ahead of me in this pregnancy. Any plan of the enemy over me is broken in the name of Jesus.

- Lord, every agent of darkness waiting for the day my baby will be delivered to torment me. I ask that the angel of death visit such an agent today in the name of Jesus.

- For the scripture says, Let God arise, Let His enemies be scattered; Let those also who hate Him flee before Him. I decree lord arise over my situation, let my enemies be scattered. Let those who hate me flee before me today in the name of Jesus.

- Lord, as the sword melt in the heat of the burning furnace, let the wicked be destroyed before me in the name of Jesus. Let those who want me dead with pregnancy eat their flesh, let them be drunk on their blood like sweet wine. Let the earth know that you are my God and my redeemer.

- For it has been written But thus says the LORD: "Even the captives of the mighty shall be taken away, and the prey of the terrible be delivered; for I will contend with him who contends with you, and I will save your children. Lord, I pray for the release of my womb from the coven of the witches.

- Lord, in any way my unborn child has been held captive by the power of darkness, I decree his Freedom today in the name of Jesus. Your word declared that even the captive would be taken away, and the prey of the terrible shall be delivered. You said you would contend with those that contend with me, and you will save my children. I decree by the authority of heaven, every demon or human that wages war against this pregnancy will receive the wrath of God.

- Lord, I pray for smooth delivery on the day this child will be coming to the world. I ask that the host of heaven will assist me during the process and ease my pain in the name of Jesus. The baby shall not die from terrible complications, neither shall the mother be mourned in the name of Jesus.

CHAPTER 3

FAMILY PRAYER:
POWERFUL PRAYER POINTS FOR PROTECTION OVER FAMILY

Today we will be dealing with powerful prayer points for protection over family. A family is a group of people related by birth or by marriage. Family is a social and spiritual institution designed by God to teach people the ways of the Lord. One of the institutions the enemy is always quick to lay attacks on is the family. When the family is in turmoil it won't be able to fulfill the core purpose of its existence.

Most times, the attack of the enemy is always focused on the children and infant of the family who still rely largely on the prayer of their parents to survive. The scripture said in the book of Psalm 127:3-5 Behold, children are a heritage from the Lord, the fruit of the womb a reward. Like arrows in the hand of a warrior are the children of one's youth. Blessed is the man who fills his quiver with them! He shall not be put to shame when he speaks with his enemies in the gate. The devil understands that children are the heritage of God that why most times he attack the family through the children.

Other times, it could be an attack in the life of the breadwinner of the family which is the father. It could be a plot to end his source of living to throw the family into poverty. Or it could be a plot to take the life of the homemaker which is the woman of the home. Whatever it is the enemy is planning for your family, I cancel it by the power in the name of Jesus. I ask by the authority of heaven that the counsel of the Lord alone shall stand over your family in the name of Jesus.

PRAYER POINTS

- The scripture says in the book of Psalm 91:1-16 He who dwells in the shelter of the Most High will abide in the shadow of the Almighty. I will say to the Lord, "My refuge and my fortress, my

God, in whom I trust. I hide my family under the secret place of the most high today in the name of Jesus. I decree that no harm shall come upon any member of my family in the name of Jesus.

- Lord, for it has been written in the book of Isaiah 41:10 Fear not, for I am with you; be not dismayed, for I am your God; I will strengthen you, I will help you, I will uphold you with my righteous right hand. I pray that you will continue to be with my family in the name of Jesus. The eyes of the Lord is always upon the righteous, I decree by the authority of heaven that your eyes will always be upon every member of my family and you will keep us away from evil in the name of Jesus.

- I come against every evil that is fashioned against me and any member of my family. The scripture said in the book of Isaiah 54:17

- No weapon that is fashioned against you shall succeed, and you shall confute every tongue that rises against you in judgment. This is the heritage of the servants of the Lord and their vindication from me, declares the Lord. I destroy every evil that is fashioned against me today by the fire of the Holy Ghost in the name of Jesus.

- I pray that the power of God Almighty will rescue my family from every plot of the enemy. He will bring us all to safety by the strength of His right hand in the name of Jesus. I pray that the Lord continue to guard every member of my family and keep us all away from every evil in the name.

- Lord, for it has been written that a thousand may fall at your side, and ten thousand at your right hand; but it shall not come near you. You promise that with our eyes shall we see and behold the reward of the wicked but none will come to us or come near our dwelling place. I decree by the authority of heaven, that no harm shall come upon my Children in the name of Jesus. I decree by the authority of heaven, no harm shall come upon my spouse in the name of Jesus.

- You promised in your word that he who was born of God protects him, and the evil one does not touch him. Lord, my children, my spouse and I are born of God, I pray that your hands of protection be upon each and everyone of us in the name of Jesus. Our going in is blessed, our coming out is blessed in the name of Jesus. I pray that the angel of the Lord take charge over our lives, they shall continue to guard us in our ways in the name of Jesus.

- Lord, it has been written in your word But thus says the LORD: "Even the captives of the mighty shall be taken away, and the prey of the terrible be delivered; for I will contend with him who contends with you, and I will save your children. I pray that the vengeance of the Lord be upon those who seek evil against my family in the name of Jesus.

- I set the Lord God at the right hand of every member of my family we shall not be shaken in the name of Jesus. I decree by the authority of heaven that no harm shall come upon any of us in the name of Jesus. Every plan of the enemy to end the life of my spouse is broken in the name of Jesus. Every plan of the enemy to harm any of children is destroyed by the authority of heaven.

- The scripture said for I carry the mark of Christ let no man trouble me. I pray by the authority of heaven, I shall not be troubled in the name of Jesus. None of my family members shall be troubled in the name of Jesus. Ever plot of the enemy to make me toil over my children, I destroy such plans in the name of Jesus.

- I confess today that my family and I are for signs and wonders, so shall it be in the name of Jesus.

PRAYER POINTS AGAINST EVIL FAMILY PATTERN

Today we will be dealing with prayer points against evil family pattern. The Lord wants to deliver people from generational and evil ancestral protocols that have confined their life to a particular demonic pattern. Some families do not have a college graduate, and anyone who tries to break that yoke by going to school, such individuals will be disgracefully rusticated from school.

In other families, people don't attain some certain age. They die when they are about to clock that age. In some families, barrenness is the order of the day. Let's draw reference from the scripture. Abraham was barren for years before he had Isaac.

Similarly, Isaac was barren before he had Jacob. In Jacob's time, his beloved wife, Rachel, was barren for years before her womb was opened. This analogy is a clear example of an evil family pattern. I don't know the structural pattern in your family, but God is set to destroy every evil pattern limiting your progress in life. I decree in the name of Jesus. Every evil pattern is destroyed in the name of Jesus.

This prayer guide will focus more on God destroying the generational curse. There are so many families of African descent that have one curse or the other. Once you are a member of that family, you will be troubled by that curse, and it will become a limiting factor until you break it. Goliath was a limiting factor to the championship of David. Until Goliath was defeated, David was just another young shepherd. Until King Saul was taken away, David would have only been another great warrior who was supposed to be King. God is destroying every limiting factor, every agent of darkness; every generational curse will be destroyed in the name of Jesus.

PRAYER POINTS

- Lord Jesus, I thank you for the grace to be alive. Let your name be exalted.

- I come against every evil Family pattern of failure in life, every evil pattern that has rendered the people ahead of me useless. I decree such a pattern fail over me in the name of Jesus. Every demonic family pattern of death at the point of breakthrough, be broken in the name of Jesus.

- I come against every evil pattern of marital failure. The demon that hindered the people in my family from settling marital, I decree that you will lose your power over me in the name of Jesus.

- O you power of failure that dealt with my parents, I come against you by the blood of the lamb. For it has been written by the anointing every yoke shall be destroyed. Every yoke of family failure, be broken concerning me in the name of Jesus. For I have set the Lord God at my right hand, I will not be shaken, every ancestral protocol in my family is broken before me in the name of Jesus.

- I come against every evil animal that has been assigned to monitor the progress of my family, let such animals be destroyed in the name of Jesus. Every pattern of witchcraft in my family, catch right now in the name of Jesus.

- Every demonic plantation that has refused to die, I come against you by the name above all other names, die in the name of Jesus.

- O you agent of death operating in my family, I come against you by the fire in the name of Jesus.

- Lord arise and set every generational garment or robe that is used for recognition by the enemies tormenting my family, set such robes or garments ablaze in my life today.

- From today, I anoint myself with the precious blood of Jesus, the anointing that will set me aside for excellence, the anointing that will set me aside for greatness, let it come upon me in the name of Jesus.

- Every satanic giant in my father's house, every strongman in my mother's house limiting the Success of people, catch fire right now in the name of Jesus.

- O Lord, arise and let your enemies be scattered. Every man and woman assigned by the devil to monitor my family's growth die right now in the name of Jesus.

- I break into pieces every evil chain that the enemy used in holding my family members down that no one in the family has been able to excel more than the other. I set such a chain on fire in the name of Jesus.

- Lord, I decree that from today, I become unstoppable for every power of darkness in my family in the name of Jesus.

- All you agent of poverty in my family, planning to attack me fall and die in the name of Jesus.

- For I carry the mark of Christ, let no man trouble me. I refused to be troubled by any evil family pattern in the name of Jesus.

- Father Lord, I want you to anoint me with the oil of greatness, that no power or principalities will be able to hold me down in the name of Jesus.

- Lord God, let the grace of excellence come upon me today in the name of Jesus. The grace that will set me aside for greatness let it come upon me today by your mighty hands.

- Every evil pattern of family infirmities, I exempt myself from it in the name of Jesus. For the scripture says Christ has carried all my infirmities, and he has healed all my diseases. I cancel every form of infirmities in my life in the name of Jesus.

- I receive the power that breaks every form of generational curse in the name of Jesus. For the scripture says Christ has been made a curse for us, I destroy every form of curse in my life in the name of Jesus.

- I come against every ancestral protocol in my lineage that has held people down. I destroy it by the fire of the Holy Ghost. Every evil pattern that frustrate people at the point of breakthrough, every agent of distraction that allows blessings of people slip away, I destroy you by the fire of the Holy Ghost.

- The scripture says how God anointed Jesus Christ with the Holy Spirit and power, and he went about doing well. Lord, I pray that you will anoint me with the Holy Spirit and power that no agent of darkness will be able to stop me. I want you to anoint me that no generational curse or evil family pattern will have power over me in the name of Jesus.

PRAYER FOR PROTECTION OF HOME AND FAMILY

Today we will be dealing with a prayer for the protection of Home and Family. Until a man understands the difference between a house and a home, such an individual might not know the essence of Family. The family is a structural institution that was established by God. In the book of Genesis chapter 2:4, the scripture says, for this reason, a man shall leave his father and mother and is united with his wife, and the two shall become one flesh. That is the word that necessitated the ministry of marriage to form a family. There is a covenant that accompanies every union that a family must stay together.

A man may have a house, but until he is joined with his woman and they become one flesh will the house transient into a home in which family could be raised. As spiritually inclined as the family is, it is also an agent of socialization. God intentionally orchestrated the ministry of marriage to ensure that there is an institution that takes of socializing every child that is born. When a family stays together, there is a little to what cannot be achieved. Little wonder, the devil is always waging a bitter war against the family. Every member of a family must say the prayer for the protection of Home and Family so that the devil doesn't find means into the family. When there is a laxity in the place of prayer, the devil will not be far from to strike; the devil might decide to take the breadwinner of the home to destroy the prayer life of the family.

The family must be spiritually alert all the to resist the devil. Sometimes, the devil might bring some form of disunity in a family, and when the family is not United, there is a little to what is achievable in the realms of the spirit. The devil understands that there is power in holding hands during prayer; that is why the family is the first ministry that is under the attack of the devil. I pray that by the mercies of God, the devil will not find a way into your home in the name of Jesus. I seal every opening entrance that the enemy might capitalize on to gain access to your home in the name of Jesus. Once the family is destroyed, the mission has been accomplished. There is no ministry to nurture every new child in the right way that is acceptable by the Lord. Many destinies have been destroyed because the enemy gained entry into the family. Many people failed purpose not because they wish to fail, but because they don't have a strong backup, which is the family. I decree by the mercies of the Most High, the devil will not find a way into your home on the name of Jesus. As you study this prayer article, may the protection of God Almighty be upon your home and family in the mighty name of Jesus. The scripture says the devil doesn't come unless to steal, kill, and destroy, may the devil never find its way into your family in the name of Jesus. Ensure that you practice this prayer article with all diligence and share it with other people. May God strengthen our homes and families against the vices of the devil in the name of Jesus?

PRAYER POINTS

1. Lord Jesus, I come before you concerning my home and family. Just like you have made the family the first ministry to put us in the way of righteousness, I pray that the family will not miss the true reason for its establishment in the name of Jesus. I pray for the protection of God Almighty upon my home and family. I pray concerning every member of my family. I decree that the hands of God Almighty will be upon every one of them in the name of Jesus. I pray that none of them shall become a victim of an accident; they shall not fall victim of death; they shall not fall victim of rape or kidnap in the name of Jesus.

2. I pray that you sanctify the heart of all of my family members. I come against every evil in their heart. I pray that you will dominate their mind, and the thoughts that come from the river of their hearts will be holy in the name of Jesus. I pray that by your mercy, you will not allow the enemy to gain access to their hearts, the devil will not influence their mind in the name of Jesus. Your word said that you would carry us in your hands so that we do not hot our foot against the rock. I pray that you will carry every member of my family in your hands that we may not hit our foot against the rock of life in the name of Jesus.

3. I pray over my family and everyone in it that you will guide us as we journey through life. The scripture says they rod and thy staff comforts me. You prepared a table before me in the presence of my enemies, and you anointed my head with oil. I pray that you will comfort us in the name of Jesus. I decree by the mercy of the most high that your spirit will journey with us as we go in life in the name of Jesus.

4. Lord Jesus, I pray that for every member of my family that are sick or heavily ladder, I pray that your hands of healing will come upon them today in the name of Jesus. For the scripture say that you have taken upon yourself all our infirmities and you have healed all our diseases, Lord, I decree that you will heal every sick one in my family in the name of Jesus.

5. Lord Jesus, the essence of our journey in life as a family, is to reign with you in eternal glory. I pray that as we approach life each day differently as family, you will grant us all the grace always to stay alert and conscious of our heavenly home in the name of Jesus. For it has been written that what shall it profit a man that gains the whole world and lose his soul. We do not want to lose our soul as a home and family, Lord, help us return home safely in the name of Jesus.

SPIRITUAL WARFARE PRAYER FOR THE FAMILY

Today we will be dealing with spiritual warfare prayer for the family. A family is a distinct unit among the agents of socialization. From the time a child is born, up until he grows into a man, he will be nurtured by the family. God has given so much power into the hands of a family. They could save one of their own from destruction, and they could also be the architect of decay to another.

Many people believe that a family is a union of people who are related by blood or by marriage. However, as against this general belief, a family is higher than that. It is not just blood or marriage that joins people together to become a family. A family could mean a group of people who shares the same interest, beliefs, norms, and values. That is why when we become one with Christ, we automatically join the family of Christ, and we see everyone in the family as brethren. While being in the body of Christ can join people together to become one, so also can being in the world join people together. For instance, an ardent drunkard will always ally with fellow drunkards. And then those who are being ruled and controlled by the devil are also one family.

When a family is united, there is a little to what they cannot achieve. That is why the scripture said one would pull a thousand, and two will pull ten thousand. Family is all about unity and togetherness. The devil is a great manipulator, understands this. That is why the devil will do everything to ensure that the family is not in good shape. When there is a problem in the family, the product of that family, i.e., the children, will have a problem.

Needless to say, there are so many families that have been manipulated and by the devil. They no longer see things from the same visual lens, the devil has created a disparity between them, and this had become a significant advantage for the enemy to penetrate. Once we come to the consciousness that things are not going the way they should, the onus is on us to rectify it. We owe our family a duty of prayer as a member of the family. When Apostle Peter was thrown into prison, the other Apostles knowing fully well that there is nothing they could do, they turn to God in prayers to rescue Peter, who was cast into the cell. The end of that story is a familiar gist.

We have compiled a list of spiritual warfare prayers to rescue the family from the devil and destroy the plans and agenda of the enemy to destroy the family.

PRAYER POINTS

- Lord God, I pray for your understanding that surpasses the wisdom of men, grants it upon each and every member of my family. The grace for us to understand ourselves with thoroughness and charm give it upon us in the name of Jesus.

- I come against every plan and agenda of the enemy to destroy my family with a dispute. Every plan and agenda of the enemy to create a disparity in my family, I destroy it by the blood of the lamb.

- For it has been written that I know the thoughts I have towards you, they are the thought of good and evil to give you an expected end. Lord Jesus, I pray that my family will not fail purpose in the name of Jesus.

- I come against every plan of the enemy to inflict my family and me with an incurable illness. Because it has been written that Christ has bare upon himself all our infirmities, and he has healed all our diseases. I destroy every form of the disease in my family in the name of Jesus.

- I decree by the authority of heaven that my family will continually work on the part of righteousness. Every plan of the enemy to cause us to fall away from the part is destroyed by fire.

- I anoint every member of my family with the blood of Christ. I destroy every form of death. I come against every scheme of kidnap, rape, or assassination in the name of Jesus.

- The Bible says, and they overcame him by the blood of the lamb and by the words of their testimony. I spill the blood of the lamb over every member of my family in the name of Jesus. I decree that your counsel alone will stand over my family in Jesus name.

- It has been written that my children and I are for signs and Wonders. Every plan of the enemy to make a laughing stock is destroyed. I counter their plans by the blood of the lamb in the name of Jesus.

- I announce our territorial authority over the devil and all his angels. The Bible says for we have been given a name that is above all other names. That at the mention of the name every knee must bow and every tongue shall confess that he is God. In the name of Jesus, I destroy the works of the enemy over my family.

- Just like Joshua announced to the people of Isreal that Choose ye this day the God you will serve, but as for my family and me, we will serve the Lord. I reiterate this assertion on behalf of my family. Lord Jesus, help us to serve you to the end.

- I decree that the purpose for the existence of every member of my family, the reason for our creation, will not be defeated in the name of Jesus Christ. I announce our liberty from the sweltering heat of iniquity, I announce our freedom from the shackles of slavery, and I declare our authority over sin through the blood of the lamb that washes away our sins.

- It has been written, declare a thing, and it shall be established, I decree success upon my family in the name of Jesus.

- The Bible says, one shall pull a thousand, and two shall pull ten thousand, I claim this by the unity of faith in my family, from now our harvest shall be higher in the name of Jesus. Amen.

POWERFUL PRAYERS FOR UNITY IN THE FAMILY

Family is structured on the principle of unity, and Unity is capable of birthing a family. Whether or not people are related by blood or marriage, they can become family when there is a unity of purpose. Reasonably, powerful prayer for unity in the family hence becomes one of the most important prayers to say for the family. A family is an essential unit in the sight of God. As much as the family could be regarded as a social institution, it can also be seen as a spiritual entity.

When a child is born into this world, they have no religion, no language, identity, or belief. It is the sole function of the family to bring up the child. The family gives the child identity, religion, helps them craft a belief, and provides them with a language.

Judging by this, it is, therefore, important that the family is united to achieve all these functions that the society and God want them to perform. When there is no unity in the family, there is no way it won't affect the upbringing of every child born into that family.

There is nothing as fulfilling as a family that stands together in unity. The merits of this great deed cannot be overemphasized. Recall that the Bible says one will pull a thousand, and two will pull ten thousand. This established the fact that families would achieve more when they are united. However, two cannot work together unless they agree. What this means is that the success or failure of any family will be based on the unity that exists that family or the lack of it.

Amazingly, when families hold hands and pray together, it spells a great doom on the kingdom of darkness. God respects a unity in purpose, the devil also knows this, and that's why the first thing he tries to steal from a family is the spirit of unity.

Even in the body of Christ, when each compartment is broken into fragments, the devil will not be too far to strike.

The book of Joshua chapter 24 – 15 And if it seems evil to you to serve the Lord, choose for yourselves this day whom you will serve, whether the gods which your fathers served that were on the other side of the River, or the gods of the Amorites, in whose land you dwell. But as for me and my house, we will serve the Lord. The only reason Joshua could authoritatively say this was because there is a unity of purpose in his family.

The unity in the family of Joshua made it easy for him to tell the elders of Isreal that they can go ahead and chose another God for themselves if they see evil in serving the Lord. However, for him and his family, they would serve the Lord.

Do not allow the devil to take away one of the greatest assets that God has given to your family. You must do everything to protect the unity that exists in your family. We have compiled a list of powerful prayers for unity in the family to help your family stay United.

PRAYERS

- Father Lord, I pray to you today concerning my family. I ask that you will teach us to be united in the name of Jesus.

- I come against every power and scheme that may want to create a disparity in our midst; I destroy such powers in the name of Jesus.

- I pray Lord that you will cause us to have a unity of purpose, you will make the vision clear to each of us that we may uniformly run by it in the name of Jesus.

- Lord God, I pray for your undiluted love, teach us how to love ourselves dearly in the name of Jesus.

- Father Lord, I pray that you will block every access that the devil is creating to cause dispute in my family. I pray that you will prevent it in the name of Jesus.

- Lord God, I pray that you will give us all the spirit to tolerate ourselves. I know that we are different people despite being family, but I pray that you will grant unto us the grace to be able to tolerate one another in the name of Jesus.

- Father Lord, I ask that you will grant us the privilege and grace to forgive ourselves whenever we cross one another in the name of Jesus.

- Lord Jesus, by your mercy, I pray that you will teach us silent when we are angry, you will give us utterance when we are furious.

- Lord God, the scripture says a house divided against itself will not stand. I come against every power of division in our family by the blood of the lamb

- Father Lord, the Bible says how good and pleasant it is for brothers to work in unity. I ask that you will help us to continue working in unity in the name of Jesus.
- Lord God, we do not want to fail our purpose as a family, help us to stand and live in love forever in the name of Jesus.
- The blood of the lamb destroys Father Lord, whatever the enemy is planning to use as an instrument to create enmity in our family.
- The scripture says that my children and I are for signs and wonders, I destroy every power that might want to use my children to cause disunity in my family, and I destroy such power in the name of Jesus.
- Father, we don't just want to be united, we also want to be blinded by love so strong, and we want to be united in godliness, help us to achieve this in the name of Jesus.
- Lord Jesus, I pray that you will mend all broken hearts in my home. I ask that by your mercy, you will heal every emotional injury in my family, I pray that you will restore the first love our hearts in the name of Jesus.
- I come against every spirit of malice, envy, jealousy, and bitterness that may want to dwell in the heart of my family members. I pray that you will destroy it in the name of Jesus.
- I pray that you will grant every lost one in my family the grace to find you, help them rediscover their place in you in the name of Jesus.
- I pray Lord Jesus that you will make our offspring's be a blessing unto others everywhere they find themselves. Help them always to be a good ambassador of the family of Christ in the name of Jesus.
- Lord God, I pray that you will bless every member of my family with a heart that will continually thirst after you in the name of Jesus.

3 DAY PRAYER AND FASTING TO BREAK THE CYCLE OF FAMILY CURSES

2 Kings 5:25 But he went in, and stood before his master. And Elisha said unto him, whence comest thou, Gehazi? And he said, Thy servant went no whither.

5:26 and he said unto him, Went not mine heart with thee, when the man turned again from his chariot to meet thee? Is it a time to receive money, and to receive garments, and olive yards, and vineyards, and sheep, and oxen, and menservants, and maidservants?

5:27 the leprosy therefore of Naaman shall cleave unto thee, and unto thy seed for ever. And he went out from his presence a leper as white as snow.

Life is full of mysteries, and nothing happens in life by accident. Everything that happens, it's because there is a cause to the effect of that happening. Therefore, for you as an individual to make progress in life, you must crave to understand how things operates in life. Today we shall be engaging in a 3 day prayer and fasting to break the cycle of family curses.

These prayer and fasting will open your eyes to the mystery of family curse and you will be empowered to break free from every form of curses working against your life and family. I encourage you to read every piece of this article by faith today and expect to see the hand of God set you free from every legal hold of the devil in your life in Jesus Christ name.

Are Curses Real?

Before we answer that question, let us first of all define what a curse is. A curse is a negative proclamation open a person, a group of people or a thing, which takes effect immediately and begins to control that person or thing. Curses can be placed upon animate and inanimate object. A person can be cursed, a tree can be cursed.

When a person is cursed, that person becomes exposed to the devil. Curses gives the devil a legal hold to operate in your life. Suffice to say that when one is cursed, he or she is handed over to the devil for torment. This torment continues until the curse is lifted. Now back to our question, are curses real?

This is a very valid question a lot of people wonder if curses are real, do they really work? The answer to this question is an emphatic YES! Curses are very real. Infect from the beginning, in Genesis 3:17, we see God curse the ground for man's sake. In case you didn't know, this is where struggles started from. That is why till date, you must work hard and sweat before you can make a living in life. That curse is still in effect till today.

Also in Deuteronomy 28:14-68, we see what the bible calls the Curse of the law. We see all the various curses attached to disobeying the commands of God. This curse is activated by sin.

In the bible we also see Noah place a curse on Canaan one of his sons, Genesis 9:25, and Jacob place a curse on Reuben his first son, Genesis 49:3. This type of curse is called parental curse.

In the book of Joshua 6:26, we saw Joshua place a curse on whosoever attempts to rebuild the walls of Jericho and in 1 Kings 16:34, we see the curse of Joshua come to pass.

In the New testament, we see Jesus Christ our Lord place a curse on a fig tree, Mark 11:12-25, Peter placed a curse on Simeon, Acts 8:20, Paul placed a curse on Elymas the sorcerer, Acts 13:8.

All this are clear indication, that curses are real. A curse placed in one generation can affect the generations after it, the same way, a curse placed on a family will remain in that family until it is broken.

Types of Curses

1. Curse of The Law: This curse is the greatest curse that ever exists, and if Christ can deliver us from this curse, then all other curses are a piece of cake to Him. This curse is triggered by sin, and the curse is death, the second death. This means as long as you are not born again this curse is still at work in your life, only believers have been set free from it through Christ. **Galatians 3:13.**

2. Parental Curse: This curses are placed on an individual by their parents, or any other elder person. When you maltreat your parents, and treat them like trash, they can place a curse on you. The same way when you maltreat older people, you can attract a curse in your life. There are also situations where evil parents and elders place a curse on an innocent child. The good news is that through the Power in the name of Jesus Christ, all these curses can be broken. However, if you offended your parents and they are still alive, you must go to them and ask for their mercy, the same goes for any elderly person you have offended. Also when you go to apologize, don't go empty handed, go with a lot of goodies as much as you can afford.

3. Generational Curse: This is a type of curse that moves from generation to generation. It can only stop in the generation that decides to break the curse. A perfect example is Gehazi 1 Kings 5:20-27.

4. The Curse of a Man Of God: This are curses released upon a person by a man of God. These men of God, can be pastors, prophets, evangelist or any believer. Every man of God has the power to proclaim blessings and curses, while the New Testament admonishes us not curse, when a man of God places a curse on you, it sticks. You must treat men of God with respect, do not maltreat them or make life miserable for them, I am talking about men God has sent your way to bless you. Treat them with respect, so that you can only attract blessings and never curses. Examples of this type of curses are; Elijah 1 Kings 17:1, Elisha 2 Kings 5:20-27, Peter Acts 8:20, Paul Acts 13:8.

5. Curses from Witch Doctors: This is a cursed place on someone by a native doctor, witch or wizard, sangoma etc. A perfect example is when King Balak summoned the sorcerer Balaam to curse the Children of Isreal, so that he will destroy them. Numbers 22, Numbers 23.

6. Family Curse: This is a curse that affects the entire family of a person, including that person. Many families today a under a curse because of the sins there ancestors committed. Examples in the bible are Gehazi 2 kings 5:20-27, Achan, Joshua 7, Korah, Dathan, and Abiram, Numbers 16.

7. Self-Inflicted Curse: This is a curse you put on yourself. This curse comes upon you when you enter a wrong covenant, or you engage on an evil act. Judas Iscariot brought himself under a curse by betraying Jesus Christ Matthew 27:1-10. He hanged himself on the tree, and Galatians 3:13-14 tells us that cursed is he that hangeth himself on the tree. Also every thief and wicked person has placed a curse upon himself, Zachariah 5:4, Proverbs 3:33.

But What About Christ Sacrifice?

Galatians 3:13 Christ hath redeemed us from the curse of the law, being made a curse for us: for it is written, Cursed is every one that hangeth on a tree: 3:14 that the blessing of Abraham might come on the Gentiles through Jesus Christ; that we might receive the promise of the Spirit through faith.

This is the word of God, Christ has delivered us from the Curse of the Law through His sacrifice on the cross. This means that we are no longer subject to the law of sin and death, Romans 8:1-2. Sin and death no longer has power over us. However, we must Use the name of Jesus Christ through prayers and fasting to break free from every other curses at work in our lives. My beloved, make no mistakes about this, the devil will still come after you even after you are saved, remember that pharaoh still ran after the Israelites when they left Egypt, despite the fact that Jesus is The Son Of God, the devil still tempted Jesus continually.

That you are redeemed from the law of sin and death, does not exempt you from the attacks of the devil, you must continuously resist the devil in all areas of your life and destiny in other to enjoy a victorious life in Christ. Before Jesus ascended to heaven, He gave us Power, in the person of the Holy Ghost, we must continually engage that power if we must keep dominating in life, Acts 1:8.

This means, that you don't assume that you are free, you possess your freedom by faith on the altar of prayer and fasting. You don't go to sleep because you are redeemed, you enforce your redemption by continually marching on the head of Satan and his angels. If there is an evil cycle in your family break it by the force of prayer and fasting.
How Do I Break the Cycle of Family Curses
Prayer and fasting is the key to breaking every cycle of family curses. Fasting empowers your spirit man to be super sensitive to wage spiritual warfare while prayers releases the hosts of Angels to destroy every legal hold of the devil over your family. I have carefully selected powerful 3 day prayer and fasting to break the cycle of family curses in your family. Engage this prayers with faith, gather your entire family together as you all embark on a 3 day fast, praying this prayer points. I see your family set free forever in Jesus name.

PRAYER POINTS

1. Father, I thank you for delivering me and my family from the curses of the law in Jesus Christ name.

2. I curse every curse in my life in Jesus Christ name.

3. Every curse hanging on my family tree be destroyed now in Jesus Christ name.

4. Every curse of witchcraft targeted on my family be destroyed now in Jesus Christ name.

5. Every curse of bondage in my family break now in Jesus Christ name.

6. Every self-inflicted curse in my family break now in Jesus Christ name.

7. Every cycle of untimely death in my family break now in Jesus Christ name.

8. I renounce every curse spoken against my family members, knowingly and unknowingly in Jesus Christ name.

9. I renounce all unholy covenant which my ancestors made on my behalf in Jesus Christ name.

10. I release my family from every form of collective captivity in Jesus Christ name.

11. Every inherited bondage in my family be destroyed in Jesus Christ name.

12. I break and lose my family from every evil covenant in Jesus Christ name.

13. I silence the voice of any curse speaking against my family in Jesus Christ name.

14. Let the rod of the wicked rising up against my family be destroyed now in Jesus Christ name.

15. Let every gates opened to the enemy as a result of curses in my family be destroyed in Jesus Christ name.

16. Once and for all I release myself and my entire family from all the authority of every curse in Jesus Christ name.

17. I render powerless every activity of sorcerers against my family in Jesus Christ name.

18. I render powerless every charm targeted against me and my family in Jesus Christ name.

19. I render powerless every strange power targeted against me in Jesus Christ name.

20. Enough is enough of curses in my life and family, I must make progress this year in Jesus Christ name.

21. I mock every problem that mocks me in Jesus Christ name.

22. I destroy every power that attempts to destroy me in Jesus Christ name.

23. I humiliate every agent of Satan that wants to humiliate me in Jesus Christ name.

24. I release calamity upon all those who trouble my life in Jesus Christ name.

25. By the blood of Jesus, I am washed from all curses in Jesus Christ name.

26. Every demonic switch designed to put off my light be destroyed now in Jesus Christ name.

27. Me and my entire family are set free now in Jesus Christ name.

28. From today, the hand of God shall never depart from my family in Jesus Christ name.

29. I declare that I am free in Jesus Christ name.

30. Thank You Jesus Christ.

3 DAYS FASTING AND PRAYERS FOR FAMILY DELIVERANCE

Esther 4:16 Go, gather together all the Jews that are present in Shushan, and fast ye for me, and neither eat nor drink three days, night or day: I also and my maidens will fast likewise; and so will I go in unto the king, which is not according to the law: and if I perish, I perish.

Many families are under the siege of the enemy, the devil and his demons have trapped those families and placed them in their demonic prison. There are many families today that no one succeeds from there, because the devil have blocked all their progress. For any family to break free from the shackles of the enemy, that family must come together for a family deliverance. Today we shall be engaging in 3 days fasting and prayers for family deliverance. This fasting and prayers is to be done by the entire family as the pray there way out of the entrapments of the devil.

Family curses are real, these are recurrent evil patterns that are continually seen in many families. There are some families where the women don't marry, they only have children out of wedlock, some others nobody goes beyond the secondary education level, some families are plagued with terminal sicknesses, while some are plagued with poverty, all these are not of natural causes, they are spiritual arrows targeted at families to keep them under the power of darkness. But today, as you engage this 3 days fasting and prayers for family deliverance, both you and your household shall be set free in Jesus name. As you and your family members engage this fasting and prayers, every evil stronghold holding your family down shall be destroyed in Jesus name. I encourage you to pray this prayers with your family members, pray those with faith and you shall testify of your freedom in Jesus name.

PRAYER POINTS
1. I repent of all ancestral idol worship, in the name of Jesus.

2. Every strongman of my father's house, loose your hold over my life, in the name of Jesus.

3. Every strongman of my father's house die, in the name of Jesus.

4. I silence the evil cry of the evil powers of my father's house, fashioned against me, in the name of Jesus.

5. All consequences of the worship of evil powers of my father's house upon my life, I wipe you off, by the blood of Jesus.

6. Holy Ghost fire, burn down all spiritual shrines of my father's house, in the name of Jesus.

7. Oppressive agenda of the evil powers of my father's house, die, in the name of Jesus.

8. Any blood, speaking against my generational line, be silenced by the blood of Jesus.

9. Every evil power of my father's house, speaking against my destiny, scatter, in the name of Jesus.

10. I break all ancestral covenants with the evil powers of my father's house, in the name of Jesus.

11. Every bitter water, flowing in my family from the evil powers of my father's house, dry up; in the name of Jesus.

12. Any rope, tying my family line to any evil power of my father's house, break, in the name of Jesus.

13. Every landlord spirit, troubling my destiny, be paralysed, in the name of Jesus.

14. Every outflow of satanic family name, die in the name of Jesus.

15. I recover every benefit stolen by the evil power of my father's house, in the name of Jesus.

16. Where is the God of Elijah, arise, disgrace every evil power of my father's house, in the name of Jesus.

17. Every satanic priest, ministering in my family line, be retrenched, in the name of Jesus.

18. Arrows of affliction, originating from idolatry, loose your hold, in the name of Jesus.

19. Every influence of the evil powers of my father's house on my life, die, in the name of Jesus.

20. Every network of the evil powers of my father's house in my place of birth, scatter, in the name of Jesus

21. Oh Lord, activate your high call on my life, in the name of Jesus.

22. Oh Lord, anoint me to recover the wasted years in every area of my life, in the name of Jesus.

23. Oh Lord, if I have fallen behind in many areas of my life, empower me to recover all lost opportunities and wasted years, in the name of Jesus.

24. Any power, that says I will not go forward, be arrested, in the name of Jesus.

25. Any power, that wants to keep me in want in the midst of plenty, die, in the name of Jesus.

26. Any power, that wants to draw me away from the presence of the Lord to destroy me, die, in the name of Jesus.

27. I will get to my promised inheritance, in the name of Jesus.

28. Any power that wants me to fulfil my destiny only partially, die, in the name of Jesus.

29. Oh Lord, anoint me with power to destroy all foundational covenants, in the name of Jesus.

30. Oh Lord, use my substance for the furtherance of the gospel, in the name of Jesus.

31. Oh Lord, arise and bless my inheritance, in the name of Jesus.

32. All my stolen virtues, be returned to me, in the name of Jesus.

33. O Lord, let my release bring revival, in the name of Jesus.

34. Oh Lord, reveal all ignorant ways in me by Your Holy Spirit, in the name of Jesus.

35. Today, you my spirit man, you will not bewitch me, in the name of Jesus.

36. Power in the blood of Jesus, redeem my destiny, in the name of Jesus.

37. Every satanic weapon, formed against my destiny, backfire, in the name of Jesus.

38. Arrows of deliverance, locate my destiny, in the name of Jesus

39. Every spiritual cobweb on my destiny, burn, in the name of Jesus.

40. Every serpent in my foundation, swallowing my destiny, die, in the name of Jesus.

30 PRAYER POINTS FOR FAMILY DELIVERANCE

Acts 16:31

And they said, Believe on the Lord Jesus Christ, and thou shalt be saved, and thy house.

There is no family on earth that doesn't suffer one challenge or another. As a matter of fact, the institution called the family is the most attacked institution on earth. Families across the world are in bondage and oppression in the form of poverty, troubled marriages, failure at the edge of success, and untimely death. Dearly beloved, the purpose of these prayer points for family deliverance is to invoke fire against all strongholds, all strange altars and every strongman that has held you and your family captive and just the way God delivered the children of Israel from Pharaoh and his hosts, after these prayers God will deliver your family with the speed of lightning: if only you believe.

Every winning family is a praying family, and every praying family cannot be a victim of demonic influence. As believers, we must understand that when we invite God into our families, we overcome all the challenges that comes to us, the purpose of these prayer points for family deliverance is to reintroduce God back to our families, is to bring down the presence of God into our families. When the presence of God is manifested in a family, every mountain standing before that family is moved. Every satanic yoke is broken and everyone under the siege of the devil is set free in Jesus name. My prayer for you today is this; as you pray this prayer points for family deliverance today, you and your household shall be delivered in Jesus name. Pray these prayers with faith today and receive your own deliverance. God bless you.

PRAYER POINTS

1. Father in the name of Jesus I thank you for the salvation of my soul today.

2. Father in the name of Jesus I thank you because before I say this prayer points for my family you have already heard me.

3. Father in the name of Jesus I thank you for fighting and winning my battles on the cross of Calvary.

4. I release myself from every household bondage in my lineage.

5. Fire of the living God, like you, came down in the days of Elijah, consume every chain of poverty, addiction, oppression, and limitation in my life today. 1kings 18:38

6. Holy ghost fire, just like the days of Elisha send down strange animals to consume every agent that have held down my finances and the finance of my family. 2 kings 2:23-24

7. Heavenly Father, just like the angel rolled away the stone from the tomb of Jesus, let my angel roll away every stone trapping the destiny of my family and me in a tomb. Matthew 28:2.

8. I release confusion and destruction into the camp of every kidnapper of my family's destiny today.

9. Heavenly father as the sea opened up and swallowed the enemies of your people who held them in captivity for years. Let the sea swallow every ancestral spirit that has held my family bond.

10. Let the mighty arm of God which broke the chains of Paul and Silas in the prison break every chain connecting me to my past and restricting me from the future God has planned for my family and me. Acts 16:25-34.

11. Heavenly Father, as you delivered Daniel and the three Hebrew children from the hands of their oppressors, deliver my family and me from the bondage of poverty, penury, and failure. Daniel 6:1-28.

12. Ballistic missiles from the heavenly places begin to bombard every coven where the glory of my family is being hidden.

13. Sporadic missiles begin to fall on every cage where my family's destiny is being kept.

14. Let the trumpets from heaven deafen the ears of my captors so that they will release my family and me without delay

15. As I say this prayer points for family, I command the hosts of heaven to begin to break free every member of my family that has been tied to a tree of failure.

16. As I pray this prayer points for family let chains begin to fall from the hands of my children, my husband, wife, parents, and relatives in the mighty name of Jesus.

17. As I pray this prayer points for family, because I am a son/daughter of Abraham, connected to the seed of David, let all that I have lost and all that have been captured from me be released, and recovered in double portion. Luke 13:16.

18. Fire of the living God, like you, consumed Sodom and Gomorrah, consume the captors of my marital life as I pray this prayer points for family. Genesis 19:24.

19. As the grave could not hold back Lazarus at the sound of the voice of Jesus. Because I am joint-heirs with Christ, as I pray this prayer points for family let the grave release everything it has held back from my family. John 11:38-44

20. Let there be mysterious earthquakes and tornados that will shake the foundations of where the success of my family has been kept as I pray this prayer points for family.

21. Because there is nothing too hard for the lord that I serve, I declare that from today, every impossible situation that has been associated with my family is destroyed in the mighty name of Jesus. Jeremiah 32:27.

22. I command the angels that were assigned to me to comb the length and breadth of the earth and release every wealth that has the name of my family on it and deliver it to me today. Psalm91:11.

23. Today, my family and I are delivered from the snare of the fowler and every noisome pestilence. Psalm 91:3.

24. This year every strong man from my father's house or every strong woman from my mother's side who have locked me in the room of failure open the gates and be disgraced in the name of Jesus. Matthew 12:29.

25. Hailstones and fire for above begin to fall on every philistine that have captured, tortured, and ruptured the finance of my helpers today. Joshua 10:11

26. Because Jesus, my savior, and lord, was resurrected and delivered from the hold of death after three days. I decree that within three days, my family and I are delivered from every strange spirit of death, haunting and trailing my family.1 corinthians 15:4.

27. Every territorial force of delay that is responsible for tying my family and me to a spot, thereby preventing us from being promoted and elevated, let thunder from heaven scatter them in the name of Jesus.

28. Let the arrows from God begin to slay the guardians of every strange calabash, causing childlessness in my family.

29. In the name of Jesus, let every principality and power standing on the way to my success, wealth, and financial dominion this year be destroyed and put to shame.

30. Let ballistic missiles visit the camp of any strange man or strange woman that has captured the hearts of my husband/wife/children and let them be bound with the same chains by which my family was bound.

Father, I thank you because as you said in your world, that if I ask anything in your name, it will be done. I thank you because you have answered all the prayer points for family. In your mighty name, I have prayed.

PRAYER AGAINST STRONGMAN IN THE FAMILY

Isaiah 49:24-25. Shall the prey be taken from the mighty, or the lawful captive delivered? 25 But thus saith the Lord, Even the captives of the mighty shall be taken away, and the prey of the terrible shall be delivered: for I will contend with him that contendeth with thee, and I will save thy children.

Today we shall be engaging in prayers against strongman in the family. Who is a strongman? A strongman is a superior demon, in charge of other evil spirits, they are dominant spirits in control of an environment, territory and family. A demonic strongman can hold a community bound with its demonic influence, it can also hold a family captive for generations. Whenever you notice a dominant plague or issue in a given family, you know that, that is the handiwork of a demonic strongman. For instance, in some families you notice a long line of marital delay, all the ladies never get married, in some families you notice that they have issues of child bearing or barrenness, in some families, you notice issues of alcoholism, some poverty, the list goes on and on. While some of these issues may be from natural causes, it is very wise you take care of the spiritual roots first. As the spiritual controls the physical. Now let's quickly look at the signs of a strongman in a family.

Signs of a Strongman in the Family.

When you see these signs in your family, you know that it's obviously the work of a demonic strongman. You must rise up and engage in prayers against strongman in the family. Below are some of the signs.
1. Little or no progress in spite of hard efforts
2. Chain problems in families
3. Prayer resistance by dark forces
4. Unpardonable errors
5. Demons overcoming the person with ease
6. Nothing going smoothly
7. Planting much but reaping little

8. The whole of life becomes a struggle

9. Profitless hard work

10. Problems remain the same after deliverance ministrations

11. Labour so much but achieve nothing

12. Devourers working against you.

13. Acidic poverty

14. Prayer become ordinary noise

I have good news for you today, these prayers against strongman in the family will set you loose from every form of satanic resistance today. As you engage it in faith every strongman in your family shall be disarmed and destroyed in Jesus name. Your freedom is guaranteed today. Remain blessed

PRAYER POINTS

1. I consume the shrine of the strongman in my family with the fire of God, in the name of Jesus.

2. Let stones of fire pursue and dominate all the strongmen in my life, in the name of Jesus.

3. I smash the head of the strongman on the wall of fire, in Jesus' name.

4. I cause open disgrace to all strongmen in my family, in Jesus' name.

5. The strongman from my father's side; the strongman from my mother's side, begin to destroy yourselves in the name of Jesus.

6. I bind and I render to nothing all the strongmen that are currently troubling my life, in the name of Jesus.

7. You strongman of body destruction, loose your hold over my body, fall down and die, in the name of Jesus.

8. Every demon, strongman and associated spirits of financial collapse, receive the hailstones of fire and be roasted beyond remedy, in Jesus' name.

9. Let the finger of God unseat my household strongman, in the name of Jesus.

10. I bind you the strongman in my life and I clear my goods from your possession, in the name of Jesus.

11. You strongman of mind destruction, be bound, in Jesus' name.

12. You strongman of financial destruction, be bound, in Jesus' name.

13. Every strongman of bad luck, attached to my life, fall down and die, in Jesus' name.

14. I bind every strongman, militating against my home, in the name of Jesus.

15. I bind and paralyse every strongman of death and hell, in the name of Jesus.

16. You evil strongman, attached to my destiny, be bound, in Jesus' name.

17. Every strongman of my father's house, die, in the name of Jesus.

18. Every strongman, assigned by the evil powers of my father's house against my life, die, in the name of Jesus.

19. Every strongman, assigned to weaken my faith, catch fire, in the name of Jesus.

20. I bind and I render to nought, all the strongmen that are currently troubling my life, in the name of Jesus.

21. Let the backbone of the stubborn pursuer and strongman break, in the name of Jesus.

22. I bind every strongman, having my goods in his possessions, in the name of Jesus.

23. I clear my goods from the warehouse of the strongman; in the name of Jesus.

24. I withdraw the staff of the office of the strongman delegated against me, in the name of Jesus.

25. I bind every strongman, delegated to hinder my progress, in the name of Jesus.

26. I bind the strongman behind my spiritual blindness and deafness, and paralyze his operations in my life, in the name of Jesus.

27. Let the stubborn strongman delegated against me fall down to the ground and become impotent, in Jesus' name.

28. I bind the strongman over myself, in the name of Jesus.

29. I bind the strongman over my family, in the name of Jesus.

30. I bind the strongman over my blessings, in the name of Jesus.

31. I bind the strongman over my business, in the name of Jesus.

32. I command the armour of the strongman to be roasted completely, in the name of Jesus.

33. I release myself from the hold of any religious spiritual strongman, in the name of Jesus.

34. I release myself from the hold of any evil strongman, in the name of Jesus.

35. I bind and plunder the goods of every strongman, attached to my marriage, in the name of Jesus.

36. I release my money from the house of the strongman, in the name of Jesus.

37. Let the backbone of the strongman in charge of each problem be broken, in the name of Jesus.

38. Any satanic strongman, keeping my blessings as his goods fall down and die, I recover my goods now.

39. Every jinx upon my _ _ _, be broken, in the name of Jesus.

40. Every spell upon my _ _ _, be broken, in the name of Jesus.

41. Let the rod of the wrath of the Lord come upon every enemy of my_ _ _, in the name of Jesus.

42. Let the angels of God invade them and lead them into darkness, in the name of Jesus.

43. Let the hand of the Lord turn against them day by day, in the name of Jesus.

44. Let their flesh and skin become old, and let their bones be broken, in the name of Jesus.

45. Let them be compassed with gall and travail, in the name of Jesus.

46. Let Your angels hedge them about and block their paths, in the name of Jesus.

47. O Lord, make their chains heavy.

48. When they cry, shut out their cries, in the name of Jesus.

49. O Lord, make their paths crooked.

50. O Lord, make their ways to be strewn with sharp stones.

51. Let the power of their own wickedness fall upon them, in the name of Jesus.

52. O Lord, turn them aside and cut them into pieces.

53. O Lord, make their ways desolate.

54. O Lord, fill them with bitterness and let them be drunken with wormwood.

55. O Lord, break their teeth with gravel stones.

56. O Lord, cover them with ashes.

57. O Lord, remove their souls far from peace and let them forget prosperity.

58. I crush under my feet, all the evil powers trying to imprison me, in the name of Jesus.

59. Let their mouth be put in the dust, in the name of Jesus.

60. Let there be civil war in the camp of the enemies of my _ _ _, in the name of Jesus.

61. Let the power of God pull down the stronghold of the enemies of my_ _ _, in the name of Jesus.

62. O Lord, persecute them and destroy them in anger, in the name of Jesus.

63. Let every blockage in my way of _ _ _ clear off by fire, in the name of Jesus.

64. Every demonic claim of the earth over my life, be dismantled, in the name of Jesus.

65. I refuse to be chained to my place of birth, in Jesus' name.

66. Any power pressing the sand against me, fall down and die, in the name of Jesus.

67. I receive my breakthroughs, in the name of Jesus.

68. I release my money from the house of the strongman, in the name of Jesus.

69. I break and loose myself from every inherited evil covenant of the earth, in the name of Jesus.

70. I break and loose myself from every inherited evil covenant of the earth, in the name of Jesus.

71. I break and loose myself from every inherited evil curse of the earth, in the name of Jesus.

72. I break and loose myself from every form of demonic bewitchment of the earth, in the name of Jesus.

73. I release myself from every evil domination and control from the earth, in the name of Jesus.

74. Let the blood of Jesus be transfused into my blood vessel.

75. I release panic upon my full time enemies, in the name of Jesus.

76. Let stubborn confusion come upon the headquarters of my enemies, in the name of Jesus.

77. I loose confusion upon the plans of my enemies, in the name of Jesus.

78. Every stronghold of darkness, receive acidic confusion, in the name of Jesus.

79. I loose panic and frustration on satanic orders issued against me, in the name of Jesus.

80. Every evil plan against my life, receive confusion, in the name of Jesus.

81. All curses and demons programmed against me, I neutralise you through the blood of Jesus.

82. Every warfare prepared against my peace, I command panic upon you, in the name of Jesus.

83. Every warfare prepared against my peace, I command havoc upon you, in the name of Jesus.

84. Every warfare prepared against my peace, I command chaos upon you, in the name of Jesus.

85. Every warfare prepared against my peace, I command pandemonium upon you, in the name of Jesus.

86. Every warfare prepared against my peace, I command disaster upon you, in the name of Jesus.

87. Every warfare prepared against my peace, I command confusion upon you, in the name of Jesus.

88. Every warfare prepared against my peace, I command spiritual acid upon you, in the name of Jesus.

89. Every warfare prepared against my peace, I command destruction upon you, in the name of Jesus.

90. Every warfare prepared against my peace, I command hornets of the Lord upon you, in Jesus' name.

91. Every warfare prepared against my peace, I command brimstone and hailstone upon you, in the name of Jesus.

92. I frustrate every satanic verdict issued against me, in Jesus' name.

93. Let the finger, vengeance, terror, anger, fear, wrath, hatred and burning judgment of God be released against my full time enemies, in the name of Jesus.

94. Every power, preventing the perfect will of God from being done in my life, receive failure and defeat, in the name of Jesus.

95. Let the warring angels and Spirit of God arise and scatter every evil gathering sponsored against me, in the name of Jesus.

96. I disobey any satanic order, programmed by inheritance into my life, in the name of Jesus.

97. I bind and cast out every power causing internal warfare, in the name of Jesus.

98. Every demonic doorkeeper, locking out good things from me, be paralysed by fire, in the name of Jesus.

99. I command every evil power fighting against me to fight against and destroy one another, in Jesus' name.

100. Every breakthrough hindering, delaying, preventing, destroying and breaking demons, receive confusion, in the name of Jesus.

101. Let divine power and control attack the spirits of violence and torture, in the name of Jesus.

102. Let the spirit of witchcraft attack familiar spirits fashioned against me, in the name of Jesus.

103. Let there be a civil war in the kingdom of darkness, in the name of Jesus.

104. Lord, loose judgment and destruction upon all stubborn, disobedient and reluctant spirits that fail to follow my commands promptly.

80 DELIVERANCE PRAYER FROM FAMILY BONDAGE

Exodus 7:1-4: 1 And the Lord said unto Moses, See, I have made thee a god to Pharaoh: and Aaron thy brother shall be thy prophet. 2 Thou shalt speak all that I command thee: and Aaron thy brother shall speak unto Pharaoh, that he send the children of Israel out of his land. 3 And I will harden Pharaoh's heart, and multiply my signs and my wonders in the land of Egypt. 4 But Pharaoh shall not hearken unto you, that I may lay my hand upon Egypt, and bring forth mine armies, and my people the children of Israel, out of the land of Egypt by great judgments.

Every child of God is constantly under the attack of the devil and his agents. As believers we cannot afford to be ignorant of the devices of the devil against our lives. Life is a battle ground and only the spiritually weak, ends up as a scape goat. Today we shall be engaging in 80 deliverance prayer from family bondage. This deliverance prayer is a prayer for family. That is we are standing in the gap for our loved ones as we engage this deliverance prayers for their release from bondage. To be in bondage is to held captive by satanic forces. A lot of families today under the captivity of the devil. The devil has held them bound with all manner of evil traps. This deliverance prayer will empower you to break to pieces every evil chains that the devil has used to tie down your family in Jesus name.

Types of Bondages

There are different types of bondages, in fact time and space will not permit us to mention all of them. The list is endless, however we are going to be looking at some of the types of spiritual bondages that the devil uses to hold down families captives. Below are types of bondages:

A). Bondage Of Poverty: This is a state where in a family no one succeeds, no matter how hard the try, no one makes it to the top in the family. Many families are under this bondage of poverty, the devil has block their progress, such that whatsoever they lay their hands on do not prosper. But today, as you engage this deliverance prayers from family bondage, your family will be delivered in Jesus name.

B). Bondage of Unfruitfulness: This is when a family have been plagued with barrenness. This is not the will of God for any family. There are many families today that are struggling to have children because of the evil works of the devil in their lives. Barrenness is not of God and as you pray this prayer for family today, your family shall be delivered in Jesus name.

C). Bondage of Sin: This is when sin has taken over your family. There are many families today where you cannot find one saved soul in it. Everyone is just living a sinful life. The devil has blocked their ears and their hearts that they cannot hear the gospel that can save them. Such a family is heading for destruction unless serious deliverance prayers is made on their behalf.

D). Bondage of Stagnation: This is when the progress of a family comes to a full stop. When all doors becomes closed and no one is making progress anymore. This is another sign that the family needs serious deliverance prayers.

E). Bondage of Evil Pattern: An evil pattern is a recurrence of evil in a family from generation to generation. That is to say, what your great grandfather, suffered, your grandfather suffered it, your father suffered it and now you are already seeing the same signs in your life. You must reject it in prayers.

F). Bondage of Ancestral Curses: These is when the sins of your ancestors brings a curse upon your family. This can be very frustrating because a lot of families are suffering from what they know nothing about. That is why you need to ask questions, find out about your background and no why you are going through what you are going through. Only deliverance prayers a break family curses.

G). Bondage of Addiction: This is when a family has a history of addiction, either addiction to alcohol, cigarettes, drugs or other harmful substances. Thank God for therapies and rehabilitation centres but a deliverance prayer for such a family will destroy that addiction from the roots.

H). Bondage of Failure: This is when a family is used to failure and always being behind in everything. This is not the will of God, God promised us in Deuteronomy 28:13, that we shall be on top only and never at the bottom.

I). Bondage of Disappointments: This is when a family is suffering from the affliction of disappointments. Broken promises, broken friendships, and broken relationships. This affliction is also the cause of what is popularly called" near success syndrome". Which is failure almost at the edge of success. You must pray yourself and your entire family out of this bondage

J). Bondage of Slavery: This is when the devil has reduced your entire family members to servants. When you and your family are seen as the least in all things. When people treat you like rags in the society. You must rise up and reject that status. You are not meant to be a slave, but a king. God has ordained you to reign in life and not beg to survive. You must stand in the gap and pray yourself and your entire family out of this evil status. These prayer for family shall bring you lasting deliverance as you engage them in Jesus name.

All these forms of bondages are used by the devil to hold families bound perpetually. But today you are going to take your deliverance by force. You are going to engage this deliverance prayer with every passion and holy anger you have in you. It's time to tell the Devi," enough is enough" your family must be set free today. Until you resist the devil, he will never flee away from your family. This deliverance prayer will make your life and entire family too hot for the devil to handle. I recommend that you gather as many of your family members that are available to you and all of you should join together and pray this deliverance prayers. Remember it is a prayer for family. As you come together and pray this deliverance prayer in agreement, I see God destroying every yoke of bondage in your family in Jesus name. Pray this prayer today with faith, and your Faith shall make you free.

PRAYER POINTS

1. Thou power of God, penetrate my spirit, soul and body, in the name of Jesus.

2. Association of demons, gathered against my progress, roast by the thunder fire of God, in the name of Jesus.

3. Blood of Jesus, redeem me, in the name of Jesus.

4. Every satanic decision, taken against my progress, be nullified, in the name of Jesus.

5. Every evil deposit in my spirit, soul and body, be flushed out by the blood of Jesus, in the name of Jesus.

6. Oh Lord my God, promote me in the spiritual and in the physical, in the name of Jesus.

7. Every stranger in my body (ministry, life and calling), jump out, in the name of Jesus.

8. Any satanic arrow, fired at me, go back, locate and destroy your sender, in the name of Jesus.

9. Holy Ghost, arise and destroy the habitation and works of the wicked in my life (home, finances, ministry), in the name of Jesus.

10. Every serpentine spirit, spitting on my breakthrough, roast, in the name of Jesus.

11. Every enemy of the perfect will of God for my life, die, in the name of Jesus.

12. The anointing of joy and peace, replace heaviness and sorrow in my life, in the name of Jesus.

13. O Lord, let abundance replace lack and insufficiency in my life, in the name of Jesus.

14. Every Pharaoh in my life, destroy yourself, in the name of Jesus.

15. Garment of Pharaoh that is upon my life, be removed by fire, in the name of Jesus.

16. Thou power of impossibility in my destiny, die, in the name of Jesus.

17. Every task master, assigned against me, somersault and die, in the name of Jesus.

18. I refuse to continue eating the crumbs from the task master's table, in the name of Jesus.

19. Any man or woman, who wouldn't let me prosper, oh Lord, write his/her obituary, in the name of Jesus.

20. Oh Lord, give me a new inner man, if I have been altered, in the name of Jesus.

21. Oh Lord, activate your high call on my life, in the name of Jesus.

22. Oh Lord, anoint me to recover the wasted years in every area of my life, in the name of Jesus.

23. Oh Lord, if I have fallen behind in many areas of my life, empower me to recover all lost opportunities and wasted years, in the name of Jesus.

24. Any power, that says I will not go forward, be arrested, in the name of Jesus.

25. Any power, that wants to keep me in want in the midst of plenty, die, in the name of Jesus.

26. Any power, that wants to draw me away from the presence of the Lord to destroy me, die, in the name of Jesus.

27. I will get to my promised inheritance, in the name of Jesus.

28. Any power that wants me to fulfil my destiny only partially, die, in the name of Jesus.

29. Oh Lord, anoint me with power to destroy all foundational covenants, in the name of Jesus.

30. Oh Lord, use my substance for the furtherance of the gospel, in the name of Jesus.

31. Oh Lord, arise and bless my inheritance, in the name of Jesus.

32. All my stolen virtues, be returned to me, in the name of Jesus.

33. O Lord, let my release bring revival, in the name of Jesus.

34. Oh Lord, reveal all ignorant ways in me by Your Holy Spirit, in the name of Jesus.

35. Today, you my spirit man, you will not bewitch me, in the name of Jesus.

36. Power in the blood of Jesus, redeem my destiny, in the name of Jesus.

37. Every satanic weapon, formed against my destiny, backfire, in the name of Jesus.

38. Arrows of deliverance, locate my destiny, in the name of Jesus

39. Every spiritual cobweb on my destiny, burn, in the name of Jesus.

40. Every serpent in my foundation, swallowing my destiny, die, in the name of Jesus.

41. Every red candle, burning against my destiny, catch fire, in the name of Jesus.

42. Song: "God of deliverance, send down fire . . ." (sing for about 15 minutes clapping your hands).

43. Every lid the enemy has put on my destiny, jump up, and die, in the name of Jesus.

44. Every serpent in my blood, die, in the name of Jesus.

45. Every serpent, caging my destiny, die, in the name of Jesus.

46. Every power of darkness, following me about, die, in the name of Jesus.

47. Evil cord of wickedness, sin or iniquity, blocking my communication with heaven and God, be cut off, in the name of Jesus.

48. Every power, spirit or personality, listening to my prayers in order to report them to the demonic world, Father, scatter them, in the name of Jesus.

49. Every authority of darkness upon which wealth and blessings are based, crumble suddenly in one day, in the name of Jesus.

50. Father, expose and destroy the workers of iniquity in Jesus' name.

51. Father, let the mystery and secret of my fulfilment be revealed, in the name of Jesus.

52. O Lord, let the heaven open, let the anointing speak, let my hidden blessings be revealed and released, in Jesus' name.

53. Oh Lord, forgive me, where I have judged others out of ignorance and pride, in the name of Jesus.

54. Oh Lord, remove the penalty of judgment upon my life and calling, in the name of Jesus.

55. Oh heavens, fight for me today, in Jesus' name.

56. Oh Lord, increase me so that your name may be glorified, in the name of Jesus.

57. Any power, diverting the will of God out of my life, somersault and die, in Jesus' name.

58. Oh Lord, arise and let every poison in my life be arrested, in Jesus' name.

59. I declare the obituary of all the opposition powers, attacking my glory and calling, in Jesus' name.

60. Holy Spirit, activate the will of God in my life and calling, in the name of Jesus.

61. I decree the will of my enemies against me to backfire, in the name of Jesus.

62. Every plot of the enemy against me, be reversed, in Jesus' name.

63. I command the confidence of my enemies to be dashed to pieces, in Jesus' name.

64. Every spiritual manipulation, against my glory and calling, fail, in Jesus' name.

65. Oh Lord, destroy the personalities of all those who live to destroy my personality, in Jesus' name.

66. Oh Lord, vindicate my position in this city (company, country, nation, etc.), in Jesus' name.

67. Oh Lord, reveal to me what you have called me to be in life (in this city, country, company), in Jesus' name.

68. Every strange god, assigned to attack my destiny, personality, glory or calling, attack your sender, in Jesus' name.

69. Ark of God, pursue every dragon assigned against me, in Jesus' name.

70. You hosts of heaven, pursue those who are raging against me, in Jesus' name.

71. Ark of God, come into my house today to locate and fight the power of the opposition against me, in the name of Jesus.

72. Ark of God, wherever I have been accepted in the past and they are now rejecting me, arise and fight for me, in Jesus' name.

73. Lion of Judah, devour every opposition, raging against me now, in Jesus' name.

74. Wherever they have rejected me, let my spirit man be accepted now, in Jesus' name.

75. I resist and refuse the sale of my glory and calling for a pair of shoes or for silver, in the name of Jesus.

76. Wine of condemnation, drunk against me, become poison for my enemies, in Jesus' name.

77. Oh Lord, let the mighty among my enemies flee from me naked, in Jesus' name.

78. Every power of darkness, that has arrested my ministry and calling, release me now, in the name of Jesus

20 DELIVERANCE PRAYER TO REMOVE FAMILY CURSE

Numbers 23:23; surely there is no enchantment against Jacob, neither is there any divination against Israel: according to this time it shall be said of Jacob and of Israel, What hath God wrought!

A family curse can be defined as a satanic hold or entrapment over a family. This satanic hold can be in a family for generations, until the hold is broken, the family and her members will remain in perpetual bondage. Today we shall be engaging 20 deliverance prayer to remove family curse. This deliverance prayer is your ticket to freedom from every form of family bondage. A lot of people suffer a lot of setback, and all kinds of calamity simply because of the curse on their families. For instance the generation of Gehazi suffered from leprosy as a result of the curse in the family, 2 Kings 5:27. You may be suffering from a curse in your family that you don't know anything about, it might even be as a result of the sins of your ancestors that your family is in bondage, but today, as you engage this deliverance prayer to remove family curse, I see all curses in your family broken forever in Jesus name.

The greatest form of deliverance is self-deliverance, this is deliverance by the word of God and through prayers. Before we go into the deliverance prayers, I want you to know some things about your status in Christ and also about curses. Below are biblical facts that establishes the fact that you cannot be under a curse.

10 BIBLE VERSES THAT CAN SET YOU FREE FROM FAMILY CURSES

1). You cannot Be Cursed. Galatians 3:13.

2). You cannot be Under A Spell. Numbers 23:23

3). You have power over devils. Luke 10:19

4). You are seated with Christ in High Places. Ephesians 2:6

5). We are far above principalities and powers. Ephesians 1:21

6). We have been transferred from darkness to light. Colossians 1:13.

7). We have the Holy Ghost in us. Acts 1:8

8). The greater one lives inside us. 1 John 4:4

9). We can do the impossible. Mark 9:23

10). We are born of God. John 1:13.

The above bible verses and knowledge is what you need to know to be free from family curses. When you prayer with understanding, you get outstanding results. My prayer for you today is this as you engage this deliverance prayer to remove family curse, armed with these understanding, you shall be unstoppable in Jesus name. I declare that as you engage in this deliverance prayer with faith today all the curses of the devil holding your family down shall be destroyed forever in Jesus name.

PRAYER POINTS

1. Father, I thank you for delivering my family by the Blood of your Son Jesus Christ.

2. Father, by your mercy and through the blood of Jesus Christ, wash away every sin in my family in Jesus name.

3. Father, let your mercy overrule every judgment of the devil against my family in Jesus name.

4. I overrule every curse of hell against my life in Jesus name

5. I decree null and void every evil pronouncement upon my family in Jesus name

6. I decree an end to every enchantments working against my family in Jesus name

7. I deliver myself from every form of generational curse and bondage in Jesus name

8. I deliver myself from every consequences of the sins of my fathers in Jesus name

9. The wicked shall die for his wickedness, I declare that I and my family shall not suffer for the wickedness of our fathers in Jesus name

10. Every tongue that rises against me in judgment today, I condemn it in Jesus name

11. I and my family we rise above curses in Jesus name

12. I declare total family deliverance from the spirit of poverty in Jesus name

13. I declare total family deliverance from the spirit of barrenness in Jesus name

14. I declare total family deliverance from the spirit of stagnation in Jesus name

15. I declare total family deliverance from the spirit of near success syndrome in Jesus name

16. I declare total family deliverance from the spirit of premature death in Jesus name

17. I declare total family deliverance from the spirit of ups and downs in Jesus name

18. I declare total family deliverance from the spirit of sicknesses and diseases in Jesus name

19. I declare total family deliverance from all forms of curses in Jesus name

20. Father, I thank you for my total deliverance and that of my entire family in Jesus name.

20 DELIVERANCE PRAYER POINTS AGAINST FAMILY ALTARS

Exodus 34:13-14; 13 But ye shall destroy their altars, break their images, and cut down their groves: 14 for thou shalt worship no other god: for the Lord, whose name is Jealous, is a jealous God:

Today, we shall be engaging 20 Deliverance Prayer Points against Family Altars. What is a family Altar? Before we define that, let's first define what an altar is. An altar is a place of worship, in the Old Testament, we see that Gods children always built altars for the lord to worship him from time to time. (See Genesis, 8:20, Genesis 22:9, Exodus 17:15, Leviticus 7:5.). The altar is where God dwell, today our body have become the altar of the Lord, and He dwells in us as believers through the Holy Spirit. Now what is a family altar? , a family altar is a place where the family worship there God or gods. This deliverance prayer points is focusing on evil altars. Evil altars are altars dedicated to idols or idol worship. This altars are dedicated to evil spirits in the name of gods. This evil spirits remain in this families even long after the idols have been destroyed by civilization.

Africa as a continent was given to idol worship, long before Christianity came, a lot of families where worshiping different gods before civilization. This demonic spirits still torments there great grandchildren today. Many families are under the bondage of family altars, this satanic altars keep speaking evil in the lives of the members of the families. Many families are suffering from issues like untimely death, barrenness, poverty, sicknesses and diseases, this are all issues from evil altars. Child of God, you must separate yourselves from this satanic covenants. You are a new creation, old things are passed away. This deliverance prayer points against family altars will destroy every altar that is speaking against you and your family members in Jesus name. As you rise up in prayers, every demonic stronghold in your family shall bow in the name of Jesus.

Engage this prayers with faith today, and you will see victory in your life in Jesus name. No matter what the devil is doing in your life, no matter the hold of the devil over your finances, you shall delivered today in Jesus name. Whoever Jesus sets free, its free forever, you are free forever, God bless you.

PRAYER POINTS

1. Father, I thank you for delivering me from every evil altar, in the name of Jesus.

2. I curse you spirit enforcing evil altars in my life and I command you to release me, in the name of Jesus.

3. Let everything that has been transferred into my life by demonic laying of hands, loose its hold right now, in the name of Jesus.

4. Let every serpentine poison that has been passed into my life, get out now, in the name of Jesus. I flush you out with the blood of Jesus.

5. Let fire fall on every spirit of death and hell fashioned against my life, in the name of Jesus.

6. I break the head and crush the tail of every serpentine spirit, in the name of Jesus.

7. Let every satanic altar that have been introduced into my family, receive the fire of God in Jesus name.

8. Let the sword of fire begin to cut off every evil parental attachment, in the mighty name of Jesus.

9. Father Lord, reveal to me any hidden covenant that the devil has arranged against me, in the name of Jesus.

10. Every tree that the Father did not plant in my life, be uprooted, in the name of Jesus.

11. Father Lord, I electrify the ground of this place now. Let every evil altar begin to shatter now, in the name of Jesus.

12. Let every evil hidden covenant break, in the mighty name of Jesus.

13. I refuse to drink from the fountain of sorrow, in Jesus name.

14. I take authority over all curses issued against my life from evil altars, in the name of Jesus.

15. Father, by the blood of Jesus, wash away every curse placed upon my life by evil altars in Jesus name.

16. I command any demon attached to any curse to depart from me now, in the mighty name of our Lord Jesus Christ.

17. Let all curses issued against me be converted to blessings, in the name of Jesus.

18. Every curse of mental and physical sickness be broken, be broken, be broken, in the name of Jesus. I release myself from you, in the name of Jesus."

19. There shall be no more poverty, sickness, etc. in my life, in Jesus' name.

20. Father, I thank you for answering my prayers in Jesus name

20 WARFARE PRAYERS FOR CONFLICT WITH FAMILY

Amos 3:3: Can two walk together, except they be agreed?

Conflicts in families are simply unresolved issues existing in families. In the Last days conflicts in families have become a normal phenomenon. The rate of hatred amongst family members are on the increase. This is the work of the devil. The spirit of conflict is the spirit of the devil, it spreads hate and remorse against family members and their other family members. However to overcome this spirit, you must engage in warfare prayers. Today we are engaging 20 warfare prayers for conflicts with family. This warfare prayers will bind and cast out every plantings of the devil that has been fuelling the crises in your family.

Many families have become perpetual enemies because of little arguments of things are were so insignificant. This is the work of the devil, this warfare prayers will place the devil tormenting your family under your feet in Jesus name. You must resist the devil and he will flee. As you engage this warfare prayers for conflict with family, I see your entire family say test to Jesus in Jesus name

PRAYERS FOR CONFLICT WITH FAMILY

1. Make a list of all the things that are presently wrong in your family
2. Now take these items one by one and pray aggressively as follows:
You . . ., (e.g. weakness, faults or problems) in my home, I root you out, I pull you down and I destroy you, in the name of Jesus.
3. Let all the enemies of progress in my family be rendered impotent, in the name of Jesus.
4. I silence every architect of conflict in my family in the name of Jesus.
5. Let every satanic factor leading to conflict in my family be dissolved by the fire of the Holy Spirit.
6. I decree that divine character be planted and built in my family in the name of Jesus.
7. I separate my marriage from the hands of evil designers, in the name of Jesus.

8. Let every evil power trying to destroy my marriage be put to shame, in the name of Jesus.

9. I refuse to pattern my marriage contrary to God's original design, in the name of Jesus.

10. Household wickedness, release my family now!!!, in the name of Jesus.

11. Let every demonic influence on my family by parents from both sides be nullified, in the name of Jesus.

12. Every disease of our family altar, be healed, in the name of Jesus.

13. I break every curse affecting my family negatively, in Jesus' name.

14. Devil, I command you to take all your properties and be gone from my family in the name of Jesus.

15. Lord, restore all that the enemies have stolen from my family in Jesus name

16. Father Lord, convert all my marital failure to success, in the name of Jesus.

17. Lord, keep the wall of defence of my family constantly strong, in the mighty name of Jesus.

18. Lord, heal all broken and sore family relationships, in the mighty name of Jesus.

19. I receive deliverance from every evil plantation designed to bring myself and my children under the bondage of the devil, in the name of Jesus.

20. I deliver myself from bondage that my sins and those of my ancestors have provoked, in the name of Jesus.

10 DELIVERANCE PRAYER TO BREAK FAMILY CURSES

Galatians 3:13-14. 13 Christ hath redeemed us from the curse of the law, being made a curse for us: for it is written, Cursed is every one that hangeth on a tree: 14 that the blessing of Abraham might come on the Gentiles through Jesus Christ; that we might receive the promise of the Spirit through faith.

All curses can be broken, it only requires faith filled deliverance prayer and a good understanding of the word of Christ. Today we have compiled 10 deliverance prayer to break family curses, these prayers will empower you to scatter every evil declaration sent in your direction. In Isaiah 54:17 the bible encouraged us to condemn every tongue that rises up against us, until you open your mouth in prayers, the embargo of the enemy may never leave your life.

Family curses are real, they are ancestral curses warring against the progress of innocent family members. These curses are as a result of demonic idol worships by our ancestors, evil dedication of one's entire family to a god or deity, certain oaths and vows that have been made by our ancestors to their gods. These evil practices don't just disappear like that, even after many years the generations of these our fore father's will continue to battles these evil spirits. For instance, when a man dedicates himself and his entire lineage to a deity, and he makes declarations like this" I and my children will forever serve you" he has handed over all his offspring to the devil. The problem now begins when his great grandchildren who don't know anything about the ancestral covenant stops worshipping the gods of their fathers, then the curse begins to work against them, the curse of a broken ancestral covenant. This is a major reason why many families are in ruins today. A lot of families are suffering under the bondage of the devil because of a broken ancestral covenant.

But the good news is these, as a child of God, You have been delivered from the curses of the law, you have been set free from all ancestral curses, by the blood of Jesus, you have been totally delivered from sin and every form of ancestral curses. As you engage these deliverance prayer to break family curses, I see your life become curse free in Jesus name. Know these today, you are UNCURSABLE!!! No devilish curse can prevail in your life anymore in Jesus name. Pray this deliverance prayer today and be totally free from the devil in Jesus name.

DELIVERANCE PRAYER TO BREAK FAMILY CURSES

1. I confess the sins of my ancestors (list them if you know any) in Jesus name
2. O Lord let your mercy prevail over every family curse attacking my life in Jesus name
3. Let the power in the blood of Jesus separate me from the sins of my ancestors, in the name of Jesus.
4. I renounce any evil dedication placed upon my life, in Jesus' name.
5. I break every satanic ordination with my names on it, in the name of Jesus.
6. I renounce and loose myself from every negative dedication placed upon my life, in the name of Jesus.
7. I command all demons behind the curses in my family to leave now, in the name of Jesus Christ.
8. I take authority over all the family curses fighting against me, in Jesus' name.
9. Lord, cancel the evil consequences of any broken demonic covenant or dedication in Jesus name.
10. I take authority over all the curses emanating from broken dedication and covenant, in the name of Jesus.

40 PRAYER POINTS AGAINST FAMILY CURSES

Numbers 23:23; surely there is no enchantment against Jacob, neither is there any divination against Israel: according to this time it shall be said of Jacob and of Israel, What hath God wrought!

Today every enemy of your family shall be put to shame. The devil's plan is to destroy and scatter families. Micah 7:6: tells us that a man's enemy shall be from his own house. This 40 prayer points against family curses shall expose every Balaam in your family, it shall turn there curses to blessings and also God shall destroy them permanently in Jesus name.

You must pray this prayer with all seriousness, the devil is wicked, many families are strangling today because of these satanic agents, they place curses on families. These curses can also be ancestral, that is from your forefathers. You must rise up and wage spiritual warfare. This 40 prayer points against family curses is the right weapon of warfare. As you pray these prayers, I see God destroying every evil opposition in your family in Jesus name.

40 Prayer points against family curses.

1). Oh Lord! By the blood of Jesus, erase every curse following me in Jesus name.

2). Oh Lord, uproot all curses that have been linked to my name and wash it away with your blood in Jesus name.

3). Oh Lord! Let your blood wash away every satanic pronouncement I have made, that is working against my life in Jesus name.

4). Anyone among my father's children or my mother's children that my blessings has been given to, retrieve them back to me now in Jesus name.

5). Oh Lord! If there anything my fore-fathers have done that will not let me reach my promised land, I separate myself from it today, for I am a new creation in Jesus name.

6). Because my God did not sanction it, every curses on my life is null and void and of no effect in Jesus name.

7). I prophesy that those who trouble my life shall die by fire in Jesus name

8). Oh Lord, deliver me by fire from every ancestral curses that I have been initiated into in Jesus name.

9). Oh Lord, deliver me from the curse of the sword in my generation and cancel any death by sword (or gun) in my family in Jesus name.

10). Oh Lord, deliver me from famine due to the bloodshed of this nation in Jesus name

11). Oh Lord! Every curse of hatred and blood shedding in my family are washed by the blood of the Lamb in Jesus name.

12). Oh Lord, remove the curse of famine from my life and family in Jesus name.

13). Oh Lord, I refuse to share of the curses of my family for your word said that the soul that sinneth it shall die. Therefore, every generational curses hanging over my head is null and void in Jesus name.

14). Every sure evil covenant that will not favor me is consumed by the Holy Spirit fire in Jesus name.

15). Every curse and oath that my parents entered into but did not keep and am bearing the consequences are washed away by the blood of Jesus in Jesus name.

16). The Lord my shield, protect me, the Lord my glory, bring forth my glory, the Lord my lifter, lift up my head in my family in Jesus name.

17). I prophesy into my life that every curse fighting my foundation and that of my family members shall collapse in Jesus name.

18). Oh the glorious God, overturn every curses in my family to blessings to the glory of your name in Jesus name.

19).Oh Lord, save me totally from the enemies within my family in Jesus name.

20). Lord, arise and attack every evil member attacking us with curses in Jesus name.

21). Oh Lord, I re-claim myself from the hands of whoever I have been handed to from birth and I hand over my life to you in Jesus name.

22). All demonic charms that is embedded in the name of my family is destroyed right now in Jesus name.

23). Oh Lord, scatter all those that hate me with cruel hatred in Jesus name.

24). Oh Lord, all demonic charms in my life that bring setback to me is destroyed by fire in Jesus name.

25). Oh Lord, redeem all those good things that has been spoilt in my life in Jesus name.

26). Every family battles either from my father's, mother's or inlaw's house shall be defeated by the blood of the lamb in Jesus name.

27). I declare that my head shall be lifted up above my enemies all around me in Jesus name.

28). Oh Lord, use your voice of thunder to pass judgment on all negative powers that work contrary in my family in Jesus name.

29). Oh Lord, let the strange powers of bad luck fly away from my life in Jesus name.

30). Oh Lord, pull me out of the web of family curses in Jesus name

31). All those that have labeled me a forgotten vessel in my father's and mother's house shall come back to crown me their King in Jesus name.

32). Oh Lord, bring to confusion all those who plot against my life in Jesus name.

33). I decree that those who knew my root and are blocking my progress shall be like chaff and be blown away from the land of the living in Jesus name.

34). Every mouth that curse my family inwardly shall be judged outwardly in Jesus name.

35). I prophesied that my family shall not share of the curse that devour the earth because we are redeemed by the blood of the lamb in Jesus name.

36). Oh Lord, cancel every curse on this land that will make my family suffer in Jesus name.

37). Oh Lord, every self-inflicted curse working against my family is overruled by the blood of Jesus in Jesus name

38). I claim redemption from the curse of the law in Jesus name.

39). I declare that my sins are washed by the blood of Christ, therefore I cannot be under any curse in Jesus name.

40). Father thank you for redeeming me from every family curses in Jesus name.

PRAYERS FOR PARENTS AND CHILDREN

Today we will be dealing with prayers for parents and children. The journey of every child into this world starts with the parent. It starts with a man and woman coming together as husband and wife. The scripture makes us understand that when God created man, he told them to be fruitful and multiply the earth. Marriage is a step towards fulfilling this mandate of multiplication. Meanwhile, the duty of every parent goes beyond producing offspring. They owe their children a duty of care both physically and spiritually.

The scripture in the book of Psalm 127:4 says like arrows in the hand of a warrior, so are the children of one's youth. The parents must take care of the children. Train your child in the way to go so that when he grows, he will not depart from it. This was the instruction of God to every parent. Parents have no excuse for laxity in bringing up their children. Let's take into account the life of Eli the Priest.

Eli was perfect as a priest, but he was as perfect as a parent. He was busy with things of the lord that he forgot to bring his children in the right way. The consequence was, however devastating as such, that Eli lost his life. While the parents owe their children a duty of care, the children also owe their parents a duty of care. Children must endeavour to obey their father and mother so their days may belong. It also goes beyond obeying their parents. They must endeavour to take care of their aged parents when they can no longer fend for themselves.

Within this prayer article, we will give several prayers that every parent and child must pray to God. We have only come to this world once. We must live right and fulfil our purposes.

Prayer Points for Parents

- Father Lord, I thank you for the gift of children that you have blessed me with. May your name be highly exalted in the name of Jesus.
- Lord Jesus, I pray that you will give me the wisdom and understanding to raise my children in the right way. I refuse

to fail on my children. I pray that you will equip me with the understanding to bring them up in the right way they should be in the name of Jesus.

- Lord, I pray that you will provide everything needed to bring up my children in the name of Jesus. The scripture says God will supply all my needs according to His riches in glory through Christ Jesus. I ask that you supply them all in the name of Jesus.

- Lord, the scripture says, here am I and the children whom the LORD has given me! We are for signs and wonders in Israel from the LORD of hosts, who dwells in Mount Zion. I pray that my children will signs and wonders for good in the name of Jesus.

- Lord, I pray for protection over my children. For it has been written, the eyes of the Lord are always upon the righteous, and his ears are always attentive to their prayers. Father Lord, I pray that your protection will always be upon my children, everywhere they go on this planet's surface, and your eyes will always be upon them in the name of Jesus.

- Lord, I pray that death shall not have power over my children in the name of Jesus. The death that take young people when they are at the corridor of greatness, I come against it over the lives of my children in the name of Jesus.

- I ask that the angel of the Lord will equip my children with the right power to overcome the devil in the name of Jesus. They shall not be swayed away from the lord in the name of Jesus. I ask for the grace for them to stand with you to the end; lord release it upon them in the name of Jesus.

- Lord, I know bad company corrupt sound mind, I ask for divine separation between my children and every evil friend that the enemy has programmed for them in the name of Jesus. Just like you cause a separation between Abraham and Lot, I pray that you shall separate my children from every evil friend in the name of Jesus.

- Lord, I come against every destiny hunter over my children. I curse them to death in the name of Jesus. Every arrow that destiny hunter has planned to shoot into my children's lives to kill their destiny, I pray that such arrow will not hit them in the name of Jesus.

Prayer Points for Children

- Father Lord, I thank you for the gift of life, I thank you particularly for the family you made me come through, I thank you for my mother and father, I thank you for how far you have helped them, may your name be highly exalted in the name of Jesus.

- Father Lord, I pray that you will help me to remain an excellent child to my parent and my community in the name of Jesus. I refuse to become a tool in the hands of the enemy to tarnish the image of my parents in the name of Jesus. I shall not become an object of ridicule to God and my parents in the name of Jesus.

- Lord, I pray that you will continue to bless my parents beyond measures. I ask that every of their heart desires shall be fulfilled in the name of Jesus. The scripture says the expectations of the righteous shall not be caught off, and I pray that their heart desires and every good thing they expect from the Lord shall be fulfilled in the name of Jesus.

- Lord, I pray that you shall bless my parents will good health and you will preserve their lives to witness my good deeds in the land of the living. I pray that they shall not be found wanting when it's time for them reap the fruits of their labour. This I pray in the name of Jesus.

PRAYER POINTS FOR AN ADULTEROUS HUSBAND

Today we will be dealing with prayer points for an adulterous husband. Adultery is a great sin before God. The Bible recorded in the book of Exodus 20:14 you shall not commit adultery. This was one of the commandments God gave to Moses. God practically instructed Moses to tell the people to desist from Adultery. There is always a punishment for people that indulged in adultery.

Sexual immorality is one of the most severe sins before God. The book of Hebrews 13:14 Let marriage be held in honour among all and let the marriage bed be undefiled, for God will judge the sexually immoral and adulterous. God will judge the sexually immoral and adulterous. Let's take into account the life of King David. Trouble started for the great king of Isreal when he laid with the wife of his servant, and a seed was conceived from the adulterous act. David didn't just stop at that. He went ahead to make a plot that will take out Uriah to have Bathsheba to himself.

He, however, didn't know that God desists evil, and He has a way of punishing the evil act of men. Bathsheba gave birth, and the child died. The evil seed was taken away. This practically explains to us that nothing good will come out of adultery.

3 Reasons Must Pray For Your Adulterous Husband

You don't have to keep fighting your adulterous husband. Fighting or reporting him to few persons that matters won't change him from that act. And if care is not taken, he is already on the path to damnation. It is vital to pray for your husband due to the following reasons:

The two of you are one

Genesis 2:24: "Therefore a man shall leave his father and his mother and hold fast to his wife, and they shall become one flesh."

Although it is your husband that is indulging in this treacherous act, however, the consequences of his actions are not for him alone to bear. There is a supernatural kind of covenant that gains power when a man and woman get married. It is the covenant of oneness, the covenant of togetherness. Whatever happens to him will directly or indirectly affect you, and it won't end at that; it will significantly affect the children.

Because you love him

Romans 13:8: Owe no one anything, except to love each other, for the one who loves another has fulfilled the law.

Another reason you must pray for your adulterous husband is that you love him. Regardless of the pit the devil has thrown him into, he is still your husband, and the two of you are together as one. Love supersedes judgment. It always leads above wrath or vengeance.

The day you accept to be his wife, you accepted to be his intercessor. You are not expected to give up on him. Pray for him because you love him.

The consequence will affect your children

Sexual immorality is one of the fastest breakers of homes. When the home is broken, it affects the children. If you allow the devil to destroy your home, your kids will suffer the brunt of a broken family. You have to take back your family from the hands of the devil. It is your duty not to allow the enemy to break your home; else, your children will suffer it.

To this end, we will be offering prayer points for an adulterous husband. The Lord will bring home your husband, and he will be free from sexual sin.

PRAYER POINTS

- Lord, I know that my husband has been having secret affairs with other women, and this has caused a broken heart for me. Gracious God, I ask you to mend my broken heart and grant me the grace not to give up on him. I refuse to allow the devil to win his soul. I pray that you will cause him to have a revelation of the consequences of his action. I pray that your holy spirit that quickens mortal body will give him the strength to overcome the temptations of adultery in the name of Jesus.

- Father of mercy, your word says he that fined a wife find a good thing and obtain favor from God. I pray that your power will help bring my husband home. I ask that the mightiness of your Will drive him home so he can obtain favor from you. The spirit of God, I ask that you will reignite the blissful covenant that existed between my husband and me on the day we were joined together as one. I ask that you will help him to fulfill his vows in the name of Jesus.

- Lord, as you have joined us together to become one body, I offer a prayer based on that covenant. I ask that you will not allow my husband to have rest, take away sleep from his eyes and his immoral partner. Until he changes and he returns home, do not let him have peace of mind. I decree that a great restlessness will come upon him. Until he returns to his senses and comes back home to his better half, let him not have peace of mind. This I ask in the name of Jesus.

- Father Lord, I pray for divine intervention in this matter that troubles the peace of my marriage. The scripture says what the Lord has joined together; let no man put asunder. I refuse to bow to the pain and heartbrokenness caused by an unfaithful husband. I ask that you will intervene in this matter and bring my list husband home. I ask for the grace to forgive him when he returns.

- Lord, I come against every demon that is against our togetherness as husband and wife. I rebuke the power of the enemy over this union today in the name of Jesus. I decree freedom for my husband from the power of sexual immorality that has taken over him. I ask that by the authority of heaven, he is free today in the name of Jesus.

10 PRAYER POINT AGAINST UNREST IN MARRIAGE

Today we will be dealing with prayer points against marriage unrest. Genesis 2:24: "Therefore a man shall Leave his father and his mother and hold fast to his wife, and they shall become one flesh." Forever is too long to spend in a toxic relationship with the wrong person. Nothing kills a man or woman faster than having a toxic marriage. It can ruin the promising visions of both parties. God's original plan is for man and woman to live happily after marriage. That's why God gave   the   principle   of   marriage.

When there is unrest in a marriage, it counters the initial plan of marriage as established by God. Marriage is for communion, koinonia with one another; it is of love and agreement. However, when the enemy finds his way into the marriage, he can create enmity between the man and the woman, such that they are happy this minute and the next minute they are biting each other's tongue.

One of the reasons the enemy often attacks marriages is because he wants to destroy the unity between the two-person involved. The scripture says in Ecclesiastes 4:12: "Though one may be overpowered, two can defend themselves. When there is unity between husband and wife when they pray, heaven listens. When they speak, it comes to pass because of the love and unity between them. However, when the enemy enters, he destroys the unity and love that exist between the two.

Consequently, when the enemy succeeds in doing destroying the love and unity, the two persons involve in marriage will begin to live their lives like cat and rat. At this moment, the marriage is on the verge of destruction. This article will focus on peace. God doesn't dwell in a place where there is no peace. If God is to dwell in a place, the peace of such an environment must not be threatened. This assertion emphasizes that when there is unrest in marriage, the spirit of God goes farther away from that home. And you know what happens when god is nowhere near us? The enemy strike at the given a chance.

How to Avert Unrest in Marriage
Marry a Godly Partner
2 Corinthians 6:14 Do not be unequally yoked together with unbelievers. For what fellowship has righteousness with lawlessness? And what communion has light with darkness?

The first step you must take to avoid unrest in marriage is to settle with a Godly partner. Ensure that the person you settle with knows God and doesn't only know Him but fear Him. The scripture says the fear of the Lord is the beginning of wisdom.

Settling with a Godly partner cannot be overemphasized. It saves you whole lots of stress. A Godly partner identifies the voice and signs of God, and they are not ignorant of the devil's devices. They obey and love God to the end, and this helps a lot in marriages.

Learn To Love and Forgive

Matthew 22:36-40 Teacher, which is the great commandment in the law?" Jesus said to him, "'You shall love the LORD your God with all your heart, with all your soul, and with all your mind. 'This is the first and great commandment. And the second is like it: 'You shall love your neighbour as yourself.'

Of the greatest commandment, Jesus stated that love is the greatest. Christ understands that when there is love, there is unity. Where there is unity, the enemy will not be able to have a place there. To avoid unrest in marriage, learn to love and forgive your partner wholeheartedly.

When they wrong you, let them know, chastise them with love and forgive them.

Ask God for Help

John 14:13-14 whatever you ask in my name, this I will do, that the Father may be glorified in the Son. If you ask me anything in my name, I will do it.

When you feel things are not going well with your union, do not keep quiet about it. Ask God for help. The scripture says, whatever you ask in my name, I will do that the Father may be glorified in the Son.

Ask for help, invite the presence of God into the marriage. Ask God to take away the bitterness in the heart of you and your partner. God is faithful to help you.

PRAYER POINTS

- Father Lord, I thank you for your grace over this home, over this marriage. I thank you because you have not let the enemy wreck this marriage; may your name be highly exalted in the name of Jesus.

- Lord, I pray for your everlasting peace to come and reign in this marriage. Every form of violence, every form of bitterness, is taken away in the name of Jesus.

- Lord Jesus, I pray that you teach us to love ourselves just like you loved the church. I pray that you will guide our hearts with the light of your words in the name of Jesus.

- Father Lord, I pray that your power will restore unity into our midst. I pray that your mercy restores the broken love in this marriage in the name of Jesus.

- Lord, we pray as one family. We decree that your power will send the devil out of this union in the name of Jesus.

- Lord Jesus, where ever the devil is lurking around in this marriage to destroy it, I pray that the fire of the Holy Ghost will chase it out in the name of Jesus.

- Lord Jesus, every unwanted visitor in this marriage, every stranger in this union causing havoc, I pray that the fire of the Holy Ghost will burn them to ashes in the name of Jesus.

- Lord Jesus, the scripture peace and be still. I speak the peace of God Almighty into this union in the name of Jesus. Every form of restlessness or tension caused by the enemy is taken away in the name of Jesus.

- Lord, I pray that you will teach us how to stop the enemy of peace from having a place in our marriage. I lock the door of this marriage against the enemy of peace in the name of Jesus.

- Lord, I pray that your power will heal every broken heart. Every heart that is hurt is healed in the name of Jesus. I pray that you will grant us the strength to keep going, grant us the spirit to discern the enemy's antics in the name of Jesus.

PRAYER POINTS TO REVIVE SICK MARRIAGE

Today we will be dealing with prayer points to revive sick marriage. The institution called marriage was designed by God for the multiplication of the earth as explained in the book of Genesis 1:28 Then God blessed them, and God said to them, "Be fruitful and multiply; fill the earth and subdue it; have dominion over the fish of the sea, over the birds of the air, and over every living thing that moves on the earth." Marriage is the coming together of a man and woman to make husband and wife.

Some of the reasons why God designed this institution aside from multiplying the earth is also to have dominance and populate the Kingdom of heaven here on earth. When a man and a woman come together in holy matrimony, they sign a live contract for better for worse. This means that regardless of the situation the marriage find itself, the two parties will stay with one another. Marriage is a blissful when it is with the right person and the devil has not strike yet. When the devil began to see the union as a threat, the enemy will begin to strike from all angles.

We have heard cases of great men of God divorce their wives. What the enemy do is inflict the marriage with terrible sickness. This sickness will gradually reduce the love and respect that both partners have for one another. If care is not taken, the marriage will go cold in death and that will be the end of the union. If you are in a marriage and your mind is not at peace, it is a perfect indication that the union is sick. You deserve to be happy, you have to be happy. If your union is not giving you peace of mind, it is a sign that the marriage is sick. Also, if the marriage has not fulfilled the purpose of God, whether in making children or bringing them up in the way of the lord, they are all signs that the marriage is sick.

Today, we will raise an altar of prayer against every sick marriages. The lord wants to revive the health of different marriages. That union that has not given you peace of mind will begin to make you happy after these prayers. The lost love in your union will be restored after these prayers in the name of Jesus.

PRAYER POINTS

1.   Lord Jesus, I thank you for a beautiful day like this. I thank you for your grace and favour. I thank you for your mercy that endure forever, I thank you particularly for your protection over my life. The scripture says it is by the mercy of the Lord that we are not consumed, I magnify you Lord Jesus for your grace, may your name be exalted in the name of Jesus.

2.   Lord, I commit my marriage into your hands. The scripture says and the lord blessed them and said to them, be fruitful and multiply. Lord, I stand upon the command in this word that we should be fruitful and multiply, I decree that this word become effective in my marriage in the name of Jesus.

3.   Father, I pray for good children. The fruit of the womb that are signs and wonders, I pray that you shall bless this marriage with them in the name of Jesus. I come against every form of barrenness in this marriage, for it has been written, ask and it shall be given unto you. Lord, I pray for fruitfulness in this marriage in the name of Jesus.

4.   Lord Jesus, everything about this marriage that is making me to shed tears secretly, I pray that you turn it around in the name of Jesus. I know you are the only one that can change evil to good, it is only you that can convert shame to celebration. Lord, in every ways that the enemy has been tormenting me in this marriage, I pray that you will turn it around in the name of Jesus.

5.   Lord Jesus, you taught us that of all commandments, the greatest one is love. I pray that you will restore the first love into this

marriage. Lord, you are the God of restoration. I pray that you will restore the lost love in this marriage in the name of Jesus. I pray that you will teach us to love ourselves in the right way in the name of Jesus.

6.   Lord Jesus, every stone heart in my partner and I, I pray that they are made flesh in the name of Jesus. I come against every spirit of pride and stubbornness that has possessed this marriage, I destroy it by the power in the name of Jesus. I

7.   Pray that you will give us the heart of humility in the name of Jesus.

8.   Lord, I pray for a total healing upon this union in the name of Jesus. In every way that this relationship is suffering from one sickness or the other, I pray for speedy recovery in the name of Jesus. The scripture says, He sent forth His words and healed their diseases. I decree by the authority of heaven that you will send forth your words this moment and heal every sickness upon this marriage in the name of Jesus.

9.   Lord, every heart filled with anguish, pain and resentment, I pray that they are healed today in the name of Jesus. I pray that you will heal every broken heart in this marriage. Every heart that is filled with pain and burn for revenge, I pray that you will heal it with love and acceptance in the name of Jesus.

10.   Lord, I pray that you will teach the two partner the essence of love and marriage and you will equip their mind to know the antics of the devil in the name of Jesus. Lord, every crack wall in the relationship that allows the devil to have an undeniable access to this marriage, I pray that they are blocked in the name of Jesus.

Thank you lord for answered prayers, I magnify you because you have changed the story of this marriage, and may your name be highly exalted in the name of Jesus.

PRAYER POINT FOR GOD FEARING WIFE

Today we will be dealing with prayer points for God-fearing wife. As with every woman to settle down with a God-fearing woman, so also is the dream of every man to settle down with a God-fearing wife. The struggle of a man and woman is quite different in marriage. While a woman wants a man that will be faithful to their marriage vows, provide for the family and never turn his back on his family. A man also wants a woman that will not forsake him when the ships are down, a woman whose tongue is guarded and whose character shows God.

Marriage is a blissful union when you are with the right partner. However, it can be a hell on earth for other people when they get into it with the wrong people. Among all partners, the kind of a partner anyone should not settle is one that doesn't have the fear of God. When a woman doesn't have the fear of God, evil becomes permissible. This explains why it necessary for every man to settle with a God-fearing woman. There are things that a man must do when searching for a God-fearing wife, let quickly highlight some of these things before we proceed into prayer.

3 Things to Do To Get God-fearing Wife

Give Your Life to Christ

The first step to take is becoming a believer. You can't be searching for a treasure in an aisle that you don't belong to. The first step towards getting a God-fearing wife is giving your life to Christ Jesus. You must surrender your all to the supremacy of Christ Jesus, only then will you know the man called God better.

There is no knowledge of God outside Christ Jesus. The portal to which you know the deep things of God is through believing that Christ is the way to the father. Once you give your life to live and you have had genuine repentance, you have become eligible to start your search and prayer for a God-fearing wife.

Join a Church

This might sound funny, but it is what it is. You don't go looking for a God-fearing wife in the club or bar. The best place to find a woman whose life and being is centered towards God is in the Church. It would interest you to know that the biggest number of people that goes to the church is the female gender.

When you are praying for a God-fearing wife, you don't just sit back at home everyday including Sundays waiting for the woman to come knocking at your door. The scripture says in the book of Proverbs 18:22 He who finds a wife finds a good thing, and obtains favor from the LORD. There is a place of searching. You must go all out to search for the woman. Once you have given your life to Christ, you begin to grow in Christ. The place of growing demands that you feed yourself with the word of God. One of the best ways to get the word of God is by attending a Bible believing Church.

Be a God-fearing Man

You will attract the kind of person you are. If you are a God-fearing man, you will attract a God-fearing woman as wife. The Bible says the fear of the lord is the beginning of wisdom. One you fear God, you will have the wisdom to identify the type of woman that fears God too.

PRAYER POINTS

- Father Lord, I thank you for a blissful day like this one. I thank you for the grace you have bestowed on me to see this day, I thank you for giving me another chance, another opportunity to serve you more, another opportunity to right my wrongs, another opportunity to pursue and know you better, Lord, may your name be highly exalted. Lord, I pray this day that you will bless me with good husband. I refuse to settle for less. I pray that you will send my way the man whom you have prepared, the man whom you have equipped to be the priest of the family, the one who will stand upon the watch for the family, I pray that you will send him my way in the name of Jesus.

- Lord, just like the scripture says, the fear of the Lord is the beginning of wisdom. I pray for the right woman with the right wisdom whose source is from God. I pray for a woman that will know you more than I do, a woman like Deborah, and woman like Ruth. The one that will fear you than I do, a woman that will serve and love the things of God better, I pray that you will send him my way in the name of Jesus.

- Lord Jesus, I come against every form of deceit, every form of Jezebel that the enemy has planned to send my way, I rebuke them in the name of Jesus. I pray that the power of God Almighty will reveal the identity of every deceitful creature that the enemy might send my way to waste my time and show me hell torment on earth, I pray that he shall not have a place in my heart in the name of Jesus.

- Lord God, I pray for a woman that is fruitful to me and vessel unto of honour unto you. I ask that you will divinely connect me with the woman you have destined for my life. Lord God, I pray that you will give me the right kind of wisdom to deal with the woman you have destined for me. I pray that you will teach me the right kind of response to give, I pray that you will guard my tongue with all diligence, I pray that you will fill my mouth with the wisdom that is needed to give the right response in the name of Jesus.

- Lord, I pray that you will equip this God-fearing woman with right kind of wisdom that he needs to be a great wife. I overcome the spirit of anger in him, I rebuke the spirit of violence in him by the authority in the name of Jesus.

- Lord, I pray this day that you will bless me with good husband. I refuse to settle for less. I pray that you will send my way the woman whom you have prepared, the woman whom you have equipped to be the priest of the family, the one who will stand upon the watch for the family, I pray that you will send him my way in the name of Jesus. Lord, just like the scripture says, the fear of the Lord is the beginning of wisdom. I pray for the right woman with the right wisdom whose source is from God. I pray for a woman that will know you more than I do, a man that will fear you than I do, a woman that will serve and love the things of God better, I pray that you will send him my way in the name of Jesus.

- Lord Jesus, I come against every form of deceit, every form of disguise that the enemy has prepared to come my way. I pray that the power of God Almighty will reveal the identity of every deceitful creature that the enemy might send my way to waste my time and show me hell torment on earth, I pray that he shall not have a place in my heart in the name of Jesus.

- Lord God, I pray that you will teach me on things to do. I pray that you will direct my steps, I pray for a divine connection between me and that man, I pray that you will cause one to happen between us in the name of Jesus.

- Lord God, I pray that you will give me the right kind of wisdom to deal with the woman you have destined for me. I pray that you will teach me the right kind of response to give, I pray that you will guard my tongue with all diligence, I pray that you will fill my mouth with the wisdom that is needed to give the right response in the name of Jesus.

PRAYER FOR GOD FEARING HUSBAND

Today we will be dealing with prayer points for a God-fearing husband. The institution of marriage as orchestrated by God is such that would last for lifetime. You will agree with me that forever is too long to spend with the wrong man. One of the many features or things that a woman prays for in the man they want to settle down with is the fear of God. This is because they believe when he has the fear of God, he would not indulge in any evil activities that would hurt the family.

Every lady wants a man that would treat her like she is the only woman in the world. A man who will be with her in thick and thin moment, a man who will act as the priest and prophet of the house. However, only a few are ready to do what it takes to have that kind of a man. One thing that is important to know is that everything about life is sacrifice. If you want something so bad you must be willing to sacrifice something in return. It would interest you to know that most women that wants a God-fearing husband does not even dear God too. They fail to understand that the deep calleth the deep.

In most cases, we attract people that share almost the same attributes or similar characteristics with us. Just before we delve into prayer points, let's quickly highlight some of the things to do get a God-fearing husband as a woman.

Things to Do To Get God-fearing Husband

Give Your Life to Christ

The first step towards having a God-fearing husband is giving your life to Christ as a woman. You can't have anything from the kingdom when you are not a member of the kingdom. You must identify that Christ is Lord and savior. You must recognize the fact that Christ was sent by God to propagate the salvation of man. Knowing this and accepting it makes you a member of the kingdom.

Then you must be broken, forsake your old ways and cling unto the cross.

Be a Godly Woman

It is not just enough for you to sit back and pray for a God-fearing husband when you barely know God yourself. The first thing you must do is to become a Godly woman too. Being a Godly woman goes beyond being called a Christian for the sake of name. Your character, attributes and everything about you must portray Christ Jesus.

Be a God-fearing Woman

One thing we must all understand is that we are a perfect replica of the people we settle with. When you fear God as a woman, the works of the Lord is designed in such a way that you will only attract men who are almost like you. When you have the feat of God, you will be equipped with the knowledge to identify a man who has the fear of God when suitors start coming. With this, you would not settle for less because you know who you are in Christ Jesus.

PRAYER POINTS

- Father Lord, I thank you for a blissful day like this one. I thank you for the grace you have bestowed on me to see this day, I thank you for giving me another chance, another opportunity to serve you more, another opportunity to right my wrongs, another opportunity to pursue and know you better, Lord, may your name be highly exalted. Lord, I pray this day that you will bless me with good husband. I refuse to settle for less. I pray that you will send my way the man whom you have prepared, the man whom you have equipped to be the priest of the family, the one who will stand upon the watch for the family, I pray that you will send him my way in the name of Jesus.

- Lord, just like the scripture says, the fear of the Lord is the beginning of wisdom. I pray for the right man with the right wisdom whose source is from God. I pray for a man that will know you more than I do, a man that will fear you than I do, a man that will serve and love the things of God better, I pray that you will send him my way in the name of Jesus.

- Lord Jesus, I come against every form of deceit, every form of disguise that the enemy has prepared to come my way. I pray that the power of God Almighty will reveal the identity of every deceitful creature that the enemy might send my way to waste my time and show me hell torment on earth, I pray that he shall not have a place in my heart in the name of Jesus.

- Lord God, I pray that you will teach me on things to do. I pray that you will direct my steps, I pray for a divine connection between me and that man, I pray that you will cause one to happen between us in the name of Jesus. Lord God, I pray that you will give me the right kind of wisdom to deal with the man you have destined for me. I pray that you will teach me the right kind of response to give, I pray that you will guard my tongue with all diligence, I pray that you will fill my mouth with the wisdom that is needed to give the right response in the name of Jesus.

- Lord, I pray that you will equip this God-fearing man with right kind of wisdom that he needs to be a great husband. I overcome the spirit of anger in him, I rebuke the spirit of violence in him by the authority in the name of Jesus.

- Lord, I pray this day that you will bless me with good husband. I refuse to settle for less. I pray that you will send my way the man whom you have prepared, the man whom you have equipped to be the priest of the family, the one who will stand upon the watch for the family, I pray that you will send him my way in the name of Jesus. Lord, just like the scripture says, the fear of the Lord is the beginning of wisdom. I pray for the right man with the right wisdom whose source is from God. I pray for a man that will know you more than I do, a man that will fear you than I do, a man that will serve and love the things of God better, I pray that you will send him my way in the name of Jesus.

- Lord Jesus, I come against every form of deceit, every form of disguise that the enemy has prepared to come my way. I pray that the power of God Almighty will reveal the identity of every deceitful creature that the enemy might send my way to waste my time and show me hell torment on earth, I pray that he shall not have a place in my heart in the name of Jesus.

- Lord God, I pray that you will teach me on things to do. I pray that you will direct my steps, I pray for a divine connection between me and that man, I pray that you will cause one to happen between us in the name of Jesus.

- Lord God, I pray that you will give me the right kind of wisdom to deal with the man you have destined for me. I pray that you will teach me the right kind of response to give, I pray that you will guard my tongue with all diligence, I pray that you will fill my mouth with the wisdom that is needed to give the right response in the name of Jesus.

- Lord, I pray that you will equip this God-fearing man with right kind of wisdom that he needs to be a great husband. I overcome the spirit of anger in him, I rebuke the spirit of violence in him by the authority in the name of Jesus.

- Lord Jesus, I rebuke every form of spirit husband that may try to torment my marriage even after I had gotten the right man that you have destined for me. I rebuke every evil vices that such spirit husband may want to use to frustrate the marriage in the name of Jesus.

CHAPTER 4

PRAYER FOR NEW JOBS
10 PRAYER POINTS FOR JOB SEEKERS

Here are 10 prayer points for job seekers, the earth is the lords and its fullness thereof. Anything we ask the Lord for I. Faith He is able to do it for us. Do you desire a job? Are you an unemployed graduate? it's time for you to go on your knees and ask the Lord for his favour before men and great institutions as you go out in search for your dream jobs.

You must also pray against every obstacle from the devil or even mistakes from yourself that can hinder you from getting your own miracle job. I encourage you to pray this prayers in faith. You can add fasting to it as you are lead and you will share your job testimonies.

10 prayer points for job seekers

1). Oh Lord, pull me out of the web of joblessness and unemployment in Jesus name.

2). All reproach of joblessness in my life shall come to an end this month in Jesus name.

3). I cast out every spirit of near success syndrome in my life in Jesus name

4) I declare that everywhere I place my CV, I shall receive good news in Jesus name.

5) I decree concerning my job, I shall receive phone calls and text messages of good news in Jesus name.

6). Oh Lord, favour me before every job interview panel in Jesus name.

7). Oh Lord direct my steps to the right job offers and opportunities in Jesus name.

8). Oh Lord, in my desperation, do not let me fall victim of fraudulent job opportunities in Jesus name.

9). Oh Lord! You are make a way where there is no way, create job opportunities for me in Jesus name.

10). Oh Lord, show me what I need to do to get a job this month in Jesus name.

10 Bible Verses for Job Seekers

Below are 10 bible verses for job seekers that will bless you. This bible verses will encourage you in your journey to finding your dream job. Meditate on them and pray with them.

1). Psalm 31:24: 24 be of good courage, and he shall strengthen your heart, all ye that hope in the Lord.

2). Philippians 4:4-7: 4 Rejoice in the Lord always: and again I say, Rejoice. 5 Let your moderation be known unto all men. The Lord is at hand. 6 Be careful for nothing; but in everything by prayer and supplication with thanksgiving let your requests be made known unto God. 7 And the peace of God, which passeth all understanding, shall keep your hearts and minds through Christ Jesus.

3). Joshua 1:9: 9 have not I commanded thee? Be strong and of a good courage; be not afraid, neither be thou dismayed: for the Lord thy God is with thee whithersoever thou goest.

4). Proverbs 3:5-6: 3 Let not mercy and truth forsake thee: bind them about thy neck; write them upon the table of thine heart: 4 so shalt thou find favour and good understanding in the sight of God and man. 5 Trust in the Lord with all thine heart; and lean not unto thine own understanding. 6 In all thy ways acknowledge him, and he shall direct thy paths.

5). Psalm 46:10: 10 be still, and know that I am God: I will be exalted among the heathen, I will be exalted in the earth.

6). Isaiah 40:30-31: 30 Even the youths shall faint and be weary, and the young men shall utterly fall: 31 But they that wait upon the Lord shall renew their strength; they shall mount up with wings as eagles; they shall run, and not be weary; and they shall walk, and not faint.

7). Psalm 119:114: 114 Thou art my hiding place and my shield: I hope in thy word.

8) Romans 12:12: 12 rejoicing in hope; patient in tribulation; continuing instant in prayer;

9). Psalm 42:11: 11 why art thou cast down, O my soul? And why art thou disquieted within me? Hope thou in God: for I shall yet praise him, who is the health of my countenance, and my God.

10). John 14:27: 27 Peace I leave with you, my peace I give unto you: not as the world giveth, give me unto you. Let not your heart be troubled, neither let it be afraid.

300 PRAYER POINTS FOR FINANCIAL BLESSINGS

Deuteronomy 8:18: 18 But thou shalt remember the Lord thy God: for it is he that giveth thee power to get wealth, that he may establish his covenant which he swore unto thy fathers, as it is this day.

Financial blessings is the birth right of every believer in Christ. God wants all His children to enjoy abundance according at their own levels, 3 John 2. Today, we have compiled 300 prayer points for financial blessings. This prayer points will grant you strange order of wisdom to create wealth in Jesus name. But what is financial blessings? It is the state of having abundant finances to cater for your day to day activities. Financial blessings is when you have control over money and its equivalents. In this end times money is more important in the church than ever.

Money is simply a means of exchange of goods and services. As believers, a lot can be achieved in our lives and ministries with money. The bible tells us that money answereth all things, Ecclesiastes 10:19. Without money, we don't have a voice, without money we can't spread the gospel far and wide, without money we will be oppressed by money driven issues and finally without money we are not truly free to live our dreams in this life. A lot of believers are trapped in dead end jobs simply because the need money. They have dreams but the lack of money or financial freedom will not allow them live their dreams. But as you engage this prayer points for financial blessings today, I see you having dominion over your finances in Jesus name.

Five Keys to Financial Blessings

It's important to note that money does not grow on trees, neither does it fall down from heaven. Money is the creation of man. God made man and manmade money. If you want to enjoy financial blessings, you must learn how to make money. To help us maximize this prayer points for financial blessings, we are going to be examining 5 keys to financial blessings. This keys will further strengthen our faith and empower us to take actions after our prayers in order to get the desired results.

1). **Think Money:** As a man thinketh in his heart so is he. You are a product of your thought. You cannot think like a pauper and end up a wealthy man. A lot of believers expect God to bless them but they have a poverty mentality. How can you be an employer of labour when you think continually like an employee? You must first of all conceive prosperity in your mind, believe it in your heart, declare it with your mouth and take the necessary action steps to bring your dreams to pass.

2). **Make Money:** Money is manmade. If you want money, then make money. For you to enjoy financial blessings, you must spend time to learn how to make money legally. Working for money is not the same as making money. To make money means to look for a human problem and find solution to it. When you solve problems, you make money. But when you work for money, you are simply working for those who are solving problems. Every Christian must be creative. We must invest time in learning money making skills, we must go for financial seminars, business seminars, and seminars that we expose us to genuine money making ideas, this ventures will equip our minds to create wealth. There are many money making opportunities both online and offline, prayerfully pick one and start making money.

3). **Manage Money:** Financial management is a very powerful tool in wealth Creation. It's not enough to make money, you must learn to manage money. When you lack money management skills, you end up being a waster. A lot of believers today make a lot of money but they end up spending more than they earn, no planned expenditure, no budget for the month, no savings and investment plans. You can never prosper this way. You must learn to plan all your expenses. You must learn to have a monthly budget and also a savings and investment plan. This will guarantee your success in life.

4). Multiply Money: Money in your hands must multiply for you to be rich. Learn to put your money to work. Let money work for you. This can be done by investing your earnings into other profitable ventures. Multiplication of money is the secret to great wealth. When you have multiple sources of income, you are said to be prosperous. Don't let money in your hands be stagnant, multiply it and enjoy great wealth.

5). Give Money: The only reason why God is blessing you is so that you can be a blessing. Learn to give money at every stage of your life. What you can't let go becomes your idol. A lot of Christians worship money, they can betray anyone for money, and this is not cool. Learn to be a blessing at whatever level you find yourself. In your church, pay your tithes and offerings, in your neighbourhood give to the poor and needy around you, as you do so, God will enrich you abundantly in Jesus name. 2 Corinthians 9:8.

The above five keys is to prepare you to engage this prayer points with understanding. This prayer points for financial blessings will open unlimited financial doors for you in your business and careers and engaging those 5 keys will help you maximize those financial doors. Engage them in faith today and see God changing your story in Jesus name.

300 PRAYER POINTS FOR FINANCIAL BLESSINGS

1. O Lord, concerning my finances, give me a new name in Jesus name.

2. Let the rain of your blessings begin to rain down on my dry business now! in the name of Jesus.

3. Let every evil conspirator gathering against my blessings be disbanded by fire, in the name of Jesus.

4. Let evil arrows against my finances be rendered null and void, in the name of Jesus.

5. You powers of darkness fighting against my businesses and career, I destroy you now by fire in the name of Jesus.

6. Every deeply-rooted problem in my life, be uprooted by fire, in the name of Jesus.

7. I reject every evil domination of poverty in my life, in the name of Jesus.

8. My angel of blessings will locate me today, in the name of Jesus.

9. My angel of blessing will not go unless he blesses me, in the name of Jesus.

10. Lord, let my cries provoke angelic assistance today.

11. Lord, give me the name that would bless me today in Jesus name

12. Let every satanic hindrance targeted against my business be destroyed in Jesus name

13. O Lord, deliver me from evil stones thrown at me by unfriendly friends.

14. Every evil riot and rage against me, be disgraced, in Jesus' name.

15. O Lord, deliver me from every satanic pit of backwardness in Jesus name

16. O Lord, deliver me from the powers of business stagnation in Jesus name

17. Let every evil crowd seeking to take my life be scattered unto desolation, in the name of Jesus.

18. Let all sicknesses costing me money come out with all their roots now, in the name of Jesus.

19. Let the poison of sickness draining my finances come out of my system now, in the name of Jesus.

20. Let every abnormality within my body receive divine healing now, in the name of Jesus.

21. Let every fountain of infirmity dry up now, in the name of Jesus.

22. Every hunter of my health, be disappointed, in the name of Jesus.

23. Let every stubborn pursuer of my health fall down and die now, in the name of Jesus.

24. My head will not be anchored to any evil, in the name of Jesus.

25. Let evil pursue all unrepentant evil workers, in the name of Jesus.

26. I neutralize every power of tragedy, in the name of Jesus.

27. No evil shall overtake me, in the name of Jesus.

28. Every evil preparation against me, be frustrated, in Jesus' name.

29. Let every dead area of my blessings receive resurrection now, in the name of Jesus.

30. Let the resurrection power of the Lord Jesus come upon the works of my hands now, in the name of Jesus.

31. O Lord, bless me to a dumbfounding degree in Jesus name

32. O Lord, enlarge my coast in Jesus name

33. Let every embargo on my progress fall down and scatter, in the name of Jesus.

34. I reject satanic restrictions in every area of my life, in Jesus' name.

35. Let the mighty hands of God be upon me for good, in Jesus' name.

36. Lord, keep me from all evil wisdom and manipulation in Jesus name

37. I reject any invitation to appointment with sorrow, in Jesus' name.

38. I scatter evil multitudes gathered against me, in the name of Jesus.

39. Let God be God against my oppressors, in the name of Jesus.

40. The Lord will not be a spectator in my affairs, but a participant, in the name of Jesus.

41. Lord, save me from sinking in the sea of life in Jesus name

42. My head will not be anchored to doubt, in the name of Jesus.

43. I refuse any evil diversion, in the name of Jesus.

44. I will not take my eyes off the Lord Jesus, in the name of Jesus.

45. O Lord, anchor your mercy to my head in Jesus name

46. Lord Jesus, let me receive the touch of signs and wonders now.

47. Let God be God in my Red Sea situation, in the name of Jesus.

48. O God, let it be known that you are God in every department of my life, in the name of Jesus.

49. O Lord, do a new thing to my enemies that would permanently dismantle their power in Jesus name

50. O Lord, let uncommon techniques be utilised to disgrace any opposition against my life in Jesus name.

51. Let the earth open up and swallow every stubborn pursuer in my life, in the name of Jesus.

52. O Lord God of Abraham, Isaac and Jacob, manifest yourself in your power to bless me.

53. O Lord, begin to answer every evil strongman that fights against my financial progress by fire and roast them to ashes.

54. Every power challenging the power of God in my life, be disgraced now, in the name of Jesus.

55. Let every rage of the enemy against my financial breakthroughs be disgraced now, in the name of Jesus.

56. Let every evil imagination fashioned against me be frustrated and be disgraced by fire, in the name of Jesus.

57. Let every satanic plan against my financial future glory be rendered useless, in the name of Jesus.

58. Evil rulers assembled against me, be scattered unto desolation, in the name of Jesus.

59. O Lord, behold the threatening of my enemies, give unto me divine boldness to prosper over them in Jesus name

60. O Lord, stretch your mighty hand to perform signs and wonders in my life in Jesus name

61. I speak destruction unto every desert spirit of poverty in my life, in the name of Jesus.

62. I speak disgrace unto the spirit of failure in my life, in Jesus' name.

63. I speak failure unto spirit of impossibility in my life, in Jesus' name.

64. Let every spirit of fruitlessness in my life, be paralysed, now, in the name of Jesus.

65. I reject every spirit of debt and bankruptcy in my life. Be paralysed now, in the name of Jesus.

66. I reject every spirit of business and work failure in my life. Be paralysed now, in the name of Jesus.

67. Spirit of infirmity in my life, be paralysed now, in Jesus' name.

68. Spirit of marriage destruction in my life, be paralysed now, in the name of Jesus.

69. Every desert security man assigned against my life, fall down and die now, in the name of Jesus.

70. I release every faculty of my life from the dominion of desert spirit, in the name of Jesus.

71. I paralyse the activities of desert spirit in my life, in Jesus' name.

72. Every evil load of desert spirit in my life, go back to your sender, in the name of Jesus.

73. Every anointing of desert spirit upon my life, dry up by the fire of the Holy Ghost, in the name of Jesus.

74. Blood of Jesus, block every doorway of poverty in Jesus name

75. All the powers assisting poverty in my life, be bound, in the name of Jesus.

76. My life, receive the anointing of fruitfulness, in the name of Jesus.

77. My life, refuse to be anchored to any evil, in the name of Jesus.

78. My head, refuse to bear any evil burden, in the name of Jesus.

79. I refuse to walk into any problem, in the name of Jesus.

80. My hands, refuse to magnetise problems to me, in Jesus' name.

81. Every satanic architect of problems assigned against me, be roasted, in the name of Jesus.

82. I break the backbone of any problem associated with every second of my life, in the name of Jesus.

83. Any power that has been supplying strength to problems in my life, be wasted, in the name of Jesus.

84. I refuse to swim in the ocean of problems in my life, in the name of Jesus.

85. Every remotely controlled problem energised by household wickedness, be devoured by the Lion of Judah, in Jesus' name.

86. I sack and disband any power behind the problems of my life, in the name of Jesus.

87. Lord Jesus, I refuse to be kept busy by the devil.

88. I receive power to convert failures designed for my life to outstanding successes, in the name of Jesus.

89. I receive power to close down every satanic factory designed for me, in the name of Jesus.

90. Angels of blessings, begin to locate me for my own blessings in this programme now, in the name of Jesus.

91. Powers behind accidental problems, I am not your candidate. Fall down and die, in the name of Jesus.

92. I receive the power to break every circle of problems, in the name of Jesus.

93. Every attempt being made by destiny killers against my destiny, be frustrated unto death, in the name of Jesus.

94. I command the fire of God to come upon every destiny killer working against my destiny, in the name of Jesus.

95. I remove my destiny from the camp of destiny killers, in the name of Jesus.

96. I use the fire of God and the blood of Jesus to surround my destiny, in the name of Jesus.

97. Every power working against the fulfilment of my destiny, be disgraced, in the name of Jesus.

98. I command my destiny to reject every bewitchment, in the name of Jesus.

99. I deliver my destiny from the grip of destiny killers, in Jesus' name.

100. Every evil done to my destiny by household wickedness, be reversed now, in the name of Jesus.

101. Every vessel of destiny killers fashioned against my financial destiny, fall down and die, in the name of Jesus.

102. Let the ground open now and swallow all destiny killers working against my finances, in the name of Jesus.

103. Every evil gathering against my financial destiny, be scattered, in the name of Jesus.

104. My destiny, you will not manage poverty, in the name of Jesus.

105. My destiny, you will not manage failure, in the name of Jesus.

106. I command my destiny to begin to change to the best now, in the name of Jesus.

107. My head will not carry evil load, in the name of Jesus.

108. Every enemy of progress in my life, fall down and die now, in the name of Jesus.

109. I reject every evil manipulation against my destiny, in the name of Jesus.

110. I paralyse every activity of destiny killers in every area of my life, in the name of Jesus.

111. I smash every giant of 'almost there' to pieces, in Jesus' name.

112. I destroy every castle of backwardness, in the name of Jesus.

113. I receive the anointing to destroy every destiny killer, in the name of Jesus.

114. Let every satanic guard organised against my life and finances be paralysed, in the name of Jesus.

115. I frustrate every evil network designed against my life, in the name of Jesus.

116. The enemies shall not understand the issues of my life, in the name of Jesus.

117. The enemies shall not understand the issues of my finances and blessings, in the name of Jesus.

118. Anything that has been done with snail to slow down my life, be destroyed by the blood of Jesus, in the name of Jesus.

119. I reject every spirit of backwardness, in the name of Jesus.

120. I reject caged life, in the name of Jesus.

121. I reject caged finances, in the name of Jesus.

122. I reject caged health, in the name of Jesus.

123. I reject caged marriage, in the name of Jesus.

124. I reject every spirit of stagnation, in the name of Jesus.

125. Every satanic chain on my legs, break now, in the name of Jesus.

126. Let every hole in my hands be blocked by the blood of Jesus, in the name of Jesus.

127. My life shall not be hung on the shelf, in the name of Jesus.

128. The hair of my Samson shall not be shaved, in the name of Jesus.

129. Every anti-progress spirit, be bound by chains of fire, in the name of Jesus.

130. Every satanic prison warden keeping me in the prison of poverty, fall down and die, in Jesus' name.

131. I shall not crash in the race of life, in the name of Jesus.

132. My progress shall not be terminated, in the name of Jesus.

133. Let my life be too hot for the enemy to handle, in Jesus 'name.

134. Every power set up to pull me down spiritually, be disgraced, in the name of Jesus.

135. Every power set up to pull me down physically, be disgraced, in the name of Jesus.

136. Every power set up to pull my marriage down, be disgraced, in the name of Jesus.

137. Every power set up to pull my finances down, be disgraced, in the name of Jesus.

138. No weapon of financial destruction shall prevail over my life, in Jesus' name.

139. I receive power to excel in every area of my life, in Jesus' name.

140. I shall mount up on wings as the eagles, in the name of Jesus.

141. I withdraw my wealth from the hand of the bond woman and her children, in the name of Jesus.

142. I will not squander my divine opportunities, in the name of Jesus.

143. I must pray to get results in this programme, in Jesus' name.

144. I dismantle any power working against my efficiency, in the name of Jesus.

145. I refuse to lock the door of blessings against myself, in the name of Jesus.

146. I refuse to be a wandering star, in the name of Jesus.

147. I refuse to appear to disappear, in the name of Jesus.

148. Let the riches of the Gentiles be transferred to me, in the name of Jesus.

149. Let the angels of the Lord pursue every enemy of my prosperity to destruction, in the name of Jesus.

150. Let the sword of the Goliath of poverty turn against it, in the name of Jesus.

151. Let wealth change hands in my life, in the name of Jesus.

152. O Lord, make a hole in the roof for me for my prosperity in Jesus name

153. Let the yoke of poverty upon my life be dashed to pieces, in the name of Jesus.

154. Let every satanic siren scaring away my helpers be silenced, in the name of Jesus.

155. Let every masquerading power swallowing my prosperity be destroyed, in the name of Jesus.

156. Let every grave dug against my prosperity swallow the owner, in the name of Jesus.

157. Let the ways of the evil angels of poverty delegated against me be dark and slippery, in the name of Jesus.

158. Lord Jesus, enlarge my purse in Jesus name.

159. Every demonic scarcity, be dissolved by fire, in Jesus' name.

160. By the wealthy name of Jesus, let heavenly resources rush to my door.

161. I attack my lack with the sword of fire, in the name of Jesus.

162. Satanic debt and credit, be dissolved, in the name of Jesus.

163. O Lord, be my eternal cashier in Jesus name

164. I bind the spirit of debt. I shall not borrow to eat, in Jesus' name.

165. Every evil meeting summoned against my prosperity, scatter without repair, in the name of Jesus.

166. Every arrow of wickedness fired against my prosperity, be disgraced, in the name of Jesus.

167. Let my life magnetize favour for breakthroughs, in Jesus' name.

168. I arrest every gadget of poverty, in the name of Jesus.

169. I recover my blessings from any water, forest and satanic banks, in the name of Jesus.

170. Let all my departed glory be restored, in the name of Jesus.

171. Let all my departed virtues be restored, in the name of Jesus.

172. Let God arise and let all my stubborn pursuers scatter, in the name of Jesus.

173. Every attack by evil night creatures, be disgraced, in the name of Jesus.

174. Let the wings of every spirit flying against me be dashed to pieces, in the name of Jesus.

175. Angels of the living God, search the land of the living and the land of the dead and recover my stolen properties, in the name of Jesus.

176. Every gadget of frustration, be dashed to pieces, in Jesus' name.

177. I break every curse of poverty working upon my life, in the name of Jesus.

178. I bind every spirit drinking the blood of my prosperity, in the name of Jesus.

179. O Lord, create new and profitable opportunities for me in Jesus name

180. Let ministering angels bring customers and favour to me, in the name of Jesus.

181. Anyone occupying my seat of prosperity, clear away in the name of Jesus.

182. Lord, make a way for me in the land of the living in Jesus name

183. I bind the spirit of fake and useless investment, in Jesus' name.

184. All unsold materials, be sold with profit, in the name of Jesus.

185. Let all business failures be converted to success, in Jesus' name.

186. Every curse on my hands and legs, be broken, in Jesus' name.

187. O Lord, embarrass me with abundance in every area of my life in Jesus name

188. Every effect of strange money affecting my prosperity, be neutralized, in the name of Jesus.

189. Let brassy heavens break forth and bring rain, in Jesus name.

190. I break the control of every spirit of poverty over my life, in the name of Jesus.

191. Lord Jesus, anoint my eyes to see the hidden riches of this world.

192. Lord Jesus, advertise your breakthroughs in my life.

193. Let the riches of the ungodly be transferred into my hands, in the name of Jesus.

194. I will rise above the unbelievers around me, in the name of Jesus.

195. O Lord, make me a reference point of divine blessings in Jesus name

196. Let blessings invade my life, in the name of Jesus.

197. Let the anointing of excellence fall on me, in the name of Jesus.

198. I disarm Satan as king and authority over my prosperity, in the name of Jesus.

199. Let harvest over take harvest in my life, in the name of Jesus.

200. Let harvest overtake the sower in my life, in the name of Jesus.

201. Every curse pronounced against my source of income, be broken, in the name of Jesus.

202. Let my breakthroughs turn around for good, in Jesus' name.

203. Curses working against my destiny, break, in the name of Jesus.

204. O Lord, network me with divine helpers in Jesus name

205. Let life-transforming breakthroughs overtake me, in Jesus' name.

206. Let divine ability overtake me, in the name of Jesus.

207. O Lord, lead me to those who will bless me in Jesus name

208. Let my favour frustrate the plans of the enemy, in Jesus' name.

209. I will witness the downfall of my strongman, in Jesus' name.

210. I will be a lender and not a borrower, in the name of Jesus.

211. My labour shall not be in vain, in the name of Jesus.

212. Let the embarrassing blessings overtake me, in Jesus' name.

213. O Lord, plant me by the rivers of prosperity in Jesus name

214. Unknown evil seeds in my life, I command you to refuse to germinate, in the name of Jesus.

215. I refuse to get stuck on one level of blessing, in Jesus' name.

216. I shall possess all the good things I pursue, in the name of Jesus.

217. Every effect of cursed house and land upon my prosperity, break, in the name of Jesus.

218. Every power shielding me away from breakthroughs, fall down and die, in the name of Jesus.

219. Let the garden of my life yield super abundance, in Jesus' name.

220. Every desert spirit, loose your hold upon my life, in Jesus' name.

221. Holy Spirit, plug my life into divine prosperity, in Jesus' name.

222. Every satanic agent in the camp of my breakthroughs, be exposed and be disgraced, in the name of Jesus.

223. Every power operating demonic gadget against my prosperity, fall down and die, in the name of Jesus.

224. Every power passing evil current into my finances, loose your hold, in the name of Jesus.

225. I break every circle of financial turbulence, in the name of Jesus.

226. I smash the head of poverty on the wall of fire, in Jesus' name.

227. Ugly feet of poverty, walk out of my life now, in Jesus' name.

228. Every garment of poverty, receive the fire of God, in Jesus' name.

229. I reject financial burial, in the name of Jesus.

230. Every garment of poverty, receive the fire of God, in Jesus' name

231. I reject financial burial, in the name of Jesus.

232. I reject every witchcraft burial of my goodness, in Jesus' name.

233. Woe unto every vessel of poverty pursuing me, in Jesus' name.

234. Let the fire of God burn away evil spiritual properties, in the name of Jesus.

235. Poverty-identification marks, be rubbed off by the blood of Jesus.

236. O Lord, heal every financial leprosy in my life in Jesus name

237. Let my foundation be strengthened to carry divine prosperity, in the name of Jesus.

238. Every stolen property and satanical transfer of virtue, be restored, in the name of Jesus.

239. Let every ordination of debt over my life be cancelled, in the name of Jesus.

240. O Lord, create newer and profitable opportunities for me in Jesus name

241. Every strange fire ignited against my prosperity, be quenched, in the name of Jesus.

242. Let those sending my money to spiritual mortuary fall down and die, in the name of Jesus.

243. Every power scaring away my prosperity, be paralysed, in the name of Jesus.

244. Every familiar spirit sharing my money before I receive it, be bound permanently, in the name of Jesus.

245. Let every inherited design of poverty melt away by fire, in the name of Jesus.

246. Let every evil re-arrangement of prosperity be dismantled, in the name of Jesus.

247. Lead me O Lord, to my own land that flows with milk and honey in Jesus name.

248. Let satanic giants occupying my Promised Land fall down and die, in the name of Jesus.

249. O Lord, empower me to climb my mountain of prosperity in Jesus name

250. Strongman of poverty in my life, fall down and die, in the name of Jesus.

251. Spirits of famine and hunger, my life is not your candidate, in the name of Jesus.

252. I remove my name from the book of financial embarrassment, in the name of Jesus.

253. Every power reinforcing poverty against me, loose your hold, in the name of Jesus.

254. I release myself from every bondage of poverty, in Jesus' name.

255. The riches of the gentiles shall come to me, in the name of Jesus.

256. Let divine magnets of prosperity be planted in my hands, in the name of Jesus.

257. I retrieve my purse from the hand of Judas, in the name of Jesus.

258. Let there be a reverse transfer of my satanically transferred wealth, in the name of Jesus.

259. I take over the wealth of the sinner, in the name of Jesus.

260. I recover the steering wheel of my wealth from the hand of evil drivers, in the name of Jesus.

261. I refuse to lock the door of blessings against myself, in the name of Jesus.

262. O Lord, restore my blessings in Jesus name

263. O Lord, return my stolen blessings in Jesus name

264. O Lord, send God's angels to bring me blessings in Jesus name

265. O Lord, let everything that needs change in my life to bring me blessings be changed in Jesus name.

266. O Lord, reveal to me the key to my prosperity in Jesus name

267. Every power sitting on my wealth, fall down and die, in the name of Jesus.

268. O Lord, transfer the wealth of world to my possession in Jesus name

269. Let all those who hate my prosperity be put to shame, in the name of Jesus.

270. Every evil bird swallowing my money, fall down and die, in the name of Jesus.

271. Every arrow of poverty, go back to where you came from, in the name of Jesus.

272. I bind every word spoken against my breakthroughs, in the name of Jesus.

273. Every business house energised by Satan, fold up, in the name of Jesus.

274. I destroy every clock and timetable of poverty, in Jesus' name.

275. Every water spirit, touch not my prosperity, in the name of Jesus.

276. Let men and women rush wealth to my doors, in Jesus' name.

277. I reject temporary blessings, in the name of Jesus.

278. Every arrow of poverty energised by polygamy, fall down and die, in the name of Jesus.

279. Every arrow of poverty energised by household wickedness, fall down and die, in the name of Jesus.

280. Let power change hands in my finances, in the name of Jesus.

281. Every serpent and scorpion of poverty, die, in the name of Jesus.

282. I refuse to eat the bread of sorrow. I reject the water of affliction, in the name of Jesus.

283. Let divine explosion fall upon my breakthroughs, in Jesus' name.

284. The enemy will not drag my finances on the ground, in the name of Jesus.

285. O Lord, advertise your wealth and power in my life in Jesus name

286. Let promotion meet promotion in my life, in the name of Jesus.

287. I pursue and overtake my enemy and recover my wealth from him, in the name of Jesus.

288. Holy Spirit, direct my hands into prosperity, in the name of Jesus.

289. Father, endue me with divine ideas to command great wealth in Jesus name

290. Father order my steps to the right business opportunities in Jesus name

291. Father, do not let money be my idol in Jesus name.

292. Father, make me a kingdom financier in Jesus name

293. Father, make me a lender to nations in Jesus name

294. I declare that money shall be my slave in this life in Jesus name

295. I declare that through the use of money, I shall move the gospel of Jesus to the ends not the earth in Jesus name

296. I declare that money shall work for me in Jesus name

297. I declare that I shall be a financial blessing in Jesus name

298. I thank you Lord for giving me supernatural financial breakthrough in Jesus name

299. I thank you Lord for opening doors of financial blessings to me in Jesus name

300. Thank you Lord for answering my prayers in Jesus name.

COVENANT PRAYER FROM THE SPIRIT OF BADLUCK

Today we will be dealing with deliverance prayers from the spirit of bad luck. Sometimes you feel like you are unlucky when it comes to doing some great things. Many times, this trial is from God to build our faith in Him. Abraham must have felt the same way, too, after God promised to make him the father of many nations. Meanwhile, Abraham doesn't even have a single child at that time. Other times, bad luck could come as a result of spoken words into the life of a man or the torment of the enemy.

Let's examine the life of Jabez. The scripture made us understand that Jabez was more honourable than his men. However, his mother, due to the pain she experienced during his birth, named him Jabez, which is quite synonymous with sorrow. 1 Chronicles 4: 9-10 Jabez was more honourable than his brothers. His mother had named him Jabez, saying, "I gave birth to him in pain." Jabez cried out to the God of Israel, "Oh that you would bless me and enlarge my territory! Let your hand be with me, and keep me from harm so that I will be free from pain." And God granted his request.

Before Jabez cried out to God for blessing, there was a mark on him. This mark resists blessing or favour from the life of Jabez. When Jabez discovered this, he had to cry to the God of Isreal to separate him from the curse associated with his birth. A curse often causes Bad luck. This curse could be from parents. It could be a generational curse affecting a particular family or household, and once you are from that family, you get affected too.

Good to know, the scripture already made us understand that Christ has saved us from the curse of the law because cursed is he that is hanged on the tree. The death and resurrection of Christ have removed our name from the list of cursed people. When a man is affected by the spirit of bad luck, he will be exempted from the list of successful people. If every other person is doing something and getting it right, a man tormented by the spirit of bad luck will find it difficult to do good things. You will go for a job interview, all other applicants will be employed, and only you will be rejected.

The spirit of bad luck will also affect your helper or everyone who has promised to help you won't be able to fulfil their pledge to you. Most times it is not that they don't want to fulfil it, but the spirit of bad luck has held them down. The moment they promise to help you, things will no longer go well for them like it used to be; because of this, they won't be able to help you. Also, it could hide you from your helper or create enmity between you and the person destined to help you. In such a case, you will only discover that whenever people get to your helper, they get help. When someone enters his house in tears, they always come out smiling. Unfortunately, the story will change the moment you step your feet into the house.

If the spirit of bad luck has tormented you, I have good news for you today. God has promised to destroy that spirit. And I speak as an oracle of God, every demon of bad luck affecting your life, I pray for divine separation between you and it today in the name of Jesus. Every spirit of bad luck tormenting your life, the fire of God burn it down today in the name of Jesus.

PRAYER POINTS

- Father Lord, I bless you for this great day. I magnify you because you are God. I thank you for your grace and protection over my life. May your name be highly exalted in the name of Jesus?

- Lord, I come against every spirit of bad luck causing problems in my life today. I decree that the fire of the Holy Ghost will destroy that spirit in the name of Jesus.

- Lord, every curse that is working against my growth in life, every curse working against my destiny, I destroy you today in the name of Jesus.

- From today, I free myself from every curse of the law in the name of Jesus. The scripture said, Christ redeemed us from the curse of the law by becoming a curse for us. I free myself from every demonic curse tormenting my life in the name of Jesus.

- For it has been written, if God is for us, who can be against us. I decree by the authority of heaven, every spirit of bad luck that has made my helper hate me, I rebuke you today in the name of Jesus. You spirit of bad luck that is against, I destroy you today in the name of Jesus.

- Lord, every demonic utterance that has been proclaimed into my life, I nullify them by the fire of the Holy Ghost. The scripture said, who speaks, and it comes to pass when God has not spoken? I decree that over my life, the plans and agenda of God alone shall stand in the name of Jesus.

- The scripture said the spirit you receive doesn't make you a slave. I decree by the power of the Most High; I'm no more slave to the spirit of bad luck in the name of Jesus.

- Lord, every form of misrepresentation affecting my life, every spirit that change my identity where I'm supposed to get help, I decree that the fire of God burn such demons today in the name of Jesus.

- Lord, every evil garment placed on me making it difficult for my destiny helper to find me; I set that garment on fire today in the name of Jesus. Every garment of hatred that has been put on me by the enemy creating enmity between my helper and me; I set that garment on fire today in the name of Jesus.

- Father, I destroy every garment of evil implications over my life today in the name of Jesus.

- I decree by the authority of heaven, when I go in search of good things, I shall find them. When I knock, doors shall be opened unto me; when I ask, I shall receive in the name of Jesus.

- From today, I prophesy no more disappointment in the name of Jesus. From today, promise and fail are destroyed over my life in the name of Jesus.

- From today, no more failures in the name of Jesus. I prophesy success into my being today in the name of Jesus.

PRAYER POINTS FOR EXCEEDING MERCY

Today we will be dealing with prayer points for exceeding mercy. There are so many verses in the scripture that talked about the mercy of God. The book of Romans 9:15 For He says to Moses, "I will have mercy on whomever I will have mercy, and I will have compassion on whomever I will have compassion." This portion of the Bible explains that the mercy of God is not for all and sundry that is why it is important to pray to God for His mercy over our lives.

Have you ever wondered why some people achieve great success in life even when they only invested little effort? Whereas, there are some other set of people that invested all their time, money and energy into something and they didn't get half the result of those that only did little. That is the concept of mercy. The scripture says, it is not of he that willeth or runneth, but of God that sheweth mercy. This means the effort of a man is not sufficient enough for the accomplishment of goals.

Another concept of mercy is that some people will do some grievous activities and their punishment will be minimal while other people will just do a little and it will seem like the mercy of God has departed completely from them. Example in the scripture is the life of King Saul and King David. The mercy of the lord is upon the live of King David. King Saul did not do half of the atrocities that were perpetrated by King David, God still named King David a man after His heart. When the exceeding mercy of God is at work in the life of a man, things becomes easy.

For proper understanding and for you to know how well to pray, let's quickly run you through the benefits of exceeding mercy.

Things That Would Happen When Exceeding Mercy is working in the Life of a Man

Things Will Become Easy

The first sign you would see in the life of man that the grace of exceeding mercy is working is that everything will become easy for such a person. The scripture in the book of 1 Samuel 2:9 He will guard the feet of His saints, but the wicked shall be silent in darkness. "For by strength no man shall prevail. A man shall not prevail or excel by strength but by the proportion of grace and mercy that works over his life.

When the mercy of God is upon a man, even when he venture into a business that he knows nothing about, he would still excel in it.

Protocols Will Be Broken

Have you gone to an interview for a job and a man that clearly has no qualifications is considered ahead of those that have all the requirements. There is something that is working in the life of such a person, it is called Mercy. When mercy speaks, protocols becomes obsolete. The natural standard or mode of operation of an organisation will fall face flat in presence of man that the mercy of God is speaking over his life.

Even the constitution of a nation will bow at the face of mercy in the life of man. The scripture made us understand that mercy prevail over judgement. Even when the person has been condemned for death, the mercy of God will speak over the life of such a man and constitution will not mean anymore.

People Blesses Such Person

Even you are a very tough person that hardly like people, when you meet a man that mercy is working in his life, you will naturally like the person and always want to bless the person with substance. The book of proverbs 16:7 when a man's ways please the LORD, He makes even his enemies to be at peace with him. This portion of the scripture further explains the concept of mercy. When the life of a man pleases God, He cause his enemy to be at peace with him.

A man that the grace of exceeding mercy is upon will have no enemy.

Prayer Points for Exceeding Mercy

- Lord Jesus, I thank you for your grace over my life. I thank you for the gift of life that you bestowed on me to see a new day that you have made. Lord, let your name be exalted in the name of Jesus.

- Lord Jesus, the scripture says I will have mercy on whom I will have mercy on and compassion on whom I will have it on. I pray that among the people you will show mercy, lord count me worthy in the name of Jesus.

- Lord Jesus, I pray against any form of sin in my life that will hinder your mercy over my life, Lord forgive me in the name of Jesus. The scripture says, we cannot continue to be in sin and ask grace to abound. I pray that by the reason of the blood that was shed on the cross of Calvary, wash away my sins and iniquities in the name of Jesus.

- Lord I decree by your power, anywhere I turn to now let your mercy speak for me in the name of Jesus. Over my career, I decree that your mercy begins to speak in the name of Jesus.

- Lord Jesus, because of your steadfast love and unending loving kindness I pray that you will have mercy upon me in the name of Jesus.

- I refuse to go without your mercy. Your mercy that replaces the judgment of man, lord let it speak over my life in the name of Jesus.

- I decree by the mercy of the Most High, in all my endeavors, let your exceeding mercy speak for me in the name of Jesus.

- Lord God, it was your mercy for mankind that brought Christ as a sacrificial lamb to die for the sin of man. I pray that the mercy of God will not come to a halt over my life in the name of Jesus.

- I pray that by your mercy, I shall be established in the name of Jesus. Everything that I have always admire, every good thing according to your will for my life is released to me today by your mercy.

- Lord I pray that by your mercy over my life, sickness is taken away in the name of Jesus. I decree that death is wiped away in the name of Jesus.

- Lord Jesus, I pray that every door of blessings that has been closed against me, u decree that the mercy of God Almighty open them today in the name of Jesus.

- I pray for grace to accomplish good thing with ease, I pray that such grace begin to speak over my life in the name of Jesus.

20 PRAYER POINTS FOR PROFITABLE EMPLOYMENT

Psalm 113:7-8: 7 He raiseth up the poor out of the dust, and lifteth the needy out of the dunghill; 8 that he may set him with princes, even with the princes of his people.

We serve a God of profitable employment that is why we are engaging this 20 prayer points for profitable employment. This prayer points will change your employment status if only you pray them in faith. Our God is a miracle working God, He knows how to change our situations from grass to grace. When we call on Him in prayers He arises up to our defense and turn our situations around for good. Do you desire a profitable job? Are you tired of your existing Job? If yes, go on your knees and pray. Understand that you need the hand of God to secure favour in your life and destiny. Thank God for your academic qualifications, those are great but it takes God to connect you to the kings of the earth. Joseph never had credentials but God connected him, to the top. God can also connect you to the top only if you trust Him and call on Him in prayers.

This prayer points for profitable employment will open doors of favour for you in your career life. As you engage this prayer points, I see the God of profitable employment, connect you to a great height in your career life. Do not give up on God, no matter how down you are now, you may not even have a job to hold on to right now, but as you engage in these prayer points today, God will arise on your behalf and cause men and women that matter to favour you. You shall have your own miracle job today and the name of God shall be glorified. I look forward to reading your testimonies.

20 PRAYER POINTS FOR PROFITABLE EMPLOYMENT
1. Father, I thank you for my miracle Job in Jesus name.
2. O Lord, cause me to have favour with all those who will decide on my employment in Jesus name

3. O Lord, unseat anyone that is seating in my position of employment today, let there be divine substitution in Jesus name.

4. I reject the spirit of the tail and I claim the spirit of the head, in the name of Jesus.

5. I declare that anyone who will disapprove of my employment to be shattered be removed and relocated elsewhere, in Jesus' name.

6. O Lord, transfer, remove or change all human agents that are bent on stopping my employment.

7. I receive the anointing to excel above my contemporaries, in the name of Jesus.

8. Lord, take me to the top as you did for Joseph in the land of Egypt in Jesus name.

9. I bind every strongman delegated to hinder my progress, in the name of Jesus.

10. O Lord, despatch your angels to roll away every stumbling block to my profitable employment in Jesus name.

11. I bind and render to naught the spirit of near success syndrome in the mighty name of Jesus.

12. I claim the position of (mention your desired position by faith) in the mighty name of Jesus

13. Lord, hammer my matter into the mind of those who will assist me so that they do not suffer from a demonic loss of memory in Jesus name

14. I paralyse the handiwork of house hold enemies and demonic agents in my career, in the name of Jesus.

15. Let all the adversaries of my profitable employment be put to shame, in the name of Jesus.

16. I claim the power to overcome and to excel amongst all competitors, in the name of Jesus.

17. Let any decision by any job interview panel be favourable unto me, in the name of Jesus.

18. All competitors with me in this issue will find my defeat unattainable, in the name of Jesus.

19. Father, I thank you for the testimony of my profitable employment

20. Father thank you for answering my prayers in Jesus name.

40 THANKSGIVING PRAYERS FOR SUCCESS AFTER JOB INTERVIEW

Psalm 8:1-9: O Lord our Lord, how excellent is thy name in all the earth! Who hast set thy glory above the heavens? 2 Out of the mouth of babes and suckling's hast thou ordained strength because of thine enemies, that thou mightest still the enemy and the avenger. 3 When I consider thy heavens, the work of thy fingers, the moon and the stars, which thou hast ordained; 4 what is man, that thou art mindful of him? And the son of man, that thou visitest him? 5 For thou hast made him a little lower than the angels, and hast crowned him with glory and honour. 6 Thou madest him to have dominion over the works of thy hands; thou hast put all things under his feet: 7 All sheep and oxen, yea, and the beasts of the field; 8 the fowl of the air, and the fish of the sea, and whatsoever passeth through the paths of the seas. 9 O Lord our Lord, how excellent is thy name in all the earth!

Success is our heritage as Gods children. Today, we have compiled 40 Thanksgiving prayers for success after job interview. 1 Thessalonians 5:18 tells us that in everything we should give thanks. We must recognize that thanks giving is an application for more. We our Thanksgiving goes up, Gods favour comes down. In Psalms 67:5-7, the bible tells us that when we praise God, the earth will yield her increase to us. This thanksgiving prayers is for those who just came back from a job interview, submitted there quotation for a contract or wrote a professional exams etc. One may be wondering why I must give God thanks.

We give God thanks because we cannot overcome the battles of life on our own, we need the divine intervention from above Exodus 14:14.

We give God thanks because thanksgiving leads to multiplication. When Jesus gave thanks he multiplied the 2 loaves and fishes to feed the five thousand.

We give thanks, because we want God himself to come down and give us flawless victory. Acts 16:25

we give thanks because we want God to ambush the enemies of our destiny and give us the victory. 2 Chronicles 20:22-24.

We give thanks because we want God to increase us in our jobs, businesses and careers. Psalm 67:5-7

Finally and more importantly, we give thanks because irrespective of what happens to us, we know our God will save and deliver us. Habakkuk 3:17-19.

My dear friend, I don't know what you are worried about, I don't know where you desire success in your life and destiny, just give God thanks concerning that area of your life. Pray this thanksgiving prayers for success after job interview with all your heart and believe God for his intervention in your life today. God will bring you success today in Jesus name.

☐

40 THANKSGIVING PRAYERS FOR SUCCESS AFTER JOB INTERVIEW

1. Father, I thank you for sending your Angels to me to help me succeed in my career in Jesus' name.

2. Father, I thank you for paralysing every aggressive force fighting my destiny n Jesus' name.

3. Father, I thank you for taking over the battles of my life in Jesus' name.

4. Father, I thank you for neutralizing every problems originating from my father's house, in the name of Jesus.

5. Father, I thank you for helping me fix my past errors in the name of Jesus.

6. Father, I thank you for giving me strange order of success this month.

7. Lord, I thank you for opening all the good doors in my life that the enemy has shut in Jesus name

8. Father, I thank you for destroying all the powers of darkness fighting me in my business and career in the name of Jesus.

9. Father, I thank you for the grace to overcome all obstacles standing on my way to success in the name of Jesus.

10. Father, in thank you for unseating every evil powers siting on my promotions, in the name of Jesus.

11. O Lord, thank you for enlarging my coast beyond my wildest dream.

12. Father, thank you for helping me retrieve all my inheritance in wrong hands, in the name of Jesus.

13. O Lord, I thank you for uprooting every evil things that are against my advancement from my life.

14. O lord, thank you for removing every evil plantings of the devil in my Life in Jesus name.

15. Father, I thank you for terminating every spiritual wickedness against my life in the name of Jesus.

16. Father, I thank you for terminating every financial failure in my life in the name of Jesus.

17. Father, thank you for terminating every sickness standing on my way to success in the name of Jesus.

18. Father, I thank you for exposing and humiliating all those behind the challenges of my life in the name of Jesus.

19. Father, I thank you for terminating near success syndrome from my life in the name of Jesus.

20. Father, I thank you for terminating all spiritual wolves working against my life, in the name of Jesus.

21. Father, I thank you for rolling away every stone of hindrance to my success in the mighty name of Jesus.

22. Father, I thank you for helping me discover my hidden and God given potential in the name of Jesus.

23. Father, I thank you for connecting me to my destiny helpers in the name of Jesus.

24. Father, I thank you for rendering null and void every evil conspiracy of evil men and women against my life in the name of Jesus.

25. Father, I thank you for binding every strongman standing on my way to success, in the name of Jesus.

26. Father, I thank you for breaking every curse of automatic failure in my life in the name of Jesus.

27. Father, I thank you for engracing me with the anointing to excel in all areas of my life in the name of Jesus.

28. Father, I thank you for eliminating every anti progress altar fighting against my destiny in the name of Jesus.

29. Father, I thank you for oppressing my oppressors in the name of Jesus.

30. Father, I thank you for destroying the power of delay over my life in the name of Jesus.

31. Father, I thank you for causing the enemy to restore 7 fold what the enemy has stolen from me in the name of Jesus.

32. O Lord, thank you for giving me the power to overcome every obstacle to my breakthroughs.

33. Father, I thank you for breaking every curses of leaking blessings, in the name of Jesus.

34. Father I thank you for the restoration of all my possessions from the warehouse of the strongman, in the name of Jesus.

35. Father, I thank you for frustrating and disappointing every instrument of the enemy fashioned against my advancement, in the name of Jesus.

36. Father, I thank you for giving me every authority over every satanic attack on my advancement, in the name of Jesus.

37. Father, I thank you for causing every opposition to my breakthroughs crash into pieces, in the name of Jesus.

38. Father, I thank you for rendering all evil attacks against my advancements impotent, in the name of Jesus.

39. Father, I thank you for giving me victory over every faith destroyer in my life, in Jesus' name.

40. I bulldoze my way into breakthroughs this month, in Jesus' name. Thank you father for answering my prayers in Jesus name.

PRAYER POINTS FOR STRENGTH WHEN FAILING

Today we will be dealing with prayer points for strength when failing. Failure is one of the demons that we have to contend with. In this context, failure doesn't only apply to academic excellence or the lack of it. Failure could be a difficult time in the life of a believer. It is a moment of our life when nothing is working. This face of life is inevitable, and the early we accept its certainty, the better for us as believers.

The book of John 16:33 these things I have spoken to you, that in me you may have peace. In the world, you will have tribulation, but be of good cheer, I have overcome the world." God has assured us of victory regardless of the situation we may find ourselves in. Your friends are married; you are the only one single, be rest assured that God has a plan for you. On no account should you allow your present predicament to sway you away from God. You have been trying to secure admission for years. Meanwhile, virtually all your mates are done with school, do not fret.

The scripture has promised us that these difficult times will not stay with us forever. It will be our undoing to be defeated by temporary failure. How do you stay afloat when failing? This is where prayer for strength comes to play. Job must have spent more time praying to God for strength than he asked for healing or recovery. God will undoubtedly restore every good thing that he has lost in due time. Job only needed to maintain good faith in the Lord.

Prayer is the secret weapon for defeating moments of failure. The scripture says in the book of Jeremiah 29:11 For I know the thoughts that I think toward you, says the LORD, thoughts of peace and not of evil, to give you a future and a hope. The plan of God is not for us to be consumed by failure. He has a better plan for us. We just need to maintain good faith in Him. He will surely make everything beautiful in his time.

When you feel like nothing is working for you, these prayers of strength should be on your lips. It is an affirmation that gives you the strength to keep believing that God will perform His wonders in due time.

PRAYER POINTS

- Lord Jesus, I come before you this day. The time is hard for me. It seems nothing is working for me, and sometimes I feel I have been left behind by the time of things. I ask that you will strengthen me during this difficult time. Grant me the strength to keep my faith in you burning.

- Lord God, the scripture says let the weak say I'm strong, let the poor say I'm rich. I prophesy strength into my being today. I decree by the authority of heaven, the strength of God Almighty come upon me today in the name of Jesus.

- The scripture says I will lift my head to hills. Where will my help come from? My help will come from the Lord, the maker of heaven and earth. Righteous Father, I ask that you will help me in my moment of great need. In this moment of terrible weakness, I pray that you will fly me your strength in the name of Jesus.

- Lord, I lift my head to the throne of grace, and I draw strength from it today. The scripture says, let us, therefore, and come boldly to the throne of grace that we may obtain mercy. I ask for strength in this moment of distress, and I pray that you release it to me in the name of Jesus.

- Lord Jesus, I believe firmly in your death and resurrection. I'm a testimony of your victory over sin and death. I key into the covenant of victory over failure in the name of Jesus. If the grave cannot hold the body of Christ beyond three days, I speak success into my life today in the name of Jesus.

- Lord God, I refuse to be defeated by this trying time. Your word says surely we will face tribulations, but we should be of good fate because you have conquered the world. Lord, I rely on the promise of your word. I rely on your strength today.

- The scripture said When the LORD brought back the captivity of Zion, We were like those who dream. Lord, I pray for restoration upon my life today. Every year wasted in the toxic battle to failure. I restore them today in the name of Jesus.

- Lord, I come against every spirit of fear in my life today in the name of Jesus. For it has been written, I have not given you the spirit of fear but of adoption to cry Abba father. Lord, in any way fear is trying to consume my faith, I pray that you shall destroy my fear in the name of Jesus.

- Father Lord, my heart has been broken by failure. The terrible pain of failure has plunged my heart. I ask that by your strength, you will mend my broken heart. I pray that your holy spirit will come upon me and minister to my wounded heart in the name of Jesus.

- Lord, I pray for the supernatural strength to set my gaze upon the cross. I don't want to run in the time of another man. I don't want my life to be a reflection of another's shadow. I want to be what you have destined me to be. I'm trusting the process. Give me the strength to focus on the cross in the name of Jesus.

- Come to me, all you who labor and are heavily laden, and I will give you rest. I ask that you will give me rest today. I cast all my cares on you. I pray that you will grant a soul to my troubled mind in the name of Jesus.

- The scripture says declare a thing, and it shall be established. I decree by the authority of heaven; failure is no longer my portion. The power of God removes every arrow of failure in my life in the name of Jesus. From today, I speak success into my life and existence. Everything I lay my hands upon shall be fruitful. My land shall no longer be addressed as desolate. My men shall be victorious, and anywhere the sole of my feet touch will be taken in possession for me in the name of Jesus. Amen.

PRAYER POINTS TO LAND YOUR DREAM JOB

Today we will be dealing with prayer points to land your dream job. My educated opinions tells us that most people settle for the job they don't really like. They only do jobs to get food on their table. Many people can boast of having their dream job. Sometimes, we could blame it on the bad state of the country's economy and in other way, we could blame it on the laxity of prayer on the part of the individual looking for job.

The truth remains, we are spiritual beings and the spiritual controls the physical. We can change the tide of moment in the realm of the spirit and have protocols broken for our sake in the physical. I have seen so many people get a job they do not merit, that's the position of grace. While other people lavish away in hardship simply because the jobs they do can't cater for their needs. God is still in the business of giving people their dream jobs. The job that will be sufficient enough to take care of your all needs, God is still capable of giving them out.

One thing is peculiar to having a dream job, happiness will be eminent in the life of such person. A man that wakes up early in the morning and returns home late in the night for a job that he is only doing because he doesn't wants to stay idle, such a man will never be happy. However, when you have your dream job, there is a level of happiness that comes with that. God is able to give job. No one receive something unless it is given from above. God will grant you that job. You only need to be intentional in your request.

This is not to say that the economy is not in the shambles. However, the concept of God's Grace is such that can be overemphasized. Grace opens door that has been closed for year. It makes human rules and regulations bow in the face of another man. If you so much desire a certain type of Job, let's pray together, God will surely make it happen. The scripture says the expectations of the righteous shall not be cut short. Your expectations will not be destroyed in the name of Jesus. The book of Matthew 7:7 Ask, and it will be given to you;

seek, and you will find; knock, and it will be opened to you. All you need to do is ask and it shall be given unto you.

I ask by the authority of heaven, your dream job shall locate you in the name of Jesus. I decree that God will connect you to the right source, men of substance shall locate you in the name of Jesus. If you feel you need to pray for a particular kind of job, let's pray the following prayers together.

PRAYER POINTS

- Lord Jesus, I thank you for the grace you have given me to see another new day. I thank you because you have been my shield and buckler. It is by your grace that we are not consumed. I magnify you Lord Jesus for your grace over my life, I say let your name be exalted in the name of Jesus.

- Father Lord, I come before you this day to ask for the provision of a job. I ask that your mercy will open new doors of opportunity for me. I pray that even as I go out in search of job, your spirit will go before me and level up exalted places in the name of Jesus.

- Lord Jesus, I know that no man receives unless it is given from above. I pray that you will release a blessing into my life. Your blessing that``` will suspend the protocol of man, your blessing that will disband the rules and regulations that has been fashioned by men, I pray that such blessing begin to follow me today in the name of Jesus.

- Lord God, I decree that you power will forth and announce me for excellence in all the places that I have been rejected me pray that your power will give me a reason to be celebrated in the name of Jesus. I refuse rejection, the grace that will make me a moon among stars, I pray that you release it to me today in the name of Jesus.

- Lord Jesus, I pray that you will connect me to the right people. The people that you have prepared to elevate me in life, I pray for a divine connection between us in the name of Jesus. I pray that you will possess such men with restlessness until they find me and help me in the name of Jesus.

- Father Lord, I pray that as I will go out in search of job, I pray that you presence go with me in the name Jesus.

- Lord Jesus, I pray that you will equip me with wisdom and grace to stand out in the midst of the multitude. Your word says we should ask and we shall receive, we should seek and we shall find, we should knock and it shall be opened. Lord as I'm going out in search of a better job, I pray that you will let me find one in the name of Jesus. I ask that your grace and power go with me. Every door that has been locked against me, I open them by the power in the name of Jesus.

- Father Lord, I ask that you will grant me favour. The scripture says if the way of a man pleases God, He cause him to find favour in the sight of men. I pray that your favour will go with me in the name of Jesus. When people see me, let them see your glory. I speak my dream job into a reality in the name of Jesus.

- Heavenly Lord, I thank you for the grace you have bestowed on me. I thank because you have heard my prayers, I thank you because I will share my testimony very soon, and Lord let your name be exalted in the name of Jesus. Lord I use this prayer as point of contact to other people who have similar issue, I pray that you shall come to their aid and answer them when they call you in the name of Jesus.

PRAYER POINTS FOR MIRACLE AND WONDERS

Today we will dealing with prayer points for miracle and wonders. Miracle is a supernatural turnaround of an event or situation that is beyond the comprehension of man. Wonders are quite similar to miracle, wonders can sometimes create confusion in the mind of people because in most cases, it defies every knowledge of man. There are some situations in our lives that what we need is just miracle and wonders. The scripture say how God anointed Jesus Christ of Nazareth with Holy Spirit and power who went about doing well.

God still perform wonders, God is still in the business of doing miracles. Christ Jesus understood the nature of human. He said without signs and wonders people will not believe. John 4:48 Then Jesus said to him, "Unless you people see signs and wonders, you will by no means believe." Some situations in our lives also need miracle and wonders for people to believe that truly we are God's people. God can also go length and do almost anything for people to believe that He is indeed God. When God will free the children of Isreal from captivity in Egypt, God performed a lot of miracle and wonders through the hands of Moses.

Also in our lives God is ready to perform His miracles and wonders just so people can believe that we serve a true God. I don't care what the situation of your life is, I don't care what people have said about you, I only care about what God will do in your life that will change the perception people have about you. Have you been struck with incurable disease? Or you are being tormented by a sickness that won't go away. Verily I say unto you, God is the great healer and He is capable of solving every situation. Or is it a job that you are not qualified for? The grace of God also wrath wonders such that you will get blessings that you do not even merit. If wonders and miracles seem like what you need in your life, let's pray together and trust that God will arise and do what only Him Can do.

PRAYER POINTS

• Heavenly father, I thank you for your blessings over my life. I thank you for the gift of life, I magnify you for your grace and mercy. The scripture says it is by the mercy of the lord that we are not consumed. I thank you because you have been my shield and buckler, I thank you because you are God over my life, let your name be exalted in the name of Jesus. Lord, I pray, you are the God of signs and wonders, I pray that you will wrath your wonders in my life in the name of Jesus. Lord Jesus, I commit my health into your hands. I know the situation has defied every medical care that I have gotten so far, but I take refuge in the fact that you are God and you are able to heal me completely. I pray that by your mercy you will perform your wonders over my health in the name of Jesus. Lord Jesus, I pray for divine miracle over this court case. You are the defender or the helpless I pray that you will bring me out of this case miraculously in the name of Jesus. Lord, I pray that you will miraculously vindicate me in the name of Jesus. I know that all odds stand against me as of now, but I take refuge in the fact that you are the God of all flesh and there is nothing impossible for you to do, I strongly believe in the die minute miracle. I pray that you will allow your miracle to happen over my life in the name of Jesus. That everyone who have tongue lash me may believe that truly I serve a living God is capable of saving His own. I pray that you will save me with the strength of your right hand in the name of Jesus. Father Lord, I pray for a miracle over my dream job. Your word says we should ask and we shall receive, we should seek and we shall find, we should knock and the door shall be open for us. Lord I know that I'm not qualified for this job, but I take solace in the fact that your grace is sufficient. I pray that your grace will miraculously set me aside for greatness in the name of Jesus. I pray that your presence will go before me and wrath wonders in the name of Jesus. Lord Jesus, there is no barren woman in Isreal. I pray that you will open my womb in the name of Jesus. Lord, I know for sure that medically I have passed the age of childbearing, I know the circumstances surrounding me conceiving is quite slim, but I strongly believe in the efficacy of your power. I believe there is nothing impossible for you to do. I pray that you will answer me in the name of Jesus. Just like you miraculously blessed Sarah with a covenant child, just like you wondrously open the womb of Hannah, I pray that you will shine your eye of mercy upon me and you will answer me in the name of Jesus. I pray for the miracle that will make my talk become topic on the lips of people, I pray that you will arise and do that which only you can do in the name of Jesus. Lord, the book of Romans 8:26 Likewise the Spirit also helps in our weaknesses. For we do not know what we should pray for as we ought, but the Spirit Himself makes intercession for us with groaning's which cannot be uttered. I pray that the spirit of the lord will intercede for me. God you know all the situations I look up to you for, you know every area of my life that needs miracle, I pray that you will perform your wonders in the name of Jesus.

- Lord, I pray, you are the God of signs and wonders, I pray that you will wrath your wonders in my life in the name of Jesus. Lord Jesus, I commit my health into your hands. I know the situation has defied every medical care that I have gotten so far, but I take refuge in the fact that you are God and you are able to heal me completely. I pray that by your mercy you will perform your wonders over my health in the name of Jesus. Lord Jesus, I pray for divine miracle over this court case. You are the defender or the helpless I pray that you will bring me out of this case miraculously in the name of Jesus. Lord, I pray that you will miraculously vindicate me in the name of Jesus. I know that all odds stand against me as of now, but I take refuge in the fact that you are the God of all flesh and there is nothing impossible for you to do, I strongly believe in the die minute miracle. I pray that you will allow your miracle to happen over my life in the name of Jesus. That everyone who have tongue lash me may believe that truly I serve a living God is capable of saving His own. I pray that you will save me with the strength of your right hand in the name of Jesus. Father Lord, I pray for a miracle over my dream job. Your word says we should ask and we shall receive, we should seek and we shall find, we should knock and the door shall be open for us. Lord I know that I'm not qualified for this job, but I take solace in the fact that your grace is sufficient. I pray that your grace will miraculously set me aside for greatness in the name of Jesus. I pray that your presence will go before me and wrath wonders in the name of Jesus. Lord Jesus, there is no barren woman in Isreal. I pray that you will open my womb in the name of Jesus. Lord, I know for sure that medically I have passed the age of childbearing,

I know the circumstances surrounding me conceiving is quite slim, but I strongly believe in the efficacy of your power. I believe there is nothing impossible for you to do. I pray that you will answer me in the name of Jesus. Just like you miraculously blessed Sarah with a covenant child, just like you wondrously open the womb of Hannah, I pray that you will shine your eye of mercy upon me and you will answer me in the name of Jesus

I pray for the miracle that will make my talk become topic on the lips of people, I pray that you will arise and do that which only you can do in the name of Jesus. Lord, the book of Romans 8:26 Likewise the Spirit also helps in our weaknesses. For we do not know what we should pray for as we ought, but the Spirit Himself makes intercession for us with groaning's which cannot be uttered. I pray that the spirit of the lord will intercede for me. God you know all the situations I look up to you for, you know every area of my life that needs miracle, I pray that you will perform your wonders in the name of Jesus.

PRAYER POINTS TO SAY BEFORE GOING FOR INTERVIEW

Today we will be dealing with prayer points to say before going for interview. There are hundreds of thousands of graduates in Nigeria who don't have job. Quite a number of job adverts fly across the internet on daily basis, but only few people are able to secure an employment from the job adverts. There are graduates who has lost count on the number of times they have heard this popular sentence, you may go now we will get back to you.

While it is important to study hard and make necessary preparations before the interview, one must not neglect the place of prayer. There are quite a number of jobs that you one can't get by means of qualifications except for grace. The grace of God is such that long time existing protocols will be broken just because of an individual. When you understand the concept of grace, you will hold it dear and never take it for granted again.

When you want to go for an interview, it is important to know that you are not the only one who has got the invite for the job interview. Also, you are going there to meet a panel of expert who will be studying you with four eyes so they can know your area of strength and weaknesses. In a situation where there are multiple options to select from, you can't afford to be the less. You just have to be the best that you can be at that time. Meanwhile, the scripture says in the book of Isaiah 45:2 'I will go before you and make the crooked places straight; I will break in pieces the gates of bronze And cut the bars of iron. Regardless of the number of people who have been called out for the interview, when God goes before you, success is sure.

So many youths have experienced nothing but rejection all their life. Even in places where it seems their education qualification match the requirements needed for the position, they still meet disappointment. God is about to turn your story around. He will give you victory over rejection. I decree as an oracle of God, in every place that you have been rejected, may the hands of God change your story in the name of Jesus. Before you go out for that interview, use the following Bible verse and prayer points for prayers and expect miracle like never before.

PRAYER POINTS

- Lord, I thank you for a new day. This is the day the lord has made and I will rejoice and be glad in it. I commit this day into your hands lord, let it end with joy in the name of Jesus.

- Father Lord, the scripture says for by grace you have been saved through faith. And this is not your own doing; it is the gift of God. Lord I pray that you will bless me with the gift of your grace in the name of Jesus.

- Father Lord, just like Esther saw favour in the sight of the king, I pray that you will let me find grace in the sight of the interviewee in the name of Jesus. I pray that your spirit will go before me and level up all the mountains that may want to arise against me at the interview in the name of Jesus.

- The scripture says if any man lacks wisdom let him ask from God that gives liberally without blemish. Lord, I pray that you will bless me with the wisdom to answers correctly in the name of Jesus. I pray that you will guard my tongue with diligence and grace to express myself with thoroughness and charm in the name of Jesus.

- Lord, regardless of my education qualification, I pray that your grace will speak for me today in the name of Jesus. As I open my mouth to utter words in response to the questions that I will be asked, I pray that you will bless the words of my mouth with power in the name of Jesus.

- Lord God, for it has been written in the book of Psalm 5:12 For You, O LORD, will bless the righteous; with favor you will surround him as with a shield. Lord I pray that you bless me with

269

favour in the name of Jesus. I pray that your favour will be eminent in my life as I step out for the interview in the name of Jesus.

- Lord, I pray that among everyone that will be coming for the interview today, I pray that your mercy will single me out in the name of Jesus. I pray for the grace that will make me a moon among stars, I pray that you equip me with the grace in the name of Jesus.

- Lord, I come against every form of mistake in my response today. I rebuke the spirit of mistakes in the name of Jesus. I come against every demon of rejection today in the name of Jesus. The scripture says the sea saw it and fled, Jordan drew back, the young mountains, the little hills like lambs. I pray that problem will flee from my way in the name of Jesus.

- I pray that among people that will be called for the job, I pray that grace that will count me worthy to be on the list in the name of Jesus.

- For it has been written in the book Proverbs 16:7 when a man's ways please the LORD, He makes even his enemies to be at peace with him. Lord, I pray that you will make my way please you in the name of Jesus. I pray for divine favour in the sight of the interviewers in the name of.

- For it has been written, the heart of man and king is in the hands of the lord and He direct it like the glow of waters. I pray that you will touch the heart of the interviewers in the name of Jesus. I pray for a divine attraction of their hearts towards me in the name of Jesus.

10 POWERFUL PRAYER POINTS FOR DIVINE FAVOUR

Psalm 103:8-13: The Lord is merciful and gracious, slow to anger, and plenteous in mercy. 9 He will not always chide: neither will he keep his anger for ever. 10 He hath not dealt with us after our sins; nor rewarded us according to our iniquities. 11 For as the heaven is high above the earth, so great is his mercy toward them that fear him. 12 As far as the east is from the west, so far hath he removed our transgressions from us? 13 Like as a father pitieth his children, so the Lord pitieth them that fear him.

I love this song; 'Jesus loves me this I know 'that song reminds me of the unconditional love of God in my life. Today we are going to be looking at 10 powerful prayer points for divine favour. Favour simply means Gods partiality towards His children. The truth is this, the title of this post is kind of misleading, we don't pray for divine favour as Gods children, rather we walk in divine favour, we are Gods favourite children therefore His endless, boundless, and unconditionally favour surrounds us constantly. Then why did I use the above topic instead? Simple answer is to get as much traffic as possible, this is because most believers think that they must beg God for His favour, they believe that God only favour certain of His children and refuse to favour others. They also believe that favour is a thing of merit and not unconditional. These are wrong believes of favour. Before we go into the prayer points, we shall be looking at some facts about the divine favour of God.

2 Biblical Facts about Gods Divine Favour

1). Favour Is Unconditional: If it was conditional ,then it won't be called favour, favour is when God gives us what we do not deserve, David was made king by the favour of God, he never deserved it, he wasn't the best choice, at least not according to Prophet Samuel, 1 Samuel 16:1-13, 2 Samuel 6:21. God chose Gideon, not because he deserved it or that he was the best choice but favour picked him and made him the judge of Isreal, Judges 6:11-23. We serve a God of unconditional favour, there is no amount of merit that can but Gods favour, God chose us in Christ, we didn't do anything to deserve it, He chose us, loved us and blessed us hallelujah.

2). Favour Comes to Us by Grace through Faith: We are saved by grace through faith, not of our own efforts let no man boost about it, Ephesians 2:8-9. Grace simply means unmerited favour. Unmerited means it's not a product of your own efforts or obedience. We receive Gods favour by believing in Christ Jesus. The day you believed in Christ, you became a candidate of Gods unending favour. Favour began to follow you everywhere you go. The unfortunate thing is that a lot of Christians do not realize that they are practically favored of God, they still go about crying to God to favour them, they keep praying and fasting for Gods favour, don't get me wrong, it is good to pray and fast, but favour is a product of faith and not of works. You must be conscious of the fact that you a Gods own favored child, He has showered you with his divine favour because of Jesus Christ. Believe this and you shall see his favour always in your life. My prayer for you today is that as you believe the is words and pray this prayer points for divine favour, Gods favour will always be visible in your life in Jesus name.

PRAYER POINTS

1. I receive the goodness of the Lord, in the land of the living, in the name of Jesus.

2. Everything done against me to spoil my joy this year, be destroyed, in the name of Jesus.

3. O Lord, as Abraham received favour from you, I also receive your favour so that I can excel, in the name of Jesus.

4. Lord Jesus, deal bountifully with me this year, in the name of Jesus.

5. It does not matter, whether I deserve it or not, I receive unquantifiable favour from the Lord, in the name of Jesus.

6. Every blessing God has earmarked for me this year will not pass me by, in the name of Jesus.

7. My blessing will not be transferred to my neighbor, in the name of Jesus.

8. Father Lord, disgrace every, power, that is out to steal your programme for my life, in the name of Jesus.

9. Every step I take this year shall lead to outstanding success, in the name of Jesus.

10. I shall prevail with man and with God, in the name of Jesus.

Father, Thank you for encompassing me with your endless favour in Jesus name.

30 PRAYER POINTS FOR FAVOUR AND GRACE

Psalms 5:12 for thou, LORD, wilt bless the righteous; with favour wilt thou compass him as with a shield.

Every child of God is ordained to walk in the realms of favour and grace. A day of favour is far better than a hundred years of labour. When one begins to enjoy favour and grace, what others struggle for, you begin to enjoy them without stress. Today we shall be engaging in prayer points for favour and grace. This prayer points will open you up to a whole new realm of supernatural favour and grace. As you engage this prayer points today, you shall not lack favour and grace in all areas of your life, you shall see the mighty hand of God manifested in every facet of your life in Jesus name.

What Is Favour and Grace?

Favour is when God adds flavour to your labour. Favour is when God make happen for you what others are struggling to make happen for themselves. Grace means unmerited favour, it means undeserved favour, God giving you things that you don't merit, God blessing you in ways that you don't deserve. We serve a God of unmerited favour, a God who blesses us unconditionally. God does not bless His children because they are perfect, He blesses us because we are His children, who believe in Him and His Son Jesus Christ. This prayer points for favour and grace shall usher you into that realm of favour in Jesus name.

How Do I Enjoy Favour and Grace?

There are two ways you can enjoy favour and grace, they are by New Birth and Prayers. New birth or salvation ushers you to the realm of undeserved and unmerited favour. The day you gave your heart to Jesus, from that day you became a beneficiary of Gods unlimited favour, You became a child of God, a child of favour, all your struggling comes to an end as the favour of God comes into your life. Secondly you can pray your way into the realms of favour. A lot of Christians still struggle in life despite the fact that they are Gods children. This is because the devil will still contend with your salvation and favour. Satan knows you are blessed, but he will still resist you, that is why you must resist him with faith and prayers. You must declare your favour on the altar of prayers. Every time you pray for favour and grace, you are reminding God of His word and letting the devil know that you know your rights from the scriptures. Today as you engage this prayer points for favour and grace, you shall never lack favour and grace in your life in Jesus name.

PRAYER POINTS

1. I receive the goodness of the Lord, in the land of the living, in the name of Jesus.

2. Everything done against me to spoil my joy this year, be destroyed, in the name of Jesus.

3. O Lord, as Abraham received favour from you, I also receive your favour so that I can excel, in the name of Jesus.

4. Lord Jesus, deal bountifully with me this year, in the name of Jesus.

5. It does not matter, whether I deserve it or not, I receive unquantifiable favour from the Lord, in the name of Jesus.

6. Every blessing God has earmarked for me this year will not pass me by, in the name of Jesus.

7. My blessing will not be transferred to my neighbour, in the name of Jesus.

8. Father Lord, disgrace every, power, that is out to steal your programme for my life, in the name of Jesus.

9. Every step I take this year shall lead to outstanding success, in the name of Jesus.

10. I shall prevail with man and with God, in the name of Jesus

11. I declare that I am delivered from demonic cage, in the name of Jesus.

12. I fire back every arrow of poverty in every department of my life, in the name of Jesus.

13. I come against every hidden and clever devourer in every department of my life, in the name of Jesus.

14. I bind the spirit of poverty, in the name of Jesus.

15. I disconnect myself from every financial trap, in the name of Jesus.

16. I uproot every seed of failure in my life with the fire of God, in the name of Jesus.

17. I nullify every spirit of leaking pocket in my finances, in the name of Jesus.

18. I nullify and destroy every activity of success polluters, in the name of Jesus.

19. Financial embarrassment will never continue to be my lot, in the name of Jesus.

20. I will not follow evil pattern of failure, in the name of Jesus.

21. Oh Lord! Let me find grace in your sight so that you will grant me all my request of (mention your request) in Jesus name.

22. Oh Lord, let me receive favour wherever I am in Jesus name.

23. Oh Lord, show yourself as a gracious God in my situations in Jesus name.

24. I confess today that my redeemer lives and will cause His Grace to make me stand on this earth in glory in Jesus name.

25. The God of favour! Show me favour today and let your grace snatch me from those who seek my death in Jesus name.

26. Let the Lord cut off all flattering lips around me so that they will not destroy my life in Jesus name.

27. Oh Lord! Use everything around me to my advantage in Jesus name

28. Oh Lord! I seek your face as the child seek the face of the parents. Cause your favour and grace to shower on me in Jesus name.

29. Oh Lord, I call on you in my distress today. Hear me and show me favour and grace in Jesus name.

30. Lord, let joy follow my prayers according to your favour in Jesus name.

30 PRAYER POINTS FOR DIVINE CONNECTION

Psalms 60:11 give us help from trouble: for vain is the help of man.

Divine connection is God linking you to men and women that are relevant to your glorious destiny in Life. No one succeeds in life without help. Everyone needs the help of God, and God helps people through destiny helpers, He sends you the right people that will catapult you to where He has ordained you to be. Today we shall be looking at 30 prayer points for divine connection. This prayer points will attract supernatural help your way in Jesus name. As you engage this prayers, any demonic veil shielding you from your destiny helpers will be erased and removed forever in Jesus name.

Divine connection is real, every child of God is entitled to divine connection. There are men and women that you need to connect with in life in order to get to the top in Life. This prayer points for divine connection is not a man dependent prayer, it is a God dependent prayer, and it is a prayer we pray when we depend on God to connect us to our destiny helpers. No man can help you, only God can. Man is created to disappoint, he does not have the capacity to be faithful that is why if you depend on man for help, you will be familiar with disappointments. On the other hand, when your faith is absolutely dependent on God, He will lead you to the right people to work with. This prayer points for divine connection is what you need to connect to the right people. Jesus prayed to God all through the night before He was led to pick the 12 apostles, Luke 6:12. As you pray this prayers today, God is going to lead you to your divine helpers in Jesus name.

PRAYER POINTS

1. Holy Spirit, do the work of deliverance in my life today, in the name of Jesus.

2. Every destiny destroyer, assigned against me, disappear, in the name of Jesus.

3. Blood of Jesus, remove every curse in my life, in the name of Jesus.

4. Holy Spirit, connect me with my destiny helpers in the name of Jesus.

5. Fire of God, explode in my life, in the name of Jesus.

6. Every satanic veil covering me from my destiny helpers, be burnt by fire in the name of Jesus.

7. Anointing for prosperity, fall upon me now, in the name of Jesus.

8. Grace for divine connection locate me now!!! In the name of Jesus.

9. Every demonic authority fighting my destiny be destroyed now! in the name of Jesus.

10. O Lord, let the heaven open upon me now, in the name of Jesus.

11). Oh Lord, I have no one here on earth that will help me.Help me for trouble is near. Deliver me so that my enemies will not cause me to weep in Jesus name.

12). Oh Lord, do not delay in helping me, send me help speedily and silent those who mock me in Jesus name.

13). Oh Lord! Do not hide your face from me at this trying period. Be merciful to me my God, arise and defend me in Jesus name.

14). Oh Lord, show me your loving kindness, raise helpers for me at this period of my life in Jesus name.

15). Oh Lord, a hope deferred makes the heart sick, there lord send me help before it's too late for me in Jesus name.

16). Oh Lord! Take hold of shield and buckler and stand up for my help in Jesus name.

17). Oh Lord, help me and use me to help others in Jesus name.

18). Oh Lord, fight against those who are fighting against my destiny helpers today in Jesus name.

19). Oh Lord, because of the glory of your name, help me on this issue (mention it) in Jesus name.

20). Oh Lord, from today, I declare that I shall never lack help in Jesus name.

21. I have come to Zion, my destiny must change, in Jesus' name.

22. Every power derailing my destiny, fall down and die, in the name of Jesus.

23. I refuse to miss my destiny in life, in the name of Jesus.

24. I refuse to accept satanic substitute for my destiny, in the name of Jesus

25. Anything programmed against my destiny in the heavenliest, be shaken down, in the name of Jesus.

26. Every power, drawing powers from the heavenliest against my destiny, fall down and die, in the name of Jesus.

27. Every satanic altar, fashioned against my destiny, crack asunder, in the name of Jesus.

28. O Lord, take away my destiny from the hands of men.

29. I revoke every satanic ownership of my destiny, in Jesus' name.

30. Satan, you will not settle down on my destiny, in Jesus' name. Thank You Jesus.

BREAKING THE YOKE OF DISFAVOUR PRAYER POINTS

Psalms 102:13 Thou shalt arise, and have mercy upon Zion: for the time to favour her, yea, the set time, is come.

It is your turn to be favoured. Every yoke of disfavour in your life is broken to pieces now!!! In Jesus name. Today we shall be looking at breaking the yoke of disfavour prayer points. To be disfavoured means to lack favour in your life. Favour simply means God doing for you good things that you don't deserve or even work for. When the favour of God is in your life, you make great progress with minimal efforts. When the hand of the Lord is upon your life, what affects others, don't affect you. No devil can afflict a favoured child of God, because God encompasses him/her with His favour as a shield. As you engage this prayer points today, you shall begin to see the unmerited favour of God at work in your life in Jesus name.

Breaking the yoke of disfavor prayer points is all about countering every attacks of the devil in your life. The devil will always throw different arrows at believers, arrows of death, failure, disappointments, setbacks etc., this are all arrows that contend with the favour of God in our lives. We must resist the devil and through the power of prayers break and destroy every yoke of disfavor placed upon our lives by the devil. We must send all those evil arrows back to the sender and put the devil where he belongs by force. Luke 10:19, tells us that we have power to trample and crush serpents and scorpions, therefore we must use that authority to scatter every gathering of devils and there angels to bring disfavor into our lives. As you engage this prayer points today, is see you breaking free and enjoying Gods favour in Jesus name.

PRAYER POINTS

1. I receive the goodness of the Lord, in the land of the living, in the name of Jesus.

2. Everything done against me to spoil my joy this year, be destroyed, in the name of Jesus.

3. O Lord, as Abraham received favour from you, let me also receive your favour so that I can excel, in the name of Jesus.

4. Lord Jesus, deal bountifully with me this year, in the name of Jesus.

5. It does not matter, whether I deserve it or not, I receive unquantifiable favour from the Lord, in the name of Jesus.

6. Every blessing God has earmarked for me this year will not pass me by, in the name of Jesus.

7. My blessing will not be transferred to my neighbour, in the name of Jesus.

8. Father Lord, disgrace every, power, that is out to steal your programme for my life, in the name of Jesus.

9. Every step I take this year shall lead to outstanding success, in the name of Jesus.

10. I shall prevail with man and with God, in the name of Jesus.

11. Lord, give me the name that would bless me today in Jesus name

12. Let every satanic hindrance targeted against my business be destroyed in Jesus name

13. O Lord, deliver me from evil stones thrown at me by unfriendly friends.

14. Every evil riot and rage against me, be disgraced, in Jesus' name.

15. O Lord, deliver me from every satanic pit of backwardness in Jesus name

16. O Lord, deliver me from the powers of business stagnation in Jesus name

17. Let every evil crowd seeking to take my life be scattered unto desolation, in the name of Jesus.

18. Let all sicknesses costing me money come out with all their roots now, in the name of Jesus.

19. Let the poison of sickness draining my finances come out of my system now, in the name of Jesus.

20. Let every abnormality within my body receive divine healing now, in the name of Jesus.

21. Let every fountain of infirmity dry up now, in the name of Jesus.

22. Every hunter of my health, be disappointed, in the name of Jesus.

23. Let every stubborn pursuer of my health fall down and die now, in the name of Jesus.

24. My head will not be anchored to any evil, in the name of Jesus.

25. Let evil pursue all unrepentant evil workers, in the name of Jesus.

26. I neutralize every power of tragedy, in the name of Jesus.

27. No evil shall overtake me, in the name of Jesus.

28. Every evil preparation against me, be frustrated, in Jesus' name.

29. Let every dead area of my blessings receive resurrection now, in the name of Jesus.

30. Let the resurrection power of the Lord Jesus come upon the works of my hands now, in the name of Jesus.

PRAYER POINTS AGAINST DELAY

Today we will be dealing with prayer points against delay. You must have heard the popular parlance that says delay is not denial. Truthfully, delay is not denial, however, there are blessings attached to each time and season of a man on earth. There is a certain time that childbearing is befitting. There is a time that gaining admission into tertiary institution is regarded as a success, and there are time when it won't be considered as success. Delay can be said to be a slowdown in the pace to achieve a set goal, objectives or fulfil purpose.

Abraham and Sarah experienced delay. They stayed years without a child. It got to a time that their faith were terribly tortured by their delay to have a child of their own. Sarah was forced to tell Abraham to take her maid as a wife just so he can have a child. Meanwhile, God's promise for Abraham is that he will be the father of many Nations. However, when there was a delay in Abraham having one child, he began to lose hope and his faith became weary. This is one of the things that delay would cause in the life of a man.

When we expect a thing for too long, we begin to lose hope that the thing will come. The scripture says God is not a man to lie and He is not a son of man to repent. This means that whatever thing that God says He will, will do it. Nevertheless, when we get a promise from God, our hope that it will be done is intensified. This further strengthen our faith in God. However, when delay set in, sometimes we begin to doubt if that promise is truly from God and if the delay tarry, our hope and faith in the Lord begins to reduce. And this is exactly what the devil wants that is why he often uses delay to fight the faith of a man in God.

Negative Effects of Delay in Life of Christian

Some of the things that delay causes in the life of a Christian include:

It Creates Doubt

Delay can make a believer doubt the existence of God. It can make a believer doubt if God truly exist and speak to people. When we get

282

promises from God, the natural instinct of man begins to expect. At that stage, the faith in God is high, because God has just promised us something great. Unfortunately, when delay set in, a time will come when we begin to doubt if it was God that truly spoke to us.

It is bad that some people doubt the existence of God. That is what delay will do.

It Causes the Faith of a Man Reduce

Abraham was a very faithful man. However, his inability to make baby with his wife Sarah began to have a negative effect on his faith in the promises of God.

Abraham was forced to bow to the pressure mounted on him by his wife Sarah when they could not have a child of their own. Abraham had to take Sarah's maid as a wife and impregnate her. The inability of Abraham and Sarah played an integral role in their decision to forget the promise of God and look for another means of having a child.

When a promise stay too long before it becomes manifest, our faith in God will be swindled by our expectations.

It Create Room for Satan to Penetrate

Delay create doubt in the mind of a believer. It causes the faith of a believer to reduce drastically. When the faith of a man or troubled, Satan is not far from there to strike.

Sometimes when we are in great tribulation, and we are looking up to God for breakthrough. Yet, solution failed to arrive. The devil begin to bring different temptation. It was because Prophet Samuel delayed in coming back in time that was why King Saul made a sacrifice and went to battle. Whereas, he has been warned by the prophet to refrain from going to the battle in the absence of the prophet.

For our faith not to be tested, we will pray against every form of delay of good things in our lives.

PRAYER POINTS

- Lord Jesus, I come against every arrow of delay that has been shot into my life from the kingdom of darkness. I break such arrows with the fire of the Holy Ghost in the name of Jesus.

- Father Lord, I come against every agent of delay in my life that the enemy has sent to frustrate me. I rebuke you today in the name of Jesus. I decree by the authority of heaven that you lose your place in my life today in the name of Jesus.

- Lord, I receive a spiritual acceleration of blessing. Every long age promise that is due for the fulfillment, I decree by the authority of heaven, the power of manifestation come upon them in the name of Jesus.

- For it has been written that by the anointing, every yoke shall be destroyed. Lord, I break every yoke of stagnation in my life by the blood that was shed on the cross of Calvary.

- Father, every vices of the devil in my life that is hindering the manifestation of God's promises and covenants over my life, I destroy you today by the authority of heaven. Father Lord, I rebuke every spirit of disappointment in my life by the fire of the Holy Ghost in the name of Jesus.

- Lord God, every demonic agent of darkness that has been sent into my life to cause a setback catch fire today in the name of Jesus. I make the ground of my life unbearable for every evil spirit in my life, working against my growth in life in the name of Jesus.

- Lord Jesus, every form of unstable blessing that rises and falls at intervals, get out of my life today in the name of Jesus. From today, I command the long-lasting blessings of Jehovah to locate me today in the name of Jesus.

- Lord, I decree that every hall of Jericho in my way to success, every prince of Persia delaying my blessing, die today in the name of Jesus.

20 WARFARE PRAYER POINTS AGAINST FAILURE AND DISAPPOINTMENT

This 20 warfare prayer points against failure and disappointment are for those who always meet failure at the point of success. Some people call it near success syndrome. This is not the will of God for His children. This are the works of evil satanic forces fighting against the destinies of Gods children. As a child of God, you must tackle spiritual problems from the root. You must learn to pray violent prayers, if you want to see yourself set free from the powers of darkness.

This warfare prayer points against failure and disappointment will empower you to send spiritual missiles to every enemy of your destiny. It will empower you to fight against any enemy that stands on your way to success in life. As you pray it, everyone that has said you will not make it in life must be put to shame and destroyed in Jesus name. They God of heaven will arise and judge your enemies today and forever. Pray this prayers with faith and watch the Lord fight your battles. Exodus 14:14.

PRAYER POINTS

1. Father, by your everlasting mercy, blot out every sin in my life that may stand on the way of my prayers this day in Jesus name.

2. Father, release your warring angels to remove every evil stone blocking my blessings in Jesus' name.

3. I bind every spirit manipulating my destiny helpers against me, in the name of Jesus.

4. Father, I rebuke every spirit of failure and disappointment in my life, in the name of Jesus.

5. Let God arise and let all the enemies of my breakthrough be scattered, destroyed and buried forever in the name of Jesus.

6. Let the fire of God melt away the stones hindering my blessings, in the mighty name of Jesus.

7. Oh God, let every evil cloud, blocking my progress rollaway now! in the name of Jesus.

8. All secrets of the enemy in the camp of my life that are still in the darkness, let them be exposed to me now, in Jesus' name.

9. My Father, My Father, arise and trouble all those who are troubling me, in Jesus' name.

10. Lord, I reject every evil heavy load in my life, in the name of Jesus.

11. All keys to my goodness that are still in the possession of the enemy, I declare their instant release now!!! In the name of Jesus.

12. Open my eyes, O Lord, and let the spirit of confusion be far from me in Jesus name...

13. Oh Lord, I declare this day that my labour shall never be in vain in the name of Jesus.

14. The pregnancy of good things within me will be not be aborted by any contrary power, in the name of Jesus.

15. Lord, turn me to untouchable coals of fire.

16. Lord, let miracles begin to happen in my life every week in the name of Jesus.

17. Lord, remove covetousness from my eyes.

18. Lord, fill the cup of my life to the brim.

19. Let every power stepping on my goodness receive God's arrow of fire now, in the name of Jesus.

20. I reject every spirit of promise and fail in the name of Jesus.

Thank you Jesus for answering me.

100 PRAYER POINTS AGAINST FAILURE AND DISAPPOINTMENT

Philippians 4:13; I can do all things through Christ which strengtheneth me.

No matter the challenges that come your way as a Christian, you will surely overcome. The word of God says, you shall be the head only and not the tail that is the word of God concerning you today and forever. We have compiled 100 prayer points against failure and disappointment. Failure is not the end of your life, disappointment is not the end of the road, and they are all components of your testimonies. Every child of God is a target from the kingdom of darkness, Satan will always fight you to bring you down, but you must never give up, you must have a die hard faith and never take "no" for an answer. For you to emerge a giant, you must rise up and resist failure and disappointment with the force of prayer.

I don't know where you may be experiencing failure today, I don't know where you may be experiencing disappointment today, I want to let you know that you are never a failure until you give up. You can never end up a loser in the game of life until you stop playing. Failure is just an event, it will come to pass, therefore do not let it weigh you down. The bible says a righteous man falls seven times but he still rises up again Proverbs 24:16. There is nothing wrong with failing or falling, but something is wrong when you refuse to rise up again or you give up. This prayer points against failure and disappointment will endue you with the spirit of faith and perseverance as you run the race of your life and destiny. As you pray this prayer points, the Holy Spirit will strengthen your faith and help you overcome the forces of darkness that is trying to bring you down.

This is your new beginning, I see God giving you a turnaround testimony as you engage this prayer points. As you rise up from your failures and setbacks and call on God today, I see Him raising you up from the dust and causing you to feast with the Kings and queens of the earth. You shall not fail in life, you shall make it, just believe in God and also believe in yourself and the God of testimonies shall give you a mega testimony in Jesus name. See you at the top.

PRAYER POINTS

1. Let every imagination of failure and disappointment against me wither from the source, in the name of Jesus.

2. Those laughing me to scorn shall be dumbfounded at my glorification in the name of Jesus.

3. Let the destructive plan of the enemies aimed against me blow up in their faces, in the name of Jesus.

4. Let my point of ridicule be converted to a source of promotion, in the name of Jesus.

5. Let all powers sponsoring evil activities against me be disgraced, in the name of Jesus.

6. Let the stubborn strongman delegated against me fall down to the ground and become impotent, in the name of Jesus.

7. Let the stronghold of every evil agents militating against me be smashed to pieces, in Jesus' name.

8. Let every sorcerer, enchanter or soothsayer behind the failures and disappointments of my life be dethroned and humiliated now!!! In the name of Jesus.

9. Let every evil counsellor hindering my progress receive the stones of fire, in the name of Jesus.

10. Let every spirit of Egypt militating against me fall after the order of Pharaoh, in the name of Jesus.

11. Let every strongman from my foundation planning my fall be disgraced, in the name of Jesus.

12. Let every evil man boasting against me receive the stones of fire, in the name of Jesus.

13. Let every demonic spirit of oppression pursuing me fall into the Red Sea of their own making, in the name of Jesus.

14. Let all satanic manipulations aimed at reversing my divine destiny be frustrated, in the name of Jesus.

15. Let all destructive broadcasters of my goodness be silenced, in the name of Jesus.

16. Let all leaking bags and pockets be sealed up, in Jesus' name.

17. Let all evil monitoring eyes fashioned against me receive blindness, in the name of Jesus.

18. Let every evil effect of strange touches be removed from my life, in the name of Jesus.

19. Let all my blessings confiscated by witchcraft spirits be released, in the name of Jesus.

20. Let all my blessings confiscated by familiar spirits be released, in the name of Jesus.

21. Let all my blessings confiscated by ancestral spirits be released, in the name of Jesus.

22. Let all my blessings confiscated by envious enemies be released, in the name of Jesus.

23. Let all my blessings confiscated by satanic agents be released, in the name of Jesus.

24. Let all my blessings confiscated by principalities be released, in the name of Jesus.

25. Let all my blessings confiscated by rulers of darkness be released, in the name of Jesus.

26. Let all my blessings confiscated by evil powers be released, in the name of Jesus.

27. Let all my blessings confiscated by spiritual wickedness in the heavenly places be released, in the name of Jesus.

28. I command all demonic machinations devised to hinder my progress to be roasted, in the name of Jesus.

29. Any evil sleep undertaken to harm me should be converted to dead sleep, in the name of Jesus.

30. Let all weapons and devices of oppressors and tormentors be rendered impotent, in the name of Jesus.

31. Let the fire of God destroy the power operating any spiritual weapon working against me, in the name of Jesus.

32. Let all evil advice given against my favour crash and disintegrate, in the name of Jesus.

33. Let all the eaters of flesh and drinkers of blood, stumble and fall, in the name of Jesus.

34. I command stubborn pursuers to pursue themselves, in the name of Jesus.

35. Let the wind, the sun and the moon run contrary to every demonic presence in my environment, in Jesus' name.

36. You devourers, vanish from my labour, in the name of Jesus.

37. Let every tree planted by fear in my life dry up to the roots, in the name of Jesus.

38. I cancel all enchantments, curses and spells that are against me, in the name of Jesus.

39. Let all iron-like curses break, in the name of Jesus.

40. Let divine tongue of fire roast any evil tongue against me, in the name of Jesus.

41. I declare that I shall prosper in life in Jesus name

42. Every enemy of my destiny is declare impotent forever in Jesus name

43. No weapon forged to make me a failure shall prosper in Jesus name

44. I shall rise above all my enemies in Jesus name.

45. I declare that all those who want me down shall fall down for my sakes in Jesus name

46. I declare that all those who are sitting on my progress be unseated in Jesus name

47. Every pit of failure and disappointment dug for me, the diggers will all be buried inside in Jesus name

48. I declare that I am u stoppable in Jesus name

49. I declare that I am too much for the devil in Jesus name

50. I declare that I have dominion over the forces of darkness trying g to pull me down I Jesus name

51. I declare that the spirit of stagnation has no power over me in Jesus name.

52. Every satanic poison targeted at me will have no effect on me in the name of Jesus

53. I rise above failure in Jesus name

54. I rise above disappointment in Jesus name

55. I rise above setbacks in Jesus name

56. I rise above stagnation in Jesus name

57. I rise above shame in Jesus name

58. I rise above my opposer's in Jesus name

59. I rise above situations and circumstances in Jesus name

60. I rise above all my enemies in Jesus name.

61. I rise above every demonic strong man in Jesus name

62. I rise above witches and wizards in Jesus name

63. I rise above familiar spirits in Jesus name

64. I rise above marine powers in Jesus name

65. I rise above the power of sin in Jesus name

66. I rise above ancestral powers in Jesus name

67. I rise above ancestral curses in Jesus name

68. I rise above parental limitations in Jesus name

69. I rise above environmental limitations in Jesus name

70. I rise above geographical limitations in Jesus name

71. Let the wrath of God be upon every enemy of my life, in the name of Jesus.

72. Let me be filled with all the fullness of God, in the name of Jesus.

73. I render every divination and enchantment of hell against my life impotent, in the name of Jesus.

74. I forbid the storm of the world from troubling my dwelling place, in the name of Jesus.

75. Let every false allegation and accusation against me fall down to the ground and die, in the name of Jesus.

76. Let there be a divine cover of the glory of God upon me, in the name of Jesus.

77. Lord, let the eyes of my understanding be enlightened, in the name of Jesus.

78. I decree all diseases of Egypt out of my life, in the name of Jesus.

79. Begin to command all afflictions to depart, in the name of Jesus.

80. O Lord, perfect what is lacking in my life in Jesus name.

81. I revoke every satanic decree issued against my promotion, in the name of Jesus.

82. I silence every evil dog barking against my breakthroughs, in the name of Jesus.

83. Let the finger of God unseat my household strongman, in the name of Jesus.

84. Every evil bird flying for my sake, be trapped, in the name of Jesus.

85. Every agent of disgrace, backward movements and shame, release me, in the mighty name of Jesus.

86. I overthrow every evil throne installed against my life, in the name of Jesus.

87. Every agent of disorder in my life, be scattered unto desolation, in the name of Jesus.

88. Every power fuelling my problems, fall down and die, in Jesus' name.

89. I release myself from any curse working in my family, in the name of Jesus.

90. Let every spiritual vulture delegated against me eat its own flesh, in the name of Jesus.

91. I trample upon serpents and scorpions, in the name of Jesus.

92. Every cleverly concealed problematic root, be uprooted, in the name of Jesus.

93. I disgrace every evil wisdom working against my breakthroughs, in the name of Jesus.

94. By the power of the Holy Spirit, I crush all my enemies, in the name of Jesus.

95. By the power of the Holy Spirit, I put every evil under my feet, in the name of Jesus.

96. Lord, let me be extraordinary in Jesus name

97. Holy Spirit, deposit your wonders in my life, in the name of Jesus.

98. Lord Jesus, break my infirmity and destroy my disease.

99. Lord Jesus, destroy satanic foundations and build me upon your word.

100. Lord Jesus, set me ablaze with Your Spirit.

Father, I thank you for answering my prayers in Jesus name

PRAYER POINTS FOR EXCEEDING GRACE

Today we will be dealing with prayer points for exceeding grace. When you hear the word exceeding grace what comes to mind? Exceeding grace can be said to be miraculous grace. In the scheme of God, there are levels to things. Grace also has levels. Exceeding grace is a supernatural one, one that is unexplainable, such that cannot be explained via the knowledge of any man.

Grace is the gift of God given to mankind. It could also mean an unmerited favour that one enjoy from God. The exceeding grace of God is a gift that knows no boundary or limitations. We live in the era of grace and for ones greatness in life, exceeding grace of God is greatly needed. For us to do great exploit on earth, we need the grace of God. This is the age when grace is exceedingly needed for triumph in life.

The book of Ephesians 2:7 so that in the ages to come He might show the surpassing riches of His grace in kindness toward us in Christ Jesus. That he will show surpassing riches of his grace. The scripture understands that a time is coming in life that nothing will count anymore, degree qualifications, social status, age, Language or culture will not amount to something anymore, only the grace of God will separate men.

Abraham enjoyed the grace of God in his life. How that a mere mortal man become the friend of God and God would tell him anything that's about to happen. When God wanted to destroy the people do Sodom and Gomorrah, Abraham through the grace of God upon his life was told about the plans of God for the people of Sodom.

Similarly, Noah also found grace in the sight of God. The book of Genesis 6:9 Noah found grace in the eyes of the LORD." God destroyed the people on the surface of the earth due to the wickedness in their heart. But grace saved Noah and his people from the wrath of God.

Most times, people have misconception about grace or how to get it. For the purpose of emphasis, let's list some of the misconceptions about grace.

Grace is merited through the effort of man
It is not the effort of a man that brings the grace. The scripture says it is not of him that willeth and runneth but of God that show mercy. By strength shall no man prevail. The grace of God is an unmerited gift of God to man.
Sometimes, we feel some people don't merit the blessings or gift of God over their lives simply because we feel we are better than them. God is in the capacity to determine who earns His grace.
Grace is not based on Righteousness
The scripture made us understand that our righteousness is like a filthy rag before God. We don't earn grace by the works of our righteousness. If God make Iniquity, who can stand?
God's Grace is an unmerited blessing, this means that you don't worth it neither have you worked for it.

How to Work in the Grace of God

Key into the Covenant of The Cross

Christ didn't just die on the cross, there was a covenant that was made with the death of Christ. The death of Christ on the cross brought grace. The book of Romans 6:14 for sin shall not have dominion over you, for you are not under law but under grace. The grace of God was made sufficient for us through the death of Christ on the cross of Calvary.

PRAYER POINTS

- Lord Jesus, I thank you for the gift of Jesus Christ that came to die for me, I thank you for saving me under the curse of the law, thank you for the marvelous blood of your son Jesus Christ that brought the new Covenant of grace, let your name be exalted in the name of Jesus.

- Lord God, the book of Ephesians 1:7 In Him we have redemption through His blood, the forgiveness of our trespasses, according to the riches of His grace. Father, I seek forgiveness for my sins and iniquities by the precious blood of Christ Jesus. I pray that by the grace of God Almighty all my sons are taken away in the name of Jesus.

- Lord God, I pray for your exceeding grace over my life. The grace of Lord Jesus Christ that will distinct me amongst many people. The grace that dignified the three Hebrews from the midst of several Hebrews, I pray that such grace begin to work over my life in the name of Jesus.

- The scripture says and Esther found favour in the sight of all that saw her. I decree by the authority of heaven, the grace of God over my life is activated in the name of Jesus. Lord, every man and woman shall begin to favour me in the name of Jesus.

- The scripture says if any man will speak, let him speak as an oracle of God. Lord every door that has closed against me, I decree that the grace of God begins to open them in the name of Jesus. The undiluted grace of Jehovah God will go before me today and make every rough way smooth in the name of Jesus.

- Lord I decree by the reason of the exceeding grace of Christ Jesus, I shall be celebrated in all places that I have be rejected. Let the grace of excellence begins to announce me for greatness in every corners of the earth in the name of Jesus.

- Lord God, I decree by the authority of heaven, everything I lay my hands on from today shall prosper. The exceeding grace of Christ will cancel all my errors at work. In every places that punishment awaits me, let grace speak for me in the name of Jesus.

- Lord Jesus, the type of grace that distinct Daniel among all his contemporaries, I pray that in the name of Jesus, let such grace begin to work over my life today. The grace that will set me aside for excellence, I activate it today in the name of Jesus.

COVENANT PRAYERS FOR FAVOR

Today we will be dealing with covenant prayers for favour. The favour of God terminates labour in the life of humans. Favour could be said to be an unmerited blessing, mercy, promotion, or recognition. One of the factors that separate men is the favour of God. When favour begin to speak in the life of a man, he works with speed and direction. There is a level of spiritual acceleration that works with a man that is highly favoured.

Also, when God favours a man, mercy speaks for such a person. Such is the story of Queen Esther. She saved the nation through the favour of God. Esther was not invited into the king's court, and it is an abominable act with death consequence for anyone to enter the king's court without being invited by the king. On the account that her people were about to be destroyed, Esther entered the king's court without being invited. However, rather than judgment she was favoured and the king listened to her.

Recall that the scripture says in the book of Proverbs 16:7, when a man's ways please the LORD, He makes even his enemies to be at peace with him. We all need the favour of God in our lives. Those battles you contend with, that problem and tribulations that you encounter now and then at work, would all be solved when the favour of God is activated upon your life. This explains why covenant prayers for favour is very important for everyone.

What does the covenant prayers of favor means? It means we will be praying for the activation of God's covenant for favor through His words. There are many places in the scripture where the Lord promises to favor us, we will be entering into that agreement through prayers. I decree by the mercy of the Lord; you will be favored in the name of Jesus.

PRAYER POINTS

• Lord, I thank you a beautiful day like this. I thank you for your grace and protection over my life. The scripture says it is by the mercy of the Lord that we are not consumed. I thank you because you have been my shield and buckler, may your name be exalted in the name of Jesus.

- Lord, I thank you because you will favor me today. I magnify you because you will cause even my enemies to be at peace with me. I magnify you because labour and hardship will be removed from my life today, may you name be highly exalted in the name of Jesus.

- Father, for it has been written, Surely, LORD, you bless the righteous; you surround them with your favor as with a shield. You have promised to surround me with your favor, I activate this promise over my life today in the name of Jesus.

- Lord, I pray that your favour will be upon me. Everywhere I turn to from today, let your favor begin to speak for me in the name of Jesus. In every places that I have been rejected, every good place that I have been ridiculed, I decree that you favor begin to speak for me in the name of Jesus.

- Lord, every door of blessing that has been closed against me making me work like an elephant with little or no results to show for it, I pray that favor replace my struggle today in the name of Jesus.

- Lord, the scripture says, for his anger lasts only a moment, but his favor lasts a lifetime; weeping may stay for the night, but rejoicing comes in the morning. Lord, my tears has come to an end. My pain and reproach are over today in the name of Jesus.

- Father, it has been written, For the LORD God is a sun and shield; the LORD bestows favor and honor; no good thing does he withhold from those whose walk is blameless. I pray that no good thing shall be withhold from me. I pray that the favor of the Lord begin to release every blessing that has been locked away, every breakthrough that has been covered, in the name of Jesus.

- The scripture says, May the favor of the Lord our God rest on us; establish the work of our hands for us— yes, establish the work of our hands. Lord, the work of my hands is lifted by the favor of the Lord. I decree by the authority of heaven my business receive supernatural speed in the name of Jesus. I decree that the favor of God will elevate my business today in the name of Jesus.

- Father Lord, I ask that you remember me when you are showing favor to your people. I refuse to continue in hardship. I refuse to continue living in pain, I decree that the favor of the Lord separate me from hardship in the name of Jesus.

- Lord, I pray that you will cause men to favor me. Just like Esther became the Favourite of the king, I ask that your favor will plant my love in the heart of great people that can help my destiny in the name of Jesus.

- The scripture says you show favor to the humble. Father, I humble myself before you today that I may find favor in your sight, I pray that your favor shall locate me today in the name of Jesus.

- Lord, just like you favored Daniel making him better than his mates, I pray that your favor will make me better than all my competitors in the name of Jesus. Lord, over my business, I pray for the grace to stand out among many. The grace that will announce me to the world, I ask that you grant it to me in the name of Jesus.

- Lord, from today, nothing shall be impossible for me to do. No good thing will be too hard for me to accomplish because I serve you. You are the God of all flesh and there is nothing impossible for you to do. Father, from today, through your favor, nothing will be impossible for me to do in the name of Jesus.

20 MFM PRAYER POINTS FOR DIVINE FAVOUR

Deuteronomy 28:13:

13 And the Lord shall make thee the head, and not the tail; and thou shalt be above only, and thou shalt not be beneath; if that thou hearken unto the commandments of the Lord thy God, which I command thee this day, to observe and to do them:

Today we have compiled 20 MFM prayer points for divine favour. This MFM prayer points are inspired by Dr. Odukoya of mountain of fire and miracle ministries. Favour is God giving you what your labour cannot give to you. When they favour of God is upon you, strange and impossible doors are opened before you. Favour took Joseph from the prison to the palace, favour took David from the bush to the palace, favour distinguished Daniel and his three Hebrew friends, favour made Nehemiah to move from an ordinary cup bearer to a governor.

My prayer for you is that, that same favour will answer for you today in Jesus name. Every child of God is a favoured child, but many Christians are still in bondage today because the devil is a thief who comes to steal the word of God from our hearts. When you lack the word of God in your life, you lack favour and when you lack favour, you suffer reproach. This MFM prayer points for divine favour will power you up spiritually to take your God ordained spiritual blessings of favour. As you pray these prayer points, your spirit man will be energized and your study life will increase also every word of declaration that you declare in this prayer points they shall come to pass in Jesus name. Don't be weary, my friend, pray this prayer today and receive your divine favour.

PRAYER POINTS

1.   Father I thank you for your favour upon my life in Jesus name

2.   I declare today that the favour of God will reflect in all my labour in Jesus name.

3.   I declare that the hand of God is upon me in all I do in Jesus name.

4.   Because of your favour, impossible doors of success will be opened to me in Jesus name.

5.   By your unmerited favour, I declare that I shall be the head only and not the tail in Jesus name.

6.   I declare that I have favour with all men, including kings in Jesus name.

7.   Because of your favour, no weapon formed against me shall prosper in Jesus name.

8.   I declare that every evil gang up against me, shall backfire on the head of my enemies in Jesus name

9.   As it was in the days of Joseph, let everyone planning evil against my life, let that same evil return back to them and turn to me to a testimony in Jesus name.

10.   Just like the days of Daniel and his friends, let favour distinguish me from my peers in Jesus name.

11.   I declare that because of your favour, I am 10 times better than my peers

12.   I declare that because of your favour, I have more understanding than my teachers.

13.   I declare that because of your favour, everything I do prospers in Jesus name.

14.   Because of your favour, I walk in supernatural victory in Jesus name.

15.   Because of your favour, I have supernatural wisdom in Jesus name.

16.   Because of your favour my Father, all my sins, past, present and future are forgiving in Jesus name.

17.   Father, let all those who seek my downfall fall for my sakes in Jesus name.

18.   Father, let all those who bless me be blessed forever.

19.   Let anyone who curse me be cursed by you in the name of Jesus.

20.   Father thank you for your never ending favour upon my life in Jesus name

CHAPTER 5

PRAYER AGAINST ENEMIES AT WORK PLACE
COVENANT PAYERS FOR FAVOUR

Today we will be dealing with covenant prayers for favour. The favour of God terminates labour in the life of humans. Favour could be said to be an unmerited blessing, mercy, promotion, or recognition. One of the factors that separate men is the favour of God. When favour begin to speak in the life of a man, he works with speed and direction. There is a level of spiritual acceleration that works with a man that is highly favoured.

Also, when God favours a man, mercy speaks for such a person. Such is the story of Queen Esther. She saved the nation through the favour of God. Esther was not invited into the king's court, and it is an abominable act with death consequence for anyone to enter the king's court without being invited by the king. On the account that her people were about to be destroyed, Esther entered the king's court without being invited. However, rather than judgment she was favoured and the king listened to her.

Recall that the scripture says in the book of Proverbs 16:7, when a man's ways please the LORD, He makes even his enemies to be at peace with him. We all need the favour of God in our lives. Those battles you contend with, that problem and tribulations that you encounter now and then at work, would all be solved when the favour of God is activated upon your life. This explains why covenant prayers for favour is very important for everyone.

What does the covenant prayers of favour means? It means we will be praying for the activation of God's covenant for favour through His words. There are many places in the scripture where the Lord promises to favour us, we will be entering into that agreement through prayers. I decree by the mercy of the Lord; you will be favoured in the name of Jesus.

PRAYER POINTS

- Lord, I thank you a beautiful day like this. I thank you for your grace and protection over my life. The scripture says it is by the mercy of the Lord that we are not consumed. I thank you because you have been my shield and buckler, may your name be exalted in the name of Jesus.

- Lord, I thank you because you will favour me today. I magnify you because you will cause even my enemies to be at peace with me. I magnify you because labour and hardship will be removed from my life today, may you name be highly exalted in the name of Jesus.

- Father, for it has been written, Surely, LORD, you bless the righteous; you surround them with your favour as with a shield. You have promised to surround me with your favour, I activate this promise over my life today in the name of Jesus.

- Lord, I pray that your favour will be upon me. Everywhere I turn to from today, let your favour begin to speak for me in the name of Jesus. In every places that I have been rejected, every good place that I have been ridiculed, I decree that you favour begin to speak for me in the name of Jesus.

- Lord, every door of blessing that has been closed against me making me work like an elephant with little or no results to show for it, I pray that favour replace my struggle today in the name of Jesus.

- Lord, the scripture says, for his anger lasts only a moment, but his favour lasts a lifetime; weeping may stay for the night, but rejoicing comes in the morning. Lord, my tears has come to an end. My pain and reproach are over today in the name of Jesus.

- Father, it has been written, For the LORD God is a sun and shield; the LORD bestows favour and honour; no good thing does he withhold from those whose walk is blameless. I pray that no good thing shall be withhold from me. I pray that the favour of the Lord begin to release every blessing that has been locked away, every breakthrough that has been covered, in the name of Jesus.

- The scripture says, May the favour of the Lord our God rest on us; establish the work of our hands for us— yes, establish the work of our hands. Lord, the work of my hands is lifted by the favour of the Lord. I decree by the authority of heaven my business receive supernatural speed in the name of Jesus. I decree that the favour of God will elevate my business today in the name of Jesus.

- Father Lord, I ask that you remember me when you are showing favour to your people. I refuse to continue in hardship. I refuse to continue living in pain, I decree that the favour of the Lord separate me from hardship in the name of Jesus.

- Lord, I pray that you will cause men to favour me. Just like Esther became the Favourite of the king, I ask that your favour will plant my love in the heart of great people that can help my destiny in the name of Jesus.

- The scripture says you show favour to the humble. Father, I humble myself before you today that I may find favour in your sight, I pray that your favour shall locate me today in the name of Jesus.

- Lord, just like you favoured Daniel making him better than his mates, I pray that your favour will make me better than all my competitors in the name of Jesus. Lord, over my business, I pray for the grace to stand out among many. The grace that will announce me to the world, I ask that you grant it to me in the name of Jesus.

- Lord, from today, nothing shall be impossible for me to do. No good thing will be too hard for me to accomplish because I serve you. You are the God of all flesh and there is nothing impossible for you to do. Father, from today, through your favour, nothing will be impossible for me to do in the name of Jesus.

PRAYER FOR EXCEEDING MERCY

Today we will be dealing with prayer points for exceeding mercy. There are so many verses in the scripture that talked about the mercy of God. The book of Romans 9:15 For He says to Moses, "I will have mercy on whomever I will have mercy, and I will have compassion on whomever I will have compassion." This portion of the Bible explains that the mercy of God is not for all and sundry that is why it is important to pray to God for His mercy over our lives.

Have you ever wondered why some people achieve great success in life even when they only invested little effort. Whereas, there are some other set of people that invested all their time, money and energy into something and they didn't get half the result of those that only did little. That is the concept of mercy. The scripture says, it is not of he that willeth or runneth, but of God that sheweth mercy. This means the effort of a man is not sufficient enough for the accomplishment of goals.

Another concept of mercy is that some people will do some grievous activities and their punishment will be minimal while other people will just do a little and it will seem like the mercy of God has departed completely from them. Example in the scripture is the life of King Saul and King David. The mercy of the lord is upon the live of King David. King Saul did not do half of the atrocities that were perpetrated by King David, God still named King David a man after His heart. When the exceeding mercy of God is at work in the life of a man, things becomes easy.

For proper understanding and for you to know how well to pray, let's quickly run you through the benefits of exceeding mercy.

Things Will Become Easy

The first sign you would see in the life of man that the grace of exceeding mercy is working is that everything will become easy for such a person. The scripture in the book of 1 Samuel 2:9 He will guard the feet of His saints, but the wicked shall be silent in darkness. "For by strength no man shall prevail. A man shall not prevail or excel by strength but by the proportion of grace and mercy that works over his life.

When the mercy of God is upon a man, even when he venture into a business that he knows nothing about, he would still excel in it.

Protocols Will Be Broken

Have you gone to an interview for a job and a man that clearly has no qualifications is considered ahead of those that have all the requirements. There is something that is working in the life of such a person, it is called Mercy. When mercy speaks, protocols becomes obsolete. The natural standard or mode of operation of an organisation will fall face flat in presence of man that the mercy of God is speaking over his life.

Even the constitution of a nation will bow at the face of mercy in the life of man. The scripture made us understand that mercy prevail over judgement. Even when the person has been condemned for death, the mercy of God will speak over the life of such a man and constitution will not mean anymore.

People Blesses Such Person

Even you are a very tough person that hardly like people, when you meet a man that mercy is working in his life, you will naturally like the person and always want to bless the person with substance. The book of proverbs 16:7 when a man's ways please the LORD, He makes even his enemies to be at peace with him. This portion of the scripture further explains the concept of mercy. When the life of a man pleases God, He cause his enemy to be at peace with him. A man that the grace of exceeding mercy is upon will have no enemy.

PRAYER POINTS FOR EXCEEDING MERCY

- Lord Jesus, I thank you for your grace over my life. I thank you for the gift of life that you bestowed on me to see a new day that you have made. Lord, let your name be exalted in the name of Jesus.
- Lord Jesus, the scripture says I will have mercy on whom I will have mercy on and compassion on whom I will have it on. I pray that among the people you will show mercy, lord count me worthy in the name of Jesus.
- Lord Jesus, I pray against any form of sin in my life that will hinder your mercy over my life, Lord forgive me in the name of Jesus. The scripture says, we cannot continue to be in sin and ask grace to abound. I pray that by the reason of the blood that was shed on the cross of Calvary, wash away my sins and iniquities in the name of Jesus.
- Lord I decree by your power, anywhere I turn to now let your mercy speak for me in the name of Jesus. Over my career, I decree that your mercy begins to speak in the name of Jesus.
- Lord Jesus, because of your steadfast love and unending loving kindness I pray that you will have mercy upon me in the name of Jesus.
- I refuse to go without your mercy. Your mercy that replaces the judgement of man, lord let it speak over my life in the name of Jesus.
- I decree by the mercy of the Most High, in all my endeavours, let your exceeding mercy speak for me in the name of Jesus.

- Lord God, it was your mercy for mankind that brought Christ as a sacrificial lamb to die for the sin of man. I pray that the mercy of God will not come to a halt over my life in the name of Jesus.
- I pray that by your mercy, I shall be established in the name of Jesus. Everything that I have always admire, every good thing according to your will for my life is released to me today by your mercy.
- Lord I pray that by your mercy over my life, sickness is taken away in the name of Jesus. I decree that death is wiped away in the name of Jesus.
- Lord Jesus, I pray that every door of blessings that has been closed against me, u decree that the mercy of God Almighty open them today in the name of Jesus.
- I pray for grace to accomplish good thing with ease, I pray that such grace begin to speak over my life in the name of Jesus.

PRAYER AGAINST EVIL BOSSES

Today we have been led by the spirit of God to engage ourselves with prayer points against evil bosses. A wicked is no different from a slave master and can be likened to a modern-day Pharaoh that will hold his employees captive as long as they work for him.

Your work under an evil will be less productive as you will be overwhelmed with the fear of making mistakes that will get your boss angry. Practically, you will worship your boss and adore him. If care is not taken, such a boss will almost take the place of God in your life. But you know, the scripture makes us understand that the heart of man and king is in the hands of the Lord, and he directs them like a flow of water. Remember the story of Esther, how God changed the heart of the king towards her. God can equally change the heart of your evil boss against you.

Unless there is a change, you will be badly oppressed at the workplace by that boss of yours. God will break down every evil enchantment upon your boss that makes him/her act the way they do, and you will see a noticeable change. When God promises to do something, He will stop at nothing until he gets that thing done. I pray by the grace of the most high, God will touch the heart of your boss, and he will soften his hardened heart against you in the name of Jesus.

As you begin to study this prayer guide, God will visit that boss in his sleep, he will see God in every way, and this will birth a new turnaround in the way and manner he treats his workers.

PRAYER POINTS:

- Lord God, I thank you for the grace to secure this job. I thank you for granting me the rare privilege to be able to secure employment with an esteemed organization like this. Let your name be exalted in the name of Jesus.

- Lord God, I pray to you today over the life of my boss. I pray that you will touch him by your power in the name of Jesus. Every evil counsel on him to work against me in that organization, I break such counsel today in the name of Jesus. Father, I pray that you will touch the heart of my boss. For the scripture says you have the heart of man and king in your hands, and you direct it like the flow of water. I pray by the authority of heaven that you will touch the heart of my boss today in the name of Jesus. Give him a loving heart for him to treat his employees well in the name of Jesus.

- Every projection of the enemy in the life of my boss to frustrate, I come against you by the power of the Holy Ghost. Every plan of the enemy to use my boss as a means of frustration for me in this organization, I destroy such plans in the name of Jesus. I nullify every plan of the enemy against me in the name of Jesus. I announce by the power of the Most High that the counsel of the Lord alone will stand over my life.

- Every strongman or giant that has enchanted my boss against me, I frustrate your plans today in the name of Jesus. I decree that the power of the Most High will touch my boss today and break every evil veil that has been used to cover his eye unto sanity, every chain of slavery that has been given to him to hold his employees captive, I break such chain today in the name of Jesus. I come against every covenant of witchcraft upon my life in this organization. I destroy their plans by the fire of the Holy Ghost.

- I come against every demonic power that my evil boss is using to intimidate me at the workplace. I set them ablaze today in the name of Jesus. I set myself from the stronghold of my evil boss, I break down all his demonic powers over me, from now, and I take my freedom by force. I decree absolute liberation for me in the name of Jesus. Never again will I be intimidated by his scheme or powers in the name of Jesus.

- I paralyze every evil power that is used against me at the workplace. For it has been written, no weapon fashioned against me shall prosper. Every power that is used against me by my evil boss is nullified in the name of Jesus. The blood of the lamb destroys all powers of my evil boss in the name of Jesus.

- Lord Jesus, by reason of the blood that you shed on the cross of Calvary, I break every evil covenant that I have unknowingly signed with my evil boss. Every evil covenant that I have ignorantly entered with my evil boss, which he is now using against me, I come against it by the blood of the lamb. By virtue of the blood of the lamb that speaks righteousness than the blood of Abel, I break every evil covenant between my boss and me today in the name of Jesus.

- Lord, I break every Influence of my evil boss on my career in the name of Jesus. I free myself from his influence in the name of Jesus. For it has been written, he that the son set free is free. Indeed, I announce my freedom today in the name of Jesus.

- Lord, arise and let your enemies be scattered. Let every evil man and woman that surrounds me be consumed by the fire of the Holy Ghost. Lord, arise for my sake today and free me from the stronghold of my boss in the name of Jesus.

- Every diabolical power used against me at the workplace ceases to work from today in the name of Jesus. For I carry the mark of Christ, let no man trouble me, I come against every power that has been stationed to harm me in the name of Jesus.

PRAYER POINTS AGAINST POWER OF DARKNESS

We have been led by the spirit of God to engage our readers with prayer points against the power of darkness. In the book of 1 Peter 5:8 Be sober, be vigilant; because your adversary the devil, as a roaring lion, walketh about, seeking whom he may devour: If you ever wonder why we come every day with a prayer guide, it is because the devil doesn't rest, the scripture says he goes about like a wounded lion looking for whom to devour. So, if the power of darkness is not at rest day and night, why should you their target rest? Little wonder the scripture instructed that we pray without season.

The power of darkness are the rulers of the world, powers, and principalities in high places. And if you think they are physical enemies that you can overcome with your physical strength, remember the scripture says by strength shall no man prevail. The book of Ephesians 6:12 says for our struggle is not against flesh and blood, but against the rulers, against the authorities, against the powers of this dark world and against the spiritual forces of evil in the heavenly realms. They are rulers of darkness, immeasurable numbers of unseen spirits terrorizing the lives of people.

There are so many people whose life has been disturbed by the power of darkness; the Lord is about to set you free today. The scripture John 1:5 and the light shineth in darkness; and the darkness comprehended it not. The light of God will shine eminently in your life today, and the stronghold of darkness tormenting your life will flee today. You must put on your spiritual warfare because we are fighting a spiritual battle. I decree by the authority of heaven that God will crush your enemy to death in the name of Jesus. People are walking in darkness. The life of many people have been characterized by gross darkness, but listen today, the scripture says in the book of Isaiah 9:2 The people who walk in darkness will see a great light; Those who live in a dark land, The light will shine on them. You will see a great light today; heaven will announce you to your helper who has not been able to locate due to the gross darkness upon you.

I announce to you today that the fire of the Holy Ghost will destroy the power of darkness working in your life. As you begin to study this prayer guide, the power of the most high will come upon you, and you will become unstoppable to every power of darkness tormenting your life in the name of Jesus.

PRAYER POINTS

- Lord God, the great monarch of Isreal and the world. I pray that you will stretch out your mighty hands, and you will destroy the power of darkness tormenting my life with your mighty hands in the name of Jesus.

- The authority of heaven destroys Father Lord, every cloud of darkness over my life. For it has been written, the light shine and darkness comprehended it not. Father Lord, let your light illuminate the darkness of my life in the name of Jesus.

- The power of darkness that has made me hidden to every destiny helper fall to death right now in the name of Jesus. From now, I become obviously visible to every man and woman that will help me grow physically, mentally, spiritually, and financially.

- Every arrow of sickness that has been sent into my life from the kingdom of darkness, catch fire in the name of Jesus. Oh power of darkness that won't let me walk into my Canaan land die right now in the name of Jesus.

- Every animal of darkness hovering around my environment, catch fire in the name of Jesus. I declare my freedom from the power of darkness in the name of Jesus.

- The scripture says Psalms 114:1-4 When Israel went out of Egypt, the house of Jacob from a people of strange language; Judah was his sanctuary, and Israel his dominion. The sea saw it and fled: Jordan was driven back. The mountains skipped like rams, and the little hills like lambs. I decree by the authority of heaven, every power of darkness in my way flee from now on in the name of Jesus.

- I become a consumable fire to the kingdom of darkness today in the name of Jesus. Every power of darkness, trying to inflict me with sickness, fall to death in the name of Jesus. I decree the healing of God upon every organ in my body; I speak my healing into existence in the name of Jesus.

- Every ruler of darkness, controlling my finances fall to death in the name of Jesus. I free my purse from your hold in the name of Jesus. From now, my finances is free in the name of Jesus.

- Lord, every demon of failure in my life catch fire in the name of Jesus. The scripture says as He is, so am I. This means that as Christ is, so also I am. I pray that by the authority of heaven, I shall not fail because failure is and cannot be found in the name of Jesus. From now, everything I lay my hands on shall prosper in the name of Jesus.

- Oh, you kingdom of darkness scaring me, I free myself from you today by the blood of Christ. Every angel of a demon tormenting me in my sleep, the fire of the Holy come upon you today in the name of Jesus. It has been written for we have not been given the spirit of fear but of sonship to cry Abba Father. Lord, every spirit of fear from the pit of hell is destroyed in the name of Jesus.

- The scripture says, and they overcome him by the blood of the lamb and by the words of their testimony. I crush the power of darkness in my life by the blood of the lamb.

PRAYER POINT AGAINST CHARM

Today we will be dealing with prayer points against charm. As believers, we must learn to build our prayer life, and the best way to do is by not stop Praying. There are men and women of the devil that can use evil charms like enchantment and incantations to inflict us with sickness, pain, or bewitchment, which could cause us to do something against our plans. Anyone the devil sees as a threat, such vices can be used against them. Little wonder, the scripture says we wrestled not against flesh and blood for against powers and rulers of darkness in high places. This explains why our spiritual life must be too notch.

The enemy never stops attacking us. Several charms have been used against us, but most times, it is God that rescues us from various attacks. However, it is also in our own place to stand tall in the place of prayer and destroy the works of the devil. The altar of prayer we raise during our good days will help us against evil charms during the bad days. I decree by the authority of heaven; every evil charm and enchantment that has been designed against you are destroyed in the name of Jesus.

People can go to any length to ensure that we fall. Sometimes they go to the grave, stay under the moon, or stand naked under the sun just to ensure that we fail. Little wonder the scripture says many are afflictions of the righteous, but God delivers him from them all. I have heard cases of people inflicted with terrible sickness after they stepped on something like a charm on the ground, but I decree in the name of Jesus, every evil charm and enchantment that has been set for you, I destroy them by the fire of the Holy Ghost. As you begin to study this prayer guide, the Holy Ghost will destroy every evil charm that has been designed against you in the name of Jesus.

PRAYER POINTS

- Lord Jesus, I decree, everyone standing naked under the sky to use the power of the air and son against me, to cause me not to achieve the height you destined for me, I destroy such person in the name of Jesus. Lord Jesus, just like the sword melt in the face of an inferno, let evil people be destroyed in the name of Jesus.

- Oh, ye Moon, hear the voice of the Lord; you are one of the things God created for my good. I decree whoever is standing under you to inflict me with pains and sorrow, let them be destroyed in the name of Jesus. Every man and woman whose heart bare great evil against me, I destroy them in the name of Jesus.

- For it has been written, no weapon fashioned against me shall prosper. Every tongue that rises against me in judgment let them be consumed in the name of Jesus. Every evil hand sending arrows of sorrow into my life go back to the sender in sevenfold in the name of Jesus.

- I come against every form of enchantment every form of evil that has been done against me, destroy them in the name of Jesus. Father Lord, let the plans of my enemy be destroyed in the name of Jesus. Lord, let my enemies die by the wickedness of their hearts in the name of Jesus.

- Every man or woman that has spilled the blood of an animal in order to harm me, render their efforts useless in the name of Jesus. Let their plans and work go against them in the name of Jesus. Every evil charm that has been placed on the floor for me to match, I destroy them by the blood of the lamb.

- Every evil covenant that the enemy has entered into because of me, I destroy such covenant in the name of Jesus. By reason of the new covenant that was made eminent by the blood of Jesus, let every covenant against me be destroyed in the name of Jesus.

- I decree by the authority of heaven; the sun should stand against every man and woman who bare evil in heart for me in the name of Jesus. Let the sun from the East, North, West, and South rise and scorch my enemy to death in the name of Jesus.

- Lord Jesus, every evil charm that has been buried in the ground to harm me, I destroy them in the name of Jesus.

- Every evil charm that has been designed by the enemy to create great havoc in my life, I send them back to the sender in the name of Jesus. Let the evil of their hearts consume them towards me in the name of Jesus.

- Every giant in my father's house, every demonic woman in my mother's house, creating havoc in my life with charm, let such a man and woman fall to death in the name of Jesus.

- Every evil charm that has been buried in the ground at my workplace, to cause me to lose my position, I destroy them in the name of Jesus.

- Every enchantment used against me to cause my decrement, I destroy it by the power in the name of Jesus. Lord, I crush every charm of failure, every charm of sickness in my life the fire of the Holy Ghost.

- Arise O Lord and let your enemies be scattered, let every man and woman who rise against me in judgment be condemned before me in the name of Jesus.

- Oh, ye earth hears the voice of the Lord, the scripture says the ground is the Lord and the fullness thereof, world and they that dwell therein. Every man and woman that is standing on the earth thinking of evil against me let them be destroyed in the name of Jesus.

- I cover myself and family with the blood of Jesus, every evil enchantment and power of sorcery or magic against me is destroyed in the name of Jesus.

- Lord Jesus, every evil trap that the enemy has set for me, I destroy them in the name of Jesus.

PRAYER POINTS AGAINST BUSINESS FAILURE

Today we will be dealing with prayer points against business failure. If you have been experiencing consistent failure in your business, then this prayer guide is for you. If after developing every nice strategy for building your business empire, you have consulted season business experts, yet your business has not experienced any breakthrough, there is a need for you to turn to God. The scripture makes us understand that every good idea comes from God.

The enemy would not want us to succeed because he doesn't want us to live comfortably while in Christ Jesus. So be sure to know that the enemy will frustrate your efforts, especially on that business. Still, I have good news for you today, God is about to look into the situation of that business, and He is ready to help you out of that business failure. For it has been written in Deuteronomy 8:18 remember the LORD your God. He is the one who gives you the power to be successful in fulfilling the covenant he confirmed to your ancestors with an oath. There are so many people whose power to make riches has been taken away by the devil, and that is why they had so many failures to contend with in their businesses.

I bring good news to you today, behold I will do a new thing, now shall it spring forth, for you know it not, I will make a way in the wilderness and a river in the desert. God will do a new thing over that your business, and you will sing a new song. As you begin to study this prayer guide, I pray the power of God will crush the demon of failure to death over your business. From now, you will begin to experience a great turn around in the name of Jesus. That crumbling business is made strong by the power of heaven.

PRAYER POINTS

- Lord Jesus, I come before you today to pray over my business. I have experienced too many failures in setting up my business. I take solace in your words that say it is God that gives the power to be successful. I pray that you will grant me the power to be successful in my business in the name of Jesus.

- I decree by the authority of heaven that the angel of failure, that agent of hardship over my business, is destroyed in the name of Jesus. Lord Jesus, I decree by the power in the name of Jesus that every stronghold of darkness over my business is taken away in the name of Jesus.

- Every dark cloud of failure over my business is removed in the name of Jesus. For it has been written that anything I lay, my hands shall be proper. I decree by the power in the name of Jesus that everything I lay my hands upon from now will begin to prosper in the name of Jesus.

- The scripture says for every good idea comes from God, I decree by the authority of heaven that every good idea that I need to stand tall in my business God begin to make provisions for it in the name of Jesus.

- Lord God, I seek your divine wisdom to go about my normal business, the wisdom to structure my business in the right part to become successful; I pray that you will grant it unto me in the name of Jesus. The scripture says if any man lacks wisdom, let him ask from God that gives liberally without blemish. I seek your wisdom that doesn't have blemish; Lord grants it to me in the name of Jesus.

- I pray that everything I need to stir the ship of my business to a successful end, I pray that God begins to supply in the name of Jesus. I stand on the promises of the word that says my God will supply all my needs according to His riches in glory through Christ Jesus. Father Lord, I pray that you will supply everything I need to become successful in my business in the name of Jesus.

- Every agent of darkness that has been assigned to my business to clout it with failure falls down and die right in the name of Jesus. Every agent of failure that wants to frustrate my efforts with immeasurable failure let the fire of the Holy Ghost burn you to death in the name of Jesus.

- I pray that every strong man and woman that is standing in my way of success be destroyed by fire because I know that the fire of the Lord will go before me and burn all my enemies.
- I declare by the power in the name of Jesus that from now, I will begin to experience another dimension of successful business in the name of Jesus. In every place that I have failed before in my trial, may the angel of success become my new companion in the name of Jesus.
- Look back the Egyptians you see today you shall see them no more, in the same vein; I decree that the failure I see today I shall see them no more in the name of Jesus. The scripture says, declare a thing, and it shall be established; I declare business success in the name of Jesus.
- Oh, ye angel that guides every successful business to success, I pray that from now on, you have become my new friend in the name of Jesus.
- The scripture says the devil has been evil from the beginning, and that is why the son of God manifest to destroy the works of the enemy. I blame my business failure on the enemy; I decree that you will destroy the works of the enemy over my business in the name of Jesus.
- I anoint my business with the oil of gladness gotten from the precious blood of Christ that when the angel of failure sees my business, it will pass over in the name of Jesus.

WARFARE PRAYERS TO DESTROY THE PLANS OF THE ENEMY

Today we will be dealing with warfare prayers to destroy the plans of the enemy. The enemy never rests, mostly when a man has decided to go on and pursue the purpose of his existence. Jacob never had issues in life until he started aspiring to become great like he has been destined to be. Joseph never has any problems in life until he began having dreams where God showed him a revelation of who he is to become.

It is worthy to note that just as God has plans for our lives, the enemies also have a plan for our lives. It is now our doing or undoing that will destroy the works of the enemy over our lives.

The enemy succeeded in the life of Samson. The strength of Samson became useless after the enemy got him. He has been warned not to marry from a strange land, a community of people that don't serve the holy one of Isreal, he took Delilah from their midst, and that led to his fall. I decree that whoever the enemy has staged to enter your life at one point in time to destroy you, I decree that the fire of most high will burn such person in the name of Jesus. Every wrong man or woman that the enemy has planned for you, may God cause a divine separation between you and that person.

Similarly, as God has designed his plans for Joseph, so also did the enemy design his plans too. Joseph was destined to become great. He was destined to lead the children of Isreal out of. Meanwhile, the enemy also has his plans for Joseph. His brothers fell into the perfect image of the enemy, and they were used against him to ensure that the plans of God concerning him were defeated. I pray that by the mercies of the most high, every agenda of the enemies to destroy the purpose of God for your life shall be destroyed today in the name of Jesus.

The enemy planned that Joseph should the killed, but God saved him. The enemy also made provision for how Joseph would sacrifice his destiny on the altar of immoralities with his master's wife. Still, God also helped Joseph overcome the plan of the enemy, by the mercies of the most high, may God destroy the plans of the enemies concerning your life.

Ensure that you study this prayer guide and say all the prayers in it. As you begin to use this guide, may God reveal the plans of the enemy to you in the name of Jesus.

PRAYER POINTS:

- Father Lord, I come before you this day, I need your help Lord Jesus, and I need your power over my enemies. The ones that have vowed that I will never amount to something in life, the one whose plans and agenda for my life is for destruction, I pray that you will destroy their plans over my life in the name of Jesus.

- Lord God, I pray that by your mercies, your counsel alone will stand in my life. Every other and agenda of the evil ones over my is scattered by fire. I call on the fire of the most high to descend into the camp of the enemies and burn them to ashes in the name of Jesus.

- Father Lord, I pray that the archangels of glory will descend mightily into the territory of enemies and destroy their agenda for my life in the name of Jesus. Lord, I want you to scatter the language of my enemies. I pray that you will cause mighty disunity to erupt in their midst, and you will cause them to destroy themselves in the name of Jesus.

- I decree that from now on, the spirit of truth, the spirit of divinity from the throne of the holy of Isreal will descend upon me in the name of Jesus. I pray that the holy spirit of God will begin to guide me in all my ways. I pray that you will not cover the secret of the enemies over my life. I pray that you will always reveal their plans over my life in the name of Jesus.

- Lord Jesus, I pray that by your death and resurrection, you will not let my enemy triumph over me. I pray that in all ways and all ramifications, you will grant me victory over my enemies. Do not let them rejoice in victory over me. Every of their plans is revealed to me in the name of Jesus. For the scripture says the secret of the Lord is with those that fear him, I pray that you will reveal the secret of dark places to me in the name of Jesus.

- Lord God, just like you helped Joseph escape all the traps and craftiness of the enemies over his life, just like you take him from the point of zero to the point of hero, I pray that you will help me overcome the trap of my enemies in the name of Jesus.

- I pray that the fire of the most high will go right now, because the scripture says, the fire will go before the army of the Lord and consume his enemies. I pray that the fire of the most high God before and destroy all my enemies. All the evil seer that sees the destiny of a man even before the time of manifestation, I pray that you will remove their sights in the name of Jesus.

- I decree by the power of the most high, every sense of consciousness of my enemies is taken away in the name of Jesus. I pray that you will cause my enemies to go blind for my sake, I decree by the power in the name of Jesus, you will cause my enemies to go deaf over my matter in the name of Jesus. Each of their plans and agenda over my life is cancelled in the name of Jesus

POWERFUL PRAYER POINTS AGAINST EVIL IMPLICATIONS

Today we will be dealing with powerful prayer points against evil implications. Evil implications could mean false accusations or an incriminating connection with another person. There are so many inmates in the prison who are innocent of the charges that led them to prison, but because they were implicated, there is nothing they could do to save themselves. Evil implications can happen anywhere. It could be at your workplace, it could be in school, your community, and it could also happen in the church.

You must know that sometimes before evil implication is perpetrated, there must be an evil alliance against the victim. In the book of Numbers 16:3, they gathered together against Moses and Aaron, and said to them, "You take too much upon yourselves, for all the congregation is holy, every one of them, and the LORD is among them. Why then do you exalt yourselves above the assembly of the LORD?" Korah had formed an alliance with the elders of Isreal against Moses and Aaron. They were accused of trying to take over the rule. If not for a divine and timely intervention of God, Moses would have been implicated.

Also, let's study the life of Joseph. The wife of his master Potiphar implicated him after she requested that Joseph come to her bedroom. This implication landed Joseph in prison. This is how evil implications work. It doesn't work against someone who doesn't have potential, the focus is always on someone with huge potentials. For instance, you are doing well at your place of work, and you are voted as the most likely to be promoted

The enemy can recruit people to implicate you at work, thereby leading to your unceremonious exit.

Furthermore, it could happen in school. We have heard cases of a bright and intelligent student expelled from school because of examination malpractices. It is evident that they were implicated. Today, we will be praying against every demonic alliance that has been formed to implicate you or bring you down. The Lord will visit the coven of your enemies with his hand of vengeance, and he will destroy every demonic implication that has been programmed to work against you.

I decree by the authority of heaven, every evil implication programmed against you is destroyed today in the name of Jesus. Every man and woman who have designated themselves to be a tool in the hands of the enemy to implicate you, I pray that the Lord shall judge them today in the name of Jesus.

For you to know that the devil is implicating you, you will discover that only a few people that matters truly believed that you did what you have been accused of. Also, the process is very fast that you are unable to think it through. You may also discover that you are being hated at the same place you were loved unconditionally. You are being rejected at the same place you were once celebrated. When you notice any of this, you should know that evil implication is at work against you. Don't relent to say the following prayers

PRAYER POINTS:

- Father Lord, I thank you because you listen to me all the time. I thank you for your blessing and provision. I thank you because you have not let the plans of the enemy triumph over my life; may your name be highly exalted in the name of Jesus.

- Lord, I come against every agent of implication from the enemy. I decree by the authority of heaven, the fire of the Holy Ghost destroys every form of implication against me.

- Lord, every man and woman who has made his or herself a tool in the hands of the enemy to implicate me, I destroy them today by fire in the name of Jesus.

- Lord, every evil conspiracy against me is rendered futile in the name of Jesus. Lord, every conspiracy against me at the place of work to ruin my years of service, I destroy them today in the name of Jesus.

- Father, every evil conspiracy against me in my community to tarnish my image, I decree by the authority of heaven they shall be an effort of futility in the name of Jesus.

- Lord, the scripture says you have the heart of man and kings, and you direct them like the flow of water. Lord, I decree, every man and woman of substance whose hearts has been poisoned against me, I pray that you shall change their thoughts today in the name of Jesus.

- Lord, I stand by the promises of your word. I become a terror to the power of evil implications in the name of Jesus.

- Lord God, every gathering of conspiracy against me, I visit their camp today with the fire of the Holy Ghost. I pray that you shall create confusion in their midst today in the name of Jesus.

- Lord, for it has been written, no weapon fashioned against me shall prosper. I pray by the authority of heaven, every plan and agenda of the enemy against me to land me in trouble is destroyed in the name of Jesus.

- Every incriminating substance that has been secretly placed in my space to implicate me at work, I pray that the power of God will destroy them in the name of Jesus.

- Father Lord, in every way the enemy has made me a target to be implicated, I seal it up today in the name of Jesus.

- Lord, I break down every stronghold of darkness hovering around me to land me in trouble. I destroy every linking channel between me and evil implications in the name of Jesus.

- Lord, I silent the mouth of an evil accuser against me today in the name of Jesus. In every way that the accuser is planning to implicate me, I destroy that way in the name of Jesus.

- Lord, I destroy every evil covenant of evil implication over my life and destiny today. I declare that I shall not be implicated in the name of Jesus.

DAILY EFFECTIVE PRAYER FOR SUCCESS AT WORK

Today we will be dishing out daily Effective Prayer for success at work. Prayer should be a thing that will be done daily; irrespective of how much you prayed yesterday; it must not affect your prayers today because each new day has its blessings and evil. We have heard different stories of how someone will close from work in a day and return to work another day only for him to be sacked.

Most importantly, when an employee is less productive, an employer would not be making a mistake to release such an employee. So, it is important to have some effective daily prayer for success at work to increase the productivity of every employee and also prevent some of the catastrophic work hazards from happening.

There is no man, no matter how little or he is, that would not want success at work. Whether you are a self-employed individual or you are working someone, everyone always wants to be successful at what they do. And often, people mistake effort for success; we tend to rate success by the magnitude of effort that we had invested in the work. Whereas, it is not of he that willeth or runneth but of God that showeth mercy, so we must understand that success is not guaranteed even when we invest all the efforts in this world into it.

Therefore, even when you are certified professional in what you do, you still need the blessings of God to be successful in work. More so, there are some successes that we so much desire in our work that we cannot get them unless God gives us.

Drawing reference from the Bible where it says no one receives anything unless it is given from God. Little wonder, the bible admonished that we ask and it shall be given unto us, knock, and it shall be open, seek and we shall find. Having known this, we have compiled a list of effective daily prayer for success at work. These prayers are not to be taken jokingly, and you must make it a point of duty to say these prayers daily to have a miraculous turn around at work.

PRAYER POINTS

- King of Heaven, I appreciate you for giving me the grace to witness another beautiful day, I thank you for this priceless gift of life you have bestowed on me to do better today, let your name be exalted in Jesus name.

- As the bible as admonished us that we should treat every unforgiveness before praying, I forgive every man and woman that crossed me yesterday, I release them from the snare of my anger, and I pray that God will forgive me my sin in the name of Jesus.

- I bind every demonic power that always robs people of their sweat at work; I destroy every power that frustrates people's hard work with failure, I decree that such demon is destroyed in my part in the name of Jesus.

- I decree by the authority of heaven that every power that causes people to make unimaginable blunder in the place of work should cease operation over my life in the name of Jesus.

- I commit into the hands of the Almighty everything I will be doing today, and I pray that your hands will be upon them in the name of Jesus.

- I anoint every of my work tool with your precious blood. I pray that your hands be upon every piece of equipment that I will be using today in the name of Jesus.

- For the Bible says it is not of he that willeth or runneth but of God that showeth mercy. I decree that today you will have mercy upon me. I pray for the grace of spiritual acceleration that will make me succeed beyond the imagination of everyone at work; Lord gives it to me in the name of Jesus.

- Lord God, I pray that today, you will help me to complete all my tasks. I pray for strength not to grow weary at the place of work. I decree that you give it to me in the name of Jesus.

- You said in your word that we should come all those that are heavy laden, and you will give us rest. I pray for your rest today, and I ask that by your mercy, you will help me carry my workload today in the name of Jesus.

- Lord God, it is a thing of joy to be an example of a great worker, I decree that you will fly me the strength to always complete my task excellently well in the name of Jesus.

- The Bible says the glory of the latter shall surpass the former, Lord, more than the exploit I made yesterday, in double folds, I decree that you will help me accomplish more today in the name of Jesus.

- Every power that has vowed to frustrate me at work today, I decree that you catch fire in the name of Jesus.

- I come against every power of negativity at work today. I decree that they cease operation in the name of Jesus.

- Lord, I shall never fail because Jesus never experienced failure. I decree success upon my work in the name of Jesus.

- The scripture says those that wait upon the Lord their strength shall be renewed. I pray for a renewed strength more than that of yesterday, I pray that you send it upon me in the name of Jesus.

- Jesus, I want you to teach and nuture me, fly me the spirit of excellence more than that which was given to Daniel and the three Hebrews, I decree that you will give it to me in the name of Jesus.

- The scripture says wisdom is profitable to direct, Lord Jesus, I pray that you will grant me the wisdom to escape work stress, I decree that you give it to me in the name of Jesus.

- The scripture made me understand that every good idea comes from God. I decree that you will grant me the wisdom and the idea to move my company forward, the idea that I need to fly my company to the next level, I decree that you give it to me in the name of Jesus.

- I decree in the name of Jesus, that my work is secured in by the blood of Christ. No power, Scheme or principalities will snatch away my work in the name of Jesus.

POWERFUL PRAYERS FOR PROTECTION AT WORK

Psalm 32:7: 7 Thou art my hiding place; thou shalt preserve me from trouble; thou shalt compass me about with songs of deliverance. Selah

We will be highlighting some of the powerful prayers for protection at work, and we pray that God will listen to our voices and give a response to our prayers. Have you heard of work hazards? Work hazards are the types of dangers that workers encounter at the place of work. For instance, it has been broadcasted and published that quite a number of health workers have lost their lives while trying to save others from the novel Covid-19. This is a perfect example of work hazards.

In our place of work, we are often faced with lots of dangerous encounters that are life-threatening, whereas it is our line of duty, and we cannot shy away from it. We must carry out our duty diligently, hence, avoiding the work because of its dangers is not an option for us. As we continue to do our job to benefit ourselves and the populace, we must say some specific prayers for protection against work hazards.

One of the notable people in the scripture that died in active duty was one of the stewards of King David, named Uzza, the angel of the Lord struck him to death for touching the Ark of the Covenant. What is worthy of knowing is that Uzza was not the only servant that accompanying King David and the Ark of Covenant at that time, why is it that only him died during the encounter?

We must understand that every day is filled with evil. However, we can redeem each day by the blood of the lamb. Little wonder, the Bible instructed that we should always pray without season. With this in mind, it is pertinent that we always pray for protection, especially in our workplace. Remember that the scripture revealed to us that no man receives anything unless it is given from above. Our protection shall come from heaven, from He that protected the children of Isreal in the land of Egypt.

Before you set out for work each morning, find time to say the following powerful prayers for protection at work.

PRAYER POINTS

- Father in Heaven, I pray for your undiluted protection as I'm about to set out for my workplace this morning, I pray that your hands of protection will be upon me. Lord, you are my rock and refuge, my present help in times of need. I ask that your eyes will always be upon me in the name of Jesus.

- Father Lord, I pray that your spirit of love and faithfulness will overshadow my life as I begin my journey to work today. I come against those plans and schedules of the enemy to cause me sorry, pain, or death today in the name of Jesus.

- Lord Jesus, Your goodness and Mercy shall continue to follow me all the days of my life. Father, as I'm preparing to go out today, let your goodness and mercy continue to go with me. Lord, I want you to be my eyes, and you will order my step. You will lead and guide me in the name of Jesus.

- The Bible says, the eyes of God is always upon the righteous, and His ears are still attentive to their prayers. Father I pray that your eyes will be upon me today even as I prepare to go to work, I ask that your hands of protection will not cease to operate in my life in the name of Jesus.

- Father in heaven, I seek protection under the wings of your hands, I come against every scheme of the enemy to make me a victim of work hazard in the name of Jesus. I refuse to fall victim to any evil circumstances in the name of Jesus.

- Father Lord, I pray that your right hand will guide me into your strength, and your spirit will ignite my inner man that I will continually work with the ambiance of your spirit and power in the name of Jesus.

- Lord Jesus, I pray that your power and glory will go with me as I journey through the world today. I pray that your spirit will help me take on all my spiritual armour to chase away every evil thing that may want to come my way today.

- Father Lord, I ask that your power will go ahead of me and sanctify my workplace with the precious blood of Christ. I speak with authority that the power destroys anything that has been scheduled or planned by the enemy to cause me pain or regret at work today in the name of Jesus.

- Jehovah, I entrust my life into your able hands as I set out today. I pray that your spirit will set me aside and exempt me from any evil thing that has been destined to happen today. I ask that you give your angels charge over me that they will guide me in all my ways today in the name of Jesus.

- Father Lord, I cover myself with the blood of Jesus. I cover my work desk with the blood of Jesus. No incriminating file will be submitted at my desk today. I destroy the scheme of the enemy to implicate me at my workplace. I pray that you will throw confusion into the camps of the enemy concerning me, and you will cause every tongue that rises against me in condemnation to be destroyed in the name of Jesus.

- Lord Jesus, for my weapon of warfare, are not carnal but spiritual, I utilize your power and strength to take on the full amour of God that will chase evil away from me in the name of Jesus. I put my hope and trust in you for victory over the enemy that wants to put me condemnation and death, and I nullify their plans in the name of Jesus.

- Lord God, I pray for both your spiritual and physical protection in my work today. I decree that my work is secured in the name of Jesus. I pray that you will guide my mouth with your word and wisdom, and you will let me know when to speak the right time to be quite. You will teach me in your wisdom the best response during every conversation in my workplace in the name of Jesus.

60 DAILY MORNING PRAYER BEFORE WORK

Psalm 63:1-3: O God, thou art my God; early will I seek thee: my soul thirsteth for thee, my flesh longeth for thee in a dry and thirsty land, where no water is; 2 to see thy power and thy glory, so as I have seen thee in the sanctuary. 3 Because thy loving-kindness is better than life, my lips shall praise thee.

Starting your morning with prayers, is the best way to kick start your day. God will only walk with those that invite Him into their hearts. Today we shall be looking at 60 daily Morning Prayer before work. We can also title it as daily Morning Prayer before school, for those of us who are students. The purpose for this prayers is to help you take charge of your day. Jesus said" every day has enough evil of its own" Matthew 6:34. Therefore we must pray that the evil of each day shall not come near us and our loved ones. We must commit our days to God every morning in order for him to lead us to the right path. Psalm 91: 5, tells us that there are arrows that flies by that day, it will only take prayers to overcome those arrows. It could be arrows of failure, arrows of disappointment, arrows of sicknesses, arrows of death, and arrows of wrong business partners etc., which ever arrows the devil is targeting at you, you must return it back to him on the altar of prayers.

When we start our day with Morning Prayer, our strength is renewed, our day is secured as the host of angels walk with us. This daily Morning Prayer before work, will empower us with the grace of God to maximize our days. I encourage you this today, never leave your house without committing your ways to God, always pray about everything to God, prayer is simply talking to God as one would talk to a friend. Commit your ways to Him and He will direct your path. When God is leading you, you will be unstoppable. No devil can ruin your day when you start it with Jesus. The reason I compiled up to 60 daily Morning Prayer is so that you will have more than enough things to pray about. When you hand over your mornings to Him in prayers, He takes care of the rest of your days. Today shall be a great day for you in Jesus name.

PRAYER POINTS

1. Father, I thank you for waking me up this morning, in Jesus' name.
2. O Lord, cause my whole heart to be at rest, trusting in you as I go about my day to day activities in Jesus name
3. O Lord, keep me from leaning and relying on my own understanding and intelligence in Jesus name
4. O Lord, deliver me from what seems right to me and deliver me to what is right to you in Jesus name
5. O Lord, I pull down every imaginations and every high thing in my life that are not of You in Jesus name
6. O Lord, purify my lips with your holy fire in Jesus name
7. O Lord, reveal to me those things that give my enemies advantage over me in Jesus name
8. O Lord, let my fellowship with you become greater in Jesus name
9. I draw upon heavenly resources today, in the name of Jesus.
10. O Lord, engrace I to become the person you created me to be in Jesus name
11. I surrender myself completely in every area of my life, in the name of Jesus.
12. I stand against every satanic operation that will attempt to hinder my blessings today, in the name of Jesus.
13. Satan, I refuse your involvement in my prayer life, in Jesus' name.
14. Satan, I command you, to leave my presence with all your demons, in the name of Jesus.
15. I bring the blood of the Lord Jesus Christ between me and you Satan in Jesus name
16. Father Lord, open my eyes to see how great you are, in the name of Jesus.
17. I declare that Satan and his wicked spirits are under my feet, in the name of Jesus.
18. I claim the victory of the cross for my life today, in Jesus' name.

19. Every satanic stronghold in my life, be dismantled by fire, in the name of Jesus.

20. I put off all forms of weakness, in the name of Jesus.

21. Lord Jesus, come into my life by fire. Break down every idol, and cast out every foe.

22. Every wicked spirit planning to rob me of the will of God for my life, fall down die, in the name of Jesus.

23. I tear down the stronghold of Satan against my life, in the name of Jesus.

24. I smash every plan of Satan formed against me, in Jesus' name.

25. I smash the stronghold of Satan formed against my body, in the name of Jesus.

26. O Lord, let me be the kind of person that would please you.

27. Holy Spirit, bring all the work of resurrection and Pentecost into my life today, in the name of Jesus.

28. Every witchcraft power, I cast you into outer darkness, in the name of Jesus.

29. I confound every stubborn pursuer, in the name of Jesus.

30. I bind every power cursing my destiny into ineffectiveness, in the name of Jesus.

31. I strike every evil power siphoning my blessing with chaos and confusion, in the name of Jesus.

32. I nullify the incantations of evil spiritual consultants, in Jesus' name

33. I turn the evil devices of household witchcraft upside down, in the name of Jesus.

34. I render every local satanic weapon harmless, in the name of Jesus.

35. I receive deliverance from the spirit of anxiety, in Jesus' name.

36. I bind every spirit of mental stagnation, in the name of Jesus.

37. I release myself from the power and authority of any curse, in the name of Jesus.

38. I renounce any unholy covenants involving my life, in Jesus' name.

39. I grab every stubborn problem and smash it against the Rock of my salvation, in the name of Jesus.

40. I nullify every sacrifice to demons used against me, in Jesus' name.

41. Every power cursing my destiny, be silenced, in the name of Jesus.

42. I break the power of any incense burnt against me, in Jesus' name.

43. Every serpentine spirit, go into the hot desert and be burned, in the name of Jesus.

44. Let the blood of Jesus poison the roots of all my problems, in the name of Jesus.

45. I go back to Adam and Eve on both sides of my bloodline, and I cut of every evil root, in the name of Jesus.

46. I reverse every improper operation of body organs, in Jesus' name.

47. Every evil contract working against my life, be rewritten by the blood of Jesus.

48. I reverse every satanic calendar for my life, in the name of Jesus.

49. Anything my ancestors have done to pollute my life, he dismantled now, in the name of Jesus.

50. I refuse to be in the right place at the wrong time, in Jesus' name.

51. I bind every negative energy in the air, water and ground working against me, in the name of Jesus.

52. Anything from the kingdom of darkness that has made it their business to hinder me, I single you out right now and bind you, in the name of Jesus.

53. I command every satanic opposition in my life to be bound with chains that cannot be broken, in the name of Jesus.

54. I strip off all the spiritual armor of every strongman militating against my destiny, in the name of Jesus.

55. I destroy the hold of every evil powers, standing on my way in the name of Jesus.

56. I separate myself from evil today and forever in the name of Jesus.

57. Lord Jesus, I thank you for the victory.

58. I renounce any signing of my name over to Satan, in Jesus' name.

59. I announce that my name is written in the Lamb's book of life, in the name of Jesus.

60. Father, I thank you for answering my prayers in Jesus name.

16 PRAYERS AGAINST SLAVERY AT WORK

Are you tired of your job? Are you labouring for nothing? Are you unsatisfied with your job? This 16 prayers against slavery at work will free you from slavery at your work place. Use them as a guide to pray and pray them with faith.

16 Prayers Against Slavery At Work

1). Oh Lord, whoever is depriving me of my salary at my place of work shall be removed from
his/her position in Jesus name.

2). Oh Lord, teach me how to retrieve all my salary in my place of work so that others will not reap wherever I have sown in Jesus name.

3). All merciless taskmasters in my place of work shall loose their position today in Jesus name.

4). Oh Lord, open business doors for me so that I will be free from total dependence on my salary in Jesus name.

5). Oh God replace all the evil and merciless taskmasters in my place of work with good leaders in Jesus name.

6). Oh Lord, I know that you can do everything. Deliver me from this dead end job in Jesus name.

7). Oh Lord, don't let my hope of divine intervention fades away, come to my rescue and save me from this work slavery in Jesus name.

8). Oh Lord, I receive mercy for my work today in Jesus name.

9). Oh Lord, remember me in this hole of hardship because I want to give testimony in your house in Jesus name.

10). Oh Lord, grant me wisdom to know how to manage my salary and resources every month thereby maximizing my financial destiny.in Jesus name.

11). Oh Lord, break all slavery in my work as you broke the yoke of burden and the rod of oppressor in the days of Gideon in Jesus name.

12). Oh Lord, by your anointing this day, destroy the yoke of over labour in my work in Jesus name.

13). Oh Lord, I eradicate all bonds of wickedness, heavy burden and oppression in my place of work in Jesus name.

14). Oh Lord, I break every yoke of financial bondage in my place of work, I set myself free in Jesus name.

15). Oh Lord, Remove all those who are making work a living hell for me, or change my level and take me to a better place in Jesus name.

16). I prophesy today that I receive freedom from all forms of slavery in Jesus name.

Thank you Jesus

PRAYER POINTS FOR DOUBLE PROMOTION

2 Kings 2:9 and it came to pass, when they were gone over, that Elijah said unto Elisha, Ask what I shall do for thee, before I be taken away from thee. And Elisha said, I pray thee, let a double portion of thy spirit be upon me.

Every believer has the authority to make demands and see them come to pass. It doesn't matter the state you find yourself now, you can change level by the power of prayer. Today we shall be engaging in Prayer points for double promotion. This prayer points are for those who are long overdue for promotion in their work place, businesses and careers. You have hovered around this mountain of slow progress long enough, it's time for you to make progress, and it's time for you to receive your double promotion. This prayer points will move the heart of kings to favour you in the name of Jesus. As you engage this prayers in faith today, the God of promotion will open your heavens and rain down on you double promotions in all areas of your endeavour in Jesus name.

Elijah asked Elisha, "what do you want" and Elisha said, I want double portion of your spirit, in other wards, I want double portion of your grace and achievements to rest upon me. Elisha made a specific demand from Elijah and He got it. In the same way, you must pray this prayer points with a specific demand in your heart. You don't just say Lord promote me, you must tell Him where you want him to take you to. You must let God know the kind of double promotion that you desire. The purpose of this prayer points is to enable you destroy every satanic oppositions that will stand against your double promotion. This prayer points will clear the air for you to receive your desired specific double promotion expectation. I encourage you to pray this prayers with passion and great expectation. These prayer points for double promotion was carefully selected for your own breakthrough. No man shall hold you down anymore in Jesus name.

PRAYER POINTS

1. I revoke every satanic decree issued against my double promotion, in the name of Jesus

2. I silence every evil dog barking against my breakthroughs in the name of Jesus

3. Let the finger of God unseat my household strongman, in the name of Jesus.

4. Let every evil bird flying for my sake be trapped, in the name of Jesus

5. Every agent of stagnation, backwardness and shame, release me now!!! In the name of Jesus

6. I overthrow every evil throne installed against my life, in the name of Jesus

7. Every agent of disorder in my life, be scattered unto desolation in the name of Jesus

8. Every power fuelling my problems, fall down and die in the name of Jesus

9. I release myself from any curse working in my family, in the name of Jesus

10. Let every spiritual vulture delegated against me eat their own flesh and drink their own blood in the name of Jesus

11. I trample upon every serpents and scorpions fighting against my promotion in the name of Jesus.

12. I claim the power to overcome and to excel among all other competitors, in the name of Jesus.

13. Lord, let every decision by any panel be favourable unto me, in the name of Jesus.

14. Every negative word and pronouncement against my success, be completely nullified, in Jesus' name.

15. All competitors with me in this issue will find my defeat unattainable, in the name of Jesus.

16. I claim supernatural wisdom to answer all questions in a, way that will advance my cause, in the name of Jesus.

17. I confess my sins of exhibiting occasional doubts.

18. I bind every spirit manipulating my beneficiaries against me, in the name of Jesus.

19. I remove my name from the book of those who see goodness without tasting it, in the name of Jesus.

20. You the cloud, blocking the sunlight of my glory and breakthrough, disperse, in the name of Jesus.

21. O Lord, let wonderful changes begin to be my lot from this week.

22. I reject every spirit of the tail in all areas of my life, in the name of Jesus.

23. Oh Lord, bring me into favour with all those who will decide on my advancement.

24. Oh Lord, cause a divine substitution to happen move me ahead.

25. I reject the spirit of the tail and I claim the spirit of the head, in the name of Jesus.

26. All evil records, planted by the devil in anyone's mind against my advancement, shatter to pieces, in the name of Jesus.

27. Oh Lord, transfer, remove or change all human agents that are bent on stopping my advancement.

28. Oh Lord, smoothen my path to the top by your hand of fire.

29. I receive the anointing to excel above my contemporaries, in the name of Jesus.

30. O Lord, catapult me into greatness as you did for Daniel in the land of Babylon.

31. O Lord, help me to identify and deal with any weakness in me that can hinder my progress.

32. I bind every strongman, delegated to hinder my progress, in the name of Jesus.

33. Oh Lord, despatch your angels to roll away every stumbling block to my promotion, advancement and elevation.

34. O Lord, let power change hands in my place of work to the hands of the Holy Spirit.

35. Fire of God, consume any rock, tying me down to the same spot, in the name of Jesus.

36. All demonic chains, preventing my advancement, break, in the name of Jesus.

37. All human agents, delaying / denying my advancement, I bind the evil spirits controlling your minds in this respect, in the name of Jesus.

38. Holy Spirit, direct the decisions of any panel in my favour, in the name of Jesus.

39. I refuse to fail, at the edge of my miracle, in the name of Jesus.

40. O Lord, release your angels to fight my battle.

Thank you Jesus for my double promotion is sure in Jesus name

PSALM 35 PRAYER POINTS AGAINST UNJUST ENEMIES

Psalms 35:1 Plead my cause, O LORD, with them that strive with me: fight against them that fight against me.

Today we shall be looking at psalm 35 prayer points against unjust enemies. This prayer points are for those who have been attacked by the enemy without cause, those who have been paid back with evil for the good they have shown, those who have been treated unjustly by evil people. If you fall into any of this category today, then you have come to the right place. Through this psalm 35 prayer points, God will give you justice over all your adversaries in Jesus name. As Christians, we must understand that our real enemy is the devil, he only operates through possessed human vessels. This human vessels carry out the devils evil acts against innocent people. My beloved brethren, there is wickedness in this world, you don't need to provoke the devil for him to attack you, the fact that you are a Christian is enough reason for all hell to be against your life. In Matthew 16:18, Jesus said 'the gates of hell shall not prevail against the church'. This simply means that if you are a child of God, the gates of hell will always contend with your destiny. As you engage this psalm 35 prayer points against unjust enemies today, every gates of hell shall bow before you in Jesus name.

Psalm 35 prayer points is a warfare prayer points. It's a prayer points to put you as a Christian in an offensive mood. I always tell believers that do not let the devil attack you before you defend yourself, rather, be always on spiritual alert, be a prayer watch man, a believer that prays always. Through consistent prayers we keep our Christian life on fire and when we are on fire, no enemy shall prevail over us. This is my prayer for you today, as you engage this psalm 35 prayer points, every wickedness of the wicked over your life shall return to their heads in Jesus name. All those who have treated you unjustly shall be judged by your Father in Heaven in Jesus name. Through this prayer points, every enemy in your life shall bow in Jesus name. I encourage you to engage this psalm 35 prayer points with faith and with all your heart. You shall overcome in Jesus name.

PSALM 35 PRAYER POINTS

1. Father, plead my cause with those who strive with me in Jesus name
2. Father arise and fight against those who fight against me in Jesus name
3. Arise O Lord and defend me from those who are too strong for me in Jesus name
4. Father draw out also the spear, and stop the way against them that persecute me in Jesus Name
5. Father, I declare today that you are my salvation in Jesus name
6... Let them be confounded and put to shame that seek after my soul in Jesus name.
7. Let them be turned back and brought to confusion that devise my hurt in Jesus name.
8. Let them be as chaff before the wind: and let the angel of the LORD chase them in Jesus name.
9. Let their way be dark and slippery: and let the angel of the LORD persecute them in Jesus name.
10. Let destruction come upon him at unawares; and let his net that he hath hid catch himself: into that very destruction let him fall in Jesus name.
11. Let them be ashamed and brought to confusion together that rejoice at mine hurt: let them be clothed with shame and dishonour that magnify themselves against me in Jesus name.
12. Let them shout for joy, and be glad, that favour my righteous cause: yea, let them say continually, let the LORD be magnified, which hath pleasure in the prosperity of his servant In Jesus name.
13. Let those that bless me be blessed, and let anyone that curses me be cursed in Jesus name
14. Let the law of divine partiality begin to operate to my favour, in the name of Jesus.

15. Every demonic establishment in my work-place and business, fighting against my progress, crash and disintegrate, in the name of Jesus.

16. Every stronghold of the devil over my life, be broken now, in the name of Jesus.

17. I pull down every external stronghold that is working against my progress, in the name of Jesus.

18. Every satanic plan to embarrass me, be dissolved by fire, in the name of Jesus.

19. Every gathering of the ungodly against me, physically or spiritually, be scattered unto desolation, in the name of Jesus.

20. I cancel every report brought against me in the kingdom of darkness, in the name of Jesus.

21. I cancel every charge brought against me in the kingdom of darkness, in the name of Jesus.

22. I cancel every accusation brought against me in the kingdom of darkness, in the name of Jesus.

23. I revoke and nullify every judgement passed upon me in the kingdom of darkness, in the
name of Jesus.

24. I cancel every decision passed upon me in the kingdom of darkness, in the name of Jesus.

25. I cancel every condemnation passed upon me in the kingdom of darkness, in the name of Jesus.

26. I paralyze evil hands to perform their enterprise against me, in the name of Jesus.

27. I sabotage the operations of the enemy commissioned against my life, in the name of Jesus.

28. I scatter every satanic efforts of the enemy commissioned against my life, in the name of Jesus.

29. Every labour of the enemy on my prosperity, receive double failure, in the name of Jesus.

30. Every war waged against my life by enemies, receive double disgrace, in the name of Jesus

Thank you Father for answering my prayers in Jesus name.

107 SPIRITUAL WARFARE PRAYERS TO TRIUMPH OVER YOUR ENEMIES

Psalm 18:37-40: 37 I have pursued mine enemies, and overtaken them: neither did I turn again till they were consumed. 38 I have wounded them that they were not able to rise: they are fallen under my feet. 39 For thou hast girded me with strength unto the battle: thou hast subdued under me those that rose up against me. 40 Thou hast also given me the necks of mine enemies; that I might destroy them that hate me.

The arch enemy of man is the devil, but the devil mostly operates through human agents. Just as no one has ever seen God, but we see His goodness through His children that believe in Him, in the same way no one has seen the devil, but we also see his evil acts through his children that believe in him. In John 8:44, Jesus told the Pharisees that "they are of their father, the devil". This simply implies that the devil has his own children among men, whom he uses to cause havoc in this world. All the evils we here in the world today, wickedness among men are all product of the works of the devil through his children. But today we are going to be engaging 107 spiritual warfare prayers to triumph over your enemies. This spiritual warfare prayers will give you permanent victory over all your enemies.

Who are your enemies? Simple, those who oppose you. Those who have vowed that it will never be better for you and your household. Your enemies are those who are standing on your way to progress, either physically or spiritually. Your enemies are also those who smile at you openly but their hearts is filled with bitterness towards you. You must arise today and pray your way to safety. Life is a battle ground, if you don't stop your enemies, they will stop you. Spiritual warfare prayers is the way to stop the enemy. Remember the story of the Apostles in the book of Acts 12:1-23, How that when King Herod killed James the Apostle, and he saw that it pleased the Jews, he went ahead and arrested Peter, that was when the eyes of the church opened, they realized that as long as they kept quiet, they all would have died one after the other. So they went into spiritual warfare prayers for peter and suddenly, the angel of the Lord appeared to peter (Acts 12:7), and Peter was delivered. It didn't stop there, that same angel went ahead to stop the enemy King Herod by Killing Him, Acts12:23.

Look child of God, we serve a God of War, we don't pray that our enemies should die, we only asked the lord to stop them, He alone knows how to stop them and which means to use. I declare to you today, that as you engage this spiritual warfare prayers every enemy standing on your way must bow today in the name of Jesus. Everyone that says you will not succeed in life, they shall be put to perpetual shame in Jesus name. The God of Heaven will arise and scatter all your enemies today in Jesus name. I see you walking in victory as you engage this spiritual warfare prayers in Jesus name. Pray this prayers with faith today and I see your victory established in Jesus name.

PRAYER POINTS

1. Thou King of glory, arise, visit me and turn around my captivity in the name of Jesus.

2. I shall not regret; I will become great, in the name of Jesus.

3. Every habitation of humiliation and demotion, fashioned against me, be battered, shattered and swallowed up by the power of God.

4. O Lord, station and establish me in your favour.

5. God of restoration, restore my glory, in the name of Jesus.

6. As darkness gives up before light, O Lord, let all my problems give up before me, in the name of Jesus.

7. Thou power of God, destroy every trouble in my life, in Jesus' name.

8. O God, arise and attack every lack in my life, in the name of Jesus.

9. Thou power of liberty and dignity, manifest in my life, in the name of Jesus.

10. Every chapter of sorrow and slavery in my life, close forever, in the name of Jesus.

11. Thou power of God, usher me out of the balcony of disgrace by fire, in the name of Jesus.

12. Every obstacle in my life, give way to miracles, in Jesus' name.

13. Every frustration in my life, become a bridge to my miracles, in the name of Jesus.

14. Every enemy, exploring devastating strategies against my progress in life, be disgraced, in the name of Jesus.

15. Every residential permit for me to stay in the valley of defeat, be revoked, in the name of Jesus.

16. I prophesy that bitter life shall not be my portion; better life shall be my testimony, in the name of Jesus.

17. Every habitation of cruelty, fashioned against my destiny, become desolate, in the name of Jesus.

18. All my trials, become gateways to my promotions, in the name of Jesus.

19. You anger of God, write the obituary of all my oppressors, in the name of Jesus.

20. O Lord, let your presence begin a glorious story in my life.

21. Every strange god, attacking my destiny, scatter and die, in the name of Jesus.

22. Every horn of Satan, fighting against my destiny, scatter in the name of Jesus.

23. Every altar, speaking hardship into my life, die, in the name of Jesus.

24. Every inherited battle in my life, die, in Jesus' name.

25. All my blessings that have been buried with dead relatives come alive and locate me, in Jesus' name.

26. All my blessings that are presently not in this country arise and locate me, in the name of Jesus.

27. Every stronghold of my father's house, be dismantled, in Jesus name.

28. Father, let all my proposals find favour in the sight of . . . in the name of Jesus.

29. O Lord, let me find favour, compassion and loving-kindness with . . . concerning this matter.

30. All demonic obstacles that have been established in the heart of . . . against this matter be destroyed, in Jesus' name.

31. O Lord, show . . . dreams, visions and restlessness that would advance my cause.

32. My money, being caged by the enemy, be released, in Jesus' name.

33. O Lord, give me supernatural breakthroughs, in all my present proposals.

34. I bind and put to flight, all the spirits of fear, anxiety and discouragement in the name of Jesus.

35. O Lord, let divine wisdom fall upon all who are supporting me, in these matters.

36. I break the backbone of any further spirit of conspiracy and treachery, in the name of Jesus.

37. O Lord, hammer my matter into the mind of those who will assist me so that they do not suffer from demonic loss of memory.

38. I paralyse the handiwork of household enemies and envious, agents in this matter, in the name of Jesus.

39. You devil, take your legs away from the top of my finances, in the mighty name of Jesus.

40. Fire of the Holy Spirit, purge my life from any evil mark put upon me, in the name of Jesus.

41. Every jinx upon my _ _ _, break, in the name of Jesus.

42. Every spell upon my _ _ _, break, in the name of Jesus.

43. You rod of the wrath of the Lord, come upon every enemy of my _ _ _, in the name of Jesus.

44. Angels of God, invade them and lead them into darkness, in the name of Jesus.

45. Thou hand of the Lord, turn against them day by day, in the name.

46. O Lord, let their flesh and skin become old, and let their bones break, in the name of Jesus.

47. O Lord, let them be compassed with gall and travail, in the name of Jesus.

48. O Lord, let your angels hedge them about and block their paths, in the name of Jesus.

49. O Lord, make their chains heavy.

50. When they cry, O Lord, shut out their cries, in the name of Jesus.

51. O Lord, make their paths crooked.

52. O Lord, make their ways to be strewn with sharp stones.

53. O Lord, let the power of their own wickedness fall upon them, in the name of Jesus.

54. O Lord, turn them aside and pull them into pieces.

55. O Lord, make their ways desolate.

56. O Lord, fill them with bitterness and let them be drunk with wormwood.

57. O Lord, break their teeth with gravel.

58. O Lord, cover them with ashes.

59. O Lord, remove their souls far from peace and let them forget prosperity.

60. I crush under my feet, all the evil powers trying to imprison me, in the name of Jesus.

61. O Lord, let their mouths be buried in the dust, in the name of Jesus.

62. O Lord, let there be civil war in the camp of the enemies of my _ _ _, in the name of Jesus.

63. Power of God, pull down the stronghold of the enemies of my _ _ _, in the name of Jesus.

64. O Lord, persecute and destroy them in anger, in the name of Jesus.

65. Every blockage, in my way of _ _ _ clear away by fire, in the name of Jesus.

66. Every demonic claim of the earth over my life, be dismantled, in the name of Jesus.

67. I refuse to be chained to my place of birth, in Jesus' name.

68. Any power, pressing the sand against me, fall down and die, in the name of Jesus.

69. I receive my breakthroughs, in the name of Jesus.

70. I release my money from the house of the strongman, in Jesus' name.

71. Blood of Jesus and the fire of the Holy Ghost, cleanse every organ in my body, in the name of Jesus.

72. I break loose from every inherited evil covenant of the earth, in the name of Jesus.

73. I break loose from every inherited evil curse of the earth, in the name of Jesus.

74. I break loose from every form of demonic bewitchment of the earth, in the name of Jesus.

75. I release myself from every evil domination and control from the earth, in the name of Jesus.

76. Blood of Jesus, be transfused into my blood vessel.

77. I release panic upon my full-time enemies, in the name of Jesus.

78. O Lord, let stubborn confusion come upon the headquarters of my enemies, in the name of Jesus.

79. I loose confusion upon the plans of my enemies, in the name of Jesus.

80. Every stronghold of darkness, receive acidic confusion, in the name of Jesus.

81. I loose panic and frustration on satanic orders issued against me in the name of Jesus.

82. Every evil plan against my life, receive confusion, in the name of Jesus.

83. All curses and demons, programmed against me, I neutralise you by the blood of Jesus.

84. Every warfare, prepared against my peace, I command panic upon you, in the name of Jesus.

85. Every warfare, prepared against my peace, I command havoc upon you, in the name of Jesus.

86. Every warfare, prepared against my peace, I command chaos upon you, in the name of Jesus.

87. Every warfare, prepared against my peace, I command pandemonium upon you, in the name of Jesus.

88. Every warfare, prepared against my peace, I command disaster upon you, in the name of Jesus.

89. Every warfare, prepared against my peace, I command confusion upon you, in the name of Jesus.

90. Every warfare, prepared against my peace, I command spiritual acid upon you, in the name of Jesus.

91. Every warfare, prepared against my peace, I command destruction upon you, in the name of Jesus.

92. Every warfare, prepared against my peace, I command hornets of the Lord upon you, in Jesus' name.

93. Every warfare, prepared against my peace, I command brimstone and hailstone upon you, in the name of Jesus.

94. I frustrate every satanic verdict issued against me, in Jesus' name.

95. You the finger, vengeance, terror, anger, fear, wrath, hatred and burning judgment of God, be released against my full-time enemies, in the name of Jesus.

96. Every power, preventing the perfect will of God from being done in my life, receive failure, in the name of Jesus.

97. You warring angels and Spirit of God, arise and scatter every evil gathering sponsored against me, in the name of Jesus.

98. I disobey any satanic order, programmed by inheritance into my life, in the name of Jesus.

99. I bind and cast out every power causing internal warfare, in the name of Jesus.

100. Every demonic doorkeeper, locking out good things from me, be paralysed by fire, in the name of Jesus.

101. Every evil power, fighting against me, fight and destroy yourselves, in Jesus' name.

102. Every breakthrough hindering, delaying, preventing, destroying and breaking demons, receive confusion, in the name of Jesus.

103. O Lord, let divine power and control attack the spirits of violence and torture, in the name of Jesus.

104. O Lord, let the spirit of witchcraft attack familiar spirits fashioned against me, in the name of Jesus.

105. O Lord, let there be a civil war, in the kingdom of darkness, in the name of Jesus.

106. O Lord, loose judgment and destruction upon all stubborn, disobedient and reluctant spirits who fail to follow my commands promptly.

Thank the Lord, for answered prayers

100 PRAYER FOR PROTECTION FROM BLACK MAGIC AND WITCHCRAFT POWERS

Numbers 23:23: 23 Surely there is no enchantment against Jacob, neither is there any divination against Israel: according to this time it shall be said of Jacob and of Israel, What hath God wrought!

Black magic, are dark forces of the devil. These forces are responsible for the evil we see in the world today. The devil does not operate alone, he operates with the help of his demonic agents, such as witches and wizards, voodoo priests, necromancers, soothsayers, stargazers, palm readers, tarot card players, diviners, mediums, psychics, etc. All this people are agents of the devil used to manipulate and harm naive people including Christians. My dear friend, do not be deceived, demonic forces are real, and if you are not protected, you can be a victim of the devil. But I am not here to put fear in you today, rather I am here to expose you to the power that can silent all the powers of darkness. The power of prayer. Today we are going to be looking at prayer for protection from black magic and witchcraft powers.

Every child of God that is given to prayers cannot be a victim of spells and enchantment, your prayer life makes you too hot for the devil to tamper with. Even demons recognize Christians that are on fire for God. When your prayer life is active, you are on fire for God. The devil is constantly stealing, killing and destroying lives on a daily basis, every evil we see in the world today has its root in the demonic world, the terrorists attacks, the violence in our schools, the crimes on our streets etc. this are all manipulations of demonic powers, aiming to kill and take as many souls to hell as possible. We must pray this prayer for protection against this evil forces and evil arrows. We must pray for our own protection on a daily basis, because when God is with you, no devil can be against you, God will always protect you like He protected the children of Isreal in the wilderness. He will be a wall of fire round about you, making it impossible for any devil to afflict you. Even when the agents of darkness come against you, they will all be destroyed in a heartbeat. That is what you experience when you are a prayerful Christian. I encourage you to pray this prayers in faith and pray them always, they may be long but, they are powerful. You can break them down in smaller groups and pray it intensively and see the Lords hands continually on your life in Jesus name.

PRAYER POINTS

1. O Rock of Ages, smash every foundation of witchcraft in my family into pieces, in the name of Jesus. Thou foundation of witchcraft in my father's house/mother's house, die, in the name of Jesus.

2. O Lord, let witchcraft powers eat their own flesh and drink their own blood, in the name of Jesus.

3. Every seat of witchcraft, receive the thunder fire of God, in the name of Jesus.

4. Every habitation of witchcraft powers, become desolate, in the name of Jesus.

5. Every throne of witchcraft, be dismantled by fire, in the name of Jesus.

6. Every stronghold of witchcraft powers, be pulled down by fire, in the name of Jesus.

7. Every refuge of witchcraft, be disgraced, in Jesus' name.

8. Every network of witchcraft, disintegrate, in the name of Jesus.

9. Every communication system of witchcraft powers, be destroyed by fire, in the name of Jesus.

10. Every transportation system of witchcraft powers, be disrupted, in the name of Jesus.

11. O Lord, let the weapons of witchcraft powers turn against them, in the name of Jesus.

12. I withdraw my blessings from every bank or strong room of the enemy, in the name of Jesus.

13. O altar of witchcraft, break, in the name of Jesus.

14. Every witchcraft padlock, fashioned against me, break by fire, in Jesus' name.

15. Every trap of witchcraft, catch your owners, in Jesus name.

16. Every witchcraft utterance, and projection made against me, backfire, in the name of Jesus.

17. I reverse, every witchcraft burial fashioned against me, in Jesus' name.

18. I deliver my soul from every witchcraft bewitchment, in the name of Jesus.

19. I reverse the effect of every witchcraft summons to my spirit, in Jesus' name.

20. Every witchcraft identification mark, be wiped off by the blood of Jesus.

21. I frustrate every witchcraft exchange of my virtues, in the name of Jesus.

22. Blood of Jesus, block the flying route of witchcraft powers, targeted at me.

23. Every witchcraft curse, break and be destroyed, in Jesus' name.

24. Every covenant of witchcraft, melt by the blood of Jesus.

25. I withdraw every organ of my body from any witchcraft altar, in the name of Jesus.

26. Anything planted in my life by witchcraft, come out now and die, in the name of Jesus.

27. Blood of Jesus, cancel every witchcraft initiation, fashioned against my destiny, in the name of Jesus.

28. Every witchcraft poison, be destroyed, in the name of Jesus.

29. I reverse every witchcraft pattern, fashioned against my destiny, in the name of Jesus.

30. Every witchcraft cage, fashioned against my life, be destroyed, in the name of Jesus.

31. Every problem in my life that originated from witchcraft receive divine and instant solution, in Jesus' name.

32. All the damages done to my life by witchcraft, be repaired, in the name of Jesus.

33. Every blessing, confiscated by witchcraft spirits, be released, in Jesus' name.

34. Every witchcraft power, assigned against my life and marriage, be destroyed in Jesus' name.

35. I loose myself from any power of witchcraft, in Jesus' name.

36. Every camp of witchcraft, gathered against my prosperity, fall down and die, in Jesus' name.

37. Every witchcraft pot, working against me, I bring the judgment of God upon you, in the name of Jesus.

38. Every witchcraft pot, using remote control against my health, break into pieces, in Jesus' name.

39. Witchcraft opposition, receive the rain of affliction, in the name of Jesus.

40. Spirit of witchcraft, attack the familiar spirits fashioned against me, in Jesus' name.

41. I retrieve my integrity from the hands of household witchcraft, in Jesus' name.

42. I break the power of the occult, witchcraft and familiar spirits, over my life, in Jesus' name.

43. In the name of Jesus, I break and loose myself from all evil curses, chains, spells, jinxes, bewitchments, witchcraft or sorcery, which may have been put upon me.

44. Thunder of God, locate and dismantle the throne of witchcraft in my household, in the name of Jesus.

45. Every seat of witchcraft in my household, roast by the fire of God, in Jesus' name.

46. Every altar of witchcraft in my household, roast in the name of Jesus.

47. Thunder of God, scatter the foundation of witchcraft in my household beyond redemption in Jesus' name

48. Every stronghold or refuge of my household witches, be destroyed, in Jesus' name.

49. Every hiding place and secret place of witchcraft in my family, be exposed by fire, in the name of Jesus.

50. Every local and international witchcraft network of my household witches, shatter to pieces, in Jesus name.

51. O Lord, let the communication system of my household witches be frustrated in Jesus' name.

52. Terrible fire of God, consume the transportation of my household witchcraft, in the name of Jesus.

53. Every agent, ministering at the altar of witchcraft in my household, fall down and die, in the name of Jesus.

54. Thunder and the fire of God, locate the storehouses and strong rooms of the household witchcraft harbouring my blessings and pull them down, in the name of Jesus.

55. Any witchcraft curse, working against me, be revoked, by the blood of Jesus.

56. Every decision, vow and covenant of household witchcraft affecting me, be nullified by the blood of Jesus.

57. I destroy with the fire of God, every weapon of witchcraft used against me, in Jesus' name.

58. Any material, taken from my body and now placed on a witchcraft altar, roast by the fire of God, in Jesus' name.

59. I reverse every witchcraft burial, fashioned against me, in the name of Jesus.

60. Every trap, set for me by witches, begin to catch your owners, in the name of Jesus.

61. Every witchcraft padlock, fashioned against any area of my life, roast, in Jesus' name.

62. Every wisdom of household witches, be converted to foolishness, in Jesus' name.

63. Every wickedness of household enemies, overtake them, in the name of Jesus.

64. I deliver my soul from every witchcraft bewitchment, in the name of Jesus.

65. Any witchcraft bird, flying for my sake, fall down, die and roast to ashes, in Jesus' name.

66. Any of my blessings, traded with by household witches, be returned to me, in Jesus' name.

67. Any of my blessings and testimonies, swallowed by witches, be converted to hot coals of fire of God and be vomited, in the name of Jesus.

68. I break loose from every bondage of witchcraft covenants, in Jesus' name.

69. Any witchcraft coven, where any of my blessings is hidden, be roasted by the fire of God, in the name of Jesus.

70. (Lay your right hand on your head) every witchcraft plantation, pollution, deposit and material in my body, melt by the fire of God and be flushed out, by the blood of Jesus.

71. Every evil ever done to me through witchcraft attack, be reversed, in the name of Jesus.

72. Every witchcraft hand, planting evil seeds in my life through dream attacks, wither and burn to ashes, in Jesus' name.

73. Every witchcraft obstacle, put on the road to my desired miracle and success, be removed by the east wind of God, in Jesus' name.

74. Every witchcraft chant, spell and projection made against me, I bind you and turn you against your owner, in Jesus' name.

75. I frustrate every plot, device, scheme and project of witchcraft, designed to affect any area of my life, in the name of Jesus.

76. Any witch, projecting herself into the body of any animal, in order to do me harm, be trapped in the body of such an animal forever, in Jesus' name.

77. Any drop of my blood, sucked by any witch, be vomited now, in the name of Jesus.

78. Any part of me, shared out among household/village witches, I recover you, in the name of Jesus.

79. Any organ of my body that has been exchanged for another through witchcraft operation be replaced now, in Jesus' name.

80. I recover any of my virtues/blessings, shared out among village/household witches, in the name of Jesus.

81. I reverse the evil effect of any witchcraft invocation or summon to my spirit, in the name of Jesus.

82. I lose my hands and feet from any witchcraft bewitchment or bondage, in Jesus' name.

83. Blood of Jesus, wash away every witchcraft identification mark on me or on any of my properties, in Jesus' name.

84. I forbid any re-union or regrouping of household and village witches, against my life, in the name of Jesus.

85. O Lord, let the entire body system of my household witches begin to run amok until they confess all their wickedness, in Jesus' name.

86. O Lord, let the mercies of God be withdrawn from them, in Jesus' name.

87. O Lord, let them begin to grope in the daytime as if in the thickness of a dark night, in the name of Jesus.

88. O Lord, let everything that has ever worked for them begin to work against them, in Jesus' name.

89. O Lord, let them not have any garment to cover their shame, in Jesus' name.

90 O Load let as many as are stubbornly unrepentant be smitten by the sun in the day and by the moon at night, in Jesus' name.

91. O Lord, let each step they take lead them to greater destruction, in Jesus' name.

92. But as for me, O Lord, let me dwell in the hollow of your hand, in the name of Jesus.

93. O Lord, let your goodness and mercies overwhelm me now, in the name of Jesus.

94. Any witchcraft operation against my life, under any water, receive immediate judgment of fire, in Jesus' name

95. Every witchcraft power, that has introduced spirit husband/wife or an evil child into my dreams, roast by fire, in the name of Jesus.

96. Every agent of witchcraft power, posing as my. Husband/wife or child. In my dreams, roast by fire, in Jesus' name.

97. Every agent of witchcraft power, physically attached to my marriage to frustrate it, fall down now and perish, in Jesus' name.

98. Every agent of witchcraft power, assigned to attack my finances through dreams, fall down and perish, in Jesus' name.

99. O Lord, let your thunderbolts locate and destroy every witchcraft power coven, where deliberations and decisions were fashioned against me, in the name of Jesus.

100. Any water spirit from my village or place of birth, practising witchcraft against me and my family, be amputated by the word of God, in Jesus' name.

Thank you Jesus for my protection.

30 WARFARE PRAYERS FOR ENEMIES TO LEAVE ME ALONE

Exodus 7:1-4: 1 And the Lord said unto Moses, See, I have made thee a god to Pharaoh: and Aaron thy brother shall be thy prophet. 2 Thou shalt speak all that I command thee: and Aaron thy brother shall speak unto Pharaoh that he send the children of Israel out of his land. 3 And I will harden Pharaoh's heart, and multiply my signs and my wonders in the land of Egypt. 4 But Pharaoh shall not hearken unto you, that I may lay my hand upon Egypt, and bring forth mine armies, and my people the children of Israel, out of the land of Egypt by great judgments.

In life there are stubborn problems and stubborn situations, this are issues that linger in your life longer than necessary, refusing to go, like Pharaoh in the bible they are hardened problems. This issues are as a result of stubborn spirits that resists you and prevents you from moving forward. The devil attacks people not only with circumstances, but also with demonic human agents. People who have vowed that they will never let you go in life, people who are desperately after your downfall in life. They attack you because they envy you, even when you have not offended them, the plot evil against you to see to it that you are humiliated. This category of enemies are enemies that will not leave you alone. They are like Pharaoh in the Old Testament. Today, I have compiled 30 warfare prayers for enemies to leave me alone, this is not a prayer of begging the enemy, and this is a prayer of commanding the enemy to leave you alone.

There is only one word the devil understands and that is the word violence, the devil does not give in to reasoning, he has no respect for dialogue, all he knows is violence, violence, violence, when he sees your violent faith in action, he bows and gives way. As you engage this warfare prayers for enemies to leave me alone prayer points today, I see every devil bowing out of your life in Jesus name. Every stubborn pharaoh shall release you by fire in Jesus name. Pray this prayers in faith and see your God deliver you today in Jesus name.

PRAYER POINTS

1. Thou power of God, penetrate my spirit, soul and body, in the name of Jesus.

2. Association of demons, gathered against my progress, roast by the thunder fire of God, in the name of Jesus.

3. Blood of Jesus, redeem me, in the name of Jesus.

4. Every satanic decision, taken against my progress, be nullified, in the name of Jesus.

5. Every evil deposit, in my spirit, soul and body, be flushed out by the blood of Jesus.

6. Oh Lord my God, promote me in the spiritual and in the physical, in the name of Jesus.

7. Every stranger, in my body, ministry, life and calling, jump out, in Jesus' name.

8. Any satanic arrow, fired at me, go back, locate and destroy your sender, in the name of Jesus.

9. Holy Ghost, arise and destroy the habitation and works of the wicked in my life, in the name of Jesus.

10. Every serpentine spirit, spitting on my breakthrough, roast, in the name of Jesus.

11. Every enemy of the perfect will of God for my life, die, in the name of Jesus.

12. Thou anointing of joy and peace, replace heaviness and sorrow in my life, in Jesus' name

13. O Lord, let abundance replace lack and insufficiency in my life, in Jesus' name.

14. Every Pharaoh in my life, destroy yourself, in the name of Jesus.

15. Garment of Pharaoh that is upon my life, be removed by fire, in Jesus' name.

16. Thou power of impossibility in my destiny, die, in the name of Jesus.

17. Every task master, assigned against me, somersault and die, in the name of Jesus.

18. I refuse to continue eating from the crumbs of the task master's table, in the name of Jesus.

19. Any man or woman, who wouldn't let me prosper, Oh Lord, declare his/her obituary, in the name of Jesus.

20. Oh Lord, give me a new inner man if I have been altered, in Jesus' name.

21. Oh Lord, activate your high calling in my life, in the name of Jesus.

22. Oh Lord, anoint me to recover the wasted years in every area of my life, in Jesus' name

23. Oh Lord, if I have fallen behind in any area of my life, empower me to recover all lost opportunities and wasted years, in the name of Jesus.

24. Any power that says I will not go forward, be arrested, in the name of Jesus.

25. Any power that wants to keep me in want in the midst of plenty, die, in Jesus' name.

26. Any power that wants to draw me away from the presence of the Lord to destroy me, die, in the name of Jesus.

27. I prophesy that I will get to my promised inheritance, in the name of Jesus.

28. Any power that wants me to fulfil my destiny partially, die, in the name of Jesus.

29. Oh Lord, anoint me with power, to destroy all foundational covenants, in the name of Jesus.

30. Oh Lord, use my substance for the furtherance of the gospel, in the name of Jesus.

60 DAILY MORNING PRAYER BEFORE WORK

Psalm 63:1-3: O God, thou art my God; early will I seek thee: my soul thirsteth for thee, my flesh longeth for thee in a dry and thirsty land, where no water is; 2 to see thy power and thy glory, so as I have seen thee in the sanctuary. 3 Because thy loving-kindness is better than life, my lips shall praise thee.

Starting your morning with prayers, is the best way to kick start your day. God will only walk with those that invite Him into their hearts. Today we shall be looking at 60 daily Morning Prayer before work. We can also title it as daily Morning Prayer before school, for those of us who are students. The purpose for this prayers is to help you take charge of your day. Jesus said" every day has enough evil of its own" Matthew 6:34. Therefore we must pray that the evil of each day shall not come near us and our loved ones. We must commit our days to God every morning in order for him to lead us to the right path. Psalm 91: 5, tells us that there are arrows that flies by that day, it will only take prayers to overcome those arrows. It could be arrows of failure, arrows of disappointment, arrows of sicknesses, arrows of death, and arrows of wrong business partners etc., which ever arrows the devil is targeting at you, you must return it back to him on the altar of prayers.

When we start our day with Morning Prayer, our strength is renewed, our day is secured as the host of angels walk with us. This daily Morning Prayer before work, will empower us with the grace of God to maximize our days. I encourage you this today, never leave your house without committing your ways to God, always pray about everything to God, prayer is simply talking to God as one would talk to a friend. Commit your ways to Him and He will direct your path. When God is leading you, you will be unstoppable. No devil can ruin your day when you start it with Jesus. The reason I compiled up to 60 daily Morning Prayer is so that you will have more than enough things to pray about. When you hand over your mornings to Him in prayers, He takes care of the rest of your days. Today shall be a great day for you in Jesus name.

PRAYER POINTS

1. Father, I thank you for waking me up this morning, in Jesus' name.

2. O Lord, cause my whole heart to be at rest, trusting in you as I go about my day to day activities in Jesus name

3. O Lord, keep me from leaning and relying on my own understanding and intelligence in Jesus name

4. O Lord, deliver me from what seems right to me and deliver me to what is right to you in Jesus name

5. O Lord, I pull down every imaginations and every high thing in my life that are not of You in Jesus name

6. O Lord, purify my lips with your holy fire in Jesus name

7. O Lord, reveal to me those things that give my enemies advantage over me in Jesus name

8. O Lord, let my fellowship with you become greater in Jesus name

9. I draw upon heavenly resources today, in the name of Jesus.

10. O Lord, engrace I to become the person you created me to be in Jesus name

11. I surrender myself completely in every area of my life, in the name of Jesus.

12. I stand against every satanic operation that will attempt to hinder my blessings today, in the name of Jesus.

13. Satan, I refuse your involvement in my prayer life, in Jesus' name.

14. Satan, I command you, to leave my presence with all your demons, in the name of Jesus.

15. I bring the blood of the Lord Jesus Christ between me and you Satan in Jesus name

16. Father Lord, open my eyes to see how great you are, in the name of Jesus.

17. I declare that Satan and his wicked spirits are under my feet, in the name of Jesus.

18. I claim the victory of the cross for my life today, in Jesus' name.

19. Every satanic stronghold in my life, be dismantled by fire, in the name of Jesus.

20. I put off all forms of weakness, in the name of Jesus.

21. Lord Jesus, come into my life by fire. Break down every idol, and cast out every foe.

22. Every wicked spirit planning to rob me of the will of God for my life, fall down die, in the name of Jesus.

23. I tear down the stronghold of Satan against my life, in the name of Jesus.

24. I smash every plan of Satan formed against me, in Jesus' name.

25. I smash the stronghold of Satan formed against my body, in the name of Jesus.

26. O Lord, let me be the kind of person that would please you.

27. Holy Spirit, bring all the work of resurrection and Pentecost into my life today, in the name of Jesus.

28. Every witchcraft power, I cast you into outer darkness, in the name of Jesus.

29. I confound every stubborn pursuer, in the name of Jesus.

30. I bind every power cursing my destiny into ineffectiveness, in the name of Jesus.

31. I strike every evil power siphoning my blessing with chaos and confusion, in the name of Jesus.

32. I nullify the incantations of evil spiritual consultants, in Jesus' name

33. I turn the evil devices of household witchcraft upside down, in the name of Jesus.

34. I render every local satanic weapon harmless, in the name of Jesus.

35. I receive deliverance from the spirit of anxiety, in Jesus' name.

36. I bind every spirit of mental stagnation, in the name of Jesus.

37. I release myself from the power and authority of any curse, in the name of Jesus.

38. I renounce any unholy covenants involving my life, in Jesus' name.

39. I grab every stubborn problem and smash it against the Rock of my salvation, in the name of Jesus.

40. I nullify every sacrifice to demons used against me, in Jesus' name.

41. Every power cursing my destiny, be silenced, in the name of Jesus.

42. I break the power of any incense burnt against me, in Jesus' name.

43. Every serpentine spirit, go into the hot desert and be burned, in the name of Jesus.

44. Let the blood of Jesus poison the roots of all my problems, in the name of Jesus.

45. I go back to Adam and Eve on both sides of my bloodline, and I cut of every evil root, in the name of Jesus.

46. I reverse every improper operation of body organs, in Jesus' name.

47. Every evil contract working against my life, be rewritten by the blood of Jesus.

48. I reverse every satanic calendar for my life, in the name of Jesus.

49. Anything my ancestors have done to pollute my life, he dismantled now, in the name of Jesus.

50. I refuse to be in the right place at the wrong time, in Jesus' name.

51. I bind every negative energy in the air, water and ground working against me, in the name of Jesus.

52. Anything from the kingdom of darkness that has made it their business to hinder me, I single you out right now and bind you, in the name of Jesus.

53. I command every satanic opposition in my life to be bound with chains that cannot be broken, in the name of Jesus.

54. I strip off all the spiritual armour of every strongman militating against my destiny, in the name of Jesus.

55. I destroy the hold of every evil powers, standing on my way in the name of Jesus.

56. I separate myself from evil today and forever in the name of Jesus.

57. Lord Jesus, I thank you for the victory.

58. I renounce any signing of my name over to Satan, in Jesus' name.

59. I announce that my name is written in the Lamb's book of life, in the name of Jesus.

60. Father, I thank you for answering my prayers in Jesus name. 30

PRAYERS AGAINST ENEMIES OF PROGRESS

Psalm 35:1-28: 1 Plead my cause, O Lord, with them that strive with me: fight against them that fight against me. 2 Take hold of shield and buckler, and stand up for mine help. 3 Draw out also the spear, and stop the way against them that persecute me: say unto my soul, I am thy salvation. 4 Let them be confounded and put to shame that seek after my soul: let them be turned back and brought to confusion that devise my hurt. 5 Let them be as chaff before the wind: and let the angel of the Lord chase them. 6 Let their way be dark and slippery: and let the angel of the Lord persecute them. 7 For without cause have they hid for me their net in a pit, which without cause they have digged for my soul. 8 Let destruction come upon him at unawares; and let his net that he hath hid catch himself: into that very destruction let him fall. 9 And my soul shall be joyful in the Lord: it shall rejoice in his salvation. 10 All my bones shall say, Lord, who is like unto thee, which deliverest the poor from him that is too strong for him, yea, the poor and the needy from him that spoileth him? 11 False witnesses did rise up; they laid to my charge things that I knew not. 12 They rewarded me evil for good to the spoiling of my soul. 13 But as for me, when they were sick, my clothing was sackcloth: I humbled my soul with fasting; and my prayer returned into mine own bosom. 14 I behaved myself as though he had been my friend or brother: I bowed down heavily, as one that mourneth for his mother. 15 But in mine adversity they rejoiced, and gathered themselves together: yea, the abjects gathered themselves together against me, and I knew it not; they did tear me, and ceased not: 16 with hypocritical mockers in feasts, they gnashed upon me with their teeth. 17 Lord, how long wilt thou look on? Rescue my soul from their destructions, my darling from the lions. 18 I will give thee thanks in the great congregation: I will praise thee among much people. 19 Let not them that are mine enemies wrongfully rejoice over me: neither let them wink with the eye that hate me without a cause. 20 For they speak not peace: but they devise deceitful matters against them that are quiet in the land. 21 Yea, they opened their mouth wide against me, and said, Aha, aha, our eye hath seen it. 22 This thou hast seen, O Lord: keep not silence: O Lord, be not far from me. 23 Stir up thyself, and awake to my judgment, even unto my cause, my God and my Lord. 24 Judge me, O Lord my God, according to thy righteousness; and let them not rejoice over me. 25 Let them not say in their hearts, Ah, so would we have it: let them not say, we have swallowed him up. 26 Let them be ashamed and brought to confusion together that rejoice at mine hurt: let them be clothed with shame and dishonour that magnify themselves against me. 27 Let them shout for joy, and be glad, that favour my righteous cause: yea, let them say continually, let the Lord be magnified, which hath pleasure in the prosperity of his servant. 28 And my tongue shall speak of thy righteousness and of thy praise all the day long.

Everyone who has dug a pit for you shall fall into it in Jesus name!!! Child of God, enemies of progress are real, they are those that openly laugh with you but in the secret the attempt to resist your progress. Enemies of progress are those who are comfortable with you as long as you are not making headway in life, but becomes uncomfortable once you start showing signs of success. Enemies of progress are those who are okay with the fact that you depend on them for survival but becomes uneasy when you start to take care of yourself. Every enemy of progress in your life today shall receive instant judgment from your God in Jesus name. I have compiled 30 prayers against enemies of progress. This prayers is your weapon of spiritual warfare. Please note that this enemies are very dangerous, they are satanic human agents who will stop at nothing to bring you down. A lot of believers have died in the hands of unsuspecting enemies of progress, you think they are with you, but they strike you from behind, that shall not be your portion. As you pray this prayers today, I see God exposing, all your enemies and destroying them by fire in Jesus name.

Every Christian that must overcome must be prayerful, the world we live in is full of wickedness, and it takes the force of prayer to make the wickedness of the wicked fall back on their heads. Arise from your slumber and pray this prayers against enemies of progress. As you pray this prayers you don't have to mention names, the Holy Spirit knows those that are working against your progress, both physically and spiritually, as you engage this prayers, the Lord will continue to frustrate all their efforts, He will constantly destroy all their evil devices targeted against you. Prayer is the force that brings deliverance from enemy attack, until you cry to the Lord, your enemies will never cry for their lives. Rise up today and defend yourself in prayers, I see you delivered from all your enemies today in Jesus name.

30 PRAYERS AGAINST ENEMIES OF PROGRESS

1. Let every satanic human agent standing on the way of my breakthroughs, clear away now, in Jesus' name.

2. I command every anti-progress friend around me to be exposed and cleared out of my life, in the name of Jesus.

3. Every power of the enemy keeping me low, fall down and die, in Jesus' name.

4. Every power of the enemy tying me down, fall down and die, in Jesus 'name.

5. Every power of the enemy stealing from me, fall down and die, in Jesus' name.

6. Every power of the enemy scattering my resources and blessings, fall down and die, in the name of Jesus.

7. Let the rock and fire of God destroy every weapon of demotion fashioned against me, in the name of Jesus.

8. Every power of the enemy suppressing my elevation, fall down and die, in the name of Jesus.

9. Every demonic panel set up against me, scatter unto desolation, in the name of Jesus.

10. Let every spell and enchantments directed against my progress turn against its owner, in the name of Jesus.

11. I overrule every demonic decision made against my progress, in the name of Jesus.

12. Let my youth be renewed like the eagle's, in the name of Jesus.

13. No evil weapon formed against me shall prosper, in the name of Jesus.

14. Let the law of divine partiality begin to operate to my favour, in the name of Jesus.

15. Every demonic establishment in my work-place and business, fighting against my progress, crash and disintegrate, in the name of Jesus.

16. Every stronghold of the devil over my life, be broken now, in the name of Jesus.

17. I pull down every external stronghold that is working against my progress, in the name of Jesus.

18. Every satanic plan to embarrass me, be dissolved by fire, in the name of Jesus.

19. Every gathering of the ungodly against me, physically or spiritually, be scattered unto desolation, in the name of Jesus.

20. I cancel every report brought against me in the kingdom of darkness, in the name of Jesus.

21. I cancel every charge brought against me in the kingdom of darkness, in the name of Jesus.

22. I cancel every accusation brought against me in the kingdom of darkness, in the name of Jesus.

23. I revoke and nullify every judgement passed upon me in the kingdom of darkness, in the name of Jesus.

24. I cancel every decision passed upon me in the kingdom of darkness, in the name of Jesus.

25. I cancel every condemnation passed upon me in the kingdom of darkness, in the name of Jesus.

26. I paralyze evil hands to perform their enterprise against me, in the name of Jesus.

27. I sabotage the operations of the powers of darkness commissioned against my life, in the name of Jesus.

28. I scatter the assignments of the powers of darkness commissioned against my life, in the name of Jesus.

29. Every labour of the enemy on my prosperity, receive double failure, in the name of Jesus.

30. Every war waged against my progress in life, receive double disgrace, in the name of Jesus

Thank you Father for answering my prayers in Jesus name.

100 PRAYER POINTS AGAINST FAILURE AND DISAPPOINTMENT

Philippians 4:13: I can do all things through Christ which strengtheneth me.

No matter the challenges that come your way as a Christian, you will surely overcome. The word of God says, you shall be the head only and not the tail that is the word of God concerning you today and forever. We have compiled 100 prayer points against failure and disappointment. Failure is not the end of your life, disappointment is not the end of the road, and they are all components of your testimonies. Every child of God is a target from the kingdom of darkness, Satan will always fight you to bring you down, but you must never give up, you must have a diehard faith and never take "no" for an answer. For you to emerge a giant, you must rise up and resist failure and disappointment with the force of prayer.

I don't know where you may be experiencing failure today, I don't know where you may be experiencing disappointment today, and I want to let you know that you are never a failure until you give up. You can never end up a loser in the game of life until you stop playing. Failure is just an event, it will come to pass, therefore do not let it weigh you down. The bible says a righteous man falls seven times but he still rises up again Proverbs 24:16. There is nothing wrong with failing or falling, but something is wrong when you refuse to rise up again or you give up. This prayer points against failure and disappointment will endue you with the spirit of faith and perseverance as you run the race of your life and destiny. As you pray this prayer points, the Holy Spirit will strengthen your faith and help you overcome the forces of darkness that is trying to bring you down.

This is your new beginning, I see God giving you a turnaround testimony as you engage this prayer points. As you rise up from your failures and setbacks and call on God today, I see Him raising you up from the dust and causing you to feast with the Kings and queens of the earth. You shall not fail in life, you shall make it, just believe in

God and also believe in yourself and the God of testimonies shall give you a mega testimony in Jesus name. See you at the top.

100 PRAYER POINTS AGAINST FAILURE AND DISAPPOINTMENT

1. let every imagination of failure and disappointment against me wither from the source, in the name of Jesus.

2. Those laughing me to scorn shall be dumbfounded at my glorification in the name of Jesus.

3. Let the destructive plan of the enemies aimed against me blow up in their faces, in the name of Jesus.

4. Let my point of ridicule be converted to a source of promotion, in the name of Jesus.

5. Let all powers sponsoring evil activities against me be disgraced, in the name of Jesus.

6. Let the stubborn strongman delegated against me fall down to the ground and become impotent, in the name of Jesus.

7. Let the stronghold of every evil agents militating against me be smashed to pieces, in Jesus' name.

8. Let every sorcerer, enchanter or soothsayer behind the failures and disappointments of my life be dethroned and humiliated now!!! In the name of Jesus.

9. Let every evil counsellor hindering my progress receive the stones of fire, in the name of Jesus.

10. Let every spirit of Egypt militating against me fall after the order of Pharaoh, in the name of Jesus.

11. Let every strongman from my foundation planning my fall be disgraced, in the name of Jesus.

12. Let every evil man boasting against me receive the stones of fire, in the name of Jesus.

13. Let every demonic spirit of oppression pursuing me fall into the Red Sea of their own making, in the name of Jesus.

14. Let all satanic manipulations aimed at reversing my divine destiny be frustrated, in the name of Jesus.

15. Let all destructive broadcasters of my goodness be silenced, in the name of Jesus.

16. Let all leaking bags and pockets be sealed up, in Jesus' name.

17. Let all evil monitoring eyes fashioned against me receive blindness, in the name of Jesus.

18. Let every evil effect of strange touches be removed from my life, in the name of Jesus.

19. Let all my blessings confiscated by witchcraft spirits be released, in the name of Jesus.

20. Let all my blessings confiscated by familiar spirits be released, in the name of Jesus.

21. Let all my blessings confiscated by ancestral spirits be released, in the name of Jesus.

22. Let all my blessings confiscated by envious enemies be released, in the name of Jesus.

23. Let all my blessings confiscated by satanic agents be released, in the name of Jesus.

24. Let all my blessings confiscated by principalities be released, in the name of Jesus.

25. Let all my blessings confiscated by rulers of darkness be released, in the name of Jesus.

26. Let all my blessings confiscated by evil powers be released, in the name of Jesus.

27. Let all my blessings confiscated by spiritual wickedness in the heavenly places be released, in the name of Jesus.

28. I command all demonic machinations devised to hinder my progress to be roasted, in the name of Jesus.

29. Any evil sleep undertaken to harm me should be converted to dead sleep, in the name of Jesus.

30. Let all weapons and devices of oppressors and tormentors be rendered impotent, in the name of Jesus.

31. Let the fire of God destroy the power operating any spiritual weapon working against me, in the name of Jesus.

32. Let all evil advice given against my favour crash and disintegrate, in the name of Jesus.

33. Let all the eaters of flesh and drinkers of blood, stumble and fall, in the name of Jesus.

34. I command stubborn pursuers to pursue themselves, in the name of Jesus.

35. Let the wind, the sun and the moon run contrary to every demonic presence in my environment, in Jesus' name.

36. You devourers, vanish from my labour, in the name of Jesus.

37. Let every tree planted by fear in my life dry up to the roots, in the name of Jesus.

38. I cancel all enchantments, curses and spells that are against me, in the name of Jesus.

39. Let all iron-like curses break, in the name of Jesus.

40. Let divine tongue of fire roast any evil tongue against me, in the name of Jesus.

41. I declare that I shall prosper in life in Jesus name

42. Every enemy of my destiny is declare impotent forever in Jesus name

43. No weapon forged to make me a failure shall prosper in Jesus name

44. I shall rise above all my enemies in Jesus name.

45. I declare that all those who want me down shall fall down for my sakes in Jesus name

46. I declare that all those who are sitting on my progress be unseated in Jesus name

47. Every pit of failure and disappointment dug for me, the diggers will all be buried inside in Jesus name

48. I declare that I am u stoppable in Jesus name

49. I declare that I am too much for the devil in Jesus name

50. I declare that I have dominion over the forces of darkness trying g to pull me down I Jesus name

51. I declare that the spirit of stagnation has no power over me in Jesus name.

52. Every satanic poison targeted at me will have no effect on me in the name of Jesus

53. I rise above failure in Jesus name

54. I rise above disappointment in Jesus name

55. I rise above setbacks in Jesus name

56. I rise above stagnation in Jesus name

57. I rise above shame in Jesus name

58. I rise above my opposer's in Jesus name

59. I rise above situations and circumstances in Jesus name

60. I rise above all my enemies in Jesus name.

61. I rise above every demonic strong man in Jesus name

62. I rise above witches and wizards in Jesus name

63. I rise above familiar spirits in Jesus name

64. I rise above marine powers in Jesus name

65. I rise above the power of sin in Jesus name

66. I rise above ancestral powers in Jesus name

67. I rise above ancestral curses in Jesus name

68. I rise above parental limitations in Jesus name

69. I rise above environmental limitations in Jesus name

70. I rise above geographical limitations in Jesus name

71. Let the wrath of God be upon every enemy of my life, in the name of Jesus.

72. Let me be filled with all the fullness of God, in the name of Jesus.

73. I render every divination and enchantment of hell against my life impotent, in the name of Jesus.

74. I forbid the storm of the world from troubling my dwelling place, in the name of Jesus.

75. let every false allegation and accusation against me fall down to the ground and die, in the name of Jesus.

76. Let there be a divine cover of the glory of God upon me, in the name of Jesus.

77. Lord, let the eyes of my understanding be enlightened, in the name of Jesus.

78. I decree all diseases of Egypt out of my life, in the name of Jesus.

79. Begin to command all afflictions to depart, in the name of Jesus.

80. O Lord, perfect what is lacking in my life in Jesus name.

81. I revoke every satanic decree issued against my promotion, in the name of Jesus.

82. I silence every evil dog barking against my breakthroughs, in the name of Jesus.

83. Let the finger of God unseat my household strongman, in the name of Jesus.

84. Every evil bird flying for my sake, be trapped, in the name of Jesus.

85. Every agent of disgrace, backward movements and shame, release me, in the mighty name of Jesus.

86. I overthrow every evil throne installed against my life, in the name of Jesus.

87. Every agent of disorder in my life, be scattered unto desolation, in the name of Jesus.

88. Every power fuelling my problems, fall down and die, in Jesus' name.

89. I release myself from any curse working in my family, in the name of Jesus.

90. Let every spiritual vulture delegated against me eat its own flesh, in the name of Jesus.

91. I trample upon serpents and scorpions, in the name of Jesus.

92. Every cleverly concealed problematic root, be uprooted, in the name of Jesus.

93. I disgrace every evil wisdom working against my breakthroughs, in the name of Jesus.

94. By the power of the Holy Spirit, I crush all my enemies, in the name of Jesus.

95. By the power of the Holy Spirit, I put every evil under my feet, in the name of Jesus.

96. Lord, let me be extraordinary in Jesus name

97. Holy Spirit, deposit your wonders in my life, in the name of Jesus.

98. Lord Jesus, break my infirmity and destroy my disease.

99. Lord Jesus, destroy satanic foundations and build me upon your word.

100. Lord Jesus, set me ablaze with Your Spirit.

Father, I thank you for answering my prayers in Jesus name.

CHAPTER 6

PRAYER FOR SALVATION
PRAYER POINTS FOR SALVATION

Today we will be dealing with prayer points for Salvation. The salvation of every man is an important business. God doesn't toy with the salvation of man, so man must endeavor to hold it dear. Christ had to come to the earth in human form, subjected to hunger and pain, loved by few and hated by many. He was ridiculed, taken, beaten and killed. If salvation was not important God would not have subjected His only begotten Son to suffer that much. If it was not important, even Christ would not have allowed himself to be greatly humiliated to that extent.

Salvation means being saved from the power of sin and slavery. It takes a conscious effort from a man to be saved from sin. This is because the devil will do everything possible to ensure that man continue to remain slave to sin so that the soul of a man can be lost. However, we give glory to father in heaven for giving us the precious gift of Christ that whoever believe in Him should not perish but have life everlasting.

The scripture says in the book of John 3:16-17 For God so loved the world that he gave his one and only Son, that whoever believes in him shall not perish but have eternal life. For God did not send his Son into the world to condemn the world, but to save the world through him. Salvation was brought to mankind from the immeasurable love of God. For God didn't want the man to perish that's why He sent His son to die for the sin of man.

For us to have salvation, we must confess Christ as our personal Lord and savior. We must believe in the power of his resurrection and we must desist from our sin. Salvation is not a one-time-all thing, it is something that must be maintained all the time. The fact that you are saved today doesn't mean that you are saved forever. That's why the scripture says in the book of 1 Corinthians 10:12 therefore let him who thinks he stands take heed lest he fall. That's why we must always check ourselves at all time to ensure we are still standing with God.

We will be offering these prayer points for as many who have missed it, for as many who have been swayed away by the temptations of life. Now is the time to return to God finally. Say the following prayers for your salvation.

PRAYER POINTS

- Lord Jesus, I thank you for the grace you have given me to see a new day. I thank you for your mercy and provision over my life, may your name be highly exalted in Jesus name.

- Lord, I pray for the forgiveness of my sin. I ask that by the reason of the blood that was shed on the cross of Calvary, you wash away my sins and iniquities in the name of Jesus. For it has been written, if my sin are as red as scarlet, they shall be made whiter than snow, if they are as red as crimson, they shall be made whiter than wool. Lord, I ask that by your mercy you wash me thoroughly from my sins.

- Lord Jesus, I confess today that you are my personal lord and saviour. I pray that you will come into my life. Today, I rededicate my life to you. Come into my life. I make the entrance of my life accessible for you Lord Jesus, I ask that you will make my life your home.

- I invite you into my home, I pray that you come and take charge of my home today. I ask that you dwell in my home and you chase out every negative spirit, every demonic spirit that has been living with me to drive me to hell, I pray that you will chase them out in the name of Jesus.

- Lord Jesus, I pray that you will visit me today with the mightiness of the Holy Spirit. I pray that the power of the Holy Ghost will from today dwell in my heart. I refuse to continue living my life based on my mortal knowledge. I ask that by your mercy you will make my life the new home of the Holy Spirit. The spirit of the lord that will guide me and direct me on which way to go, I ask that it dwells in my life today in the name of Jesus.

- Lord, for it has been written Stand fast therefore in the liberty by which Christ has made us free, and do not be entangled again with a yoke of bondage. I refuse to be a slave to sin anymore. I pray that the spirit of the lord that will guide me and nurture me in the right part to go dwell in me from today. I refuse to live life by myself. I want to be led by the spirit of God.

- The scripture says for as many as are led by the Spirit of God, these are sons of God. I want to be your son. I pray that your spirit will lead me from today. I will go only where you ask me to go, I don't want to return to slavery again. Every power and principality planning to steal this new gift from me, fall to death in the name of Jesus.

- Lord Jesus, I come against every form of temptation that may want to take me back into sin. For it has been written in the book of 1 Corinthians 10:13 No temptation has overtaken you except such as is common to man; but God is faithful, who will not allow you to be tempted beyond what you are able, but with the temptation will also make the way of escape, that you may be able to bear it. You have promised that you will not allow any temptation to overcome me, I ask for the fulfillment of this word by the mercy of Christ.

- Lord, as I continue to grow in Christ Jesus, let me begin to experience an impeccable level of relationship with you. Every area of my life that the enemy has destroyed the relationship that exist between us, I mend those areas in the name of Jesus.

PRAYER POINTS FOR SOMEONE WHO NEEDS SALVATION

Today we will be dealing with prayer points for someone that needs salvation. Salvation only comes to people who are prepared for it. Those who are tired of living in the bondage of sin and slavery. Those who have found passion to come into the marvelous light of God, these are the people that will receive salvation.

How Do I Get Salvation?

Salvation comes through faith. When you have faith in the only begotten son of God, salvation comes to you. The scripture says in book of Romans 10:17 so then faith comes by hearing, and hearing by the word of God. We build our faith by hearing the word of God.

Biblical Verses That Speaks About Salvation

Acts 4:12 "Neither is there salvation in any other: for there is none other name under heaven given among men, whereby we must be saved."

John 5:24 "Truly, truly, I say to you, whoever hears my word and believes him who sent me has eternal life. He does not come into judgment, but has passed from death to life."

Matthew 6:9-13 "Pray then like this: "Our Father in heaven, hallowed be your name. Your kingdom come, your will be done, on earth as it is in heaven. Give us this day our daily bread, and forgive us our debts, as we also have forgiven our debtors. And lead us not into temptation, but deliver us from evil."

Romans 10:9-10 "That if you confess with your mouth, "Jesus is Lord," and believe in your heart that God raised him from the dead, you will be saved. For it is with your heart that you believe and are justified, and it is with your mouth that you confess and are saved."

These are some of the Bible verses that talks about salvation or being saved. Let's proceed to prayers for salvation of our soul.

PRAYER POINTS

- Lord Jesus, I thank you for the gift of life, I thank you for the gift of your son Jesus Christ whose blood was shed for the atonement of our sin, I thank you for the redemption of my soul, let your name be exalted in the name of Jesus.

- Lord Jesus, I confess that you are God over all. I ask that you will take over my life. I submit my life to you as a living sacrifice. I beg that you will become the king of my life. I want to go where you ask me to go, I want to do things that please you, Lord take over my life in the name of Jesus.

- Lord, I confess my sins to you. To you have I sinned and done great evil in your sight. I pray that you forgive me in the name of Jesus. The scripture made me understand that God doesn't take pleasure in the death of a sinner but repentance through Christ Jesus. I pray that you help me to repent genuinely in the name of Jesus.

- Lord God, the scripture says it is for freedom that Christ has set us free, therefore let us stand firmly in our Freedom that we may not become slave to sin anymore. Lord, I pray for the grace to remain steadfast in your presence. I come against every form of distraction that may drive me away from you, I destroy every monitoring spirit that has been assigned to snatch my salvation away in the name of Jesus.

- Father Lord, I pray that you anoint me with your Holy Spirit and power. The spirit of the Lord that will ignite my spirit man when temptation comes, I pray that you give it to me today in the name of Jesus.

- I ask Lord Jesus, that you will bless me with wisdom to live differently from today. I refuse to go back to my old way of life, I want to continue living in the light of your word and command. I refuse to be a slave to sin anymore, in the name of Jesus.

- Lord Jesus, thank you for this grace to know you. I thank you for the salvation of my soul. I thank you for calling out of darkness with the strong light of your righteousness. I pray for everyone who needs to know you, I pray that you reveal yourself to them in the name of Jesus.

PRAYER FOR CHILDREN SALVATION

Children's salvation. Train up a child in the way he should go: and when he is old, he will not depart from it.

We would be praying for our children. Glory to God this cuts across every individual, couples with children and expectant couples, singles who are looking forward to settling down as well. Irrespective of our status, we have one thing in common as Believers which is Christ.

We should not be so concerned about our children's pursuit in education, their future ambitions, their feeding, well-being and all that pertains to them that we forget to take responsibility for their Spiritual upbringing.

To abandon our children to external influence would do more harm than good. Taking a good look at the society we live in today. Times are changing and technology keeps evolving rapidly. We come across parents who are shocked at their children's behavioral pattern and wonder how and where they might have come across such.

As God empowers us in businesses and grants us career success on the long run, that we bear fruits financially, how they grow up, what they know, what they're being taught from home lies upon us.

They should not be left out during morning devotion. Talk to them about Jesus. Get them children Bible materials. Let them come to know God from home. The effect of this that, when there's a solid foundation, where children can strongly point to the love of God being taught and seen between their parents, nothing will be able to shake the foundation of the knowledge they have.

Values form in their hearts. Parents ought to teach godly values that would leave indelible mark on them. It forms how they choose their friends in school, it forms how they respond to ungodliness on the outside. Why? Because they have been trained and taught from home.

We can never run out of what to teach. There are Bible Personalities to study, to examine and learn from. King David, for example, let him get to know who that Bible personality is. These are conversations that could come up in the car, back from school, during their break time, after meals etc. It does not become a thing as there is never a time for such discussions, tiny bits here and there are seeds you plant in their hearts that would germinate into fruits, on the long run. They should not be asked outside the home who Esther is from the Bible and they are blank. In teaching and praying, we are setting our children on the right pedestal to go through life with boldness because they are equipped.

JESUS should never be a strange name to children. The Bible records that Jesus welcomed children during his incarnate ministry.

Mark 10:13-16

13.And they brought young children to him, that he should touch them: and his disciples rebuked those that brought them.14 But when Jesus saw it, he was much displeased, and said unto them, Suffer the little children to come unto me, and forbid them not: for of such is the kingdom of God.15 Verily I say unto you, Whosoever, shall not receive the kingdom of God as a little child, he shall not enter therein.,16 And he took them up in his arms,, put his hands upon them, and blessed them.

Let them get to know that Jesus loves them, that He cares about them. Teach them to know that Jesus would always care for them every day.

John 3:16,"For God so loved the world, that he gave his only begotten Son, that whosoever believeth in him should not perish, but have everlasting life.

Teach about the works of Jesus and how saved their soul is in believing what He did for them. The Bible says that Faith comes by hearing and hearing by the Word of God. It is the Word they hear that they will be inclined to.

Acts 4:12, "Neither, is there salvation in any other: for there is none other name under heaven given among men, whereby, we must be saved." Teach children about Salvation.

Matt.18:3-4

And, Verily I say unto you, Except ye be converted, and become as little children, ye shall not enter into the kingdom of heaven.4 Whosoever therefore shall humble himself as this little child, the same is greatest in the kingdom of heaven.

Jesus Christ speaking here was explaining that the hearts of children can be so tender and simple unlike the adults who might infuse rigidity into accepting the Goodness of Our Lord Jesus Christ. The child's mind from birth is a clean slate. The responsibility is on us to put in the work, talk to them about Jesus and the Love of the Father.

The strength to do all that is needed for us as Parents and intending Parents, the Lord will grant unto us in Jesus Name.

That is why it is important to pray for them. Prayer works. As we pray, we see remarkable results. Halleluiah.

PRAYER POINTS

- Father we thank you because over us, your goodness and your Mercy endures forever.
- Father we thank you for your unfailing love over our families, thank you because nothing can separate us from the love of the Father, in Jesus name.
- Father in the name of Jesus, we pray over our children, we declare the blessings and wisdom of God upon them in the name of Jesus.
- Heavenly Father, we thank you for the blessings of wonderful children that we have received from you in Jesus name.
- Father we pray that our children will come to know you better, day by day.
- Father we pray for wisdom for our children, we pray that they will make the right choices, do the right thing at the right time in Jesus name.
- Father we pray that you help them to grow in the knowledge of you every day as their desire and zeal to know you increases daily in Jesus name.

- Father in the name of Jesus, we pray that the hearts of our children are yielded to you, they respond to your love correctly in Jesus name.

- Heavenly Father we pray that our children are delivered from bad influences, evil association and ungodly company. They make the right choice of friends at each state of their lives in Jesus name.

- Father Lord we pray for every word taught, the Spirit of God will impart it upon their hearts in Jesus name.

- Father Lord, let Christ be continually formed in the lives of our children in the name of Jesus.

- Father we thank you for every seed that has proceeded and will proceed out of our wombs, we thank you because they are yours, thank you because you take charge of their lives from beginning to the end in Jesus mighty name.

28 PRAYER POINTS FOR SALVATION OF LOVED ONES

2 Corinthians 5:18-21:

16 Wherefore henceforth know we no man after the flesh: yea, though we have known Christ after the flesh, yet now henceforth know us him no more. 17 Therefore if any man be in Christ, he is a new creature: old things are passed away; behold, all things are become new. 18 And all things are of God, who hath reconciled us to himself by Jesus Christ, and hath given to us the ministry of reconciliation; 19 To wit, that God was in Christ, reconciling the world unto himself, not imputing their trespasses unto them; and hath committed unto us the word of reconciliation. 20 Now then we are ambassadors for Christ, as though God did beseech you by us: we pray you in Christ's stead, be ye reconciled to God. 21 For he hath made him to be sin for us, who knew no sin; that we might be made the righteousness of God in him.

Why do we need this 28 prayer points for salvation of loved ones? As Christ ambassadors, God expects us to reconcile the world of sinners to himself. Because of the sacrifice of Christ, the world no longer has a sin problem, but it now has a sinner problem. A lot of sinners don't know that their sins have been paid for. They don't know that Jesus died for the absolute forgiveness of their sins, past, present and future, because they don't know, they don't get saved, and because they don't get saved, they go to hell. This is a very sad circle in the world we live in. If you are born again, your primary assignment is to be an ambassador of Christ. It's to share the gospel of Jesus to all who need it around you. This includes your loved ones who are yet to be born again. Do not let them die in their sins, let them know that Jesus loves them, even in the midst of their sins. Let them know that the love of God can change them and break the yoke of so in their lives. Also pray for them.

These 28 prayer points for salvation of loved ones will make their hearts ripe for the harvest of salvation. When we pray for salvation of loved ones, the Holy Spirit begins to convict them of sin, he begin to show them the errors of their ways and these can lead to their salvation. Prayer is an effective tool for soul winning, when we pray we set the atmosphere for the harvest. It is effective prayers that

397

leads to effective evangelism. When the prayer alter is on fire, the souls will be saved when the word is preached to them. Therefore, if you want to see your loved ones saved, engage these 28 prayer points for salvation of loved ones with strong faith. Pray for them, mention them by name and command them to be saved in the name of Jesus Christ. As you pray these prayer points today, I see your entire household saying yes to Jesus amen.

28 prayer points for salvation of loved ones

1. Father, I thank you for the grace of salvation, thank you Father for sending your son Jesus to die for our sins.
2. Father, in the name of Jesus, grant (Mention the name of the loved one) revelation in the knowledge of you.
3. Let every stronghold of the enemy resisting the mind of (mention the name of the loved one) from receiving the Lord be pulled down, in the name of Jesus.
4. Let all hindrances coming between the heart of (mention the name of the loved one) and the gospel be melted away by the Fire of the Holy Spirit, in the name of Jesus.
5. In the name of Jesus, I bind the strongman attached to the life of (mention the name of the loved one), for keeping him from receiving Jesus Christ as his Lord and Saviour.
6. Lord, build a hedge of thorns around (mention the name of the person), so that he turns to the Jesus.
7. I command all the children who have been dedicated to the Lord and have become bound by the devil be loosed, in the name of Jesus.
8. In the name of Jesus, I break the curse placed on. (Mention the name of the loved one), binding him from receiving the Lord.
9. You spirit of death and hell, release (mention the name of the loved one), in the name of Jesus.
10. Every desire of the enemy on the soul of (mention the name of the loved one) will not prosper, in the name of Jesus.
11. You spirit of destruction, release (mention the name of the loved one), in the name of Jesus.

12. I bind every spirit of mind blindness in the life of (mention the name of the loved one), in the name of Jesus.

13. Let there be no peace or rest in the mind of (mention the name of the loved one) until he surrenders to the Lord Jesus Christ.

14. Spirit of bondage, Luke warmness and perdition, release (mention the name of the loved one), in the name of Jesus.

15. Lord, open the eyes of (mention the name of the loved one) to his own spiritual condition, in the name of Jesus.

16. I bind the strongman shielding (mention the name of the loved one) from receiving the gospel, in the name of Jesus.

17. Lord, send people across the path of (mention the name of the loved one) who can share the gospel with him.

18. Father, let spiritual blindness be erased from the life of (mention the name of the loved one), in the name of Jesus.

19. Father, grant (mention the name of the loved one) repentance leading to a personal relationship with Jesus.

20. I come against the powers of darkness blinding and holding (mention the name of the loved one) back from receiving the gospel, in the name of Jesus.

21. I command you spirit of the power of the air to loose your hold on (mention the name of the loved one) so that he will be free to accept Jesus as Lord and Saviour, in the name of Jesus.

22. I tear down and smash every stronghold of deception keeping (mention the name of the loved one) in the enemy's camp, in the name of Jesus.

23. Holy Spirit, reveal to me other strongholds that need to be broken in the life of (mention the name of the loved one), in Jesus' name.

24. Father, Let (mention the name of the loved one) come from the kingdom of darkness into the kingdom of light, in the name of Jesus.

25. Lord, let your plan and purpose for the life of (mention the name of the loved one) prevail.

26. Lord, let your mercy and your grace overwhelm (mention the name of the loved one) so that he may be saved.

27. Father let the Holy Spirit, the lord of the harvest, convict (mention the name of the loved one) thereby leading him/her to the Lord in Jesus name.

28. Father thank you for answering my prayers in Jesus name.

12 PRAYER POINTS FOR LIBERTY

Today, we have been led by the spirit of God to deal with prayer for liberty. This is why we are offering 12 prayer points for liberty. God wants to set His people free from the power of darkness tormenting their lives. As a believer, the importance of liberty cannot be overemphasized. If you must carry out your obligations effectively as a believer, you must be liberated from certain things.

A believer can't serve God better when they are in slavery. For years the children of God could not serve Jehovah. Not because they choose not to, but because they were held in captivity. Their abductors don't serve Jehovah, so they were compelled to stop calling on Jehovah. God understands that a man needs some level of liberty to serve well. That was why God told Moses to go to Egypt and tell Pharaoh to let my people go that they may serve him better.

Similarly, many believers are still in Egypt today. They are not free yet. Some so many believers are slaves to sin. Some believers can do without committing adultery, telling lies, fornicating, and all manner of evil things. They have been made a prisoner of sin. Some believers are slaves to sickness. They have tried everything possible, but that sickness won't go away. This has held them incapacitated to discharge their duties effectively as Christians.

Regardless of what is holding you down today, the good news is that God wants to grant liberty to people. God wants to deliver his people that they may serve him well. I announce to you today that your day of freedom is here. Though your trouble and bondage may last for a night by morning, your liberty will shine like the morning stars. I declare by the authority of heaven, every power that is holding down as slaves, such powers should lose their powers today in the name of Jesus.

For it has been written, he that the son has set free is free indeed. I speak your liberty into a reality in the name of Jesus. From today, no power will be able to hold you down. You have strengthened to move from strength to strength in the name of Jesus.

PRAYER POINTS

- Father Lord, I thank you for the grace of your son Jesus Christ. I thank you for the love that has called us out of darkness into the marvelous light of God. I thank you for the redemption of our life from the pit of death and the salvation of our souls. May your name be highly exalted in the name of Jesus?

- Father Lord, I pray that you will help me establish my liberty in the name of Jesus. Every power of darkness threatening my freedom falls to death today in the name of Jesus.

- I cancel every power bondage over my life, catch fire in the name of Jesus. I free myself from every shackle of slavery. Every ring and chain of bondage that has been used to hold me down are broken in the name of Jesus.

- The fire breaks, Lord, every bondage of sickness in my life in the name of Jesus. I free myself from any bondage of sickness in the name of Jesus. The scripture says by his stripe; we are healed. I speak my healings to reality today in the name of Jesus.

- Lord, I receive liberty against the power of sin. For it has been written for one who has died has been set free from sin. I die with Christ in the name of Jesus, and I'm renewed in the name of Jesus.

- Father Lord, I come against every shackle of sin and iniquity. The scripture says it is for freedom that Christ has set is greet. Let us, therefore, stand firm in the calling that we may not be slaves to sin anymore. Lord, I refuse to be a slave to sin in the name of Jesus. I speak my freedom to reality by the power in the name of Jesus.

- Father Lord, I pray that your spirit will overshadow my life in the name of Jesus. The scripture says if the spirit of Him that raised Christ from death dwells in you, it will quicken your mortal body. Lord, I pray that your spirit will come mightily in the name of Jesus.

- Lord Jesus, for it, has been written, Now the Lord is the Spirit, and where the Spirit of the Lord is, there is freedom. From now, I begin to walk in the shadow of the spirit in the name of Jesus. The

Bible says where the spirit of God is; there is liberty. I begin to walk in the power of the Holy Ghost in the name of Jesus.

- Lord Jesus, I receive the power to know the truth. The scripture says I shall know the truth, and the truth shall set me free. Father Lord, I refuse to work in lies or ignorance of who Christ is. From today, I pray for insight and revelation of God in the name of Jesus.

- Lord, the scripture says Out of my distress, I called on the Lord; the Lord answered me and set me free." Lord, answer me today in the name of Jesus. I pray that you will set me free by your mighty hands in the name of Jesus.

- The Spirit of the Lord God is upon me because the Lord has anointed me to bring good news to the afflicted; He has sent me to bind up the brokenhearted, to proclaim liberty to captives and freedom to prisoners." From today, I proclaim liberty in the name of Jesus.

- For it has been written, decree a thing, and it shall be established. Lord, I speak my liberty into reality in the name of Jesus. I refuse to continue to wallow in toxic slavery in the name of Jesus. The Bible says if the son set you free, you are free indeed. I seal my liberty with the blood of Christ in the name of Jesus.

10 BIBLE VERSES YOU MUST NOT FORGET WHEN PRAYING FOR FORGIVENESS

Today we will be dealing with 10 Bible verses you must not forget when praying for forgiveness. Forgiveness is a deliberate decision to let go of resentment or anger against another person. There are so many Christians that find it difficult to forgive other people, whereas they want God to forgive them their shortcomings. The Lord's Prayer stated that forgive us this day as we forgive those who trespass against us.

God is merciful and His truth extend from generations to another. He has promised to forgive our sin because Christ has paid for them on the cross of Calvary. However, when praying or seeking for forgiveness, we must remember some scriptural verses in the Bible. Some of them includes:

Mark 11:25

And whenever you stand praying, if you have anything against anyone, forgive him that your Father in heaven may also forgive you your trespasses.

You must always remember that God will most like treat us the same way we treat other people. When you go on your knees to pray for forgiveness, search your heart deep to know if there are people you have not forgiven yet. Try to forgive everyone that has crossed you in one way or another. The scripture admonish that when we pray for forgiveness, we must endeavor to forgive people that has offended us so that our father in heaven can forgive us too.

Mathew 6:15

But if you do not forgive men their trespasses, neither will your Father forgive your trespasses.

This is to further emphasize the previous verse of the scripture. If you do not forgive men their trespasses, neither will your father forgive your trespasses. The Lord's Prayer states that forgive us this day as we forgive those that trespass against us. When we are kind enough to forgive those who trespass against us, our father in heaven is kind enough to forgive us our sins.

1 John 1:9
If we confess our sins, He is faithful and just to forgive us our sins and to cleanse us from all unrighteousness.

When praying for forgiveness, it is important to confess our sin. The scripture makes us understand that the sacrifices of God are a broken spirit, a broken and contrite heart will God not despise. He that hides his sin will not prosper but he that confess and forsake them shall find mercy.

When we confess our sins and iniquities, God will forgive us our sins.

Hebrews 8:12
For I will be merciful to their unrighteousness, and their sins and their lawless deeds I will remember no more."

This is a promise from God. He has promised to be merciful to our unrighteousness. The love of God for humanity is not for those that has been saved but for those that are yet to receive the gift of salvation. God has promised to be merciful to us and He will not judge us by our sins and lawless deeds.

Ephesians 1:7
"In him we have redemption through his blood, the forgiveness of sins, in accordance with the riches of God's grace."

The blood of Jesus has been shed for us already. The blood speak righteousness than the blood of Abel. The blood speak for us in our moment of need. The blood speak righteousness. And in the blood we have redemption. The blood of Christ intercede for us when we cry to God for mercy.

The blood of Christ still flows in Calvary and it still works wonder till date. All we need to do is key into the covenant of the blood.

Daniel 9:9

"The Lord our God is merciful and forgiving, even though we have rebelled against him."

Although we have rebelled against God on several occasions, but God is merciful to us and He still show compassion. Praise be the lord that doesn't treat us as a result of our shortcomings. The love of God is abundant to us. We are no longer under the law, grace has saved us.

The scripture says we have not a high priest that can't be touched with the feeling of our infirmity. We therefore come boldly to the throne of mercy that we may obtain grace from God the father.

Isaiah 1: 18

"Come now, let us settle the matter," says the Lord. 'Though your sins are like scarlet, they shall be as white as snow; though they are red as crimson, they shall be like wool.'"

How big is your sin that cannot be forgiven? Regardless of how big our sins are God is great enough to forgive us our sins and iniquity. The scripture says even if our sin as red as scarlet they shall be made whiter than snow, even if they are red as crimson they shall be made whiter than wool.

Jeremiah 31: 34

"For I will forgive their wickedness and will remember their sins no more."

God has promised to forgive our wickedness. You have heard that God doesn't want the death of a sinner but repentance through Christ Jesus. He doesn't want us to die, he wants our repentance and we can obtain our repentance through Christ Jesus.

Matthew 6: 14-15

"For if you forgive other people when they sin against you, your heavenly Father will also forgive you. But if you do not forgive others their sins, your Father will not forgive your sins."

Forgiveness is a give and take something. When you hoard kindness, you might not obtain mercy too. But when you forgive other people of their shortcomings, the lord is merciful to forgive you. When you don't forget other people their sins, God in heaven will not forgive your sins.

Ephesians 4: 31-32
"Get rid of all bitterness, rage and anger, brawling and slander, along with every form of malice. Be kind and compassionate to one another, forgiving each other, just as in Christ God forgave you."
When you want mercy and forgiveness from God, you must ensure you are not bittered, filled with rage or anger against another person. Be kind to other people, show mercy to others and forgive those that trespass against you. Then your father in heaven will forgive you

POWERFUL PRAYERS FOR UNSAVED WIVES

Today we shall be engaging in powerful prayers for unsaved wives. Being in a marriage where your wife does not share the same faith in Christ with you can be a very tough experience. If the way you live your life is based on the principles of your faith in Christ, then there will be a problem because not being able to share that with your Wife can be trying at times. More so, your love for your Wife will mean that you are concerned for her spiritual well-being. One of the greatest acts of love you can show to someone is praying for them, and one of the most powerful things you can do for your marriage is to pray regularly for your Wife.

You are the one person that loves your Wife more than anyone else in the world and, if you don't pray for them, who will? You need to bear in mind that praying for your unsaved wife without referring to God's word is no more effective than wishful thinking. To pray effectively, you need to pray with God's word. God's promises are your guarantee for answered prayers. Don't be random in your approach to prayer. And remember, God is not depending on you to bring your unsaved wife to salvation. He is quite capable of orchestrating that Himself. What he does need you to do is to bring the matter to Him and persist in intercession.

No matter how hard your unsaved wife's heart is, God has a formula for softening it, so don't lose hope, even if it takes longer than you would have liked. Therefore, base your prayers on specific promises from God's word and see His will unfold in the life of your Wife. Below is a guide on how to pray for your unsaved wife with relevant scriptures.

PRAYER POINTS

- Lord, I thank you because you always hear and answer the prayer that is asked in faith and by your will.
- Lord Jesus, I lift my Wife to You now, knowing that she has not accepted you as her Saviour, and we are drifting apart from each other, as our whole outlook on life has become so very different.

- Lord, You are full of mercy and goodness, and I pray that You Lord in Your mercy would change the heart of my Wife so that she develops a deep desire to know You, to trust You and to follow You for the rest of her Life

- Lord, each time I look at my Wife, and how rebellious she is, it makes me sad on you will feel, I know You love her, and I implore You Lord to take over her life for Yourself and let her will be subject to Your will alone In Jesus Name.

- Lord Jesus, I have tried all my best to win my Wife for you, but it didn't work out. I pray to you, Lord that you send someone that his or her faith will influence her and let her change to serve you always in Jesus name.

- O Lord, I pray that give me wisdom and let your spirit guide me in all my conduct so that I may not behave in a way that will harden the heart of my Wife in receiving You into her life

- You, God, are a shield around us. You protect us from the enemy who seeks to destroy, and you will not let us be put to shame. Your arm is mighty, and Your Word is powerful (Psalm 3:3, 12:7, 25:20; Exodus 15:9; Luke 1:51; Hebrews 1:3). I pray Lord that You shield her from the pestilence fowlers and every attack of the enemy in Jesus Name

- I pray Lord that you help my wife to grow her love for you. May she be increasingly in awe of your power, beauty, and grace? May she know more each day about the depth and width of Your love and respond with increasing love of her own in Jesus name (Psalm 27:4; Ephesians 3:18).

- Lord, may your wise and knowing Spirit rest on my wife. Be her counselor. May she delight in you and obey your commands. (Isaiah 11:2-3)

- God, you will fulfill the purpose in each of our lives. Your love endures forever. Do not abandon the works of your hands. Do not leave her. Draw her to you always (Psalm 138:8).

- I pray that you, Lord endow her with the ability to find and fulfill your purpose for her life before it too late.
- Lord, I pray that you bring her into a living, vital, intimate, overpowering relationship with you. Open her eyes that she may see beautiful things in your law in Jesus Name (Psalm 119:18).
- Your hands made my wife and formed her; Lord I Pray you to give her understanding to learn Your commands always in Jesus Name (Psalm 119:73)
- Lord please bless my wife, Your Word says that your kindness leads to repentance. Do not allow her to continue to store up wrath for herself (Romans 2:4-6).
- Lord give my wife a singleness of heart and action so that she will always fear you for her good and the good of our children. (Jeremiah 32:39)
- Lord instruct her and teach her in the way she should go. Counsel her Lord and watch over her always because your unfailing love surrounds the one who trusts in you. (Psalm 32:8, 10)
- Lord help her to humble herself under your mighty hand, that you may lift her up in due time (1 Peter 5:6).
- I pray a hedge of thorns around my wife that those with evil influence will lose interest and leave her alone (Hosea 2:6).
- I pray that you would use me to be an example to my wife, Lord. Give me the wisdom to know how to respond to some of her negativity.
- Lord give me the mind of Christ I pray, so that I may respond in spirit and love, accordance with your will. Lord, I pray that my wife will one day be saved. In Jesus name. Amen

PRAYER POINTS AGAINST THE BLINDNESS OF THE HEART

Today we will be dealing with prayer points against the blindness of the heart. One of the worst things that can happen to a man is blindness. It is a state where the sight of a man is not functioning. Imagine a blind man walking through the street without help. Such is the life of a man who is blinded spiritually. The blindness of the heart is a form of repellent that the enemy put in people's minds, making it difficult for them to believe the gospel of Christ.

The book of 1 Corinthians 1:8 stated that for the preaching of the cross is to them that perish foolishness, but unto us which are saved, it is the power of God. You only believe in the gospel of Christ because you are saved. Those whose heart has been blinded by heresy and vices of the enemy will count it as foolishness. The enemy understands this; that is why he often inflict people with a blindness of the heart. Regardless of how much preaching you do, how much evangelism you do, they will not believe Christ is the way, the truth, and the light.

The scripture further explains the nemesis of this type of blindness in the book of 2 Corinthians 4:3-6,"But if our gospel be hid, it is hid to them that are lost: In whom the god of this world hath blinded the minds of them which believe not, lest the light of the glorious gospel of Christ, who is the image of God, should shine unto them. For we preach not ourselves, but Christ Jesus the Lord; and ourselves your servants for Jesus' sake. For God, who commanded the light to shine out of darkness, hath shined in our hearts, to give the light of the knowledge of the glory of God in the face of Jesus Christ."

A man with the blindness of the heart is a lost sheep. He is a lost sheep because he can't hear the shepherd's voice. Even when he hears it, he won't still yield to it. This is because the enemy has put a veil of darkness upon his mind, which affects his understanding. The blindness of the heart is a severe disease because anything that affects the heart of a man affects the whole body. The scripture says from the abundance of the heart the mouth speaketh. It means every word, action, and reaction that a man exudes results from the thoughts in his heart. Little wonder the enemy focuses on the heart of men inflicting it with great evil.

We will be raising a standard against every spiritual darkness, against every blindness of the heart. One last thing that happens to a man with a blind heart is the lack of presence of God. Such a person will be devoid of the spirit of God. And when a man lacks the spirit of God, such a person becomes prey to the devil.

Prayer is the only cure for this sickness. This prayer will be a prayer of deliverance. Many Christians wallow in the toxic of spiritual blindness. They need to be freed from this demon. The scripture says the effectual prayer of the righteous avail. If you have someone who doesn't want to listen to the gospel of Christ or doesn't believe in the death and resurrection of Christ Jesus, do well to pray for them. If your spouse doesn't attend church anymore or believes in Jesus Christ, do not keep silent on this prayer. Pray it fervently.

PRAYER POINTS

- Lord, I thank you for the grace to see another day. I magnify you for giving me the privilege to pray over this matter again. I thank you for your loving kindness; may your name be highly exalted in the name of Jesus.

- Father Lord, I pray for the forgiveness of my sin, in any way that I have sinned and fall short your glory, I pray that you will forgive me in the name of Jesus. Because of the bloodshed on the cross of Calvary, I pray that you wash away my sins entirely in the name of Jesus.

- Lord, every satanic veil covering my heart making it difficult for the gospel of Christ to penetrate. I remove such veils with the fire of the Holy Spirit in the name of Jesus.

- Lord, every form of blindness that is troubling me, I decree healings upon myself in the name of Jesus. I decree that the healing of God will come upon me in the name of Jesus.

- Lord, I break every demonic shackle that has been used to hold me down. I destroy them today in the name of Jesus. I pray for listening ears and a contrite heart, a spirit of brokenness. I pray that you grant it to me in the name of Jesus.

- Lord, I pray that you will search my heart, and you will heal every blindness on it today in the name of Jesus. I refuse to continue to walk in darkness. I want to start manifesting in the marvelous light of God. Lord, I pray that every blindness in my heart is healed today in the name of Jesus.

- Every Power that has blocked my heart against the gospel of Christ, I destroy you today in the name of Jesus. I pray for a supernatural type of encounter with the father. I pray that it happens in the name of Jesus.

- I pray for an encounter. An encounter that will remove every demonic veil that has been used to cover my eyes, I pray that you will let it happen in the name of Jesus. The type of encounter that you caused Apostle Paul to have on his way to Damascus, I pray that you will let me have it in the name of Jesus.

- Lord, every evil arrow that has been fired to destroy my spiritual eyes and ears, I come against such arrows by the blood of the lamb. I rebuke every form of confusion in my heart about the Son of man. Lord, I pray that you will visit me today with your mighty hands in the name of Jesus.

- I pray for a special kind of revelation that will clear my doubt about the cross and the man called Jesus Christ. I pray that you let it happen to me in the name of Jesus.

- Lord, I pray that you will set me free from every form of blindness in the name of Jesus. From today, I activate my spiritual sense organ. My eyes are opened in the name of Jesus.

My ears are opened in the name of Jesus. I decree that my heart is sanctified in the name of Jesus.

- Lord, every evil veil that has been used to cover my sight catch fire today in the name of Jesus.

PRAYERS FROM THE BONDAGE OF SIN

Psalms 66:18 If I regard iniquity in my heart, the Lord will not hear me: 66:19 But verily God hath heard me; he hath attended to the voice of my prayer.

The greatest challenge any believer will face is the temptation to sin. No genuine child of God will ever be comfortable living in Sin. Sin in this context is the transgression of the laws of God. When we walk contrary to the dictates of the word of God, we are headed in the direction of sin. Also, sin in these contexts talks about our trespasses that is our day to day wrong doings. Finally sin in these context talks about some stubborn sinful addictions that will not let believers go. Today we shall be engaging in deliverance prayers from the bondage of sin. This deliverance prayers shall empower you spiritually to overcome the temptations and urges to sin. It will engrace you to bear spiritual fruits and because you're light to shine before men and your good works will lead them to Jesus Christ.

For every believer, Jesus has paid for your sins, past, present and future. 1 John 2:1-2. He has given us His Spirit to enable us live Like Him in righteousness. The Holy Spirit in Us empowers us to live like Christ, He helps us to bear godly spiritual fruits and empowers our light to shine brighter and brighter. We must understand that as believers, Satan will not just let us go like that. We must know that Satan is constantly after us to drag us away from God through sin. We must guard our salvation, putting on the whole armour of God. We must be sensitive to the temptations of the devil. As believers we must allow the Spirit of God lead us all the time, we usually fall into sin when we become careless. While God will always forgive us for our sins, the devils goal is to make us go back to living a sinful life, thereby dragging us back to the world. This deliverance prayers from the bondage of sin will indeed delivers us from all evil.

Who is this prayers for? This prayers are for those believer's who are struggling with sin, those whom the devil have trapped in one form of addiction or the other, it could be smoking, lust, fornication, adultery, envy etc. God will be setting you free today, as you engage this prayers in faith today, you shall be totally set free from all the trappings of sin in Jesus name. God loves you unconditionally and he shall indeed deliver you today in Jesus name.

PRAYER POINTS

1. Father, thank You for your saving grace and Eternal Salvation that you have blessed me with In Jesus name.

2. Father, I thank you for sending me the Holy Spirit to teach me how to live right in Jesus name.

3. As the walls of Jericho came tumbling down, let every sinful habits in my life be destroyed in Jesus name.

4. Every sin putting a question mark in my salvation be destroyed now in Jesus name

5. You powers of darkness, lose your hold from my life now in Jesus name

6. Oh Lord, by Your Spirit, engrace me to walk in obedience in Jesus name

7. Oh Lord deliver me from all appearance of evil in Jesus name

8. Oh Father, lead me not into temptation in Jesus name

9. Oh Lord empower me to produce the fruits of the Spirit in Jesus name

10. Give me the grace to flee from youthful lusts in Jesus name.

11. Father, by your grace cover my weaknesses from the eyes of men until I am totally delivered in Jesus name

12. By the Blood of Jesus, flush out every evil deposits of Sin in my Life in Jesus name

13. I command every hidden arrows of wickedness in my life to come out now in Jesus name

14. Every power harboring, enchantment against me, is destroyed now in Jesus name

15. Every demonic force causing me to sin, is neutralized now in Jesus name

16. Every plan of the devil to ruin my ministry through sin is frustrated now in Jesus name.

17. I disgrace every altar of sin in my life in the name of Jesus

18. I separate myself from the sins of my Fathers now In Jesus name.

19. Father, by your mighty hand, break every yoke of sin in my life in Jesus name

20. The Spirit of death shall not overtake me in Jesus name

21. Let every yoke of flesh be destroyed in my life in Jesus name

22. Blood of Jesus, remove any unprogressive label from every aspect of my life.

23. O Lord, create in me a clean heart by your power.

24. O Lord, let the anointing of the Holy Spirit break every yoke of backwardness in my life

25. O Lord, renew a right spirit within me.

26. O Lord, teach me to die to self.

27. Thou brush of the Lord, scrub out every dirtiness in my spiritual pipe, in the name of Jesus.

28. O Lord, ignite my calling with your fire.

29. O Lord, anoint me to pray without ceasing.

30. O Lord, establish me as a holy person unto you.

30 PRAYERS FOR FORGIVENESS AND GUIDANCE

John 1:8 if we say that we have no sin, we deceive ourselves, and the truth is not in us. 1:9 if we confess our sins, he is faithful and just to forgive us our sins, and to cleanse us from all unrighteousness.

We serve a loving and merciful Father. Who is ever willing to forgive us of all our sins and cleanse us from all unrighteousness? There's no sin that God cannot forgive, there is no trespass that God cannot cleanse, all you need to do I to accept Jesus perfect sacrifice for your sins and you will be made right with God and before Him. Today we shall be looking at 30 prayers for forgiveness and guidance, these prayer points will open your eyes to the fathers love as you receive His mercies and grace in Jesus name. Pray this prayers with faith today and trust that God will forgive you of all your sins in Jesus name.

Sin is a nature of the devil in the flesh of man. Whenever we sin, we act according to our human nature, no man can please God working in the flesh, we need the grace and mercy of God to overcome sin in the flesh. Every child of God is made righteous before God through His/her faith in Christ, when one gets born again, the Holy Spirit comes into the life of that person, the Holy Spirits mission in the life of a believer is to teach that believer how to live like Christ. Every newly born again child of God must grow in his/her salvation. Spiritual growth is a continuous process, and while we are at it, we make mistakes here and there, we commit sin from time to time, and this is where God's forgiveness comes in. Whenever you make a mistake or commit sin as a child of God, you just run to His throne of Grace to receive mercy and grace to keep running the race, Hebrew 4:16. This prayers for forgiveness and guidance will input the Spirit of boldness inside you in Jesus name.

Forgiveness is a gift of God to all born again believers. There is no reason for you to backslide or run away from God because of sin. Running away from God because of sin is just like a sick person running away from the Hospital because of His sickness. Christ have died for sins, He has paid the price for every sin or mistake you will ever make and He has sent His Holy Spirit to teach you to live right. He has also provided an unlimited room for improvement, this room is called forgiveness. I encourage you to pray this prayers with faith today, receive God's forgiveness and guidance in your life, and also receive the grace to always live like Christ in Jesus name. Be Blessed

PRAYER POINTS

1. Oh Father, have mercy on me according to your Loving Kindness

2. Father, by your mercies and goodness, blot out every handwriting of sin against me in Jesus name

3. Father, lead me not into temptation but deliver me from all evil in Jesus name

4. Father, deliver me from sins that are too powerful for me.

5. Father, deliver me from sinful addictions in Jesus name

6. Father, do not let my sins bring public embarrassment to your name in Jesus name

7. Father, silence the voice of every accuser pointing accusing finger at me in Jesus name

8. Father, let your, mercies prevail over every judgment against me in Jesus name

9. Empower me Oh Lord to live Holy in Jesus name

10. Empower me Oh Lord to live righteously in Jesus name

11. Father, my salvation is not based on my performance, but on Christ performance, empower me to keep showing Christ to others in Jesus name.

12).Oh Lord that is full of grace and mercy, pardon all my sins so that I will see your face today in Jesus name.

13). Oh Lord, let your mercy cover up my sins today and forever in Jesus name.

14).Father, I come against every evil spirit of deceit that bring iniquity into my life, let them be destroyed today in Jesus name

15). Oh Lord, save me from every iniquity in my life that make me rise and fall in Jesus name.

16). Oh Lord, every work of iniquity in my life that will bring me back to the world I destroy them in the name of Jesus.

17). Oh Lord, let me receive your thorough cleansing by your Blood from all my sins today so that I will be victorious in my prayers in Jesus name.

18). Oh Lord, deliver me from the spirit of lying in Jesus name.

19). Oh Lord, deliver me from the sin of fornication in Jesus name.

20). Oh Lord deliver me from the sin of the lust of the eyes in Jesus name.

21). Lord, forgive my sins today so that I will be preserved from all wickedness in Jesus name.

22). Oh Lord, erase all mark of iniquity away from my life in Jesus name

23). Oh Lord, let the lot of sinners not be my portion in Jesus name.

24). Oh Lord, because I am now a new creation, do not judge me according to all my sins today in Jesus name.

25). Oh Lord, because you have power to forgive sins on earth, forgive me today and grant me my needs in Jesus name.

26).Oh Lord, plead my cause and do not let man prevail over me because of my sins into my life in Jesus name.

27). as a faithful and just God, forgive all my sins as I confess them today in Jesus name.

28). Father, Let men begin to see your light in me and glorify you In Jesus name

29. Father, I receive the grace to be a vessel of Honour unto you in Jesus name

30. Thank you Jesus for forgiving me in Jesus name

20 PRAYER POINTS FOR DELIVERANCE FROM ADULTERY

1 Corinthians 6:18: Flee fornication. Every sin that a man doeth is without the body; but he that committeth fornication sinneth against his own body.

Adultery is extramarital sex that willfully and maliciously interferes with marriage relations. The situation where a man or woman goes out of marital vows to keep a sexual affair with another partner. The scripture even preached against the act of adultery. In the book of 1st Corinthians 6:18-20 the Bible says, he who fornicates sin against his own body because our body is the temple of the living God. Today we shall be engaging in prayer points for deliverance from adultery.

Quite a number of married men and women are caught up in the act of adultery, they have tried several methods or means of breaking free but they keep failing because it is a spiritual problem. Many married couples are dying in silent, they can't speak out because of the fear of damnation from people. Whereas, even those who are swift in condemning others are also caught in that mess too.

The act of adultery is actually demonic, most people are fast becoming addicted to adultery, they cannot explain how or when they got into it, but all they know is that they are weak in fighting the temptations of adultery.

Meanwhile, I have a piece of good news for you today, whether you have been in the act for long or you just get into it. Prayer is a way out of it, God is willing to save you from the mess, and He will give you the strength to overcome the temptations whenever it rises again. But before we go into the prayers deliverance, let us see some steps to avoid adultery.

5 STEPS TO ESCAPE FROM ADULTERY

1. Repent: To repent means to acknowledge your faults and make a decision to turn right. Lasting change starts from the heart, it is with the heart that man believes and repents. If you are caught in the web of adultery, the first step to your deliverance is to acknowledge your sins, and go to God for forgiveness. There is no sin that God will not forgive, God hates adultery, but he loves those who are trapped in it. When we go to God in repentance, acknowledging our sins, He is faithful and just to forgive us and He will cleanse us from all unrighteousness.1 John 1:9.

2. Confront Your Partner: Whatever you don't confront, will remain. The moment you repent from the sin of adultery, call your partner immediately and tell him or her that you are no longer interested in the affair, tell them that you have acknowledge your wrongs and that you are ready to go in the right direction from today. This is a very bold step, and it is not an easy one. Some partners will not leave you because you tell them to, some partners may even go as far as trying to blackmail you or threating to ruin your marriage if you don't give in to them. But at this time you must be strong in the Lord, and resist the devil. Also when you find yourself in this kind of situation, it will be wise you confess to your pastor and to your spouse, by so doing, you get spiritual support from your pastor, forgiveness from your spouse and also support from him or her. Remember, a threefold cord cannot be easily broken.

3. Disconnect From Wrong Company: Evil communication corrupts good manners, 1corinthians 15:33. You must disconnect from every ungodly association that leads you into the sin of adultery. This also includes, avoiding wrong places, and sinful environments. For instance, if you found your partner in a bar, then you must avoid hanging out in bars. Disconnect yourself from any friend of yours that is still in the sin of adultery.

4. Be committed to God: Be prayerful, attend your local church regularly, serve God from your heart, be a student of the Word of God. You need to desire the word of God, so that you will grow in the faith. The word of God renews your mind daily, while prayers empowers you to do the will of God in your life.

5. Keep Running: The bible tells us to flee from sexual sins, flee means to run away from every appearance of evil. When you are fleeing, you are not looking back. Avoid unnecessary attachment to the opposite sex, as a married man, avoid giving single ladies lifts in your car. I know this may look extreme to some of us, but sexual sins starts with little things like this. As a pastor, when you are counselling ladies, keep your office door open, or better still let all the office doors be transparent doors. You must device means to protect your from adultery at all cost. Please not, that this doesn't meant that you are to be sin conscious, no, it only means that you are desperate and willing to please God, it also means that you are guarding your heart will all diligence.

20 PRAYER POINTS TO BREAK FREE FROM ADULTERY

- Heavenly Father, I know that my flesh has made me sinned against you, and to you alone have I done this great evil, by your mercy, I ask that you will forgive me of my sins and wash them away with the blood of Christ.

- Righteous King, the Bible says even if our sin is as red as scarlet they shall be made whiter than snow and if our sin is as red as crimson, they shall be made whiter than wool, I ask that you will by your mercy never bring my son to remembrance again, in Jesus name.

- Heavenly Father, I come to you with a broken and a shattered heart. The scripture says a broken and a contrite heart will you not despise, I ask that you will give me the grace to overcome the temptations of adultery in Jesus name.

- Heaven Father, I'm vulnerable to adultery without your spirit and power. Most times when I repent in my heart they don't last for long. I ask that by your power, you will send your Holy Spirit into my life, your spirit that will always ignite my mortal body to fight against sin, Lord let that spirit dwell me

- Lord, by your powers, I destroy every yoke of adultery that has been embedded in my blood. The Bible says that by the anointing every yoke shall be destroyed. Every yoke of adultery that is holding me bound is destroyed in Jesus.

- Father of Heaven, I come against every demonic man or woman sent from the pit of hell to destroy the union that you God have ordained. I destroy such women and men by fire in the name of Jesus.

- Lord, I lose whatever chains that held me bond to adultery, I break them by the fire of most high, I decree my freedom from the snare of adultery in the name of Jesus

- Father Lord, the scripture says anyone who is in Christ is now a new creature and old things are passed away. Lord, as I rededicate my life to you today grant unto the power to flee from my old lifestyle in Jesus name.

- Lord, I give all my life to you in total submission, I give my spirit, body, and soul unto you, and I ask that you will take control of it in Jesus name.

- Lord, I announce my liberation from sexual immorality in Jesus name. I ask that you will grant me the grace to respect my marital vows, privilege to lovey partner dearly in the name of Jesus.

- Lord God, put upon me the full armor of God that I may resist the devil completely in the name of Jesus. The scripture says resist the devil and he will flee, Lord today, I take upon myself your full armor and I resist sexual immorality in its entirety in the name of Jesus.

- Lord, at the mention of Jesus every knee must bow and every tongue shall confess, I decree my dominance over sexual sins in the name of Jesus. I receive the grace to respect my marital vows that I may not sin unto you and to my own body in Jesus name.

- Lord, for it has been written that our body is the temple of the living God, hence, nothing must defile it, I pray that you will come and make my heart your new home in the name of Jesus.

- I decree, that you will make everything that I ever had your own, Lord, I ask that you will search me to and through and my life will be a replica of your identity in Jesus name.

- I command you Satan in the name of Jesus get your hands off this marriage. This marriage belongs to the Lord, I send you packing from this union in the name of Jesus.

- Lord, every string of adultery, sexual immorality and sins that have been orchestrated by the devil to make me fall from this righteous part, I destroy them in the name of Jesus.

- The Bible says let him that thinks he stands to be careful, or else, he falls. Lord, I seek for your spiritual stamina that comes what may, I will not fall, and I ask that you release it unto me in Jesus.

- Lord, I decree that you will break every spiritual contamination that may cause me to return to my sin, I destroy them by the virtue and power in the name of Jesus.

- I receive my victory over adultery by the blood of the lamb, and it will never conquer me anymore in the name of Jesus.

- Thank you, heavenly King, for the freedom, thank you for the chains that you have broken, thanks for the victory, let your name be exalted in the name of Jesus.

Amen.

10 BIBLE VERSES TO PRAY WHEN WE WANT FORGIVENESS

Today we will be dealing with 10 Bible verses to pray when you want forgiveness. One thing people fail to understand about forgiving other people is that it is not a kindness towards the people that have offended, rather it is a kindness to oneself. When we sin to God, we have retribution and go back to him in prayers. Sometimes we bare the guilt for so long until we finally find the courage to seek God for forgiveness.

Similarly, we must learn to forgive other people just as Christ has forgiven us. Sin can take us far away from God. Until we seek His face for forgiveness, we might bare the guilt for long. Let's take the life of Peter and Judas for example. The two Apostles betrayed Christ. Peter denied Christ while Judas Iscariot gave Christ away for money. Apostle went on to seek forgiveness while Judas Iscariot could not bare the guilt, he eventually committed suicide.

It is not the Will of God that sinners should die, heaven rejoice when a sinner is converted. The book of Ezekiel 33:11 Say unto them, as I live, saith the Lord GOD, I have no pleasure in the death of the wicked; but that the wicked turn from his way and live: turn ye, turn ye from your evil ways; for why will ye die, O house of Israel? This makes us to understand that God takes no pleasure in the death of a sinner.

Hebrews 4:15-16 For we have not an high priest which cannot be touched with the feeling of our infirmities; but was in all points tempted like as we are, yet without sin. Let us therefore come boldly unto the throne of grace that we may obtain mercy, and find grace to help in time of need. Despite our sin and iniquities, God is ever faithful to forgive us. However, we must endeavor to forgive other sin when it is needed.

If you are in a situation where you feel your sin is too cumbersome to warrant forgiveness. God takes no delight in the death of a sinner, neither does He want your sacrifice. The book of Psalm 51 stated that the sacrifices of the Lord are a broken spirit, a broken and a contrite heart will God not despise.

We will supply ten bible verses to seek forgiveness from God.

Bible Verses

Isaiah 1:18 Come now, let us settle the matter,' says the Lord. 'Though your sins are like scarlet, they shall be as white as snow; though they are red as crimson, they shall be like wool.'

This book of the Lord stated that regardless of how big we think our sins are, God is able to forgive us. Even if our sins are as red as Scarlett, they shall be made whiter than snow, even if they are red as crimson they shall be made whiter than wool. Christ has shared his blood on the cross of Calvary for the atonement of our sin.

Ephesians 1:7 in him we have redemption through his blood, the forgiveness of sins, in accordance with the riches of God's grace."

The bible make to understand that God is rich in grace and glory. The grace of the Lord abound. However, we cannot continue to live in sin and ask that grace should abound. The scripture made us understand that in Christ Jesus, we have been redeemed from sin. The blood of Christ was all that was needed to redeem man from the bondage of sin.

Daniel 9:9 The Lord our God is merciful and forgiving, even though we have rebelled against him"

The book of Daniel chapter 9:9 is laying emphasis on the mercy of God. The scripture recorded that God is merciful and forgiving. Even though we have disobeyed him, even though we have gone against his ruling, His steadfast love remains forever and forever.

Micah 7:18-19 who is a God like you, who pardons sins and forgives the transgression of the remnant of his inheritance? You do not stay angry forever but delight to show mercy. You will again have compassion on us; you will tread our sins underfoot and hurl all our iniquities into the depths of the sea."

We must understand that God is not a man to lie, neither is he a son of man to repent. Even in our sin and unrighteousness, God is still faithful. He shows mercy even in face of anger. There is none like God when it comes to compassion and mercy. Regardless of how enormous our sins are, God is faithful to forgive us.

Matthew 26:28 this is my blood of the covenant, which is poured out for many for the forgiveness of sins."

The main essence of Christ death and resurrection is to give us everlasting forgiveness. The scripture made it known that there is no other blood that can bring redemption for man. Before Christ, people use the blood of lamb and other animals for atonement of sin. However those bloods were not sufficient enough to wash out our sin completely, that was why God sent Christ to the world.

Christ's blood is a covenant poured for the forgiveness of sin.

Numbers 14:18 The LORD is slow to anger and abounding in steadfast love, forgiving iniquity and transgression, but he will by no means clear the guilty."

God is slow to anger. His steadfast love knows no limit. Meanwhile, this is not to say that he doesn't have a means of punishing sinners, however, forgiveness of sin is guaranteed. Regardless of how big your sins are, know that God just need your genuine repentance.

Luke 6:37 Judge not, and you will not be judged; condemn not, and you will not be condemned; forgive, and you will be forgiven."

This is for those that are rigid towards forgiving other people. Most believers today are judgmental. Whereas the scripture admonished that we should judge not. Also, we should forgive others so we can be forgiven. If unforgiveness lies in our hearts, it is impossible for us to find forgiveness in the sight of the Father.

Luke 17:4 if he wins against you seven times in the day, and turns to you seven times, saying, 'repent,' you must forgive him."

This passage is teaching us how many times we must forgive the same person. This also shows us that our forgiveness before God has no limit. For as many times we go to him for forgiveness, he is graceful enough to forgive us of all-out sins.

1 John 1:9 if we confess our sins, he is faithful and just to forgive us our sins and to cleanse us from all unrighteousness."

Confession is the first step towards seeking repentance. The only way to find forgiveness from God is through the confession of our sin. Confessing our sins means we are tired of wallowing in the toxic of sin. This is our first step towards redemption from Sin.

Conclusively, we have learned some bible passages for forgiveness. Meanwhile, let it be known that this is not a reason for us to continue sin. God is faithful, and He is merciful, His grace endureth from generation to generation. However, our forgiveness is certain through genuine

REPENTANCE.

5 WAYS TO GAIN CONTROL OVER SIN

Today we will be teaching on five ways to gain self-control over sin. Besides death, sin is the common enemy of man. The devil, having understood the nature of God long before human existence, strives to take the man away from his original position and rob him of his inheritance through sin. For the face of God is too righteous to behold sin. When sin finds its way into the life of man, its ominous aura drives the spirit of God away from a man.

Isaiah 59:1-2 Behold, the LORD's hand is not shortened, that it cannot save, nor His ear heavy, that it cannot hear. But your iniquities have separated you from your God, and your sins have hidden His face from you So that He will not hear. Sin creates differences between man and God. After God created man in His image and likeness, the scripture recorded that God will come down in the cool of the evening to chat with Adam. God cherishes the company of man, but when sin came in, the presence of God was retrieved from man, and Adam could no longer see God the way he used. Until a man can overcome sin, they will continue to be slaves to the devil.

Gaining control over sin goes beyond praying. Before we delve into ways you can gain control over sin, let's highlight some of the adverse effects of sin in a man's life.

3 Things That Happens When Man Sin

1. The presence of God goes farther from man

The first thing that happens when a man falls into sin is that the presence of God will go farther from man. Man will no longer feel the presence of God because of the nature of sin in his life. And when this happens, the devil becomes the closest ally of man.

Man is a spiritual being. A spirit must control him. Either he is controlled by the spirit of God or by the one from the devil. When Saul sinned against God, the spirit of God was withdrawn from him, and evil spirits from the enemy came upon him.

2. The Devil Becomes the Lord

The more a man continues to wallow in sin, the more the devil becomes lord over him. As time goes on, he will not feel the presence of God anymore. The devil will take full possession of his being.

And you need not be told what will happen when the devil becomes lord in the life of man. The consequences are pretty devastating.

3. Prayers Will Not Be Answered

Romans 6:1 what shall we say then? Shall we continue in sin that grace may abound?

A sin is a dividing object that separates us from the love of the father. The scripture makes us understand that the eyes of the lord are too righteous to behold. And in the book of Isaiah 59:1-2 Behold, the LORD's hand is not shortened, that it cannot save, nor His ear heavy, that it cannot hear. But your iniquities have separated you from your God, and your sins have hidden His face from you So that He will not hear.

Often, sin can cause a man to keep praying under a closed heaven. Having known the harmful effects of sin, would it not be nice for you to know how to overcome it? I know you have prayed tirelessly, but still, you are unable to overcome sin completely. By the grace of God, we will highlight five ways you can gain control over sin.

5 Ways You Can Gain Control Over Sin

1. Confess Your Sin

Proverbs 28:13 He who covers his sins will not prosper, but whoever confesses and forsakes them will have mercy.

The first step towards gaining control over sin is the confession of sin. There is no true repentance unless sins have been confessed. The scripture says he that confess his sin shall find mercy. When you hide your sin, you give the enemy more leverage to ride you.

However, confession of sin tells the devil you are a step towards repentance. And God is merciful enough to forgive your sins.

2. Submit Yourself to the Will of God

Luke 22: 41-42 And He was withdrawn from them about a stone's throw, and He knelt and prayed, saying, "Father, if it is your will, take this cup away from me; nevertheless not my will, but yours, be done."

You must learn to submit yourself to the will of God. When Christ was about to be taken, for some moments, he thought about the pain and agony he will go through. He begged God to allow the cup to pass over him.

Christ was quick enough to know that his flesh was leading him. He resubmitted himself to the will of the father. The will of the father must be done, and you must submit yourself to that will.

3. Ask For Grace

1 Samuel 2:9 He will guard the feet of His saints, But the wicked shall be silent in darkness. "For by strength, no man shall prevail.

You can't overcome sin by self-righteousness. The scripture makes us understand that our righteousness is like a filthy rag before God. Instead of glorifying self-righteousness, why not pray for grace. The grace of God will help you in moments of great need.

Whenever temptations arise, the grace of God will help you overcome them.

4. Stay Away From the Things That Makes You Sin

James 4:7 therefore submit to God. Resist the devil and he will flee from you.

You must first identify the things that makes you sin. If your weakness is gossip, stay away from it. Do not go near anything that makes you sin. The scripture says let he that thinks he stand take heed unless he falls.

You must not be ignorant of the devices of the enemy to make you fall into sin. Identify it and stay away from it.

5. Ask For the Power of the Holy Spirit

Acts 1:8 but you shall receive power when the Holy Spirit has come upon you, and you shall be witnesses to Me in Jerusalem, and in all Judea and Samaria, and to the end of the earth."

The power of the Holy Spirit cannot be overemphasized when it comes to overcoming sin or gain control over it. Indeed the spirit is willing, but the flesh is weak. However, if the power of him that raised Christ from the dead dwells in you, it will quicken your mortal body. You will have the power to overcome sin when the spirit of the Lord is upon you.

PRAYER FOR REPENTANCE WITH BIBLE VERSES

In our Christian Life, After Salvation and Redemption, Repentance is no doubt one of the most used words. Because there is no way, a sinner can be converted without repentance. The word Repentance means to turn or change from some specific ways or styles of doing things. What is worthy of note is that if there were no sin, there would not be any need for repentance. And a man cannot repent unless he has seen and admitted the bad things he has done. It takes a man who has a broken and a contrite heart to walk through the part of repentance.

Meanwhile, the book of Ezekiel 18 – 23, Have I any pleasure in the death of the wicked, declares the Lord GOD, and not instead that he should turn from his way and live? God made it known that He takes no pleasure in the death of a sinner. This means God doesn't have joy in seeing a sinner die, but he takes more pleasure when a sinner is converted.

Little wonder, Jesus told the story of the prodigal son. The parable of the prodigal son describes how God takes delight in a sinner who repented from his evil ways. Recall that the prodigal son went away with his inheritance and spent everything lavishly when he got broke, he remembered his rich father. He made way to return home to his father, but not a child, but to seek his mercy to be made one of his slaves. Jesus narrated how the father celebrated the return of the prodigal son and even reinstated him to his rightful position as a son and not slave. This illustration explains that heaven rejoices at the return of a lost sheep.

Furthermore, Jesus also told the story of a shepherd that left his herds of cattle to go in search of a lost sheep. All these stories are to make us see how much God values repentance. The original design of man is sinful, and it takes a conscious effort with help from the Holy Spirit to overcome sin and see it as an abomination.

Some people want to repent, but they have no clue how to do that, worry less, this article is for you. We will be highlighting some prayer for repentance with Bible verses. Your time for salvation has just come, remember, the first step is to confess your sin to God, remember the Bible says he that hides his sin shall not prosper, but he that confesses them shall find mercy.

Once you have confessed your sin, make a conscious decision not to do them again that is your first step towards repentance. After making a decision not to return to your mess, you must adopt a new culture and style of living which can be found in Christ Jesus.
Let me take you through some prayer for repentance with Bible verses.
Lord Jesus, I feel sorry for all my evil deeds. I have never felt this guilty until. I learned about you and how much you detest the evil things that I used to do. I was so scared that I may die as a punishment for my evil deeds. However, I gained strength from your word that says that you delight not in the death of a sinner, but you are happy when they repent. Because of this, I ask that you will create in me a clean heart, and you will renew the right spirit within me. Grant me your Holy Spirit and power that will help me to stay away from sin in the name of Jesus.

James 4:8 Draw near to God, and He will draw near to you. Cleanse your hands, you sinners; and purify your hearts, you double-minded.
Father Lord, I have listened to the loud voice of the enemy, and I turned a deaf ear to your spirit. I'm sorry for all I have done. I allowed myself to be deceived by the devil, and I was carried away by the things of the world. I lost my gaze upon the cross as I wallow in toxic of impurity. Sin has overcome me, and by every standard, I have been condemned. My heart is so bitter that I fear that I might not be forgiven, but this is my plea, Christ has died. He has spilled the blood on the cross of Calvary for my sake, on this, have I stand as I announce my permanent retirement in the workforce of sin and

iniquity. I confess my sin before you, Lord, because to you alone have I sinned and done a great evil in your sight. Lord, I ask that you will forgive me and receive back into your palace in the name of Jesus.

Acts 3 vs. 19 Repent, then, and turn to God so that your sins may be wiped out, that times of refreshing may come from the Lord.

Father Lord, nothing is as painful as me knowing that my sin hurts you badly. When I remember the price you paid at the cross of Calvary, I cannot resist the pain and anguish in my heart for disappointing you after you invested so much trust in me that even caused you to lay down your life for me. And yes, I know that your love to us knows no boundary, I have realized my faults, and I'm greatly pained for doing them. I pray that you will wash with the blood of Christ, and I shall be clean, wash me, and I shall be whiter than snow. I pray that you will cause me to be dead to sin from now and be alive to righteousness.

Joel 2-13 so rend your heart, and not your garments; Return to the Lord your God, for He is gracious and merciful, Slow to anger, and of great kindness; And He relents from doing harm.

Lord God, I thank you for the grace you have given us always to find our way back to you when we sin. Thank you because sin doesn't disqualify us from getting back to you.

Father Lord, I can't hide the fact that I'm a sinner who needs help, and I confess my sin before you this day that I may find compassion before you. You are the God of restoration. I ask that you will restore me. The scripture says he that hides his sin shall not prosper, but he who confesses them shall find mercy. All I seek is your mercy, as my soul is plunged unto repentance, I ask that you will have mercy on me, and you will show me kindness in the name of Jesus.

Proverbs 28: 13 He who covers his sins will not prosper, but whoever confesses and forsakes them will have mercy

BIBLE VERSES FOR THE BROKEN HEARTED

Today we shall be exploring bible verses for the broken hearted. Have you ever been broken-hearted? Have you ever felt some sort of pain or sorrow after being disappointed probably from someone you love? This article is just for you. It is almost impossible for us not to have experienced heartbreak, especially in relationships. A scholar once argued humans could not be trusted and that many people do make a lifetime decision based on temporary feelings. So when the feelings stop, their choice also stops.

On several occasions have heard the gist of people who left their Fiancé they have been dating for years to get married to someone they met just a few months ago. At times, it could be cheating in a relationship, and there is no doubt that in every relationship, one party will love than the other. The other party that has been investing so much love in the relationship will end up being heartbroken or down casted when they finally discover they have been alone all the while.

A relationship is more complicated than we all envisaged, even the man himself sometimes disrupts even man to God relationship God could repent in his heart for creating man, how much more man to man relationship if you have ever experienced heartbreak in any relationship, you will understand the pain and trauma it can cause. And I'm sure you would not want ever to experience something like that anymore. In this article, we have compiled a list of bible verses that will help us heal the pain in our hearts, especially the ones we suddenly develop due to heartbreak. All you need do is study these bible verses for the broken hearted and read them repeatedly until you find strength and peace.

Bible Verses

Matthew 11:28-30 come unto me, all ye that labour and are heavy laden, and I will give you rest. Take my yoke upon you, and learn of me; for I am meek and lowly in heart: and ye shall find rest unto your souls. For my yoke is easy, and my burden is light.

Psalms 55:22-23 cast thy burden upon the LORD, and he shall sustain thee: he shall never suffer the righteous to be moved. But thou, O God, shalt bring them down into the pit of destruction: bloody and deceitful men shall not live out half their days; but I will trust in thee.

Proverbs 3:5-8 Trust in the LORD with all thine heart; and lean not unto thine own understanding. In all thy ways acknowledge him, and he shall direct thy paths. Be not wise in thine own eyes: fear the LORD, and depart from evil. It shall be health to thy navel, and marrow to thy bones.

Romans 5:1-5 therefore being justified by faith, we have peace with God through our Lord Jesus Christ: By whom also we have access by faith into this grace wherein we stand, and rejoice in hope of the glory of God. And not only so, but we glory in tribulations also: knowing that tribulation walketh patience; and patience, experience; and experience, hope: And hope maketh not ashamed; because the love of God is shed abroad in our hearts by the Holy Ghost which is given unto us.

Philippians 3:13-14 Brethren, I count not myself to have apprehended: but this one thing I do, forgetting those things which are behind, and reaching forth unto those things which are before, I press toward the mark for the prize of the high calling of God in Christ Jesus.

Psalms 34:17-20 the righteous cry, and the LORD heareth, and delivereth them out of all their troubles. The LORD is nigh unto them that are of a broken heart; and saveth such as be of a contrite spirit. Many are the afflictions of the righteous: but the LORD delivereth him out of them all. He keepeth all his bones: not one of them is broken.

Romans 8:18 For I reckon that the sufferings of this present time are not worthy to be compared with the glory which shall be revealed in us.

Jeremiah 29:11 for I know the thoughts that I think toward you, saith the LORD, thoughts of peace, and not of evil, to give you an expected end.

Ezekiel 36:26 a new heart also will I give you, and a new spirit will I put within you: and I will take away the stony heart out of your flesh, and I will give you and heart of flesh.

Revelation 21:4 And God shall wipe away all tears from their eyes; and there shall be no more death, neither sorrow, nor crying, neither shall there be any more pain: for the former things are passed away.

Isaiah 41:10 Fear thou not; for I am with thee: be not dismayed; for I am thy God: I will strengthen thee; yea, I will help thee; yea, I will uphold thee with the right hand of my righteousness.

Deuteronomy 31:6 be strong and of a good courage, fear not, nor be afraid of them: for the LORD thy God, he it is that doth go with thee; he will not fail thee, nor forsake thee.

Isaiah 43:18-19 Remember ye not the former things, neither consider the things of old. Behold, I will do a new thing; now it shall spring forth; shall ye not know it? I will even make a way in the wilderness, and rivers in the desert.

Romans 15:13 Now the God of hope fill you with all joy and peace in believing, that ye may abound in hope, through the power of the Holy Ghost.

Psalms 9:9-10 The LORD also will be a refuge for the oppressed, a refuge in times of trouble. And they that know thy name will put their trust in thee: for thou, LORD, hast not forsaken them that seek thee.

Psalms 9:13-14 Have mercy upon me, O LORD; consider my trouble which I suffer of them that hate me, thou that liftest me up from the gates of death: That I may shew forth all thy praise in the gates of the daughter of Zion: I will rejoice in thy salvation.

BIBLE VERSES ABOUT REPENTANCE

Today we will be exploring bible verses about repentance. Firstly, repentance is being remorseful or having a bad feeling about something and making an effort to stop doing it. Repentance is the first step we take toward reconciliation with God.

The scripture noted in the book of Psalms 51:17 the sacrifices of God are a broken spirit: a broken and a contrite heart, O God, thou wilt not despise. God doesn't take pleasure in any sacrifices, and God prefers that we confess our sin and make amends not to do them again. Little wonder the book of Proverbs said He that covers his sin should not prosper, but he that confesses them shall find mercy.

Many times in our lives, we cover our sins like God is not seeing them. We are the holy brothers and sister on the surface, but in our closets, we do terrible God forsaken things. We must understand that God doesn't want the death of a sinner, but repentance is what the Lord is asking from us. We do not have to perish with our sins when we can confess them and repent from them. Our repentance starts when we identify that we have been doing the wrong things when we come to the knowledge that the things we are doing don't interest God. We begin to detest those things and start avoiding them, and we turn to God for mercy to overcome the temptation of the devil that may want to force us into doing them again.

We have compiled a list of bible verses that talk about repentance. You will do yourself a great favor by studying some of these bible verses repeatedly so you can find your part unto repentance and thereby reconciling with God.

Bible Verses

Hosea 13:14 I will ransom them from the power of the grave; I will redeem them from death: O death, I will be thy plagues; O grave, I will be thy destruction: repentance shall be hid from mine eyes.

Matthew 3:8 Bring forth therefore fruits meet for repentance:

Matthew 3:11 I indeed baptize you with water unto repentance: but he that cometh after me is mightier than I, whose shoes I am not worthy to bear: he shall baptize you with the Holy Ghost, and with fire:

Matthew 9:13 but go ye and learn what that meaneth, I will have mercy, and not sacrifice: for I am not come to call the righteous, but sinners to repentance.

Mark 1:4 John did baptize in the wilderness, and preach the baptism of repentance for the remission of sins.

Mark 2:17 When Jesus heard it, he saith unto them, They that are whole have no need of the physician, but they that are sick: I came not to call the righteous, but sinners to repentance.

Luke 3:3 and he came into all the country about Jordan, preaching the baptism of repentance for the remission of sins;

Luke 3:8 Bring forth therefore fruits worthy of repentance, and begin not to say within yourselves, We have Abraham to our father: for I say unto you, That God is able of these stones to raise up children unto Abraham.

Luke 5:32 I came not to call the righteous, but sinners to repentance.

Luke 15:7 I say unto you, that likewise joy shall be in heaven over one sinner that repenteth, more than over ninety and nine just persons, which need no repentance.

luke 24:47 and that repentance and remission of sins should be preached in his name among all nations, beginning at Jerusalem.

Acts 5:31 Him hath God exalted with his right hand to be a Prince and a Saviour, for to give repentance to Israel, and forgiveness of sins.

Acts 11:18 When they heard these things, they held their peace, and glorified God, saying, Then hath God also to the Gentiles granted repentance unto life.

Acts 13:24 When John had first preached before his coming the baptism of repentance to all the people of Israel.

Acts 19:4 then said Paul, John verily baptized with the baptism of repentance, saying unto the people, that they should believe on him which should come after him, that is, on Christ Jesus.

Acts 20:21 Testifying both to the Jews, and also to the Greeks, repentance toward God, and faith toward our Lord Jesus Christ.

Acts 26:20 but shewed first unto them of Damascus, and at Jerusalem, and throughout all the coasts of Judaea, and then to the Gentiles, that they should repent and turn to God, and do works meet for repentance.
Romans 2:4 Or despisest thou the riches of his goodness and forbearance and longsuffering; not knowing that the goodness of God leadeth thee to repentance?

Romans 11:29 for the gifts and calling of God are without repentance.

2 Corinthians 7:9 Now I rejoice, not that ye were made sorry, but that ye sorrowed to repentance: for ye were made sorry after a godly manner, that ye might receive damage by us in nothing.

2 Corinthians 7:10 for godly sorrow worketh repentance to salvation not to be repented of: but the sorrow of the world worketh death.

2 Timothy 2:25 in meekness instructing those that oppose themselves; if God peradventure will give them repentance to the acknowledging of the truth;

Hebrews 6:1 Therefore leaving the principles of the doctrine of Christ, let us go on unto perfection; not laying again the foundation of repentance from dead works, and of faith toward God,

Hebrews 6:6 if they shall fall away, to renew them again unto repentance; seeing they crucify to themselves the Son of God afresh, and put him to an open shame.

Hebrews 12:17 for you know how that afterward, when he would have inherited the blessing, he was rejected: for he found no place of repentance, though he sought it carefully with tears.

2 Peter 3:9 The Lord is not slack concerning his promise, as some men count slackness; but is longsuffering to us-ward, not willing that any should perish, but that all should come to repentance.

Matthew 4:17 from that time Jesus began to preach, and to say, Repent: for the kingdom of heaven is at hand.

Numbers 23:19 God is not a man that he should lie; neither the son of man that he should repent: hath he said, and shall he not do it? Or hath he spoken, and shall he not make it good?

Luke 13:5 I tell you, Nay: but, except ye repent, ye shall all likewise perish.

BIBLE VERSES ABOUT NEW BEGINING

Today we shall be engaging in bible verses about new beginning. Who doesn't want a new beginning after a moment of toil and hardship? We all deserve a new start when we finally realize that we have been wrong all the while. A new beginning comes right after repentance and accepting Christ as our Lord and Savior, from then, we start a new life, a life devoid of sin and iniquity. A unique experience that will be nurtured and tutored by Christ Jesus.

A new beginning could be when God wants to start his covenant in the life of a man. Father Abraham, for instance, had a new beginning after God told him to walk before him and the perfect, and he will establish his covenant with him. His name was changed from Abram to Abraham, and God began to establish the long-term covenant that he has had concerning Abraham.

We also in our individual lives deserves a new and better beginning, a life that is filled with the glory and presence of God Almighty. The bible says he that is in Christ Jesus has become a new creature and old things are passed away, behold everything is now new. That is what the life of Christ in us could do for us. We will forget old things while looking unto Jesus. Whether you are a grievous sinner, a rapist, armed robber, prostitute, hired assassin or whatever, come into Jesus, and you will have a new life.

The old being will be laid to the cross the day we truly accept Jesus as our personal Lord and savior, and we will begin to express a different character in new Jesus. The more we grow in God's wisdom, the better we will exhibit a Godly character. People will be confused, like is this not the old you. Also, economically, someone who has been very poor, God can turn a story around in no time, and it will amaze everyone that they will find it difficult to believe that it is the old you.

If you want a new beginning, we have compiled a list of bible verses for you to read and study well. Read thoroughly and study it repeatedly until you notice obvious changes in your life.

Bible Verses

2 Corinthians 5:16-20 wherefore henceforth know we no man after the flesh: yea, though we have known Christ after the flesh, yet now henceforth know us him no more. Therefore if any man be in Christ, he is a new creature: old things are passed away; behold, all things are become new. And all things are of God, who hath reconciled us to himself by Jesus Christ, and hath given to us the ministry of reconciliation; To wit, that God was in Christ, reconciling the world unto himself, not imputing their trespasses unto them; and hath committed unto us the word of reconciliation. Now then we are ambassadors for Christ, as though God did beseech you by us: we pray you in Christ's stead, be ye reconciled to God.

Luke 7:47 – Wherefore I say unto thee, her sins, which are many, are forgiven; for she loved much: but to whom little is forgiven, [the same] loveth little.

Isaiah 42:16 And I will bring the blind by a way that they knew not; I will lead them in paths that they have not known: I will make darkness light before them, and crooked things straight. These things will I do unto them, and not forsake them.

Isaiah 43:18-20 Remember ye not the former things, neither consider the things of old. Behold, I will do a new thing; now it shall spring forth; shall ye not know it? I will even make a way in the wilderness, and rivers in the desert. The beast of the field shall Honour me, the dragons and the owls: because I give waters in the wilderness, and rivers in the desert, to give drink to my people, my chosen.

Ephesians 4:22-24 That ye put off concerning the former conversation the old man, which is corrupt according to the deceitful lusts; And be renewed in the spirit of your mind; And that ye put on the new man, which after God is created in righteousness and true holiness.

Job 8:6-7 if thou wert pure and upright; surely now he would awake for thee, and make the habitation of thy righteousness prosperous. Though thy beginning was small, yet thy latter end should greatly increase.

Luke 7:47 wherefore I say unto thee, her sins, which are many, are forgiven; for she loved much: but to whom little is forgiven, the same loveth little.

1 Peter 1:3 blessed be the God and Father of our Lord Jesus Christ, which according to his abundant mercy hath begotten us again unto a lively hope by the resurrection of Jesus Christ from the dead.

Ecclesiastes 3:11 He hath made everything beautiful in his time: also he hath set the world in their heart, so that no man can find out the work that God maketh from the beginning to the end.

Philippians 3:13-14 Brethren, I count not myself to have apprehended: but this one thing I do, forgetting those things which are behind, and reaching forth unto those things which are before, I press toward the mark for the prize of the high calling of God in Christ Jesus.

Psalms 40:3 and he hath put a new song in my mouth, even praise unto our God: many shall see it, and fear, and shall trust in the LORD.

Isaiah 65:17 for, behold, I create new heavens and a new earth: and the former shall not be remembered, nor come into mind.

Ezekiel 11:19 And I will give them one heart, and I will put a new spirit within you; and I will take the stony heart out of their flesh, and will give them and heart of flesh:

Psalms 98:1-3 O sing unto the LORD a new song; for he hath done marvellous things: his right hand, and his holy arm, hath gotten him the victory. The LORD hath made known his salvation: his righteousness hath he openly shewed in the sight of the heathen. He hath remembered his mercy and his truth toward the house of Israel: all the ends of the earth have seen the salvation of our God.

PRAYER FROM DELIVERANCE FROM SIN

We have been led by the spirit of God to give some specific prayers for deliverance from sin. As much as God would love that man rise and live the pure Creed of their creation, sin has become a hindering factor to that. When God created Adam in the Garden of Eden, the plan of God was for man to have a consistent koinonia with Him, for man to have dominance over everything that was created.

It was inevitable that God created the heavens and the earth. However, God, in his holy majestic, cannot stay on earth. Hence, he needed to put some people in charge of the earth to have dominion over the earth on behalf of God and the host of heaven. Little wonder, God will always descend during the cool of the evening to have a chat with Adam and know how his day went.

The relationship between Adam and God made God realize that Adam needed something very important, a companion. God then created Eve to be the supporting system of a man. Meanwhile, the creation of Eve did not alter the relationship that had existed between God and Adam. God maintains His relationship with a man until sin broke in. Immediately man sinned, God couldn't help but went away from a man simply because his face is too righteous to behold iniquity.

The creation would have been perfect if not for sin, and up until now, sin is still thriving among men. To some, it is like sin is inevitable; the purpose of Christ's death is to rescue from the curse of the law, which condemns any sinner to death without giving a chance for repentance. However, the death of Christ did not abolish sin but only gave us a means of escape from sin and iniquity by giving us the Holy Spirit.

The power that the Holy Spirit gives us will liberate us from the power of sin and iniquity, which has been made to limit our progress in life. Sin will cause the spirit of God to depart from us and make us void of the spirit. It is capable of clearing our path to ensure that we never find our way to the cross again, and in all, it will bring eternal death. All these consequences of sin is imperative for every man to try as much he/she can to break free from the power of sin. To this effect, prayer for deliverance from sin is therefore, compulsory for every believer who still battle with sin in the secret.

PRAYER POINTS

- Lord Jesus, the essence of your death and resurrection is to free me from sin. You took the cross, went through the street of shame, and paid the capital price with your precious blood that I may be saved from the curse of the law. Lord, how bad will it be, that thousands of years, even after your death, I'm still wallowing deep in the toxic of sin? I take solace in the scriptural text that emphasized that we shall know the truth, and the truth shall set us free. Jesus, I have known the truth that genuinely you died that I may be saved from sin, I launch into the covenant of freedom that was made with your blood in Calvary, and I announce my total deliverance from sin in the name of Jesus.

- Father in heaven, my heart is greatly bittered when I learned that sin has no good it does to a man except to put one into bondage. Jesus, I'm tired of being a slave unto sin, and I have made my resolution to walk on the path of righteousness. However, this will be difficult if the shackles of sin have not been broken yet from the back, I pray for mercy that will give me victory over sin, Lord I ask that you will give it unto me in the name of Jesus.

- The Bible says we cannot be in sin and ask grace to be surplus. Lord God, you reign because your mercy over man endureth forever. I beg for your mercy over my sins and iniquities that you will make me see you. The Bible made it known that the face of a sinner will not see Christ, Lord Jesus, I pray that by virtue of the blood that was shed in Calvary, you will wash me entirely from my sin in the name of Jesus.

- Father in heaven, your word made it known that you do not want the death of a sinner but repentance through Christ Jesus. Also, you have not sent your son to the world to condemn the world, but for us to find salvation through his death. I confess all my sins before you today, I'm a glorified liar, a thief, and I indulge in sexual immoralities. As much as I'm not proud of all these bad things I do, my repentance away from it doesn't last long either. This is why I need your help to assist me in overcoming the flesh that has to want to take over my entire being. I pray for mercy that will lift me above sin. Lord have mercy on the name of Jesus.

- Father Lord, sin has overridden my life. It has become inevitably impossible for me to do without it. Bad enough, I cannot even boast of them outside, whereas I can't confess them to man instead because of shame and reproach. I take strength in the book of Psalm that says unto you have I done this iniquity and done this evil in your sight. And the book of proverbs says he that hides his sin will not prosper, but he that confess and repent will find mercy. I seek for total repentance, and the everlasting Lord gives me the grace to overcome sin completely in the name of Jesus.

- For Christ has died, this is my plea, truly sin has overpowered, but Christ has died to save me entirely from it. I seek your strength to eradicate sin in the name of Jesus.

PSALM 51 MEANING VERSE BY VERSE

Today we will be exploring Psalm 51 meaning verse by verse and we trust that the Holy Spirit will help us do justice to this scripture. Just before we commence, let us pray. Our heavenly father, we exalt you for this wonderful moment that you have bestowed on us to see a great day like this, we thank you because you have been our shield and buckler, and may your name be exalted. Lord, as we are going into your word, we pray that the Holy Spirit will minister your word to us in the name of Jesus. We put ourselves under the leading of the Holy Ghost, we ask that you will teach us and break things down for us in the name of Jesus. Father, at the end, do not let this word stand against us, instead through it, let us be liberated from the power of sin in the name of Jesus.

Have mercy upon me, O God,

According to Your loving kindness;

According to the multitude of your tender mercies,

Blot out my transgressions. Wash me thoroughly from my iniquity,

And cleanse me from my sin. For I acknowledge my transgressions,

And my sin is always before me. Against You, You only, have I sinned,

And done this evil in your sight—

That you may be found just when you speak,

And blameless when you judge. Behold, I was brought forth in iniquity,

And in sin my mother conceived me. Behold, you desire truth in the inward parts,

And in the hidden part you will make me to know wisdom. Purge me with hyssop, and I shall be clean;

Wash me, and I shall be whiter than snow. Make me hear joy and gladness,

That the bones you have broken may rejoice. Hide your face from my sins,

And blot out all my iniquities. Create in me a clean heart, O God,

And renew a steadfast spirit within me. Do not cast me away from your presence, and do not take Your Holy Spirit from me. Restore to me the joy of your salvation,

And uphold me by your generous Spirit. Then I will teach transgressors your ways,

And sinners shall be converted to you. Deliver me from the guilt of bloodshed, O God,

The God of my salvation,

And my tongue shall sing aloud of your righteousness. O Lord, open my lips,

And my mouth shall show forth your praise. For you do not desire sacrifice, or else I would give it;

You do not delight in burnt offering. The sacrifices of God are a broken spirit, a broken and a contrite heart—

These, O God, You will not despise. Do well in your good pleasure to Zion;

Build the walls of Jerusalem. Then you shall be pleased with the sacrifices of righteousness,

With burnt offering and whole burnt offering;

Then they shall offer bulls on your altar.

Psalm 51 speaks volume of someone who have been wallowing in the toxic of sin for long. Someone whose life and existence has been marred by the power of sin. This Psalm speak volume of someone who desire righteousness in it raw form, someone who doesn't see himself as a worthy person before God. This Psalm reflect the life of someone begging God for mercy.

For better understanding, let's analyses this book of Psalm in verses.

Have mercy upon me, O God,

According to Your loving kindness;

According to the multitude of your tender mercies,

Blot out my transgressions. Wash me thoroughly from my iniquity,

And cleanse me from my sin.

This first few verses of the scripture reflect the life of someone pleading for mercy. Have mercy upon me according to your loving kindness, according to the multitude of your tender mercies. The mercy of the lord is unending. The book of Psalm 136 says give thanks to the lord for He is good and His mercy endure forever. The mercy of the lord have no ending.

The second verse depict that only God is capable of washing away our sin through the blood of His only begotten Son Jesus Christ. It is the blood of Christ that is sufficient to wash away out iniquities. This verse recognizes that nothing else can wash away the sin of man except God.

For I acknowledge my transgressions,

And my sin is always before me. Against You, You only, have I sinned,

And done this evil in your sight—

That you may be found just when you speak, and blameless when you judge.

The scripture says in the book of proverbs, he that hide his sin shall perish but he that confess and forsake them shall find mercy. The first step towards getting forgiveness is by acknowledging that you have sinned. Our sin is before God and against Him have we all sinned.

God is fair and just. He doesn't punish or reprimand people for doing nothing. That you be found just when you speak and blameless when you judge.

Behold, I was brought forth in iniquity,

And in sin my mother conceived me. Behold, you desire truth in the inward parts,

And in the hidden part you will make me to know wisdom.

This is to emphasize the fact that we inherit sin from our parents, just like the world inherited sin from the first man Adam. Even the womb that bears a child for nine month is contaminated and filled with sin. The book of Romans says for all have sinned and fall short of the glory of God.

God takes delight in truth even in the inward part. This means our genuinely should not be a public thing alone, we should be genuine and real with our confessions even when no one is watching.

Purge me with hyssop, and I shall be clean;

Wash me, and I shall be whiter than snow. Make me hear joy and gladness,

That the bones you have broken may rejoice. Hide your face from my sins,

And blot out all my iniquities.

Until there is a purging, there is no cleansing. Meanwhile, the hyssop means the blood of Jesus. Nothing else can wash away our sin but the blood of Jesus. Nothing can makes us whiter than the snow except the blood of Jesus.

When we are purged by the blood of Christ we become a new creation and old things are passed away. The face of the of lord will be hidden from our sin as they have been washed by the precious blood of Christ.

Do not cast me away from your presence,

And do not take Your Holy Spirit from me. Restore to me the joy of your salvation,

And uphold me by your generous Spirit. Then I will teach transgressors your ways, and sinners shall be converted to you.

When the load of sin is too much in the life of a man, such a person will be cast away. This is because the eyes of the lord is too righteous to behold sin. Saul began to have problem when he deep his hands into sin. The spirit of God was with Saul, but when sin entered, the spirit of the lord vacated his life and he was tormented by an evil spirit.

Uphold me with your generous spirit here means uphold me with your holy spirit. The scripture says when the power that raised Christ from the dead dwells in you, it will quicken your mortal body. Our body needs to be strengthened by the power of the Holy Spirit.

Deliver me from the guilt of bloodshed, O God,

The God of my salvation,

And my tongue shall sing aloud of your righteousness. O Lord, open my lips,

And my mouth shall show forth your praise.

When we are weighed down by the power of sin, most times what the devil do is bring guilt into our heart. This guilt will even stop us from pursuing salvation in Christ Jesus because we feel the load of our sin is too much than what God can forgive.

This was what happened to Judas Iscariot. He was consumed by guilt of what he has done and at the end, instead of him to seek forgiveness, he took his own life.

For you do not desire sacrifice, or else I would give it;

You do not delight in burnt offering. The sacrifices of God are a broken spirit, a broken and a contrite heart—

These, O God, You will not despise.

Gone are the days when God take delight in burnt offering. The blood of the ram or bullock is not precious anymore. There is a blood that is more precious than the blood of ram or bullock, it is the blood of Jesus.

The scripture says the sacrifices of God are a broken spirit, broken and a contrite heart God will not despise. This means, when we beg God for forgiveness, we must have a broken heart, and heart that feel sober for the evil that has been committed and a genuine repentance must follow. These are the sacrifices that God take delight in, remember the scripture says God doesn't want the death of sinner, but repentance through Christ Jesus.

Do well in your good pleasure to Zion;

Build the walls of Jerusalem. Then you shall be pleased with the sacrifices of righteousness,

With burnt offering and whole burnt offering;

Then they shall offer bulls on your altar.

This is a plea to God not to hinder good things in our life because of sin. There are times that sin stop the manifestation of God's glory in the life of a man. This portion of the Psalm is pleading that God should do well in his pleasure to Zion.

Your life is the Zion, you career, education, marriage, relationship and everything that concern you is the Zion. The sacrifice that you will offer on the altar of the Lord is Thanksgiving.

BIBLE VERSES ABOUT VICTORY

We all want victory over every threatening challenge and that is why we need some bible verses about victory. We can have victory in any form; it could be over court cases, over sickness, or land dispute as the case may be. However, the greatest type of victory we can have is in Christ Jesus. Our Victory in Christ Jesus gives us liberty over sin.

It could be recalled that Christ told his disciples that in life, they would face tribulations and challenges, but they should be of good faith because He has conquered the world. The victory of Christ is what we believers exhibit today. At the same time, many other people will toil and exhaust themselves trying to be victorious, our victory has been settled in Christ Jesus. All we need to do is just attest to our victory in Christ Jesus, although, we may face challenges in life, although the storm of life will come raging at us, we should be of good faith because Christ has conquered all.

Meanwhile, victory in Christ Jesus has a lot to do with our relationship with God. When the relationship between God and us is undisturbed, then our victory is certain. That is why we must always find our way back to the cross whenever we miss it. Also, we need to know that believing in Jesus Christ doesn't automatically translate into a spontaneous victory. There are times that our victory will come bit by bit. Even while we are in the waiting room for our victory to manifest, we must exhibit a good character, and the bible says nothing can separate us from the love of God. Even when it seems the victory will not, we must trust in God and keep believing.

Bible Verses

2 Samuel 19:2 and the victory that day was turned into mourning unto all the people: for the people heard say that day how the king was grieved for his son.

2 Samuel 23:10 He arose, and smote the Philistines until his hand was weary, and his hand clave unto the sword: and the LORD wrought a great victory that day; and the people returned after him only to spoil.

2 Samuel 23:12 but he stood in the midst of the ground, and defended it, and slew the Philistines: and the LORD wrought a great victory.

1 Chronicles 29:11 Thine, O LORD, is the greatness, and the power, and the glory, and the victory, and the majesty: for all that is in the heaven and in the earth is thine; thine is the kingdom, O LORD, and thou art exalted as head above all.

Psalms 98:1 O sing unto the LORD a new song; for he hath done marvellous things: his right hand, and his holy arm, hath gotten him the victory.

Isaiah 25:8 He will swallow up death in victory; and the Lord GOD will wipe away tears from off all faces; and the rebuke of his people shall he take away from off all the earth: for the LORD hath spoken it.

Matthew 12:20 A bruised reed shall he not break, and smoking flax shall he not quench, till he send forth judgment unto victory.

1 Corinthians 15:54 So when this corruptible shall have put on incorruption, and this mortal shall have put on immortality, then shall be brought to pass the saying that is written, Death is swallowed up in victory.

1 Corinthians 15:55 O death, where is thy sting? O grave, where is thy victory?

1 Corinthians 15:57 But thanks be to God, which giveth us the victory through our Lord Jesus Christ.

1 John 5:4 for whatsoever is born of God overcometh the world: and this is the victory that overcometh the world, even our faith.

Revelation 15:2 And I saw as it were a sea of glass mingled with fire: and them that had gotten the victory over the beast, and over his image, and over his mark, and over the number of his name, stand on the sea of glass, having the harps of God.

1 Corinthians 15:57 But thanks be to God, which giveth us the victory through our Lord Jesus Christ.

Deuteronomy 20:4 For the LORD your God is he that goeth with you, to fight for you against your enemies, to save you.

Romans 6:14 for sin shall not have dominion over you: for ye are not under the law, but under grace.

Ephesians 6:10-18 finally, my brethren, be strong in the Lord, and in the power of his might. Put on the whole armour of God that ye may be able to stand against the wiles of the devil. For we wrestle not against flesh and blood, but against principalities, against powers, against the rulers of the darkness of this world, against spiritual wickedness in high places. Wherefore take unto you the whole armour of God that ye may be able to withstand in the evil day, and having done all, to stand. Stand therefore, having your loins girt about with truth, and having on the breastplate of righteousness; And your feet shod with the preparation of the gospel of peace; Above all, taking the shield of faith, wherewith ye shall be able to quench all the fiery darts of the wicked. And take the helmet of salvation, and the sword of the Spirit, which is the word of God: Praying always with all prayer and supplication in the Spirit, and watching thereunto with all perseverance and supplication for all saints

1 John 4:4 ye are of God, little children, and have overcome them: because greater is he that is in you, than he that is in the world.

1 John 5:5 who is he that overcometh the world, but he that believeth that Jesus is the Son of God?

Revelation 2:7 He that hath an ear, let him hear what the Spirit saith unto the churches; to him that overcometh will I give to eat of the tree of life, which is in the midst of the paradise of God.

Revelation 2:11 He that hath an ear, let him hear what the Spirit saith unto the churches; He that overcometh shall not be hurt of the second death.

Revelation 2:17 He that hath an ear, let him hear what the Spirit saith unto the churches; To him that overcometh will I give to eat of the hidden manna, and will give him a white stone, and in the stone a new name written, which no man knoweth saving he that receiveth it.

Revelation 2:26 and he that overcometh, and keepeth my works unto the end, to him will I give power over the nations:

Revelation 3:5 He that overcometh, the same shall be clothed in white raiment; and I will not blot out his name out of the book of life, but I will confess his name before my Father, and before his angels.

Revelation 3:12 Him that overcometh will I make a pillar in the temple of my God, and he shall go no more out: and I will write upon him the name of my God, and the name of the city of my God, which is new Jerusalem, which cometh down out of heaven from my God: and I will write upon him my new name.

Revelation 3:21 To him that overcometh will I grant to sit with me in my throne, even as I also overcame, and am set down with my Father in his throne.

Revelation 11:7 and when they shall have finished their testimony, the beast that ascendeth out of the bottomless pit shall make war against them, and shall overcome them, and kill them.

Revelation 13:7 and it was given unto him to make war with the saints, and to overcome them: and power was given him over all kindred's, and tongues, and nations.

Revelation 17:14 these shall make war with the Lamb, and the Lamb shall overcome them: for he is Lord of lords, and King of kings: and they that are with him are called, and chosen, and faithful.

Revelation 21:7 He that overcometh shall inherit all things; and I will be his God, and he shall be my son.

CHAPTER 7

PRAYER FOR HEALING
PRAYER FOR HEALING WITH BIBLE VERSE

Today we will be dealing with a prayer for healing and bible verses. God has promised to heal us of all our infirmities and diseases. What we need to do is pray and believe that God is capable of healing us. This is a period when the entire world is going through an awkward situation. Many people are even skeptical of visiting health centers because they feared that people would think the deadly Covid-19 infects them.

As much as the virus has refused to evacuate the planet Earth, we must understand that God is still on the throne, and his eye is still gazed upon the earth to rescue the world from this pandemic. One of the way ways God wants to heal the world is through the prayers of the saints. That is why this prayer for healing and bible verses is very important. In this article, we will be dealing with healing prayers for ourselves, our country, and the world at large.

Healing was one of the most important activities of Christ's missionary on earth. He went from one place to another, healing all manner of diseases and casting out demons. Little wonder the scripture says The Spirit of the Lord GOD is upon Me Because the LORD has anointed Me To preach good tidings to the poor; He has sent Me to heal the brokenhearted, To proclaim liberty to the captives, And the opening of the prison to those who are bound. Just the same way Christ was sent to raise the dead, heal the sick, so also do we have the power to pray for healing, and it will come to pass, for the scripture says, as he is so we are. We will be giving some prayer for healing with bible verses for our use.

PRAYER POINTS

1.   Lord Jesus, I believe that you are the great healer, and you are capable of healing all manner of illnesses. I pray to you today that you will, by your power, heal me from all my sickness in the name of Jesus. I cry to you today concerning this cancer, brain tumor,

diabetics, and all because I believe that your name is stronger, bigger, and more powerful than all of these diseases, and the scripture says at the mention of the name Jesus, every knee must bow. Every tongue shall confess that he is God. I decree in the name of Jesus that the hold of cancer, diabetics, and brain tumor is destroyed.

2.   Deuteronomy 7:15, "And the LORD will take away from thee all sickness, and will put none of the evil diseases of Egypt, which thou knowest, upon thee; but will lay them upon all [them] that hate thee.

3.   Lord Jesus, I stand in the gap for every man and woman who is currently sick, everyone going through pain as a result of one disease or another, the scripture says the effectual prayer of the righteous avail much. I pray that God, by your mercy, you will heal their illnesses in the name of Jesus. The scripture made me understand that God will take away tears from the faces of people; he will replace pain with happiness and tears with laughter. Lord, on your promises, do I stand as I decree that you heal me of my illness in the name of Jesus.

4.   James 5:15, "And the prayer of faith shall save the sick, and the Lord shall raise him up; and if he have committed sins, they shall be forgiven him.

5.   The Bible says, if my people who are called by my name can humble themselves before me, if they can turn away from their sin, I will hear their prayers from heaven, and I will heal their land. Father Lord, the land of the earth is sick, and the entire world is going through a moment of turbulence, Lord we pray that you will have mercy upon the world in the name of Jesus. Lord God, we understand that even in your wrath, you will be merciful, especially when you see the blood that flows on the cross of Calvary. You are a gracious God, and we pray that you will wipe out this pandemic from the surface of the earth in the name of Jesus.

6.   2 chronicle 7:14 My people who are called by My name will humble themselves, and pray and seek My face, and turn from their

wicked ways, then I will hear from heaven, and will forgive their sin and heal their land

7.   Lord Jesus, the scripture admonishes that we pray for the peace of Jerusalem and those that love it shall prosper. Lord Jesus, we decree your healings upon the earth, your peace upon Africa, your peace upon Asia, we decree your peace upon Europe, we decree your peace upon, South America, your peace upon North America, we decree the peace of God upon Australia, in the name of Jesus. We pray that the angel of healing, the angel of good health, will visit the four corners of the earth today in the name of Jesus.

8.   Psalm 122:6 Pray for the peace of Jerusalem: "May they prosper who love you.

9.   The scripture made me understand your plans for me. It says it is the plans of good and not evil to give me an expected end. Lord on this promise I stand, I refuse to be cut off my malaria, I refuse to be hindered by kidney failure, I refuse to be stopped by heart failure. I pray that in the name of Jesus Christ of Nazareth, every form of sickness or disease inside of me is destroyed in the name of Jesus. I decree that the hands of healings of God Almighty should rest upon me right now in the name of Jesus. Everything that needs to be touched in my body, everything that needs to be fixed, I decree that by the mercy of God Almighty, you will begin to fix them in Jesus's Name.

10.   Matthew 10:8, "Heal the sick, cleanse the lepers, raise the dead, cast out devils: freely ye have received, freely give.

URGENT PRAYER FOR HEALING

Today we will be dealing with an urgent prayer for healing. There are times in our lives that what we need to survive at that time is the quick hands of God. During this time, we might not even have much to say in place of prayers because we have been troubled, and that is why we must build ourselves up in the place of prayer and in place of studying the word.

When we are in a critical state, it is often common among people to talk back at God for letting such a catastrophe happen to them, however, what we need at that time is not to blame God, we need to talk to God using his words, remembering him of his promises and all our sacrifices before him. Remember the story of King Hezekiah when the prophet of God brought a message of death to him that he will die. At that critical state being in sickness, King Hezekiah could not do much rather than to talk to God in prayers. He reminded God of all his promises to him and reminded God of all his sacrifices to the things of God. God changed his mind and added to his years.

Similarly, in our lives, there are some moments of our lives that, instead of talking back at God, asking if he was blind or deaf to have allowed evil happens to us, what we need is to talk to God in prayers. We must learn to remind God of his promises for us. In this article, we will be exploring some urgent prayer for healing, which will be backed up with the word of God because we also need the word of God. Meanwhile, the word of God in this context will be some of the promises of God to humankind to grant us good health. Many times, these words wrath wonders; it causes God to change his mind and save us. The Bible makes us understand that God honors his word even more than his name. The scripture says though the heavens and earth will pass, none of his words will go without fulfilling the purpose for which it was sent.

This makes us know that one of the best ways to get God to work is through his words. Let quickly brake you through some of the urgent prayers for healing that you need when in critical situations.

PRAYER POINTS:

1.　　The scripture says that I will not die but live to declare the works of the Lord in the land of the living. I rebuke every form of death in the name of Jesus. I decree by the authority of heaven that I'm healed in the name of Jesus. Lord, for your mercy that endureth forever, I pray that you will heal me in the name of Jesus. I Believe that you are capable of setting me free from this diseases, I know that once you touch me everything about my health will change, Lord Jesus, I need your touch, your divine touch Lord Jesus.

2.　　Heal me, O Lord, and I will be healed; save me, and I will be saved, for you are the one I praise." Jeremiah 17:14

3.　　Father Lord, I know that there is nothing impossible for you to do. I ask that you will prove your supremacy over my health. You said you are the God of all flesh, and there is nothing impossible for you to do. You that spoke to the dry bone, and it gains life again, you that spoke to the dry leaf, and it became alive again, I know that when you hold my hands, everything becomes possible, Lord Jesus, I pray that you will touch me in the name of Jesus.

4.　　So do not fear, for I am with you; do not be dismayed, for I am your God. I will strengthen you and help you; I will uphold you with my righteous right hand." -Isaiah 41:10

5.　　Father in heaven, I come against every power of sickness over my life, every demonic agent that has been assigned to me by the enemy to frustrate my healings, every ancestral power that has been assigned to me to slow down my healing process, I call the fire of God upon you today in the name of Jesus. May the consumable fire of Jehovah be unleashed upon you all in the name of Jesus?

6.　　Father Lord, I break free from every and shackle of sickness. The scripture says that by the anointing, every yoke shall be destroyed. I come against every yoke of sickness and diseases in my life, and I destroy them by the anointing in the name of Jesus. For it has been written that my body is the temple of the living God; hence, nothing evil should have a place in it. I send you packing you power of sickness in my life, and I destroy you in the name of Jesus.

7.   For it has been written, every tree that my father has not planted shall be uprooted, every tree of sickness, every tree of diseases, I decree that you lose your life in the name of Jesus. I announce my liberty from the power of sickness, I declare my free from the pain of disease in the name of Jesus.

8.   The scripture says Christ has bared upon Himself all our infirmities, and he has healed all our diseases, I decree in the name of Jesus that all of my ailments are healed in Jesus. I stand in alignment with the word of God that says he knows the plans he has for me; they are the plan of good and not of evil to give me an expected end. Lord God, untimely death is never an expected end. I know that it is never your plans for my life to be bedridden by a sickness that has refused to go, I pray that by the power in the name of Jesus, such sickness is dead. I regain my freedom from the power of sickness in the name of Jesus.

SHORT PRAYER FOR HEALING AND RECOVERY

Today we will be dealing with short prayer for healing and recovery. There is a clear difference between healing and recovery. Sickness might stop, but it takes the grace of God before a man can get back to his former state before the illness. Sometimes, it will take God to cause a miracle for something like that to happen.

Let's take a look at the life of Job in the scripture. After God allowed the devil to torment Job, thereby killing these children and losing all his wealth in a jiffy, after he got his healing, Job would have probably ended up dying of depression due to his loss. Someone who used to be very prosperous, he can travel to any city of his choice, he is so wealthy that he could afford anything. Also, he was blessed with beautiful children. In essence, Job was just a perfect replicate of Prosperous. Being inflicted with terrible sickness is not as catastrophic as losing all his possession within the twinkle of an eye, Job was devastated, his healing process would not have completed if he had not recovered all that was lost.

We can say recovery is the final stage of healing; some healings will never come unless there is a recovery of that which has been lost. Take, for instance, someone who has been barren for years only for the person to have a child and lose the child to the cold hands of death again. Such an individual might not be bedridden, but he or she will carry the pain and burden with them everywhere they go, and the wound will not heal until there is a restoration. There are so many people today that all they need is a restoration of lost blessings, the years that locust and cankerworm have stolen from them to be recovered, that is just the healing that they need. The bible recorded that when the Lord restored the captivity of Zion, they were like those that dream their mouth was filled with Thanksgiving.

God wants to restore the years that locust and cankerworm have stolen away from people, he wants to heal people from their sickness and infirmities completely, there will recovery of stolen glory, wasted years will be restored, and the power will recover the glory that has been stolen away in the name of Jesus. That is why you must share the following prayer points with your family and loved ones. We all need the healing of God Almighty, and many to recover from the pain and wound caused by sickness.

PRAYER POINTS

1.   Father in heaven, I appreciate you for facilitating my healing process. I thank you for saving the clutch of death, and I magnify you for protecting from the deadly pit of hard drugs. I magnify you because you have always proven yourself to be God over my life. I thank you because you are faithful despite all my unfaithfulness. Your faithfulness is a thing of your power and strength, even when I do not merit your mercy, but you still moved by compassion to save me.

2.   Lord, I appreciate your majesty, let your name be exalted in the name of Jesus.

3.   Father in heaven, I pray for the recovery of the stolen years when I was in the bondage of sin and iniquity, Lord Jesus, I pray that by your mercy, you will restore me all the lost blessings by your holy name. Father Lord, I pray for a total recovery from sickness. I pray for a speedy recovery from diseases, let it be made manifest in the name of Jesus.

4.   Lord Jesus, you are the God of restoration, you restored the blessings of Abraham and made it manifest in the lives of the Israelites. Father Lord, in the same vein, I pray for a recovery of all the lost years, restoration of the stolen glory. I pray that you restore them to me in the name of Jesus. The scripture says when the Lord restores the captive of Zion, they were like those that dream. Lord Jesus, I pray that you will restore my possession in double folds in the name of Jesus.

5.   Everything that has been lost in my life, every glory that has been stolen away through sin, Lord, I pray for a total recovery of all in the name of Jesus.

6.   Father Lord, I use this as a point of contact to every man and woman who are currently on the sickbed, I pray for a total recovery, I pray that by your power you will facilitate their healing process, I

decree that the angel of healing will visit them on their sickbed today. I decree a speedy recovery upon their lives in the name of Jesus.

7.   Father Lord, we pray for the world at large, as we are journeying through this critical time, I pray that God will heal the world in the name of Jesus. For every man and woman that is currently battling for their lives due to the novel Covid-19, I pray that they are healed in the name of Jesus. Lord Jesus, as life has been halted for several weeks due to the emergence of this deadly pandemic, I pray that you will make a recovery for every man in the name of Jesus.

8.   Lord God, I pray that by your power you will have mercy upon the earth, you will cause your angels in charge of the earth to drive away this pandemic out of the land in the name of Jesus. The scripture says, and Jesus was moved with compassion, Lord, we pray that you will be moved with compassion today and will send this pandemic away from the surface of the earth in the name of Jesus.

PRAYER FOR HEALING AND PREVENTION OF CORONAVIRUS

Exodus 15:26 "And said, If thou wilt diligently hearken to the voice of the LORD thy God, and wilt do that which is right in his sight, and wilt give ear to his commandments, and keep all his statutes, I will put none of these diseases upon thee, which I have brought upon the Egyptians: for I am the LORD that healeth thee."

In a time like this, there is a need for us all to put sentiments and all our differences aside and pray for a better world, a world free the snare of Corona virus. Our land has been badly affected by the virus, it is important that we say a prayer for healing and prevention of Coronavirus. God is so much concerned about our wellbeing; His plans is not for the entire world to wipe out by a deadly and incurable epidemic. This is clearly the work of the devil because God never does anything evil. While scientists all over the globe are working round the clock in a bid to get a cure for this disease it is important that we also at the corridor of spirituality do all we can to salvage the situation. Just before we go into prayers, for the benefit of those have little or no knowledge about the virus, it is impeccable that we write about it for you to know how deadly it is so that you will know how to pray well.

Coronavirus outbreak is the most recent and deadliest epidemic that has attacked the world, the worst the world has ever seen. It was first discovered in Wuhan, a city in the Republic of China back in December 2019. At first, when the virus started in China, the rest of the world turned blind eyes and deaf ears to it, not until it was transported into Europe, Africa, America and the rest.

Within three months, more than 100 countries have been greatly affected by the virus and more than 4000 people have been declared dead. Our fear increases in Africa when the virus flourishes abundantly in the western world. And now, sport activities all over the globe have been put to a stop due to the deadly virus. Also, many trade centers across the globe have stopped business because of the outbreak.

The coronavirus disease also known as COVID-19 is characterized by mild symptoms. People who are infected by this disease may experience the following:

Runny nose

Sore Throat

Cough

Fever

Difficulty Breathing (Severe Cases)

The World Health Organization (WHO) while still struggling to find a cure to the virus gave some tips on how to prevent ourselves from contracting the virus.

Read steps To Prevention of Corona Virus below

Regularly and thoroughly wash your hands with soap and water, and use alcohol-based hand sanitizer.

Maintain at least 1 & half meters (5 feet) distance between yourself and anyone who is coughing or sneezing.

Persons with persistent cough or sneezing should stay home or keep a social distance, but not mix in the crowd.

Make sure you and people around you, follow good respiratory hygiene, meaning cover your mouth and nose with a tissue or into your sleeve at the bent elbow or tissue when you cough or sneeze. Then dispose of the used tissue immediately.

Stay home if you feel unwell with symptoms like fever, cough, and difficulty in breathing. Please call Medical emergency toll free number in your country which is available day and night, for guidance. Do not engage in self-medication

After we have equipped ourselves with enough information about the virus, it is important to know that God can heal the land, he can take away the effect of COVID-19 and restore peace back to the world.

What Do We Pray For?

As we call on God in prayers, we should focus on the following areas and expect speedy answers from the Lord.

For The Spread to Stop

The virus is spreading like a wildfire in the Harmattan and if it should persist, no corner of the world would be saved. There is a need to pray that God should stop the virus from spreading further. Since the knowledge of medical practitioners has proved abortive, all measures to prevent the spread have proved abortive, is it not about time that we turn back to God in prayers? We will pray for the spread of the virus to stop, the virus should lose its power. The rate at which the virus spread is alarming, any contact with an infected person the virus will be transmitted. Little wonder, it is becoming almost uncontrollable in Europe especially in the world of Football and business empires. God is a supreme being, He has power over everything, and our prayer of healing and prevention of Coronavirus would cause God to put a stop to it.

For God to Give Our Doctors Solution

Also, we will be praying that God should give the doctors and scientists the knowledge and wisdom to come up with a cure. Up until now, there has not been a shred of concrete evidence to what could have been the cause of the virus, it just sprang up from the blue. The scripture made us understand that every good idea comes from God, we will be praying that God should give them the wisdom to come up with a cure.

For The Death Toll to Stop

The death toll has increased from one to over 4000 within three months and if care is not taken, it will increase more than that. Our prayer will also focus on stopping the death toll from increasing any further. A virus that started in one city has extended to over 100 countries, the death toll must stop, and before the virus successfully kills us all and there will be nobody to pray, won't you advise that we start praying now that we are still alive?

For speedy recovery of all infected patients worldwide

No fewer than 144,078 people have been infected with the virus about 70,920 have recovered and the rest are still battling with the virus. While praying, we should pray for those that have been affected by the virus that God Himself should heal them. The Bible made us understand that God is a powerful healer, He can stretch forth His hands and heal millions of people in a second. Enough of people dying from the virus, we will be praying God should heal everyone that has been affected by the virus.

For divine protection for the uninfected

While saying a prayer for healing and prevention of coronavirus, we must also pray that God protects those that are not infected yet from contracting the virus. The only way we are working as reinforcement against the virus is because we have not been affected by it yet. We must pray that while God is stopping the virus from spreading further and healing those that has been affected, His hands of protection should be upon those that are not affected yet.

The scripture says for we bear the mark of Christ let no man trouble us. We must pray that the hands of God be upon each and every one of us and protect us from the virus.

PRAYER POINTS

1.   Father Lord, we come against every power of Coronavirus in the name of Jesus

2.   We pray that the virus will lose its potency in the name of Jesus

3.   We destroy every stronghold of Coronavirus in the world in the name of Jesus.

4.   Lord, we ask that by your power, you will stop the spread of the virus in the name of Jesus.

5.   Lord by your mercy, we ask that you will give the medical team all around the world the wisdom to come up with a cure in the name of Jesus.

6.   Father in heaven, we pray that by your power, you will expose the cause of this deadly epidemic in the name of Jesus.

7.   The scripture says every good idea comes from you Lord, we ask that you will give them the idea to get a cure in the name of Jesus.

8.   Father Lord, we pray that you will stop the death toll of the virus in the name of Jesus.

9.   Father in Heaven, we ask that by your power, you will curb its spread from moving further in the name of Jesus.

10.   Every power of Coronavirus is destroyed in the name of Jesus

11.   We careless if it is a virus or it was orchestrated by the devil, Jehovah, we ask that you will heal the world in the name of Jesus.

12.   For it has been written that Christ has taken upon himself all our infirmities and He has healed all our diseases. We speak our healings to being in the name of Jesus.

13.   We pray for every man and woman all around the globe that has been struck with the wipe of the virus, we pray that you will heal them in the name of Jesus.

14.   The Bible says our body is the temple of God, hence, something of immorality would find a place in us. We come against the virus in their body in the name of Jesus.

15. For it has been written, strangers shall be afraid, and shall run out of their hiding places? We command Coronavirus to run out of the body of the affected people in the name of Jesus.

16. We decree by the authority of Heaven that the end has come for Coronavirus in the world in the name of Jesus.

17. Every demon of Coronavirus is destroyed by fire in the name of Jesus.

18. We decree that in the name of Jesus, the right of God that gives liberation should rest upon every man and woman affected by the deadly syndrome in the name of Jesus

19. For it has been written, we carry the mark of Christ, let no one trouble us. We decree out freedom from Coronavirus in the name of Jesus.

20. Lord Jesus, we ask that you will look down upon the earth from heaven and you will heal our land in the name of Jesus.

21. The Bible says by His stripe we are healed, we decree our healings in the name of Jesus.

22. We speak our liberation into reality in the name of Jesus.

23. Father, we ask that you will go to the source of Coronavirus and you will destroy its power from the root in the name of Jesus.

24. Lord God, we decree that there shall be no more death caused by Coronavirus in the name of Jesus.

25. We decree that the virus will no longer have power over the life of people in the name of Jesus.

26. For it has been written that you know the thoughts that you have for us, they are the thoughts of good and not of evil to give us an expected end. We decree that Coronavirus will not have power over us anymore in the name of Jesus.

27. It has been written, that if any man will speak, let them speak like an oracle of God, we join our Faiths and we decree uniformly that the virus will lose its potency in the name of Jesus.

28. We decree the healings of God Almighty upon our land in the name of Jesus.

29. We decree that the end has come for it in the name of Jesus.

30. Father by the authority of heaven, you will enlighten the understanding of medical practitioners that will help them get cure in the name of Jesus.

31. Lastly, we pray Lord, the book of 2 Chronicles 7:14 says If my people who are called by my name humble themselves, and pray and seek my face and turn from their wicked ways, then I will hear from heaven and will forgive their sin and heal their land. We are your people redeemed by your blood, we are called by your name Lord, and we ask that you will forgive our sins and iniquities in the world. Our land is in turmoil, the pain, fear, and death caused by the deadly coronavirus has done more than enough harm to your people Lord, we ask that you will hear our prayers from Holy Heaven and with the strength of your right hand you will liberate us from the disease, we ask that you will give healings to those affected and you will protect hundreds of billions that are not infected yet, in the name of Jesus. Amen.

100 POWERFUL PRAYERS FOR HEALING

Psalms 103:3:

Who forgiveth all thine iniquities; who healeth all thy diseases

We serve a God who is ultimately interested in our well-being, which includes your healing. God loves us very much and He will always he will always heal us when we ask Him in prayers. Today we are going to be engaging in 100 powerful prayer for healing. This prayers are powerful because they are word based and scripturally inspired. All through the earthly ministry of Jesus, He spent a lot of time healing the sick, raising the dead and casting out devils, Acts 10:38. Jesus paid the ultimate price for our healing; he took upon Himself all our sicknesses and diseases and nailed them to the cross. Isaiah 53:4, Matthew 8:17. Jesus paid the price for our healing, therefore sickness is not permitted to be in your body. You are not permitted to be a victim of sicknesses and diseases. Today as we engage this powerful prayer for healing, every sickness in your life shall disappear forever in Jesus name.

The Power of Faith for Our Healing

For us to be healed, we must understand that God operates in the realms of faith that is we must believe in His healing virtues for us to be healed. Until our faith is in place, Gods healing power may not work effectively in your life. Everyone God healed in the bible exercised their faith in the healing power of God. Jesus always told them," your faith has made you whole", Luke 17:19, Mark 5:34, Luke 8:48. Our Faith is the magnetic force that attracts the power of God in our direction.

The Prayer of Faith for Healing

To enjoy God's healing power, we must learn to pray the prayer of faith. The prayer of faith is an authoritative prayer. In this prayer, you command the sicknesses in your body to come out in Jesus name. Every sickness is an operation of the devil, therefore when you are praying a prayer of faith to heal the sick, you must command that sickness in the name of Jesus. Call the sickness by name and rebuke it in Jesus name. Any sickness you pamper and tolerate can never leave your body, whatever you tolerate, you cannot terminate, stop pampering sicknesses in your body, reject them and command them to come out of your body in the name of Jesus. When it comes to your healing, be serious and be violent about it. When the devil sees your faith, he will depart from your life instantly. As you engage in this powerful prayer for healing, engage it with violent faith and resist the spirit of infirmity from your life in Jesus name. I see God perfecting your healing in Jesus name.

PRAYER POINTS

1. Every power, planning to kill, steal and destroy my body, release me by fire, in the name of Jesus.
2. Every spirit of tiredness, release me, in the name of Jesus.
3. Every spirit of hypertension, come out of my body with all your roots, in the name of Jesus.
4. Every bondage of diabetic spirits, break by fire, in Jesus' name.
5. Any evil power, running through my body, loose your hold, in the name of Jesus.
6. Every evil power, hooking on to my brain, release me, in Jesus' name.
7. Every spirit with tentacles moving about in my body, come out by fire, in the name of Jesus.
8. Every spirit of migraine and headache, come out by fire, in the name of Jesus.
9. Every dark spirit, working against the kingdom of God in my life, come out by fire, in the name of Jesus.
10. Every power, working on my eyes and reducing my vision, be eliminated completely, in the name of Jesus.
11. Every demon of insulin deficiency, depart from me by fire, in Jesus' name.
12. Every spirit of hypertension, release my liver, in Jesus' name.

13. Every evil power, planning to amputate my leg, I bury you alive, in the name of Jesus.

14. Every spirit of hypertension, release my bladder, in Jesus' name.

15. Every spirit of excessive urination, release me, in Jesus' name.

16. Every spirit of hypertension, release my skin and ears, in the name of Jesus.

17. Every spirit of itching, depart from me, in the name of Jesus.

18. Every spirit of hypertension, release my lungs, in Jesus' name.

19. Every spirit of hypertension, release my reproductive areas, in the name of Jesus.

20. I release myself from every spirit of drowsiness, tiredness and impaired vision; I bind you and cast you out, in Jesus' name.

21. Every spirit of infirmity, generating tiredness, loose your hold, in the name of Jesus.

22. Every spirit of excessive thirst and hunger, I bind you and cast you out, in the name of Jesus.

23. I bind every spirit of weight loss, in the name of Jesus.

24. I bind every spirit of rashes, in the name of Jesus.

25. I bind every spirit of slow healing of cuts and bruises, in the name of Jesus.

26. I bind every spirit of bed-wetting, in the name of Jesus.

27. I bind every spirit of enlargement of the liver, in Jesus' name.

28. I bind every spirit of kidney disease, in the name of Jesus.

29. I bind every spirit of blockage, in the name of Jesus.

30. I bind every spirit of hardening of the arteries, in Jesus' name.

31. I bind every spirit of confusion, in the name of Jesus.

32. I bind every spirit of convulsion, in the name of Jesus.

33. I bind every spirit of loss of consciousness, in the name of Jesus.

34. You spirit of fear of death, depart from my life, in Jesus' name.

35. You evil doorkeeper of insulin, loose your hold, in Jesus' name.

36. Every power, destroying insulin in my body, I bind you and cast you out, in the name of Jesus.

37. Every power, hindering the co-ordination between my brain and my mouth, I bind you and cast you out, in the name of Jesus.

38. Every spirit of torment, release me, in the name of Jesus.

39. Every power, attacking my blood sugar, loose your hold, in the name of Jesus.

40. I break every curse of eating and drinking blood from ten generations backward on both sides of my family line, in the name of Jesus.

41. Every door, opened to diabetic spirits, close by the blood of Jesus.

42. Every inherited blood disease, loose your hold, in Jesus' name.

43. All bloodline curses, break, in the name of Jesus.

44. Every curse of breaking my skin unrighteous, break, in the name of Jesus.

45. I bind and cast out every demon in my pancreas, in Jesus' name.

46. Any power, affecting my vision, I bind you, in Jesus' name.

47. Every satanic arrow in my blood vessel, come out by fire, in the name of Jesus.

48. Every demon of stroke, come out of my life with all your roots, in the name of Jesus.

49. Every spirit of confusion, loose your hold over my life, in the name of Jesus.

50. Anything inhibiting my ability to read and meditate on the word of God, be uprooted, in the name of Jesus.

51. I bind and cast out every spirit of (convulsion – abdominal problems – fear – guilt – hopelessness – impotence – palsy – animal – candor – swelling – stress – worry – anxiety – deafness – high blood pressure -nerve destruction – kidney destruction), in Jesus' name.

52. I bind and cast out, familiar spirits travelling through family bloodlines to afflict me with hypertension and other sickness, in Jesus' name.

53. Every evil plantation in my life: Come out with all your roots in the name of Jesus! (Lay your hands on your stomach and keep repeating the emphasized area.)

54. I cough and vomit any food eaten from the table of the devil, in the name of Jesus. (Cough and vomit them in faith. Prime the expulsion.)

55. All negative materials, circulating in my blood stream, be evacuated, in the name of Jesus.

56. I drink the blood of Jesus. (Physically swallow and drink it in faith. Keep doing this for some time.)

57. (Lay one hand on your head and the other on your stomach or navel and begin to pray like this): Holy Ghost Fire, burn from the top of my head to the sole of my feet. (Begin to mention every organ of your body; your kidney liver, intestines, etc. You must not rush at this level, because the fire will actually come, and you may start feeling the heat).

58. Blood of Jesus, be transfused into my blood vessels; in the name of Jesus.

59. Every agent of disease in my blood and body organs, die, in the name of Jesus.

60. My blood, reject every evil foreign entity, in Jesus' name.

61. Holy Spirit, speak deliverance and healing into my life, in the name of Jesus.

62. Blood of Jesus, speak disappearance unto every infirmity in my life.

63. I hold the blood of Jesus against you spirit of . . . (mention what is troubling you). You have to flee.

64. O Lord, let your healing hand be stretched out upon my life now.

65. O Lord, let your miracle hand be stretched out upon my life now.

66. O Lord, let your deliverance hand be stretched out upon my life now.

67. I annul every engagement with the spirit of death, in Jesus' name.

68. I rebuke every refuge of sickness, in the name of Jesus.

69. I destroy the grip and operation of sickness upon my life, in the name of Jesus.

70. Every knee of infirmity in my life, bow, in Jesus' name.

71. O Lord, let my negativity be converted to positivity.

72. I command death upon any sickness in any area of my life, in the name of Jesus.

73. I shall see my sickness no more, in the name of Jesus.

74. Father Lord, let the whirlwind of God scatter every vessel of infirmity fashioned against my life, in the name of Jesus.

75. Every spirit, hindering my perfect healing, fall down and die now, in the name of Jesus.

76. Father Lord, let all death contractors begin to kill themselves, in the name of Jesus.

77. Father Lord, let every germ of infirmity in my body die, in the name of Jesus.

78. Father Lord, let every agent of sickness working against my health disappear, in the name of Jesus.

79. Every fountain of discomfort in my life, dry up now, in the name of Jesus.

80. Every dead organ in my body, receive life now, in the name of Jesus.

81. Father Lord, let my blood be transfused with the blood of Jesus to effect my perfect health, in the name of Jesus.

82. Every internal disorder, receive order, in the name of Jesus.

83. Every infirmity, come out with all your roots, in the name of Jesus.

84. I withdraw every conscious and unconscious cooperation with sickness, in the name of Jesus.

85. O Lord, let the whirlwind of God blow every wind of infirmity away.

86. I release my body from every curse of infirmity, in the name of Jesus.

87. O Lord, let the blood of Jesus flush out every evil deposit from my blood.

88. I recover, every organ of my body from every evil altar, in Jesus' name.

89. I withdraw body from the manipulation of every caldron of darkness, in the name of Jesus.

90. Holy Ghost fire, destroy every stubborn agent of disease in my body, in the name of Jesus.

91. I arrest every demon of terminal disease, in Jesus' name.

92. I cancel every clinical prophecy concerning my life, in the name of Jesus.

93. Holy Ghost fire, boil every infirmity out of my system, in the name of Jesus.

94. I cancel every witchcraft verdict on my life, in Jesus' name.

95. O earth, vomit anything that has been buried inside you against my health, in the name of Jesus

96. Every tree that infirmity has planted in my blood, be uprooted by fire, in the name of Jesus.

97. Every witchcraft arrow, depart from my _ _ _ (spinal cord – spleen – navel – heart – throat – eyes – nose – head), in the name of Jesus.

98. I bind every evil presence in my (reproductive, digestive, respiratory, nervous, skeletal, muscular, circulatory, endocrine, excretory) system, in the name of Jesus.

99. I break the backbone and destroy the root of every spirit speaking against me, in the name of Jesus.

100. Begin to thank God for your healing.

PRAYER FOR HEALING STRANGE SICKNESSES

Job 5:12 12 He disappointeth the devices of the crafty, so that their hands cannot perform their enterprise.

Not all sicknesses are from natural causes, there are many illnesses that are demonically engineered. Acts 10:38, tells us that Jesus Christ was busy healing all that were oppressed of the devil that is to tell us that the devil is behind sicknesses and diseases. Today we are going to be engaging in prayer for healing strange sicknesses. In this healing prayer, we are going to be focusing on strange sicknesses, sicknesses that defile medical science. Sicknesses that the doctors cannot diagnose even after running several tests in their medical labs.

Such kind of sicknesses are called strange sicknesses, they are caused by spiritual poison, planted by demonic agents and witchcraft forces. When a person is suffering from a strange sickness, no medical expertise can save such a person, it doesn't matter how experienced that doctor is in his or her field. This is because, the sickness is caused by a spiritual force and only a spiritual force can cure it. We fight spiritual with spiritual. There are many people today, suffering from unidentified illnesses, even the doctors cannot explain it medically, and these classes of sicknesses must be addressed with prayers.

Prayers is the force that brings down the supernatural into the affairs of the natural, when we pray in the name of Jesus, we release the power of God in us to destroy every plantings of the devil in our lives. This prayer for healing strange sicknesses will flush out every spiritual poison of the devil in the life of every sick person as it is prayed in faith. Nothing can be hidden from God. As you call forth the power of God through these prayer for healing, the anointing of the Holy Spirit will move through your body, destroying all the satanic poisons and evil plantings in your body in Jesus name. You can pray this prayer for yourself, for spiritual cleansing and you can also pray this prayer over a loved one and watch God cleanse that person in Jesus name. I am waiting for your testimonies.

PRAYER POINTS

1. My body, reject every poisonous arrow, in Jesus' name.

2. Every spiritual poison that has entered into my system be neutralized by the blood of Jesus.

3. Holy Ghost fire, purge away every handwriting of wickedness, in the name of Jesus.

4. Fire of God, burn to ashes every power programmed into my life to poison me, in the name of Jesus.

5. Every evil plantation in my life come out with all your roots, in the name of Jesus! (Lay your hands on your stomach and keep repeating the emphasized area.)

6. Evil strangers in my body, come out of your hiding places, in the name of Jesus.

7. I disconnect any conscious or unconscious link with demonic caterers, in the name of Jesus.

8. All avenues of eating or drinking spiritual poisons, be closed, in the name of Jesus.

9. I cough and vomit any food eaten from the table of the devil, in the name of Jesus. (Cough and vomit it by faith. Prime the expulsion)

10. All negative materials, circulating in my blood stream, be evacuated, in the name of Jesus.

11. I drink the blood of Jesus. (Physically swallow it by faith. Do this for some time.)

12. All evil spiritual feeders, warring against me, drink your own blood and eat your own flesh, in the name of Jesus.

13. All demonic food utensils, fashioned against me, be destroyed in the name of Jesus.

14. Holy Ghost fire, circulate all over my body.

15. All physical poisons, inside my system, be neutralized, in the name of Jesus.

16. All evil assignments, fashioned against me through the mouth gate, be nullified, in the name of Jesus.

17. All spiritual problems, attached to any hour of the night, be cancelled, in the name of Jesus. (Pick the period from midnight to 6:00 a.m. GMT)

18. Bread of heaven, fill me till I want no more.

19. All catering equipment's of evil caterers, attached to me, be destroyed, in the name of Jesus.

20. My digestive system, reject every evil command, in the name of Jesus.

Father, thank you for answering my prayers in Jesus name.

20 POWERFUL PRAYER FOR HEALING A FRIEND

Jeremiah 30:17: 17 For I will restore health unto thee, and I will heal thee of thy wounds, saith the Lord; because they called thee an Outcast, saying, this is Zion, whom no man seeketh after.

Today we shall be engaging 20 powerful prayer for healing for a friend. As a child of God, the greatest gift you can give a dear friend is the gift of prayer. Sicknesses and diseases are not the will of God for His children. Therefore we as Christians should always reject sicknesses and pray for the sick around us. Do you have a friend that is suffering from any sickness? Today we are going to be engaging on a prayer for healing for them. While Jesus Christ was on earth, He went about doing good and healing all that where oppressed of the devil, Acts 10:38. This people where oppressed by sicknesses, this implies that sicknesses are oppressions of the devil. For us to overcome sicknesses, we must command it to disappear in the name of Jesus.

I want you to know that, as a child of God, God has given us power over all forms of sickness and disease, and He said in His name we shall heal the sick, Acts 16:18-20. He has given us authority over sicknesses of all kinds. Therefore you are going to be rebuking that sickness that has been tormenting your friend today in the name of Jesus. Every sickness has a name and everything name bows down to the name of Jesus Christ. So as you lay your hand on that your friend today, command that sickness by name to disappear from that body in Jesus name. Pray this prayer with faith, because it's a prayer of faith that will heal the sick, James 5:15. As you pray over your sick friend today, as you use this powerful prayer for healing for a friend today, I see your friend being healed immediately in Jesus name. Looking forward for your testimony.

PRAYER POINTS

1). Father, I thank you for I know you always hear me.

2). Take all the glory Father, for you always answer prayers

3). Father, let your mercy begin to speak over this my friend (mention his name and ask him to also join you in praying for mercy).

4). Father, in the name of Jesus, I command this sickness (mention name) to disappear from this body in Jesus name

5). Father, let your healing power begin to move round this body in Jesus name

6). Father, let your healing power flow all through his/her blood now in the name of Jesus

7). I curse this sicknesses and diseases from the roots today in Jesus name

8). This body has been bought by Christ, therefore, I command this strange sickness to be removed from this body in Jesus name.

9). I declare that these sickness shall not be unto death in Jesus name

10). I declare that this my friend (mention name) shall be delivered from this sickness today in Jesus name.

11). You foul spirit of infirmity, I command you to let go of this person now!!! In Jesus name

12). You foul spirit of terminal disease, be flushed out of this body completely in Jesus name.

13). I command healing in your body now in the name of Jesus Christ

14). I command healing in your soul now in the name of Jesus Christ

15). I command healing in your blood now in the name of Jesus Christ

16). I command healing in your bones and joints now in the name of Jesus Christ

17). I declare your total freedom from sicknesses and diseases in Jesus name

18). I declare that in the next seven days, you shall be absolutely healed in Jesus name

19). Father I thank you for the healing of this my friend (mention name) Jesus name

20). Father, I thank you for answering my prayers in Jesus name.

MIRACLE PRAYER FOR HEALING AND RECOVERY

Acts 10:38:38 How God anointed Jesus of Nazareth with the Holy Ghost and with power: who went about doing good, and healing all that were oppressed of the devil; for God was with him.

Healing is one of God's greatest desires for His children. It is not the will of God that we live a sickness ridden life. Exodus 23:25, tells us that God will take away sickness from all that serve Him, that is He will take sickness away from all His children. Jesus spent most of His ministry healing the sick, in fact He was either preaching or healing all manner of sicknesses. Jesus never cared what name or type of sicknesses they were, the bible said he healed them all. Today we are going to be engaging miracle prayer for healing and recovery. This prayer for healing will place you above sicknesses and diseases in Jesus name.

We serve a God of miracles, Hebrews 13:8, tells us that Jesus Christ is the same yesterday, today and forever. He has not changed, if he healed yesterday, he will heal today and forever. However, for one to receive his or her healing, we must have faith. God will not work in a faithless environment. God will not force healing on you. You must believe in his healing power in the name of His son Jesus .Jesus kept telling the people He healed, 'your faith has made you whole ', ' be it unto you according to your faith'. This is because for us to receive our healing, we must pray for the prayer for healing to work in our lives, we must believe in the healing power of God through Christ. This miracle prayer for healing and recovery are prayers you can pray for yourself and also for someone who needs healing, pastors can pray it for their individual members who are sick or they can pray it generally over the church. Remember that only God heals, doctors may treat but only God heals, you and I are not the healers or miracle workers, only God heals and today as you engage this Prayer for healing, you shall see the healing power of God at work in your life in Jesus name.

PRAYER POINTS

1). Father, I thank you for you are the healer of all kinds of sicknesses and diseases in Jesus name

2). Father, by the blood of Jesus Christ, wash clean sins of anyone that may hinder your healing power from reaching them in Jesus name.

3). Father, let your healing power touch anyone that is sick in the body today in Jesus name

4). Father, let every blood disease be flushed out by the blood of Jesus in Jesus name.

5). Father, let everyone, that has been appointed for death by sicknesses receive their total deliverance now in Jesus name.

6). Father, I don't care the kind of type of sicknesses that your children are plagued with by the devil, heal them all in Jesus name.

7). I command every pains in the body to be healed in Jesus name

8). I command every headaches to be healed in Jesus name

9). I command every form of fever to be gone in the name of Jesus

10). I command diabetes to be destroyed in Jesus name

11). I command sickle cell anemia to be turned to AA now!!! In Jesus name

12). I command malaria to be healed now in Jesus name

13). I command every form of weakness in the body to be gone Now in Jesus name

14). I command internal heat to disappear now in Jesus name

15). I command all forms and kinds of STDs to disappear now!!! In Jesus name

16). I command blind eyes to be open now in Jesus name

17). I command every terminal disease to be terminated in Jesus name

18). I command every mental illness to be healed now in Jesus name

19). I command every other form of sicknesses and diseases holding your children bound is destroyed in Jesus name.

20). Father, I thank you for your healing power at work already in Jesus name.

20 POWERFUL PRAYERS FOR HEALING CANCER

Matthew 4:23-24:23 And Jesus went about all Galilee, teaching in their synagogues, and preaching the gospel of the kingdom, and healing all manner of sickness and all manner of disease among the people. 24 And his fame went throughout all Syria: and they brought unto him all sick people that were taken with divers diseases and torments, and those which were possessed with devils, and those which were lunatic, and those that had the palsy; and he healed them.

While Jesus Christ was on earth, He healed all manner of sicknesses and diseases, Jesus never cared about name or the serious nature of the sicknesses, and He just healed them all. Today I have compiled 20 powerful prayer to heal cancer. Cancer is a name, and the name of Jesus is higher than it. Do not be afraid of cancer, do not be afraid of the stage your cancer may have gotten to, just take a step of faith today, and pray this prayer for healing with every strength you have. Cancer has killed countless people all round the world, but the power of God will subdue that satanic plague of cancer fighting Gods children in Jesus name.

Are you suffering from cancer, or do you know anyone that is? This is the time to arise and rebuke that satanic affliction. What kills people faster than sickness is the fear of it. Do not let fear overcome you, it doesn't matter what the doctors are saying concerning the cancer, just be strong and believe I the report of the Lord. Christ has taken away all our sicknesses, he has paid the ultimate price for our freedom from sickness and disease. You must hold on the Word of God and command the spirit of cancer to be gone from your body now in Jesus name. No matter where the cancer is located in your body, begin to curse it and command it to disappear in Jesus name. The name of Jesus is superior to cancer, therefore refuse to lose faith, you shall not die but live, and that cancer in your body or the body of your loved ones will be destroyed forever in Jesus name.

PRAYER POINTS

1). Father, I thank you for giving us the name of Jesus to heal every form of sickness and diseases

2). Father, I thank you for your salvation in my life, qualifying me to be free from sicknesses and diseases in Jesus name

3). Father, I thank you for through Christ all my sicknesses have been erased forever in Jesus name.

4). Father, as I am a new creation, I declare that cancer has no power over my life in Jesus name.

5). You Bladder Cancer, I command you in the name of Jesus, be gone from my body (or this body) now!!! In Jesus name

6). You Breast Cancer, I command you in the name of Jesus Christ be gone from this body in Jesus name

7). You Colon and Rectal Cancer, I command you in the name of Jesus Christ be gone from this body in Jesus name

8). You Endometrial Cancer, I command you in the name of Jesus Christ be gone from this body in Jesus name

9). You Kidney Cancer, I command you in the name of Jesus Christ be gone from this body in Jesus name

10). You Leukemia, I command you in the name of Jesus Christ be gone from this body in Jesus name

11). You Liver Cancer, I command you in the name of Jesus Christ be gone from this body in Jesus name

12). You Lung Cancer, I command you in the name of Jesus Christ be gone from this body in Jesus name

13). You Melanoma Cancer, I command you in the name of Jesus Christ be gone from this body in Jesus name

14). You Non-Hodgkin Lymphoma Cancer, I command you in the name of Jesus Christ be gone from this body in Jesus name

15). You Pancreatic Cancer, I command you in the name of Jesus Christ be gone from this body in Jesus name

16). You Prostate Cancer, I command you in the name of Jesus Christ be gone from this body in Jesus name

17). You Thyroid Cancer, I command you in the name of Jesus Christ be gone from this body in Jesus name

18). Father, I thank you for I am free from cancer in the name of Jesus Christ.

19). Father, I thank you for your total deliverance in the name of Jesus Christ

20). Thank you Lord for answering my Prayers in Jesus name.

20 DAILY EFFECTIVE PRAYER FOR HEALING EYES

This 20 daily effective prayer for healing eyes will restore your partial blindness when you pray them in faith. Our God is called Jehovah raphe the God that healeth. Are you struggling with the spirit of blindness, are you afraid of losing your total sight? Fear not and be strong. The God who me you serve is a God that answers prayers.

Pray this prayer points with great faith, believing that you're God will intervene. Remember the story of blind bartemaus in the bible, he cried for mercy believing that Jesus will heal him and he got his sight. As you cry for mercy praying this daily effective prayer for healing eyes The God of heaven will intervene and your sights shall be restored instantly. Receive your miracle today in Jesus name Amen.

20 Daily Effective Prayer for Healing Eyes

1). Oh Lord, let your healing light shine on my eyes henceforth and cause my sight to become clearer in Jesus name.

2). Oh Lord, you restored the sights of blind bartemaus and the two blind men, my Father restore my sight this day in Jesus name.

3). Have mercy on me oh Lord! Grant it today that my eyes shine brightly. Remove any form of scales covering my eyes in Jesus name.

4). Oh Lord, Just as you commanded light to come out of darkness, I command every darkness covering my eyes to disappear in Jesus name.

5). Oh God of mercy, don't let me grope in the dark all the days of my life. Heal my eyes in Jesus name.

6). I decree that my night has been changed into morning and the darkness that cover my sight is destroyed in Jesus name.

7). Jesus, thou son of David and the Son of the Living God, have mercy on me and heal my sight instantly today in Jesus name.

8). Oh Lord, I know that you can do everything. Touch my eyes and heal it miraculously in Jesus name.

9). Oh Lord, I reject this blindness, I declare that I shall see the goodness of the lord in the land of the living in Jesus name.

10). Oh Lord, do not judge me by the measure of my faith over my eye problem. Let the rain of mercy fall on me today in Jesus name.

11). Oh Lord, I have absolute faith in you. Heal my eyes in Jesus name.

12). Oh Lord, you are the creator of all things, heal me lord and restore my sights permanently in Jesus name.

13). Oh Lord, intervene on my failing eye sight today in Jesus name.

14). Oh Lord, open my physical eyes so that I will see wonderful things you have created clearly once again in Jesus name.

15). Oh Lord, unto you I lift up my eyes. Touch it and heal me today in Jesus name.

16). Oh Lord, you are the God that calleth those things that be not as though they were, recreate my eyes and cause it to see clearly in Jesus name

17). Oh Lord, I command this darkness that is gradually overtaking my body to disappear and let light come in Jesus name.

18). I receive my sight today to the glory of God and all that see me shall join me to give God thanks in Jesus name.

19). Oh Lord, let my eyes work perfectly with other parts of my body in Jesus name.

20). Father, thank you for healing me, I declare that now I can see, thank you Jesus, thank you Jesus

12 Scriptures for healing eyes

Here are 12 scriptures for healing eyes, study them, meditate on them and pray with them.

1). Psalm 146:8:

8 The Lord openeth the eyes of the blind: the Lord raiseth them that are bowed down: the Lord loveth the righteous:

2). Isaiah 35:5:

5 Then the eyes of the blind shall be opened, and the ears of the deaf shall be unstopped.

3). Isaiah 29:18:

18 And in that day shall the deaf hear the words of the book, and the eyes of the blind shall see out of obscurity, and out of darkness.

4). Isaiah 42:18:

18 Hear, ye deaf; and look, ye blind, that ye may see.

5). Isaiah 42:7:

7 To open the blind eyes, to bring out the prisoners from the prison, and them that sit in darkness out of the prison house.

6). Luke 7:22:

22 Then Jesus answering said unto them, Go your way, and tell John what things ye have seen and heard; how that the blind see, the lame walk, the lepers are cleansed, the deaf hear, the dead are raised, to the poor the gospel is preached.

7). Luke 4:18:

18 The Spirit of the Lord is upon me, because he hath anointed me to preach the gospel to the poor; he hath sent me to heal the brokenhearted, to preach deliverance to the captives, and recovering of sight to the blind, to set at liberty them that are bruised,

8). John 9:39:

39 And Jesus said, for judgment I am come into this world, that they which see not might see; and that they which see might be made blind.

9). John 9:32:32 since the world began was it not heard that any man opened the eyes of one that was born blind.

10). John 10:21:21 others said, these are not the words of him that hath a devil. Can a devil open the eyes of the blind?

11). John 11:27:27 she saith unto him, Yea, Lord: I believe that thou art the Christ, the Son of God, which should come into the world.

12). Acts 26:18:18 To open their eyes, and to turn them from darkness to light, and from the power of Satan unto God, that they may receive forgiveness of sins, and inheritance among them which are sanctified by faith that is in me.

10 POWERFUL CATHOLIC PRAYER FOR HEALING STOMACH PAIN

Catholic here means the universal body of Christ. We have compiled powerful catholic prayer for healing stomach pain. This prayers are powerful and most be prayed with faith. We serve a God that heals and he heals everyday those who call on him in prayers. If you are suffering from stomach problems such as ulcers, abdominal pains, severe menstrual pains, stomach infections etc. This prayers can healing you today.

Here at prayer guide, we don't discourage people from taking medications, but we encourage them to put their trust in God more than medicine. We have seen from experience that many afflictions of our health are spiritual, so why you may take your medications, see to it that you also pray this prayer to destroy the sicknesses from the root in order to avoid recurrence. Keep praying this prayers until you see results in your life. My prayer for you is as you engage this powerful catholic prayer for healing stomach pain that pain will disappear from your life forever in Jesus name.

10 Powerful catholic prayer for healing stomach pain

1). Father in the name of Jesus, I declare that by your stripes I am healed, therefore I command this stomach pain to come out!! Of my body in Jesus name.

2). Father, I command every pain in my upper and lower abdomen to cease now in Jesus name

3). Father, I command that sore in my intestines that causes me unbearable pains to heal permanently now in Jesus name.

4). Father I declare that I am totally healed from ulcers in Jesus name.

5). Father, I rebuke any stomach upset in my belly, I command it to stop forever in Jesus name.

6). Father, every stomach related infection that is causing this pains, I command it to disappear in Jesus name.

7). Father I declare that every pain in my stomach as a result of food poisoning is totally healed in Jesus name

8). Oh pains, here the word of the lord, get out of my stomach now in Jesus name.

9). Oh Lord, let your healing power overwhelm me and heal me totally in Jesus name.

10). Father thank you for healing me of this stomach pain in Jesus name.

THANKSGIVING PRAYER FOR HEALING

Today, we shall be engaging in thanksgiving prayers for healing. Have you ever being healed from any diseases, infirmities, or weakness? You will surely know how to give thanks. Many times, the reason why some people never experience breakthroughs is that they don't know how to give thanks for what they have received and the ones they have not received yet.

Thanksgiving time is a period to gather families together to give thanks to God for the great things that He has done. As a believer, we must learn how to give thanks to God. Recall the Bible says we should be a worry for nothing but in everything through prayers supplication and thanksgiving, we should make our request known unto God.

Even when we pray and have not received yet, we must still endeavor to thank God. Thanksgiving moves God to compassion for Him to arise for our help. Healing is something that many of us pray for. There are so many of us who have been healed from different diseases and infirmities. If you have been healed from one disease or the other, you must endeavor to give thanks to God.

Thanksgiving Prayer for Life

Lord God, I looked around me and I discover that it is by your mercy that I'm still standing. If it were left to the will of my enemies I would have been long forgotten, I magnify you because you have been the protector of my Goshen, you have been my shield and buckler. Lord, I appreciate your majesty for the wonderful gift of life that you have bestowed unto me, I thank you because you have not let my enemies sing a song of victory over my life, and I appreciate you because you are God. I appreciate you because you kept to the promises of your word, your word says no evil shall befall me or any danger come to my dwelling place. I appreciate you because you have kept your promises, Lord I say to let you name be exalted in the name of Jesus.

Thanksgiving Prayer for Healing of Cancer

Lord Jesus, I thank you because you are the great healer. When I was first diagnosed with cancer, I had lost hope, with the excruciating pain and exhaustion from different chemotherapy I thought my end has come. But I appreciate you for your kindness. Although it always seems to be like you will not come to my aid until you did. I thank you because you have put the devil to shame over my Hath challenges. I magnify you because you made a way when it seemed to be no, I appreciate you because you took away all my reactions and evacuate all my pain from that fiery ailment.

I thank you for the Supernatural hands of healings that you extended unto me, Lord I exalt your holy name.

Thanksgiving Prayers for Healing of Malaria

Only those who have lost their lives to this biggest killer of men in Africa can know what it takes to survive it. Lord, I thank you for seeing me through my moment of terrible sickness with Malaria. Lord, I thank you because you didn't let me add up the cases of who people died as a result of Malaria. I thank you, Lord, for facilitating my being and recovering process.

Your word says, that you have taken upon yourself all our infirmities and you have healed all our diseases. I thank you because you have made the clarity of this word manifest in my life. I appreciate my health status now, I thank you for all your loving-kindness over my, let your name be exalted.

Thanksgiving Prayer for Healing of Kidney Problem

Lord Jesus, I appreciate you for this loving-kindness. Men may truly not understand how much I mean to you, but I appreciate you for never leaving me in my moment of great needs. The fear of living with kidney disease is more tormenting and kills faster than the disease itself. Lord, I thank you because you have me strength in my terrible moment of weakness.

Thank you for giving me the strength never to lose hope even as my recovery process seemed slow, I thank you for giving your strength to never lose my faith in you. Yeah, because I know that when you finally arise for my help, it will be nothing short of a miracle. Thank you, Lord, for giving me the grace to exhibit character even as I wait upon you. Lord Jesus, I thank you for helping the doctors and nurses who were attending to me, I appreciate you for not forsaking me when I needed you most, and Lord I appreciate your holy name.

Thanksgiving Prayer for Good Health

In our moment of terrible sickness that is when we truly appreciate your loving-kindness for the good health that you have given to us. Lord, we thank you because you didn't let our faith be tested with a terrible sickness. We thank you for taking care of all our health needs and giving us sound health.

Lord Jesus, we thank you for loving us so much that you didn't let anyone of my family and friends fall victim to an untreatable disease or ailment. Lord, I thank you for being the protector of our Goshen, I magnify you for being God over our lives, and Lord let your holy name be exalted in the name of Jesus.

Thanksgiving Prayer for anticipated healing

Lord God, your word says that we should be a worry for nothing; but in everything, through supplication, prayers, and Thanksgiving we should make out request known unto you. Lord, I thank you because you will perfect my healings. I thank you because you have been helping my health situation from scratch and I thank you because you never leave your work undone, I'm thanking you in anticipation for total healing. I understand that we cannot be condemned on something that we have given thanks for and this is why I'm thanking you for healing, let your name be exalted in the name of Jesus.

I thank you because all my pain is gone, my fever is healed, and all my infirmities have been taken away, Lord I magnify your name, may your name be praised forever and ever.

PRAYER FOR EMOTIONAL HEALING FOR A FRIEND

Prayer for the emotional healing of a friend

Exodus 15:26 King James Version (KJV)

And said, If thou wilt diligently hearken to the voice of the Lord thy God, and wilt do that which is right in his sight, and wilt give ear to his commandments, and keep all his statutes, I will put none of these diseases upon thee, which I have brought upon the Egyptians: for I am the Lord that healeth thee.

In our daily life, we often encounter people who are heartbroken, down casted, or depressed. These people must have suffered some form of emotional problems, which has led them into a state of depression. All we need to do is pay attention to people's behavior; then we can tell what they are going through and find a way to help them out of their troubles. In this article, we will be dealing with a prayer for emotional healing for a friend. It would interest you to know that many people who have committed suicide would not have done that if there was someone to pray for them.

A man who suffers from emotional trauma will wish the world end at the very minute the trauma started, and they will lose hope on life itself and begin seeking a passage to the world beyond. At that time, to them, death is the only option that can bring a solution to all their troubles.

Emotional pain or trauma can be caused by a huge disappointment, betrayal, and loss that an individual has experienced. Quite a number of Biblical figures also experienced this type of ailment. Among the notable biblical figures that encountered such a traumatic situation was the great King of Isreal and Psalmist, David.

King David, most times in his Psalm, is always expressing his loneliness, pain, and anguish. The book of 2nd Samuel 15 verse 1 to the end explained how the kingdom was taken away from David by Absalom. David fell into depression not because his enemy took the Kingdom but because his son took it. The pain of betrayal took a heavy turn on King David that he almost lost himself to it.

Emotional pain is not an ailment that just comes overnight, but it is something that is caused by an event.

Meanwhile, not everyone is strong enough to overcome the trauma by themselves, while we stay around them to comfort them with kind words of inspiration, we must also raise an altar of prayer for them. Our words of hope can only raise them a bit, but only God can cause them to have a reason to stay alive.

You must read this prayer article because your friend might just need one or two prayers from it to get him/her out of emotional pain.

PRAYER POINTS

1.   Lord Jesus, I thank you for the Grace you have given unto me to discover the emotional demon my friend has been battling with for a while. I thank you because you have kept him this far by your power and didn't let him be overwhelmed by the emotional wound, Lord let your name be exalted in the name of Jesus.

2.   Lord, I pray that you will, by your mercy, give him victory over his emotional trauma. Do not let him be overwhelmed by it. I pray that you will have a fellowship of friendship with him, that he may see a friend in Christ Jesus.

3.   Lord, you are the great healer, I ask that you will take away his pains and will not bring them to remembrance anymore in the name of Jesus.

4.   The scripture says you bear upon yourself all our infirmity and heed all our diseases. I decree that his emotion pain is healed in the name of Jesus.

5.   I speak the word of comfort and healings to his pain and trauma. I decree that they are taken away in the name of Jesus.

6.   Father in heaven, emotional pain could lead to depression, which can cause any man to attempt to take his own life. Father Lord, I ask that you will my friend from all his pains, the power of healing of God Almighty should rest upon him in the name of Jesus.

7.   Father Lord, I pray that you will teach him to cast all of his burden upon you. You will teach him to put all his hopes and trust in

you alone. You cause him to do away with all the disappointments and betrayal that he has experienced and move on with life.

8. Lord Jesus, I ask that you will give him the grace to on the brighter side of life that he may give life another chance and never give up on living.

9. Father Lord, I pray that my friend would find your peace during hard times, whenever the pain and torment of the disappointments and betrayal put him down, I ask that you will fly him your strength that he may find a sense of inner peace in the name of Jesus.

10. I pray that by your mercy, you will connect him with men and women who will alleviate his sufferings. That by your grace, you will join him with people that would lift his spirit in the name of Jesus.

11. The Bible says that you sent forth your word and heal their diseases. Lord today, I pray that you will send forth your words to emotionally heal my friend in the name of Jesus.

12. Lord God, I ask that by your mercy, you will make yourself a source of inspiration, encouragement, and motivation. I ask that you will build a sustainable relationship that will strengthen his faith in you.

13. Father Lord, I pray that you will give him the strength he needs it, you will grant him healing where it is required, and you will speak to him when and where he needs to hear you. I pray that your spirit will not depart from him, and you will continue to be with him during this moment and forever.

14. Father, I pray that you will teach him to accept things that he cannot change in the name of Jesus.

15. Lord God, before you formed him you have known him, and you created him for a specific purpose, father in heaven, I ask that you will grant him the grace to fulfill the purpose of his existence. Take away every pain that the emotional wound has caused him and give him a favor so that he can look beyond the scar, in the name of Jesus.

16.   Heavenly Father, I pray that you will teach him to always bask in his contentment, you will teach him how to be satisfied with little things until you bring a greater and better one.

17.   Father Lord, you will never set out on a project and let it half done, I ask that you complete his healing process, and you will make him whole again in the name of Jesus.

18.   I pray that on his path, you cause every rough patch smooth, and you will remove every hindrance from his way. I pray that your light of love and peace will illuminate the darkness of her life, and you uproot every pain, blame, anguish, and bitterness in his life in the name of Jesus.

19.   Lord Jesus, I pray that you will give her the needed wisdom for him to make the right choice as he set out today. Give him your understanding to when you say NO, grant him the grace of spiritual alertness to identify when you say YES.

20.   Thank you, Lord, for answered prayers, thank you because you have responded to his prayers. Thank you because this prayer of emotional healing for my friend won't go without answers, thank you, Lord, let your name be exalted in the name of Jesus.

50   DELIVERANCE   PRAYERS   FOR   HEALING HYPERTENSION

Psalms 107:20 **He sent his word, and healed them, and delivered them** *from their destructions.*

Hypertension also known as High blood pressure is a long term medical condition in which the long-term force of the blood against your artery walls is high enough that it may eventually cause health problems, such as heart disease. Medical experts agree that Hypertension is a chronic disease, and if not properly checked can lead to the demise of the victim. Today we shall be engaging in deliverance prayers for healing hypertension. Every sickness has its spiritual root from the devil. Acts 10:38 tells us the sicknesses and diseases are the oppressions of the devil. Therefore we as believers must not see sicknesses and diseases as ordinary, but rather we must see them as evil arrows and tackle them spiritually through prayers.

These deliverance prayers for healing hypertension, will destroy every trace of heart disease in your body. It will empower you to be strong, and as you pray them in faith, you shall see your blood pressure normalize in Jesus name. You can chose to pray them yourself or have someone pray them over you. Sickness and diseases is not our portion as believers, we are ordained to live in soundness of health and vitality. Divine health is our heritage as believers. Exodus 23:25, tells us that as we serve the Lord, sickness shall be far away from us, Isaiah 53:5 tells us that by the stripes of Jesus, we are healed. I pray for you today, as you pray this prayers, every trace of hypertension shall disappear from your life forever in Jesus name. Remain Blessed.

Deliverance Prayers

1. Every power, planning to kill, steal and destroy my body, release me by fire, in the name of Jesus.
2. Every spirit of tiredness, release me, in the name of Jesus.
3. Every spirit of hypertension, come out of my body with all your roots, in the name of Jesus.
4. Every bondage of diabetic spirits, break by fire, in Jesus' name.

5. Any evil power, running through my body, loose your hold, in the name of Jesus.

6. Every evil power, hooking on to my brain, release me, in Jesus' name.

7. Every spirit with tentacles moving about in my body, come out by fire, in the name of Jesus.

8. Every spirit of migraine and headache, come out by fire, in the name of Jesus.

9. Every dark spirit, working against the kingdom of God in my life, come out by fire, in the name of Jesus.

10. Every power, working on my eyes and reducing my vision, be eliminated completely, in the name of Jesus.

11. Every demon of insulin deficiency, depart from me by fire, in Jesus' name.

12. Every spirit of hypertension, release my liver, in Jesus' name.

13. Every evil power, planning to amputate my leg, I bury you alive, in the name of Jesus.

14. Every spirit of hypertension, release my bladder, in Jesus' name.

15. Every spirit of excessive urination, release me, in Jesus' name.

16. Every spirit of hypertension, release my skin and ears, in the name of Jesus.

17. Every spirit of itching, depart from me, in the name of Jesus.

18. Every spirit of hypertension, release my lungs, in Jesus' name.

19. Every spirit of hypertension, release my reproductive areas, in the name of Jesus.

20. I release myself from every spirit of drowsiness, tiredness and impaired vision; I bind you and cast you out, in Jesus' name.

21. Every spirit of infirmity, generating tiredness, loose your hold, in the name of Jesus.

22. Every spirit of excessive thirst and hunger, I bind you and cast you out, in the name of Jesus.

23. I bind every spirit of weight loss, in the name of Jesus.

24. I bind every spirit of rashes, in the name of Jesus.

25. I bind every spirit of slow healing of cuts and bruises, in the name of Jesus.

26. I bind every spirit of bed-wetting, in the name of Jesus.

27. I bind every spirit of enlargement of the liver, in Jesus' name.

28. I bind every spirit of kidney disease, in the name of Jesus.

29. I bind every spirit of blockage, in the name of Jesus.

30. I bind every spirit of hardening of the arteries, in Jesus' name.

31. I bind every spirit of confusion, in the name of Jesus.

32. I bind every spirit of convulsion, in the name of Jesus.

33. I bind every spirit of loss of consciousness, in the name of Jesus.

34. You spirit of fear of death, depart from my life, in Jesus' name.

35. You evil doorkeeper of insulin, loose your hold, in Jesus' name.

36. Every power, destroying insulin in my body, I bind you and cast you out, in the name of Jesus.

37. Every power, hindering the co-ordination between my brain and my mouth, I bind you and cast you out, in the name of Jesus.

38. Every spirit of torment, release me, in the name of Jesus.

39. Every power, attacking my blood sugar, loose your hold, in the name of Jesus.

40. I break every curse of eating and drinking blood from ten generations backward on both sides of my family line, in the name of Jesus.

41. Every door, opened to diabetic spirits, close by the blood of Jesus.

42. Every inherited blood disease, loose your hold, in Jesus' name.

43. All bloodline curses, break, in the name of Jesus.

44. Every curse of breaking my skin unrighteously, break, in the name of Jesus.

45. I bind and cast out every demon in my pancreas, in Jesus' name.

46. Any power, affecting my vision, I bind you, in Jesus' name.

47. Every satanic arrow in my blood vessel, come out by fire, in the name of Jesus.

48. Every demon of stroke, come out of my life with all your roots, in the name of Jesus.

49. Every spirit of confusion, loose your hold over my life, in the name of Jesus.

50. Anything inhibiting my ability to read and meditate on the word of God, be uprooted, in the name of Jesus.

50 DELIVERANCE PRAYERS FOR HEALING DIABETICS

Isaiah 53:5 but he was wounded for our transgressions, he was bruised for our iniquities: the chastisement of our peace was upon him; and with his stripes we are healed.

Today we shall be engaging in miracle prayers for healing diabetes. According to medical experts, diabetes is a disease in which the body's ability to produce or respond to the hormone insulin is impaired, resulting in abnormal metabolism of carbohydrates and elevated levels of glucose in the blood. Diabetes is a terrible sickness and it has cost many people there lives. Diabetes is not the will of God for any of His Children. Exodus 23:25, God said, when we serve Him, He shall take sickness far away from us. Jesus our Lord and saviour, died for our sins and rose again for our Justification, He took upon himself 39 stripes for our sicknesses. The bible said, by His stripes, we are healed. The stripes of Jesus Christ was for our health and wholeness. Therefore as you pray this miracle prayers today, I see you taking you're healing by force in Jesus name.

Diabetes is not your portion, Jesus took it, and therefore you don't have it. Jesus took all your sicknesses upon himself and nailed it to the cross and today you are set free in His name. Therefore sickness has no right to reside in your body. Your body is the temple of the Lord, and the temple of the Lord cannot accommodate sickness. This miracle prayers for healing diabetes shall destroy every trace of diabetes in your blood and make you whole again, it shall cleanse your blood and by the power in the name of Jesus make you new again. Pray this prayers in faith today and receive your miracle.

PRAYER POINTS

1. Every power planning to kill, steal and destroy my body, release me by fire, in the name of Jesus.
2. Every spirit of tiredness, release me, in Jesus' name.
3. Every spirit of diabetes, come out with all your roots, in Jesus name

4. Every bondage of diabetic spirits, come out with all your roots, in the name of Jesus.

5. Any evil power running through my body, loose your hold, in the name of Jesus.

6. Every evil power touching my brain, release me, in Jesus' name.

7. Every tentacle spirit moving about in my body, come out by fire, in the name of Jesus.

8. Every spirit of migraine and headache, come out by fire, in the name of Jesus.

9. Every dark spirit working against the kingdom of God in my life, come out by fire, in Jesus' name.

10. Every power working on my eyes and reducing my vision, be eliminated completely, in the name of Jesus.

11. Every demon of insulin deficiency, depart by fire, in Jesus' name.

12. Every spirit of diabetes, release my liver, in the name of Jesus.

13. Every evil power planning to amputate my leg, I bury you alive, in the name of Jesus.

14. Every spirit of diabetes, release my bladder, in Jesus' name.

15. Every spirit of excessive urination, release me, in Jesus' name.

16. Every spirit of diabetes, release my skin and ears, in the name of Jesus.

17. Every spirit of itching, depart, in the name of Jesus.

18. Every spirit of diabetes, release my lungs, in the name of Jesus.

19. Every spirit of diabetes, release my reproductive areas, in the name of Jesus.

20. I release myself from every spirit of drowsiness, tiredness and impaired vision, I bind you and cast you out, in Jesus' name.

21. Every spirit of infirmity generating tiredness, loose your hold, in Jesus' name.

22. Every spirit of excessive thirst and hunger, I bind you and cast you out, in the name of Jesus.

23. I bind every spirit of loss of weight, in Jesus' name.

24. I bind every spirit of rashes, in the name of Jesus.

25. I bind every spirit of slow healing of cuts and bruises, in the name of Jesus.

26. I bind every spirit of bedwetting, in the name of Jesus.

27. I bind every spirit of enlargement of the liver, in Jesus' name.

28. I bind every spirit of kidney disease, in the name of Jesus.

29. I bind every spirit of gangrene, in Jesus' name.

30. I bind every spirit of hardening of the arteries, in Jesus' name.

31. I bind every spirit of confusion, in Jesus' name.

32. I bind every spirit of convulsion, in Jesus' name.

33. I bind every spirit of loss from ten generations of consciousness, in Jesus' name

34. The spirit of the fear of death, depart from my life, in the name of Jesus.

35. The evil doorkeeper of insulin, loose your hold, in Jesus' name

36. Every power destroying insulin in my body, I bind you and cast you out, in Jesus' name.

37. Every power hindering the co-ordination between my brain and my mouth, I bind you and cast you out, in Jesus' name.

38. Every spirit of torment, release me, in Jesus' name.

39. Every power attacking my blood sugar, loose your hold, in the name of Jesus.

40. I break every curse of eating and drinking blood from ten generations backward on both sides of my family lines, in the name of Jesus.

41. Every door opened to diabetic spirits, be closed by the blood of Jesus.

42. Every inherited blood disease, loose your hold, in Jesus' name.

43. All bloodline curses, be broken, in Jesus' name.

44. Every curse of breaking the skin of my body unrighteously, be broken, in Jesus' name.

45. I bind every demon in my pancreas and I cast them out, in the name of Jesus.

46. Any power affecting my vision, I bind you, in the name of Jesus.

47. Every satanic arrow in my blood vessel, come out by fire, in the name of Jesus.

48. Every demon of stroke, come out with all your roots, in the name of Jesus.

49. Every spirit of confusion, loose your hold, in Jesus' name

50. Anything inhibiting my ability to read and meditate, on the word of God, be uprooted, in the name of Jesus

30 INSTANT MIRACLE PRAYERS FOR HEALING

Mark 2:5 When Jesus saw their faith, he said unto the sick of the palsy, Son, thy sins be forgiven thee. 2:6 but there were certain of the scribes sitting there, and reasoning in their hearts, 2:7 why doth this man thus speak blasphemies? Who can forgive sins but God only? 2:8 and immediately when Jesus perceived in his spirit that they so reasoned within themselves, he said unto them, why reason you these things in your hearts? 2:9 weather is it easier to say to the sick of the palsy, Thy sins be forgiven thee; or to say, Arise, and take up thy bed, and walk? 2:10 But that ye may know that the Son of man hath power on earth to forgive sins, (he saith to the sick of the palsy,) 2:11 I say unto thee, Arise, and take up thy bed, and go thy way into thine house. 2:12 And immediately he arose, took up the bed, and went forth before them all; insomuch that they were all amazed, and glorified God, saying, We never saw it on this fashion.

We serve a miracle working God, with our God there is no impossible situation. No matter what your challenge is, all you need to do is believe, and you will see His performance in your life. Today we shall be looking at instant miracle prayers for healing. Jesus Christ the healer is here, and He heals instantly for those who believe. I want you to understand today that there is no incurable sickness with God, what men call incurable or terminal is nothing before Jesus. Everyone in the bible that came to Jesus with faith received there total healing and restoration. I believe that you too shall receive your healing today in Jesus name.

Jesus Paid the Price for Your Health

Isaiah 53:4 surely he hath borne our grieves, and carried our sorrows: yet we did esteem him stricken, smitten of God, and afflicted. 53:5 but he was wounded for our transgressions, he was bruised for our iniquities: the chastisement of our peace was upon him; and with his stripes we are healed.

Jesus took our sicknesses, pains and our sorrows upon Himself, and He nailed them on the cross, he took the stripes so that you and I can be healed. Jesus Christ our Lord has paid the price for our health and wholeness, therefore sickness is not our portion. You are not meant to be sick as a Christian, sickness has become a stranger in your life. Anytime you experience symptoms of sicknesses in your body, rebuke it in the name of Jesus and claim you're healing. Do not be moved by body symptoms, stand on the word of God concerning your healing, let the devil know that Jesus took it, therefore I cannot have it. Declare your faith in the word of God and receive your healing in Jesus name. This instant miracle prayers for healing will guide you as you rebuke sicknesses and diseases in your life.

What about Drugs?

I always tell people everywhere I am privileged to preach about healing that, God is not against taking drugs, He is not against doctors either. The wisdom of medical science is also from God. The decision of whether to take drugs or not is a matter of personal conviction. I advise sick people to see a doctor even after I have prayed with them. Many of them go to the Doctors to certify them healed and free of symptoms. When Jesus healed the ten lepers, He told them to go and show themselves to the priest. Why did Jesus send them to the priest? He did that because in those days, the priest are the only people authorized by the law to declare a leprous person clean and fit to mix with the crowd. The priest then are like the Doctors today (See Luke 17:11-19). So even if you have been prayed for, and you receive your healing, you can still go and see your doctor to verify the healing works of Christ. Supernatural healing is not afraid of medical verification. Also if you are on medication when you received your healing, it is still advisable to finish your medication.

My prayer for you is that this instant miracle prayers for healing will take you to the realms of divine health in Jesus name. As you pray this prayers by faith today, you shall never visit the Hospital for sickness again in Jesus name. Pray it with faith and receive your miracles.

PRAYER POINTS

1. Every power, planning to kill, steal and destroy my body, release me by fire, in the name of Jesus.

2. Every spirit of tiredness, release me, in the name of Jesus.

3. Every spirit of hypertension, come out of my body with all your roots, in the name of Jesus.

4. Every bondage of diabetic spirits, break by fire, in Jesus' name.

5. Any evil power, running through my body, loose your hold, in the name of Jesus.

6. Every evil power, hooking on to my brain, release me, in Jesus' name.

7. Every spirit with tentacles moving about in my body, come out by fire, in the name of Jesus.

8. Every spirit of migraine and headache, come out by fire, in the name of Jesus.

9. Every dark spirit, working against the kingdom of God in my life, come out by fire, in the name of Jesus.

10. Every power, working on my eyes and reducing my vision, be eliminated completely, in the name of Jesus.

11. I drink the blood of Jesus. (Physically swallow it by faith. Do this for some time.)

12. All evil spiritual feeders, warring against me, drink your own blood and eat your own flesh, in the name of Jesus.

13. All demonic food utensils, fashioned against me, be destroyed in the name of Jesus.

14. Holy Ghost fire, circulate all over my body.

15. All physical poisons, inside my system, be neutralized, in the name of Jesus.

16. All evil assignments, fashioned against me through the mouth gate, be nullified, in the name of Jesus.

17. All spiritual problems, attached to any hour of the night, be cancelled, in the name of Jesus. (Pick the period from midnight to 6:00 a.m. GMT)

18. Bread of heaven, fill me till I want no more.

19. All catering equipment's of evil caterers, attached to me, be destroyed, in the name of Jesus.

20. My digestive system, reject every evil command, in the name of Jesus.

21. I command every evil plantation in my life, come out with all your roots, in the name of Jesus!

22. You evil strangers of sicknesses and disease in my body, I command you to come out now!!! In the name of Jesus.

23. I cough out and vomit any food eaten from the table of the devil causing continuous sicknesses in my body, in the name of Jesus.

24. Let all negative materials circulating in my bloodstream be evacuated, in the name of Jesus.

25. I cover myself with the blood of Jesus and by this blood, in am shielded from all forms of sicknesses in the name of Jesus.

26. Holy Ghost fire, burn from the top of my head to the sole of my feet, deliver me from all forms of sicknesses in Jesus name.

27. I separate myself off from every strange sicknesses in the name of Jesus.

28. I separate myself off from every genetic sickness, in Jesus' name.

29. I cut myself off from every recurring sicknesses, in the name of Jesus.

30. Father I thank you for totally delivering me from sicknesses and diseases in Jesus name.

50 PRAYER POINTS FOR HEALING CANCER

Proverbs 4:20-22. KJV

20 My son, attend to my words; incline thine ear unto my sayings. 21 Let them not depart from thine eyes; keep them in the midst of thine heart. 22 For they are life unto those that find them, and health to all their flesh.

Every Sickness is an oppression of the devil, Acts 10:27. Today we shall be engaging in 50 prayer points for healing cancer. Cancer is a terrible disease and it is not the will of God for any of His children to be afflicted with cancer. In 3 John 1:2, God made His will for man clear, He wants us to enjoy good and soundness of health. Our God is a loving Father and He will never afflict any of His children with cancer. Today you shall be free from every form of cancer in Jesus name.

We serve a God whose name is called Jehovah Rapha, He is the God that healeth. In Matthew 15:30, the bible tells us that Jesus healed all that came to him for healing. There is no sickness and disease that our God cannot heal, but we must come to him in faith. Our faith is key to our healing. What we don't believe he cannot perform it in our lives. For you to be totally healed from cancer you must come to God in faith. As you engage this prayer points for healing cancer, your faith will produce results in Jesus name

Someone may ask, but how do I come to God? Through prayers. Prayers is the only ways we express our faith before God. The cancer you don't pray against, you cannot see it disappear from your body. But as you rise up in faith today and rebuke that demonic cancer in the name of Jesus the Christ, you shall see it no more in your life in Jesus name This prayer points today shall set you free from all forms of cancer, whether breast, prostate or any form of cancer in your body, they shall be gone forever in Jesus name. You must pray them in faith and be expectant. I see you totally free today in Jesus name.

PRAYER POINTS

1. All the activities of silent killers in my body, die, in the name of Jesus.

2. You the symptom of cancer in any area of my body, die, in the name of Jesus.

3. Every evil growth in my body, I curse you to die, in Jesus' name.

4. I fire back every arrow of cancer, in the name of Jesus.

5. Every abnormal production and uncontrollable behavior of cells in my body, stop, in the name of Jesus.

6. I bind every spirit of death and hell, in the name of Jesus.

7. Every negative consequence of abnormal production of cells in my body, die, in the name of Jesus.

8. I shall not die but live to declare the works of God, in Jesus' name,

9. You mass of extra tissue/tumour that has become malignant in my breast, be melted by the fire of God, in the name of Jesus.

10. Every demon of cancer, I bind you and cast you out, in Jesus' name,

11. Every break away cancer cell from malignant tumour that has entered my bloodstream (Lymphatic system), be flushed away by the blood of Jesus.

12. Every vampire spirit, release my life, in the name of Jesus.

13. You the malignant tumour, go back to your own kind by fire, in the name of Jesus.

14. O Great Physician, deliver me now.

15. Every spread of cancer (metastasis) in my body, stop and I command normalcy to my body system, in the name of Jesus.

16. Lay your hands on the affected parts and pray like this:

– Evil growth, dry up and die, in the name of Jesus.

– Satanic instructions to my body, be dismantled, in Jesus' name.

– Every poison in my body, come out through the mouth and through the nose, in the name of Jesus.

– Every spirit behind this cancer, come out with all your roots, in the name of Jesus.

– Every cancer anchor in my body, be dismantled, in Jesus' name.

– Every vehicle of cancer, crash, in the name of Jesus.

– Power of cancer, die, in the name of Jesus.

– Holy Ghost fire, burn away every cancer, in the name of Jesus. Caldron of witchcraft cooking my flesh, die, in the name of Jesus.

– Let the fire of God kill bewitched cells in my body, in the name of Jesus.

– Blood of Jesus, move upon every area of my life.

– I dismantle every hand of witchcraft, in the name of Jesus.

17. The power of cancer, die, in the name of Jesus.

18. Every threat to my life, my God shall threaten you to death, in the name of Jesus.

19. Holy Ghost, break the yoke of cancer in my life, in Jesus' name.

20. Every devastating attack on my beauty through the attack on my breast, die, in the name of Jesus.

21. Every power behind unprofitable growth, die, in the name of Jesus.

22. Every cancer initiation beginning from the duct in my breast, die, in the name of Jesus.

23. The spirit of cancer, loose your hold and die, in the name of Jesus.

24. You cancer of any kind, I am not your candidate, therefore, leave me alone, in the name of Jesus.

25. Cancer of _ _ _, I command you to dry up and die, in the name of Jesus.

26. Every power jingling the bell of untimely death on my life, you, your bell and pronouncements, die, in the name of Jesus.

27. I curse every cancerous cell to die, in the name of Jesus.

28. Every disease of Egypt, I am not your candidate, in Jesus' name

29. You demon of unprofitable growth and cell multiplication, I bind you and cast you out, in the name of Jesus.

30. Every re-occurrence of breast cancer in my life, die, in the name of Jesus.

31. Father Lord, let your power move away every mountain of infirmity in my life, in the name of Jesus.

32. Every sign of inflammatory of breast cancer, die, in the name of Jesus.

33. I receive deliverance from every inherited spirit, in the name of Jesus.

34. Every unusual change in size, shape or colour of my breast, die in the name of Jesus.

35. Holy Ghost arise and kill every satanic agent in my life, in the name of Jesus.

36. Every satanic discharge from my nipple, dry up to source, in the name of Jesus.

37. By the power that divided the Red Sea, let every evil growth dry up, in the name of Jesus.

38. Every solid lump or thickening in any area of my body, be melted away by fire, in the name of Jesus.

39. Every circulating serpent in my body, come out by fire, in the name of Jesus.

40. Any stage breast cancer has reached in my life, today, I terminate your advancement and I command a reversal now, in the name of Jesus.

41. I decree you will not spread to any other part of my body, in the name of Jesus.

42. Let my body reject every handwriting of darkness, in Jesus' name.

43. There shall be no reinforcement or regrouping of any cancer attack against me anymore, in the name of Jesus.

44. Let the arrow of darkness release my blood and my organs, in the name of Jesus.

45. Satan, hear me and hear me very well, I am not a death carrier but I am a life carrier, in the name of Jesus.

46. I speak destruction unto every cancerous cell, in the name of Jesus.

47. Blood of Jesus, mop up all the poison of cancer, in the name of Jesus.

48. Every arrow of cancer, came out now, in the name of Jesus.

49. Every power battling my health, receive the fire of God, in the name of Jesus.

50. By the power in the striped of Jesus, I kill every power of cancer, in the name of Jesus.

51. The power of pain, be dissolved by fire, in the name of Jesus.

52. O God arise and let every enemy of my sound health scatter, in the name of Jesus.

53. O cancer, hear the power of the Lord, I command you to dry up, in the name of Jesus.

54. Poison and insects programmed into my body, come out now, in the name of Jesus.

55. I cancel by fire the evil instructions given to my body, in Jesus' name.

56. I received deliverance from the grip of destructive spirit, in the name of Jesus.

57. Holy Ghost fire and blood of Jesus, destroy every contrary handwriting of infirmity.

58. Begin to thank God for your healing.

HEALING PRAYERS FOR DIABETICS

Psalm 103:3: Who forgiveth all thine iniquities; who healeth all thy diseases;

Today we are going to be engaging on Healing prayers for diabetes. Diabetes is not the will of God for any believer. As you pray these healing prayers today, every trace of diabetes in your blood shall be flushed out in Jesus name. The name of Jesus is the name above all names, and diabetes is a name, by the name of Jesus every form of diabetes in your blood shall be flushed out in Jesus name.

But for you to be free from this sickness, you must pray in faith. It is only a prayer of faith that can heal the sick. This healing prayers for diabetes can only answer in your life by faith. You must believe that the God you are praying to have the capacity heal you and set you free. God's presence is everywhere, but He will only manifest himself in an atmosphere of faith. I encourage you to pray this healing prayers for diabetes with faith today and watch God heal all your diseases in Jesus name

PRAYER POINTS

1. Every power planning to kill, steal and destroy my body, release me by fire, in the name of Jesus.

2. Every spirit of tiredness, release me, in Jesus' name.

3. Every spirit of diabetes, come out with all your roots, in Jesus name

4. Every bondage of diabetic spirits, come out with all your roots, in the name of Jesus.

5. Any evil power running through my body, loose your hold, in the name of Jesus.

6. Every evil power touching my brain, release me, in Jesus' name.

7. Every tentacle spirit moving about in my body, come out by fire, in the name of Jesus.

8. Every spirit of migraine and headache, come out by fire, in the name of Jesus.

9. Every dark spirit working against the kingdom of God in my life, come out by fire, in Jesus' name.

10. Every power working on my eyes and reducing my vision, be eliminated completely, in the name of Jesus.

11. Every demon of insulin deficiency, depart by fire, in Jesus' name

12. Every spirit of diabetes, release my liver, in the name of Jesus.

13. Every evil power planning to amputate my leg, I bury you alive, in the name of Jesus.

14. Every spirit of diabetes, release my bladder, in Jesus' name.

15. Every spirit of excessive urination, release me, in Jesus' name.

16. Every spirit of diabetes, release my skin and ears, in the name of Jesus.

17. Every spirit of itching, depart, in the name of Jesus.

18. Every spirit of diabetes, release my lungs, in the name of Jesus.

19. Every spirit of diabetes, release my reproductive areas, in the name of Jesus.

20. I release myself from every spirit of drowsiness, tiredness and impaired vision, I bind you and cast you out, in Jesus' name.

21. Every spirit of infirmity generating tiredness, loose your hold, in Jesus' name.

22. Every spirit of excessive thirst and hunger, I bind you and cast you out, in the name of Jesus.

23. I bind every spirit of loss of weight, in Jesus' name.

24. I bind every spirit of rashes, in the name of Jesus.

25. I bind every spirit of slow healing of cuts and bruises, in the name of Jesus.

26. I bind every spirit of bedwetting, in the name of Jesus.

27. I bind every spirit of enlargement of the liver, in Jesus' name.

28. I bind every spirit of kidney disease, in the name of Jesus.

29. I bind every spirit of gangrene, in Jesus' name.

30. I bind every spirit of hardening of the arteries, in Jesus' name.

31. I bind every spirit of confusion, in Jesus' name.

32. I bind every spirit of convulsion, in Jesus' name.

33. I bind every spirit of loss from ten generations of consciousness, in Jesus' name.

34. The spirit of the fear of death, depart from my life, in the name of Jesus.

35. The evil doorkeeper of insulin, loose your hold, in Jesus' name

36. Every power destroying insulin in my body, I bind you and cast you out, in Jesus' name.

37. Every power hindering the co-ordination between my brain and my mouth, I bind you and cast you out, in Jesus' name.

38. Every spirit of torment, release me, in Jesus' name.

39. Every power attacking my blood sugar, loose your hold, in the name of Jesus.

40. I break every curse of eating and drinking blood from ten generations backward on both sides of my family lines, in the name of Jesus.

41. Every door opened to diabetic spirits, be closed by the blood of Jesus.

42. Every inherited blood disease, loose your hold, in Jesus' name.

43. All bloodline curses, be broken, in Jesus' name.

44. Every curse of breaking the skin of my body unrighteously, be broken, in Jesus' name.

45. I bind every demon in my pancreas and I cast them out, in the name of Jesus.

46. Any power affecting my vision, I bind you, in the name of Jesus.

47. Every satanic arrow in my blood vessel, come out by fire, in the name of Jesus.

48. Every demon of stroke, come out with all your roots, in the name of Jesus.

49. Every spirit of confusion, loose your hold, in Jesus' name

50. Anything inhibiting my ability to read and meditate, on the word of God, be uprooted, in the name of Jesus.

51. I bind and cast out every spirit of _ _ _

- Convulsion
- Abdominal Problems
- Fear
- Guilt

- Hopelessness
- Impotence
- Palsy
- Candor
- Swelling
- Stress
- Worry

52. I bind and cast out familiar spirits travelling through family bloodlines to cause diabetes and other sickness, in Jesus' name.

53. I cast out _ _ _ (pick from the under listed), in Jesus' name.

- Demons in abdomen
- Acute pain
- Amputation
- Animal spirits
- Bed wetting
- Anger
- Beta cell destroyer
- Demons in bladder
- The fear of death
- Accelerated hardening of the arteries
- Anxiety
- Beef insulin
- Blackwell
- Blood diseases
- blood restricting
- Demons in blood vessels.
- Bondage
- Bowel disease
- Brain migraine

Father, I thank you for healing me in Jesus name.

25 PRAYER POINTS FOR HEALING ALL MANNER OF SICKNESS

> *Acts 10:38:38 How God anointed Jesus of Nazareth with the Holy Ghost and with power: who went about doing good, and healing all that were oppressed of the devil; for God was with him.*

Today we are looking at 25 Prayer Points for Healing All Manner of Sicknesses and Diseases. We serve a God that heals, He is called Jehovah raphe, and no matter your sickness he will heal you when you call unto him. Sicknesses and diseases are oppressions of the devil, it is not the will of God for any of His children to be sick. No good father will punish his children with sicknesses and diseases, our God in heaven is a good God, and He will never afflict or harm us with sicknesses and diseases. Therefore, do not think that God is punishing you with sickness because of your sins, or that God is afflicting you with sickness because of the wayward life which you led in the past, no, God is a merciful God, and when he forgives, he forgets, what you are suffering from is the consequences of your wrong decisions, and the mercies of God can heal you of all the consequences of your wrong decisions.

Are you sick in your body today, God will heal you, it doesn't matter how you got sick, or what the name of the sickness is, God will heal you and deliver you from all afflictions. Engage this Prayer Points for Healing All Manner of Sicknesses and Diseases with faith today and expect you're healing to come instantly. I see God perfecting all that concerns your health in Jesus name.

PRAYER POINTS

1. Father, I thank you for your mighty power that is able to heal all sickness.
2. Father, I thank you for you are the Lord God that heals me.
3. Let the blood of Jesus be transfused into my blood vessels, in the name of Jesus.
4. I command every agent of disease in my blood and body organs to disappear, in the name of Jesus.

5. Let my blood reject every form of sicknesses and diseases, in Jesus' name.

6. Holy Spirit, speak deliverance and healing into my life, in the name of Jesus.

7. Let the blood of Jesus speak healing of every infirmity in my life.

8. I hold the blood of Jesus against you spirit of (mention what is troubling you). Disappear from my body now!!! In Jesus name

9. O Lord, let your healing hand be stretched out upon my life now in Jesus name.

10. O Lord, let your miracle hand be stretched out upon my life now in Jesus name.

11. O Lord, let your deliverance hand be stretched out upon my life now.

12. I disannul every engagement with the spirit of death, in the name of Jesus.

13. I rebuke every refuge of sickness, in the name of Jesus.

14. I destroy the grip and operation of sickness upon my life, in the name of Jesus.

15. Every knee of infirmity in my life, bow, in the name of Jesus.

16. O Lord, let every weakness in my body be converted to strength in Jesus name

17. I command death upon any sickness in any area of my life, in the name of Jesus.

18. I shall see this sickness no more, in the name of Jesus.

19. Father Lord, let the whirlwind of God scatter every vessel of infirmity fashioned against my life, in the name of Jesus.

20. Every spirit hindering my perfect healing, fall down and die now, in the name of Jesus.

21. Father Lord, let all death contractors begin to kill themselves, in the name of Jesus.

22. Father Lord, let every germ of infirmity in my body die, in the name of Jesus.

23. Father Lord, let every agent of sickness working against my health disappear, in the name of Jesus.

24. Fountain of discomfort in my life, dry up now, in the name of Jesus.

25. Every dead organ in my body, receive life now, in Jesus' name.

Thank You Jesus

PRAYER FOR THE GIFT OF HOLY GHOST
30 PRAYER POINTS ON SANCTIFICATION AND CLEANSING OF THE HOLY SPIRIT

Acts 26:18 to open their eyes, and to turn them from darkness to light, and from the power of Satan unto God, that they may receive forgiveness of sins, and inheritance among them which are sanctified by faith that is in me.

Sanctification is a major requirement to be accepted by God. Until you are sanctified, you may not be qualified to be in the presence of God. Our God is a Holy God, He cannot operate in a filthy environment, and also He cannot operate with unholy and unsanctified people. The good news have for you today is this, you can be sanctified. No matter your sins and shortcomings, the God of grace and unlimited mercies shall show you mercy, justify you and sanctify you. Today we shall be engaging in 30 powerful prayer points on sanctification and cleansing of the Holy Spirit. These powerful sprayer points will set you apart for a profitable work with God.

What Is Sanctification?

Sanctification is to be set apart, it means to be separated from the World unto God. When you are born again, God separates you from the world, He calls you to himself, and justifies you, that is to declare you righteous by faith. Haven been justified, you need the word of God and prayers to continue to cleanse your mind and your thoughts. Romans 12:1-2 tells us that we need to continually renew our mind with the word of God in order not to conform to this world and also to be transformed by God. This powerful prayer points on sanctification and the cleansing of the Holy Spirit, will empower us to serve God effectively, as we engage this prayers the grace to live like Christ will be lavished on us in Jesus name.

Nothing blesses like sanctification, in Acts 20:32, we see that only the sanctified receive their inheritance, I encourage you to pray these prayer points with passion today. Ask God to sanctify you for His use, ask the Holy Spirit to cleanse you and purge you of every evil in your heart. This prayer points for sanctification shall surely improve your walk with God.

PRAYER POINTS

1. Father, thank you for sending your Holy Spirit to me in Jesus name.

2. O Lord, fill me afresh with the power of your spirit in Jesus name

3. O Lord, heal every wounded part of my life, through the power of the Holy Spirit

4. O Lord, help me subdue every fleshly manifestation of sin in my body by the power of your spirit

5. O Lord, re-align my life and set me on the right track by the help of the Holy Spirit

6. O Lord, let the fire of the Holy Spirit come afresh upon my life today in Jesus name.

7. O Lord, by the help of your spirit, let my life reflect the life of God in Jesus name

8. O Lord, kindle in me the fire of love through the help of the Holy Spirit in Jesus name

9. Sweet Holy Spirit, I want to be connected to you forever in Jesus name

10. Dear Holy Spirit, enrich me with your gifts in Jesus name

11. I decree the joy of the oppressors upon my life to be turned into sorrow, in the name of Jesus.

12. Let all multiple strongmen operating against me be destroyed, in the name of Jesus.

13. Lord, open my eyes and ears to receive wondrous things from you.

14. Lord, grant me victory over temptation and satanic device.

15. Lord, ignite my spiritual life so that I will stop fishing in unprofitable waters.

16. Lord, release your tongue of fire upon my life and burn away all spiritual filthiness present within me.

17. Father, make me to hunger and thirst for righteousness, in the name of Jesus.

18. Lord, help me to be ready to do your work without expecting any recognition from others.

19. Lord, give me victory over emphasizing the weaknesses and sins of other people while ignoring my own.

20. O Lord, give me depth and root in my faith

21. Thou power in the blood of Jesus, separate me from the sins of my ancestors.

22. Blood of Jesus, remove any unprogressive label from every aspect of my life.

23. O Lord, create in me a clean heart by your power.

24. O Lord, let the anointing of the Holy Spirit break every yoke of backwardness in my life

25. O Lord, renew a right spirit within me.

26. O Lord, teach me to die to self.

27. Thou brush of the Lord, scrub out every dirtiness in my spiritual pipe, in the name of Jesus.

28. O Lord, ignite my calling with your fire.

29. O Lord, anoint me to pray without ceasing.

30. O Lord, establish me as a holy person unto you.

Thank You Jesus

PRAYER TO BE FILLED WITH THE HOLY SPIRIT
Acts 1:8:

8 But ye shall receive power, after that the Holy Ghost is come upon you: and ye shall be witnesses unto me both in Jerusalem, and in all Judaea, and in Samaria, and unto the uttermost part of the earth.

The Holy Spirit is the Source of Gods power. The Holy Spirit is the Spirit of God sent to us to enable us Live like Christ. As Christians, we serve God through the help of the Holy Spirit. Today we are going to be engaging in prayer to be filled with the Holy Spirit. Before we go into these Holy Spirit prayers, it is important we know a little about the Holy Spirit and His mission in our lives as Christians. I pray for you that after you finish reading this article and engaging in the prayers, the fire of God which only the Holy Spirit brings shall never depart from your life in Jesus name.

Who Is The Holy Spirit?

John 14:16:16 And I will pray the Father, and he shall give you another Comforter, that he may abide with you forever;

The Holy Spirit is a person, He is not wind, or fire or a force, and He is the third person of the Godhead. The Holy Spirit is God Himself lives in us. When Jesus was about to leave His disciples on earth, He promised to send them another comforter, this comforter shall not only be with us, but he shall be in us, John 14:17. This comforter is the Holy Spirit. Every child of God needs the help of the Holy Spirit to succeed in his/her Christian life. Without the Holy Spirit, we cannot serve God effectively. The Holy Spirit is our helper, we cannot help ourselves that is why we need the holy spirits help. Let's look at the mission of the Holy Spirit in our lives.

Mission of the Holy Spirit in Our Lives

Below are the roles of the Holy Spirit in our lives.

1. Helper: The Holy Spirit is our Helper. The Spirit of God is the one that helps us to serve God effectively, He helps us also in our prayer life. When you have the Holy Spirit in your life, you can never lack divine help.

2. Comforter: A comforter is an encourager, a lifter of your head, the holy spirit, is not a kill joy, he is not a judgmental spirit, he comforts, he encourages, he loves and lifts. While the devil condemns your conscience, the holy spirits comforts you always. When you are filled with the Holy Spirit, you can never lack comfort.

3. Advocate: An advocate is someone who publicly supports you. The Holy Spirit is always on your side, He will never leave you or abandon you. He will always be there for you. When you do something wrong by omission, run to the Holy Spirit, he knows how to defend you and protect you from harm, will empowering you not make same errors again.

4. Intercessor: The Holy Spirit is our intercessor, He intercedes for us. An intercessor is someone who intervenes on behalf of another, especially in prayer. The Holy Spirit prays for us according to Romans 8:26. When you are filled with the Holy Spirit, you will always be in Gods mind because He through His Spirit will always intercede for you.

5. Counselor: The Holy Spirit is our counselor, he is our chief adviser, and he guides us in the affairs of our lives. Jesus said the Spirit will teach us all things, John 14:26. The Holy Spirit teaches and counsels us so that we can fulfill our purpose in life. The Holy Spirit is our life time coach.

6. Strengthener: The Holy Spirit gives us strength. He strengthens us on every side. When you are filled with the Holy Spirit, you can ever be weak. You will always walk in divine strength. Also the Holy Spirit strengthens us in the inner man, through the word of God that we listen daily.

7. Standby: The Holy Spirit is our standby that is he is ever present with us. The Holy Spirit will never leave us or forsake us. He will ever be by your side. The Holy Spirit does not give up on us, but unfortunately many of us give up on him. The Holy Print is ever present with us to help us, councounsel us, strengthen us, intercede for us and much more. Infact the Holy Spirit is to us a friend indeed.

How to Be Filled With the Holy Spirit.

There are certain steps to take to be filled with the Holy Spirit, below are the steps:

1. Be Born Again. To know more about salvation and being born again, click here

2. Have Faith. Believe in the Holy Spirit. Hebrews 11:6

3. Pray to be filled with the Holy Spirit

Prayer to Be Filled With the Holy Spirit:

Below, we are going to be looking at some prayers to be filled with the Holy Spirit. As you engage these prayer, pray them with faith and receive a fresh baptism of fire in Jesus name.

PRAYER POINTS

1. Father, I thank you for my salvation in Jesus name

2. Father, I thank you for the power of the Holy Spirit.

3. Father, by the blood of Jesus wash me of all my sins and strengthen me by your spirit in Jesus name.

4. Father, let the Holy Spirit fill me afresh.

5. Father, let every unbroken area in my life be broken, in the name of Jesus.

6. Father, incubate me with the fire of the Holy Spirit, in Jesus' name.

7. Every anti-power bondage in my life, break, in Jesus' name.

8. O Lord, let all strangers flee from my spirit and let the Holy Spirit take control, in the name of Jesus.

9. O Lord, catapult my spiritual life to the mountaintop.

10. Father, let heavens open and let the glory of God fall upon me, in the name of Jesus.

11. Father, let signs and wonders be my lot, in the name of Jesus.

12. Every joy of the oppressors upon my life, be turned into sorrow, in the name of Jesus.

13. All multiple strongmen, operating against me, be paralyzed, in the name of Jesus.

14. O Lord, open my eyes and ears to receive wondrous things from you.

15. O Lord, grant me victory over temptations and satanic devices.

16. O Lord, ignite my spiritual life so that I will stop fishing in unprofitable waters.

17. O Lord, release your tongue of fire upon my life and burn away all spiritual filthiness present within me.

18. Father, make me to hunger and thirst for righteousness, in the name of Jesus.

19. Lord, help me to be ready to do your work without expecting any recognition from others.

20. O Lord, give me victory, over emphasizing the weaknesses and sins of other people, while ignoring my own.

21. O Lord, heal every area of backsliding in my spiritual life.

22. Lord, help me to be willing to serve others, rather than wanting to exercise authority.

23. Lord, help me to be willing to serve others, rather than wanting to exercise authority.

24. O Lord, open my understanding concerning the scriptures

25. O Lord, help me to live each day, recognizing that the day will come when you will judge secret lives and innermost thoughts.

26. O Lord, let me be willing to be the clay in your hands, ready to be moulded as you desire.

27. O Lord, wake me up from any form of spiritual sleep and help me to put on the armour of light.

28. O Lord, give me victory over all carnality and help me to be at the center of your will.

29. I stand against anything in my life that will cause others to stumble, in the name of Jesus.

30. O Lord, help me to put away childish things and put on maturity.

31. O Lord, empower me to stand firm against all the schemes and techniques of the devil.

32. O Lord, give me a big appetite for the pure milk and solid food in your word.

33. O Lord, empower me to stay away from anything or anybody, whom might take God's place in my heart.

34. O Lord, I thank you for the testimonies that will follow.

35. I declare that I am called of God; no evil power shall cut me down, in the name of Jesus.

36. O Lord, give me the power to be faithful to my calling, in the name of Jesus.

37. I receive the anointing to remain steady, committed and consistent in my ministerial life, in Jesus' name.

38. I declare that I shall not be lured into politics, church rivalry or rebellion, in the name of Jesus.

39. O Lord, give me the wisdom to respect my teachers and seniors who have trained me, in the name of Jesus.

40. O Lord, give me the heart of a servant, so that I can experience your blessings every day, in the name of Jesus.

41. I receive power to rise with wings as eagles, in the name of Jesus.

42. I decree that the enemy will not waste my calling, in the name of Jesus.

43. By the power of the living God, the devil will not swallow my ministerial destiny, in Jesus' name.

44. Power for effective development in my calling, come upon me now, in the name of Jesus.

45. I declare war against spiritual ignorance, in the name of Jesus.

46. I bind and cast out every unteachable spirit, in the name of Jesus.

47. I receive the anointing for success in my ministry, in the name of Jesus.

48. I shall not be an enemy of integrity, in Jesus' name.

49. I shall not steal God's money, in the name of Jesus.

50. I shall not disgrace the call of God upon my life, in Jesus' name.

51. I shall walk in holiness every day, in Jesus' name.

52. I bind the spirit of sexual immortality, in Jesus' name.

53. I receive the culture of loyalty in my ministry, in the name of Jesus.

54. I shall not become an old king that is resistant to advice, in the name of Jesus.

55. I shall not live a wasteful and extravagant life, in the name of Jesus.

56. I shall not serve my wonderful Saviour for filthy financial gain, in the name of Jesus.

57. I prevent every spirit of quarrel and opposition from my wife/husband, in the name of Jesus.

58. My wife/husband shall not scatter my church members, in the name of Jesus.

59. Every Judas in my ministry, fall into your own trap, in the name of Jesus.

60. My ministry will not destroy my marriage, in the name of Jesus.

61. My marriage will not destroy my ministry, in the name of Jesus.

62. My children will not become misfired arrows in my ministry, in the name of Jesus.

63. I claim progress and excellence for my ministry, in the name of Jesus.

64. My church shall experience prosperity, in the name of Jesus.

65. O Lord, let my ministry reach the unreached, in the name of Jesus.

66. A multitude of people will go to heaven because of my ministry in the name of Jesus.

67. I kill every attack on my ministry. I shall prevail, in the name of Jesus.

68. I shall not bite the fingers that fed me, in Jesus' name.

69. I shall not engage in rebellion, in the name of Jesus.

70. Every power of my father's house, working against my calling, die, in the name of Jesus.

Father, I thank you for answering me in Jesus.

50 PRAYERS FOR THE HOLY SPIRIT POWER

Acts 1:8:

8 But ye shall receive power, after that the Holy Ghost is come upon you: and ye shall be witnesses unto me both in Jerusalem, and in all Judaea, and in Samaria, and unto the uttermost part of the earth.

The Holy Spirit is the person and power of God. It is impossible to serve God without His Holy Spirit. Today we are going to be engaging 50 prayers for the Holy Spirit power. This prayers will enable you as a born again Christian activate the power and presence of the holy spirit in you. But before we go into the prayers, let us get acquainted with some facts about the Holy Spirit.

Who Is The Holy Spirit?

The Holy Spirit is a Person. He is the third Person of the God head. We have God the Father, the Son and the Holy Spirit, see 1 John 5:7, Mathew 28:19-20. The Father is the Almighty God, The Son is our Lord Jesus Christ, and The Holy Spirit, is the one that Jesus sent to us, Acts 1:8. The Holy Spirit is the carrier of God's presence and Power. In Genesis 1:1-2, we see that God began to recreate the whole world through His Spirit. Jesus could not have fulfilled His ministry on earth without the Holy spirit, Acts 10:38 tells us that God empowered Him with the Holy Spirit and Power to do great miracles. The Holy Spirit is not the Power of God, the Holy Spirit carries the Power of God. As a Christian, you cannot manifest or feel Gods presence without the Holy Spirit, it is the Holy Spirit that separates Christianity from every other religion in the world. Let's look at some Characteristics of the Holy Spirit.

Characteristics of the Holy Spirit

1. Salvation: The Holy Spirit is the Lord of the Harvest, Matthew 9:38. It is the Holy Spirit that convicts sinners of their sins, without the Holy Spirit one cannot be born again. The Holy Spirit is the author of our salvation.

2. Godliness: The Holy Spirit enables us to live a holy and righteous life. Just as He convicts sinners of their sins, He also convicts believers of their righteousness John 16:8-9. The Holy Spirit helps us to serve God in words and in deeds, you cannot live right before God by your own human strength, the arm of flesh will always fail you, but you must constantly depend on the Holy Spirit to live a godly life. Remember, it's not by power, nor by might, but by my Spirit says the Lord, Zechariah 4:6.

3. Supernatural: We command the Supernatural through the Holy Spirit inside us. Through the power of the Holy Spirit, we can heal the sick, raise the dead, cast out devils etc. We can control events from the realms of the spirit through the power of the Holy Ghost. Mark 16:17-18

4. Answered Prayers: The Holy Spirit helps us to pray, Romans 8:26-27. The Holy Spirit gives us utterances in our prayers. The Holy Spirit in us guarantees answers to our prayers. He is our advocate before God. Learn to pray in the Holy Ghost, Jude 1:20.

5. Direction: It is the voice of the Spirit in us that gives us direction. The Holy Spirit is our helper, as a believer, get to know the person of the Holy Spirit, He will guide you and teach you all things you need to know. Jesus said, He will even bring back to you things you may have forgotten. The Holy Spirit is our teacher, guide and shepherd. He is the Spirit of Truth, John 14:26. John also tells us that the anointing (Holy Spirit) in us teaches us all things. 1 John 2:27.

How Do I Get Filled With Holy Spirit

I believe that by now you are more aware of the holy spirit and what He can do in your life, before we begin to engage the prayers for the holy spirit power, I want to answer one more question, How do I receive the Holy spirit, the simple answer is this, you pray for the infilling of the Holy Spirit. The prayers we are engaging is just the prayers you need to be filled with the Holy Spirit. I encourage you to engage this prayers by faith, get acquainted with the person of the Holy Spirit and see you Christian life change to a higher level in Jesus name.

50 Prayers for the Holy Spirit Power

1. Father, thank you for sending your Holy Spirit to me in Jesus name.

2. O Lord, fill me afresh with the power of your spirit in Jesus name

3. O Lord, heal every wounded part of my life, through the power of the Holy Spirit

4. O Lord, help me subdue every fleshly manifestation of sin in my body by the power of your spirit

5. O Lord, re-align my life and set me on the right track by the help of the Holy Spirit

6. O Lord, let the fire of the Holy Spirit come afresh upon my life today in Jesus name.

7. O Lord, by the help of your spirit, let my life reflect the life of God in Jesus name

8. O Lord, kindle in me the fire of love through the help of the Holy Spirit in Jesus name

9. Sweet Holy Spirit, I want to be connected to you forever in Jesus name

10. Dear Holy Spirit, enrich me with your gifts in Jesus name

11. Dear Holy Spirit, quicken me and increase my desire for the things of heaven.

12. By Your ruler ship, sweet spirit of God, let the lust of the flesh in my life be subdued in Jesus name

13. Sweet Holy Spirit, increase daily in my life in Jesus name.

14. Dear Holy Spirit, maintain your gifts in my life in Jesus name

15. Holy Spirit, my refiner, refine and purge my life by your fire in Jesus name

16. Holy Spirit, inflame and fire my heart, in the name of Jesus.

17. Dear Holy Spirit, lay your hands upon me and quench every rebellion in me in Jesus name

18. Holy Ghost fire, begin to burn away every self-centeredness in me, in the name of Jesus.

19. Sweet Holy Spirit, breathe your life-giving breath into my soul, in the name of Jesus.

20. Sweet Holy Spirit, make me ready to go wherever you send me in Jesus name.

21. Sweet Holy Spirit, never let me shut you out in Jesus name

22. Sweet Holy Spirit, never let me try to limit you to my capacity in Jesus name

23. Dear Holy Spirit, work freely in me and through me in Jesus name

24. Dear Holy Spirit, purify the channels of my life in Jesus name

25. Let your heat O Lord, consume my will, in the name of Jesus.

26. Let the flame of the Holy Spirit blaze upon the altar of my heart, in the name of Jesus.

27. Holy Spirit, let your power flow like blood into my veins.

28. Dear Holy Spirit, order my spirit and fashion my life in your will in Jesus name

29. Sweet Spirit Of God, let your fire burn all that is not holy in my life in Jesus name

30. Dear Holy Spirit, let your fire generate power in my life in Jesus name.

31. Sweet Holy Spirit, impart to me thoughts higher than my own thoughts in Jesus name

32. Holy Spirit, come as dew and refresh me, in the name of Jesus.

33. Holy Spirit, guide me in the way of liberty, in the name of Jesus.

34. Holy Spirit, blow upon me such that sin would no more find place in me, in the name of Jesus.

35. Holy Spirit, where my love is cold, warm me up, in Jesus' name.

36. Dear holy spirit, continue to show forth your manifest presence in my life in Jesus name

37. Let my hand become the sword of fire to cut down evil trees, in the name of Jesus.

38. Let my feet become the thunder of God, as I stamp them. Let them deafen the enemy, in the name of Jesus.

39. Let the spiritual rag of poverty in my life be destroyed by the fire of the Holy Spirit in the name of Jesus.

40. Every enemy of excellence in my life, be consumed by the power of the Holy Spirit in Jesus' name.

41. Dear Holy Spirit, Let every past satanic achievements in my life be converted to my promotion, in the name of Jesus.

42. Dear Holy Spirit, help me, let the shame of my enemies be multiplied greatly in Jesus name

43. Dear Holy Spirit, help me, let the defeat and disgrace of enemy of my progress be multiplied beyond measure in Jesus name

44. Dear Holy Spirit, help me, let every power planning to turn my life upside down, fall down and die now, in the name of Jesus.

45. Dear Holy Spirit, help me, I destroy every satanic inspiration targeted against me, in the name of Jesus.

46. With the Power of the Holy Spirit at work in me, I barricade my life from every satanic opinion, in the name of Jesus.

47. Holy Spirit, trouble let all my divinely-appointed helpers begin to locate me from now, in the name of Jesus.

48. Dear Holy Spirit, thank you for causing me to ride above principalities and powers in the name of Jesus.

49. Father thank you for the empowerment of the Holy Spirit.

50. Thank God for answers to your prayer.

SCRIPTURAL PROOF THAT THE SPIRIT OF GOD IS LEADING YOU

Today we will be teaching the scriptural proof that the spirit of God is leading you. The Christian life is a life of power and dominance. That's why often than not, the scripture emphasized being led by the spirit of God. The scripture stated in the book of Acts 1:8 but you shall receive power when the Holy Spirit has come upon you, and you shall be witnesses to Me in Jerusalem, and in all Judea and Samaria, and to the end of the earth."

The Holy Spirit empowers us as believers. The New Testament writer explained that the flesh is weak. That's why most believers find it difficult to do things of the spirit. However, when the spirit of Him that raised Christ dwells in us, it will quicken our mortal body. When the spirit of God dwells in us, our lives no longer become ours, we no longer control ourselves, but the spirit does. We are transformed into a better version of ourselves through the help of the spirit of God.

When the spirit of God is leading you, some signs would be eminent in you. These signs will show your difference and separate you from others. Here are some of the signs that you would notice.

5 signs the spirit of God is leading you
1. You Become Courageous

ACTS 2:13 others mocking said, "They are full of new wine." But Peter, standing up with the eleven, raised his voice and said to them, "Men of Judea and all who dwell in Jerusalem, let this be known to you, and heed my words. For these are not drunk, as you suppose, since it is only the third hour of the day. But this is what was spoken by the prophet Joel:

And it shall come to pass in the last days, says God,

That I will pour out of My Spirit on all flesh; your sons and your daughters shall prophesy, your young men shall see visions, your old men shall dream dreams. And on My menservants and my maidservants I will pour out My Spirit in those days, and they shall prophesy.

This was Apostle Peter courageously preaching the gospel to thousands of people. Meanwhile, the old Apostle Peter could not stand with Christ when he was taken. He had denied Christ thrice because he lacked the courage to stand with Christ in the face of tribulation.

However, when the spirit of God came upon him, he spoke with courage amid several people. The fire of the Holy Ghost had just baptized the people, and they were speaking in diverse tongues. When they were seen, people argued that they are being intoxicated by sweet wine. Immediately, Apostle Peter stood to his feet and debunked the allegation.

He could not have done this without courage. Indeed, when the spirit of God is leading you, fear becomes a thing of the past.

2. You Show the Fruits of the Spirit

Galatians 5:22-23 But the fruit of the Spirit is love, joy, peace, patience, kindness, goodness, faithfulness, gentleness, self-control; against such, there is no law..''

When the spirit of God is leading you that means the Holy Spirit dwells in you. When the Holy Spirit dwells in you, the following signs will be eminent in your life, goodness, kindness, self-control, gentleness, peace, patience, love, and faithfulness. There is an unexplainable peace that comes with those who are led by the spirit of God. Even when the storm of life is raging at them, they are calm because they know God.

The scripture says those that know their God shall be strong, and they shall do exploit. When the spirit of God is leading a man, what bothers other people will not affect him. Their gaze is set on things on high. Such persons have inner peace even in the face of trouble.

3. You Walk In Faith

Hebrews 11:6 But without faith, it is impossible to please Him, for he who comes to God must believe that He is and that He is a rewarder of those who diligently seek Him.

When you no longer walk by sight but by faith. Abraham didn't walk by sight. He walked by faith simply because he trusted God. He obeyed every instruction that God gave to him. Whether or not the instructions defy the common sense of man, Abraham would still obey.

When the spirit of God leads you, you trust God to a level that every instruction that comes from Him becomes mandatory for you. Even when it doesn't seem pleasant in the sight of men, you would not care. If God has commanded it, that means there is something He wants to achieve through it. God will never abandon us amid the storm; His help will always come through for us at the moment we need it most.

4. You Seek God First

James 1:5 if any of you lacks wisdom, let him ask of God, who gives to all liberally and without reproach, and it will be given to him.

The moment you no longer rely on your wisdom to do things. The moment you only look up to God for a direction that means you have been able to subdue the flesh through the power of the Holy Ghost.

The scripture says if any man lack wisdom, let him ask from God that gives liberally without blemish. What this means is that when you speak, you expend wisdom that supersedes the understanding of men. That baby Jesus has more knowledge and understanding of the scripture than scholars who are way older than him. This can only be possible by the power of the Holy Spirit.

5. You Have Power over Sin

Acts 1:8 but you shall receive power when the Holy Spirit has come upon you, and you shall be witnesses to Me in Jerusalem, and in all Judea and Samaria, and to the end of the earth."

Man in his natural state is powerless against sin and principalities. But when the spirit of God comes upon a man, he receives power to do the impossible. Remember Apostle Peter that could not calm the storm when the boat was about to wreck, he prayed for a lame man, and he walked. Acts 3:6 Then Peter said, "Silver and gold I do not have, but what I do have I give you: In the name of Jesus Christ of Nazareth, rise up and walk."

When the spirit of God is leading you, it gives you the power to do things that are considered impossible.

PRAYER POINTS FOR FRUIT OF THE SPIRIT

Today we will be dealing with prayer points for fruit of the spirit. According to the book of (Galatians 5:22-23) But the fruit of the Spirit is love, joy, peace, forbearance, kindness, goodness, faithfulness, gentleness and self-control. Against such things there is no law." These are nine fruits that every believer who have accepted Christ as their personal Lord and savior should have. Fruit is an evidence of something. The fruits of the spirit are the behavioral evidences that would prove the genuinity of one's repentance.

There are believers who claim to have accepted Christ as their Lord and savior but yet they lack love. Christ never called the apostles Christian throughout his stay on earth. It was after the death of Christ that the apostles have been fully initiated into the kingdom of heaven that people began to call them Christians. The meaning of Christian is Christ Like that means people that look like Christ. Meanwhile, one of the reasons why Christ came to the earth is to teach people how to be like him.

It is important to know that all fruits of the spirit were eminent in the life of Christ and until we bear all this the fruits our spiritual race on earth is not complete yet. If you notice that you lack one or two of these fruits of the spirit, there is a need for you to pray.

PRAYER POINTS

- Father Lord, I thank you for another moment like this, I thank you for the grace to witness a new day, let your name be exalted in the name of Jesus.

- Lord Jesus, I pray that you baptize me with the fruit of the spirit. I want to be like you Christ Jesus, in humility. I come against every spirit of pride in me, I destroy every atom of self-exaltation in me in the name of Jesus.

- Lord Jesus, you stated in your word that we should love our neighbors as ourselves. Christ made emphasis that of all the laws, love is the greatest. Father Lord, I pray that you will teach me how to love. I come against every spirit of hatred in my heart, let it be destroyed in the name of Jesus.

- Lord, I ask that you will break me down and remold me to the shape and size that you want. I ask that by your mercy you will take away every negative spirit inside of me, I pray Lord that you will take over my entire being in the name of Jesus.

- Lord Jesus, I pray that you will let your love reign in my heart. The grace to overlook the wrongdoings of other people, the grace to shun every negative things that people have done to me, I pray that you will give it to me in the name of Jesus.

- Lord, I pray that you will baptize me with your Holy Spirit and power. The spirit of the love that will quicken my mortal body. The spirit of God that will assist me to live in the true standard that God wants, I pray that you give it to me in the name of Jesus.

- Father Lord, grant me the grace to be kind to other people. I rebuke every spirit of resentment and anger inside of me. Anger and resentment belongs to the devil, I rebuke them inside me in the name of Jesus.

- The grace to control myself, I pray that you give it to me in the name of Jesus. Lord, I don't want to be driven around by temptations of the devil. The grace to hold myself, I pray that you give it to me in the name of Jesus.

- Lord, restore unto me the joy of thy salvation and uphold me with thy free spirit. I pray that you will feel my heart with your joy. The joy of the Holy Ghost, I pray that you feel my heart with it in the name of Jesus.

- Father Lord, I pray that by your mercy, you will help me to love other people genuinely. Regardless of their religious beliefs, doctrine, tribe or language, I pray that you will help me to look beyond all the things that separate us, in the name of Jesus.

- Father Lord, I pray for the grace to remain faithful to you alone Lord give it to me in Jesus name. I know it is hard for man to be faithful, but I pray that by your mercy, you will grant me the grace to be faithful in all my dealings. The grace to fear you and obey all your instructions, I pray that you give it to me in the name of Jesus.

- Lord, I pray for the grace to be kind to other people, Lord give it to me in the name of Jesus. I come against every spirit of bias and nepotism, the grace to see everyone equally and the grace to treat people with kindness and humility, Lord give it to me in the name of Jesus.

- Father Lord, from now, I want to start exhibiting the fruit of the spirit in a greater dimension. The scripture made me understand that we have been redeemed to be like you. Lord, I begin to operate in another dimension in the name of Jesus.

- Father Lord, I come against every demonic powers that is hindering me from exhibiting my full potentials as a child of God. Every Power that is limiting me from attaining a new level in the realm of the spirit, I come against it today in the name of Jesus.

- I rebuke every power that is hindering me from hearing the fruits of the spirit. I pray that you will heightened my spiritual maturity to grow beyond every limiting factors in the name of Jesus.

- I pray that you will feel my heart with love, joy and peace. The grace to be at peace with all men, I pray that you give it to me in the name of Jesus.

PRAYER POINTS FOR THE SPIRIT OF FORGIVENESS

Today we will dealing with prayer points for the spirit of forgiveness. Unforgiving spirit is one thing that has hindered most people from finding mercy, favour and grace in the sight of God. The Lord's Prayer emphasize on the need to forgive other people. Forgive this day as we forgive those that trespass against us this means, as much as we offend God and he forgive us, we must also learn to forgive others.

In the book of Ephesians 4:32 and be ye kind one to another, tenderhearted, forgiving one another, even as God for Christ's sake hath forgiven you. The scripture admonish us to be kind to one another, forgive another as God has forgiven us. There are pains and reproach that we must learn to let go. Recall the story of the prodigal son that was forgiven by his father.

The prodigal had taken all his birth right from his father in an unripe time and walk away into a distant land to enjoy his wealth. Although the father was not happy to let him leave, however, he could not stop him either. The prodigal son spent everything that was given to him by his father and he came broke. It was not long before he became destitute in a strange land. One day, he got tired of the whole situation and decided to return to his father to beg him for forgiveness and allow him work as one of his service.

Surprisingly, his father took him in with celebration. This parable explains our life before God and how God has continued to forgive us all our sins. God expects that we forgive on another too. There are some people who find it very difficult to forgive completely. No matter how hard they try, they can't just let go completely. You must understand that Christ wants us to be exactly like him in all our dealings. One of the fruit of the spirit is Forgiveness. When we the power of the holy ghost in our lives, it becomes very easy for us to forgive other people when they offend us.

Why Must You Forgive

We must forgive for the following reasons:

For our happiness

If you have ever been angry, you will understand that unhappiness comes whenever you see that person that has offended you. This means the presence of that person would determine if you will angry or happy. But when you let go and forgive completely, the pain, anger and resentment goes away and your happiness will be restored.

Esau knew no happiness until the day he forgave Jacob. For every time Esau remember Jacob, he was always filled with anger and rage. But he began to experience a new dimension of happiness and joy the day he forgave Jacob.

Forgiveness let you forget painful past

To move forward in life quickly, we must have a forgiving spirit. When you hold on to the pain and anger, you will continue to live in the past. Until the day you decide to let go, it unlocks the stage for you immediately.

Do not let unforgiveness lock you up in the prison of the past. The scripture says do not remember the things of the old for everything has been made new. You will not experience newness until you learn to forgive.

For God to forgive us our sins too

The easiest way to earn God's forgiveness is by forgiving others. The scripture in the book of Matthew 6:14-15 for if ye forgive men their trespasses, your heavenly Father will also forgive you: But if ye forgive not men their trespasses, neither will your Father forgive your trespasses. God cherish the heart that forgive others. There is a level of spiritual maturity that we must get to before can understand how to forgive people of their sin.

Forgiveness heals our wound

You get hurt when someone offend you. Meanwhile, retribution will not cure the pain that you go through. You will discover that even when you take revenge on that person that has offended you, it still doesn't cure the pain.

However, the pain can be cured by forgiving that person. When you forgive people, you free yourself from the shackles of pain and slavery that anger has kept you and once more you become a free man.

PRAYER POINTS

- Lord Jesus, I exalt you for the gift of life that you have given to me to witness this day. I thank you because you have been the protector of my Goshen and it is by your mercy that I'm not consumed. Lord, let your name be exalted in the name of Jesus.

- Lord Jesus, I pray for the spirit of Forgiveness. I ask that you will bless me with the spirit of forgiveness in the name of Jesus. Lord, I don't want to be destroyed by the pain, anger and resentment, I want to be freed by forgiving other people. Lord, please grant me the spirit of forgiveness in the name of Jesus.

- Lord Jesus, I pray that you will unlock all the blessings that unforgiveness has denied me from, I pray that you will release them to me today in the name of Jesus.

- Lord, I pray for the spirit of obedience to your word that says we should forgive others just as God has forgiven us all our sins. Father Lord, I pray for spiritual maturity to attain this stage in the name of Jesus.

- Father Lord, I come against every spirit of stubbornness. Every satanic spirit of captivity that wants to keep me in bondage through the unforgiven spirit, I destroy it by the fire of the Holy Ghost.

- Lord Jesus, I pray for deliverance from the power of captivity. Every form of slavery that I have been thrown into by the spirit of unforgiveness, I break them today in the name of Jesus.

- Lord from now, I receive grace to forgive and forget. I receive grace to begin to operate in a greater dimension in the name of Jesus. The grace not to harbour pain, anger or resentment, I pray you give it to me in the name of Jesus.

PRAYER POINTS FOR THE POWER OF HOLY GHOST

Today we will be dealing with prayer points for the power of the Holy Ghost. The holy spirit is the comforter as Christ has explained in book of John 14:16-18 And I will pray the Father, and he shall give you another Comforter, that he may abide with you forever; Even the Spirit of truth; whom the world cannot receive, because it seeth him not, neither knoweth him: but ye know him; for he dwelleth with you, and shall be in you. I will not leave you comfortless: I will come to you.

It was evidently displayed that Christ promised never to leave us void of a guiding spirit. When the spirit of the Lord (Holy Spirit) is absent in the life of a man, such a person will have no direction for their life. The ministry of Christ could not have been completed without the coming of the Holy Ghost.

Throughout the ministry of Christ on earth, the apostles learned about kingdom goals and rules. However, they have no sufficient power to run the ministry of Christ. It was after the death and resurrection of Christ, when Christ was about to be taken to heaven, he promised the apostles a comforter. This was explained in the book of John 14. The Holy Spirit will guide and nurture us into becoming like Christ.

For clarity, we will highlight some of the benefits of the Holy Spirit when it comes upon a man. We believe this will help us intensify our prayer for the power of the Holy Spirit.

Why You Must Have the Power of Holy Ghost
The Holy Ghost Gives Power

One of the benefits of having the power of the Holy Ghost is for us to be equipped with power. The scripture made us understand that we wrestle not against flesh and blood but against powers of darkness, rulers of darkness in high places. We need power to triumph over them. And the scripture made it known in Acts 1:8 but you shall receive power when the Holy Spirit has come upon you;

and you shall be witnesses to Me in Jerusalem, and in all Judea and Samaria, and to the end of the earth. This is an evident that the Holy Spirit gives power to man.

The Power of the Holy Spirit Gives Courage

Another reason why we must pray for the power of the Holy Spirit is to find Courage and bravery to preach the gospel. Apostle Peter was the closest ally to Christ, however, he denied Christ thrice when he was about to be taken. This was because he had no courage. Fast-forward to the book of Acts 2:17 And it shall come to pass in the last days, says God, That I will pour out of My Spirit on all flesh; Your sons and your daughters shall prophesy, Your young men shall see visions, Your old men shall dream dreams.

This was an account of Apostle Peter after they have gotten the power of the Holy Ghost. The apostles began to speak in strange tongues, people thought they were drunk with new wine. Peter that couldn't find courage to stand with Christ in the face of trouble, now stood in front of several people to preach the gospel. There is a kind of supernatural strength, courage and bravery that comes with having the power of the Holy.

The Power of the Holy Ghost Tells What's To Come

The book of John 16:13 However, when He, the Spirit of truth, has come, He will guide you into all truth; for He will not speak on His own authority, but whatever He hears He will speak; and He will tell you things to come. There is nothing better than having direction in life. It makes our journey through life simple.

God promised us that when the spirit comes upon us, it will guide us and teach us things to come. Revelation is very important in the life of a believer. These and many more is what the power of the Holy Spirit will do in our lives.

PRAYER POINTS

- Lord Jesus, I thank you for the grace to know the importance of the Holy Spirit. I thank you for the privilege to study, and come to the realization that the Holy Spirit is important in the life of a man. Thank you Jesus.

- Lord God, as you have promised in the book of Acts 2:17 that you will pour your spirit upon all flesh. Lord, upon this promise we wait Lord. I wait for the manifestation of your word. Lord, pour out your spirit upon me in the name of Jesus.

- Lord, I do not want to live my life without direction. The scripture made me understand that the spirit of God will teach me things that is yet to come. I pray for spiritual revelation of my life and purpose, Lord send your spirit upon me in the name of Jesus.

- Lord God, for it has been written, if the power that raised Jesus Christ of Nazareth dwells in you, it will quicken your mortal body. Lord, I do not want to slave to sin anymore, I decree that your spirit come upon my life in the name of Jesus.

- Lord Jesus, I pray that you will grant me your spirit that will give me victory over sin and Iniquity. Lord Jesus, by your mercy, grant me your spirit in the name of Jesus.

- Lord, I pray for the forgiveness of sin, if there is any sin in my life that will hinder the manifestation of your power, Lord by your mercy, forgive me in the name of Jesus.

- Father Lord, when you spirit is upon the life of a man, your protection is guaranteed. Lord I do not want to rely on my physical strength and ability for protection, Lord I pray that you will send your spirit into my life in the name of Jesus.

- You charged us in the book of Matthew that we should go into the world and preach the gospel of Christ, baptize people in the name of the Father, Son and Holy Ghost. Lord, I need the power of the Holy Ghost to fulfill this great mandate, Lord Send down your spirit in the name of Jesus. Amen.

HOW TO PRAY IN THE SPIRIT

Today we teach ourselves how to pray in the spirit.

1 Cor 2:14, "But the natural man receiveth not the things of the Spirit of God: for they are foolishness unto him: neither, can he know them, because they are spiritually discerned."

One hallmark of the believer is that he has the indwelling of the Spirit of God. He is spiritually inclined to the things of the Spirit, on the flip side the unbeliever does not have this access. Acts 2:17, "And it shall come to pass in the last days, saith God, I will pour out of my Spirit upon all flesh: and your sons and your daughters shall prophesy, and your young men shall see visions, and your old men shall dream dreams:"

The believer has the trademark of the Spirit of God on Him. This marks him out from the Unbeliever. It is our signature, it is our seal. It is how we identify with the Heavenly Father. So we understand that there's a place where the believer does things from the Spirit because He has the Spirit of God upon Him, indwelling of the Holy Spirit. 1John 4:13," Hereby know we that we dwell in him, and he in us, because he hath given us of his Spirit." So the believer dwells in Him by the Spirit, halleluiah. That's how we access the Father.

1 Peter 2:5, "Ye also, as lively stones, are built up a spiritual house, an holy priesthood, to offer up spiritual sacrifices, acceptable to God by Jesus Christ."

1 Peter 3:18, "For Christ also hath once suffered for sins, the just for the unjust, that he might bring us to God, being put to death in the flesh, but quickened by the Spirit:"

How Believer pray in the Spirit

Giving Thanks
1Thessa. 5:18 in everything give thanks: for this is the will of God in Christ Jesus concerning you.

We must come to understand that Thanksgiving is part of our prayer life. We do the Will of the Father when we give thanks. We can draw numerous references from the scriptures where Jesus gave thanks.

Matt. 15:36, "And he took the seven loaves and the fishes, and gave thanks, and broke them, and gave to his disciples, and the disciples to the multitude."

Mark 8:6, "And he commanded the people to sit down on the ground: and he took the seven loaves, and gave thanks, and broke, and gave to his disciples to set before them; and they did set them before the people."

We see that in everything, Jesus gave thanks to the Father. Jesus did the Will of the Father.

In all situations, He gave thanks. Halleluiah.

We do the Will of the Father by giving thanks.

Also, we give thanks for the victory in Christ Jesus.

1 Cor. 15:57,"But thanks be to God, which giveth us the victory through our Lord Jesus Christ."

2Cor. 2:14 says, "Now thanks be unto God, which always causeth us to triumph, in Christ, and maketh manifest the savor of his knowledge by us in every place."

Halleluiah for the victory.

2 Cor.9:15, "Thanks be unto God for his unspeakable gift."

Further references from scriptures on Thanksgiving

Col.1:12, "Giving thanks unto the Father, which hath made us meet to be partakers of the inheritance of the saints in light:"

We give thanks for what Christ has done for us, made us partakers of the inheritance of the saints in light. That is, all that the saints should have in possession, we have become partakers of that inheritance.

Worship in the Spirit

The Believer is to worship in the Spirit. It's the right thing to do. Phil. 3:3,"For we are the circumcision, which worship God in the spirit, and rejoice in Christ Jesus, and have no confidence, in the flesh."

John 4:23-24

23 But the hour cometh, and now is, when the true worshipers shall worship the Father in spirit and in truth: for the Father (2532) seeketh such to worship him.

24 God is a Spirit: and they that worship him must worship him in spirit and in truth.

There is a manner in which the believer is to offer worship – in the Spirit. It is where our confidence lies. Halleluiah.

Eph.5:18-19

"And be not drunk with wine, wherein is excess; but be filled with the Spirit;

Speaking to yourselves in psalms and hymns and spiritual songs, singing and making melody in your heart to the Lord;"

It is not enough to just sing songs but to sing the right songs. Songs by the Spirit and of the Spirit. We do not get edified by singing the songs of the World. They are not Spirit-filled. Singing in hymns and Psalms and Spiritual songs. All these are spirit originated.

To talk about what Christ has done, what he has provided for us, to celebrate His love and show appreciation for the salvation we have received. Hallelujah!

Communication in the Spirit.

First, we understand that Prayer is pure communication with the Father. Prayer is fellowshipping with the Father. We talk to God as a Man talks to His friend-in prayer.

Prayer is the lifestyle of the believer. It's a call to duty and Responsibility. In the New Testament, Apostle Paul prayed and laid examples of how we are to pray in the Spirit. In his letters he prayed for men, and encouraged the church to do so.

In communication, we are being filled with the Spirit

Eph. 5:18

18 And be not drunk with wine, wherein is excess; but be filled with the Spirit;

In the preceding verse we see that we are to understand what the Will of God is, as stated earlier, it goes in in verse 18 as an instruction for us not to be filled with wine wherein is excess but to be filled with the Spirit.

There's an instruction in Gal. 5:16 to walk in the Spirit. It's a posture to maintain for the believer who is to be filled. So there's a walking to be done so as to be filled. When we read further to verse 16 to verse 24 of Gal.5

Verse 25 says, 25 if we live in the Spirit, let us also walk in the Spirit. So we live in the Spirit, we are filled in the Spirit to communicate in the Spirit.

By the extension of what the believer enjoys, the indwelling if the Spirit which prompts a Living and walking. The availability of these is what makes us alert at all times.

Obedience to the Spirit

1 Thessa. 5:19, "Quench not the Spirit."

There's this story of a man who was driving home and somehow he didn't know how he got home. On getting home, he met his wife asleep as opposed to her being asleep as at that time. She then asked, "How was your ride?"

He replied saying he didn't know how he got home because at some point he felt really sleeping behind the wheels. His wife answered saying," I figured, that's why I prayed for you at 4:30pm"

She received the nudge to pray at that point even though she felt sleepy also. So we use this to our advantage. The Unbelievers do not enjoy this, so if we have this in our possession, the last thing we'd want to do is quench the Spirit of God.

We pray in the Spirit in Obedience to the Spirit.

Dependence on the Spirit

Rom.8:26," Likewise the Spirit also helpeth our infirmities: for we know not what we should pray for as we ought: but the Spirit itself maketh intercession for us with groaning's which cannot be uttered.

27 And he that searcheth the hearts knoweth what is the mind of the Spirit, because he maketh intercession for the saints according to the will of God.

Here we see that the Spirit of God helps us to pray in the Spirit as we ought to which is the will of God. There are moments where our words fail us, we rely on the Spirit of God.

Praying In Other Tongues

Mark 16:17

"And these signs shall follow them that believe; in my name shall they cast out devils; they shall speak with new tongues;"

Jesus speaking here said that there's a power that we be given to the ones that believe. They shall speak with new tongues.

1 Cor. 14:2

For he that speaketh in an unknown tongue speaketh not unto men, but unto God: for no man understandeth him;

We see from the verse above that a man who prays in the Spirit prays to God. Apostle Paul in verse 18 of the same chapter which says," I thank my God, I speak with tongues more than ye all:"

So we pray in the Spirit by speaking in tongues.

We see the clarity of this in chapter 14

A man who speaks in the Spirit edifies himself and speaks to God but in a congregation there should be an interpretation for those who are without.

Glory to God, no one is left out of the Gift of the Spirit

You can desire to speak in other tongues. When there's a desire, you expect to speak. Remember, it's speaking to God in other tongues that no one understands.

In Conclusion:

Prayer is our lifestyle. Prayer works all the time and 100% of the time. If Elijah could pray how much more he who has the indwelling of the Spirit of God. We pray with understanding of what we have, we pray in the light of God's Word. We pray as the Spirit helps us only when we rely on him. We are helped in Jesus name.

30 PRAYER POINTS FOR MANIFESTATION OF SPIRITUAL FRUITS

> *Galatians 5:22 but the fruit of the Spirit is love, joy, peace, longsuffering, gentleness, goodness, faith, 5:23 Meekness, temperance: against such there is no law*

Spiritual fruits are the fruits of the Spirit that is produced by the Holy Spirit in Us. The fruit of the spirit are the roots of our righteousness. It takes a righteous person to produce a righteous fruits. The fruits of the Spirit are the virtues that flows from us that shows that we are children of God. Today we shall be looking at 30 prayer points for manifestation of spiritual gifts. This prayer points will empower you manifest righteousness not only before God, but also before men.

Different Between Spiritual Gifts and Spiritual Fruits

Spiritual gifts are endowments of the Holy Spirit, they are given randomly by Gods election of grace. You can also desire any of the spiritual gifts of your choice. You don't work for spiritual gifts, you just receive them by faith and grace empowers you to manifest them. The purpose of spiritual gifts is for evangelism and for the furtherance of the gospel. On the other hand Spiritual fruits are fruits of righteousness or the fruits of the grace of Christ in us. While gifts helps us be a blessing to others, fruits show that we are really Children of God. To explain this better, a Christian can be manifesting the gift of the spirit and still be living in Sin. For instance someone may have the gift of prophecy and still be harboring hate in her heart. The fruits of the spirit is relevant to us for our personal work with God. Any believer can manifest gifts, it's by grace, but only mature Christians manifest the fruits of the Spirit. Do not only crave for gifts, more importantly crave for the fruits of the Spirits. These prayer points for manifestation of spiritual fruits will empower you to manifest the fruits of the spirit in your everyday life. Pray them with faith and be blessed.

PRAYER POINTS

1. Father, I thank you for the Fruits of the Holy Spirit in Jesus name

2. Father thank you for your mercies that have helped me to manifest the fruits of the Holy Spirit

3. Dear Holy Spirit fill me afresh today in Jesus name.

4. Oh Lord empower me to manifests Spiritual fruits in Jesus name.

5. I receive fresh grace to manifest Spiritual fruits in Jesus name

6. Dear Holy Spirit, baptize me with the spiritual fruit of Love in Jesus name

7. Dear Holy Spirit, baptize me with the spiritual fruit of joy in Jesus name

8. Dear Holy Spirit, baptize me with the spiritual fruit of peace in Jesus name

9. Dear Holy Spirit, baptize me with the spiritual fruit of longsuffering or patience in Jesus name

10. Dear Holy Spirit, baptize me with the spiritual fruit of gentleness in Jesus name

11. Dear Holy Spirit, baptize me with the spiritual fruit of goodness in Jesus name

12. Dear Holy Spirit, baptize me with the spiritual fruit of faith in Jesus name

13. Dear Holy Spirit, baptize me with the spiritual fruit of meekness in Jesus name

14. Dear Holy Spirit, baptize me with the spiritual fruit of temperance in Jesus name.

15. Let your heat O Lord, consume my will, in the name of Jesus.

16. Let the flame of the Holy Spirit blaze upon the altar of my heart, in the name of Jesus.

17. Holy Spirit, let your power flow like blood into my veins.

18. Dear Holy Spirit, order my spirit and fashion my life in your will in Jesus name

19. Sweet Spirit Of God, let your fire burn all that is not holy in my life in Jesus name

20. Dear Holy Spirit, let your fire generate power in my life in Jesus name.

21. Sweet Holy Spirit, impart to me thoughts higher than my own thoughts in Jesus name

22. Holy Spirit, come as dew and refresh me, in the name of Jesus.

23. Holy Spirit, guide me in the way of liberty, in the name of Jesus.

24. Holy Spirit, blow upon me such that sin would no more find place in me, in the name of Jesus.

25. Holy Spirit, where my love is cold, warm me up, in Jesus' name.

26. Dear holy spirit, continue to show forth your manifest presence in my life in Jesus name

27. Let my hand become the sword of fire to cut down evil trees, in the name of Jesus.

28. Let my feet become the thunder of God, as I stamp them. Let them deafen the enemy, in the name of Jesus.

29. Let the spiritual rag of poverty in my life be destroyed by the fire of the Holy Spirit in the name of Jesus.

30. Every enemy of excellence in my life, be consumed by the power of the Holy Spirit in Jesus' name.

30 PRAYER POINTS FOR MANIFESTATION OF SPIRITUAL GIFTS

Ephesians 4:11 and he gave some, apostles; and some, prophets; and some, evangelists; and some, pastors and teachers; 4:12 for the perfecting of the saints, for the work of the ministry, for the edifying of the body of Christ:

Spiritual gifts are an essential part of our Christian walk. Spiritual gifts is an empowerment of the Holy Spirit. These gifts empowers us for quality service as we run our Christian race in life. Every child of God must desire to manifest the gifts of the spirit. Without the manifestation of this gifts, people will not see signs and wonders in your life and unbelievers are mostly attracted to God through signs and wonders. Today I have compiled carefully selected prayer points for manifestation of spiritual gifts this prayer points will empower us to discover our spiritual gifts and also to manifest those gifts in our lives. As you pray this prayers today, you Christian life shall never lack power in Jesus name.

The endowment of Spiritual gifts is by grace, not by merit, that is why it is called a gift. Also, every believer has one or more spiritual gifts operational in him or she, the only problem is that many believers are unaware of the gifts at work in them. One of the tragedies of life is to have what you need and not know. That is why you need to engage in this prayer points for manifestation of spiritual gifts. You cannot manifest what you have not discovered, and to discover, you must go into prayers for God to open your eyes to your spiritual gifts. This prayer points will also empower you to operate in any spiritual gifts that you desire, whether, it is healing, working of miracles, word of knowledge or wisdom or any of the other 9 gifts as seen in 1 Corinthians 12. As you engage this prayer points today you shall not only discover your own gifts, you shall also operate in any other gifts of your choice in Jesus name.

PRAYER POINTS

1. Father, I thank you for the Gift of the Holy Spirit in Jesus name

2. Father thank you for your mercies that had qualified me for the gifts of the Holy Spirit

3. Dear Holy Spirit fill me afresh today in Jesus name.

4. Open my eyes oh Spirit of the Lord to the gift that you have endued me with in Jesus name.

5. I receive fresh grace to manifest the gifts of the Spirit in Jesus name

6. Dear Holy Spirit, baptize me with the gift of the Word of knowledge in Jesus name

7. Dear Holy Spirit, baptize me with the gift of the Word of wisdom in Jesus name

8. Dear Holy Spirit, baptize me with the gift of faith in Jesus name

9. Dear Holy Spirit, baptize me with the gift of working of miracles in Jesus name

10. Dear Holy Spirit, baptize me with the gift of speaking in diverse tongues in Jesus name

11. Dear Holy Spirit, baptize me with the gift of interpretation of tongs in Jesus name

12. Dear Holy Spirit, baptize me with the gift of discernment of Sprits in Jesus name

13. Dear Holy Spirit, baptize me with the gift of healing in Jesus name

14. Dear Holy Spirit, baptize me with the gift of prophecy in Jesus name.

15. Holy Spirit, my refiner, refine and purge my life by your fire in Jesus name

16. Holy Spirit, inflame and fire my heart, in the name of Jesus.

17. Dear Holy Spirit, lay your hands upon me and quench every rebellion in me in Jesus name

18. Holy Ghost fire, begin to burn away every self-centeredness in me, in the name of Jesus.

19. Sweet Homey Spirit, breathe your life-giving breath into my soul, in the name of Jesus.

20. Sweet Holy Spirit, make me ready to go wherever you send me in Jesus name.

21. Sweet Holy Spirit, never let me shut you out in Jesus name

22. Sweet Holy Spirit, never let me try to limit you to my capacity in Jesus name

23. Dear Holy Spirit, work freely in me and through me in Jesus name

24. Dear Holy Spirit, purify the channels of my life in Jesus name

25. Let your heat O Lord, consume my will, in the name of Jesus.

26. Let the flame of the Holy Spirit blaze upon the altar of my heart, in the name of Jesus.

27. Holy Spirit, let your power flow like blood into my veins.

28. Dear Holy Spirit, order my spirit and fashion my life in your will in Jesus name

29. Sweet Spirit Of God, let your fire burn all that is not holy in my life in Jesus name

30. Dear Holy Spirit, let your fire generate power in my life in Jesus name.

POWERFUL PRAYER POINTS FOR SPIRITUAL GROWTH

1 Corinthians 13:11:11 When I was a child, I spake as a child, I understood as a child, I thought as a child: but when I became a man, I put away childish things.

Every healthy child is a growing child. One of the major characteristics of a living thing is growth. If you are not growing, it means you are dying. As a child of God, it's not enough to be born again, we must desire to grow in our salvation. Today we shall be engaging in powerful prayer points for spiritual growth. Spiritual growth is defined as the spiritual energy we need for growth. Just like every new born baby needs to be properly fed for strength and growth, that is how every child of God also needs to be feed spiritually for spiritual strength and growth.

If you are not spiritually strong, you cannot last in the faith, you must learn to equip yourself spiritually in order to overcome the temptations of the devil. There are two ways to grow in strength as a child of God, they are: The Word, and Prayers. We are going to be examining these two ways shortly:

Two Ways to Spiritual Growth.

1). The Word Of God: 1 Peter 2:2 , tells us that as new born babies, we must desire the sincere milk of the word of God, in order to grow in our salvation. The word of God is your spiritual food as a child of God if you desire spiritual growth, you must feed on the word of God daily. Just like a baby will be malnourished if he or she is not properly fed, you also will be malnourished spiritually if you do not feed on the word of God. The word of God is the balance diet for the soul, without it you cannot experience spiritual growth.

But how do you feed on the word of God? Simple you feed on the word of God through the following ways:

A). Daily Bible Study

B). Reading Christian Literatures

C). Listening To A Sermon

D). Attending Church Regularly

E). Putting the Word to Work in Your Life

2). Prayers: Jesus speaking in Luke 18:1, he said we should pray always and not faint. If the word is the food for the soul, then prayers is the exercise for the soul. Every time we pray we exercise our spirit man. Eating always without exercising will not make you fit, the same way studying the word without prayers will still keep you weak spiritually. We must pray always it takes prayers to overcome the temptations of the devil. Prayer is very vital in our spiritual walk with God that is why I have compiled over 100 powerful prayer points for spiritual growth. This prayer points will fire up your spirit man and increase your spiritual strength as you walk with God.

I really encourage you to invest in your spirit man by being a student if the word and also a prayer giant. As you take out time to engage this prayer points for spiritual growth, you shall never know weakness in your spiritual life again in Jesus name. You are blessed

PRAYER POINTS

1. Let my wounded parts receive healing, in the name of Jesus.

2. Let my worried parts encounter the power in the blood of Jesus, in the name of Jesus.

3. I refuse to be divided against myself, in the name of Jesus.

4. O Lord, pour your healing oil into my troubled soul, in the name of Jesus.

5. O Lord, hold me in your arms of healing, in the name of Jesus.

6. Let every weariness of the mind melt away, in Jesus' name.

7. O Lord, heal my bruised heart, in the name of Jesus.

8. Any coldness towards the Lord in my heart, let the fire of the Holy Ghost melt it away, in the name of Jesus.

9. Every power, holding me down from touching the helm of the garment of the Lord, break away, in the name of Jesus.

10. O Lord, cleanse me and sweeten the springs of my being, in the name of Jesus.

11. Let the freedom and light of the Lord flow into my mind, in the name of Jesus.

12. O Lord, let your grace and love, be my true rest, in Jesus' name.

13. In the dark places of human life, let the light of the Lord shine on me, in the name of Jesus.

14. Every wrestling match with self-pity in my life, die, in the name of Jesus.

15. Every power that is threatening to swallow me up, loose your hold, in the name of Jesus.

16. O Lord, take me in your arms and heal me, in the name of Jesus.

17. Let the power in the blood of Jesus dissolve my pride, in the name of Jesus.

18. My Jacob, arise and wrestle into your breakthroughs, in the name of Jesus.

19. In the wound of my soul, Holy Spirit, pour your healing oil, in the name of Jesus.

20. O Lord, anoint my wounds with the oil of healing, in Jesus' name.

21. Every cry of frustration, be silenced, in the name of Jesus.

22. Every anti-harvest power of my father's house, be dismantled, in the name of Jesus.

23. O Lord, remake me to enable me fulfil my destiny, in Jesus' name.

24. Thou power of self-imprisonment, die, in the name of Jesus.

25. Power of God, draw my scattered blessings together, in the name of Jesus.

26. O God arise and sharpen my senses that I may truly see what I am looking at, in the name of Jesus.

27. Let the water of my circumstances be turned into wine by the power of the Lord, in the name of Jesus.

28. O Lord, pick me up and re-arrange my life for breakthroughs, in the name of Jesus.

29. O Lord, stay at the center of my life, in the name of Jesus.

30. Every fountain of bitterness, dry up, in the name of Jesus.

31. Let the cock crow in my heart whenever I am about to go astray, in the name of Jesus.

32. Cobwebs of poverty, be melted away by the fire of God, in the name of Jesus.

33. O Lord, fill me with your love and peace, in the name of Jesus.

34. Every power, weighing me down, be dismantled, in Jesus' name.

35. Every ancestral power, tying my hands, be uprooted, in the name of Jesus.

36. O Lord, give me the power to abandon my idols, in Jesus' name.

37. Holy Ghost fire, illuminate my darkness, in the name of Jesus.

38. Thou Great Physician, heal me and make me whole, in the name of Jesus.

39. Let the oil of the anointing of the Lord penetrate every cell in my body, in the name of Jesus.

40. O God of wholeness, manifest your power in my life, in the name of Jesus.

41. Hold me, O Lord, and do not let me fall, in the name of Jesus.

42. Whenever I want to hurt others, O Lord, deflect my action, in the name of Jesus.

43. O Lord, let my desire to be true to you prevail over everything else, in the name of Jesus.

44. I receive deliverance from the bondage of unnecessary words, in the name of Jesus.

45. O Lord, teach me when to be silent, in the name of Jesus.

46. Holy Spirit, let all my words be well used, in the name of Jesus.

47. O Lord, defend your interest in my life, in the name of Jesus.

48. By Your mountain-moving power, O Lord, stay beside me to defend me, in the name of Jesus.

49. by the power that divided the Red Sea, O Lord, stay before me to lead me, in the name of Jesus.

50. by the power that changed the lot of Jabez, O Lord, stay above me to bless me, in the name of Jesus.

51. O Lord, make me open to your wisdom, in the name of Jesus.

52. O Lord, make me receptive to your will, in the name of Jesus.

53. My life will not be ruled by fear of what anyone can do to me, in the name of Jesus.

54. I shall not die inwardly, in the name of Jesus.

55. I release myself from every bondage of fear, in Jesus name.

56. O Lord, remember me as you remembered the dying man next to you at the cross, in the name of Jesus.

57. My Father, transform me in the fire of your love, in Jesus' name.

58. Thou power of God, clear away my inner rubbish, in Jesus' name.

59. O Lord, use my life to bless many people, in the name of Jesus.

60. O Lord, make my life a garden in which you can work in this world, in the name of Jesus.

61. O Lord, fill me with the spirit of healing and peace, in the name of Jesus.

62. O Lord, set my whole heart with Holy Ghost fire, in the name of Jesus.

63. O Lord, let me be a channel of blessings to others, in the name of Jesus.

64. O God, let me be employed by you, in the name of Jesus.

65. O Lord, let me be exalted by you, in the name of Jesus.

66. O Lord, let me be set aside for you, in the name of Jesus.

67. Let the Spirit of God dwell richly in me, in the name of Jesus.

68. O Lord, use me to affect my generation positively, in Jesus' name.

69. O Lord, make me part of the mystery of your presence in the world, in the name of Jesus.

70. Let every part of my life be overshadowed by You, O Lord, in the name of Jesus.

71. Ignite my cold love with your fire, O Lord, in the name of Jesus.

72. Let holy fervency come upon me, in the name of Jesus.

73. Empower me, O Lord, to be selfless in all my spiritual activities, in the name of Jesus.

74. Let the bonds of evil and death be broken, in the name of Jesus.

75. Let the light of the Lord flood the darkness in my life, in the name of Jesus.

76. O Lord, let me be your delight in this planet, in Jesus' name.

77. O Lord, simplify my life and take possession of me, in Jesus' name.

78. O Lord, forgive me for relying on my own strength, in the name of Jesus.

79. Father, empower me to climb to my mountain of fulfilment, in the name of Jesus.

80. O Lord, let your splendour shine forth in my life, in Jesus' name.

81. O God, grant me journey mercies, till my journey's end, in Jesus' name.

82. Lord, let your light radiate through me, in the name of Jesus.

83. O Lord, help me to empty myself before you, in the name of Jesus.

84. O Lord, teach me to be quiet in your presence, in Jesus' name.

85. My Father, give unto me untold riches, in the name of Jesus.

86. I thank You Lord for the unimaginable gift of the gospel.

87. O Lord, keep me thankful all my days, in the name of Jesus.

88. No matter what is going on, I shall not lose sight of hope, in the name of Jesus.

89. Thank You Lord for all the insults you have borne for me, in the name of Jesus.

90. O Lord, empower me to know you deeper, in the name of Jesus.

91. Hold me, O Lord, in the palm of your hands, in Jesus' name.

92. Hide me, O Lord, in the hollow of your hands, in Jesus' name.

93. O Lord, let me be wholly available to you on this earth, in the name of Jesus.

94. O Lord, give me a generous heart and open hands, in Jesus' name.

95. Blood of Jesus, heal every damage done to my body, soul and spirit, in the name of Jesus.

96. O Lord, pour into my heart the gentle balm of Your Spirit, in the name of Jesus.

97. O light of God, surround me always, in the name of Jesus.

98. O presence of God, envelope my life, in the name of Jesus.

99. O God, be the light in my darkness, in the name of Jesus.

100. O God, be my refuge and strength in times of fear, in the name of Jesus.

Thank you Father for answering my prayers in Jesus name.

FIVE WAYS TO PRAY IN SPIRITUAL WARFARE

Today we will be teaching the five ways to pray in spiritual warfare. Life is a warzone. We are warriors. We must not exhibit laxity. The scripture admonishes us in the book of Ephesians 6:11-12-13 Put on the whole armor of God that you may be able to stand against the wiles of the devil or we do not wrestle against flesh and blood, but against principalities, against powers, against the rulers of the darkness of this age, against spiritual hosts of wickedness in the heavenly places. Therefore take up the whole armor of God that you may be able to withstand in the evil day, and having done all, to stand.

This portion of the scripture has explained our type of Warfare. Our battle is not physical because we do not wrestle against flesh and blood but rulers, principalities, and powers in high places. Judging by this type of fight, we must not show any form of weakness. We must be prepared all the time. Good to know, God has promised us victory over every power and darkness through the power in the name of Jesus. However, this doesn't mean there is no fight. We must still engage in spiritual warfare.

Knowing how to pray in spiritual warfare goes a long way in ensuring that victory is ascertained. Spirit warfare is not like the regular prayer. These are prayers for freedom, for dominance, for restoration. They are not the type of prayer prayed solemnly. As these prayers are essential, not knowing the best ways to pray them makes them ineffective. When you pray, you must do it with understanding with consciousness.

Five Ways to Pray In Spiritual Warfare
1. Pray In the Spirit

Praying in the spirit is not just about speaking in tongues during prayer. Although speaking in the Holy Ghost is one common way of praying in the spirit, however, there is more to it. Praying in the spirit comes with knowing and understanding the word.

When you study the word, there is an interpretation through the power of the Holy Spirit. When the interpretation comes, you are ignited in your spirit to pray using the word. The word of God is a sword. The book of Hebrews 4:12 for the word of God is living and powerful, and sharper than any two-edged sword, piercing even to the division of soul and spirit, and joints and marrow, and is a discerner of the thoughts and intents of the heart.

Praying in spiritual warfare is never complete without praying in the spirit. Praying in the spirit is not effective until the word is sent forth. While praying in the spirit, it is also important to pray in the Holy Ghost. These are unknown tongues that are clear to God. When you speak in the Holy Ghost, you become a territorial commander in the realm of the spirit. You make utterances with words that are beyond the understanding of man.

2. Pray Without Ceasing

You should not launch into prayer only when you are in trouble. Learn to pray even when things seem normal. In the days of trouble, you don't get enough strength to fight back. For instance, you don't have all the strength to pray fervently when a terrible illness strikes you down. So also will you lose every hold of strength to pray when you are troubled? Your saving grace during this time will be years of fruitful praying time you have labored.

You must know that a fighter is not a champion by virtue of what happened in the fighting ring. He is a champion through the hours of preparation. He will only enter the ring to display all that has been practiced. So also is spiritual warfare. You don't become a victor when trouble comes; you become a victor through the years or days of preparations you have made. That is what will keep you going in moments of trouble.

3. Fast and Pray

Mathew 17:21 However, this kind does not go out except by prayer and fasting."

Nothing moves by itself unless there is an external force. You must not negate the place of sacrifice when fighting spiritual warfare. The adversary doesn't rest day and night; why should you linger as a believer? You should intensify your prayer life with fasting.

This was the response of Christ when the apostles asked why they could not perform certain miracles like Jesus. Miracle will not happen unless there is fasting and prayer. Even Christ the Supreme Being fasted for forty days and nights before he commenced his work here on it. You must learn how to fast as a Christian. Some victories will not come unless you have fasted.

While prayer is a force that drives answers, fasting is the energy that makes the force compelling.

4. Pray With Faith

Hebrews 11:6 But without faith, it is impossible to please Him, for he who comes to God must believe that He is and that He is a rewarder of those who diligently seek Him.

You are praying to God, but you don't have faith in Him. For you to receive from the Father, you must believe in the potency of His power. You must believe that exists, and He is powerful enough to turn that situation around.

Your faith must be strong; you must have a conviction in your heart that God can grant you victory. We are men of incredible sight. Our sight is in our faith that our heavenly father is powerful and He has conquered the world. You must first key into this faith, and then victory will come.

5. Pray With the Blood of Christ

Revelation 12:11 and they overcame him by the blood of the Lamb and by the word of their testimony, and they did not love their lives to the death.

The blood of Christ is leverage for us believers. For redemption to come, there must be a shedding of the blood. For victory over sin, Christ had to shed his blood. Similarly, for spiritual warfare, the blood is still adequate to ascertain victory.

The scripture says, and they overcame him by the blood of the lamb. When you pray spiritual warfare, always emphasize the blood. The blood of Christ has been shed, and it continues to flow in Calvary. This tells us that the potency of the blood is everlasting.

30 POWERFUL HOLY GHOST FIRE PRAYER POINTS

The Holy Ghost Fire is real. That is the fire of God that consumes all the works of the devil in your life. Today we shall be engaging in 30 powerful Holy Ghost fire prayer points. This prayer points are offensive prayer points that will shake the kingdom of darkness in your life. Our God is Love and He showers His unconditional Love to all, He also protects those that have accepted Him jealously. When Paul the Apostle was on his way to eliminate the Christians in Jerusalem, God arrested him and struck him with blindness, when King Herod killed James and made a move on Peter, God sent an Angel to release Peter and that same Angel killed Herod the next day. This Holy Ghost fire prayer points will be releasing angels into the camp of your enemies to destroy all their works against your life and destiny in Jesus name.

When we pray Holy Ghost fire prayer points, we release fiery angels to work, the Angels of the Lord are flames of fire, Hebrews 1:7 tells us. These angels are released into battle to fight for us. Whenever you see Christians praying and screaming 'holy ghost fire' they are not joking, the fire of God that destroys is real, and it is released by these fiery angels to destroy every evil planted in our lives by the devil. The best way to destroy an evidence is by fire, in the same way, whatsoever the devil has planted in your life as an evidence, the Holy Ghost fire of God shall consume it to ashes in Jesus name. I encourage you to pray this prayers by faith and with holy anger today, and you shall see all satanic oppositions against you burn to ashes by the fire of God in Jesus name.

PRAYER POINTS.

1. Father, I thank you for sending us the Holy Spirit and power in Jesus name

2. Father, I enter your throne room of grace and mercy now to receive mercy and grace to keep going in Jesus name

3. Oh God arise and scatter all my enemies and adversaries in Jesus name

4. I release the Holy Ghost Fire upon every plan of the devil against my life in Jesus name.

5. I release the Holy Ghost Fire upon every enchantment of darkness against my life in Jesus name.

6. I release the Holy Ghost Fire upon every activities of witchcraft against my life in Jesus name.

7. I release the Holy Ghost Fire upon every satanic oppositions against my life in Jesus name.

8. I release the Holy Ghost Fire upon every evil limitations against my life in Jesus name.

9. I release the Holy Ghost Fire upon every force of darkness fighting my marital destiny in Jesus name.

10. I release the Holy Ghost fire against every marine force fighting my marriage in Jesus name.

11. I release the Holy Ghost Fire upon every demonic strongman fighting my progress in Jesus name.

12. I release the Holy Ghost Fire upon every witchcraft coven fighting my marriage in Jesus name.

13. I release the Holy Ghost Fire upon every spirit of bareness in Jesus name.

14. I release the Holy Ghost Fire upon every spirit of untimely death in Jesus name.

15. I release the Holy Ghost Fire upon every Spirit of stagnation against my life in Jesus name.

16. I release the Holy Ghost Fire against every ancestral connection in my father's house in Jesus name.

17. I release the Holy Ghost Fire against every evil covenant working against my life in Jesus name.

18. I release the Holy Ghost Fire against every form of stagnation working against my life in Jesus name.

19. I release the Holy Ghost Fire against every evil utterance working against my life in Jesus name.

20. By the Fire of the Holy Ghost, return to sender every arrow of the devil targeted against my life in Jesus name

21. By the Holy Ghost Fire, I consume Poverty In my life in Jesus name

22. By the Holy Ghost Fire, I consume failure in my life in Jesus name

23. By the Holy Ghost Fire, I consume lack in my life in Jesus name

24. By the Holy Ghost Fire, I consume sickness in my life in Jesus name

25. By the Holy Ghost Fire, I consume backwardness in my life in Jesus name

26. By the Holy Ghost Fire, I consume Generational curses in my life in Jesus name

27. By the Holy Ghost Fire, I consume evil pattern in my life in Jesus name

28. By the Holy Ghost Fire, I consume bareness in my life in Jesus name

29. By the Holy Ghost Fire, I consume every evil deposits of the devil in my life in Jesus name

30. Thank you Father, for indeed you are a consuming Fire.

PRAYER POINTS FOR JOY

Today we will be dealing with prayer points for joy. To understand the meaning of joy we will we look at happiness first.

Definition of happiness

A feeling of extreme happiness or cheerfulness, especially related to the acquisition or expectation of something good. Happiness is an emotion which one experiences feelings ranging from contentment and satisfaction to bliss and intense pleasure.

Let's look at joy

Joy is a deeply rooted happiness inspired by the Holy Spirit. It is derived from the Lord. No wonder the bible says 'the joy of the Lord is my strength'. According to English context, happiness is described as a feeling or emotion, but in the kingdom joy is more than just a feeling, it is a lifestyle.

If joy is seen as a feeling alone, then we can decide to be joyous this moment and sorrowful the next moment. Of course not, as believers we are not to live our lives like that.

The kingdom lifestyle negates that of the world's,, according to kingdom principles you are to be joyful in any challenge you face, although this will look stupid to the world, they'll be fast to call you names seeing you rejoice in the face of trial instead of you to be sorrowful and hopeless.

Believers are to work by faith and not by sight (2 Cor 5; 7) which perfectly explains why we should be joyous even if the face of trails. Working by faith means that we have the assurance that Jesus is in the ship with us to calm the storm(Mark 4:35-41) Walking by faith means following God's directives for we know all things work together for good for those that love God.(Rom 8:28)

Generally today, a huge number of us mistake happiness for joy and vice versa. As much as they can be used interchangeably there are differences between them.

Some of which are explained below.

Happiness is based on an occurrence or event while joy isn't

Happiness is fickle. Something makes one become happy for e.g. your wife/husband bought you a new phone, you won a contract, you passed a scholarship examination, you just got a car, you are about to attend a wedding party or naming etc. All the happiness that comes with this are due to what happened, /happening but joy is within and isn't event based.

Happiness fades off at the face of tribulations. See Lamentations 3:17 "'My soul is bereft of peace; I have forgotten what happiness is"

Happiness is for a while, joy is everlasting

Happiness is based on an event/happening/ occurrence reason it is temporary, and according to the kingdom temporary things do not last. When someone is surprised with gifts, cars, money etc., the happiness is for a while, about two to three weeks then afterwards the happiness reduces or is totally gone.

Joy is permanent, joy is everlasting. We want you to know, brothers, about the grace of God that has been given among the churches of Macedonia, for in a severe test of affliction, their abundance of joy and their extreme poverty have overflowed in a wealth of generosity on their part. (2 Corinthians 8:1-2)

Joy is among the fruits of the spirit (Gal 5:22-23)

But the fruit of the Spirit is love, joy, peace, longsuffering, kindness, goodness, faithfulness, gentleness, self-control. Against such there is no law.

Joy exists as one of the fruits of the spirit expedient for a believer to possess. The essences of joy in a person's life cannot be over emphasized.

People give happiness, God gives joy

The bible says God gives us peace and joy. Humans can't provide joy and joy in abundance, only God can. The Holy Spirit is the giver of joy and in Him is everlasting joy found. A song says 'I have joy like a river, joy like a river, joy like a river in my soul'.

Joy cut across your spirit, soul and body. The joy of the Lord is my strength (Neh 8:10) Many others differences includes joy is internal, happiness is external.

Joy is long termed, happiness is short termed.

Prayer Points for Joy

- Father I thank you Lord for this exposition on joy, be thou exalted in Jesus name.
- More than this exposition, teach me the meaning of joy by yourself in Jesus name.
- Feel my heart with your joy in Jesus name.
- Help me to possess Joy as one of the fruits of the spirit in Jesus name.
- Make me to hear joy and gladness in Jesus name.
- Joy is deeply rooted in God, father help me to find you, and for once I find you I also find joy.
- James 1:2-3 2, Consider it pure joy, my brothers and sisters, whenever you face trials of many kinds, because you know that the testing of your faith produces perseverance. Father help me to be joyous even in the face of trials and tribulations.
- Give me the grace to have trust you in difficulties for the bible says even in the midst of the fire He will be with us...
- My Lord, restore unto me the joy of my salvation and renew your spirit within me.
- Prob 10:28, 'The prospect of the righteous is joy, but the hopes of the wicked come to nothing'.
- Father let everything I lay my hands on result to joy in Jesus name.
- Rom 15: 13 May the God of hope fill you with all joy and peace as you trust in him, so that you may overflow with hope by the power of the Holy Spirit.
- Father fill me with joy and peace that I may overflow with hope in Jesus name.

- Help my joy to be complete and bountiful.
- Isaiah 12:6 "Shout aloud and sing for joy, people of Zion, for great is the Holy One of Israel among you."
- Songs of joy will never ceases from my mouth in Jesus name.
- Isaiah 35:10 "and those the LORD has rescued will return. They will enter Zion with singing; everlasting joy will crown their heads. Gladness and joy will overtake them, and sorrow and sighing will flee away"
- I declare this my portion in Jesus name
- Thank you Jesus for answered prayers.
- In Jesus joyous name I pray. Amen

PRAYER FOR GOD TO SPEAK THROUGH ME

Today we will be dealing with a prayer for God to speak through me. God is omnipotent and he does things the way and manner which pleases him. When you hear revelation from an anointed man of God and the revelation came to pass, you cannot but envy the gift. Meanwhile, as against the belief that God only speaks through his anointed alone, God can speak through anyone and anything, remember the camel of Balaam spoke.

This prayer guide dubbed prayer for God to speak through me will heighten your prophetical ministry, people will hear God through you. The scripture says he that speaks in a tongue edifies himself, but he that prophesies edifies the church. You know what it means to say thus saith the Lord of host, this time tomorrow this will happen. God still perform such wonders through His people. Remember the story of Saul when he found himself in the midst of the Prophets, the spirit of prophecy came upon him and he did prophesy, I decree by the authority of heaven that the spirit of prophecy will come upon you right now in the name of Jesus.

God speaking through a man demands that a revelation is being revealed to a man and the man speaking of that which has been revealed unto him. Matthew 16:16-17 And Simon Peter answered and said, Thou art the Christ, the Son of the living God. And Jesus answered and said unto him, Blessed art thou, Simon Peter: for flesh and blood hath not revealed it unto thee, but my Father which is in heaven. God spoke through Simon Peter in the book of Mathew when Christ asked his disciples who they think he is, everyone was saying different things until Apostle Peter told Jesus that you are Christ, the Son of the living God.

There must be a revelation before God can speak through a man, he that prophesies speaks of what has been revealed unto him or her. I decree by the power of God Almighty that the portal of revelation is opened unto you right now in the name of Jesus. It is something very shameful for a man not to be in a position where God can speak through him that it took God to speak through an animal. If God will speak through you, prayer alone cannot do it. You must ensure that you stand in alignment with the Will of God and you are standing right with God. By doing this, God will see you as a vessel that can be used to propagate His works in the land of the living. I pray that God will continually use you in the name of Jesus, you shall not become desolate in the presence of God.

PRAYER POINTS:

- Father Lord, I submit myself to you your Will and power today. I want you to take charge of my life and use me for your Will. I decree that by your power, you will humble my hard heart and you will penetrate my being by your mighty power and you will begin to use me for your glory in the name of Jesus.

- Lord Jesus, I pray that you will descend upon me mightily your spirit for I want to be a vessel for glory I want you to use me for your work. Father Lord, I pray that you will speak through me in the name of Jesus.

- Lord God, your word says at the end you will pour upon us your spirit, our sons and daughters shall prophesy, our old men shall dream dreams and our young men shall see vision. Lord Jesus, I decree that your spirit will come upon me. Your spirit of revelation, your spirit of prophecy, I decree that you will pour it upon me in the name of Jesus.

- From today Lord Jesus, I submit myself totally to your power, I want more of you and less of me in the name of Jesus. I want you to take over my life, I want to take over my entire being in the name of Jesus.

- Lord Jesus, I do not want to end up like King Saul that started with you and ended with the devil. I don't want to be a man that used to hear from you before but suddenly started hearing from the devil. Father, help me to be diligently consistent in your presence. I don't want to be swayed away by the thrilling sight of the world. I come against every form of distraction in my way, I destroy them by the fire of the Holy Ghost.

- Father Lord, I do not want an animal or any other being that is less to take my place in your presence. I do not want to suffer the type of shame and reproach that Balaam suffered in your presence when you left him and spoke through a camel. I want to always remain your vessel, I decree that you will continually speak through me in the name of Jesus.

- Father Lord, I break every form of barrier between you and me, I come against every form of hindrances that may stop me from hearing from you, and I pray that you destroy them in the name of Jesus. From now, I activate my spiritual sense organ, my eyes and ears receive Spiritual alertness in the name of Jesus. When I open my mouth to speak, let me speak your mind in the name of Jesus.

- Lord Jesus, I want you to always reveal things to me, for the scripture says the secret of the Lord is with those that fear him. Father, because I fear you, I pray that nothing shall be hidden from me in the name of Jesus. I decree that you will open the portal of revelation for me, you will reveal to me things that are yet to come in the name of Jesus.

PRAYER FOR THE SPIRIT OF WISDOM AND DISCERNMENT

Proverbs 4:7: Wisdom is the principal thing; therefore get wisdom: and with all thy getting get understanding.

There is practically nothing as important as walking in wisdom. This is not just Sophia (human wisdom) but the wisdom that comes from above. Several scriptures in the Bible made clear expository statements that support this fact.

The great Apostle Paul in several instances while writing the epistles prayed for the people that they will receive the Spirit and workings of wisdom for them to live their lives to the fullest. The book of Proverbs from the first to the last chapter, spoke extensively about how important it was for an individual to live wisely and to discern rightly.

In fact, one of the proofs that you really have a relationship with Jesus is that you walk in a high level of wisdom, because the Bible tells us in 1 Corinthians 1:24 that Jesus is the wisdom of God therefore if He lives inside of you wisdom must be in display in your life.

Wisdom produces discernment, that is, your ability to perceive and always understand things by God's Spirit and to judge wisely. When you have wisdom, you can understand God's divine purpose for your life. Which is why Apostle Paul prayed for the church in Ephesus in the book of Ephesians 1: 17, that they may be filled with the Spirit of wisdom and revelation so that they may know the hope of God's calling for their lives. The Spirit of wisdom also helps you to act in ways that pleases God. Most times we think that because we are engaging in spiritual activities it automatically means that we are pleasing God but the book of Colossians 1:9 tells us that until we are filled with knowledge of God's will in all wisdom, we will not be able to fully please God.

Also, the Spirit of wisdom helps us to live a struggle free life because it reveals to us those great plans that God has made for our own peace. The book of 1cor: 2 tells us that there is a hidden wisdom that God has reserved for the glorification of His people, but this wisdom can only be revealed by God's Spirit to us.

Even Jesus needed the Spirit of wisdom and discernment for Him to fulfil His mission on the earth. The book of Isaiah 11 tells us that a prophecy had already come before the birth of the Messiah revealing that He was going to possess different dimensions of the Spirit, one of which was the Spirit of wisdom.

The Spirit of discernment helps you to make the right judgments and decisions in the face of challenging situations. The book of 1 Corinthians 2:14 tells us that the things that the Spirit of God says to us can only be understood by those who have the Spirit of discernment, this is because the instruction that God gives always appears foolish to the ordinary man.

If you therefore want to operate in a high-level spiritual judgment and to live based on God's will for you, then you must pray earnestly for the Spirit of wisdom and discernment. The book of James tells us that if we need wisdom, we are at liberty to ask from God, who gives to all and upbraided from none. I have compiled some personal prayers for wisdom and discernment to guide you as you seek to know the will of God for your life. As you pray this prayer by faith today, I see the spirit of wisdom and discernment working in your life in Jesus Christ name.

Prayers for Wisdom

• Heavenly Father, you said in your word, in James 1:5 that if any man lacks wisdom that he should ask of you who gives liberally to all without reproaching. Lord, I therefore acknowledge that I need the wisdom that only you can give, pour upon me your Spirit of wisdom in its fullest measure in the name of Jesus.

• Lord I ask according to the book of Ephesians 1 from verse 16, that you give me the Spirit of wisdom and revelation in the Knowledge of you, the eyes of my heart being enlightened that I may know the hope of your calling and the riches of your glorious inheritance in the saints and the immeasurable greatness of your power towards me who believe according to the working of your great might in Jesus name.

• Heavenly Father, I don't want to keep on making mistakes and wrong turns in life, give me the Spirit of wisdom and discernment so that I can know those hidden wisdom that has been prepared for my glory. Sweet Holy Spirit according to the book of 1cor 2, I ask that you search the mind of God and reveal these things to me in Jesus name.

• Father I ask according to the book of Colossians 1:9, I ask that you fill me with the knowledge of your will in all wisdom and spiritual understanding so that I may walk worthy of the lord, fully pleasing Him and increasing in the knowledge of God in Jesus name.

• Lord, I ask that you give unto me a discerning Spirit so that I can make the right decisions at all times, that even when your instructions seem foolish I will obey them nonetheless, knowing that they will help me live directly in the center of your will in Jesus name.

• The book of Luke 2:52 tells us that Jesus grew in wisdom and stature. Heavenly father I therefore ask that you will not just give me the Spirit of wisdom but that you will help me to grow continuously in it, so that I will not fall out of your leading in all seasons of life in Jesus name.

• Lord, your word records that God granted Daniel and the other three Hebrew boy's wisdom and understanding in all skills and because of this they stood out among all their peers, I therefore ask that you grant me this same spirit so that I can stand out in every sphere of life that I find myself in Jesus name.

• Scripture tells us that among the people of Israel, there was a tribe who were able to discern times and to know what the children of Israel ought to do. Lord I ask that now and at all times, you will help me to discern times and to know exactly what I ought to do in Jesus name.

• Your word says in Proverbs that with wisdom comes long life. Father fill me with your Spirit of wisdom so that I can live long to fulfill your mandate on the earth in Jesus name.

• Lord I pray for every member of the body of Christ that you will pour upon them also the Spirit of wisdom so that they will know you heart for them and they will walk in the center of your will in Jesus name.

Prayers for Discernment

• Father, I thank you for your unconditional love upon my life in Jesus Christ name

• Father, I ask that your mercy prevail over judgment in my life today in Jesus Christ name

• Father, endue me with the Spirit of discernment now in the name of Jesus Christ.

• Father, open my spiritual eyes to see what my physical eyes cannot see in the name of Jesus Christ.

• Father, by the direction of the Holy Spirit, order my steps as I walk through the Journey of life Jesus Christ name

• Father open my eyes to perceive evil before it overwhelms me in the name of Jesus Christ.

• I declare today that my days of confusion are over in the name of Jesus Christ

• I declare that my days of spiritual blindness are over in the name of Jesus Christ

• I declare that the Spirit of discernment at work in my life in the name of Jesus Christ.

• From this day henceforth I shall by the Spirit of God always know what to do at the right time in the name of Jesus Christ.

• I declare today that no weapon fashioned against me shall prosper in the name of Jesus Christ

• Every evil friend in my life shall be exposed by the gift of discernment in me in the name of Jesus Christ.

• My days of failure are over Jesus Christ name

- My days of disappointments are over Jesus Christ name
- My days of setbacks are over Jesus Christ name
- Thank you Father for baptizing me with the Spirit of Discernment Jesus Christ name

Thank you Jesus

PRAYER FOR POWER AND ANOINTING

Acts 1:8 but ye shall receive power, after that the Holy Ghost is come upon you: and ye shall be witnesses unto me both in Jerusalem, and in all Judaea, and in Samaria, and unto the uttermost part of the earth. The difference between Christianity and other religion is Power. The difference between the word of God and motivational speaking is power. Our God is a living God and Jesus Christ is alive, when He arose from the dead, He sent us the Holy Spirit. The Holy Spirit is the custodian of Power and Anointing. The Holy Spirit is not power, He is the source of power, He is not the anointing, and He carries the anointing. The Spirit of God is the source of all powers. Jesus Christ did a lot of mighty works in His earthly ministry because He was empowered by the Holy Spirit, Acts 10:38. The good news is this, if you are born again, that same Holy Spirit is in you that means the source of power is in your inside. Today we shall be engaging in prayers for power and anointing. But before we go into the prayers proper, let us see what power and anointing is.

What Is Power And Anointing?

Power is the capacity of God at work in a man and through a man. Anointing is the endowment of that power. When you are endued with the power of God, it means that you now carry the power of God inside your spirit. Every born again child of God have been endued with power. Every child of God is anointed with the power of God. As a Christian, you have the power of God on your inside and you can manifest it on the outside. However, having the power of God inside you and manifesting that same power outside you are not the same thing. It takes spiritual understanding to know what to do to manifest the power of God inside of you. A lot of Christians today are victims in life because they know not what to do to manifest power in their lives. The question now is this, how do I manifest the power of God on my inside?

The most effective way to manifest power as a believer is through Prayer and Fasting. This is without prejudice to the studying of the word of God. The word of God keeps you spiritually informed at all times, but prayers and fasting keeps you spiritually alert and sensitive, it also activates the power of God in you to make things happen in your life. There is no short cut to power, those believers that will see power in their lives are those believers that will be given to continuous fasting and prayers. It is important to note that, prayers and fasting do not give you power, you received power when you believed, but prayers and fasting enables you to activate the already existing power of God inside you. Also prayer and fasting should not be seen as a price we pay for power, no, Power was given to us by grace through our faith in Christ Jesus, rather prayer and fasting is we creating an enabling environment to connect to the power of God on our inside. It's just like having a generator filled with fuel in your house, that is power, but until you put on the generator, there will be no light or power in your life. When we pray and fast, we are putting on that generator and we are powering every area of our lives. Prayer and fasting makes our spirit man sensitive at all times to pick spiritual signals from heaven. Jesus when preparing for His earthly ministry, fasted for 40 days, Matthew 4:2. This is to let us know how important fasting and praying is. While we may not fast 40 days like Jesus Christ, we must live a fasted life and a prayerful life in order to be on fire for Jesus.

If we want to see things change in our lives, if we want to see our mountains move at our command, if we want to constantly command signs and wonders, then we must be given to regular prayers and fasting, this is a major way to be in constant command of power and the anointing. These prayers for power and anointing will guide you as you undertake your journey to the manifestation of power and anointing. As you engage them in faith today, your life will never remain the same in Jesus name.

PRAYER POINTS

1. Father, I thank you for my salvation today in the name of Jesus

2. Father I thank You for the gift of the Holy Spirit in the name of Jesus Christ

3. I lose myself now from every grip of the devil upon my life in the name of Jesus Christ

4. Holy Ghost fire, destroy every garment of reproach in my life in the name of Jesus Christ

5. Oh Lord, let every stubborn enemy fighting against my calling be destroyed now in the name of Jesus

6. Father, Let your fire in me begin to burn endlessly in the name of Jesus

7. Father baptize me afresh with unquenchable fire in the name of Jesus

8. Father empower me by the Holy Spirit to be an agent of signs and wonders in the name of Jesus.

9. Father, by your mighty hand upon my life, cause me to do great miracles that will shut the mouths of my mockers in Jesus name

10. Father, make me a battle axe in your hands in Jesus name.

11. Just as the grave could not hold Jesus, no grave can hold me in the name of Jesus

12. I receive fire to quench all satanic oppositions in the name of Jesus

13. Oh Lord give me fire that destroys death in the name of Jesus

14. Father, anoint my tongue with the coal of fire, in the name of Jesus

15. Oh Lord, let the lust of the flesh in my life be destroyed now in the name of Jesus Christ

16. Oh Lord, purge my life by your fire now in the name of Jesus

17. Father, lay your hands on me and quench every spirit of rebellion in my life in the name of Jesus

18. Holy Ghost fire, burn away all that is not holy in my Life in the name of Jesus Christ.

19. Oh Lord, let your fire generate power in my life in the name of Jesus

20. Every plan of failure fashioned against my destiny, die now in the name of Jesus Christ

21. Every plan of witchcraft against my calling be destroyed now in the name of Jesus Christ

22. Every arrow of poverty, go back to the sender in the name of Jesus Christ

23. Every serpent and scorpion working against my destiny, I trample over you now in the name of Jesus Christ.

24. I cast out the Spirit of snail out of my finances in the name of Jesus

25. I nullify every evil word spoken against my finances in the name of Jesus Christ.

26. I challenge and destroy every satanic opposition standing before me in the name of Jesus

27. Every power blocking me from the will of God, fall down and die in the name of Jesus Christ

28. I pull down every stubborn strongholds protecting my enemies in the name of Jesus Christ.

29. I arrest every spirit of confusion and failure by fire in the name of Jesus Christ

30. I declare that from this day, I shall manifest the power of God, in my spirit man in the name of Jesus Christ.

Thank You Jesus

60 PRAYER POINTS FOR FRESH ANOINTING

Acts 1:8:

8 But ye shall receive power, after that the Holy Ghost is come upon you: and ye shall be witnesses unto me both in Jerusalem, and in all Judaea, and in Samaria, and unto the uttermost part of the earth.

Every believer in Christ needs a fresh anointing, the anointing of yesterday is not sufficient for the task of today. The bible tells us that the mercies of God are new every morning, Lamentations 3:22-23. In the same way the anointing of the Holy Spirit in us can be renewed on a regular basis. What is the anointing? The anointing is the power Of God in us, this power was given to us by the Holy Spirit when we gave our hearts to Jesus that is when we became born again. This power in us must be stirred continually for maximum effectiveness. For us to stir up the anointing of God in us, and continually make it fresh, we must be given to continuous prayers. This is why I have compiled 60 prayer points for fresh anointing, this prayer points will empower us to increase in the grace of God upon our lives. The more you pray, the fresher the anointing of God upon your life and the fresher the anointing, the more powerful you become, and the more powerful you become, the more dominion you command over sin and the devil. Remember, this, you can have a working electrical system in your house and still remain in darkness, until you put on the light switch, you don't see power at work in your house. Prayer is putting on the power switch in your spirit man. As you engage this prayer points for fresh anointing today, I see you increasing from one level of grace to another level in Jesus name.

Why must you pray for fresh anointing? This prayer for fresh anointing is timely for those who desire a personal revival in their spiritual life. Those who want to always be on fire for God. If you desire that your spirit, soul and body pursue after God then this prayer points are for you. Secondly, this prayer is for those who need fresh fire to overcome the battles of life. Life is a battle field, and to overcome, you need fresh anointing, your spirit man must be updated with the latest spiritual ammunitions. Prayer is the only way to update your spirit man. Only a prayerful Christian can overcome the battles of life. Thirdly, this prayer is for those who need the anointing of the Holy Spirit to fulfill destiny. The Holy Spirit is our only destiny helper, He is called our helper because we need His help to fulfill our destiny in life. Destiny can only be fulfilled by the power of God, and that power is in you but you must keep it fresh and active on the altar of prayer. My prayer for you today is this, as you engage these prayer points for fresh anointing, I see you changing positions for greatness in Jesus name.

PRAYER POINTS

1. Father, in the name of Jesus, I thank you for your mighty power to save and to deliver me from all bondages.

2. Father, let your mercies prevail over every judgment in my life as a result of my sins and shortcomings in Jesus name.

3. I cover myself with the blood of Jesus.

4. I separate myself from any inherited bondage and limitation, in the name of Jesus

5. O Lord, send your axe of fire to the foundation of my life, and destroy every evil plantation therein in Jesus name.

6. Blood of Jesus, flush out from my system, every inherited satanic deposit, in the name of Jesus.

7. Any rod of the wicked, rising up against my family line, be rendered impotent for my sake, in the name of Jesus.

8. I cancel the consequences of any evil local name attached to my person, in the name of Jesus.

9. You evil foundational plantations, come out of my life with all your roots, in the name of Jesus.

10. I break and loose myself from every form of demonic bewitchment, in the name of Jesus.

11. I separate myself from every evil domination and control, in the name of Jesus.

12. I separate myself from the grip of any problem transferred into my life from the womb, in the name of Jesus.

13. Blood of Jesus and the fire of the Holy Ghost, cleanse every organ in my body, in the name of Jesus.

14. I break and loose myself from every inherited evil covenant, in the name of Jesus.

15. I break and loose myself from every inherited evil curse, in the name of Jesus.

16. I vomit every evil consumption that I have been fed with as a child, in the name of Jesus.

17. I command all foundational strongmen attached to my life to be paralyzed, in the name of Jesus.

18. O Lord, let the blood of Jesus, be transfused into my blood vessel.

19. Every gate, opened to the enemy by my foundation, be closed forever with the blood of Jesus.

20. Lord Jesus, walk back into every second of my life and deliver me where I need deliverance; heal me where I need healing and transform me where I need transformation.

21. Thou power in the blood of Jesus, separate me from the sins of my ancestors.

22. Blood of Jesus, remove any unprogressive label from every aspect of my life.

23. O Lord, create in me a clean heart by your power.

24. O Lord, let the anointing of the Holy Spirit break every yoke of backwardness in my life

25. O Lord, renew a right spirit within me.

26. O Lord, teach me to die to self.

27. Thou brush of the Lord, scrub out every dirtiness in my spiritual pipe, in the name of Jesus.

28. O Lord, ignite my calling with your fire.

29. O Lord, anoint me to pray without ceasing.

30. O Lord, establish me as a holy person unto you.

31. O Lord, restore my spiritual eyes and years.

32. O Lord, let the anointing to excel in my spiritual and physical life fall on me.

33. O Lord, produce in me the power of self-control and gentleness.

34. Holy Ghost, breathe on me now, in the name of Jesus.

35. Holy Ghost fire, ignite me to the glory of God.

36. O Lord, let every rebellion flee from my heart.

37. I command every spiritual contamination in my life to receive cleansing by the blood of Jesus.

38. Every rusted spiritual pipe in my life, receive wholeness, in the name of Jesus.

39. I command every power, eating up my spiritual pipe to be roasted, in the name of Jesus.

40. I renounce any evil dedication placed upon my life, in the name of Jesus.

41. I break every evil edict and ordination, in Jesus' name.

42. O Lord, cleanse all the soiled parts of my life.

43. O Lord, deliver me from every foundational Pharaoh.

44. O Lord, heal every wounded part of my life.

45. O Lord, bend every evil rigidity of my life.

46. O Lord, re-align every satanic straying in my life.

47. O Lord, let the fire of the Holy Spirit warm every satanic freeze in my life.

48. O Lord, give me a life that kills death.

49. O Lord, kindle in me the fire of charity.

50. O Lord, glue me together where I am opposed to myself.

51. O Lord, enrich me with your gifts.

52. O Lord, quicken me and increase my desire for the things of heaven.

53. By Your ruler ship, O Lord, let the lust of the flesh in my life die.

54. Lord Jesus, increase daily in my life.

55. Lord Jesus, maintain your gifts in my life.

56. O Lord, refine and purge my life, by your fire.

57. Holy Spirit, inflame my heart with your fire, in the name of Jesus.

58. Holy Ghost fire, begin to burn away every power of the bond woman in me, in the name of Jesus.

59. O Lord, make me ready to go wherever you send me.

60. Lord Jesus, never let me shut you out.

Thank you father, for your fresh grace in Jesus name.

PRAYER POINTS FOR THE SPIRIT OF HUMILITY

Today we will be dealing prayer points for Humility.

Humility is the state of being humble, the quality of having a modest or low view about one's importance. Humility means modesty, meekness, simplicity and quietness. The opposite of humility is pride which means the unreasonable overestimation of one's self.

Humility is a very good trait that should be seen in every believer even though some lack it. The importance of humility cannot be overemphasized. So many quarrels and chaos in the society and home is as a result of impatience and lack of humility/meekness.

In our world today humility has been mistaken for foolishness, but they are two different things entirely. You are humble doesn't mean you are foolish, but it is termed foolishness because you didn't take the expected step you ought to take that is retaliate/fight back.

Our leader and mentor Jesus Christ was humble and lived all His days on earth in humility and respect to God and man. Nowhere was recorded in the bible where He displayed pride or disrespect. Jesus set a standard and a legacy of humility in which He wants us to follow.

The devil who was once an angel in heaven was sent to the earth because of pride, he thought to be above God and instead he was lowered. No wonder a school of thought says 'pride goes before a fall'. God cherish humility, the bible says in 1Peter 5:5, but He giveth greater grace, therefore it says, God resists the proud but gives grace to the humble. Humility should not be a choice but rather a lifestyle. The bible admonishes us in 1Peter 5:6 'Therefore humble yourself under the mighty hands of God'.

Some bible verses on humility

The following verses lays more emphasis on why we're should live w humble life.

Colossians 3:12

As God's chosen people, holy and dearly loved, clothe yourselves with compassion, kindness, humility, gentleness and patience.

Ephesians 4:2
Be completely humble and gentle; be patient, bearing with one another in love.

James 4:10
Humble yourselves before the Lord, and he will lift you up.

2 Chronicles 7:14
If my people, who are called by my name, will humble themselves and pray and seek my face and turn from their wicked ways, then I will hear from heaven, and I will forgive their sin and will heal their land.

Luke 14:11
For all those who exalt they will be humbled, and those who humble themselves will be exalted."

Micah 6:8
He has shown you, O mortal, what is good. And what does the LORD require of you? To act justly and to love, mercy and to walk humbly with your God.

Proverbs 3:34
He mocks proud mockers but shows favor to the humble and oppressed.

Benefits of being humble
You may be wondering in your heart if humility is just a good virtue and nothing more, I am glad to tell you that there are benefits attached to it.

Makes you live a healthy life
A life of humility is a life of simplicity, which saves you the stress of having to retaliate/fight back.
Being humble saves you from stress which can affect your emotional, mental or psychological health and can lead to sickness or death.
When you live a humble life, you are not after trying to show off your wealth or other resources which will save you from a lot of headache.
Humble living makes your mind at rest and makes you happy which is good for your health.

Makes you at peace with every one
Living a humble life makes you live a peaceful life.
Being humble involves overlooking something and not negatively reacting to things around you that may lead to fight.
When you are humble, you are indirectly trying to maintain peace and harmony

Living at peace is one of the instructions from God, Heb 12:14 'follow peace with all men and holiness without which no man can see God'.

Makes you a tool of evangelism

Beyond the words of our mouth, our actions must/should portray that we are Christians.

The bible says 'be an example of a believer in your words, thoughts, in charity. 1Tim 4:12

The disciples were first called believers in Antioch not because they were pronouncing it upon themselves, but because they acted like Christ and this was evident through their actions. Acts 11:26. Meekness as part of the fruits of the spirit can be compared to humility, which is what Christ wants us to exhibit to draw more people to His kingdom.

Nowadays, believers are the bible people study, they want to see how you behave and react to things, and your life style generally passes a negative or positive message to people. A soul can be won through your simple act of humility. Live humble always!

Makes you loved and respected

This is true because nobody likes a proud person because they are so full of themselves. Jesus won the heart of many through his humility. It was even hard for people to identify him among his apostles due to his humble nature.

Humility commands respect.

PRAYER POINTS

1.   Father, I thank you for this exposition, for I know knowledge is light, be thou exalted in Jesus name.

2.   Help me to live a humble life, the kind of lifestyle you lived on earth.

3.   You washed the disciple's feet (John 13:1-17) this explains your height of humility.

4.   Father let humility find expression in me.

5.   Help me to be selfless in the mighty name of Jesus

6.   Wipe every iota of pride in my life with your precious blood.

7.   Help me to direct every praise/accolades I receive back to you.

8.   When I'm at the peak of my pursuit/career help me to acknowledge you in Jesus name.

9.   James 1:17, 'every good and perfect gift is from above and comes down from the giver of light'

10.   I come against every spirit of pride in my life, I destroy it by fire in the name of Jesus.

11.   Father help me to realize that you are the giver of all good and perfect gift.

12.   I will not think too highly of myself in Jesus name.

13.   Hold my hands and teach me how to live by yourself Lord Jesus.

14.   Help me to know when to react and when not to react in Jesus name.

15.   Thank you Lord Jesus for answered prayer, in Jesus name I pray. Amen

SPIRITUAL CLEANING PRAYER

Spiritual cleansing is a form of deliverance that must happen in the life of a person or believer for such individual to be completely free from the torment of the devil. The blood of Jesus is the perfect washer that will purge us from every evil fruit that has been deposited in us by the enemy. Many times, those who truly need spiritual cleansing are men and women who are still struggling with faith.

They do not have the man called Holy Spirit on the inside of them, hence, they are being possessed by the devil. Also, judging by the evil that inhabits the world we live in there are some demonic ancestral protocols that affect people from a particular lineage or family. Today we shall be engaging in spiritual cleansing prayers. These prayers will help you deal with all the foundational problems in your life.

Many challenges in the lives of many people today are traceable to their roots, their ancestral background. It takes spiritual cleansing to be free from such challenges.

It is important to know that this type of spiritual cleansing is not the one that an individual does by going to bath or wash from a flowing river. The Bible says the blood that speaks righteousness than the blood of Abel has been shed for us. Even while we are yet sinners, Christ had died for us, his blood has been slain from the foundation of the world.

In essence, those who are yet to receive the comforter who is the Holy Spirit may be possessed by the devil which will cause them to need spiritual cleansing.

However, as a true Christian, it is impossible to be fully possessed by the devil or evil spirit because of the Holy Spirit that dwells on the inside of every true believer. The presence of the Holy Spirit is like a light that shines in the darkness of life. However, a Christian can be tormented and hindered by the devil. The devil knowing fully well that it cannot possess or dwell in the life of a true believer can decide to inflict suffering that will oppress such a believer.

That is why many believers or Christians today are suffering from poverty, sicknesses, disappointments, marital delay, untimely deaths, stagnation and much more. As you engage this spiritual cleansing prayers today, you shall be set free

Many times, we might be oppressed by the devil and we know not until we come to the consciousness through the power of the Holy Spirit. These are some symptoms of an oppressor in the life of a believer; Sickness, Anger, Fear, Debt, inability to resist sin and many more.

Whether you have received the gift of the Holy Spirit or not, whether you are always been possess or tormented by the devil you all need the prayer for spiritual cleansing which will wipe away every iniquity, infirmities and every other vice of the devil to hold you captive as a believer.

Anytime you noticed some strange things about yourself, or you discovered that you do things that are not spiritually inclined, or things happen to you that do not represent the thoughts that God have for you, it is important you say the following spiritual cleansing prayers:

PRAYERS POINTS

• Lord Jesus, I humbly confess my sins and iniquities. Before you and you only have I sinned and done evil in your sight, Lord I ask that you will forgive my sin in the name of Jesus.

• Lord God, I detach myself from every ancestral protocol working against my life and destiny in the name of Jesus.

• Every power and principalities tormenting me and frustrating my efforts are destroyed in the name of Jesus.

• Lord Jesus, I renounce every work of the devil. The Bible says resist the devil and it will flee, I resist every work of the devil in my life in the name of Jesus.

• I claim my spiritual cleansing by the authority of heaven. I purge myself from every power and principalities and covenants working against my existence in the name of Jesus.

• I decree that by the blood of Christ, I destroy every curse working against me. The Bible says for Christ has been made a curse for us because cursed is he that is hanged on the tree. I announce my freedom from the curse of the law in the name of Jesus.

• Lord Jesus, I break every yoke of darkness upon my life. Every demonic chain that has been used to tie me to a spot is broken in the name of Jesus.

• Lord Jesus, I grant Christ the undeniable access to my life. I seal every grounds and every hole that the devil may have in my life in the name of Jesus.

• From now on, I begin to walk in the light of Christ. I decree that by the power in the name of Jesus I release the light of Christ into my life, never again will I walk in darkness in the name of Jesus.

• Lord Jesus, I decree that in the name of Jesus I equip myself with the full armor of God in the name of Jesus.

• Lord God, the Bible says by the anointing every yoke shall be destroyed. I break every yoke of the devil in my life in the name of Jesus

• The Bible says we are seated in heavenly places far above powers and principalities. I take up the spiritual alertness and authority to be seated in the heavenly realms in the name of Jesus.

• I raise myself above every power and principalities, against rulers of darkness, I decree my power of dominance in the name of Jesus.

• I cast out the power of Satan and its demons in the name of Jesus.

• The scripture says wash me and I shall wash me and I shall be whiter than, I purge myself with your precious blood and I confess my newness as bright as the morning stars in the name of Jesus.

• I decree my freedom from every marine spirit causing me to have a marital problem in the name of Jesus.

• The scripture says he that the son has set free is free indeed, I announce my freedom from the power of slavery in the name of Jesus.

• Father Lord, I ask that you will create in me a clean heart and renew a right spirit within in the name of Jesus.

• I pray for power and grace that from henceforth I will no longer conform to the world in the name of Jesus.

CHAPTER 9

PRAYER AGAINST EVIL DREAM
PRAYER POINTS AGAINST EVIL DREAM

Today we will be dealing with prayer points against evil dreams. A dream is one way through which God communicates with man. There are times in our dreams while we sleep that the portal of revelation will be opened, and we see things that are yet to come. In the book of John 33:14-18 For God speaks in one way, and in two, though man does not perceive it. In a dream, in a vision of the night, when deep sleep falls on men, while they slumber on their beds, then he opens the ears of men and terrifies them with warnings, that he may turn man aside from his deed and conceal pride from a man; he keeps back his soul from the pit, his life from perishing by the sword. In most cases, the things we see in dreams are a revelation of things that would happen.

There are times that things happen to us in life, whereas they have been revealed in the dream, but because we failed to pray against them, they eventually come to pass. I decree by the power of the most high, every evil dream is destroyed in the name of Jesus. Meanwhile, sometimes we see something terrible in the dream that affects our sleep. Some people can't even close their eyes to sleep at night because of the numerous terrible dreams. But the scripture says we have not been given the spirit of fear but of sonship to cry Abba Father. Today God will destroy every evil dream in the name of Jesus.

PRAYER POINTS

- Lord Jesus, I thank you for the good things you have done in my life, I thank you for sparing my life to witness another day like this, Lord let your name be exalted in the name of Jesus.
- Lord Jesus, I thank you for the grace and privilege that you have bestowed upon me to sleep and dream dreams. I thank you for increasing my spiritual sensitivity even while I close my eyes to see, Lord, let your name be exalted in the name of Jesus.

- Lord God, I pray concerning every evil dream that I have had. I pray that you will restore them in the name of Jesus. I pray that you will cancel every plan of the enemy to harm me. I pray that such plans is destroyed in the name of Jesus.

- I come against every power and principalities that are always bringing evil dreams in my sleep. I come against them by the blood of the lamb. Every evil force that has vowed always to spoil my night with terrible and fearful dreams, I destroy you all in the name of Jesus.

- For the scripture says I have not been given the spirit of fear but of sonship to cry Abba Father. Lord, I cry unto you today to save me from the fear of evil dreams in the name of Jesus.

- The book of Prob. 3 vs. 34 says when I lie down, I shall not be afraid, and my sleep shall be sweet. Every power that wants to make me afraid in my sleep, every power that wants to cause me to have terrible dreams, I destroy you by the fire of the Holy Ghost be consumed in the name of Jesus.

- Lord Jesus, I pray that you will grant me the grace and ability to sleep and wake up in peace in the name of Jesus. The scripture says I know the thoughts I have towards you; they are the thoughts of good and not of evil to give you an expected end. Lord Jesus, any power that wants to alter your plans for my life, let such power catch fire in the name of Jesus.

- Every evil animal that has been sent by the enemy to come appear in my dreams to scare me. I release the fire of the Holy Ghost upon you right now in the name of Jesus.

- Every satanic dog, goat, snake, or cow appearing in my dream, die right now in the name of Jesus.

- I decree that the angel of the Lord will stand watch over me when I sleep, it will guide me in my sleep that no masquerade of the devil will come near my dwelling place in the name of Jesus.

- Lord, the scripture says, and they overcome him by the blood of the lamb and by the words of their testimonies. I decree that the enemy is destroyed in the name of Jesus. Every power of the enemy that wants to contaminate my sleep with terrible dreams, you are destroyed in the name of Jesus.

- I come against every evil dream; every dream of death is canceled in the name of Jesus. For your words say I will not die but live to declare the works of the Lord in the land of the living. I decree by the mercy of God that death is destroyed over my life in the name of Jesus.

- Every evil spirit that has been assigned to my life to contaminate my dream catch fire right now in the name of Jesus. Every dream of an accident is destroyed in the name of Jesus. I decree that it shall not come to pass in the name of Jesus. For it has been written, who speaks and it comes to pass when the Lord has not spoken, the blood of the lamb cancels every evil dream.

- Every evil animal that has been assigned to monitor my sleep, I call the fire of the holy upon you right now in the name of Jesus.

- Every evil coverage, every demonic power controlling the territory where I stay, I release the fire of the Holy Ghost upon you right now in the name of Jesus. Every evil attack, for the scripture, says no weapon fashioned against me shall prosper; every evil attack is nullified in the name of Jesus.

- I decree that as from today, my sleep will be blessed with sweet dreams: no more masquerade, no more snakes in the name of Jesus. Good morning people

POWERFUL PRAYER POINTS A GOOD NIGHT SLEEP

Today we will be dealing with powerful prayer points for good night sleep. To many people, a good night sleep is a special gift from the maker to end a stressful day. However, if your night sleep has ever been tormented with dreadful dreams, you will always get frightened when is getting dark? God is about to change that story today.

Regardless of the stress you went through during the day, a good night sleep is capable of replenishing the lost energy and keeps you motivated for the next day. For all you that are scared to close your eyes in the night due to constant terrible dreams, I decree by the authority of heaven that those powers destroying your sleep are destroyed today in the name of Jesus.

PRAYER POINTS

- Heavenly father, I thank you for your grace and protection over my life today. I thank you because eyes was upon me as I journeyed throughout the world today and your mercy brought me peace and not in pieces, may your name be highly exalted.

- Lord God, I seek for the forgiveness of sin that I have committed today while I was out. The scripture says we cannot continue to live in sin and ask grace to abound. Lord, I pray that you forgive me all my sins today in the name of Jesus. I ask that by the precious blood of Christ that was shed on the cross of Calvary, you will wash away my sins completely in the name of Jesus.

- Lord Jesus, as I'm going to bed tonight, I pray that you grant me good rest. I pray that you will grant me a good night sleep. Your word made me understand that I'm like a sheep and you guard me as a shepherd. I lay my head in your bosom tonight, let your angels' minister to my spirit tonight. I come against every power that spoil sleep with evil dreams, let them be destroyed before me today in the name of Jesus.

- Lord, I pray that you grant me a splendid night sleep to rejuvenate my energy for tomorrow's business. I rebuke every demon that torment my sleep with masquerade. Lord, when I wake from sleep tomorrow, fill my heart with joy and gladness to meet a new day that you have made. Help me to have hope and assist me in building faith that tomorrow shall be better than today. For the scripture says the glory of the latter shall surpass the former, I pray that tomorrow shall be better and greater than today in the name of Jesus.

- Lord, I pray that your peace that surpass the understanding of men will be upon me as I sleep tonight. I come against every spirit of fear. For it has been written, God has not given us the spirit of fear but of adoption to cry Abba father. I prophesy that I shall not be afraid in the name of Jesus.

- It has been written, you shall not be afraid of the terror by night, Nor of the arrow that flies by day, Nor of the pestilence that walks in darkness, nor of the destruction does that lay waste at noonday. Lord, your angels shall comfort me as I sleep tonight. I shall not be disturbed by the terror of the night not by the pestilence that walks in darkness. I pray that the four corners of my house is protected in the name of Jesus.

- Father Lord, I rebuke every form of evil dream that may destroy the night. Every demonic power that appears in the dream to shatter it, I consume you by the fire of the Holy Ghost. I pray that the lord mount a pillar of fire round my home and make my environment uncomfortable for any evil power in the name of Jesus.

- I come against every evil assassination that is perpetrated in the night. I refuse every attempt on my life by the kingdom of darkness. I pray that the protection of the lord will upon me. The scripture says, for carry the mark of Christ, let no man trouble me. I decree that I shall not be troubled in the name of Jesus.

- Lord, I pray that you will encircle my life with peace and love. Do not let my soul be bothered, do not let me be troubled. Let me rest tonight with hope in you. Regardless of the trouble or problem that I face, I strongly believe you are God and you are powerful to take them away. So this night I will sleep like a champion, like a man without trouble? And tomorrow when I wake, I pray for the ability to accept a new day with huge possibilities in the name of Jesus.

- Father Lord, instead of terrible dreams, I pray for an encounter, such that I will never forget in a rush. I pray that you make it happen tonight in the name of Jesus. I pray that when I sleep tonight, let me see the angels of the lord, let them minister to me.

- Father Lord, I cast all my cares and worry on you. Tonight I will sleep without trouble. Your words says, Come to me, all you who labour and are overburdened, and I will give you rest. Shoulder my yoke and learn from me, for I am gentle and humble in heart, and you will find rest for your souls. Yes, my yoke is easy and my burden light.' Lord, I laid my problems down to the cross. Every problem that may want to disrupt me sleep tonight, I lay them down at the cross tonight in the name of Jesus.

- Lord Just like the Psalmist says in peace I will lie down and sleep, for you alone, LORD, make me dwell in safety. Lord, I believe my safety with you not compromised. For this reason I will lie down and sleep bearing in me that I'm your child and you will take care of me, you will comfort me and grant me mercy.

PRAYER POINTS AGAINST MASQUERADE IN DREAM

Today we will be dealing with prayer points against masquerades in dreams. Masquerades have powerful demons that must be defeated both physically and spiritually. When you see masquerade in the dream, it is a perfect indication that your family have a covenant with masquerade or they used to worship this deity.

Oftentimes I have heard people say they are being chased in their dream by a masquerade. Some people just see masquerade all of a sudden in their sleep and it becomes so terrifying that they don't want to close their eyes to sleep anymore. Before we go deep into this topic, let me quickly highlight some of the things that happens when you see masquerade in your sleep.

Things That Happens When You See Masquerade in Your Sleep
Marital Bad Luck

One of the numerous things that could happen to you when you see masquerade chase you in your sleep is marital bad luck especially if you are married. When you see masquerade in the dream, you can't possibly embrace it, what you will do is run and never get rest.

This could signify marital unrest for such individual unless he or she prays hard to God to destroy every covenant that existed that exist between him and masquerade.

Stagnation

Another thing that it could lead to is stagnation. Anyone who sees masquerade in the sleep could be tormented by the power of stagnation. It causes a man to be stagnant in life. Things would not move forward for anyone who is tormented by the demon of masquerade in the dream.

Unrest

The scripture says God has not given us the spirit of fear but of power, sound mind and love. However, the devil will try as much as it can to stop a believer from having strong faith in the Lord.

One of the ways the devil do this is instigating fear in the mind of a believer by tormenting them with masquerade in their dream. When this becomes so intensed, a believer can be so scared that he/she would not even want to sleep anymore. And what corrupts faith is fear.

Premature Death

Another thing that this type of dream can lead to is premature death. The enemy may be trying to attack the destiny of an individual. One of the ways the enemy hinder an individual from reaching their potential is through untimely death.

How Tackle Masquerade

Total Repentance

As stated earlier, one of the reasons we see masquerades in our dream is because our lineage have a connect with the masquerade. The best way to halt this is true genuine repentance.

The scripture says he that is in Christ is a new creature and old things are passed away. You must allow Christ to take over your existence. The life you start living after you give your life to Christ is no longer your own but Christ.

Protect Yourself with Holy Ghost

There is power in the name of Jesus. One of the ways a believer can tackle any spiritual problem is by protecting himself with the full armor of God. The book of Ephesians 6:11 Put on the whole armor of God that you may be able to stand against the wiles of the devil. One of the ways to take on the full armor of God is by the power of the Holy Spirit.

Recall that the scripture says when a man sleep his enemy comes and sow tares with wheat and went his way. The devil understands that a man is weak when he's asleep. But the power of the Holy Ghost protects us even when we are not conscious.

PRAYER POINTS

- Lord Jesus, I pray that you turn my shame to joy, I pray that by your mercy, you will turn my disgrace to glory in the name of Jesus.
- Lord, in every way that I have experienced disappointment, I pray that by your grace I will be elevated in the name of Jesus.
- I come against the spirit of fear that the demon of masquerade want to instill inside me, I replace fear with courage in the name of Jesus.
- Lord, every point in my life that the power of darkness wants to take over, I decree by the authority of heaven that is blocked in the name of Jesus.

- Lord, the scripture says, For He shall give His angels charge over you, to keep you in all your ways. I decree by the authority of heaven that even in my sleep the angel of the Lord shall guide me.
- Every stronghold of darkness in my family house working against me is destroyed in the name of Jesus.
- Every covenant that my family have with masquerade which makes it pertinent that the demon comes to torment in my dreams all the time, by the reason of the blood that was shed on the cross of Calvary, I cancel such covenants in the name of Jesus.
- Lord Jesus, I destroy every spirit of stagnation that was inherited from my lineage, I break it by the power in the name of Jesus.
- I decree by the authority of heaven, every limiting power that appears to me in my dream in form of a masquerade, I destroy you by the fire of the Holy Ghost.
- Every Calderon of darkness working against my life, break today in the name of Jesus.
- Every agenda of the enemy to kill me untimely, I destroy you by the fire of the Holy Ghost in the name of Jesus. You demon that turn into a masquerade and appear to me in my sleep, hear the word of the Lord, the Bible says in the book of Obadiah 1:17 But on Mount Zion there shall be deliverance, and there shall be holiness; the house of Jacob shall possess their possessions. I speak my deliverance into reality in the name of Jesus.
- Every form of marital bad luck is destroyed by the fire of the Holy Ghost. I rebuke every plans and agenda to destroy my relationship in the name of Jesus.

PRAYER POINTS AGAINST DOG BITE IN DREAM

Today we will be dealing with prayer points to destroy dog bite in dreams. Dog bite even in the physical realm is not a good thing, let alone in the dream. When a man is bitten by a dog in the dream, it could lead to stagnation, isolation, terrible sickness, sexual impurity and many more. What does the bible say about dogs? The book of Philippians 3:2: "Beware of dogs, beware of evil workers, beware of the concision." The scripture explained that dogs are evil workers.

One of the ways the devil penetrate into the life of people is via the use of dogs. What such an individual will just discover is that they can no longer shun sexual impurity. Others, it could have a negative effect on their health and finances. When you see people who can't stop fornicating or adultery, they could be possessed by the spirit of dog. Sometimes, it could lead to failed relationship. Whatever the case may be, you must pray fervently whenever you dream that you were bitten by dogs. The adverse effect could be minimal and it could escalate into more dangerous situation.

Dreams are spiritual reality that are showed to us. God could be telling you the cause of your problems. That's why it is important to pray always especially when something is revealed to you in your sleep. I decree by the authority every spirit of dog affecting your life is destroyed in the name of Jesus.

PRAYER POINTS

- Lord God, I ask that by your power, you will destroy every venom from dog bite affecting my life in the name of Jesus.

- Every spirit of dog causing me to fornicate or commit adultery repeatedly I rebuke you today in the name of Jesus.

- Father Lord, I decree by the authority of heaven, every Spirit of stagnation in my life brought upon me by the dog bite from my dream, I cancel you today in the name of Jesus.

- I decree by the authority of heaven, every power and principalities that appears to me in my sleep in form of a dog, you are destroyed by the fire of the Holy Ghost.

- Every ancestral powers in my lineage that is known for tormenting everyone in my generation, I cancel you over my life in the name of Jesus.

- You demon of adultery and fornication, get back from me today in the name of Jesus.

- Lord, every dog bite from the dream that is affecting my spiritual growth, let the fire of the Holy Ghost burn them in the name of Jesus.

- Lord, I rebuke sickness over my life in the name of Jesus. I saturate my sleep with the precious blood of Christ. Every time I close my eyes to sleep, I decree that the angel of Lord be with me in the name of Jesus.

- Every blood suckling demon appearing to me in the dream to create fear, I curse you today in the name of Jesus.

- For it has been written, we have not been given the spirit of fear but of sonship to cry Abba Father. I come against every form of fear in my life in the name of Jesus.

- Lord, I put on the armour of my warfare. I embodied myself with the armour of God from today. My spirit man receive supernatural power in the name of Jesus.

- Every demonic arrow that is fired into my life from the pit of hell, I send you back to the sender in seven fold in the name of Jesus.
- Let the fire of the Holy Ghost come and destroy every attack of the enemy using dog as an agent to hold me down to a spot, in the name of Jesus.
- Every demonic dog that has been sent by the enemy to bite me in my sleep to destroy my marriage, I destroy you in the name of Jesus.
- Every demonic dog that has been sent by the enemy to destroy my relationship, fall to death today in the name of Jesus.
- Lord Jesus, I pray that every evil dog that is enemy is using its bite to disfigure my life and destiny, die today in the name of Jesus.
- I decree by the authority of heaven that the strength of God come upon my spirit man. The power to fight and resist the bite of an evil dog in the dream, let it come upon me today in the name of Jesus.
- I decree by the authority of heaven that my body and spirit becomes dangerous to any dog bite in the name of Jesus. From today, I become a terror to the power of darkness in the name of Jesus.
- The scripture says touch not my anointed and do my prophets no harm. I decree from today, I'm untouchable in the name of Jesus. From today, I become a terror to the power of the enemy in the name of Jesus.
- I pray that the blood of Jesus will neutralize every power of bite was given in my dreams in the name of Jesus.
- For it has been written, I carry the mark of Christ let no man trouble me. I stand upon the efficacy of this word and I decree that I shall not be troubled in the name of Jesus.
- The power of the enemy shall have no bearing over my life in the name of Jesus. I shall not be overpowered in the name of Jesus.

- For it has been written, I will feed those who oppress you with their own flesh, and they shall be drunk with their own blood as with sweet wine. All flesh shall know that I, the LORD, am your Savior, And your Redeemer, the Mighty One of Jacob. Holy Spirit of God, arise now a take vengeance upon every demonic enemy tormenting my life with dogs in the name of Jesus.

- I come against every evil habit of sexual impurity in my life, I destroy it by the fire of the Holy Ghost. Every form of addiction in my life, I cancel it in the name of Jesus.

PRAYER POINTS TO RECOVER STOLEN BLESSING IN THE DREAM

Today we will dealing with prayer points to recover stolen blessings in the dream. The scripture has made us to understand that our adversary the devil rest not day and night. He goes about looking for whom to destroy. And the devil only comes to steal, kill and destroy. Many believers are suffering in life because of a blessing that was taken away from them by the devil in the dreams. This explains why we as believers should never let our guard down, we must pray all the time.

The scripture says in the book of Matthew 13:25 but while men slept, his enemy came and sowed tares among the wheat and went his way. The best time for the enemy to strike is when a man is asleep. The devil understands that a man is most times vulnerable when he close his eyes in sleep. This is why the devil will until darkness comes before he strikes. Many blessings has been taken away through dreams. Also, many destinies has been destroyed through evil dreams. But thanks to God the Father Almighty who is capable of restoring every lost blessing and dent destinies. When the Amalekites stole from Isreal. David went to God in prayers, saying 1 Samuel 30:8 And David enquired at the Lord, saying, Shall I pursue after this troop? Shall I overtake them? And he answered him, Pursue: for thou shalt surely overtake them, and without fail recover all. The lord has given us the power to recover every stolen blessing.

The book of Psalm 126:1 When the LORD brought back the captivity of Zion, We were like those who dream. The lord is powerful enough to restore all the years that the cankerworm has taken. God is powerful enough to take back for us all the blessings that we have lost through dreams. I decree by the authority of heaven, every good thing that the enemy has taken away from you is restored in the name of Jesus.

I want you to trust God enough. He alone has the power to restore all that has been taken away from you. He specifically told us in his word, Joel 2:25 "I will restore to you the years that the locust hath eaten, the cankerworm and the caterpillar, and the palmerworm my great army which I sent among you". If you feel there is a need for you to pray, I want you to use the following prayer points to restore all that has been taken away from you.

Prayer Points

- Lord Jesus, I thank you for your grace and protection over my life. I thank you for the gift of salvation that you made possible through your blood, I magnify you for your grace, let your name be exalted in the name of Jesus.
- I come against every evil dream that was stationed by the enemy to destroy my destiny in life. I scatter such dreams in the name of Jesus. Lord God, I pray for restoration over every good things that I have lost through dreams.
- Lord, I pray that you shall help me recover all the blessings that has been taken away through dreams in the name of Jesus. Lord Jesus,
- I cancel the power of every evil dream programmed by the devil to reduce me to nothing in life.
- I decree by the authority of heaven, such dreams will have no power over me in the name of Jesus. Lord God, I pray that every object of the enemy in my life that serves as a monitoring device for the enemy, I break them into pieces in the name of Jesus. Lord,
- I attack every demonic armed robber that always come to me in my dream to steal from me.
- I pray that the fire of the Holy Ghost burn them down in the name of Jesus. Lord God, every demonic power in my father's house that comes to me at night to steal my blessings, I destroy you by the fire of the Holy Ghost. Lord Jesus, every plan of the enemy to steal from me in the dream is cancelled by the fire of the Almighty. Lord,

- I come against every sex demon that comes to me in the sleep to steal from me through sex, I destroy you by the fire of the Holy Ghost in the name of Jesus. Lord, in every ways that the enemies have used my semen to steal my blessings, I recover them all by the power in the name of Jesus. Every demonic that uses food to steal from me in my sleep, I destroy you by fire in the name of Jesus.

- I come against every evil dream that was stationed by the enemy to destroy my destiny in life. I scatter such dreams in the name of Jesus.

- Lord God, I pray for restoration over every good things that I have lost through dreams. Lord, I pray that you shall help me recover all the blessings that has been taken away through dreams in the name of Jesus.

- Lord Jesus, I cancel the power of every evil dream programmed by the devil to reduce me to nothing in life. I decree by the authority of heaven, such dreams will have no power over me in the name of Jesus.

- Lord God, I pray that every object of the enemy in my life that serves as a monitoring device for the enemy, I break them into pieces in the name of Jesus.

- Lord, I attack every demonic armed robber that always come to me in my dream to steal from me. I pray that the fire of the Holy Ghost burn them down in the name of Jesus.

- Lord God, every demonic power in my father's house that comes to me at night to steal my blessings, I destroy you by the fire of the Holy Ghost.

- Lord Jesus, every plan of the enemy to steal from me in the dream is cancelled by the fire of the Almighty.

- Lord, I come against every sex demon that comes to me in the sleep to steal from me through sex, I destroy you by the fire of the Holy Ghost in the name of Jesus.

- Lord, in every ways that the enemies have used my semen to steal my blessings, I recover them all by the power in the name of Jesus.

- Every demonic that uses food to steal from me in my sleep, I destroy you by fire in the name of Jesus.

- Lord, I pray that from today my sleep is sanctified. I pray that the angel of the lord shall continue to guide me in my sleep. Every plan of the enemy to steal from me again is cancelled by the fire of the Holy Ghost. Lord Jesus, every demonic arrow of loss that entered my life from my sleep is removed in the name of Jesus. The scripture says no weapon fashion against me shall prosper. Lord, every arrow of damnation that the enemy shot at me from the sleep is destroyed by fire in the name of Jesus.

- Lord Jesus, every demonic arrow of loss that entered my life from my sleep is removed in the name of Jesus. The scripture says no weapon fashion against me shall prosper. Lord, every arrow of damnation that the enemy shot at me from the sleep is destroyed by fire in the name of Jesus.

- Lord God, every agenda of the enemy to use my hair against me in the sleep. Every agenda of the enemy to reduce or kill my growth in life, I cancel you by fire in the name of Jesus.

- Lord, every evil dream of me seeing myself in the village, every evil dream of me seeing myself in primary school, every evil dream of me seeing myself in my old house, I cancel you today in the name of Jesus.

- From today, the event of the dream shall have no power over me anymore in the name of Jesus. I raise a standard against every effect of evil dreams in my life in the name of Jesus.

- Every demon that suck out the fruit of my womb in the dream, vomit it now in the name of Jesus. I raise a standard against you demon of bareness that attacks me in the dream, I set you on fire in the name of Jesus.

- For it has been written who speaks and it comes to pass when the Lord has not spoken. I decree by the authority of heaven, every evil utterance that has been uttered against me in my dream, you are cancelled in the name of Jesus.

- Lord, every evil dream of me seeing myself in the village, every evil dream of me seeing myself in primary school, every evil dream of me seeing myself in my old house, I cancel you today in the name of Jesus.

- From today, the event of the dream shall have no power over me anymore in the name of Jesus. I raise a standard against every effect of evil dreams in my life in the name of Jesus.

- Every demon that suck out the fruit of my womb in the dream, vomit it now in the name of Jesus. I raise a standard against you demon of bareness that attacks me in the dream, I set you on fire in the name of Jesus.

- For it has been written who speaks and it comes to pass when the Lord has not spoken. I decree by the authority of heaven, every evil utterance that has been uttered against me in my dream, you are cancelled in the name of Jesus.

PRAYER POINTS TO CANCEL EVIL DREAMS

Today we will be dealing with prayer points to cancel evil dreams. One of the numerous ways God communicate with us is through dreams. Remember in the Acts of Apostle 2:17 And it shall come to pass in the last days, says God, That I will pour out of My Spirit on all flesh; Your sons and your daughters shall prophesy, Your young men shall see visions, Your old men shall dream dreams. God reveals things to us through our dreams. Sometimes, the spirit of God brings revelation of the enemy's plan to us in our dreams. It is left for us to act on it to prevent those things from coming to fulfillment.

Joseph was a dreamer, God revealed to him the destiny of his life. As God reveals good things to us, so also does He reveals the plans of the enemy for our lives through dreams? When we see evil things in our dreams, it is not enough for us to sit back and be consumed for fear. It is a time for us to pray fervently to God to avert every evil plans for our lives. Some of the terrible things we see in our sleep includes:

1. Sexual dream
2. Eating in the dream
3. Being pursued by masquerade
4. Being pursued by snake
5. Having severe accident in the dream
6. Visiting the village
7. Seeing blood in the dream

There are so many evil things that we see in the dream. Sometimes, we could be badly tormented in the dream and we lost the ability to shout out loud or cry for help. When we see some of these things in our dream, they are perfect indication of the devil's devices to harm us. This is why we must endeavor to pray hard when we see these events in our sleep.

In the book of Mathew 18:18 "Verily I say unto you, whatsoever ye shall bind on earth shall be bound in heaven: and whatsoever ye shall loose on earth shall be loosed in heaven." This is an assurance for us that we can decide what will happen and what will not happen in real life.

To overcome evil dreams, you must submit yourself to the leading of the Holy Spirit. Become a friend with Christ. It is, however, important to know that giving out lives to Jesus doesn't mean that we will not be faced with tribulations. It is not an assurance that we won't have trouble, but it is a seal that whatever trouble that comes up, Christ will be there to save us.

If you feel like you need prayer to cancel evil dreams over your life, let's pray together.

PRAYER POINTS

- Lord Jesus, I thank you for the gift of revelation that you have bestowed on me to know the plans and agenda of the enemy over my life. I thank you for not making the plans of the enemy hidden over my life, Lord, let your name be exalted in the name of Jesus.

- Lord, I stand on the promise of your word as written in the book of Isaiah 54:17 No weapon formed against you shall prosper, and every tongue which rises against you in judgment you shall condemn. This is the heritage of the servants of the LORD, and their righteousness is from me," Says the LORD. I decree that no weapon of the enemy shall be successful over my life in the name of Jesus.

- I decree by the authority of heaven, every evil dreams of setback, stagnation and failure, I destroy you today in the name of Jesus. I come against you by the power in the name of Jesus. Every evil dream of setback over my life, I cancel your manifestation over my life in the name of Jesus.

- I stand upon the promise of God as stated in the book of Luke 10:19 Behold, I give unto you power to tread on serpents and scorpions, and over all the power of the enemy: and nothing shall by any means hurt you." No evil dream shall come to pass over my in the name of Jesus.

- I cancel every idea of the enemy to drag failure into my life in the name of Jesus. The scripture says, for we have not been given the spirit of fear but of sonship to cry Abba Father. I cancel the spirit of fear in me today in the name of Jesus.

- I stand on the promise of word as stated in the book of Isaiah 28:18 KJV,"And your covenant with death shall be disannulled, and your agreement with hell shall not stand; when the overflowing scourge shall pass through, then ye shall be trodden down by it." Death is cancelled over my life in the name of Jesus. Every covenant of death hovering round me, I cancel you today in the name of Jesus.

- Lord God, every covenant of failure in my life, I destroy you today in the name of Jesus. For it has been written that Christ has bare upon himself all our infirmities and he has healed all our diseases. Every form of illness or disease is healed in the name of Jesus.

- Father Lord, every ancestral power in my lineage working against my life through evil dream, lose your power over me in the name of Jesus. From today, I decree that you lose your power in the name of Jesus.

- I order the fire of the Holy Ghost to go into the camp of my enemies and every demonic agent fighting my life with evil dreams. Let the fire of the Holy Ghost begin to consume them this moment in the name of Jesus.

- As it has been written in the book of Psalm 91:13, Thou shalt tread upon the lion and adder: the young lion and the dragon shalt thou trample under feet. I receive power to tread upon serpent in the name of Jesus. From today, I receive power to become unstoppable in the name of Jesus.

- I pray that the power of the Holy Spirit strengthens me against every demonic battle in my sleep in the name of Jesus.

WARFARE PRAYER TO DESTROY PLAN OF THE ENEMIES

Today we will be dealing with warfare prayers to destroy the plans of the enemy. The enemy never rests, mostly when a man has decided to go on and pursue the purpose of his existence. Jacob never had issues in life until he started aspiring to become great like he has been destined to be. Joseph never has any problems in life until he began having dreams where God showed him a revelation of who he is to become.

It is worthy to note that just as God has plans for our lives, the enemies also have a plan for our lives. It is now our doing or undoing that will destroy the works of the enemy over our lives.

The enemy succeeded in the life of Samson. The strength of Samson became useless after the enemy got him. He has been warned not to marry from a strange land, a community of people that don't serve the holy one of Isreal, he took Delilah from their midst, and that led to his fall. I decree that whoever the enemy has staged to enter your life at one point in time to destroy you, I decree that the fire of most high will burn such person in the name of Jesus. Every wrong man or woman that the enemy has planned for you, may God cause a divine separation between you and that person.

Similarly, as God has designed his plans for Joseph, so also did the enemy design his plans too. Joseph was destined to become great. He was destined to lead the children of Isreal out of. Meanwhile, the enemy also has his plans for Joseph. His brothers fell into the perfect image of the enemy, and they were used against him to ensure that the plans of God concerning him were defeated. I pray that by the mercies of the most high, every agenda of the enemies to destroy the purpose of God for your life shall be destroyed today in the name of Jesus.

The enemy planned that Joseph should the killed, but God saved him. The enemy also made provision for how Joseph would sacrifice his destiny on the altar of immoralities with his master's wife. Still, God also helped Joseph overcome the plan of the enemy, by the mercies of the most high, may God destroy the plans of the enemies concerning your life.

Ensure that you study this prayer guide and say all the prayers in it. As you begin to use this guide, may God reveal the plans of the enemy to you in the name of Jesus?

PRAYER POINTS

* Father Lord, I come before you this day, I need your help Lord Jesus, and I need your power over my enemies. The ones that have vowed that I will never amount to something in life, the one whose plans and agenda for my life is for destruction, I pray that you will destroy their plans over my life in the name of Jesus.

* Lord God, I pray that by your mercies, your counsel alone will stand in my life. Every other and agenda of the evil ones over my is scattered by fire. I call on the fire of the most high to descend into the camp of the enemies and burn them to ashes in the name of Jesus.

* Father Lord, I pray that the archangels of glory will descend mightily into the territory of enemies and destroy their agenda for my life in the name of Jesus. Lord, I want you to scatter the language of my enemies. I pray that you will cause mighty disunity to erupt in their midst, and you will cause them to destroy themselves in the name of Jesus.

* I decree that from now on, the spirit of truth, the spirit of divinity from the throne of the holy of Isreal will descend upon me in the name of Jesus. I pray that the holy spirit of God will begin to guide me in all my ways. I pray that you will not cover the secret of the enemies over my life. I pray that you will always reveal their plans over my life in the name of Jesus.

* Lord Jesus, I pray that by your death and resurrection, you will not let my enemy triumph over me. I pray that in all ways and all ramifications, you will grant me victory over my enemies. Do not let them rejoice in victory over me. Every of their plans is revealed to me in the name of Jesus. For the scripture says the

secret of the Lord is with those that fear him, I pray that you will reveal the secret of dark places to me in the name of Jesus.

- Lord God, just like you helped Joseph escape all the traps and craftiness of the enemies over his life, just like you take him from the point of zero to the point of hero, I pray that you will help me overcome the trap of my enemies in the name of Jesus.

- I pray that the fire of the most high will go right now, because the scripture says, the fire will go before the army of the Lord and consume his enemies. I pray that the fire of the most high God before and destroy all my enemies. All the evil seer that sees the destiny of a man even before the time of manifestation, I pray that you will remove their sights in the name of Jesus.

- I decree by the power of the most high, every sense of consciousness of my enemies is taken away in the name of Jesus. I pray that you will cause my enemies to go blind for my sake, I decree by the power in the name of Jesus, you will cause my enemies to go deaf over my matter in the name of Jesus. Each of their plans and agenda over my life is cancelled in the name of Jesus.

BEDTIME PRAYERS FOR KIDS

Today we will be dealing with bedtime prayers for kids. Parents must engage their kids in bedtime prayer before they retire to bed. Due to the nature of the kids, they might not remember or attach importance to bedtime prayer. It is in the doing of the parent to ensure that they get used to it.

Bedtime prayer for kids can take different forms or patterns. It can be for protection against some unseen spirit in the middle of the night to possess little children. And also, it could be a pattern for teaching the child in the way of the Lord so that when they grow up, they will not depart from it. Many children have lost their destinies simply because their parents relaxed in the place of prayer. The scripture was not making a mistake when it said that Christians should pray without season.

The Bible made it known that the devil doesn't rest. It goes about like a hungry beast looking for whom to devour. And the thief doesn't come during the day when the house owner is actively awake. The thief will instead come in the night when he is sure that the house owner has gone to sleep—our prayers as a defense mechanism to protect us from the vices of the devil. I decree as God lives and his spirit lives, the enemy shall not have power over your kids in the name of Jesus.

Another important reason why we must engage the children in bedtime prayer is to fulfill the words of the Lord that train your child in the way he should go so that when he grows up, he won't depart from it. When we continuously engage our children in prayers, it will give them a sense of consciousness that prayer is an integral part of their existence. I pray that the enemy will not have power over your kids in the name of Jesus. The evil spirit of the devil that possesses the lives of young children will never come near your children in the name of Jesus.

From now on, I assign the Seraphims of glory to take charge of your children; they shall guide and protect them in the name of Jesus. Study and use this bedtime prayer for kids, and you are sure to protect the lives of your children.

You must let your kids repeat after you during the moment of prayer. Teach them how to pray so they can learn how to communicate with God.

PRAYER POINTS

- Dear Lord, I thank you for the success of my day. I thank you because you protected me all through the day. I appreciate you, Lord Jesus, because you stood by me every single minute of the day, and you did not allow any evil to befall. I thank you, Lord Jesus, for this, let your name be exalted.

- Father in heaven, I thank you for the lives of my parents, I thank you because you taught them to teach us in your way, I appreciate you because you never left them for a single moment, I thank you because you did not let any evil happen to them, let your name be exalted in the name of Jesus.

- Father Lord, I pray for the forgiveness of sin. In every way that I have childishly sin against you, in any way that I committed a crime and I do not know, Lord, please forgive me. For the sake and death of son Jesus Christ, I pray that you forgive me. And I promise never to do them again because your word says the sacrifices of the Lord are a broken spirit and a broken and a contrite heart will you not despise.

- Lord Jesus, I pray that as I'm going to sleep this night, I pray that your hands of protection be upon me. I protect myself from every arrow that flies by night. For the scripture says, children are a gift from God. As you have made me a gift from you to my parents, Lord, please do not allow the enemy to snatch away the gift in Jesus name.

- Father Lord, I come against every form of a scary dream that may contaminate the night. Every demonic dream that the enemy has staged to bring to my sleep to scare me, I destroy those dreams in the name of Jesus. The scripture says For God has not given us the spirit of fear but of sonship to cry Abba Father. Lord, I cry unto you today that you should destroy every evil dream from coming to my sleep tonight in the name of Jesus.

- Father Lord, for it, has been written that in for signs and wonders and the scripture also made to understand that I bear the mark of Christ so no one should trouble me. I come against every attack of the enemy with your power. I pray that you destroy their attacks in the name of Jesus.

- Lord Jesus, as I will be entering into a new day tomorrow, I sanctify tomorrow with your precious blood. I pray that every evil that is loaded is the blood of Jesus nullifies tomorrow. For it has been written that and they overcame him by the blood of the lamb and by the words of their testimonies. I decree in the name of Jesus that you will destroy every evil in tomorrow in the name of Jesus.

- Lord Jesus, I commit my education into your hands. I pray that you will give me the grace to excel excellently in the name of Jesus. And I decree into my future that it shall be great in the name of Jesus. In my sleep tonight, I want you to reveal deep things to me about myself. I decree that the heaven of revelations open for me in the name of Jesus. By tomorrow morning, let me have guts to glorify your name, in Jesus I pray.

PRAYER AGAINST DREAM POLLUTION

Today we will be exploring powers that pollute the dream of a man and prayers against such dream pollution. Firstly, we must know that dream is not the sequence of events that one see in the sleep, but they are those goals and aspirations that are awaiting manifestation.

No man becomes great by accident; God has purposed it and such an individual must have seen some kind of revelation of how great he will be. God has a great plan for each and every one of us; however, the devil also has his own plans.

Albeit you will see someone who is doing well at one stage in life but change all of a sudden. I know for sure that we all must have experienced something of such. A student that has been doing so well in academics and people is already seeing him be the most successful among his peers but all of a sudden develop a deviant behavior and start constituting nuisance in the community.

Have you not seen a child with great prospects, and whenever he/she is asked what they will like to become in the nearest future, their response reveals that they have a great plan for the future? However, within a twink of an eye, that child or person will just become a social calamity. These are demons that pollute the dream of a man.

What is worthy of knowing is that the devil never challenges someone who is a non-entity, the devil has no business with any man who does not amount to anything. The devil only has problems with people with a great prospect, people whose dreams and aspirations are big enough to affect the entire world positively.

One of such similar cases in the Bible is Joseph the son of Jacob. Joseph was a dreamer, God has shown him how great he will be through his dream. He shared the dream with his family and battle arise against him among his siblings. The devil knew quite well that God was preparing Joseph to become a deliverer for the people of Egypt and Isreal in nearest future, the devil knew that Joseph's dream meant that he will be great and very successful, so the devil made move to contaminate Joseph's dream.

When the devil wants to contaminate the dream of a man, he will use familiar people to try to pull you down. To Joseph, the devil used his siblings to try to achieve his aim by possessing them to sell Joseph into slavery.

A similar thing happened to Christ Jesus, the devil knew that after the fall of man in the book of Genesis God was not too pleased with the new state of man. He knew it was God's dream that one day man will be restored to the realm of glory that God has factored for man. So, when Christ Jesus came, the devil knew this was a means for God to actualize His dreams so he made move to get Jesus killed when he was still a child.

Likewise our lives as Christians, we all have dreams and aspirations for our life and future, however, it seems we have forgotten that dream or the dream has been abated. Many people have lost the purpose of God for their lives simply because the devil polluted their dreams. Little wonder, a scholar said that the richest land on earth is the graveyard because hundreds of million people die without fulfilling God's purpose for their lives.

Whenever you feel you are experiencing laxity in pursuing that dream, you must be spiritually alert to sense that the devil is at work, we have compiled a list of prayers that you should say against dream pollution.

PRAYER POINTS

- Father Lord, I thank you for the grace that called me out of many to commit to my hands this great task, Lord I say to let you name be exalted in the name of Jesus.

- Lord Jesus, I come against every power and principalities that may want to hinder me from fulfilling my task and your purpose for my life, I destroy such powers in the name of Jesus.

- Lord God, the Bible says the expectations of the righteous shall not be cut short. Lord, each of my expectations, desires, and dreams will receive power to be made manifest in the name of Jesus.

- Lord, I destroy by fire every power that wants to contaminate my dream with nonsense, every power that want to make me lose focus on my dream, I destroy such powers in the name of Jesus.
- Lord arise and let you enemies be scattered, every power and principalities that may want to pollute my dreams and aspirations, I destroy them by the consuming fire of God Almighty in the name of Jesus.
- Lord, says that I'm for signs and Wonders, Lord I refuse to be an object of ridicule in the name of Jesus.
- Lord Jesus, I understand that it profits nothing for a man to fail the purpose of his existence, I pray that you help me to achieve all my dreams that you have factored for my life in the name of Jesus.
- Every power, demon, or scheme that may want to contaminate my mind towards achieving my goals in life, I come against them by the blood of the lamb in the name of Jesus.
- The scripture says declare a thing and it shall be established, I receive the power to manifest my dreams in the name of Jesus.
- I receive the spiritual grace to begin to operate in the office that rightfully belongs to me in the name of Jesus.
- I receive power over every power that causes a delay in the time of success, I receive my Dominion over every spirit that extends the time of success in the name of Jesus.
- Father Lord, I refuse to experience weakness, I receive the grace not to slumber until my dreams and aspirations are fulfilled in the name of Jesus.

Amen

PRAYER AGAINST BAD DREAMS DURING PREGNANCY

Today we shall be dishing out prayers against bad dreams during pregnancy. When a lady is pregnant, that is the first stage towards multiplying as God has commanded. However, so many things happen in the realm of the spirit during that stage when the baby is still in the womb.

There are numerous battles and attacks that happen to a woman when they are pregnant. You will be wondering why is it that battle often arises against pregnant women, well is, it is because pregnancy launches a family into the realm of fulfilment. Also, every child carries a blessing from God Almighty and all are made a blessing unto their generation, this is the reason why battle and attack often arise against a pregnant woman.

What is worthy of knowing is that oftentimes, the battle and attack is not against the pregnant woman but against the child. However, the battle becomes that of the pregnant woman because she is the container.

One of the forms of the battle that arises against a pregnant woman is an evil dream. It is important to know that dreams are activities of the spirit and the spiritual realm controls the physical. Whatever thing that is settled in the realm of the spirit will come to manifestation in the real world. Hence, it is very bad for a pregnant woman to experience bad dreams during pregnancy.

When a pregnant woman starts seeing evil things in the dream, it is a clear identification that war is coming. The bible says for we wrestled on against flesh and blood but against powers and principalities ruler of dark places. So, it is not enough to just trivialize dreams on the altar of mere coincidence just because it doesn't make a direct meaning to you. If it doesn't make sense to you that is more reason why you need to pray.

There are so many mothers today who have been careless while they were pregnant and the enemy has utilized that to steal something great in the life of their children. Some kids were born empty of glory because their parents exhibit laxity in the place of prayer during their pregnancy. Whenever you see something that don't add up in a dream about your unborn child, it is important that you pray against it.

Examples of Bad Dreams during Pregnancy
1. **Seeing Blood In The dream:** These can mean miscarriage, you must reject it through prayers
2. **Seeing yourself cutting meat:** These can be a sign of still birth, you must reject it through prayers
3. **Strange or familiar faces making love to you in the dream:** These connotes demonic contamination; you must pray against it.
4. **Someone pursuing you in the dream**

Other forms of Nightmares

These examples are not meant to scare you or to magnify the devil, there are even no scriptural back up for any of these dreams but they are gotten from the many experiences of people who have been a victim of satanic dreams. As a pregnant mother, you must be spiritually sensitive, when the devil shows you any strange dream, arise and reject it by faith through prayers. Remember the scripture says resist the devil and it will flee, you have a power that is hidden in the name of Jesus. When you start having bad dreams during pregnancy, for the sake of your unborn child, say this prayer more often until every hold of darkness over the fruit of your womb is broken.

PRAYER POINTS
- Lord God, I thank you for this wonderful process that you are making me go through, I appreciate your loving kindness over my life, let your name be exalted in the name of Jesus.
- Father in Heaven, I thank you for the grace that you have given unto me to dream dreams, I appreciate you because it is a fulfilling of your promises that you made for us in the book of Acts father I exalt your Holy name in the name of Jesus.

- Lord Jesus, I thank you because you have not kept the secret of the enemy over my life. I thank you for the sight that you have given unto me to behold the plans and agenda of the enemy for my life Lord I magnify you because you will destroy their plans over my life and pregnancy in the name of Jesus.

- Lord, I come in the name of beloved son Jesus Christ and I pray that every evil dreams and revelation concerning the fruit of my womb is destroyed in the name of Jesus.

- Father Lord, for it has been written that children are the heritage of God, Lord, the fruit of my womb is your heritage, a gift of goodness from the throne of mercy, let no evil befall it in the name of Jesus.

- Lord God, the Bible says who speaks and it comes to pass when the Almighty has not commanded? Lord, I pray that you will not allow that counsel to be fulfilled over my life in the name of Jesus.

- Lord Jesus, I come against every power that has vowed to always create fear in my heart by bringing me evil dreams, I destroy such power in the name of Jesus.

- Lord God according to your words in the book of Proverbs 3vs 24 that when I lie down I shall not be afraid and my sleep shall be sweet, I receive power for a sweet sleep in the name of Jesus.

- Lord God, I cover the fruit of my womb with your precious blood, let no harm befall it in the name of Jesus.

- The Bible says no weapon fashion against us shall prosper, Lord every arrow that is shot at my unborn child from the dream is destroyed in the name of Jesus.

- Lord Jesus, as I close my eye in sleep, I ask that you're Holy Spirit and power will guide me and they will close the door against every evil manipulation that may want to contaminate my sleep with evil dreams in the name of Jesus.

- Lord God, I stand upon the promise of your words that say that my children and I are for signs and Wonders. Lord, every evil contamination of the dream during pregnancy is destroyed in the name of Jesus.

- Lord God, the Bible says before I formed you in the womb I knew you before you were born I set you apart; I appointed you as a prophet to the nations." In the same vein, you have known my child even in the state of pregnancy. Lord, I pray that you will Shield him/her with your marvelous power that no evil thing from the dream shall befall him/her in the name of Jesus.

- Lord God, for myself I pray for spiritual strength, I pray for your power Lord to conquer every battle that may arise against me in the dream, Lord fly me your spiritual strength in the name of Jesus.

- Father Lord, I thank you for this gift that you are giving the world that is coming through me, I appreciate your kindness over my life, let your name be exalted in the name of Jesus.

Amen

PRAYER AGAINST MISSING HUSBAND IN THE DREAM

Today we shall be looking at prayers against missing husband in the dream. Dreams play a vital role in our lives, and our spiritual ability to interpret this dreams will help us avert a lot of potential disasters in our lives. Dreams are prophetic in nature, that is to say, what you dream can come to pass either for good or for evil. Dreams are symbolic in nature, this means what you see is not necessarily what there is. It is just a symbol of something else. For instance, the dreams of Pharaoh, about the seven slim cows, swallowing the seven fat cows, the dreams had little or nothing to do with cows, but the seven slim cow's means seven years of famine. (See Genesis 41). Today we shall be looking at the meaning of a missing husband in the dream, and what to do about such a dream.

Missing Husband in the Dream Meaning

Whenever something precious to you is missing in the dream, it is not a good sign. When you dream and see yourself looking for your husband in the dream, it means a couple of things. This could mean the death of your husband, it could mean an attack to end your marriage through divorce or separation, and generally it's a sign of something bad that is about to happen to your marriage. Now the good news is this, dreams can be cancelled or reversed, they are not final, Infact when God shows you something in the dream, it is for you to do something about it.

Any time you encounter a bad dream, you must counter it through prayers. About this dream of missing husband, you must pray seriously for your husband, you must pray against the spirit of death, and also pray for your marriage. Pray against any force that will come against your marriage. You must open your mouth to place the devil where he belongs, when he comes to attack you in your dreams you must resist him through prayers. These carefully selected prayers against missing husband in the dream will give you the right platform to intercede for your Husband. As you pray this prayers over your husband and marriage, every plan of the devil against your marriage shall be destroyed in Jesus name.

PRAYER POINTS

1). Father, I thank you for giving me a very handsome husband in Jesus name.

2). Father, I ask for your overflowing mercy upon my beloved husband in Jesus name.

3). I cover my husband with the blood of Jesus, in Jesus name

4). I declare the going out and coming in of my husband blessed in Jesus name

5). I shield my husband from the arrows that flies by day and night in Jesus name

6). I declare my husband protected from wicked and unreasonable men in Jesus name.

7). I protect my husband from husband snatchers in Jesus name.

8). No evil woman shall see my husband in Jesus name

9). No demonic agent from the marine kingdom shall see my husband in Jesus name.

10). Father I thank you for protecting my husband in Jesus name.

11). Father, I thank you for giving me a very handsome husband in Jesus name.

12). Father, I ask for your overflowing mercy upon my beloved husband in Jesus name.

13). I cover my husband with the blood of Jesus, in Jesus name

14). I surround my husband by fire in Jesus name

15). every one seeking the life of my husband shall be destroyed in the name of Jesus

16). I decree today that no weapon fashioned against my husband shall prosper in Jesus name.

17). every evil agent from the marine world trying to seduce my husband, I release the fire of God upon you now in Jesus name.

18). I scatter by fire every evil gang up against my husband in Jesus name.

19). I Declare total blindness upon every monitoring spirit, monitoring the progress of my husband in Jesus name

20). every enemy of my husband progress shall be out to permanent shame in Jesus name

Thank you Jesus.

PRAYER AGAINST WEARING BLACK CLOTH IN THE DREAM

To dream and not understand the meaning of your dream can be very tragic. This is because, through dreams we can be privileged to see things before the happen. A lot of believers today dream dreams but many of them do not know about dreams interpretation. What you don't know will always overpower you, but I believe that will not be your portion in Jesus name. Today we are going to be looking at prayers against wearing black cloth in the dream. What does this dream mean? What is the interpretation? What does black clothes mean in the dream? We shall be looking at these answers in this article. No devil shall prevail over your life in Jesus name.

Wearing Black Cloth in the Dream Meaning

Black cloth in the dream means a cloth for mourning, when you see yourself wearing a black cloth in the dream, it means someone close to you about to be attacked by the spirit of death. You must immediately begin to pray against the spirit of death in your household. You must organize a midnight prayer session to avert the spirit of death, cover all your family with the blood of Jesus and command death to carry his load out of your heart. As a child of God, you have been given the authority to have what you say, if you command death to go away from your house, it will go away, but if you keep quiet, the dream will come to pass. I have carefully selected prayers against wearing black cloth in the dream, I encourage you to pray this prayers with faith and all seriousness. You shall overcome in Jesus name.

PRAYER POINTS

1. Every power, transforming into masquerades in the night in order to attack me in the dreams, be exposed and die, in the name of Jesus.
2. Every power, transforming into animals in the night in order to attack me in the dreams, fall down and die, in Jesus' name.
3. Every coffin, prepared by the agent of death for my life, catch fire and roast to ashes, in the name of Jesus.

4. Every pit, dug for my life by agent of death, swallow the agents, in the name of Jesus.

5. Every power, oppressing my life through dreams of death, fall down and die, in the name of Jesus.

6. Every witchcraft power, tormenting my life with the spirit of death, fall down and die, in the name of Jesus.

7. Every witchcraft power, assigned to my family for untimely death, scatter and die, in the name of Jesus.

8. Every satanic agent, monitoring my life for evil, fall down and die, in the name of Jesus.

9. Every unconscious gift of death that I have received, receive the fire of God, in the name of Jesus.

10. Every stubborn pursuer of my life, turn back and perish in your own Red Sea, in the name of Jesus.

11. Every arrow of terminal sickness, come out of my life and die, in the name of Jesus.

12. Every power, enforcing terminal sickness in my life, fall down and die, in the name of Jesus.

13. Every decree of untimely death hovering over my life, catch fire and die, in the name of Jesus.

14. Every evil link between me and the spirit of untimely death is cut off by the blood of Jesus.

15. I reject and renounce every association with the spirit of death, in the name of Jesus.

16. Every inherited satanic glass on my eyes, break by the blood of Jesus.

17. Every ancestral agreement with the spirit of untimely death, break by the blood of Jesus.

18. Every agreement and covenant of hell fire in my family line, be destroyed by the blood of Jesus.

19. Every agreement with the spirit of death in my family line, break by the blood of Jesus.

20. I shall not die but live. The number of my days shall be fulfilled, in the name of Jesus.

21. Hidden sicknesses disappear now, in the name of Jesus.

22. Fountain of discomfort in any part of my body, dry up, in the name of Jesus.

23. Every dead organ in my body, receive life, in the name of Jesus.

24. Let my blood be transfused with the blood of Jesus.

25. Every internal disorder in my body, receive order, in Jesus' name.

26. Every infirmity, come out with all your roots, in the name of Jesus.

27. I withdraw every conscious and unconscious cooperation with sickness, in the name of Jesus.

28. Let the whirlwind of the Lord blow away every wind of infirmity, in the name of Jesus.

29. I release my body from every curse of infirmity, in Jesus' name.

30. Let the blood of Jesus flush out every evil deposit from my blood, in the name of Jesus.

31. I recover every organ of my body from every evil altar, in the name of Jesus.

32. Help me, O Lord, to recognize your voice.

33. Lord, where I am blind, give me sight.

34. I command my fears to evaporate now, in the name of Jesus.

35. I throw off every burden of worry, in the name of Jesus.

36. I refuse to be entangled with evil friends, in the name of Jesus.

37. I cast down every road-block hiding my progress, in Jesus' name.

38. Let my spiritual climate send terror to the camp of the enemy, in the name of Jesus.

39. O Lord, release me from evil words or evil sentences.

40. O Lord, let all my enemies be boxed to a corner.

41. I bind every jungle and desert spirit working in any area of my life, in the name of Jesus.

42. O Lord, deliver me by signs and wonders.

43. O Lord, make me a divine phenomenon.

44. Let spiritual violence that confuses the enemy be set into the camps of my enemies, in the name of Jesus.

45. Let heavenly fire ignite my prayer life, in the name of Jesus.

46. Let the divine anointing for spiritual breakthroughs fall upon me now, in the name of Jesus.

47. Let my prayer altar receive power today, in the name of Jesus.

48. O Lord, make me a prayer addict.

49. O Lord, forgive me of the sin of ingratitude.

50. Lord Jesus, make me a burning flame for you.

PRAYERS AGAINST MISSING CHILD IN THE DREAM

Isaiah 8:18 Behold, I and the children whom the LORD hath given me are for signs and for wonders in Israel from the LORD of hosts, which dwelleth in mount Zion.

Today we shall be looking at prayers against missing child in the dream. Whenever you see yourself looking for a particular child in the dream and you don't find that child until you wake up, you must rise up and pray, it is not a good dream. A missing child in a dream means the spirit of death may come for that child. When you have such dreams, do not panic, God has allowed you to see it so that you can pray against it. Call the child involved and pray over his life, make declarations of life over him and anoint that Child in the name of Jesus.

Know that as a child of God, you have the power to cancel bad dreams, Mark 11:23-24 tells us that we shall have what we say, if we don't doubt. Therefore reject the spirit of death in your family, cover all your children with the blood of Jesus and declare their freedom from death. These prayers against missing child in the dream will guide you as you engage them. Pray them with faith and do not fear, you shall overcome in Jesus name.

PRAYER POINTS

1. Every power, transforming into masquerades in the night in order to attack me in the dreams, be exposed and die, in the name of Jesus.

2. Every power, transforming into animals in the night in order to attack me in the dreams, fall down and die, in Jesus' name.

3. Every coffin, prepared by the agent of death for my life, catch fire and roast to ashes, in the name of Jesus.

4. Every pit, dug for my life by agent of death, swallow the agents, in the name of Jesus.

5. Every power, oppressing my life through dreams of death, fall down and die, in the name of Jesus.

6. Every witchcraft power, tormenting my life with the spirit of death, fall down and die, in the name of Jesus.

7. Every witchcraft power, assigned to my family for untimely death, scatter and die, in the name of Jesus.

8. Every satanic agent, monitoring my life for evil, fall down and die, in the name of Jesus.

9. Every unconscious gift of death that I have received, receive the fire of God, in the name of Jesus.

10. Every stubborn pursuer of my life, turn back and perish in your own Red Sea, in the name of Jesus.

11. Every arrow of terminal sickness, come out of my life and die, in the name of Jesus.

12. Every power, enforcing terminal sickness in my life, fall down and die, in the name of Jesus.

13. Every decree of untimely death hovering over my life, catch fire and die, in the name of Jesus.

14. Every evil link between me and the spirit of untimely death be cut off by the blood of Jesus.

15. I reject and renounce every association with the spirit of death, in the name of Jesus.

16. Every inherited satanic glass on my eyes, break by the blood of Jesus.

17. Every ancestral agreement with the spirit of untimely death, break by the blood of Jesus.

18. Every agreement and covenant of hell fire in my family line, be destroyed by the blood of Jesus.

19. Every agreement with the spirit of death in my family line, break by the blood of Jesus.

20. I shall not die but live. The number of my days shall be fulfilled, in the name of Jesus.

PRAYERS AGAINST FIGHTING IN THE DREAM

Isaiah 59:19 so shall they fear the name of the LORD from the west, and his glory from the rising of the sun. When the enemy shall come in like a flood, the Spirit of the LORD shall lift up a standard against him.

Today's prayer topic is titled: Prayers against fighting in the dream. Anytime you sleep and you see yourself fighting both familiar and unfamiliar people in the dream, you are contending with satanic oppositions, demonic resistance and violent witchcraft powers. Fighting in the dream should not be taking lightly, many people have been killed in their dreams. You must stop them before they stop you. If you are not spiritually strong, the forces can overpower you and even destroy you in the spirit realm, but that will not be your portion in Jesus name. As a child of God, you have power over all powers of darkness, whenever the devil comes raging in the dream, you have power to overcome him and place him where he belongs, which is under your feet. But to overcome the devil, there are certain spiritual exercises that you must engage. We shall looking into them shortly.

How to Overcome Satanic Oppositions

Prayers and fasting is an unbeatable weapon against all demonic oppositions anytime any day. You conquer the devil through intense prayers, every time you pray and fast, you strengthen your spirit man, and when your spirit man is energized, you will always conquer the devil whether in the dream or in the physical. I they come against you to fight you in the dream, you will beat the broad daylight out of them. Prayers and fasting strengthen you both in the spiritual and physical realm, always set time for yourself to fast and pray to build up spiritual capacity. This prayers against fighting in the dream is your spiritual offensive weapon against satanic oppositions, as you fast, pray those prayers and watch the devil bow at your feet. You shall never be a victim again in Jesus name.

PRAYER POINTS

1. I crush under my feet, all the evil powers trying to imprison me, in the name of Jesus.

2. O Lord, let there be civil war in the camp of the enemies of my destiny in the name of Jesus.

3. Power of God, pull down the stronghold of the enemies of my destiny, in the name of Jesus.

4. O Lord, persecute and destroy them in anger, in the name of Jesus.

5. Every blockage, in my way of my progress clear away by fire, in the name of Jesus.

6. Every demonic claim of the earth over my life, be dismantled, in the name of Jesus.

7. I refuse to be chained to my place of birth, in Jesus' name.

8. Any power, pressing the sand against me, fall down and die, in the name of Jesus.

9. I receive my breakthroughs, in the name of Jesus.

10. I release my money from the house of the strongman, in Jesus' name.

11. Blood of Jesus and the fire of the Holy Ghost, cleanse every organ in my body, in the name of Jesus.

12. I break loose from every inherited evil covenant of the earth, in the name of Jesus.

13. I break loose from every inherited evil curse of the earth, in the name of Jesus.

14. I break loose from every form of demonic bewitchment of the earth, in the name of Jesus

15. I release myself from every evil domination and control from the earth, in the name of Jesus.

16. Blood of Jesus, be transfused into my blood vessel.

17. I release panic upon my full-time enemies, in the name of Jesus.

18. O Lord, let stubborn confusion come upon the headquarters of my enemies, in the name of Jesus.

19. I loose confusion upon the plans of my enemies, in the name of Jesus.

20. Every stronghold of darkness, receive acidic confusion, in the name of Jesus.

21. I loose panic and frustration on satanic orders issued against me in the name of Jesus.

22. Every evil plan against my life, receive confusion, in the name of Jesus.

23. All curses and demons, programmed against me, I neutralize you by the blood of Jesus.

24. Every warfare, prepared against my peace, I command panic upon you, in the name of Jesus.

25. Every warfare, prepared against my peace, I command havoc upon you, in the name of Jesus.

26. Every warfare, prepared against my peace, I command chaos upon you, in the name of Jesus.

27. Every warfare, prepared against my peace, I command pandemonium upon you, in the name of Jesus.

28. Every warfare, prepared against my peace, I command disaster upon you, in the name of Jesus.

29. Every warfare, prepared against my peace, I command confusion upon you, in the name of Jesus.

30. Every warfare, prepared against my peace, I command spiritual acid upon you, in the name of Jesus.

31. Every warfare, prepared against my peace, I command destruction upon you, in the name of Jesus.

32. Every warfare, prepared against my peace, I command hornets of the Lord upon you, in Jesus' name.

33. Every warfare, prepared against my peace, I command brimstone and hailstone upon you, in the name of Jesus.

34. I frustrate every satanic verdict issued against me, in Jesus' name.

35. You the finger, vengeance, terror, anger, fear, wrath, hatred and burning judgment of God, be released against my full-time enemies, in the name of Jesus.

36. Every power, preventing the perfect will of God from being done in my life, receive failure, in the name of Jesus.

37. You warring angels and Spirit of God, arise and scatter every evil gathering sponsored against me, in the name of Jesus.

38. I disobey any satanic order, programmed by inheritance into my life, in the name of Jesus.

39. I bind and cast out every power causing internal warfare, in the name of Jesus.

40. Every demonic doorkeeper, locking out good things from me, be paralyzed by fire, in the name of Jesus Christ.

PRAYER AGAINST SERVING OTHERS IN THE DREAM

Deuteronomy 28:13 And the LORD shall make thee the head, and not the tail; and thou shalt be above only, and thou shalt not be beneath; if that thou hearken unto the commandments of the LORD thy God, which I command thee this day, to observe and to do them: Every child of God is ordained a King and a Priest on the Earth, Revelation 5:10. None of us are ordained to be servants of men in our life time. God speaking in Deuteronomy 28:13, He said we shall be the Head, ONLY and not the tail. The head is our porting in redemption. Today we shall be looking at prayers against serving others in the dream. If you must overcome the devil continually in your life, then you must learn to take your dreams seriously. Every dream has the power to come to pass, if it is a good dream, better for you, but if it's a bad dream, it will hurt you. Also it's important to know that as a believer, you have all what it takes to cancel every bad dream working against you. Through prayers of faith, you can cancel every bad dreams and stop them from coming to pass in your life. Also through prayers you can enforce the speedy manifestation of good dreams in your life. Now let us look at the meaning of serving others in your dreams.

Meaning of Serving Others in Your Dreams

When you dream and you see yourself serving others in the dream, this is talking about the spirit of slavery and backwardness. Please note that this does not include serving a mentor or a Great man of God in the dream. When you see yourself serving a great man of God or someone you consider as a mentor in the dream, God is showing you whom to follow and whom will impact your life and ministry. But the dream we are focusing on today, is when you see yourself as a servant or an errand boy in the dream, it connotes the spirit of slavery. You must guard against that spirit. You must resist it through intense deliverance prayers. People who are victims of this dreams never succeed in life, they spend all their active working years serving people as slaves and end up achieving nothing. A lot of highly educated people today have retired to their villages at their old age, after working for many years only to return home with nothing. That is the Spirit of slavery at work. You work like an elephant but you feed like an ant. To overcome this spirit of slavery, you must begin to resist the devil now in prayers. You must rise up at midnight and curse the spirit of slavery in the name of Jesus. This prayers against serving others in the dream will give you spiritual platform to put the devil where he belongs. Pray this prayers with faith today and receive your deliverance.

PRAYER POINTS

1. Oh Lord, as long as I am not employed as a slave in my place of work, whoever deprive me of my due shall be removed from his/her position in Jesus name.

2. Oh Lord, teach me how to retrieve all my due in my place of work so that others will not share what belongs to me in Jesus name.

3. All merciless taskmasters in my place of work shall lose their position today in Jesus name.

4. No matter how severe the condition of my work presently, I will multiply and grow and people will fear me in Jesus name.

5. All those who pattern my work after the slave masters of Egypt in my place of work, I decree that the God of Israel will replace you with merciful masters in Jesus name.

6. Oh Lord, I know that you can do everything. Deliver me from slavery in my workplace in Jesus name

7. Remember me oh Lord for good! Let your promises come alive today in Jesus name

8. Oh Lord! Make me a great nation; bless me and make my name great and I shall be a blessing in this generation in Jesus name.

9. Oh Lord! Bless those who bless me and curse him who curses me. In me all the families of the earth shall be blessed in this generation in Jesus name

10. I recover all that has been taken away from me today in Jesus name.

11. I take it back! I take back all my inheritance today in Jesus name.

12. Oh Lord, make with me a covenant of multiplication today in Jesus name.

13. Oh Lord, like Abraham, let me spend all the days of my life in great blessing in Jesus name

14. Gen. 26:13 – Oh Lord! After this prayer, I will begin to prosper, and continue prospering until I become very prosperous in Jesus name.

15. Oh Lord, give me a new name. A name that is synonymous with wealth, breakthrough and prosperity in Jesus name.

16. Oh Lord! Let my fear of you build a house for me in Jesus name.

17. Oh Lord! Let me find grace in your sight so that you will grant me all my request of breakthrough in Jesus name.

18. Oh Lord! Empower me today to get wealth so that I will continue to advance your kingdom in Jesus name.

19. Oh Lord, don't let the person that will channel my breakthrough rest until he/she has fulfil it in Jesus name.

20. Oh Lord, it is within your reach to make my glory shine. Place me to the place of the top through your mighty work so that my life will glorify your name in Jesus name.

21. The spirit of the Lord had voice through me, his word was on my tongue that my breakthrough starts now in Jesus name.

PRAYERS AGAINST SEEING TORTOISE OR SNAILS IN THE DREAM

Ezekiel 12:28 Therefore say unto them, Thus saith the Lord GOD; There shall none of my words be prolonged any more, but the word which I have spoken shall be done, saith the Lord GOD.

Dreams are prophetic in nature, it takes spiritual understanding from the Holy Spirit for us to understand dreams, and it takes understanding of your dreams to claim the blessings of it or to reverse the curses from it. Today we shall be looking at prayers against seeing tortoise or snail in the dream. A lot of people might be surprised at this topic, some may even wonder whether it is a big deal to see such creatures in the dream. The dream world is a symbolic world, a world where everything has significance. Many people who have dreams of tortoise and snails and have no idea of what it means suffer for what they know nothing about. Many of them are going through tough times and frustrations in life and they don't know that their woes is traceable to their dreams. But today we shall be examining the meaning of seeing tortoise or snail in the dream and what to do about it.

Meaning of Seeing Tortoise or Snail in the Dream

The tortoise and they snail has one thing in common, they are both slow. When you see any of these scriptures in your dream, it means you are suffering from the delay. Delay is a very bad thing; it can lead to frustration, and depression. Nothing discourages a man like delay, everything in your life moves at a slow motion; this is a very terrible state to find yourself. Delay can be experienced in any areas of your life, for instance, your job, business, careers, marriage, child birth, even answers to your prayers. To overcome delay, you must be giving to intense prayers. The good news is that what you see in your dreams is not final, if you like it, you can claim it, if you don't like it, and you can reject, reverse or cancel it. These prayers against seeing tortoise or snail in the dream are carefully selected for you to overcome the spirit of delay in your life. As you engage them in faith today, you shall receive divine speed in Jesus name.

PRAYER POINTS

1. Every power, prolonging my journey to breakthroughs, fall down and die, in Jesus' name.

2. Every problem that I brought into my life through my association with the spirit of the tortoise or snail die now, in Jesus' name.

3. I cancel the activities and powers of the snail spirit in my life, in the name of Jesus.

4. I break the covenants and curses of the snail spirit over my life, in the name of Jesus.

5. Every effect of the spirit of the snail over my life, be nullified by the blood of Jesus.

6. Every spirit of sluggishness and backwardness in my life receive the fire of God now and be destroyed, in the name of Jesus.

7. Every spirit, preventing good things in my life, be destroyed, in the name of Jesus.

8. O Lord, I reject left-over blessings.

9. By the grace of God, I will not feed from waste bins, in the name of Jesus.

10. I refuse to have boneless blessings, in the name of Jesus.

11. Every spirit of irritation in my life, be washed off by the blood of Jesus.

12. O Lord, let all the impossible begin to become possible for me in every department of my life, in Jesus' name.

13. O Lord, take me from where I am to where you want me to be.

14. O Lord, make a way for me where there is no way.

15. O Lord, grant me the power to be fulfilled, successful and prosperous in life, in the name of Jesus.

16. O Lord, break me in every department of my life, in the name of Jesus.

17. O Lord, make me to break through into dumbfounding miracles in all areas of my life, in the name of Jesus.

18. O Lord, make me to break loose from every obstacle on my way to progress in life, in the name of Jesus.

19. O Lord, establish me in the truth, godliness and faithfulness.

20. O Lord, add flavour to my work, in the name of Jesus.

21. O Lord, add increase to my work, in the name of Jesus.

22. O Lord, add profitability to my work, in the name of Jesus.

23. O Lord, promote and preserve my life, in the name of Jesus.

24. I reject the plans and agenda of the enemies for my life, in the name of Jesus.

25. I reject the assignments and weapons of the enemy against my life, in the name of Jesus.

26. Every weapon and evil designs against me, fail totally, in Jesus' name.

27. I reject premature death, in the name of Jesus.

28. I reject nightmares sudden destruction, in the name of Jesus.

29. I reject dryness in my walk with God, in the name of Jesus.

30. I reject financial debt, in the name of Jesus.

31. I reject lack and famine in my life, in Jesus' name.

32. I reject physical and spiritual accidents in my going in and coming out, in Jesus' name.

33. I reject sickness in my spirit, soul and body, in the name of Jesus.

34. I stand against every work of evil in my life, in the name of Jesus.

35. I overcome powerlessness confusion and every attack of the enemy, in the name of Jesus.

36. I command spiritual divorce between me and every power of darkness, in Jesus' name.

37. Every poison and arrow of the enemy, be neutralized, in Jesus' name.

38. I break every yoke of unfruitfulness in my life, in the name of Jesus.

39. I cancel the plans and the mark of life in the name of Jesus.

40. Lord Jesus, break all harmful genetic ties in my life, in Jesus' name.

PRAYERS AGAINST SEEING YOURSELF DEAD IN THE DREAM

Psalms 118:17 I shall not die, but live, and declare the works of the LORD.

Today we shall be looking at Prayers against seeing yourself dead in the dream.

As a child of God, your dreams should not be taken lightly, because dreams are mature ways God communicates with us, the devil can also attack us through dreams. You can only be a victim of dreams, when you don't understand the meaning of your dreams. Understanding the meaning of dreams is key to overcoming every arrows sent to you by the devil. Some dreams are symbolic, for example, the dream of Pharaoh and king Nebuchadnezzar where all symbolic. You need the wisdom of God through the power of the Holy Spirit to understand the meaning of such dreams. Today we are going to be looking at the meaning of seeing yourself dead in the dream and what to do about it. No devil shall prevail over your life in Jesus name.

Meaning Of Seeing Yourself Dead In the Dream

To die in the dream or to see yourself dead in the dream, simply means Spiritual death, this can also mean physical death, death of a loved one, death of a business, or job, it can also mean loss of some kind or bad luck. This is not a good dream at all, you must rise up and rebuke the Spirit of death, and you must cover yourself and everyone and everything you have with the blood of Jesus. You must keep making faith declarations concerning your life and destiny, you must keep rejecting death and declaring life over yourself and your loved ones. N this Kingdom, we are ordained to have what we say by faith, Mark 11:23-24. Do not be afraid of evil dreams, once you understand it, you have the power to cancel it or reverse it. No devil shall prevail over your life from this day forth in Jesus name.

PRAYER POINTS

1. I withdraw anything representing me from every evil altar, in the name of Jesus.

2. Mention the organ that you know is not behaving the way it should. When you have done this begin to say, "I withdraw you from every evil altar, in the name of Jesus. "Say these seven hot times.

3. Let the wind of the Holy Spirit bring all scattered bones together now, in the name of Jesus.

4. I use the blood of Jesus to reverse every poor record of the past about my life, in the name of Jesus.

5. I refuse to accept satanic substitute for my destiny, in Jesus' name.

6. I refuse to be caged by the enemy of good things, in Jesus' name.

7. Let every internal coffin in my life receive the fire of God and be roasted now, in the name of Jesus.

8. Every destiny-paralyzing power fashioned against my destiny, fall down and die, in the name of Jesus.

9. Every inherited evil limitation in any area of my life, depart now, in the mighty name of Jesus.

10. Every architect of spiritual coffins, I command you to fall down and die, in the name of our Lord Jesus Christ.

11. Every cloud of uncertainty, clear away now, in the name of Jesus.

12. I refuse to be converted to a living dead, in the name of Jesus.

13. Let every evil laying on of hands and shaking of evil hands be nullified, in the name of Jesus.

14. Every satanic consultation concerning my life, be nullified, in the name of Jesus.

15. Every decision taken against my life by witchcraft spirits, be nullified, in the name of Jesus.

16. I reject aborted victories in every area of my life, in Jesus' name.

17. Every caged star, be released now, in the name of Jesus.

18. My imagination and dreams will not be used against me, in the name of Jesus

19. Let every germ of infirmity die, in the name of Jesus.

20. Let every agent of sickness die, in the name of Jesus.

21. Hidden sicknesses disappear now, in the name of Jesus.

22. Fountain of discomfort in any part of my body, dry up, in the name of Jesus.

23. Every dead organ in my body, receive life, in the name of Jesus.

24. Let my blood be transfused with the blood of Jesus.

25. Every internal disorder in my body, receive order, in Jesus' name.

26. Every infirmity, come out with all your roots, in the name of Jesus.

27. I withdraw every conscious and unconscious cooperation with sickness, in the name of Jesus.

28. Let the whirlwind of the Lord blow away every wind of infirmity, in the name of Jesus.

29. I release my body from every curse of infirmity, in Jesus' name.

30. Let the blood of Jesus flush out every evil deposit from my blood, in the name of Jesus.

31. I recover every organ of my body from every evil altar, in the name of Jesus.

32. Help me, O Lord, to recognize your voice.

33. Lord, where I am blind, give me sight.

34. I command my fears to evaporate now, in the name of Jesus.

35. I throw off every burden of worry, in the name of Jesus.

36. I refuse to be entangled with evil friends, in the name of Jesus.

37. I cast down every road-block hiding my progress, in Jesus' name.

38. Let my spiritual climate send terror to the camp of the enemy, in the name of Jesus.

39. O Lord, release me from evil words or evil sentences

40. O Lord, let all my enemies be boxed to a corner.

41. I bind every jungle and desert spirit working in any area of my life, in the name of Jesus.

42. O Lord, deliver me by signs and wonders.

43. O Lord, make me a divine phenomenon.

44. Let spiritual violence that confuses the enemy be set into the camps of my enemies, in the name of Jesus.

45. Let heavenly fire ignite my prayer life, in the name of Jesus.

46. Let the divine anointing for spiritual breakthroughs fall upon me now, in the name of Jesus.

47. Let my prayer altar receive power today, in the name of Jesus.

48. O Lord, make me a prayer addict.

49. O Lord, forgive me of the sin of ingratitude.

50. Lord Jesus, make me a burning flame for you

PRAYERS AGAINST DRINKING ALCOHOL IN THE DREAM

Ephesians 5:18 and be not drunk with wine, wherein is excess; but be filled with the Spirit;

In Spiritual warfare, dreams are very vital instruments. Our dreams are often times the medium from which we get spiritual information, whether good or bad. The ability to understand dreams enable us to better know the approach we must take to overcome the devil. Some dreams are straight forward and easy to understand, while some other dreams are symbolic nature. We need to ask the Holy Spirit to empower us with grace to understand our dreams and know whether to claim it or reject it. Today we shall be looking at prayers against drinking alcohol in the dream. What exactly does this dream mean? Is it a random dream? Should I take it seriously? We shall be answering these questions shortly.

Meaning Of Drinking Alcohol in the Dream?

Drinking alcohol in the dreams means spiritual pollution. It is not a good dream, whenever you see yourself drinking alcohol in the dream, the devil is polluting your spirit, he is planting some evil deposits in your life that will definitely affect your life negatively. But you must reject such dreams and pray against it. Whenever you find yourself in this type of a dream, as soon as you wake up, you must reject the dream and ask the Holy Spirit to purge you and cleanse you perfectly in Jesus name. Command the devil to get out of your body in Jesus name, also command your body to spiritually vomit every form of evil deposits in your body in Jesus name. You are declared free in Jesus name.

PRAYER POINTS

1. Let every organized strategy of the hosts of the demonic world against my life be rendered useless, in the name of Jesus.

2. Let every demonic influence targeted at destroying my vision, dream and ministry receive total disappointment, in Jesus' name.

3. Let every demonic trap set against my life be shattered to pieces, in the name of Jesus.

4. All unfriendly friends militating against my life, receive commotion and be dis organized, in the name of Jesus

5. Father Lord, let my life, ministry and prayer life be extremely dangerous for the kingdom of darkness, in the name of Jesus

6. All demoniacally organized seductive appearances to pull me down, be rendered null and void, in the name of Jesus.

7. My Lord and my God, raise intercessors to stand in the gap for me always, in the name of Jesus.

8. I reject all uncontrollable crying, heaviness and regrets, in the name of Jesus.

9. Father Lord, help me so that my divine spiritual assignments shall not be transferred to another pet-son, in the name of Jesus.

10. I command all organized forces of darkness against my life to receive commotion, lightning and thunder, in the name of Jesus.

11. All demonically organized networks against my spiritual and physical ambition, be put to shame, in the name of Jesus.

12. I command all demonic mirrors and monitoring gadgets against my spiritual life to crack to pieces, in the name of Jesus.

13. Let every ceremony on this issue be soaked in the blood of Jesus and in the fire of the Holy Ghost.

14. I paralyze any attempt by the devil to use this ceremony as a cover-up to carry out any evil assignment against my life, in the name of Jesus.

5. Lay one hand on your head and the other on your stomach or navel and begin to pray like this: Holy Ghost fire, burn from the top of my head to the sole of my feet. Begin to mention every organ of your body: your kidney, liver, intestine, blood, etc. You must not rush at this level, because the fire will actually come and you may start feeling the heat.

16. I cut myself off from every spirit of. .. (Mention the name of your place of birth), in the name of Jesus.

17. I cut myself off from every tribal spirit and curse, in Jesus' name. I cut myself off from every territorial spirit and curse, in the name of Jesus.

18. Holy Ghost fire, purge my life.

19. I claim my complete deliverance, in the name of Jesus, from the spirit of . . . (mention those things you do not desire in your life).

20. I break the hold of any evil power over my life, in Jesus' name.

21. I move from bondage into liberty, in the name of Jesus

22. I deliver myself from every form of poverty, lack and want, from the foundation of my life, in the name of Jesus.

23. I deliver myself from every satanic trap, from the foundation of my life, in the name of Jesus.

24. I deliver myself from every bewitchment power, from the foundation of my life, in the name of Jesus.

25. I deliver myself from every idol deposits from the foundation of my life, in the name of Jesus.

26. I deliver myself from every form of sexual pollution from the foundation of my life, in the
Name of Jesus.

27. I deliver myself from every witchcraft coven, from the foundation of my life, in the name of Jesus.

28. I deliver myself from the spirit of polygamy, from the foundation of my life, in the name of Jesus.

29. I deliver myself from cultural bondage, from the foundation of my life, in the name of Jesus.

30. I deliver myself from every dream harassment, from the foundation of my life, in the name of Jesus.

PRAYERS AGAINST SNAKE BITE IN THE DREAM

Mark 16:18 they shall take up serpents; and if they drink any deadly thing, it shall not hurt them; they shall lay hands on the sick, and they shall recover.

Today, we shall be looking at prayers against snake bite in the dream. As children of God, we have power over serpents and scorpions and to crush every power of the enemy. Just like God ministers to us through dreams, and blesses us through the same, the devil can as well attack us through dreams too. Every born again child of God must be spiritually sensitive, your spiritual eyes must be open to see the attacks of the devil when it comes. We must also ask the Holy Spirit to endue us with the gift of interpretation of dreams. You cannot fight what you don't understand. Now let's look at snake bite in the dream.

Meaning of Snake Bite in the Dream

Whenever you dream and you are bitten by a snake in the dream, this means spiritual poison. It is a bad dream and you urgently need to pray your way out of it. Spiritual poison is a very serious matter; they are spiritual deposits that cannot be traceable by medical science. There are some people, who are dying of strange sicknesses, but nobody knows what is killing them, the scan cannot find it, but it's killing them. Strange movements in the body, strange movements in the private parts, are also as results of spiritual poison. With the power of prayers, you can destroy every spiritual poison in your life, you can flush out of your life by the blood of Jesus.

What to Do About This Evil Dream

You must engage in deliverance prayers to uproot every spiritual poisons from your life. These prayers are midnight prayers. They must be prayed aggressively and violently. Spiritual poison can only be erased by spiritual forces. You command spiritual forces when you engage in violent deliverance prayers. These prayers against snake bite in the dream will flush out every spiritual poison in your life. Pray them with faith today and receive your deliverance today in Jesus name.

PRAYER POINTS

1. What the enemy has programmed into my life to destroy me, Oh Lord, remove it by fire, in the name of Jesus.

2. Oh Lord my God, remove whatever the enemy has planted in my life, in the name of Jesus.

3. Every good thing that the enemy has destroyed in my life, Oh Lord my God, restore it unto me today, in Jesus' name.

4. My spiritual antenna, be connected to the kingdom of God, in the name of Jesus.

5. Every pollution in my spiritual life, be purged with holy fire, in the name of Jesus

6. Evil strangers in my body, come out of your hiding places, in the name of Jesus.

7. I disconnect any conscious or unconscious link with demonic caterers, in the name of Jesus.

8. All avenues of eating or drinking spiritual poisons, be closed, in the name of Jesus.

9. I cough and vomit any food eaten from the table of the devil, in the name of Jesus. (Cough and vomit it by faith. Prime the expulsion).

10. All negative materials, circulating in my blood stream, be evacuated, in the name of Jesus.

11. I drink the blood of Jesus. (Physically swallow it by faith. Do this for some time.)

12. All evil spiritual feeders, warring against me, drink your own blood and eat your own flesh, in the name of Jesus.

13. All demonic food utensils, fashioned against me, roast, in the name of Jesus.

14. Holy Ghost fire, circulate all over my body.

15. All physical poisons, inside my system, be neutralized, in the name of Jesus.

16. All evil assignments, fashioned against me through the mouth gate, be nullified, in the name of Jesus.

17. All spiritual problems, attached to any hour of the night, be cancelled, in the name of Jesus. (Pick the period from midnight to 6:00 a.m.)

18. Bread of heaven, fill me till I want no more.

19. All catering equipment's of evil caterers, attached to me, be destroyed, in the name of Jesus.

20. My digestive system, reject every evil command, in the name of Jesus.

21. Spirit of excellence, take control of my life, in the name of Jesus.

22. O Lord, let the gift of revelation promote my ministry, in the name of Jesus.

23. Holy Spirit, lay your hands upon me, in the name of Jesus.

24. O Lord, let the power of resurrection activate holiness and purity in me, in the name of Jesus.

25. Oh Lord, let every marriage conducted for me in the dream be destroyed, in the name of Jesus.

26. Evil marriage, that is destroying my holiness and purity, die, in the name of Jesus.

27. Evil marriage, that is destroying my ministry and calling, die, in the name of Jesus.

28. Every power that has turned my life upside-down, roast by fire, in the name of Jesus.

29. Oh Lord my God, re-arrange my destiny according to your plan, in the name of Jesus.

30. Oh Lord my God, crush every power that says I will not fulfil my destiny, in the name of Jesus.

PRAYERS AGAINST SEEING FIRE IN THE DREAM

Daniel 1:17 as for these four children, God gave them knowledge and skill in all learning and wisdom: and Daniel had understanding in all visions and dreams.

Dreams are one of the major ways God speaks to His children. Dreams are not natural experiences, they are supernatural occurrences. Any time you sleep and dream, your spirit man goes into action, a lot of information are communicated to your spirit man in the dream realm. There are different types of dreams, random dreams, godly dreams, and satanic dreams. Just as the Lord speaks to us through dreams, the devil can also speak or send attacks to us through dreams. Today we shall be engaging in prayers against seeing fire in the dream. Every evil dream can be erased through prayers. This is because dreams are prophetic in nature, if they are godly or good dreams, you can claim it, but if they are evil dreams, you must reject it on the altar of prayers.

Meaning Of Seeing Fire in the Dream

Knowing the meaning of a dream is key to understanding how to handle a dream. A lot of people are attacked through dreams and because they don't know the meaning of their dreams, they become victims of their dreams. But today we shall be looking at the meaning of seeing fire in the dream. Whenever you sleep and see fire destroying or consuming anything in the dream is a bad dream. Fire in the dream is a sign of a coming disaster, or destruction coming your way. All through the bible, we see fire as a tool for destruction, Exodus 24:17, James 3:6, Lamentation 2:4, and Luke 9:54. Anytime you see fire destroying things in the dream, you should know that destruction is around the corner and you must pray against it. It could be a destruction of life or property, but you have power in the name of Jesus to destroy that dream.

What to Do About an Evil Dream

You must pray against it. In this case, you must pray against the spirit of destruction, you must command the destroyer to depart from your household in the name of Jesus. The power of prayers can undo any evil dreams. That is why I have compiled this prayers against seeing fire in the dream. I encourage you to pray this prayers with all your heart and receive your deliverance today in Jesus name.

PRAYER POINTS

1. Every good thing that has been amputated in my life receive new life and begin to germinate and prosper, in the name of Jesus.

2. Any power of the destroyer, assigned to be swallowing my goodness like the grave, roast by fire, in Jesus' name.

2. Any spirit of death, harboring my blessings and potentials, receive the fire of God and vomit them unto me now, in the name of Jesus.

3. Any power of the grave, that had swallowed my blessings and potentials, receive the fire of God and vomit them unto me now, in the name of Jesus.

4. Any power in any water that has ever swallowed my blessings, receive the fire of God and vomit them unto me now.

5. Any spiritual animal, that has ever swallowed my blessings, melt by fire.

6. Any satanic strongman, keeping my blessings as his goods, fall down and die; I recover my goods now.

7. Any evil swallower, assigned by the destroyer against my life, vomit my blessings, fall down and die.

8. Any power of the destroyer, assigned to destroy my body organs, fall down and die.

9. Any power of the destroyer, drinking my blood and eating my flesh, fall down and die.

10. Any power of the destroyer, assigned to pollute my body, fall down and die.

11. You strongman of body destruction, loose your hold over my body, fall down and die.

12. I wash every polluted organ in my body with the blood of Jesus.

13. Any organ of my body, that has been eaten up spiritually, receive the blood of Jesus and be made whole.

14. Any power of the destroyer, specifically assigned to destroy my relationship with my God, fall down and die.

15. Any power of the destroyer, attacking my spiritual life, fall down and die.

16. Any power of the destroyer, fighting against my spiritual well-being, fall down and die.

17. Any damage, done so far to my spiritual relationship with God, be repaired.

18. All spiritual gifts, blessings, virtues and benefits that have been paralyzed, damaged or amputated, I recover them now, in the name of Jesus.

19. Every evil power, fashioned to life, be paralyzed waste my divine and opportunities, loose your hold, fall down and die, in the name of Jesus.

20. Any agent of the destroyer, assigned to waste my goods, loose your hold, fall down and die

Thank You Jesus

CHAPTER 10

PRAYER AGAINST EVIL UTTERANCES AND PROPHECY

Prayer Points Against Evil News And Utterances

Today we will be dealing with prayer points against evil news and Utterances. This prayer guide us something every parents should take serious. One of the worst nightmares of parents is to hear the news of their children's death. It can be so devastating. I decree as an oracle of God, no parent shall hear bad news about their children in the name of Jesus.

Before we go fully into the prayer topic, let's quickly draw reference from the scripture. A perfect example is the story of Eli the Priest. Eli didn't train his children well that they became evil and sinned greatly against God. This brought down the curse of God upon them and upon the house of Eli. 1 Samuel 4:17–18 so the messenger answered and said, "Israel has fled before the Philistines, and there has been a great slaughter among the people. Also your two sons, Hophni and Phineas, are dead; and the ark of God has been captured." And it came to pass, when he made mention of the ark of God, that he fell from off the seat backward by the side of the gate, and his neck brake, and he died: for he was an old man, and heavy. And he had judged Israel forty years.

Eli could not hold back the pain of losing two children at once, when the new came, he died too. I decree once more, no parent will suffer bad news on any of their children whether home or abroad. The news of children's death is not only the evil news or utterances that can create problem in the life of an individual. Evil news generally are unpleasant events that take place. Every form of evil news that the enemy has planned to bring your way is cancelled by the authority of heaven.

PRAYER POINTS

- Lord God, I cancel every form of evil news that the enemy has planned for me, I cancel it by the power in the name of Jesus. I change every evil occurrences that the enemy has put in place to break out to steal my joy away, I change it to event of joy in the name of Jesus.

- Father Lord, I cover all my children with the blood of Jesus. Anyone that the enemy wants to take in order to bring evil news to my dwelling place, I cancel it in the name of Jesus. My kids shall not die but live to declare the works of the lord in the land of the living, in the name of Jesus.

- Lord, I come against every evil utterances that has said to my life, I rebuke them by the authority of heaven. Every utterances that is bringing nothing but trouble into my life, I destroy it by the fire of the Holy Ghost in the name of Jesus.

- Lord, for it has been written who speaks and it comes to pass when the Almighty has not commanded. I come against every evil tongue spitting evil into my life in the name of Jesus. I decree that the power of God Almighty will change every evil words that has been said into my life in the name of Jesus.

- Lord God, you are the God of all possibilities, just like you compelled Balaam to bless the children of Isreal instead of curse, I pray that you will cause my enemies to bless me instead of cursing me in the name of Jesus. I pray that by your mercy you will change their evil utterances into blessing in the name of Jesus.

- Lord, the scripture made me understand that your mercy endure forever. I pray that you will cover me with your mercy and you will not allow the plan of the enemies to be fulfilled over my life in the name of Jesus. Lord, every demonic animal or agent that has been sent to me by the enemy to plant the seed of evil into my life, I pray that such animal fall to death in the name of Jesus.

- Every man born of woman waiting for bad news about me, I pray that the angel of the lord strike them dead this moment in the name of Jesus. I pray that no evil shall come near me or anyone around me. I pray that the hands of God Almighty fix everything that concerns me in the name of Jesus. I refuse to fall victim to any evil circumstances in the name of Jesus.

- Lord, I decree that I shall not fall victim to the antic of the enemy in the name of Jesus. I pray that the power of God Almighty will go before me in all my ways in the name of Jesus. I come against any form accident in my way, I come against every form of kidnapping in the name of Jesus. I pray that the mark of God will be upon everyone around me in the name of Jesus.

- Oh you agent of darkness wait for bad news to be broadcasted about me or my family, I pray the fire of God will consume you this moment in the name of Jesus. Where other people are saying there is a casting down, I pray there shall be lifting up in the name of Jesus. No harm shall come near me in the name of Jesus. I shall not become an object of ridicule in the name of Jesus.

- I come against every plan of the devil to terminate my existence in the name of Jesus. In the remaining of this year, I refuse to be a carrier of evil news in the name of Jesus and I refuse to receive one concerning the people that are close to me in the name of Jesus.

- I redeem each days remaining in this year with the precious blood of Christ. I exempt myself and everyone around me from evil arrow that will fly in the remaining months of this year in the name of Jesus.

PRAYER TO DESTROY THE EVIL PLANS OF THE ENEMY

Today we will be dealing with warfare prayers to destroy the plans of the enemy. The enemy never rests, mostly when a man has decided to go on and pursue the purpose of his existence. Jacob never had issues in life until he started aspiring to become great like he has been destined to be. Joseph never has any problems in life until he began having dreams where God showed him a revelation of who he is to become.

It is worthy to note that just as God has plans for our lives, the enemies also have a plan for our lives. It is now our doing or undoing that will destroy the works of the enemy over our lives.

The enemy succeeded in the life of Samson. The strength of Samson became useless after the enemy got him. He has been warned not to marry from a strange land, a community of people that don't serve the holy one of Isreal, he took Delilah from their midst, and that led to his fall. I decree that whoever the enemy has staged to enter your life at one point in time to destroy you, I decree that the fire of most high will burn such person in the name of Jesus. Every wrong man or woman that the enemy has planned for you, may God cause a divine separation between you and that person.

Similarly, as God has designed his plans for Joseph, so also did the enemy design his plans too. Joseph was destined to become great. He was destined to lead the children of Isreal out of. Meanwhile, the enemy also has his plans for Joseph. His brothers fell into the perfect image of the enemy, and they were used against him to ensure that the plans of God concerning him were defeated. I pray that by the mercies of the most high, every agenda of the enemies to destroy the purpose of God for your life shall be destroyed today in the name of Jesus.

The enemy planned that Joseph should the killed, but God saved him. The enemy also made provision for how Joseph would sacrifice his destiny on the altar of immoralities with his master's wife. Still, God also helped Joseph overcome the plan of the enemy, by the mercies of the most high, may God destroy the plans of the enemies concerning your life.

Ensure that you study this prayer guide and say all the prayers in it. As you begin to use this guide, may God reveal the plans of the enemy to you in the name of Jesus.

PRAYER POINTS

- Father Lord, I come before you this day, I need your help Lord Jesus, and I need your power over my enemies. The ones that have vowed that I will never amount to something in life, the one whose plans and agenda for my life is for destruction, I pray that you will destroy their plans over my life in the name of Jesus.

- Lord God, I pray that by your mercies, your counsel alone will stand in my life. Every other and agenda of the evil ones over my is scattered by fire. I call on the fire of the most high to descend into the camp of the enemies and burn them to ashes in the name of Jesus.

- Father Lord, I pray that the archangels of glory will descend mightily into the territory of enemies and destroy their agenda for my life in the name of Jesus. Lord, I want you to scatter the language of my enemies. I pray that you will cause mighty disunity to erupt in their midst, and you will cause them to destroy themselves in the name of Jesus.

- I decree that from now on, the spirit of truth, the spirit of divinity from the throne of the holy of Isreal will descend upon me in the name of Jesus. I pray that the holy spirit of God will begin to guide me in all my ways. I pray that you will not cover the secret of the enemies over my life. I pray that you will always reveal their plans over my life in the name of Jesus.

- Lord Jesus, I pray that by your death and resurrection, you will not let my enemy triumph over me. I pray that in all ways and all ramifications, you will grant me victory over my enemies. Do not let them rejoice in victory over me. Every of their plans is revealed to me in the name of Jesus. For the scripture says the

690

secret of the Lord is with those that fear him, I pray that you will reveal the secret of dark places to me in the name of Jesus.

- Lord God, just like you helped Joseph escape all the traps and craftiness of the enemies over his life, just like you take him from the point of zero to the point of hero, I pray that you will help me overcome the trap of my enemies in the name of Jesus.

- I pray that the fire of the most high will go right now, because the scripture says, the fire will go before the army of the Lord and consume his enemies. I pray that the fire of the most high God before and destroy all my enemies. All the evil seer that sees the destiny of a man even before the time of manifestation, I pray that you will remove their sights in the name of Jesus.

- I decree by the power of the most high, every sense of consciousness of my enemies is taken away in the name of Jesus. I pray that you will cause my enemies to go blind for my sake, I decree by the power in the name of Jesus, you will cause my enemies to go deaf over my matter in the name of Jesus. Each of their plans and agenda over my life is canceled in the name of Jesus.

PRAYER POINTS AGAINST EVIL PROPHECY

Today we will be dealing with prayer points against evil prophecy. Have you ever heard an evil Prophecy concerning your life? Has anyone given you a bad revelation and that got you so scared that you don't even know what to do? What about evil utterances? Has anyone condemned you even to death? Has any affirmatively told you that you cannot amount to anything significant in life?

The truth is, what people say about you doesn't matter. What people have told you God told them about you should not define you. You should not just cover your face in fear because you were given a prophecy of death. That is the best time to seek the face of God through prayers. Remember the story of King Hezekiah in the book of 2 Kings 20 in those days Hezekiah became ill and was at the point of death. The prophet Isaiah son of Amos went to him and said, "This is what the LORD says: Put your house in order, because you are going to die; you will not recover." Hezekiah turned his face to the wall and prayed to the LORD, "Remember, O LORD, how I have walked before you faithfully and with wholehearted devotion and have done what is good in your eyes." And Hezekiah wept bitterly. Before Isaiah had left the middle court, the word of the LORD came to him: "Go back and tell Hezekiah, the leader of my people, 'this is what the LORD, the God of your father David, says: I have heard your prayer and seen your tears; I will heal you. On the third day from now you will go up to the temple of the LORD. I will add fifteen years to your life. And I will deliver you and this city from the hand of the king of Assyria. I will defend this city for my sake and for the sake of my servant David.'

Sometimes evil Prophecy are a test of our faith and how fervent we are in the place of prayer. Hezekiah could have just accepted his fate and prepare for his death to come. However, he understood that nothing comes to pass unless it has been commanded by God. And he knew God was capable to change the tide of things in the slightest moment. He immediately went back to God in prayer and God changed the prophecy. Even Prophet Isaiah had not left the court yard when God told him to return to Hezekiah and tell him another fifteen years has been added to his days.

The scripture says in the book of Lamentations 3:37 who is he who speaks and it comes to pass, When the Lord has not commanded it? No one can command anything to come into reality except it has been commanded by God. So whatever people have told you doesn't hold much weight. You have an undeniable access to God through Christ Jesus. You call always go to God in prayers and change the prophecy that has been said concerning you.

PRAYER POINTS

- Lord Jesus, I thank you for the grace and privilege that you have bestowed on me to see another day like this, let your name be exalted in the name of Jesus. It is by your mercy that I'm not consumed yet, I pray that your mercy will continually be upon me in the name of Jesus.

- Lord Jesus, the scripture says who is he who speaks and it comes to pass, When the Lord has not commanded it? Lord, I stand only your promises for my life. I silent every evil word and utterances that has been said concerning my life in the name of Jesus.

- I break down every empire of evil prophecy over my life. Every wall of demonic utterances trying to work against my destiny, I rebuke you by the fire of the Holy Ghost in the name of Jesus. Every evil prophecy over my life is silenced in the name of Jesus.

- I establish a new covenant through the blood of Christ. By the virtue of the blood that was shed on the cross of Calvary, I tap into a new covenant of life in the name of Jesus. I destroy every form of old covenant over my life in the name of Jesus.

- Lord, every evil prophecy of death over my and family, I cancel it by the blood of the lamb. For it has been written that I shall not die but live to declare the works of the lord in the land of the living. I cancel every evil utterance of death over my life in the name of Jesus.

- Lord, every evil Prophecy of failure over my life, you are broken today in the name of Jesus. The scripture says as Christ is so we are. Every evil prophecy of failure over my life, hear the word of the lord, the scripture says I'm for signs and wonders, I'm too big for failure, oh spirit of failure, you are destroyed concerning me in the name of Jesus.

- Lord Jesus, every prophecy of sickness over my life and the life of my family, I cancel you today in the name of Jesus. For it has been written, Christ has taken upon himself all our infirmities and he has healed all our diseases. Every form of infirmity or disease in life is broken by the power in the name of Jesus.

- Lord, I decree that over life your counsel alone will stand in my life in the name of Jesus. I rebuke whatever Prophecy that has been said concerning me. I cancel every evil utterance and demonic curses over my life by the power in the name of Jesus. For it has been written, Christ has been curse for us because cursed is he that is hanged on the tree. I cancel every manifestation of curse over my life in the name of Jesus.
- Lord, you are the great changer. I decree that by your power you will transform every evil prophecy into blessing and upliftment for me in the name of Jesus.

PRAYER POINTS TO OVERCOME THE DEVIL

Today we will be dealing with prayer points to overcome the devil. Overcoming Satan means resisting the devil. Resisting the devil means resisting every evil thing. The scripture says in James 4: 7, "Submit yourself to the Lord resist the devil, and he will flee from you. The devil doesn't go to a place without leaving a lasting impact behind. The scripture says the thief comes to steal, kill and destroy. It is essential to know that the thief in this context is the devil. When the devil visits a place, there is always a mark left behind to show that the devil was there.

We will be praying powerful prayers to overcome the devil. When we overcome the devil, we have power over sin and iniquity. When we get power over sin and iniquity, we no longer become slaves to sin. The enemy understands that the best thing that can sway us away from the presence of God is sin. Recall in the book of Genesis how man sinned and fell short of the glory of God. The consequence was very devastating, which led to a man being sent out of the beautiful Garden of Eden. The man was not just sent out of the garden; God also cursed man and woman for disobeying Him.

Devil is the mastermind of sin. He tempts us using different vices. Little wonder the scripture admonishes us not to be ignorant of the devices of the devil. When we overcome the devil, it gives us the leverage to serve God better and do His bidding. The spirit is of the Lord; the flesh is of the devil. The book of Matthew 26:41 Watch and pray, lest you enter into temptation. The spirit indeed is willing, but the flesh is weak." When we strive to do the things of the spirit, the flesh arises with temptations that will hinder us from doing them. But when we overcome the devil, we have subdued the flesh. I decree by the authority of heaven; the flesh will have no power over you again in the name of Jesus.

PRAYER POINTS

- Lord, I thank you for grace you have bestowed on me to see a new day, I magnify you for keeping me to witness this day, may your name be highly exalted in the name of Jesus.

- Father Lord, I pray for power over sin and iniquity. The scripture says if the power of Him that raised Christ from the dead dwells in you, it will quicken your mortal body. Lord, I pray that you let there be an outpour of God's spirit into me today. The spirit of God that will help me stay dead to sin and be alive to righteousness, I ask that by the mercy of God, it is released unto me in the name of Jesus.

- Lord, I come against every form of Temptation by the enemy. You have promised in your word that I shall not be tempted beyond what I can bear. Lord, I come against every form of temptation that the enemy is planning for me, I nullify them by the power in the name of Jesus.

- Lord, I come against every demonic force that the enemy is using to attack me, I destroy such curse by the blood of the lamb. Lord, I pray that every evil covenant of the devil over my life that gives the devil power over me, I decree that such covenants are destroyed today in the name of Jesus.

- Lord, it has been written, any tree that is not planted by God shall be uprooted. I decree by the authority of heaven, every demonic tree in my life that is not of you Lord, let them be uprooted in the name of Jesus.

- From today, I receive power to resist the devil even in my sleep. In every way the devil used to torment from my sleep, I pray that the spirit of God will help me stop the devil today, in the name of Jesus.

- Lord, I cancel the plans of the enemy over my life today in the name of Jesus. Every strategy of the enemy to subdue me is destroyed by fire. I decree that the fire of God Almighty will descend into the camp of my enemies and consume them with fire in the name of Jesus.

- For it has been written, he that the son has set free is free indeed. I free myself from every shackles of the enemy in the name of Jesus. I decree by the authority of heaven, every bondage that the enemy has used to hold, every bondage that the enemy is using to hold me down, I break them into pieces by the power in the name of Jesus.

- In the name of Jesus Christ, every evil tongue of the accuser is condemned over my life in the name of Jesus. I silent the accuser over my life today by the authority of heaven, in the name of Jesus. Every power of death over my life, I destroy you by fire in the name of Jesus.

- Father Lord, every evil oppressor over my life, I destroy them today in the name of Jesus. Every demonic oppressor is destroyed today by the fire of the Holy Ghost.

- The scripture says you shall receive power when the Holy Spirit has come upon you. I receive the power of the Holy Spirit today in the name of Jesus.

- I decree that from today, my life becomes uncomfortable for every evil demon or person to toy with in the name of Jesus. I decree that my health receive power from above in the name of Jesus.

- I decree by the authority of heaven that my finances receive the power of God today in the name of Jesus. I free mu finances from the bondage of the devil in the name of Jesus.

- The scripture says Stand fast therefore in the liberty by which Christ has made us free, and do not be entangled again with a yoke of bondage. I pray that the Holy Spirit strengthen me, I refuse to be slave to the devil anymore in the name of Jesus.

20 PRAYER POINTS AGAINST SPIRITUAL ATTACK

Obadiah 1:3-4 3 The pride of thine heart hath deceived thee, thou that dwelleth in the clefts of the rock, whose habitation is high; that saith in his heart, who shall bring me down to the ground? 4 Though thou exalt thyself as the eagle, and though thou set thy nest among the stars, thence will I bring thee down, saith the Lord.

Are you under any kind or form of spiritual attack, if yes then these message is for you? Spiritual attack is real, the bible said that we wrestle not with flesh and blood, but with principalities and powers…Ephesians 6:12. In the realm of the spirit, there are demonic agents sent by the devil to attack Gods children. In Matthew 16:18-19, Jesus said, I will build my church and the gate of hell will not prevail against it. This is to tell us that the gates of hell are always contending with the salvation of the saints. Every child of God is a target of spiritual attack. But the good news is this, when your prayer altar is on fire, the devil will be too small for you. I have compiled 20 prayer points against spiritual attack. When you resist the devil, he runs away from you. How do you resist the devil, by prayers and bold declarations? As you pray these prayers today, I see the hand of God overruling every plans of the devil against your life and destiny. Please understand that these prayers points against spiritual attack cannot work for you if you do not have faith. No matter how much we pray, if we don't have faith, we might as well watch telemundo (LOL). But if our faith is intact, we can rise up and displace the devil in our life. Pray this prayers with great expectation, I see you riding in the wings of glory.

Prayer Points

1. Father, I thank you for setting me far above all principalities and powers

2. I enter into the throne of grace, my father and I receive mercies for all my sins in Jesus name.

3. I command all demonic activities against my calling to receive disgrace and commotion, in the name of Jesus.

4. Father Lord, let my life, my ministry and my prayer life be extremely dangerous for the kingdom of darkness, in Jesus' name.

5. Father Lord, let all the dormant spiritual gifts and talents in my life begin to function for your glory, in the name of Jesus.

6. I reject the spirit of heaviness and regrets, in the name of Jesus.

7. I command all organized forces of darkness against my life to receive commotion, lightning and thunder, in the name of Jesus.

8. All demonic organized network against my spiritual and physical progress, be put to shame, in the name of Jesus.

9. I command all demonic mirrors and monitoring gadgets against my life to crack to pieces, in the name of Jesus.

10. I command every demonic agent of frustration to lose its hold over my life, in the name of Jesus.

11. I command every agent of poverty to lose its hold over my life, in the name of Jesus.

12. I command every agent of debt to lose its hold over my life, in the name of Jesus.

13. I command every agent of defeat to lose its hold over my life, in the name of Jesus.

14. I command every agent of spiritual rags to lose its hold over my life, in the name of Jesus.

15. I command every agent of infirmity to loose its holdover my life, in the name of Jesus.

16. I command every agent of demonic delays to loose its hold over my life, in the name of Jesus.

17. I command every agent of demotion to loose its hold over my life, in the name of Jesus.

18. I command every agent of confusion to loose its holdover my life, in the name of Jesus.

19. I command every agent of backward movement to loose its hold over my life, in the name of Jesus.

20. I command every wicked oppressor to stumble and fall in every area of my life, in the name of Jesus.

Father I thank you for answering my prayers

30 PRAYER POINTS AGAINST EVIL PRONOUNCEMENT

Numbers 23:20-23:

20 Behold, I have received commandment to bless: and he hath blessed; and I cannot reverse it. 21 He hath not beheld iniquity in Jacob, neither hath he seen perverseness in Israel: the Lord his God is with him, and the shout of a king is among them. 22 God brought them out of Egypt; he hath as it were the strength of a unicorn. 23 Surely there is no enchantment against Jacob, neither is there any divination against Israel: according to this time it shall be said of Jacob and of Israel, What hath God wrought!

Today we are going to be engaging on prayer against evil pronouncement. Evil pronouncements are satanic verdicts released on God's children by satanic agents. This satanic verdict if not overturned, can lead to a total destruction of life and destiny. A lot of Christians today are struggling to survive because of one evil pronouncement or another that have been released upon their lives. Evil pronouncements can work against you whether you are aware or not, innocent or not, as a matter of fact, many people were placed under the spell of evil pronouncements from their mother's womb. But as you engage this prayer against evil pronouncement, they shall all be overruled now in Jesus name.

The good news is this, all evil pronouncements can be overruled, we overrule them by releasing divine pronouncements over our life and destiny, just as light dispels darkness, divine pronouncements overrules every form of evil pronouncements. Every child of God must learn to speak the blessings of God over his/her life, we must learn to condemn with our mouth every satanic verdicts released in our direction. A closed mouth is a closed destiny, we must not allow the devil to keep speaking curses over our life, and we must shut him down by speaking the blessings of God into our lives. Jesus said we shall have what we say, Mark 11:23-24. As we engage this prayer against evil pronouncement, we shall be overturning every satanic verdict spoken over our lives and we shall be returning them back to sender in Jesus name. By the end of this prayers, you shall be totally free from evil pronouncements in Jesus name.

PRAYER POINTS

1. No evil vow, decision or prophecy shall come to pass in my life, in the name of Jesus.
2. My life, you will not be used by the devil in the name of Jesus.
3. Father Lord; anoint my life to do powerful things in your kingdom.
4. Father Lord, let every curse of impossibility against me backfire to the sender, in the name of Jesus.
5. Father Lord, let every agent of impossibility, fashioned against me, receive permanent failure, in the name of Jesus.
6. I refuse to be diverted from the, path of blessings, in the name of Jesus.
7. Every hole in my hand, be sealed by the blood of Jesus.
8. Holy Spirit, help me to discover myself, in Jesus' name.
9. My life, refuse every bewitchment, in Jesus' name.
10. Every evil door that I have used my hand to open for the enemy to come into my life, close by the blood of Jesus.
11. Every evil power, drinking the milk of my life, vomit it, in the name of Jesus.
12. Light of God, shine upon my life, in the name of Jesus.

13. Holy Ghost fire, burn away every satanic deposit in my life, in the name of Jesus.

14. Father Lord, give me knowledge, wisdom and understanding, in Jesus' name.

15. I receive the power to become great in life, in Jesus' name.

16. Father Lord, baptize me with your divine favour, in Jesus' name.

17. O Lord, impress my matter into the hearts of those who will help me, in the name of Jesus.

18. In the name of Jesus, spirit of error, you will not prosper in my life.

19. Father Lord, let it be known that you are God in every situation of my life.

20. I cancel the manifestation of every satanic dream, in the name of Jesus.

21. Father Lord, anoint my prayers with your fire, in the name of Jesus.

22. O Lord, let me touch heaven today and let heaven touch me, in the name of Jesus.

23. Anything in my life that will hinder my prayer, blood of Jesus, flush it out.

24. I receive the power to mount up with wings like an eagle, in the mighty name of Jesus.

25. My Father, let the power of resurrection of our Lord Jesus Christ resurrect every dead potential and virtue in my life, in the name of Jesus.

26. I release myself from every satanic prison, in Jesus' name.

27. I paralyze every evil power working against my career in the name of Jesus.

28. Every contrary power in my family, loose your peace until you repent and leave me alone, in Jesus' name.

29. Every satanic camp, reinforcing against me, scatter, in the name of Jesus.

30. I reject every spirit of the crossroads, in the name of Jesus.

Thank you Jesus for answering my prayers.

WARFARE PRAYER TO REVOKE EVIL DECREES Isaiah 8:10 Take counsel together, and it shall come to nought; speak the word, and it shall not stand: for God is with us. Evil decrees are satanic arrows sent to destroy Gods children. With the mouth, blessings are released, and with the same mouth, curses are released. Evil decrees are curses, released from demons and their agents, upon Gods children. These curses if not revoked, becomes a stronghold in the life of many believers. The good news today is this, every evil decree can be revoked, every curses, can be returned back to the sender and tonight every evil decree upon your life shall be revoked by fire in the name of Jesus. We shall be engaging in warfare prayers to revoke evil decrees. This warfare prayers will empower you to overturn every evil declaration sent to your life and destiny in Jesus name. This prayers should be prayed aggressively and violently in order to see desired results. The devil must know that you mean business, your heart must be in the prayers. Every evil decree against your life today shall be revoked by fire in the name of Jesus!!! When King Balak wanted to destroy the children of Israel, He sent prophet Balaam to curse them, (See Numbers 22, 23). He knew the power of evil decrees, the king knew that if only he could place a curse on them, he will successfully destroy them. But anytime Balaam opened his mouth to curse the Israelites, the curse was instantly revoked to a blessing, because the hand of God was upon the Children of Israel, in the same way today, as you engage in this warfare prayers to revoke evil decrees, the Hand of God shall rest upon you and every evil decree sent upon your life and destiny shall be revoked by fire in the name of Jesus. Every evil decree sent in your direction shall be revoked and sent back to the sender in the name of Jesus. I see you overcoming the devil and claiming your victory today in Jesus name.

PRAYER POINTS

1. I reject every evil manipulation in all areas of my life in Jesus name

2. I reject every demonic family control over my destiny in Jesus name

3. Let every evil decree or curse issued against me bounce back to the enemy now in Jesus name

4. Let every impossibility fashioned against me receive permanent failure in the name of Jesus.

5. Let every evil plantation of the devil in my life be roasted in the name of Jesus Christ.

6. I refuse to be diverted from the path of blessings to curses in the name of Jesus Christ

7. Let every satanic agent deflecting my blessings, stumble and fall to rise no more in the name of Jesus Christ

8. I command every evil power drinking the milk and honey of my life to begin to vomit them now, in the name of Jesus.

9. Let every satanic prayer against my life be reversed, in the name of Jesus Christ

10. Let every access Satan has to my life be withdrawn permanently in Jesus name

11. I curse every satanic mountain problem in my life in the name of Jesus

12. Let all fake friends be exposed and disgraced in the name of Jesus

13. Let all evil conspirators in disguise be exposed and disgraced, in the name of Jesus

14. Let all Spiritual vultures in any area of my life be destroyed in the name of Jesus Christ

15. Evil family river, do not touch me, in the name of Jesus

16. Holy Spirit, help me to really discover myself in the name of Jesus

17. I release my hand from every form of bewitchment, in the name of Jesus

18. I forbid regrouping and reinforcements, of any evil decree against my life in Jesus name

19. Let every vow of the enemy against my life be nullified in the name of Jesus

20. Oh Lord, reverse all curses issued against me, in the name of Jesus

21. Let every satanic decision and judgment against me be rendered null and void, in the name of Jesus.

22. Every astral projection against me, I frustrate you, in Jesus' name.

23. I disentangle myself and my family from every witchcraft cage and pot, in the name of Jesus.

24. Every enemy that will not let go easily, I bring the judgment of death against you, in Jesus' name.

25. I prophesy that this year, my blessings will not sink, in the name of Jesus.

26. O Lord, let the spirit of salvation fall upon my family, in the name of Jesus.

27. Every grip of the evil consequences, of the ancestral worship of my forefathers' gods over my life and ministry, break by fire, in Jesus' name.

28. Every covenant with water spirits, desert spirits, witchcraft spirits, spirits in evil sacred trees, spirits inside / under sacred rocks / hills, family gods, evil family guardian spirits, family /village serpentine spirits, masquerade spirits, inherited spirit husbands / wives, break by the blood of Jesus.

29. Every unconscious evil soul-tie and covenant with the spirits of my dead grandfather, grandmother, occultist uncles, aunties, custodian of family gods/oracles/shrines, break by the blood of Jesus.

30. Every decision, vow or promise made by my forefathers contrary to my divine destiny, loose your hold by fire, in the name of Jesus.

31. Every legal ground, that ancestral/guardian spirits have in my life, be destroyed by the blood of Jesus.

32. Any ancestral bloodshed of animals or human beings affected me, loose your hold by the blood of Jesus

33. Every generational curse of God, resulting from the sin of idolatry of my forefathers, loose your hold, in Jesus' name

34. Any curse, placed on my ancestral line by anybody cheated, maltreated or at the point of death, break now, in Jesus' name.

35. Every ancestral evil altar, prospering against me, be dashed against the Rock of Ages, in the name of Jesus.

36. Every garment of ancestral infirmity, disease, sickness, untimely death, poverty, disfavor, dishonour, shame and failure at the edge of miracle, passed down to my generation, roast fire, in the name of Jesus.

37. Every ancestral placenta manipulation of my life, be reserved, in Jesus' name.

38. Every evil ancestral river, flowing down to my generation, dry up, in the name Jesus.

39. Every evil ancestral life pattern, designed for me through vows, promises and covenants, be reserved, in Jesus' name.

40. Every evil ancestral habit and weakness of moral failures, manifesting in my life, loose your grip and release me now, in Jesus' name.

41. Every hold of any sacrifice ever offered in my family or on my behalf, I break your power in my life, in the name Jesus.

42. Any power, from my family background, seeking to make a shipwreck of my life and ministry, be destroyed by the power of God, in the name Jesus.

43. Every rage and rampage of ancestral and family spirits, resulting from my being born again, be quenched by the liquid fire of God, in Jesus' name.

44. Any ancestral power frustrating any area of my life, in order to discourage me from following Christ, receive multiple destruction, in the name Jesus.

45. Every ancestral chain of slavery, binding my people from prospering in life, break in my life by the hammer of God, in the name Jesus.

46. I prophesy that I will reach the height nobody has attained in my generation, in Jesus' name.

47. I recover every good thing, stolen my ancestral evil spirits from my forefathers, my immediate family and myself, in the name Jesus.

48. Every ancestral embargo, be lifted; good things, begin to break forth in my life and in my family, in Jesus' name.

49. I release myself from any inherited bondage, in Jesus' name.

50. O lord, send your axe of fire to the foundation of my life and destroy every evil plantation therein.

PRAYER POINTS AGAINST EVIL ATTACK

Today we will be engaging ourselves in prayer points against evil attack. God wants to destroy every evil attack in our life so we can have a better life. There are so many people that have been badly wounded by the devil; their life has not known any happiness due to a series of terrible attacks from the enemy. Little wonder the scripture advised that we pray all the time because our adversary is like a roaring lion looking for who to devour.

The enemy made an evil attack on the life of Job, but God was faithful enough to save him. You must understand that sometimes even your closest family member of Friend could be an instrument in the hands of the devil to launch terrible attacks against your life. In the case of Joseph, his siblings were the instrument the devil uses. They attacked him because of his dream, and they made efforts to kill him before the manifestation of God's plan for his life.

The scripture made us understand that the enemy doesn't come unless to kill, steal, and destroy. So, you become a target for the enemy the day you accept Christ as your personal Lord and savior, and if you have great potential in you, you become their number one target. This is not to scare you; remember, the scripture says many are the afflictions of the righteous, but God is faithful to rescue him from all. The power of the Holy Ghost will destroy every evil attack over your life.

As you begin to study this prayer guide, the angel of the Lord will be your guide, and it will be on standby to destroy every evil attack on your life.

PRAYER POINTS

- Father Lord, I thank you for your grace over my life. I thank you because you have not allowed the plans of my enemies to prevail over me. Let your name be exalted in the name of Jesus.
- Father Lord, I come against every evil attack of the enemy over my life. I destroy such attacks by the fire of the Holy.

- The scripture says, declare a thing, and it shall be established. I decree by the authority of heaven that the fire of the Holy Ghost destroys every attack of the enemy over my life-threatening my wellbeing.
- Lord God, the scripture promises me that I'm for signs and wonders. Lord, any attack that wants to alter that promise, I destroy it by fire in the name of Jesus.
- Father, I refuse to live my life under the threat of the enemy. I counter every attack over my life with the armies of the Lord in the name of Jesus.
- Lord God, I destroy every attack that is aimed at my health. Every attack to create chaos in my health, I destroy it by the fire of the Holy Ghost.
- Father Lord, the scripture says my body is the temple of the Lord; hence, no infirmity should defy it. I come against every attack of sickness over my life in the name of Jesus.
- Lord Jesus, I pray that you will create confusion in the camp of my enemies, and you will cause them to kill themselves in the name of Jesus.
- Lord God, I come against every evil attack over my marriage. The scripture says what God has joined together, let no man put an asunder. I come against every attack to scatter my family in the name of Jesus.
- Lord, my family, belongs to you, Jesus; therefore, no attack of the enemy should be able to break my home in the name of Jesus.
- Every attack to create confusion between my spouse and me, I destroy such attacks by fire in the name of Jesus.
- Every demonic animal that has been sent to inflict me with sufferings catch fire right now in the name of Jesus.
- I call the fire of the Holy Ghost upon every evil dog that has been sent by the enemy to eat out my success, catch fire now in the name of Jesus.

- Every demonic snake swallowing up my success, catch fire in the name of Jesus.

- Every attack on my success, every effort of the enemy to frustrate me at the point of success, every attacks to distract me at the point of breakthrough. I destroy you all in the name of Jesus.

- Every evil attack on my children, for the scripture, says my children are for signs and wonders. Every attack of the enemy on them to turn them into a reason for my sadness, I destroy such attacks by fire in the name of Jesus.

- I decree that from now, my children will be marked with excellence in the name of Jesus.

- Lord, as you anointed Daniel with the spirit of excellence that every effort of the enemy to frustrate his breakthrough became futile, I pray that you will anoint me children for excellence in the name of Jesus.

- I destroy every attack of the enemy to inflict my children with a terrible sickness. The scripture says Christ has bare upon himself all our infirmities, and he has healed all our diseases. Every attack of the enemy on my children's health, I destroy it in the name of Jesus.

- Father Lord, every attack of failure upon my life is destroyed in the name of Jesus. Because Christ didn't fail, I shall not fail in the name of Jesus.

- Every attack of poverty over my life, I destroy it by fire in the name of Jesus.

- I open the portal of abundance over my life today in the name of Jesus.

- The scripture says God will supply all my needs according to his riches in glory through Christ Jesus. I pray for the provision of all my needs in the name of Jesus.

- Lord Jesus, I come against an attack of poverty. I break the yoke of slavery over myself in the name of Jesus.

- Lord from today, let every attack of the enemy become futile over my life in the name of Jesus.

PRAYER POINTS AGAINST EVIL PLOTS

Today we will be engaging ourselves with prayer points against evil plots. As believers, we only have one adversary: the devil, and he will stop at nothing to ensure that we suffer. As God has called us into His marvelous light through Christ Jesus, the devil is also on a rampage to ensure that many believers either suffer or return to their first derogatory state of sin and iniquity. While we must pray to God to manifest all His plans for our lives, it is also vital that we pray against the plots of the enemy over our lives. The devil gets so bittered when people who used to be his own are saved into the kingdom of heaven; he will make efforts as much as he can to ensure that they have a bitter experience. Remember the life of Daniel, as prayerful as Daniel was, the enemies used the chiefs of Babylon against Daniel until he was cast into the den of the Lions. But God who has promised in the scripture that many are the righteous afflictions, but the is faithful to rescue him from all. This prayer guide will focus more on God, destroying the evil plots of the enemy concerning our lives and destiny. And I pray that as we use this prayer guide, the Lord in His infinite mercy will destroy the enemy's plots against us in the name of Jesus. We will also focus more on the protection of God. For it has been written that eyes of the Lord are always upon the righteous, and His ears are still attentive to their prayers. When the eyes of the Lord are upon you, the plot of the enemy will not be made secret to you. The Lord will reveal all their plans to you because the scripture says the mystery of the Lord is with those that fear him. I decree by the authority of heaven, the plans of the enemies against you will be open in the name of Jesus.

PRAYER POINTS

- Father Lord, I thank you for this beautiful gift of life that you have bestowed upon me to see another day like this. I thank you because you have been my shield and buckler. I exalt your mighty name because you have kept your promises over my life, I thank you because you gave me the power to trample upon snakes and Scorpion, I exalt your holy name because you did not allow any evil to come near my dwelling place, father, let your name be exalted in the name of Jesus.

- Lord Jesus, I thank you for your protection over my life. For the scripture says it is by the mercy of the Lord that we are not consumed. I thank you because your hands of protection are upon me; let your name be exalted in the name of Jesus. I magnify you because despite my unfaithfulness, despite my unrighteousness, your steadfast love over me is always there for me; I thank you because you are God mighty Jesus.

- Father Lord, I pray to you today that you will destroy the plot of my enemies over my life by your mighty hands. I decree that by your mercy, you will let my enemies die by the sword they have planned to kill me in the name of Jesus. The scripture says, for I bear the mark of Christ, let no man trouble me. I decree by the power in the name of Jesus; I will not be troubled in Jesus name.

- Lord God, it has been written that no weapon fashioned against me shall prosper, every weapon of the enemy that has been sent to harm me, let them be destroyed in the name of Jesus. For the Bible says, we have been given a name that is above all other names, that at the mention of the name Jesus, every knee must bow and every tongue must confess that he is God. I come against every harmful weapon of the enemies that have been fashioned against me; lose your power right now in the name of Jesus.

- I anoint myself with the blood of the lamb because the scripture says when the angel of death sees the blood, it will pass over. I decree that when the angel of death sees me, it will pass over in the name of Jesus.

- For it has been written, if any man speaks, let him speak as an oracle of the living God. I decree by the power of the most high, every weapon that has been fashioned against me should return to their sender in seven folds in Jesus name.

- Lord Jesus, the scripture says the secret of the Lord is with those that fear him. I decree that you will always reveal the plans of the enemies to me in the name of Jesus. I pray for your Holy Spirit and power, the spirit of divinity; I pray that you will send it into my life in the name of Jesus. Do not let the plan of the enemy succeed over my life in the name of Jesus.

- Arise O Lord, and let your enemies be scattered. Let those that have evil plots against me be consumed with their hatred. Just like Haman took the death of Mordecai, let every wicked man and woman the devil has assigned to my life die in the name of Jesus. I decree that you will send a fire into the camp of my enemies tonight, let them have rancor and kill themselves in the name of Jesus.

- The scripture says, the fire goes before the army of the Lord and destroys His enemies. Let the fire of the Holy Ghost go before me. Everywhere my enemies are gathered, everywhere they are hiding plotting evil against me, let the fire of the Lord consume them this moment in the name of Jesus. For the scripture says, touch not my anointed and do my prophets no harm, I decree that no evil shall befall me in the name of Jesus.

PRAYER FOR PROTECTION AGAINST EVIL

Matthew 6:13: And lead us not into temptation, but deliver us from evil: For thine is the kingdom, and the power, and the glory, forever. Amen.

The fact that you clicked on this article means that it is of interest to you. This prayer is a little bit different from the prayer against the activities of the enemy, this is the prayer of protection against evil.

Why should we pray for protection against evil? The Bible made us understand that there are arrows that fly by day, pestilence that roam in darkness and destructions that strike at noon day, Psalm 91. These are winds of evil that hover around on a daily basis. As a child of God, it is very risky for you not to cover yourself in prayers before going out from your house. A prayer for protection is a defensive prayer that protects you and shields you from all the evil of the day, every time you engage this prayers, the angels of the Lord are dispatched on your behalf to see to your protection and preservation. Evil things happen every day, it is only the ones that are revealed to us that we know, people die every day, people get jailed every day. Especially in third world countries where we have poor security, you often hear of killings, robbery, and all manner of senseless attacks on innocent citizens. The developed countries are also not exempted. We must have heard several times of people taking guns and randomly killing people in America. It takes a person who is prayerful to escape all this daily horrors.

The fact remains, no one is too good to die and no one is too bad to live, there are so many people who have fell victim to evil circumstances that can actually be prevented. Therefore, it is important we always seek God's protection every day because each day is filled with evil.

However, believers should have an advantage in the word of God. The scripture says, he who sits in the secret place of the highest shall abide under the shadow of the Almighty. Any man that abides on the shadow of the Almighty will be exempted from any evil occurrences.

Such an individual will not fall, a victim of evil attacks, he or she will not become a victim of kidnappers, all these will happen only by abiding in the shadow of the Almighty.

We have compiled a list of prayer points for protection against evil, this prayer points will shield you from all satanic attacks and assaults. I encourage you to engage this prayers with all your heart and believe that the wings of the Almighty will never stop protecting and preserving you. The hand of God shall never depart from your life in Jesus Christ name.

PRAYER POINTS

• Heavenly Father, I'm not ignorant of the fact that every day is filled with evil. But the book of 2 Thessalonians 3:3 says but the Lord is faithful. He will establish you and guard you against the evil one. Your word says that you will guide me against any evil, I pray for your protection upon me. I activate your umbrella of protection over me in the name of Jesus. I ask for your grace to continually remain under your shade, grant me the undeniable access to always dwell in your shade. I ask that in every of my journey in life you will go with me, I refuse to take a step unless you go with me, I refuse to journey this life on my own, I ask that by your mercy, you will journey with me in Jesus name.

• By your mercy, I change the course of each day with your blood, I change the headline and reconstruct the evil narrative about each day in the name of Jesus. I exempt myself from any evil catastrophe of the day in the name of Jesus. The right hand of God that does great things, I call it upon the journey in life, the hands of God that turn things around, I ask that you put it in my life in the name of Jesus.

• Heavenly Lord, your word says that you will go before me and level up exalted places, you cut through bars of iron, I ask that by your power, every evil mountain in my way is made low in the name of Jesus. I counter every evil. Of the day and I change it into good tidings by the precious blood of Christ.

• Heavenly Father, I hide behind the cross that flows with the blood of Christ and I decree that the angels of the Lord always be with me in my journey through life in the name of Jesus. Your angels will put me in their arms that I may not dash my foot against the rock of life, your angel that will bear me in their arms that I may not stumble upon the stone of destruction in the name of Jesus.

• I hide under the supreme wings of the Almighty. I put my spirit, soul, and body under the protection of God Almighty and I decree that no evil shall befall me or come near my dwell place.

• I send forth the angels of God to always guide me in my ways and I will always come to consciousness wherever evil lies in the name of Jesus.

• Your angels will nurture me and always ignite my spirit man. I seek for an anointing that will distinct me, the anointing that will exempt me from every evil occurrence. Lord God, I change the course of each day with your name, the Bible says decree a thing and it shall be established, I decree that the favor of God Almighty will always be upon me.

• Lord God, I seek your mercy, your mercy that speaks in place of judgment. If a man finds mercy in your sight, he or she will not fall victim to accident, rape, kidnap, I seek that your mercy is upon me. The scripture says touch, not my anointed and do my Prophet no harm, every evil discharge, I cast and bind every evil angel assign to do the duty of each, I destroy them in the name of Jesus. For the Bible says, we have been given a name that is above every other name, that at the mention of that name every knee must bow and every tongue shall confess that he is God, I command every demonic angel that is to wreak havoc in each day to be destroyed in the name of Jesus.

• By the virtue of your blood, I redeem each day, I turn the hands of the moment from evil to good in the name of Jesus.
Amen.

PRAYER AGAINST THE EVIL INTENTION OF MEN

Today we will be dealing with prayer points against the evil intentions in the mind of men. The heart of men is filled with great evil. The book of Genesis chapter 6:5-6 Then the LORD saw that the wickedness of man was great in the earth, and that every intent of the thoughts of his heart was only evil continually. And the LORD was sorry that He had made man on the earth, and He was grieved in His heart. This portion of the scripture made us understand that God repented in His heart after the creation of man because the hearts of men is filled with great evil.

Abel could not have thought that his blood brother Cain could kill him until he was dropped dead by his brother. Every idea and action begins with a thought in the heart. Little wonder the scripture says from the abundance of the heart the mouth speaketh. Also from the abundance of the heart, action is being carried out. Before King David decided to lay with Uriah's wife, he had thought about it in his heart, before he decided to instruct his Warlord to put Uriah at the battle front where he would get killed just so he can cover his heinous act. Every evil decision that a man take begins from the heart.

The face is deceiving, if only you can know your neighbor's thought towards you? You would know that friendship most times is only a word of mouth, not from the heart. I decree by the authority of heaven every plot of the enemy to harm is destroyed in Jesus. I decree by the authority of heaven, may the angel of the Lord go to the camp of your enemy and destroy them all in Jesus name.

If you feel there is a need for you to pray against the evil intention in the mind of men, whether your friend or family, use the following praying points.

PRAYER POINTS

- Lord Jesus, I thank you because you are God over my life. I thank you for your grace and blessings. I thank you for the protection over my life and home, Lord may your name be exalted in Jesus name.

- Father Lord, I cancel every plan and evil thoughts of men against me. Every plot in their minds to harm me or kill me, Lord let it fail in Jesus name.

- Lord Jesus, as the sword melt in the face of fire, let evil men be destroyed. Let those who are planning evil against me be destroyed by their evil thoughts.

- For it has been written, I will bless those that bless you and I shall curse those who curse you. Lord God, I pray that you shall put every evil man to death in Jesus name.

- Let their own table before them become a snare; and when they are at peace, let it become a trap. I stand upon the authority in this word and I decree that every man planning evil against me shall know no peace in Jesus name.

- Lord, before the evil man in my father's house fulfill their plans over my life, I decree that the angel of the Lord shall visit them in Jesus name.

- As it has been written in the book of Psalm 69:23 Let their eyes be darkened, so that they cannot see, and make their loins tremble continually. I decree blindness upon men and women having evil thoughts against me in the name of Jesus.

- I stand upon the promise of this word that says: pour out your indignation upon them and let your burning anger come against them. I decree the burning anger upon my enemies in the name of Jesus.

- I decree upon the camp of my enemies and people have evil thoughts against me, their camp shall be desolate in the name of Jesus.

- Help me O God of my salvation, for the glory of your name; deliver me, and atone for my sins, for your name's sake, I pray that you deliver me from the hands of the enemy in the name of Jesus.

- I decree by the authority of heaven, let the anger and pain in the heart of the enemy become the cause of their death in the name of Jesus.

- Lord deliver me from my enemies and those who rise against me. I ask that by your power you create fire upon the camp of the enemy in the name of Jesus.

- Father Lord, I want you to remember your covenant over my life. You word promised that you will be ever-present help in my moment of need. I pray that you shall continue to protect me from the evil thoughts and agenda of the enemy in the name of Jesus.

- Father Lord, I pray that the evil thoughts of men shall not defeat me in Jesus name. I ask that by your power, you will lift me far above the evil agenda of the enemy over my life in the name of Jesus.

- Lord Jesus, I pray that by the authority of heaven you shall not allow the plan of the enemy to become secret over my life. I pray by the power in the name of Jesus, you will continue to reveal the plans of the enemy over my life in Jesus.

- I pray that your hands of protection shall always be upon me. The scripture says with my eyes shall I behold the reward of the wicked but none shall come upon me. I decree by the authority of heaven, every evil arrow against me is destroyed in the name of Jesus.

- Lord, I silent every evil tongue speaking evil over my life. I cancel every evil thoughts and agenda plotting evil against me.

- I decree that the angel of the Lord will go out and cancel every demonic camp built against me in the name of Jesus.

- I thank you Lord for answered prayers. I magnify you because you are God over my life. I exalt you holy name because you are the prince of peace, thank you Lord Jesus.

POWERFUL DECLARATION PRAYER TO DESTROY EVIL COVENANT

Today we will be dealing with powerful declaration prayer to destroy evil covenant. When God gives an instruction on a particular prayer topic, it means God is ready to perform wonders. God is ready to set people free from evil covenant affecting their lives for years. Covenant is an agreement between two or more persons. Most times, covenant is usually between a human and demonic powers, these are the type of covenant that affects the life of a man. In most cases, people affected by these covenant are not the one who directly entered into the covenant. Most people suffer from problems they didn't create.

Sometimes, an entire family could be in a covenant with marine spirit and these spirits will torment the life of every man and woman born into that family. Especially when you accept Christ as Lord and savior and you bid farewell to those old living. These spirits will then come after you because they want to ruin your salvation. Meanwhile, God has given us an authority through the name of Jesus and He has given us a new covenant through the blood of Jesus. Usually, a covenant is nothing until there is a spillage of blood. The blood of Christ on the cross of Calvary signifies the beginning of a new covenant.

As far as we are Christians, we have the new covenant which was made possible by the blood of Christ. This explains why the scripture says He that is in Christ is now a new creature, behold, old things have passed away and everything has become new. However, some stubborn evil covenant would still make life tough until they are destroyed. It take a deliberate plan and conscious effort to destroy evil covenant. We have an authority which is the name of Jesus and we have a new covenant which is the blood of Christ that is flowing in Calvary. We would be using our authority as heirs of salvation. I decree by the authority of heaven, every evil covenant working against your progress in life, they are destroyed today in the name of Jesus.

PRAYER POINTS

- I renounce every evil allegiance that I have knowingly and unknowingly sworn to the power of darkness. I cut every demonic chain or link between me and power of darkness today with the power in the name of Jesus.
- Every evil covenant that I have entered through sin, I break you into pieces today in the name of Jesus. I come against your manifestation over my life in the name of Jesus.
- Every evil covenant crying for blood over my life and family, I cancel you today in the name of Jesus. I direct you to the cross of Calvary where there is an abundance of blood to go and drink. I key into the new covenant that was made eminent by the blood of Christ, and I cancel every evil agreement over my life in the name of Jesus.
- Lord arise and let your enemies be scattered. Let those who rise against me be condemned in the name of Jesus.
- I come against every demonic covenant in my father's house working against my progress in life. Every demonic covenant in my father's house limiting me from attaining my full potentials, I destroy you today in the name of Jesus.
- I break into pieces every satanic agreement in my mother's house working against every member of that family, I decree that you lose your power over me in the name of Jesus.
- Lord, every covenant with the marine spirit troubling me in my sleep, I break you today in the name of Jesus.
- You power of the underworld hear the word of the Lord, but thus saith the LORD, Even the captives of the mighty shall be taken away, and the prey of the terrible shall be delivered: for I will contend with him that contendeth with thee, and I will save thy

children. I release myself from your captivity today in the name of Jesus.

- Every demonic covenant taking the life of every first child in my family, I rebuke you over the life of my child in the name of Jesus. The scripture says for I carry the mark of Christ let no man trouble me. My child carries the mark of Christ he/she shall not be troubled by you in the name of Jesus.

- Exodus 12:23 For the LORD will pass through to strike the Egyptians; and when He sees the blood on the lintel and on the two doorposts, the LORD will pass over the door and not allow the destroyer to come into your houses to strike you. I anoint myself with the blood of the lamb and I become unrecognizable for demonic covenant in the name of Jesus.

- Lord, every mark of the enemy in my life that has made me vulnerable to the evil covenant affecting my lineage, I remove such marks today in the name of Jesus. Every spiritual garment that has been put upon me that makes me recognizable for agents of satanic covenant to attack, I burn you into ashes in the name of Jesus.

- Every evil covenant that I have entered into via sexual impurity, I decree that they are broken in the name of Jesus. For it has been written, anyone in Christ has become a new creature, behold old thing have passed away and everything has been made new. I cancel every evil sexual covenant working against me in the name of Jesus.

- Every covenant with spiritual husband or wife tormenting my marriage, I break you today in the name of Jesus.

- Lord, I break every satanic covenant working against my life because of the womb I came out from, I destroy such covenant in the name of Jesus.

- The scripture says he set aside the first to establish the second. Every existing covenants in my life, I break you all into pieces in the name of Jesus. Every demonic cord or alliance between me and those covenants is destroyed by the fire of the Holy Ghost, in the name of Jesus.

20 DELIVERANCE PRAYER TO BREAK CURSES AND SPELL

2 Kings 2:18-22: 18 And when they came again to him, (for he tarried at Jericho,) he said unto them, did I not say unto you, Go not? 19 And the men of the city said unto Elisha, Behold, I pray thee, the situation of this city is pleasant, as my lord seeth: but the water is naught, and the ground barren. 20 And he said, bring me a new cruse, and put salt therein. And they bring it to him. 21 And he went forth unto the spring of the waters, and cast the salt in there, and said, thus saith the Lord, I have healed these waters; there shall not be from thence any more death or barren land. 22 So the waters were healed unto this day, according to the saying of Elisha which he spake.

Here are 20 deliverance prayer to break curses and spells. The bible tells us that we cannot be cursed or be a victim of spells, Numbers 23:23. Any Christian suffering from any form of curses is simply suffering in ignorance. The bible made it clear that no weapon fashioned against us shall prosper, Isaiah 54:17, this simply means we are above the attacks of the devil. However, the devil is a stubborn spirit, he will continue to attack you always, and you must continue to resist him steadfastly. We must be steadfast on the prayer altar, if you want to subdue the powers that stands on your way to success, you must be prayerful. Thank God for what He has done for us all in Christ, but only those who believe can benefit, and when we pray, we show God that we believe in Him and what He has given us in Christ Jesus.

Prayer is an expression of faith, and faith is the key to our breakthrough 1 John 5:4. This deliverance prayer to break every curses and spells will surely bring great deliverance to you as you pray it. You shall be delivered from all forms of enchantments from the devil and his agents that has hitherto been plaguing your life. They Lord shall give you victory from every challenges that you are battling with. The God of great deliverance shall arise to your defense and fight your battles as you engage this deliverance prayer. My dear friend, pray this prayer with faith and expect a great deliverance in your life.

☐

PRAYER POINTS

1. Father, I praise you for the redemptive power in the blood of Jesus.
2. Father, I praise you for redeeming us from the curse of the law.
3. Father, forgive me for all the sins that has given the enemy legal right to place any curse on me and my household in Jesus name.
4. Father, by your precious blood wash me clean from all sins in Jesus name
5. I take authority over every curse, spells and enchantment upon my life, in Jesus' name.
6. I command all curses issued against me to be broken, in the name of Jesus.
7. I command all evil spirits associated with any curse to leave me now, in the name of Jesus.
8. I take authority over inherited curses and command them to be broken now, in the name of Jesus.
9. I take authority over curses emanating from ancestral line and command them to be broken now, in Jesus' name.
10. In the name of Jesus, I break any curse which may be in my parents' families back to ten generations in Jesus name.
11. I renounce and break all curses put on my family line and my descendants, in the name of Jesus.
12. I command every bad spirit of any curse and spells to release me and go now, in the name of Jesus
13. I break every curse of constant failure working in my family, in the name of Jesus.
14. I take authority over every curse of stagnation in my family, in the name of Jesus.
15. I cancel the consequences and evil effects of all curses, in the name of Jesus.

16. I take authority over every unconscious or playful curse issued on me, in the name of Jesus.
17. Let the root of my life be purged by the fire of the Holy Spirit, in the name of Jesus.
18. Let the root of my life be washed in the blood of Jesus.
19. I break and cancel every curse placed on children to punish their parents in my life, in the name of Jesus.
20. I break and cancel every curse placed on me out of jealousy, in the name of Jesus.

Father thank you for delivering me from all curses, spells and enchantment in Jesus name.

☐

PRAYER POINTS AGAINST EVIL SPELL

Today we will be dealing with prayer points against evil spell. What comes to mind when you hear a spell? Spells are demonic enchantments that are used to invoke a demon or bewitch an individual. There is no apparent difference between a spell and an incantation. They are both demonic utterances for creating spiritual havoc. Spells are evil enchantments to possess an individual's being, compelling them to do things against their Will or purpose.

Sometimes, spells could come in the form of a curse on an individual. They are demonic utterances that are used to lay a curse on someone or to put someone in bondage. Anyone working under the influence of a spell or enchantment, such an individual will be possessed by an evil spirit that will be forcing them to do things that are against their Will. But God is about break every evil spell in the life of people. Every evil spell that has held you down for years, it shall be broken in the name of Jesus.

Remember the scripture says in the book of Genesis 12: 3 And I will bless them that bless thee, and curse him that curseth thee: and in thee shall all families of the earth be blessed. The power of God shall condemn any mouth speaking evil against your life.

Have you noticed anyone around you that suddenly changes from good to evil? Many times it is not their will or plans to change. It is mostly a manifestation of evil spells that have been said to hold them captive. That's why they will do things without their knowledge. I decree by the authority of heaven, every evil spell that has been holding you down to a spot, they are broken today in the name of Jesus. I declare absolute liberation upon your life today in the name of Jesus.

If you ever notice any strange thing in your life or the life of someone close to you, no better time to raise an altar of prayer for them. God commands this prayer guide to free people from an evil spell that has been tormenting their lives. As you begin to use this guide, may the angel of the Lord be with you, may the right hand of God destroy every hand of the enemy over you in the name of Jesus.

PRAYER POINTS

- Lord God, I pray to you this day to destroy every evil spell in my life. Every demonic spell of the enemy that is toying with my life and destiny, I pray that by the fire of the Holy Ghost, you will destroy them in the name of Jesus. Every evil enchantment that has been used to invoke evil demons against my life, I decree by the power of the most high, Lord destroy them today in the name of Jesus.

- Lord God, every demonic spell against my health, turning me into a perpetual stickler, I decree that the fire of the Lord will burn such spells in the name of Jesus. Every strong man in my father's house or mother's house using evil spells against my health, let such people fall to death in the name of Jesus. Lord, every tongue speaking evil enchantment over my life, I pray that you will cut that tongue in the name of Jesus.

- Father Lord, every evil spell against my marital life. Every spoken word that is aimed at destroying my home. For it has been written, who speaks and it comes to pass when the Lord has not commanded? I decree by the fire of the Holy Ghost, every tongue speaking against my marital life is cut off today in the name of Jesus. I decree by the fire of the Most High, every man speaking evil against my spouse and I, Lord, let them fall to death in the name of Jesus.

- Lord Jesus, I pray against every evil spell of failure that has been said over my life. Every word that has been spoken against my life, causing me to fail in almost every attempt in life, I destroy it by the authority of heaven. For it has been written, declare a thing, and it shall be established. Lord, every spell of failure over my life is destroyed in the name of Jesus. From now on, I begin to operate in another dimension of excellence in the name of Jesus. Every attempt to bring me down is destroyed in the name of Jesus.

- Father Lord, every evil spell against my spiritual life, I come against it by the power of the Holy Ghost. Every word that has been spoken to render my spiritual life impotent, I decree that it is destroyed in the name of Jesus. From now, I receive the grace of spiritual acceleration in the name of Jesus. I will not be stopped anymore in the name of Jesus. I refuse to be a cold-blooded Prayerist. The fire on the altar of my prayer life receives more strength to burn in the name of Jesus.

- Lord, I destroy every evil spell that has been said over the life of my children to ruin their future. For it has been written, my children and I are for signs and wonders. I come against every spoken word against their destiny in the name of Jesus. They will not fail the purpose of God for their lives in the name of Jesus.

- I pass the judgment of the Lord upon every giant in my lineage trying to ruin my life with an evil spell. Every evil curse that has been layer upon me, I destroy them by the fire of the Holy Ghost. And I will bless them that bless thee, and curse him that curseth thee: and in thee shall all families of the earth be blessed, saith the Lord of host. Every man that opens his to curse me shall be condemned in the name of Jesus. I decree that the angel of death visit every man tormenting my life with an evil spell in the name of Jesus.

☐

DESTROYING THE DESTROYER PRAYER POINTS

Isaiah 54:15 Behold, they shall surely gather together, but not by me: whosoever shall gather together against thee shall fall for thy sake. 54:16 Behold, I have created the smith that loveth the coals in the fire, and that bringeth forth an instrument for his work; and I have created the waster to destroy. 54:17 No weapon that is formed against thee shall prosper; and every tongue that shall rise against thee in judgment thou shalt condemn. This is the heritage of the servants of the LORD, and their righteousness is of me, saith the LORD.

Today we shall be engaging in destroying the destroyer prayer points. Who is a destroyer? The destroyer is the devil himself, and his agents are called destroyers. Jesus told us that the mission of the devil is to steal, kill and destroy, John 10:10. A destroyer in these context is anyone that is after your life and destiny, anyone that has vowed that you will never make it in life. A destroyer is someone who will stop at nothing to see you succeed in life. A destroyer is an unrepentant foe, they will never stop opposing you physically and spiritually until you stop them. But today we shall be destroying the destroyer through dangerous prayer points. These destroying the destroyer prayer points will take every destroyer in your life unawares, they won't know what hit them as we begin to pray. Every destroyer must bow today in Jesus name.

In the bible we see destroyers at work, in the book of Esther, we see the story of Esther, medical, Haman and the Jews, Esther 3, 7. Haman wanted to destroy the entire Jews simply because Mordechai refuse to bow down to him, but when Mordechai and Esther declared a fast and prayed, for the salvation of the Jews, Haman was destroyed. The same gallows he set for Mordechai to be hanged, was where he was hanged. We also saw the story of Herod in the book of Acts, after he arrested and killed Apostle James, he saw that he pleased the Jews, so he took peter also, but the church prayed ernestly, and the Lord sent an Angel to deliver peter and that same Angel destroyed Herod the following day. Acts 12:18-25. Destroyers must be stopped, you don't give them space, when they come against you, and you must keep attacking them spiritually through prayers until they all are eliminated. As you engage this destroying the destroyer prayer points every destroyer in your life shall meet there own doom in Jesus name.

PRAYER POINTS

1. Every cloud of untimely death, clear away now, in the name of Jesus.
2. I refuse to be converted to a living dead, in the name of Jesus.
3. Let every evil strongman of untimely death be dethroned in my life in the name of Jesus.
4. Every satanic consultation concerning my life, be nullified, in the name of Jesus.
5. Every decision taken against my life by witchcraft spirits, be nullified, in the name of Jesus.
6. I reject aborted victories in every area of my life, in Jesus' name.
7. Let all those whom seem my life be destroyed now in the name of Jesus.
8. Let every imagination of death and dreams used against me, backfire on the head of my enemies in the name of Jesus
9. Let every germ of infirmity in my body, die, in the name of Jesus.
10. Let every agent of sickness die, in the name of Jesus.
11. You Hidden sicknesses, disappear from my body now, in the name of Jesus.
12. I command every discomfort in any part of my body to dry up, in the name of Jesus.
13. Every dead organ in my body, receive life, in the name of Jesus.
14. Let my blood be transfused with the blood of Jesus.
15. I command every internal disorder in my body, to receive order, in Jesus' name.
16. I command every infirmity, to come out with all your roots, in the name of Jesus.

17. I scatter by fire every conscious and unconscious cooperation with sickness, in the name of Jesus.
18. Let the whirlwind of the Lord blow away every wind of infirmity, in the name of Jesus.
19. I release my body from every curse of infirmity, in Jesus' name.
20. Let the blood of Jesus flush out every evil deposit from my blood, in the name of Jesus.
21. I recover every organ of my body held by witches and wizards in any evil altar in the name of Jesus.
22. Help me, O Lord, to recognize your voice in my life in Jesus name
23. Lord, where I am blind, give me sight in Jesus name
24. I command my fears to evaporate now, in the name of Jesus.
25. I throw off every burden of worry, in the name of Jesus.
26. I refuse to be entangled with evil friends, in the name of Jesus.
27. I cast down every road-block hiding my progress, in Jesus' name.
28. Let my spiritual life send terror to the camp of the enemy, in the name of Jesus.
29. O Lord, deliver me from evil words or evil utterances in Jesus name
30. O Lord, let the enemies of my life be buried before me in Jesus name.

PRAYER POINTS AGAINST EVIL SPELL

Today we will be dealing with prayer points against evil spell. What comes to mind when you hear a spell? Spells are demonic enchantments that are used to invoke a demon or bewitch an individual. There is no apparent difference between a spell and an incantation. They are both demonic utterances for creating spiritual havoc. Spells are evil enchantments to possess an individual's being, compelling them to do things against their Will or purpose.

Sometimes, spells could come in the form of a curse on an individual. They are demonic utterances that are used to lay a curse on someone or to put someone in bondage. Anyone working under the influence of a spell or enchantment, such an individual will be possessed by an evil spirit that will be forcing them to do things that are against their Will. But God is about break every evil spell in the life of people. Every evil spell that has held you down for years, it shall be broken in the name of Jesus.

Remember the scripture says in the book of Genesis 12: 3 And I will bless them that bless thee, and curse him that curseth thee: and in thee shall all families of the earth be blessed. The power of God shall condemn any mouth speaking evil against your life.

Have you noticed anyone around you that suddenly changes from good to evil? Many times it is not their will or plans to change. It is mostly a manifestation of evil spells that have been said to hold them captive. That's why they will do things without their knowledge. I decree by the authority of heaven, every evil spell that has been holding you down to a spot, they are broken today in the name of Jesus. I declare absolute liberation upon your life today in the name of Jesus.

If you ever notice any strange thing in your life or the life of someone close to you, no better time to raise an altar of prayer for them. God commands this prayer guide to free people from an evil spell that has been tormenting their lives. As you begin to use this guide, may the angel of the Lord be with you, may the right hand of God destroy every hand of the enemy over you in the name of Jesus.

Prayer Points

- Lord God, I pray to you this day to destroy every evil spell in my life. Every demonic spell of the enemy that is toying with my life and destiny, I pray that by the fire of the Holy Ghost, you will destroy them in the name of Jesus. Every evil enchantment that has been used to invoke evil demons against my life, I decree by the power of the most high, Lord destroy them today in the name of Jesus.

- Lord God, every demonic spell against my health, turning me into a perpetual stickler, I decree that the fire of the Lord will burn such spells in the name of Jesus. Every strong man in my father's house or mother's house using evil spells against my health, let such people fall to death in the name of Jesus. Lord, every tongue speaking evil enchantment over my life, I pray that you will cut that tongue in the name of Jesus.

- Father Lord, every evil spell against my marital life. Every spoken word that is aimed at destroying my home. For it has been written, who speaks and it comes to pass when the Lord has not commanded? I decree by the fire of the Holy Ghost, every tongue speaking against my marital life is cut off today in the name of Jesus. I decree by the fire of the Most High, every man speaking evil against my spouse and I, Lord, let them fall to death in the name of Jesus.

- Lord Jesus, I pray against every evil spell of failure that has been said over my life. Every word that has been spoken against my life, causing me to fail in almost every attempt in life, I destroy it by the authority of heaven. For it has been written, declare a thing, and it shall be established. Lord, every spell of failure over my life is destroyed in the name of Jesus. From now on, I begin to operate in another dimension of excellence in the name of Jesus. Every attempt to bring me down is destroyed in the name of Jesus.

- Father Lord, every evil spell against my spiritual life, I come against it by the power of the Holy Ghost. Every word that has been spoken to render my spiritual life impotent, I decree that it is destroyed in the name of Jesus. From now, I receive the grace of spiritual acceleration in the name of Jesus. I will not be stopped anymore in the name of Jesus. I refuse to be a cold-blooded Prayerist. The fire on the altar of my prayer life receives more strength to burn in the name of Jesus.
- Lord, I destroy every evil spell that has been said over the life of my children to ruin their future. For it has been written, my children and I are for signs and wonders. I come against every spoken word against their destiny in the name of Jesus. They will not fail the purpose of God for their lives in the name of Jesus.
- I pass the judgment of the Lord upon every giant in my lineage trying to ruin my life with an evil spell. Every evil curse that has been layer upon me, I destroy them by the fire of the Holy Ghost. And I will bless them that bless thee, and curse him that curseth thee: and in thee shall all families of the earth be blessed, saith the Lord of host. Every man that opens his to curse me shall be condemned in the name of Jesus. I decree that the angel of death visit every man tormenting my life with an evil spell in the name of Jesus.

POWERFUL DECLARATION AGAINST UNTIMELY DEATH

Today we will be dealing with powerful declaration against untimely death. The Lord wants to deliver people from the power of untimely death. So many destinies has been abated by the power of untimely death. This type of death will cut a man short when he is yet to fulfil the purpose of his existence. So many people have died while their potentials are undiscovered. Some are the verge of fully attaining their potentials in life when death came for them.

The story of Samson is a peculiar example. Samson was born a leader to deliver the people of Isreal from the captivity of the Philistines. He was equipped with enormous physical strength that he could conquer hundred thousand men all by himself. However, he could not do much as he died at a very early stage of life especially when the children of Isreal needed him most. God has created everyone for a purpose, we are to discover the purpose in order to fulfill it. However, when untimely death comes, everything stops. Just before we delve into prayers against untimely death, let's quick highlight some of the things that could cause us to fall victim.

There are people who died untimely not because they committed a crime or they sin against God, but because of the curse ravaging in their lineage. You must have heard the popular parlance that states: The parents have eaten sour grapes, and the children's teeth are set on edge. There are families where the forefathers have done some terrible which later affects the life of the Children born into that family.

There are families that every first child die when they are about to clock 40 years. It has become a pattern in the family. Until that evil curse is broken, the pattern will remain in the family.

Sin

This is not to say that God kills those that sin or come short his glory. The scripture has made us understand that God doesn't want the death of sinners but repentance through Christ Jesus.

However, when a man fall into sin, it gives the enemy the opportunity to strike. Samson was not killed by God. He simply disobeyed God. The instruction was that he should not marry from a strange land. However, Samson decided to settle with a woman from a strange land named Delilah.

Delilah teamed up with the Philistines and found the source of Samson's power. His hair was cut and he lost his powers. At the end Samson died with his enemies. Disobedience is a sin against God. When we disobey God, it gives the enemy the right to harm us.

Broken Relationship with God

Psalm 91:15 He shall call upon me, and I will answer him; I will be with him in trouble; I will deliver him and honor him.

Even if there is a generational curse in the lineage where you come from, when there is unbroken relationship with God, no harm will come upon you. When there is a broken relationship with God, the enemy we always near to strike us.

When King Saul failed God, he could not mend his relationship with God. The spirit of God left him, the throne was taken away from him and on top of that he died. A broken relationship with God can lead to untimely death.

PRAYER POINTS

- Lord Jesus, I magnify you for your grace and protection over my life thus far. I thank you for your mercy, I thank you for how far you have kept me, and Lord may your name be exalted in the name of Jesus.

- Lord, I come against every plan of the enemy to take my life unjustly, I come against every plan of the enemy to take me out before I reach my potentials, and I destroy such plans over my life in the name of Jesus.

- Lord, I destroy every evil generational curse that has been ravaging my family for long. Every demonic curse that kills member of the family when they are about clock a certain age, I destroy such curse over my life in the name of Jesus.

- Lord, I key into the covenant of long life that you have promised me through the death and resurrection of Christ on the cross of Calvary and I rebuke every any of death over my life today in the name of Jesus.

- Lord, the scripture said I know the thoughts I have towards you, they are the thoughts of good and not of evil to give you an expected end. Lord I pray that no harm shall befall me in the name of Jesus. I declare that I shall not die but live to declare the word of the lord in the land of the living. I come against evil death in the name of Jesus.

- Every demonic altar that has been raised against me in the kingdom of darkness, I come against you by the fire of the Holy Ghost. I cancel every form of gathering against my life, I pray that God throw confusion into their midst today in the name of Jesus.

- Oh you power of death hear the word of the Lord, I destroy you over my life in the name of Jesus. I rebuke the power of hell over my life, I cancel the power of grave over my life in the name of Jesus.

- Father Lord, I decree by the grace of the Most High, your counsel alone will stand in my life. I rebuke every demonic utterances speaking evil over my life and destiny, I cancel you today in the name.

- Lord, I key into your promise that said you will satisfy me with long life and you will show me your salvation. I declare long life is ascertain for me in the name of Jesus.

- Lord Jesus, I cling to the cross of Calvary where there is an abundance of blood. I pray that by the virtue of the blood that was shed on the cross of Calvary you will redeem me from the power of death in the name of Jesus.

20 PRAYER POINTS FOR BREAKING STUBBORN CURSE

Numbers 23:23 Surely there is no enchantment against Jacob, neither is there any divination against Israel: according to this time it shall be said of Jacob and of Israel, What hath God wrought!

Whom God has blessed, no man can curse. We have compiled 20 prayer points for breaking stubborn curses. A closed mouth is a closed destiny, until you declare your freedom in Christ, you will never enjoy it. We must understand that the devil is a stubborn spirit, who will always contend with the blessings of God in our lives. The devil will always fight us to see if our faith is intact. We must resist the devil, and we do that through bible study and prayers. When we pray, we let the devil know our stand and authority in Christ Jesus. When we pray, we generate power, through the Holy Spirit to destroy all the attacks of the devil. When we pray, we exercise our faith in redemption and our faith serves as a shield that destroys all the arrows of the devil. Prayer indeed is the key to freedom from all curses.

A prayerful Christian is an uncrushable Christian. It is true that we have been delivered from the curse of the law, but we must continue to fight the right not faith on the altar of prayer, this prayer points for breaking stubborn curses will give us the platform to wage spiritual warfare against the enemy. Receive grace today to pray your way out. No matter what you are struggling with now, as you engage this prayers, I see you walking away with victory in the name of Jesus.

PRAYER POINTS

1. Father, I thank you for delivering me from every curse in Jesus name
2. I declare that I am free from the curse of the law through Christ in Jesus name
3. I declare that I am free from the curse of sin and death in Jesus name
4. I declare that I am free from every curse from my father's house in Jesus name

5. I declare that imam free from every curse from my mother's house in Jesus name
6. I declare that I am free from all forms of generational curses in Jesus name
7. I declare that I am free from every self-inflicted curse in Jesus name
8. I declare that I have been translated from darkness to the kingdom of light, where I cannot be cursed in Jesus name
9. I declare that no weapon fashioned against my life shall ever prosper in Jesus name
10. I silence every evil tongue speaking against my life today by the blood of Jesus in Jesus name.
11. I declare that I shall always be the head and not the tail in Jesus name
12. I declare that I shall be above only band not beneath in Jesus name
13. I reject the spirit of hard luck and stagnation in my life in Jesus name
14. I command every ancestral spirits fighting against my progress to be destroyed by fire in Jesus name
15. I declare that with my eyes I shall see the downfall of my enemies in Jesus name.
16. I declare that the arrows that flies by day, and the pestilence that roam in darkness cannot come near me in Jesus name.
17. I declare that I shall rise from this level I am to a higher level in my career in Jesus name
18. I declare that I am a new creation, a new species of being, therefore I have no connection any curse of the devil in Jesus name
19. As a new creation, no stubborn curse can prevail in my life in Jesus name.
20. I declare that I am absolutely free from every stubborn curse hovering around my life and destiny in Jesus name. Thank you Jesus.

PRAYER POINT AGAINST EVIL PLANS

Today we will be engaging ourselves with prayer against evil plans. Just as God has His plans for our lives, so also the devil is strategizing his plan against us. And in most cases, the plan of the enemy is always evil. Little wonder the scripture says in the book of John 10:10 the thief comes only to steal and kill and destroy. Many people have fell victim to the evil plans of the enemy because they have refused to be spiritually alert of the devil's devices.

Meanwhile, some people are just saved by grace; if not, they would have become prey in the hands of the devil. Recall the story of Haman and Mordecai in the book of Esther. Haman hated Mordecai so much that he made plans for Mordecai to be hanged from a 50-cubit high gallows that he has prepared to kill all the Jews. But God destroyed the plans of Haman and made him killed by the same trap he has set for Mordecai.

This prayer guide will focus on God destroying the evil plans of the enemy over life and making them kill themselves with their plans. Just like Haman fell to the same trap that he set for Mordecai, so shall all your enemies die by their plans to hurt you in the name of Jesus? What we must understand as believers is that the enemy doesn't rest. The scripture describes him as a roaring Lion going about looking for who to devour; that is why you must not let your guard down in the place of prayer. I pray that by the mercy of the Most High, your enemy will not triumph over you in the name of Jesus.

As you have been bought with the precious blood of Jesus, every evil plan over your life and destiny is destroyed by fire in the name of Jesus. Take your time to study this prayer guide. God is set to perform wonders. There shall be numerous miracles as you use this guide, the plans of the enemies will be revealed unto you, and you shall triumph over them in the name of Jesus.

PRAYER POINTS

- Lord God, I come before you today to destroy every evil plan that the enemy has concerning me in the name of Jesus. Father, every evil friend that is in my life that does not mean well for me, I pray that you destroy them by the fire of the Holy Ghost.

- I come against every evil plan and every manipulation of the enemy over my life; I destroy it by the fire of the Holy Ghost in the name of Jesus. Every man or woman whose heart intention towards me is evil, Lord destroy them today in the name of Jesus.

- Father Lord, I pray that you will render my enemies powerless before they strike me. Lord, before they carry their plans over my life, I pray that you will chatter them in the name of Jesus.

- Lord God, just like you destroyed the plans of Haman over Mordecai, as you caused Haman to die by his plan to kill Mordecai, I pray that all my enemies will die by their plans in the name of Jesus.

- Every evil plan of the enemies to tamper with my success, each of their plans to frustrate me at the junction of success, Lord, let such plans be destroyed by fire in the name of Jesus.

- Father Lord, every plan of the enemy to ridicule my effort, every plan to distract me at the point of breakthrough, I counter that plans by the power of the Holy Ghost.

- Father Lord, every plan of the enemy to inflict me with a terrible sickness, I come against such plans in the name of Jesus. Lord, for the scripture, says Christ has bared upon himself all our infirmities, and he has healed all our diseases. The fire of the Holy Ghost destroys Lord, every plan of the enemy to inflict me with sickness.

- Every plan of the enemy to tamper with my brain, destroy such plans in the name of Jesus.

- The scripture says, declare a thing, and it shall be established, Lord, I decree upon my life every evil plan of the enemy over my life should catch fire in the name of Jesus.

- Lord Jesus, I break into pieces every high ground that has been laid in front of me by the enemies, every evil plan against my destiny, every demonic plan to ruin my future is scattered in the name of Jesus.

- Lord, I decree that you through confusion into the camp of my enemies. Let men and women who sort after my downfall be put to shame, let them be drunk with their blood like a glass of sweet wine, let them be fed with their flesh in the name of Jesus.

- Every demonic plan of the enemy to cause me to shed tears over my children, I destroy such plans by the power in the name of Jesus. Every plan of the enemy to inflict my kids with the spirit of stubbornness, I destroy such plans by the fire of the Holy Ghost.

- Every evil plan to ruin my academic career, every evil plan channeled at me to take away my memory; I destroy it by the power in the name of Jesus. For it has been written, if any man lacks wisdom, let him ask from God that gives liberally without blemish. I seek your wisdom, grant it unto me in the name of Jesus.

- For it has been written, the earnest expectations of the creature awaits the manifestations of the sons of God. Father Lord, I decree that from now, I begin to manifest in the full capacity that you have destined for me. Every plan of the enemy to destroy your plans for my life, I destroy it by the authority of heaven.

- Lord, I decree that upon my life and family, your counsel alone will stand. I decree upon all my children and everything you have blessed me with; I decree that your counsel alone will stand upon them.

PRAYER POINTS AGAINST EVIL DREAM

Today we will be dealing with prayer points against evil dreams. A dream is one way through which God communicates with man. There are times in our dreams while we sleep that the portal of revelation will be opened, and we see things that are yet to come. In the book of John 33:14-18 For God speaks in one way, and in two, though man does not perceive it. In a dream, in a vision of the night, when deep sleep falls on men, while they slumber on their beds, then he opens the ears of men and terrifies them with warnings, that he may turn man aside from his deed and conceal pride from a man; he keeps back his soul from the pit, his life from perishing by the sword. In most cases, the things we see in dreams are a revelation of things that would happen.

There are times that things happen to us in life, whereas they have been revealed in the dream, but because we failed to pray against them, they eventually come to pass. I decree by the power of the most high, every evil dream is destroyed in the name of Jesus. Meanwhile, sometimes we see something terrible in the dream that affects our sleep. Some people can't even close their eyes to sleep at night because of the numerous terrible dreams. But the scripture says we have not been given the spirit of fear but of sonship to cry Abba Father. Today God will destroy every evil dream in the name of Jesus.

PRAYER POINTS

- Lord Jesus, I thank you for the good things you have done in my life, I thank you for sparing my life to witness another day like this, Lord let your name be exalted in the name of Jesus.

- Lord Jesus, I thank you for the grace and privilege that you have bestowed upon me to sleep and dream dreams. I thank you for increasing my spiritual sensitivity even while I close my eyes to see, Lord, let your name be exalted in the name of Jesus.

- Lord God, I pray concerning every evil dream that I have had. I pray that you will restore them in the name of Jesus. I pray that you will cancel every plan of the enemy to harm me. I pray that such plans is destroyed in the name of Jesus.

- I come against every power and principalities that are always bringing evil dreams in my sleep. I come against them by the blood of the lamb. Every evil force that has vowed always to spoil my night with terrible and fearful dreams, I destroy you all in the name of Jesus.

- For the scripture says I have not been given the spirit of fear but of sonship to cry Abba Father. Lord, I cry unto you today to save me from the fear of evil dreams in the name of Jesus.

- The book of Prob. 3 vs. 34 says When I lie down, I shall not be afraid, and my sleep shall be sweet. Every power that wants to make me afraid in my sleep, every power that wants to cause me to have terrible dreams, I destroy you by the fire of the Holy Ghost be consumed in the name of Jesus.

- Lord Jesus, I pray that you will grant me the grace and ability to sleep and wake up in peace in the name of Jesus. The scripture says I know the thoughts I have towards you; they are the thoughts of good and not of evil to give you an expected end. Lord Jesus, any power that wants to alter your plans for my life, let such power catch fire in the name of Jesus.

- Every evil animal that has been sent by the enemy to come appear in my dreams to scare me. I release the fire of the Holy Ghost upon you right now in the name of Jesus.
- Every satanic dog, goat, snake, or cow appearing in my dream, die right now in the name of Jesus.
- I decree that the angel of the Lord will stand watch over me when I sleep, it will guide me in my sleep that no masquerade of the devil will come near my dwelling place in the name of Jesus.
- Lord, the scripture says, and they overcome him by the blood of the lamb and by the words of their testimonies. I decree that the enemy is destroyed in the name of Jesus. Every power of the enemy that wants to contaminate my sleep with terrible dreams, you are destroyed in the name of Jesus.
- I come against every evil dream; every dream of death is canceled in the name of Jesus. For your words say I will not die but live to declare the works of the Lord in the land of the living. I decree by the mercy of God that death is destroyed over my life in the name of Jesus.
- Every evil spirit that has been assigned to my life to contaminate my dream catch fire right now in the name of Jesus. Every dream of an accident is destroyed in the name of Jesus. I decree that it shall not come to pass in the name of Jesus. For it has been written, who speaks and it comes to pass when the Lord has not spoken, the blood of the lamb cancels every evil dream.
- Every evil animal that has been assigned to monitor my sleep, I call the fire of the holy upon you right now in the name of Jesus.
- Every evil coverage, every demonic power controlling the territory where I stay, I release the fire of the Holy Ghost upon you right now in the name of Jesus. Every evil attack, for the scripture, says no weapon fashioned against me shall prosper; every evil attack is nullified in the name of Jesus.

- I decree that as from today, my sleep will be blessed with sweet dreams: no more masquerade, no more snakes in the name of Jesus.

Made in the USA
Las Vegas, NV
13 December 2023

82680317R00413